Fourth Workshop on Speech, Vision, and Language Technologies for Dravidian Languages (DravidianLangTech 2024)

St. Julian's, Malta
22 March 2024

ISBN: 978-1-7138-9453-7

Printed from e-media with permission by:

Curran Associates, Inc.
57 Morehouse Lane
Red Hook, NY 12571

Association for Computational Linguistics
209 N. Eighth Street
Stroudsburg, Pennsylvania 18360

Phone: 1-570-476-8006
Fax: 1-570-476-0860

acl@aclweb.org

Additional copies of this publication are available from:

Curran Associates, Inc.
57 Morehouse Lane
Red Hook, NY 12571 USA
Phone: 845-758-0400
Fax: 845-758-2633
Email: curran@proceedings.com
Web: www.proceedings.com

DravidianLangTech 2024

The Fourth Workshop on Speech, Vision, and Language Technologies for Dravidian Languages

Proceedings of the Workshop

March 22, 2024

The DravidianLangTech organizers gratefully acknowledge the support from the following sponsors.

In cooperation with

Association for Computational Linguistics (ACL)
209 N. Eighth Street
Stroudsburg, PA 18360
USA
Tel: +1-570-476-8006
Fax: +1-570-476-0860
acl@aclweb.org

Introduction

We are excited to welcome you to DravidianLangTech 2024, the 18th Conference of the European Chapter of the Association for Computational Linguistics (EACL). This year the workshop is being held hybrid (online and at Malta), on March 21, 2024 with EACL 2024 that will take place also hybrid March 17-22, 2024.

The development of technology increases our internet use, and most of the global languages have adapted themselves to the digital era. However, many regional, under-resourced languages face challenges as they still lack developments in language technology. One such language family is the Dravidian family of languages. Tamil languages are primarily spoken in south India, Sri Lanka, and Singapore. Pockets of speakers are found in Nepal, Pakistan, Malaysia, other parts of India, and elsewhere globally. The Tamil languages, which are 4,500 years old and spoken by millions of speakers, are under-resourced in speech and natural language processing. The Dravidian languages were first documented in Tamili script on pottery and cave walls in the Keezhadi (Keeladi), Madurai and Tirunelveli regions of Tamil Nadu, India, from the 6th century BCE. The Tamil languages are divided into four groups: South, South-Central, Central, and North groups. Tamil morphology is agglutinating and exclusively suffixal. Syntactically, Tamil languages are head- final and left-branching. They are free-constituent order languages. To improve access to and production of information for monolingual speakers of Dravidian (Tamil) languages, it is necessary to have speech and languages technologies. These workshops aim to save the Dravidian languages from extinction in technology.

This is the Fourth workshop on speech and language technologies for Dravidian languages.

Program Committee

Program Chairs

Bharathi Raja Chakravarthi, University of Galway, Ireland
Ruba Priyadharshini, Gandhigram Rural Institute-Deemed to be University, India
Anand Kumar Madasamy, National Institute of Technology Karnataka, India
Sajeetha Thavareesan, Eastern University, Sri Lanka
Elizabeth Sherly, Digital University Kerala, India
Rajeswari Natarajan, SASTRA University, India
Manikandan Ravikiran, Hitachi Research & Development, AI Research Group, Bangalore, India

Publication Chair

Rahul Ponnusamy, University of Galway, Ireland
Prasanna Kumar Kumaresan, University of Galway, Ireland
Saranya Rajiakodi, Central University of Tamil Nadu, India
Kathiravan Pannerselvam, Central University of Tamil Nadu, India

Program Committee

Selam Abitte, Instituto Politécnico Nacional, Mexico
Zahra Ahani, Instituto Politécnico Nacional, Mexico
Premjith B, Amrita Vishwa Vidyapeetham (Deemed University), India
Bharathi B, Sri Sivasubramaniya Nadar College of Engineering, India
Fazlourrahman Balouchzahi, Instituto Politécnico Nacional, Mexico
Sivaji Bandyopadhyay, Jadavpur University, India
Shankar Biradar, Indian Institute of Information Technology Dharwad, India
Jerin Mahibha C, Meenakshi Sundararajan Engineering College, India
Mithun Das, Indian Institute of Technology Kharagpur, India
Prajit Dhar, Universität Potsdam, Germany
Thenmozhi Durairaj, Sri Sivasubramaniya Nadar College of Engineering, India
Jyothish Lal G, Amrita Vishwa Vidyapeetham (Deemed University), India
Piyushi Goyal, Manipal University, India
Shaun Allan H, Sri Sivasubramaniya Nadar College of Engineering, India
Viktor Hangya, The Center for Information and Language Processing, University of Munich, Germany
Asha Hegde, Mangalore University, India
Nikilesh Jayaguptha, Sri Sivasubramaniya Nadar College of Engineering, India
Rohith Gowtham Kodali, asrlytics, India
Sai Koneru, Karlsruher Institut für Technologie, Germany
Yuta Koreeda, Hitachi, Ltd., California, United States
Sergey Koshelev, Institute of Linguistics of the Russian Academy of Sciences, Russia
Amrit Krishnan, Sri Sivasubramaniya Nadar College of Engineering, India
Saurabh Kumar, Indian Institute of Technology, Guwahati, India
Danni Liu, Karlsruher Institut für Technologie, Germany
Sainik Kumar Mahata, Institute of Engineering and Management, India
Aman Mahendroo, Delhi Technological University, India
Durga Prasad Manukonda, ASRlytics, India

Rajeswari Natarajan, Sri Venkateswara College of Engineering, India
Md Osama, Chittagong University of Engineering and Technology, Bangladesh
Keun Hee Park, Arizona State University Tempe Campus, United States
Sanjai R, Kongu Engineering College, India
Jairam R, Amrita Vishwa Vidyapeetham (Deemed University), India
Rohan R, Sri Sivasubramaniya Nadar College of Engineering, India
Abhishek R, Sri Sivasubramaniya Nadar College of Engineering, India
Surangika Ranathunga, University of Moratuwa, Sri Lanka
Manikandan Ravikiran, Hitachi Research & Development, AI Research Group, Bangalore, India
Koustav Rudra, Indian Institute of Technology Kharagpur, India
Richard Saldanha, National Institute of Technology Karnataka, India
Sunil Saumya, Indian Institute of Information Technology, Dharwad, India
Kogilavani Shanmugavadivel, Kongu Engineering College, India
Manish Shrivastava, International Institute of Information Technology Hyderabad, India
Samyuktaa Sivakumar, Sri Sivasubramaniya Nadar College of Engineering, India
Malliga Subramanian, Kongu Engineering College, India
Ashwin V Sundar, Sri Sivasubramaniya Nadar College of Engineering, India
Musica Supriya, Manipal University, India
Moein Shahiki Tash, Instituto Politécnico Nacional, Mexico
Fida Ullah, Instituto Politécnico Nacional, Mexico
Christeena Varghese, Technical University of Applied Sciences Würzburg-Schweinfurt, Germany
Anil Vuppala, International Institute of Information Technology - Hyderabad, India
Ivan P. Yamshchikov, Technical University of Applied Sciences Würzburg-Schweinfurt and ISEG, University of Lisbon, Germany
Mesay Gemeda Yigezu, Instituto Politécnico Nacional, Germany
Muhammad Tayyab Zamir, Instituto Politécnico Nacional, Germany
Zheng Zhao, University of Edinburgh, United Kingdom

Table of Contents

Program

Friday, March 22, 2024

09:15 - 09:30 *Opening Remarks*

09:30 - 10:00 *Keynote*

10:00 - 11:00 *Developing Models and Resources for Low Resource Applications*

A Few-Shot Multi-Accented Speech Classification for Indian Languages using Transformers and LLM's Fine-Tuning Approaches
Jairam R, Jyothish Lal G and Premjith B

Neural Machine Translation for Malayalam Paraphrase Generation
Christeena Varghese, Sergey Koshelev and Ivan P. Yamshchikov

From Dataset to Detection: A Comprehensive Approach to Combating Malayalam Fake News
Devika K, Hariprasath .S.B, Haripriya B, Vigneshwar E, Premjith B and Bharathi Raja Chakravarthi

Exploring the impact of noise in low-resource ASR for Tamil
Vigneshwar Lakshminarayanan and Emily Prud'hommeaux

11:00 - 13:00 *Poster Session*

SetFit: A Robust Approach for Offensive Content Detection in Tamil-English Code-Mixed Conversations Using Sentence Transfer Fine-tuning
Kathiravan Pannerselvam, Saranya Rajiakodi, Sajeetha Thavareesan, Sathiyaraj Thangasamy and Kishore Kumar Ponnusamy

byteSizedLLM@DravidianLangTech 2024: Fake News Detection in Dravidian Languages - Unleashing the Power of Custom Subword Tokenization with Subword2Vec and BiLSTM
Rohith Gowtham Kodali and Durga Prasad Manukonda

Fida @DravidianLangTech 2024: A Novel Approach to Hate Speech Detection Using Distilbert-base-multilingual-cased
Fida Ullah, Muhammad Tayyab Zamir, Muhammad Arif, M. Ahmad, E Felipe-Riveron and Alexander Gelbukh

Selam@DravidianLangTech 2024:Identifying Hate Speech and Offensive Language
Selam Abitte Kanta, Grigori Sidorov and Alexander Gelbukh

Wit Hub@DravidianLangTech-2024:Multimodal Social Media Data Analysis in Dravidian Languages using Machine Learning Models
Anierudh H S, Abhishek R, Ashwin V Sundar, Amrit Krishnan and Bharathi B

CUETSentimentSillies@DravidianLangTech-EACL2024: Transformer-based Approach for Sentiment Analysis in Tamil and Tulu Code-Mixed Texts
Zannatul Fardaush Tripty, Md. Arian Al Nafis, Antu Chowdhury, Jawad Hossain, Shawly Ahsan, Avishek Das and Mohammed Moshiul Hoque

Social Media Hate and Offensive Speech Detection Using Machine Learning method
Girma Yohannis Bade, Olga Kolesnikova, Grigori Sidorov and José Luis Oropeza

CUETSentimentSillies@DravidianLangTech EACL2024: Transformer-based Approach for Detecting and Categorizing Fake News in Malayalam Language
Zannatul Fardaush Tripty, Md. Arian Al Nafis, Antu Chowdhury, Jawad Hossain, Shawly Ahsan and Mohammed Moshiul Hoque

Social Media Fake News Classification Using Machine Learning Algorithm
Girma Yohannis Bade, Olga Kolesnikova, Grigori Sidorov and José Luis Oropeza

MUCS@DravidianLangTech-2024: Role of Learning Approaches in Strengthening Hate-Alert Systems for code-mixed text
Manavi K K, Sonali k, Gauthamraj k, Kavya G, Asha Hegde and Hosahalli Lakshmaiah Shashirekha

MUCS@DravidianLangTech-2024: A Grid Search Approach to Explore Sentiment Analysis in Code-mixed Tamil and Tulu
Prathvi b, Manavi K K, Subrahmanyapoojary k, Asha Hegde, Kavya G and Hosahalli Lakshmaiah Shashirekha

InnovationEngineers@DravidianLangTech-EACL 2024: Sentimental Analysis of YouTube Comments in Tamil by using Machine Learning
Kogilavani Shanmugavadivel, Malliga Subramanian, Palanimurugan V and Pavul chinnappan D

KEC_HAWKS@DravidianLangTech 2024 : Detecting Malayalam Fake News using Machine Learning Models
Malliga Subramanian, Jayanthjr J R, Muthu Karuppan P, Keerthibala A T and Kogilavani Shanmugavadivel

13:00 - 13:30 *Lunch Break*

13:30 - 15:45 *Overview and Findings of Shared Tasks at DravidianLangTech 2024*

Findings of the Shared Task on Hate and Offensive Language Detection in Telugu Codemixed Text (HOLD-Telugu)@DravidianLangTech 2024
Premjith B, Bharathi Raja Chakravarthi, Prasanna Kumar Kumaresan, Saranya Rajiakodi, Sai Prashanth Karnati, Sai Rishith Reddy Mangamuru and Chandu Janakiram

Findings of the Shared Task on Multimodal Social Media Data Analysis in Dravidian Languages (MSMDA-DL)@DravidianLangTech 2024
Premjith B, Jyothish Lal G, Sowmya V, Bharathi Raja Chakravarthi, K Nandhini, Rajeswari Natarajan, Abirami Murugappan, Bharathi B, Saranya Rajiakodi, Rahul Ponnusamy, Jayanth Mohan and Mekapati Spandana Reddy

SetFit: A Robust Approach for Offensive Content Detection in Tamil-English Code-Mixed Conversations Using Sentence Transfer Fine-tuning
Kathiravan Pannerselvam, Saranya Rajiakodi, Sajeetha Thavareesan, Sathiyaraj Thangasamy and Kishore Kumar Ponnusamy

Overview of Second Shared Task on Sentiment Analysis in Code-mixed Tamil and Tulu
Lavanya Sambath Kumar, Asha Hegde, Bharathi Raja Chakravarthi, Hosahalli Lakshmaiah Shashirekha, Rajeswari Natarajan, Sajeetha Thavareesan, Ratnasingam Sakuntharaj, Thenmozhi Durairaj, Prasanna Kumar Kumaresan and Charmathi Rajkumar

Overview of the Second Shared Task on Fake News Detection in Dravidian Languages: DravidianLangTech@EACL 2024
Malliga Subramanian, Bharathi Raja Chakravarthi, Kogilavani Shanmugavadivel, Santhiya Pandiyan, Prasanna Kumar Kumaresan, Balasubramanian Palani, Premjith B, Vanaja k, Mithunja S, Devika K, Hariprasath S.B, Haripriya B and Vigneshwar E

Findings of the First Shared Task on Offensive Span Identification from Code-Mixed Kannada-English Comments
Manikandan Ravikiran, Ratnavel Rajalakshmi, Bharathi Raja Chakravarthi, Anand Kumar Madasamy and Sajeetha Thavareesan

15:45 - 17:00 *Tea Break*

17:00 - 17:15 *Meeting, Awards, Closing (TBD)*

A Few-Shot Multi-Accented Speech Classification for Indian Languages using Transformers and LLM's Fine-Tuning Approaches

Jairam R[1, 2], Jyothish Lal G[1], Premjith B[1]
[1]Amrita School of Artificial Intelligence, Coimbatore, Amrita Vishwa Vidyapeetham, India
[2]RBG AI Research, RBG.AI, SREC Incubation Center, Coimbatore, India.
g_jyothishlal@cb.amrita.edu

Abstract

Accented speech classification plays a vital role in the advancement of high-quality automatic speech recognition (ASR) technology. For certain applications, like multi-accented speech classification, it is not always viable to obtain data with accent variation, especially for resource-poor languages. This is one of the major reasons that contributes to the underperformance of the speech classification systems. Therefore, in order to handle speech variability in Indian language speaker accents, we propose a few-shot learning paradigm in this study. It learns generic feature embeddings using an encoder from a pre-trained whisper model and a classification head for classification. The model is refined using LLM's fine-tuning techniques, such as LoRA and QLoRA, for the six Indian English accents in the Indic Accent Dataset. The experimental findings show that the accuracy of the model is greatly increased by the few-shot learning paradigm's effectiveness combined with LLM's fine-tuning techniques. In optimal settings, the model's accuracy can reach 94% when the trainable parameters are set to 5%.

Keywords : Accent-classification, few-shot, LoRA, QLoRA, LLM, Whisper, Dravidian Language

1 Introduction

In this digital era, speech data has become a valuable resource, alongside text data. In the field of speech processing, recent developments in deep learning have made it possible to create end-to-end systems for tasks like speech classification and recognition. Much of the ongoing research in speech processing focuses on constructing end-to-end devices for automatic speech recognition (ASR) capable of handling diverse input data and providing accurate transcriptions. While ASR systems have shown remarkable performance in many cases, they face challenges when it comes to generalizing and adapting to resource-poor or resource-limited languages. Even though there are multilingual ASR and classification systems that have been trained on different Indian languages like Tamil, Kannada, Malayalam, Telugu, and others, their effectiveness is still lacking. This is due to the fact that speech is highly influenced by a variety of factors, such as the speaker's accent, gender, age, and more, and the lack of data covering all these variations (Bachate and Sharma, 2019; Malik et al., 2021).

Apart from gender, the speaker's accent (Huang et al., 2001) is recognized as the second most influential speech variation that affects the performance of speech recognition systems. An accent typically refers to a unique way of speaking or pronouncing a non-native language by a native speaker, influenced by the speaker's demographic background or geographical location. Accent classification, at its core, involves the categorization of regional or demographic accents within spoken language. The speaker's accent classification is considered a preliminary task for enhancing the capabilities of multilingual ASR systems.

The primary objective of this research is to tackle the aforementioned accent variations by introducing a data-driven approach to address the challenge of multi-accented speech classification. This paper proposes a few-shot learning method for multi-accented speech classification tasks as a means to handle the diverse array of accents effectively. The few-shot learning paradigm was chosen for this work due to its ability to learn from small amounts of data, which emphasizes how important it is for successfully tackling accent classification problems. The whisper ASR model serves as the foundational framework for the task of classifying accented speech. In this work, we primarily use the encoder component of the model, to which we attached a classification head, excluding the decoder

Proceedings of the Fourth Workshop on Speech, Vision, and Language Technologies for Dravidian Languages, pages 1–9
March 22, 2024

component.

Furthermore, we used two of the most popular large language model (LLM) adapters, such as Quantized Low-Rank Adaptation (QLoRA) and Low-Rank Adaptation (LoRA), to make the training and fine-tuning processes efficient and memory-friendly. In this work, we utilized the data derived from six Indian languages, sourced from the IndicAccentDB (Darshana et al., 2022) and NISP (Kalluri et al., 2021) datasets. Both of these datasets are significant for their inclusion of multi-accented speech, featuring conversations in English among native speakers.

Our main contributions are as follows:

- The pre-trained ASR model was employed in conjunction with LLM fine-tuning adapters such as Low-Rank Adaptations (LoRA) and Quantized Low-Rank Adaptation (QLoRA) in order to categorize individuals' accents.

- Extensive experiments on the combined IndicAccentDB, NISP, and Gujarati Digits datasets have been conducted to show the efficacy of LLM's fine-tuning techniques. These experiments involve reducing the trainable parameters by setting different low-rank values ranging from 2 to 32.

- The significance of the few-shot learning paradigm was demonstrated by obtaining an average accuracy of 90% under LoRA and 93.3% under QLoRA.

- A multi-class accent classification task using few-shot learning paradigm has been demonstrated using only 2 hours and 30 minutes of training data and observed to have 94% accuracy in the optimal setting where the training parameters were reduced to 5% using LLM's adapters.

The paper contribution is detailed in the sections that follow, which are arranged as follows: Section 2 describes the related works, while Section 3 completely describes the methodology used in this work. Section 4 holds the results and discussion, and we conclude the work in Section 5.

2 Related Works

Previous research has extensively investigated how various components of speech change with accents. Notably, spectral features like formant frequencies and temporal features such as intonation and duration's exhibit variation with accent (Arslan and Hansen, 1997; Ferragne and Pellegrino, 2010). To automate accent classification, these features have been combined into different statistical models and machine learning techniques.

Historically, Hidden Markov Models (HMMs) and Gaussian Mixture Models (GMMs) have been commonly used in accent classification (Deshpande et al., 2005; Ghesquiere and Van Compernolle, 2002; Zheng et al., 2005). Some studies looked at how the number of GMM components affected the performance of classification (Chen et al., 2001), while others compared HMMs to Support Vector Machines (SVM) (Tang and Ghorbani, 2003). Further studies explored the impact of GMM component numbers on classification performance (Chen et al., 2001). In (Pedersen and Diederich, 2007), SVM has been used to classify Arabic and Indian accents using the most popular Mel-Frequency Cepstral Coefficients (MFCCs) as the speech feature. Linear models, such as linear discriminant analysis (LDA), have also found applications, as seen in the identification of accents in Australian English (Kumpf and King, 1997).

Conventional statistical models and machine learning models have played a crucial role in accented speech classification. However, deep learning frameworks like deep neural networks (DNNs) and recurrent neural networks (RNNs) have been widely used in the latest speech recognition and synthesis systems (Hinton et al., 2012; Zen and Sak, 2015; Xu et al., 2014; Jiao et al., 2016; Lalitha et al., 2019). Notably, for the accent classification task, Telugu dialect datasets were created and classified using variants of RNN models like LSTM, GRU, and BiLSTM with attention layers (Podila et al., 2022).

However, there have been fewer studies evaluating neural networks for accent identification (Chan et al., 1994) and (Rabiee and Setayeshi, 2010). Nevertheless, in related areas like language identification (LID), neural networks have been thoroughly investigated (Montavon, 2009; Cole et al., 1989; Lopez-Moreno et al., 2014). As a breakthrough, convolutional neural networks (CNNs) and gated recurrent units (GRUs) (Tzudir et al., 2021) have been combined to classify accents with approximately 6 hours of speech data for resource-poor languages. Moreover, transformers have been a crucial breakthrough in both the natural language processing (NLP) and speech processing domains.

Most of the transformer-based studies (Shi et al., 2021; Gao et al., 2021) have been mostly conducted on accented speech recognition and not on the accent classification task. Recently, the few-shot paradigm has gained more popularity among researchers because of its ability to learn from a limited amount of data, which resolves the issues with neural net networks, which require a lot of data to train the model (Shrestha and Mahmood, 2019). To the best of our knowledge, the efficacy of few-shot approaches in accent classification is still unknown, despite the fact that these approaches have been used in audio processing (Keshav et al., 2023; Chou et al., 2018; Arik et al., 2018; Anand et al., 2019).

Based on the existing literature, it is evident that while extensive research has been conducted in the field of speech processing techniques, there remains a significant gap in the development of a system that effectively addresses accent variation and performs classification. In our research, we aim to bridge this gap by introducing a novel approach that utilizes a few-shot learning paradigm for accent classification. To the best of our knowledge, this is the first work that poses multi-accented speech classification as a few-shot learning problem to address the diversity in speech variations caused by speakers' accents. This approach is designed to identify the accents of native speakers from spoken non-native English speech datasets.

3 Materials and Methodology

3.1 Datasets

The IndicAccentDB was first presented in the work MARS (Darshana et al., 2022), where a hybrid CNN was used in multi-accented English speech recognition. IndicAccentDB is comprised of audio recordings containing six English accents spoken by non-native speakers, each originating from six different Indian languages such as Tamil, Telugu, Malayalam, Hindi, Gujarati, and Hindi. Within the dataset, 19 speakers were asked to recite sentences from the Harvard sentences dataset, which is renowned for its phonetically balanced and gender-balanced content (Huang et al., 2001). There are 72 sets in the Harvard Sentences dataset, and each set has 10 moderately long sentences. Together, these 19 speakers contribute 8,180 speech utterances to the IndicAccentDB. The average length of the audio files is about 5 seconds each. The detailed data statistics for the IndicAccentDB are presented in Table 1.

IndicAccentDB	
Accents	No. of Recordings
Tamil	1,640
Malayalam	1,563
Telugu	1,614
Gujarati	298
Hindi	827
Kannada	1,486

Table 1: Data Statistics for IndicAccentDB corpus

Apart from the IndicAccentDB, we also incorporated publicly available datasets such as NISP (Kalluri et al., 2021) and Gujarati Digits (Dalsaniya et al., 2020). The NISP corpus encompasses speech recordings in five native Indian languages: Tamil, Kannada, Malayalam, Hindi, Telugu, and Indian-accented English. This corpus comprises recordings from 345 speakers, including 126 females and 219 males. It contains a total of 28,268 speech utterances, with 14,691 in English and 13,577 in native languages. In this work, we focused on a subset of the Indian-accented English utterances within this dataset.

Furthermore, the Gujarati digits (Dalsaniya et al., 2020) corpus is specifically designed to support speech recognition systems and features distinct recordings of Gujarati digits. These recordings were collected from various regions of Gujarat, including the Saurashtra, North Zone, South Zone, Central Zone, and Kutch Region, encompassing diverse environmental conditions and background noises. This dataset contains a total of 1,940 speech utterances from 20 different speakers. Table 2 provides a more detailed overview of the data statistics for both the NISP and Gujarati Digits datasets used in this work.

Corpus	Accents	No. of Recordings
NISP	Tamil	280
	Malayalam	187
	Telugu	167
	Kannada	233
	Hindi	276
Gujarati Digits	Gujarati	250

Table 2: Data Statistics for NISP and Gujarati Digits corpus

In this study, we utilized a subset of the Gujarati Digits dataset in conjunction with the IndicAccentDB and a subset of the NISP datasets. For multi-class classification, a total of six labels were employed for the six Indian languages. As part of the dataset's pre-processing, the audio files were resampled to 16 kilohertz. Then, a 400-point Fourier transform was used to make an 80-channel log Mel spectrogram for a 25-millisecond period with a 10-millisecond step. The resulting spectrogram was then used as input for the model's training.

3.2 Proposed Methodology

3.2.1 Model Architecture

Whisper (Radford et al., 2023), an advanced automatic speech recognition (ASR) model, currently stands as the state-of-the-art (SOTA) in speech recognition. Trained on an extensive dataset comprising 680,000 hours of multilingual and multitask-labeled data sourced from the web, it adopts a transformer architecture. The model involves both encoder and decoder components to process audio files and generate corresponding textual outputs.

In this study, we leveraged the pre-trained whisper-large-v2 ASR model for a classification task. This variant of the whisper is a multi-lingual model with 1550 million parameters. The encoder within the whisper model undergoes a specific architectural sequence: initial processing through a short stem consisting of two convolution layers, utilizing a filter width of 3, and activation by the GELU activation function. The second convolution layer introduces a stride of two. Following this, sinusoidal position embeddings are incorporated into the stem's output.

Subsequently, the encoder applies transformer blocks. Notably, the transformer employs pre-activation residual blocks. A concluding layer normalization step is then applied to the output of the encoder. The decoder component was omitted, as the absence of a transcription task negated its necessity. Instead, we utilized a classification head on top of the encoder to facilitate classification tasks. Then this model is optimized using the LLM fine-tuning adapters and trained as seen in Figure 1.

3.2.2 LLM's Fine-Tuning Techniques

Recently, large language models (LLMs) have gained increased attention within the research community, particularly in the field of natural language processing (NLP) applications. This surge in popularity has led to a gradual expansion of their util-

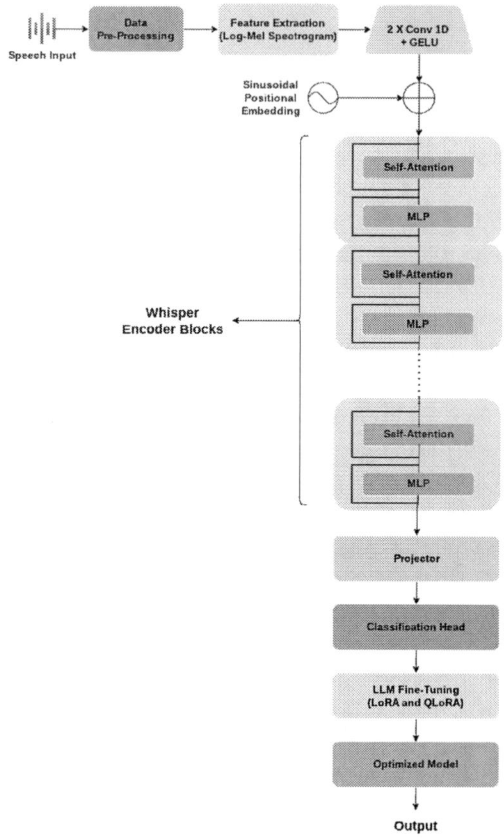

Figure 1: The proposed model includes data processing, feature extraction, encoder block of Whisper, and a classification head added on top of it, which is followed by LLM's fine-tuning techniques.

ity into other domains, including computer vision and speech. This paradigm involves large-scale pre-training on diverse web data, followed by fine-tuning for specific downstream tasks. However, fine-tuning LLMs for such tasks often necessitates substantial computing resources, rendering them inaccessible to many.

Parameter Efficient Fine-Tuning (PEFT) (Liu et al., 2022) addresses this issue by loading and fine-tuning the model in a memory-efficient manner while ensuring the model's performance. Despite the fact that these methods were initially applied to language models, they could be modified to improve the usability and accessibility of sophisticated models like Whisper in a variety of domains, including speech processing.

The PEFT methodology proves invaluable in fine-tuning LLMs. It achieves this by selectively fine-tuning only a small subset of parameters in a pre-trained model, significantly mitigating computational and storage expenses. In our work, we leverage two popular PEFT methods: LoRA (Low-Rank Adaptation) (Hu et al., 2021) and its evolution, QLoRA (Quantized Low-Rank Adaptation) (Dettmers et al., 2021), for the fine-tuning of the Whisper language model.

In the context of training the neural networks, the most fundamental procedure involves the iterative updating of weight matrices through the use of gradient descent. Nevertheless, when it comes to LLMs, the process of updating the weight matrix (*Wo*) in the pre-trained model presents challenges in terms of both compute and memory resource use.

LoRA (Hu et al., 2021) effectively addresses this by introducing two low-rank matrices (*B and A*) as an update matrix that approximates the large weight matrix. During training, *Wo* remains fixed without receiving gradient updates, while the smaller matrices *B* and *A* house the trainable parameters for LLMs fine-tuning. Consequently, when inputs are processed, they undergo multiplication by both *Wo* and the newly introduced update matrices (*B and A*), with the loss computed by aggregating the output vectors of *Wo, B, and A*.

QLoRA (Dettmers et al., 2021) is a further enhanced version of LoRA with improved memory efficiency. In QLoRA, the pre-trained model is loaded onto GPU memory using quantized 4-bit weights, a notable advancement from the 8-bit weights employed in LoRA. Importantly, QLoRA maintains comparable effectiveness to its predecessor, LoRA.

4 Results and Discussion

4.1 Experiments

The experiments were carried out in a hardware environment equipped with a T4-XLarge, 4 cores, 16 GB of RAM, 1 GPU, and 40 GB of disk space. We conducted experiments utilizing the 'whisper-large-v2' model with two Large Language Model (LLM) settings: one employing the LoRA adapter and the other employing the QLoRA adapter.

Following preprocessing, the audio files underwent segmentation into training, testing, and validation sets. The specific details of this segmentation are outlined in Table 3. The whisper-large-v2 model was loaded with 8-bit precision into memory using the INT8 and bitsandbytes Python libraries during training with LoRA. On the other hand double-quantization was used to load the model with 4-bit precision in QLoRA, and a datatype of NF4 (normalfloat4) was used to reduce perplexity.

Language	Total Recordings	Train	Test	Validation
Tamil	1,920	403	1,355	162
Malayalam	1,750	201	1,415	156
Telugu	1,781	437	1,188	134
Kannada	1,719	229	1,309	181
Gujarati	548	205	233	110
Hindi	1,103	289	674	140
Total	8,821	1,764	6,174	883

Table 3: Train, Test, and Validation split statistics

The whisper model was trained under both LoRA and QLoRA configurations, employing varying rank projections from 2, 4, 8, 16, 24, and 32 with a training epoch of 10. The training process utilized a batch size of 8 and a learning rate of 10-3. During training, around 2 hours and 30 minutes of data were used, while testing was conducted on approximately 8 hours of data.

4.2 Discussion

The effectiveness of the whisper model along with the LLM's fine-tuning techniques in multi-accented speech classification has been evaluated in this section through qualitative analysis of corpora (Darshana et al., 2022; Kalluri et al., 2021; Dalsaniya et al., 2020). Precision, Recall, F1-Score, and Accuracy are the primary metrics we use in our evaluation. Precision measures how often the model correctly predicts positive samples among all positive predictions. Recall measures the accuracy of the model's positive predictions among the actual positive samples. Accuracy measures the total number of correct predictions made by the model for the entire corpus, whereas Precision and Recall are combined to score the model's accuracy for each class in the F1-Score.

Rank	LoRA (Accuracy)	QLoRA (Accuracy)
32	93%	96%
24	91%	95%
16	90%	95%
8	85%	94%
4	89%	86%
2	**92%**	**94%**

Table 5: Accuracy comparison between LoRA and QLoRA

Rank and Trainable Parameters	Languages	LoRA			QLoRA		
		Precision	Recall	F1-Score	Precision	Recall	F1-Score
Rank - 32, Trainable Parameters-80%	Tamil	0.93	0.96	0.95	0.97	0.95	0.96
	Malayalam	0.95	0.93	0.94	0.96	0.96	0.96
	Telugu	0.93	0.92	0.92	0.96	0.96	0.96
	Kannada	0.95	0.98	0.97	0.96	0.98	0.97
	Gujarati	0.89	0.77	0.82	0.95	0.93	0.94
	Hindi	0.90	0.88	0.89	0.91	0.92	0.92
Rank - 24, Trainable Parameters-61%	Tamil	0.93	0.94	0.93	0.96	0.96	0.96
	Malayalam	0.90	0.95	0.93	0.95	0.97	0.96
	Telugu	0.90	0.89	0.90	0.96	0.93	0.95
	Kannada	0.93	0.96	0.95	0.96	0.97	0.97
	Gujarati	0.88	0.70	0.78	0.99	0.86	0.92
	Hindi	0.85	0.76	0.80	0.88	0.92	0.90
Rank-16, Trainable Parameters-40%	Tamil	0.91	0.91	0.91	0.95	0.95	0.95
	Malayalam	0.91	0.93	0.92	0.95	0.95	0.95
	Telugu	0.86	0.86	0.86	0.93	0.92	0.93
	Kannada	0.95	0.96	0.96	0.97	0.97	0.97
	Gujarati	0.84	0.58	0.69	0.95	0.93	0.94
	Hindi	0.81	0.83	0.82	0.91	0.94	0..92
Rank-8, Trainable Parameters-20%	Tamil	0.82	0.90	0.86	0.94	0.98	0.96
	Malayalam	0.88	0.96	0.92	0.96	0.94	0.95
	Telugu	0.82	0.75	0.79	0.93	0.93	0.93
	Kannada	0.90	0.94	0.92	0.96	0.97	0.96
	Gujarati	0.76	0.41	0.53	0.96	0.83	0.89
	Hindi	0.79	0.67	0.73	0.91	0.88	0.90
Rank-4, Trainable Parameters-10%	Tamil	0.86	0.91	0.89	0.90	0.91	0.91
	Malayalam	0.87	0.95	0.91	0.88	0.87	0.87
	Telugu	0.93	0.84	0.88	0.84	0.85	0.85
	Kannada	0.93	0.96	0.94	0.92	0.92	0.92
	Gujarati	0.93	0.73	0.82	0.66	0.62	0.64
	Hindi	0.86	0.77	0.81	0.69	0.70	0.70
Rank-2, Trainable Parameters-5%	Tamil	0.93	0.94	0.93	0.96	0.95	0.95
	Malayalam	0.91	0.95	0.93	0.95	0.96	0.95
	Telugu	0.94	0.86	0.90	0.93	0.92	0.93
	Kannada	0.95	0.96	0.96	0.96	0.96	0.96
	Gujarati	0.91	0.75	0.82	0.93	0.84	0.88
	Hindi	0.78	0.86	0.82	0.85	0.90	0.87

Table 4: Multiclass Classification Report for LoRA and QLoRA.

Table 4 shows the outcomes of multi-class classification using LoRA and QLoRA adapters at different rank values. Notably, the whisper model performs well in both LoRA and QLoRA settings across most rank values. Particularly, it excels when double quantized and operating in 4-bit precision under QLoRA settings.

The rank values in these adapters represent the low-rank matrix dimension learned during fine-tuning, impacting the model's trainable parameters. The rank values parameter in both LoRA and QLoRA is used to reduce the number of trainable parameters. Reducing the trainable parameters minimizes the computational cost and memory usage of the model. Optimal performance occurs at a rank value of 2 for both LoRA and QLoRA, utilizing only 5% of trainable parameters compared to the pre-trained model's total parameters.

Table 5 highlights significantly improved performance for both LoRA and QLoRA at this optimal rank value of 2, achieving an overall accuracy of 92% and 94%, respectively. Throughout the experiments, the model consistently performs better when trained on roughly two and a half hours of speech data, emphasizing the significance of the few-shot learning paradigm.

5 Conclusion and Future Works

In this work, we aimed to mitigate the impact of accent variation on speech classification systems. Our approach leveraged a data-driven method employing few-shot learning to perform multi-accented speech classification across six Indian language speakers' English accents. This was achieved by utilizing the IndicAccentDB alongside subsets from the NISP and Gujarati Digits Corpora, utilizing the pre-trained whisper ASR model.

Furthermore, we demonstrated the efficacy of LLM fine-tuning techniques such as LoRA and QLoRA, which make it possible to fine-tune large language models in a manner that is both memory-efficient and computationally efficient. As can be shown in Table 5, our studies produced remarkable overall accuracies of 92% and 94% when the settings were optimized.

Future endeavors will focus on encompassing other speech variations, such as age group and gender, using the few-shot learning paradigm. This approach will be particularly valuable in scenarios where data availability for these diverse attributes is limited, continuing to enhance the robustness of speech classification systems.

References

Prashant Anand et al. 2019. Few shot speaker recognition using deep neural networks. *arXiv preprint arXiv:1904.08775*.

S. Arik, J. Chen, K. Peng, W. Ping, and Y. Zhou. 2018. Neural voice cloning with a few samples. In *Advances in Neural Information Processing Systems*, pages 10019–10029.

L. M. Arslan and J. H. Hansen. 1997. Frequency characteristics of foreign accented speech. In *Proceedings of the IEEE International Conference on Acoustics, Speech, and Signal Processing (ICASSP)*, volume 2, pages 1123–1126, Munich, Germany. IEEE.

R. P. Bachate and A. Sharma. 2019. Automatic speech recognition systems for regional languages in india. *International Journal of Recent Technology and Engineering*, 8(2):585–592.

M. V. Chan, X. Feng, J. A. Heinen, and R. J. Niederjohn. 1994. Classification of speech accents with neural networks. In *Proceedings of the IEEE World Congress on Computational Intelligence, IEEE International Conference on Neural Networks*, volume 7, pages 4483–4486. IEEE.

T. Chen, C. Huang, E. Chang, and J. Wang. 2001. Automatic accent identification using gaussian mixture models. In *Proceedings of the IEEE Workshop on Automatic Speech Recognition and Understanding*, pages 343–346, Madonna di Campiglio, Italy. IEEE.

S.-Y. Chou, K.-H. Cheng, J.-S. R. Jang, and Y.-H. Yang. 2018. Learning to match transient sound events using attentional similarity for few-shot sound recognition. *arXiv preprint arXiv:1812.01269*.

R. A. Cole, J. W. Inouye, Y. K. Muthusamy, and M. Gopalakrishnan. 1989. Language identification with neural networks: A feasibility study. In *Proceedings of the IEEE Pacific Rim Conference on Communications, Computers and Signal Processing*, pages 525–529. IEEE.

Nikunj Dalsaniya et al. 2020. Development of a novel database in gujarati language for spoken digits classification. In *Advances in Signal Processing and Intelligent Recognition Systems: 5th International Symposium, SIRS 2019, Trivandrum, India, December 18–21, 2019, Revised Selected Papers 5*. Springer Singapore.

S. Darshana, H. Theivaprakasham, G. Jyothish Lal, B. Premjith, V. Sowmya, and K. Soman. 2022. Mars: A hybrid deep cnn-based multi accent recognition system for english language. In *Proceedings of the First International Conference on Artificial Intelligence Trends and Pattern Recognition (ICAITPR)*, pages 1–6, Hyderabad, India.

S. Deshpande, S. Chikkerur, and V. Govindaraju. 2005. Accent classification in speech. In *Proceedings of the Fourth IEEE Workshop on Automatic Identification Advanced Technologies*, pages 139–143, Buffalo, NY, USA. IEEE.

T. Dettmers, M. Lewis, S. Shleifer, and L. Zettlemoyer. 2021. 8-bit optimizers via block-wise quantization. *arXiv preprint arXiv:2110.02861*.

E. Ferragne and F. Pellegrino. 2010. Formant frequencies of vowels in 13 accents of the british isles. *Journal of the International Phonetic Association*, 40(01):1–34.

Qiang Gao et al. 2021. An end-to-end speech accent recognition method based on hybrid ctc/attention transformer asr. In *Proceedings of the IEEE International Conference on Acoustics, Speech and Signal Processing (ICASSP)*. IEEE.

P.-J. Ghesquiere and D. Van Compernolle. 2002. Flemish accent identification based on formant and duration features. In *Proceedings of the IEEE International Conference on Acoustics, Speech, and Signal Processing (ICASSP)*, volume 1, pages I–749, Orlando, FL, USA. IEEE.

G. Hinton, L. Deng, D. Yu, G. E. Dahl, A.-r. Mohamed, N. Jaitly, A. Senior, V. Vanhoucke, P. Nguyen, T. N. Sainath, et al. 2012. Deep neural networks for acoustic modeling in speech recognition: The shared views of four research groups. *IEEE Signal Processing Magazine*, 29(6):82–97.

E. J. Hu, Y. Shen, P. Wallis, Z. Allen-Zhu, Y. Li, S. Wang, L. Wang, and W. Chen. 2021. Lora: Low-rank adaptation of large language models. Preprint or Unpublished.

C. Huang, E. Chang, and T. Chen. 2001. Accent issues in large vocabulary continuous speech recognition. In *Proceedings of ACL*, Beijing, China. Microsoft Research China. Technical Report MSR-TR-2001-69.

Y. Jiao, M. Tu, V. Berisha, and J. Liss. 2016. Online speaking rate estimation using recurrent neural networks. In *Proceedings of the IEEE International Conference on Acoustics, Speech and Signal Processing*, Shanghai, China. IEEE.

Shareef Babu Kalluri et al. 2021. Nisp: A multi-lingual multi-accent dataset for speaker profiling. In *Proceedings of ICASSP*. IEEE.

S. Keshav, G. Jyothish Lal, and B. Premjith. 2023. Multimodal approach for code-mixed speech sentiment classification. In *Proceedings of Seventh ICMEET-2022: Advances in Signal Processing, Embedded Systems and IoT*, pages 553–563, Singapore. Springer Nature Singapore.

K. Kumpf and R. W. King. 1997. Foreign speaker accent classification using phoneme-dependent accent discrimination models and comparisons with human perception benchmarks. In *Proceedings of EuroSpeech*, volume 4, pages 2323–2326.

S. Lalitha, Shikha Tripathi, and Deepa Gupta. 2019. Enhanced speech emotion detection using deep neural networks. *International Journal of Speech Technology*, 22:497–510.

H. Liu, D. Tam, M. Muqeeth, J. Mohta, T. Huang, M. Bansal, and C. A. Raffel. 2022. Few-shot parameter-efficient fine-tuning is better and cheaper than in-context learning. In *Advances in Neural Information Processing Systems*, volume 35, pages 1950–1965.

I. Lopez-Moreno, J. Gonzalez-Dominguez, O. Plchot, D. Martinez, J. Gonzalez-Rodriguez, and P. Moreno. 2014. Automatic language identification using deep neural networks. In *Proceedings of the IEEE International Conference on Acoustics, Speech and Signal Processing (ICASSP)*, pages 5337–5341, Florence, Italy. IEEE.

Mishaim Malik et al. 2021. Automatic speech recognition: A survey. *Multimedia Tools and Applications*, 80:9411–9457.

G. Montavon. 2009. Deep learning for spoken language identification. In *Proceedings of the NIPS Workshop on Deep Learning for Speech Recognition and Related Applications*, pages 1–4, Whistler, BC, Canada.

C. Pedersen and J. Diederich. 2007. Accent classification using support vector machines. In *Proceedings of the 6th IEEE/ACIS International Conference on Computer and Information Science (ICIS 2007)*, pages 444–449. IEEE.

Rama Sai Abhishek Podila et al. 2022. Telugu dialect speech dataset creation and recognition using deep learning techniques. In *2022 IEEE 19th India Council International Conference (INDICON)*. IEEE.

A. Rabiee and S. Setayeshi. 2010. Persian accents identification using an adaptive neural network. In *Proceedings of the Second International Workshop on Education Technology and Computer Science*, pages 7–10, Wuhan, China. IEEE.

Alec Radford et al. 2023. Robust speech recognition via large-scale weak supervision. In *Proceedings of the International Conference on Machine Learning*. PMLR.

Xian Shi et al. 2021. The accented english speech recognition challenge 2020: Open datasets, tracks, baselines, results and methods. In *Proceedings of the IEEE International Conference on Acoustics, Speech and Signal Processing (ICASSP)*. IEEE.

Ajay Shrestha and Ausif Mahmood. 2019. Review of deep learning algorithms and architectures. *IEEE access*, 7:53040–53065.

H. Tang and A. A. Ghorbani. 2003. Accent classification using support vector machine and hidden markov model. In *Advances in Artificial Intelligence*, pages 629–631. Springer.

M. Tzudir, S. Baghel, P. Sarmah, and S. M. Prasanna. 2021. Excitation source feature based dialect identification in ao — a low resource language. In *Proceedings of Interspeech 2021*, pages 1524–1528.

Y. Xu, J. Du, L.-R. Dai, and C.-H. Lee. 2014. An experimental study on speech enhancement based on deep neural networks. *IEEE Signal Processing Letters*, 21(1):65–68.

H. Zen and H. Sak. 2015. Unidirectional long short-term memory recurrent neural network with recurrent output layer for low-latency speech synthesis. In *Proceedings of the IEEE International Conference on Acoustics, Speech and Signal Processing (ICASSP)*, pages 4470–4474, Brisbane, Australia. IEEE.

Y. Zheng, R. Sproat, L. Gu, I. Shafran, H. Zhou, Y. Su, D. Jurafsky, R. Starr, and S.-Y. Yoon. 2005. Accent detection and speech recognition for shanghai-accented mandarin. In *Proceedings of Interspeech*, pages 217–220, Lisbon, Portugal. Citeseer.

Neural Machine Translation for Malayalam Paraphrase Generation

Christeena Varghese
Technical University of Applied Sciences
Würzburg-Schweinfurt
Würzburg, Germany

Sergey Koshelev
Institute of Linguistics, RAS
Moscow, Russia
s.koshelev@iling-ran.ru

Ivan P. Yamshchikov
CAIRO,
Technical University of Applied Sciences
Würzburg-Schweinfurt
Würzburg, Germany
ivan.yamshchikov@thws.de

Abstract

This study explores four methods of generating paraphrases in Malayalam, utilizing resources available for English paraphrasing and pre-trained Neural Machine Translation (NMT) models. We evaluate the resulting paraphrases using both automated metrics, such as BLEU, METEOR, and cosine similarity, as well as human annotation. Our findings suggest that automated evaluation measures may not be fully appropriate for Malayalam, as they do not consistently align with human judgment. This discrepancy underscores the need for more nuanced paraphrase evaluation approaches especially for highly agglutinative languages.

1 Introduction

Paraphrase generation is the task of rephrasing a given text while retaining its original meaning. Paraphrase generation has attracted considerable attention in natural language processing (NLP) and computational linguistics. Alternatively, paraphrasing can be defined as rewriting a sentence in a different form without losing its semantic information. Thus automated paraphrasing is an essential component of any successful NLP system. For example, paraphrasing is essential for an NLP system to pass the Turing test.

There are several notable ideas to generate paraphrases that are relevant in the context of this paper. First, the idea to use machine translation-inspired solutions for paraphrasing dates back to Quirk et al. (2004) who developed monolingual machine translation for paraphrase generation. Second, the idea of context-aware statistical paraphrase, that, to our knowledge, was first introduced in Zhao et al. (2009).

Recently, Li et al. (2017) presented an approach that integrated deep reinforcement learning to obtain automated paraphrases. Gupta et al. (2018) showed how deep generative networks could be used for paraphrase generation. Whereas Egonmwan and Chali (2019) used transformers for paraphrase generation. Zhou and Bhat (2021) provide a more detailed view of paraphrase generation.

In the context of linguistic diversity, the focus on paraphrasing extends beyond widely spoken languages to also include regional languages with rich linguistic nuances. Salloum and Habash (2011) addressed the challenge of dialectal to standard Arabic paraphrasing to enhance Arabic-English statistical machine translation. Their work signifies a critical effort to improve translation accuracy and fluency across different Arabic linguistic variants. Additionally, Mizukami et al. (2014) made a substantial contribution by creating a free, general-domain paraphrase database for the Japanese language. Furthermore,Gao et al. (2018) explores the enhancement of English-to-Chinese neural machine translation through paraphrase-based data augmentation.

This work addresses paraphrase generation in Malayalam. Malayalam is a Dravidian language spoken predominantly in Kerala. It is also spoken in Mahe and Lakshadweep of India, altogether resulting in a population of about 34 million. Malayalam is known for its complicated grammatical structures, complex verb conjugations, and extensive vocabulary.

There are several research projects addressing paraphrases identification Malayalam language and recognizing sentence similarities, see (Mathew and Idicula, 2013b) and (Gokul et al., 2017). Recently, (K. Nambiar et al., 2023) provided a Malayalam model for machine translation, text summarization, and question-answering.

As an extension of the above-mentioned stud-

Proceedings of the Fourth Workshop on Speech, Vision, and Language Technologies for Dravidian Languages, pages 10–15
March 22, 2024 ©2024 Association for Computational Linguistics

ies, this paper aims to address the complex area of Malayalam paraphrase generation. Our investigation focuses on developing a specialized dataset tailored to Malayalam paraphrases, leveraging insights from established paraphrase generation models. The main motivation behind this research is to address the lack of resources for non-English languages and to improve the capabilities of NLP systems in the context of languages with special linguistic features.

2 Related Works

A seminal work by Dolan and Brockett (2005) emphasizes the importance of developing effective models for paraphrase generation, considering the varying syntactic and semantic expressions across different languages. These challenges become more pronounced in highly agglutinative languages, where words can be formed by stringing together multiple morphemes, adding an additional layer of complexity to the generation process. Extending paraphrase generation to Malayalam, a language with a complex linguistic structure, demands special attention.

Scientific papers on multilingual NLP, such as the work by Huang et al. (2020), emphasize the need for language-specific adaptations in paraphrase generation models. The authors discuss the impact of linguistic diversity on the performance of NLP models, underscoring the importance of addressing language-specific challenges.

Mathew and Idicula (2013a) propose four similarity measures to predict the similarity between two sentences in Malayalam. Those are cosine similarity, Jaccard similarity, overlap coefficient, and containment measure.

A shared Task on Detecting Paraphrases in Indian Languages, namely, Hindi, Tamil, Malayalam, and Punjabi are proposed by Anand Kumar et al. (2018). It consisted of two subtasks: Subtask 1 is to determine whether a sentence pair is a paraphrase or not, and Subtask 2 is to determine whether a sentence pair is a semi-paraphrase or a paraphrase or not. Different members use different features such as stop words, lemmatization, POS tagging, synonyms, overlap, cosine similarity, Jaccard similarity, etc. Due to the complexity of sentences, the F1 score and accuracy of Task 1 are comparatively high compared to the accuracy of Task 2. They concluded that the agglutinative character of Malayalam and Tamil makes paraphrasing more challenging.

3 Data

This paper uses the GYAFC dataset Rao and Tetreault (2018) in English as a start for the paraphrasing pipeline. This dataset consists of informal and formal sentence pairs which are built using the Yahoo Answers L6 corpus. The sentences in this dataset are obtained from various domains including Entertainment, Music, Family, Relationships, etc. Around 1000 English sentence pairs are available in this dataset.

Though we explore the possibility of adopting English datasets for Malayalam paraphrasing, we also provide a sample of 800 Malayalam paraphrase pairs evaluated by crowd workers with overlap of five[1]. The details on datalabelling are provided in Section 5.

4 Methods

We try to explore four approaches that could potentially leverage the knowledge that we have for English and transfer it into Malayalam paraphrase. The first approach simply uses Google Translate on a random sample of 200 GYAFC paraphrases. We evaluate all four approaches on random 200 GYAFC sentence pairs.

The first model combines the output of Google Translate with MultiIndic Paraphrase Generation, a pre-trained model for paraphrase generation Kumar et al. (2022). A prior study by Zhou et al. (2018) served as the foundation for MultiIndic Paraphrase Generation, which extracts paraphrases from a parallel corpus. The model is developed using the Samanantar corpus Ramesh et al. (2022), which contains parallel corpora between English and all 11 Indic languages. 200 pairs of English phrases from the GYAFC dataset are translated into Malayalam using Google Translate. These translated Malayalam sentences are then fed into the MultiIndic Paraphrase Generation to obtain desired Malayalam paraphrase pairs. An illustrative example pertaining to this model can be found in Figure 1.

In the second approach, we use a set of English synonym word pairs[2] to generate paraphrases in English with a simple synonym replacement heuristic approach to paraphrase. The generated paraphrases

[1]Omitted to preserve anonymity in peer reivew.

[2]`https://github.com/i-samenko/Triplet-net/blob/master/data/data.csv`

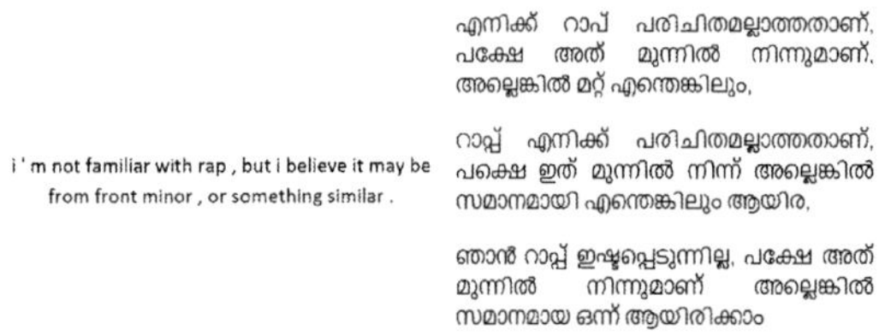

Figure 1: Result from Model 1

are then translated into Malayalam using Google Translate to obtain the Malayalam paraphrase set. Figure 2 exhibits an instance exemplifying this model, contributing to a deeper understanding.

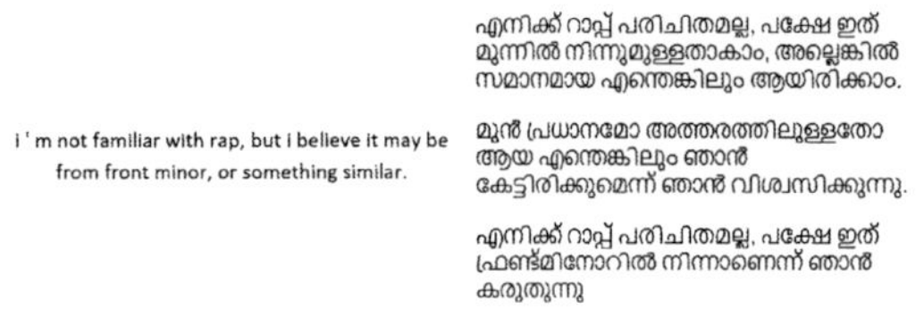

Figure 2: Result from Model 2

In the third approach, we use the bart-large-cnn model Lewis et al. (2019). Figure 3 contains an exemplar related to this model, offering additional clarity.

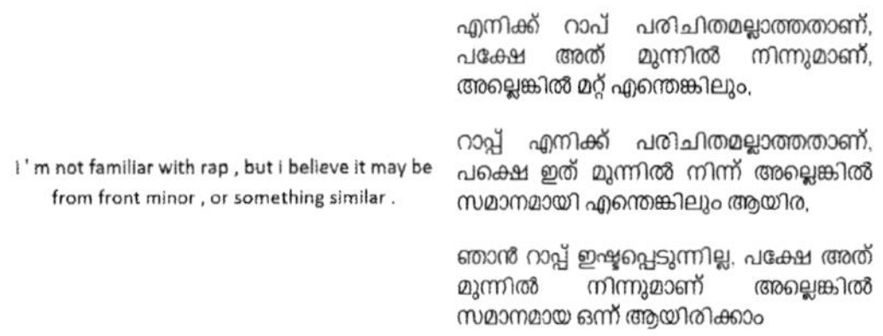

Figure 3: Result from Model 3

Finally, in the fourth model a pre-existing language translation model named, OPUS(Open Parallel Corpus) Tiedemann (2012). OPUS models are a collection of pre-trained multilingual machine translation models developed by the Helsinki NLP group. OPUS models are designed to handle translation tasks in several languages. They are trained to support translation between different language pairs, making them versatile for multilingual applications. Once again 200 pairs of sentences from the GYAFC dataset are passed to this model and Malayalam sentence pairs are generated. These translated sentences are then paraphrased by adjusting the beam-search parameters. Figure 4 includes an example associated with this model, providing supplementary clarity.

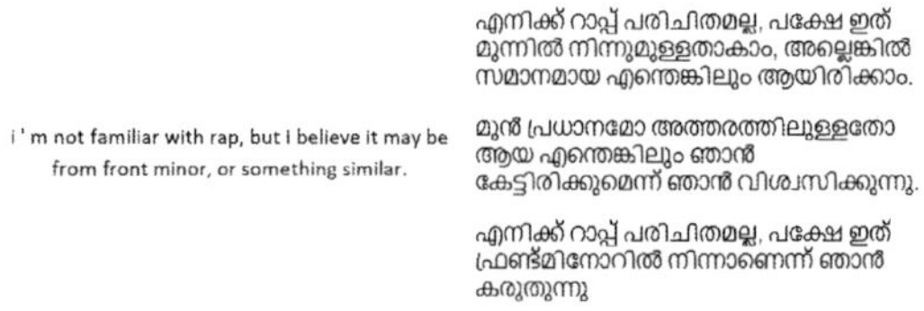

Figure 4: Result from Model 4

The num_beams parameter controls the number of beams to use in beam search. Beam search is a decoding algorithm that explores multiple possible sequences and selects the most likely ones. A larger num_beams value can increase diversity in generating phrases. Additionally, the num_return_sequences parameter determines how many different sequences to return. A higher value will result in more diverse paraphrases. Moreover, early_stopping is used to speed up the paraphrase generation process. These parameters collectively influence the diversity, quality, and speed of paraphrase generation.

Finally, we compare these paraphrase methods based on NMT with the paraphrase proposed for Malayalam in Anand Kumar et al. (2018).

5 Evaluation

Yamshchikov et al. (2021) have explored various metrics for the evaluation of paraphrases. They found BERTScore (Zhang et al., 2019) to be the most adequate metric for English paraphrases. However, there is no direct analogy of BERTScore for Malayalam and the most commonly used metrics do correlate with human judgment (Solomon et al., 2022) on par with BERTScore though not perfectly. Thus, in this work, we calculate the BLEU score (Papineni et al., 2002) and METEOR score (Lavie and Denkowski, 2009) for evaluating the phrases generated for a reference sentence. We also use cosine similarity used for paraphrase evaluation by Anand Kumar et al. (2018) to put our results in perspective, despite cosine similarity was found to have a lower correlation with the human evaluation of paraphrases. Finally, we have labelled 200 paraphrase pairs generated by each of the models with human labellers via crowd-sourcing platform. Each sentence was labelled with three or more native speakers of Malayalam. We measured a percentage of sentence pairs that were labelled as correct

[3]The self-reported evaluation metric.

Model	BLEU	METEOR	cosine similarity	human labels
MultiIndic Paraphrase (Kumar et al., 2022)	0.04	0.25	0.70	0.37
Synonym Replacement	0.05	0.28	0.60	**0.42**
BART (Lewis et al., 2019)	0.20	0.31	**0.96**	0.31
OPUS (Tiedemann, 2012)	**0.34**	**0.63**	0.83	0.23
Malayam Paraphrase (Anand Kumar et al., 2018)	-	-	0.79 [3]	-

Table 1: Average BLEU score, METEOR score, Cosine Similarity as well as the percent of paraphrases labelled as correct paraphrase by human labellers for various models.

paraphrases with high confidence. We publish the resulting human-labelled dataset of 800 sentence pairs to facilitate further research of paraphrasing in Malayalam.

Table 1 shows the results of the evaluation for 200 randomly sampled sentence pairs produced by four models that we test. It also puts these results into perspective comparing with the best result for Malayalam presented reported in Anand Kumar et al. (2018) denoted in the Table 1 as 'Malayalam Paraphrase'.

One can see that the OPUS model outperforms other models in terms of automated evaluation metrics. In the meantime, the paraphrases generated with MultiIndic Paraphrase Generation, specifically designed for Indian languages, show lower results on automated evaluation. Comparison of the proposed methods with the best Malayalam paraphrasing model described in Anand Kumar et al. (2018) also shows that on automated paraphrase evaluation metrics, direct application of machine translation methods, namely, BART or OPUS, leads to results that score higher in terms of BLEU, METEOR, and Cosine Similarity. However, this does not necessarily point at the weakness of the models but rather highlights the inadequacy of those popular evaluation metrics for Malayalam paraphrasing as well as the opportunity to leverage NMT to significantly expand the capabilities of Malayalam NLP.

Once we include human evaluation into the picture we see two crucial results. First, the most successful paraphrases, according to human judgement, as simply achieved by heuristic synonym replacement. This is not surprising. What is important is that humans also evaluate MultiIndic Paraphrase higher that BART or OPUS, despite those models higher scores on automated metrics.

6 Discussion

In this study, we check if one could use machine translation methods for paraphrasing in Malayalam. We test several methods of generating paraphrases in English, followed by their translation into Malayalam. This methodology was compared with the performance of Malayalam-specific paraphrase models.

Our findings reveal that using English for initial paraphrase generation and then translating to Malayalam can yield results that are on par with those from Malayalam-specific models. This has several important implications:

- Resource Optimization: This strategy showcases an efficient use of resources, leveraging the strengths of a high-resource language like English to benefit lower-resource languages;
- Model Versatility: The success of this approach suggests a potential shift in focus from developing language-specific models to enhancing translation-based methods;
- Expandability: such health check could be interesting for other Dravidian languages.

At the same time, one has to highlight certain limitations:

- Translation Dependence: The effectiveness of paraphrases is heavily reliant on the accuracy and nuances captured by the machine translation process;
- Evaluation Metrics Concern: A critical limitation is the potential inadequacy of automated evaluation metrics in accurately capturing the quality of paraphrases in Malayalam. This raises concerns about the reliability of any paraphrase results solely evaluated automatically without any human labels whatsoever;

- Model Reliance: The approach's success is contingent on the performance of the English paraphrase models employed.

7 Conclusion

This study evaluates how effective is the idea to apply the existing neural machine translation methods to paraphrase generation in Malayalam. The core finding of this paper is that the models specifically designed for agglutinative languages like Malayalam are showing performance on par with NMT machine translation pipelines that leverage available English resources. The study also highlights the demand for specific paraphrase evaluation metrics more suitable for Dravidian languages. Finally, we publish human-labelled dataset of paraphrases to facilitate further research on the topic.

References

M Anand Kumar, Shivkaran Singh, B Kavirajan, and KP Soman. 2018. Shared task on detecting paraphrases in indian languages (dpil): An overview. In *Text Processing: FIRE 2016 International Workshop, Kolkata, India, December 7–10, 2016, Revised Selected Papers*, pages 128–140. Springer.

Bill Dolan and Chris Brockett. 2005. Automatically constructing a corpus of sentential paraphrases. In *Third International Workshop on Paraphrasing (IWP2005)*.

Elozino Egonmwan and Yllias Chali. 2019. Transformer and seq2seq model for paraphrase generation. In *Proceedings of the 3rd Workshop on Neural Generation and Translation*, pages 249–255.

Qinghong Gao, Pengjun Xie, Hua Wu, and Haifeng Wang. 2018. Improving english-to-chinese neural machine translation through paraphrase-based data augmentation. In *Proceedings of the Conference on Empirical Methods in Natural Language Processing*, pages 3389–3398.

PP Gokul, BK Akhil, and Kumar KM Shiva. 2017. Sentence similarity detection in malayalam language using cosine similarity. In *2017 2nd IEEE International Conference on Recent Trends in Electronics, Information & Communication Technology (RTEICT)*, pages 221–225. IEEE.

Ankush Gupta, Arvind Agarwal, Prawaan Singh, and Piyush Rai. 2018. A deep generative framework for paraphrase generation. In *Proceedings of the aaai conference on artificial intelligence*, volume 32.

Zhen Huang, Shiyi Xu, Minghao Hu, Xinyi Wang, Jinyan Qiu, Yongquan Fu, Yuncai Zhao, Yuxing Peng, and Changjian Wang. 2020. Recent trends in deep learning based open-domain textual question answering systems. *IEEE Access*, 8:94341–94356.

Sindhya K. Nambiar, David Peter S, and Sumam Mary Idicula. 2023. Abstractive summarization of text document in malayalam language: Enhancing attention model using pos tagging feature. *ACM Transactions on Asian and Low-Resource Language Information Processing*, 22(2):1–14.

Aman Kumar, Himani Shrotriya, Prachi Sahu, Raj Dabre, Ratish Puduppully, Anoop Kunchukuttan, Amogh Mishra, Mitesh M. Khapra, and Pratyush Kumar. 2022. Indicnlg suite: Multilingual datasets for diverse nlg tasks in indic languages.

Alon Lavie and Michael J Denkowski. 2009. The meteor metric for automatic evaluation of machine translation. *Machine translation*, 23:105–115.

Mike Lewis, Yinhan Liu, Naman Goyal, Marjan Ghazvininejad, Abdelrahman Mohamed, Omer Levy, Ves Stoyanov, and Luke Zettlemoyer. 2019. Bart: Denoising sequence-to-sequence pre-training for natural language generation, translation, and comprehension. *arXiv preprint arXiv:1910.13461*.

Zichao Li, Xin Jiang, Lifeng Shang, and Hang Li. 2017. Paraphrase generation with deep reinforcement learning. *arXiv preprint arXiv:1711.00279*.

Ditty Mathew and Sumam Mary Idicula. 2013a. Paraphrase identification of malayalam sentences - an experience. In *2013 Fifth International Conference on Advanced Computing (ICoAC)*, pages 376–382.

Ditty Mathew and Sumam Mary Idicula. 2013b. Paraphrase identification of malayalam sentences-an experience. In *2013 Fifth International Conference on Advanced Computing (ICoAC)*, pages 376–382. IEEE.

Masahiro Mizukami, Graham Neubig, Sakriani Sakti, Tomoki Toda, and Satoshi Nakamura. 2014. Building a free, general-domain paraphrase database for japanese. In *2014 17th Oriental Chapter of the International Committee for the Co-ordination and Standardization of Speech Databases and Assessment Techniques (COCOSDA)*, pages 1–4. IEEE.

Kishore Papineni, Salim Roukos, Todd Ward, and Wei-Jing Zhu. 2002. Bleu: a method for automatic evaluation of machine translation. In *Proceedings of the 40th annual meeting of the Association for Computational Linguistics*, pages 311–318.

Chris Quirk, Chris Brockett, and Bill Dolan. 2004. Monolingual machine translation for paraphrase generation.

Gowtham Ramesh, Sumanth Doddapaneni, Aravinth Bheemaraj, Mayank Jobanputra, Raghavan Ak, Ajitesh Sharma, Sujit Sahoo, Harshita Diddee, Divyanshu Kakwani, Navneet Kumar, et al. 2022. Samanantar: The largest publicly available parallel corpora collection for 11 indic languages. *Transactions of the Association for Computational Linguistics*, 10:145–162.

Sudha Rao and Joel Tetreault. 2018. Dear sir or madam, may I introduce the GYAFC dataset: Corpus, benchmarks and metrics for formality style transfer. In *Proceedings of the 2018 Conference of the North American Chapter of the Association for Computational Linguistics: Human Language Technologies, Volume 1 (Long Papers)*, pages 129–140, New Orleans, Louisiana. Association for Computational Linguistics.

Wael Salloum and Nizar Habash. 2011. Dialectal to standard arabic paraphrasing to improve arabic-english statistical machine translation. In *Proceedings of the first workshop on algorithms and resources for modelling of dialects and language varieties*, pages 10–21.

Shaul Solomon, Adam Cohn, Hernan Rosenblum, Chezi Hershkovitz, and Ivan P Yamshchikov. 2022. Rethinking crowd sourcing for semantic similarity. In *Conference on Artificial Intelligence and Natural Language*, pages 70–81. Springer.

Jörg Tiedemann. 2012. Parallel data, tools and interfaces in opus. In *Lrec*, volume 2012, pages 2214–2218. Citeseer.

Ivan P Yamshchikov, Viacheslav Shibaev, Nikolay Khlebnikov, and Alexey Tikhonov. 2021. Style-transfer and paraphrase: Looking for a sensible semantic similarity metric. In *Proceedings of the AAAI Conference on Artificial Intelligence*, volume 35, pages 14213–14220.

Tianyi Zhang, Varsha Kishore, Felix Wu, Kilian Q Weinberger, and Yoav Artzi. 2019. Bertscore: Evaluating text generation with bert. In *International Conference on Learning Representations*.

Shiqi Zhao, Xiang Lan, Ting Liu, and Sheng Li. 2009. Application-driven statistical paraphrase generation. In *Proceedings of the Joint Conference of the 47th Annual Meeting of the ACL and the 4th International Joint Conference on Natural Language Processing of the AFNLP*, pages 834–842.

Jianing Zhou and Suma Bhat. 2021. Paraphrase generation: A survey of the state of the art. In *Proceedings of the 2021 conference on empirical methods in natural language processing*, pages 5075–5086.

Qingyu Zhou, Nan Yang, Furu Wei, Chuanqi Tan, Hangbo Bao, and Ming Zhou. 2018. Neural question generation from text: A preliminary study. In *Natural Language Processing and Chinese Computing: 6th CCF International Conference, NLPCC 2017, Dalian, China, November 8–12, 2017, Proceedings 6*, pages 662–671. Springer.

From Dataset to Detection: A Comprehensive Approach to Combating Malayalam Fake News

Devika K[1], Hari Prasath.S.B[1], Haripriya B[1], Vigneshwar E[1], Premjith B[1], Bharathi Raja Chakravarthi [2]
[1]Amrita School of Artificial Intelligence, Coimbatore
Amrita Vishwa Vidyapeetham, India
[2]School of Computer Science, University of Galway, Ireland
b_premjith@cb.amrita.edu

Abstract

Identifying fake news hidden as real news is crucial to fight misinformation and ensure reliable information, especially in resource-scarce languages like Malayalam. To recognize the unique challenges of fake news in languages like Malayalam, we present a dataset curated specifically for classifying fake news in Malayalam. This fake news is categorized based on the degree of misinformation, marking the first of its kind in this language. Further, we propose baseline models employing multilingual BERT and diverse machine learning classifiers. Our findings indicate that logistic regression trained on LaBSE features demonstrates promising initial performance with an F1 score of 0.3393. However, addressing the significant data imbalance remains essential for further improvement in model accuracy.

1 Introduction

Detecting fake news is critical to identifying false or intentionally misleading information presented as legitimate news. In today's digital age, numerous websites spread fake news, significantly influencing society. The deceptive strategies employed by fake news to appear true further complicate this problem. Fake news has far-reaching consequences, shaping public opinion, interfering with democratic processes like elections, and even inciting violence. Researchers from various disciplines recognize the significance of studying and addressing this issue (Jain et al., 2019; Baarir and Djeffal, 2021; Choudhary et al., 2021).

Although technology and social media positively impact society, they are not without limitations or defects. The spread of fake news and the threat of inaccurate data have grown, potentially leading to serious social problems. The effects of fake news can be wide-ranging, from being merely annoying to influencing and misleading entire communities or even countries. Inaccurate information has a negative impact on society, according to related research. There are many ways to identify false news, including topic-agnostic, knowledge-based, machine-learning-based, and hybrid techniques.

The importance of classifying fake news in Malayalam and other low-resource languages lies in reducing the spread of false information and promoting informed decision-making in linguistically diverse societies. This requires developing effective models for classifying fake news in various languages, especially those with limited linguistic resources, such as Malayalam. Fake news frequently exploits linguistic and cultural particulars in low-resource languages, requiring the development of language-specific detection methods. Effective models for identifying false information in languages with limited resources, as demonstrated in (Raja et al., 2023b), (De et al., 2022), and (Nair et al., 2022), can play a crucial role in nurturing acceptance of diverse perspectives. Keeping fake news detection in low-resource languages relevant and effective in the digital age.

This paper makes a significant contribution to the field by providing a dataset and baseline machine learning models designed for classifying fake news into different classes based on the degree of misinformation it contains. To the best of our knowledge, this is the first dataset in this domain focusing on combating the spread of fake news to protect society from these inhumane acts of violence.

This paper delves into the strategies for detecting fake news and the complexities of distinguishing between the types of fake news. Deception, manipulation, and polarization are among the negative impacts that detection seeks to prevent by combating the spread of misleading information across various platforms, including social media and messaging apps. This pressing issue motivates us to dedicate our efforts to this work.

The absence of relevant data made it difficult to create a large corpus to identify and categorize

Proceedings of the Fourth Workshop on Speech, Vision, and Language Technologies for Dravidian Languages, pages 16–23
March 22, 2024

false news in Malayalam. Creating a sufficiently large and diverse dataset is more challenging for Malayalam, which is the topic of extensive research due to the absence of Malayalam-specific resources. The lack of data makes developing and evaluating reliable identification algorithms more challenging and highlights the urgent need for coordinated efforts to offer datasets related to Malayalam.

In addition, we explore various machine learning and deep learning algorithms to develop methods to detect fake information effectively. The morphological complexity and the complicated structures of Malayalam words and sentences made the feature extraction and classification model development a challenging task, needing the use of advanced techniques in order to capture the complex aspects of the language effectively. The state-of-the-art multilingual BERT models were utilized to transform the input sequence into embeddings, whereas Support Vector Machine (SVM), Random Forest (RF), Logistic Regression (LR), Decision Tree (DT) and K-Nearest Neighbour (KNN) classification algorithms were employed for categorizing a fake content into different classes.

2 Literature review

(Raja et al., 2023b) employed two datasets for fine-tuning their pre-trained model. The first dataset is the English ISOT(Ahmed et al., 2018) dataset, consisting of actual and factual news articles. The second dataset is a new collection comprising regional languages such as Telugu, Kannada, Tamil, and Malayalam. For every news article represented by $(D = \{(x_1, y_1), (x_2, y_2), \ldots, (x_n, y_n)\})$, where x represents the news and y its corresponding label, the authors utilized a pre-trained mBERT or XLM-R model trained on a large, resourceful language dataset. This pre-trained model was fine-tuned for the new dataset D using an adaptive fine-tuning algorithm. The main approach involves transfer learning, taking a pre-trained model from one domain and adapting it to the target domain. The authors aimed to optimize the fine-tuning process and develop a model that maximizes the accuracy of detecting fake news in dataset D.

According to the study by (Raja et al., 2024), the Dravidian Languages, including Tamil, Telugu, Malayalam, and Kannada, have unique characteristics. The words are formed by adding affixes to the root word, making it challenging to find the meaning of the words without knowing the context in which they are used. The paper leverages the strengths of dilated temporal convolutional networks (DTCN) and integrates them with Bidirectional LSTM (BiLSTM) and a contextualized attention mechanism (CAM). The DTCN is employed to capture temporal dependencies, BiLSTM to seize long-range dependencies, and CAM to emphasize important information from the news while neglecting irrelevant content. The authors applied an adaptive cyclical learning rate with an early stopping mechanism to improve the model's convergence rate and accuracy. The dataset consists of news articles represented by (d_1, y_1), (d_2, y_2), ..., (d_n, y_n), where d represents the article and y its corresponding label. The researchers constructed a model to predict the label for each news article.

A Bala and P Krishnamurthy employed the MuRIL model in (Bala and Krishnamurthy, 2023) to detect fake news. MuRIL was refined by supervised learning on a handpicked dataset of labelled posts, comments, and keywords in Dravidian languages. The process of fine-tuning allowed the algorithm to distinguish between true and fake news. The MuRIL model examines textual information in each news to anticipate the classification and extracts semantic features. With the help of a sizable corpus of data from several Indian languages, MuRIL is a transformer-based architecture that has been pre-trained to capture linguistic subtleties and semantic correlations unique to the languages in the dataset.

(Balaji et al., 2023) proposed that data preprocessing is important for fake news detection since the appropriate form of data is required for training ML models. First data cleaning is done to eliminate punctuations, special characters and other HTML elements that don't add anything to the meaning of the news. The text is then separated into distinct words to produce a structured representation. Words are shortened to their base form using stemming processes to maintain consistency. Finally the text is vectorized before feeding it to the machine learning model. Various models like the BERT, ALBERT, XLNET, M-BERT are used in this paper and M-BERT comes out on top with an accuracy of 0.74. M-BERT is a version of BERT which supports multilingual text feasibly. It is trained on a combination of monolingual and multilingual data by which it gains the ability to produce language representations of languages from different origins. Fine-tuning the model on task-specific labelled data across many languages is a necessary step.

(Coelho et al., 2023) deployed fake news detection models for Malayalam. In this work, the punctuations and special characters were removed in data pre-processing and the text is converted into its equivalent English form which is useful for classification. An ensemble machine learning classifier was proposed in this paper to identify fake news.

(Raja et al., 2023a) developed a XLM-R model for fake detection in Malayalam. The XLM-RoBERTa model is also a multilingual variant of the BERT based transformer model. It consist of self-attention mechanisms which enables it to learn contextualized word embeddings which helps in capturing relationships between words in a sentence, ultimately tuning the model to encode the semantic information of the input text effectively. The model is fine-tuned using an annotated Malayalam fake news dataset. It allows the model to learn specific patterns and linguistic characteristics of fake news in Malayalam. The news is labelled genuine or fake by augmenting the model with a classification layer on the top. The parameters of the model are updated during the fine-tuning process. Bayesian optimizer wass used to find the optimal hyperparameters for the deep learning based model which maximizes the model's performance. The proposed XML-RoBERTa model achieved a F1-Score of 87%.

According to (Oshikawa et al., 2020), the fake news detection problem is often viewed as a classification problem rather than a regression problem since regression gives us an output of a numeric score of the integrity of the data. Pre-processing steps followed in this work includes tokenization, stemming and weighting of words. The input texts were converted into features using TF-IDF. Though various Machine Learning models were used for fake news detection, the Neural Network based model achieved the highest accuracy in detection. Attention mechanisms are incorporated into neural networks to boost their performance and accuracy.

(Thota et al., 2018) implemented three different variations of neural networks. The first model utilizes TF-IDF with Dense Neural Networks. This model takes the TF-IDF vector of the headline pair's cosine similarity, a standard practice to measure similarity between non-zero vectors, as input and predicts the output. The vectors are passed to the dense network layers, and the final dense layer predicts the output label for the text news. The second model employs a Bag of Words vector with Deep Neural Networks (DNN). It uses a simplified vector space embeddings to represent text. The third model incorporated a pre-trained word embedding model trained using neural networks. For this neural network architecture, Word2Vec was employed to represent words in a 300-dimensional vector space, and these embeddings are fed into the classification model. Among these, the TF-IDF-based model was the best-performing model. To address the potential overfitting of the neural network model, various regularization techniques such as L2 and early stopping, are deployed to improve generalization. This model has demonstrated superior performance compared to existing model architectures, achieving an accuracy of 94% on the test data.

3 Fake news dataset in Malayalam

Even though there are datasets available for checking whether news is fake, there are no datasets available in Malayalam to check how much misinformation a news carries, which motivated our research. Therefore, we refer to various fact-checking websites to prepare an authentic dataset to measure different levels of misinformation in the news. This process posed different challenges.

- **The selection of the fact-checking websites**: We addressed this issue by selecting the fact-checking pages of the mainstream media in Malayalam. The list of websites from where the data was collected are listed below
  - Newsmeter [1]
  - India Today Malayalam [2]
  - Malayalam Factcrescendo [3]
  - Asianet News [4]
- **Annotation**: Instead of manually annotating each piece of news, we select the labels provided by the fact-checking websites. This work aims to classify the different classes of fake news. Instead of labelling news as either true or fake, we decided to collect the news, which is categorized into different degrees of falseness. The labels we used to classify are False, Partly False, Mostly False, and Half True. We labelled the news as False when the entire news is untrue, Partly False when

[1] https://newsmeter.in/fact-check-malayalam
[2] https://malayalam.indiatoday.in/fact-check/
[3] https://www.malayalam.factcrescendo.com/
[4] https://www.asianetnews.com/fact-check

Classes	Train set	Test set
Half True	145	24
False	1,251	149
Partly False	44	14
Mostly False	242	63
Total	1,682	250

Table 1: Class-wise distribution of the dataset

the news contains a mixture of accurate and inaccurate information with a small portion being false, Mostly False when the news is false but contains some true information, and Half True when the news has equal true and untrue information.

- **The authenticity of the annotation**: To ensure that the labels are not biased, we cross-checked the fake category of each piece of news with different fact-checking websites.
- **Identification of the fake news**: Instead of going through every fact-checking website, we searched specific keywords and collected the fact-checking results.
- **Redundancy in data**: Data was repeated as the news was collected from various sources. The sources were limited; some were labelled as misleading rather than clearly true, partially true, or false.
- **Morphological complexity of Malayalam words**: The morphological richness and complexity of the Malayalam language made it challenging to identify keywords for news retrieval. We had to search for different word forms to collect different news sets about one particular keyword.

The collected dataset was divided into train data and test data. The class-wise statistics of the train and test datasets are given in Table 1.

4 Methodology

The Block diagram of the proposed model is shown in Figure 1 and the steps involved in the proposed methodology are described below.

The classification of fake news into distinct sub-categories was modelled as a text classification problem in which a sequence of tokens served as the input, and a class label representing a fake news category was considered the output. We employed BERT-based multilingual models to generate embeddings for the input token sequence. Besides, machine learning classifiers were utilised to determine the function that converts the embedding into the appropriate labels.

The collected data was divided into training and test sets. Both training and test datasets were converted into vector representation using BERT-based models. We used multilingual sentence transformers for transforming input text sequences into embeddings. The resultant features and their labels were used for building the classifier. Since the number of data points is less in the training data, we decided to implement a cross-validation-based grid search approach to fix the optimal hyperparameters of each classification model. The best estimators were used to train the model using the training data.

5 Experiments

This section provides an overview of the five experiments conducted. We considered four multilingual BERT models and one Malayalam-specific BERT model for generating the embeddings. The input sequences were fed into the sentence transformer designed using the abovementioned BERT models to generate the feature vector. The multilingual BERT models considered for this work are - BERT multilingual-cased, MuRIL, LaBSE, and indicBERT. The classification of news into different categories was modelled using five different classification algorithms - Support Vector Machine (SVM), Random Forest (RF), Decision Tree (DT), Logistic Regression (LR) and K-Nearest Neighbor (KNN) (Premjith et al., 2019). The following subsections explain the performance of different classifiers with each embedding model.

The first experiment uses the Malayalam BERT model (Joshi, 2022). This model is trained on publicly available Malayalam monolingual datasets. The performance of each classifier with the embeddings generated using the Malayalam BERT model is given in Table 2.

The training dataset is highly imbalanced, and most of the data belong to the FALSE category. This imbalance may force the model to be biased towards the majority class. Therefore, accuracy cannot be trusted as the best metric to evaluate the performance of a classification model. Consequently, we considered the macro F1 score as the metric to assess the prediction capabilities of each classifier. Table 2 shows that RF exhibited the high-

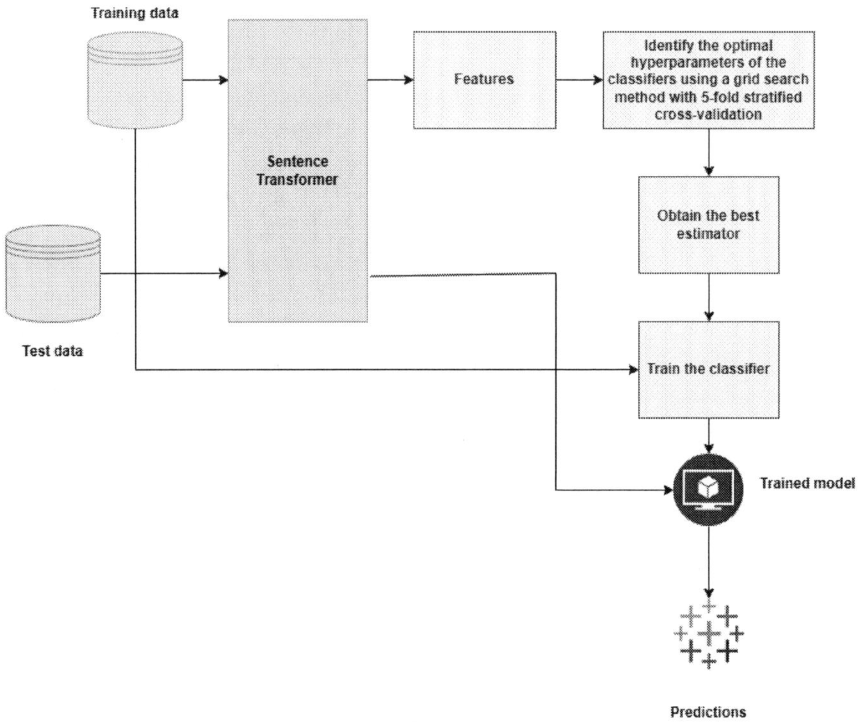

Figure 1: Flow diagram for the proposed fake news classification methodology

Classifier	Accuracy	Precision	Recall	F1 score
SVM	63.69	0.4154	0.3253	**0.3392**
RF	**74.40**	0.4358	0.2551	0.2231
LR	66.39	0.3046	0.3070	0.3052
DT	64.88	0.3235	0.3018	0.3094
KNN	72.32	0.3117	0.2638	0.2497

Table 2: Performance of the malayalam-bert model

Classifier	Accuracy	Precision	Recall	F1 score
SVM	**74.10**	0.1852	0.2500	0.2128
RF	**74.10**	0.1852	0.2500	0.2128
LR	65.17	0.3374	0.3346	**0.3353**
DT	63.69	0.2653	0.2675	0.2658
KNN	72.61	0.2615	0.2572	0.2360

Table 3: Performance of the multilingual-cased model

Classifier	Accuracy	Precision	Recall	F1 score
SVM	63.98	0.2775	0.2843	0.2799
RF	**74.40**	0.4358	0.2551	0.2231
LR	68.75	0.3310	0.3162	**0.3156**
DT	66.66	0.2875	0.2869	0.2846
KNN	73.51	0.2712	0.2561	0.2312

Table 4: Performance of the MuRIL model

Classifier	Accuracy	Precision	Recall	F1 score
SVM	**74.10**	0.1852	0.2500	0.2128
RF	**74.40**	0.4358	0.2586	0.2298
LR	67.55	0.3542	0.3308	**0.3393**
DT	62.79	0.2910	0.2909	0.2907
KNN	72.61	0.2784	0.2613	0.2442

Table 5: Performance of the LaBSE model

Classifier	Accuracy	Precision	Recall	F1 score
SVM	63.98	0.2789	0.2796	**0.2786**
RF	**74.40**	0.4358	0.2551	0.2231
LR	66.36	0.2850	0.2795	**0.2786**
DT	64.88	0.2644	0.2627	0.2600
KNN	71.72	0.2321	0.2501	0.2266

Table 6: Performance of the IndicBERT model

est accuracy of 74.40%, followed by KNN with an accuracy of 72.32%. However, SVM achieved the maximum F1 score of 0.3392. In the case of RF and KNN, the precision was higher than recall, which means that the model was more accurate in predicting the positive class but failed to capture all other relevant results. The optimal hyperparameters for building the SVM model are $C = 0.1, gamma = 1, kernel = linear$. The RF classifier was built using 200 estimators.

In the second experiment, we used the multilingual BERT base-cased model (Devlin et al., 2018) to compute the vector representation for the input data. This model is pre-trained on a large corpus of multilingual data in a self-supervised fashion. It is pre-trained with data collected from 104 languages. The performance of each classifier is shown in Table 3.

The best-performing classifiers in terms of accuracy are SVM and RF. Both models achieved an accuracy of 74.10%. Nevertheless, LR demonstrated the best performance with multilingual BERT-based features regarding the F1 score with an F1 score of 0.3353. The optimal hyperparameters for developing the LR model were $C = 0.1, penalty = L2$, whereas SVM and RF were built using the parameters $C = 10, gamma = 0.1, kernel = RBF$ and $n_estimators = 50$, respectively.

The third experiment used the MuRIL (Khanuja et al., 2021) model for generating the embedding. This model is pre-trained using 17 Indian languages. This model is pre-trained on translation and their transliterated counterparts. Table 4 describes the performance of different classifiers in categorizing the news into different classes with MuRIL embeddings. In this experiment, RF attained the highest accuracy of 74.40%, and LR exhibited the best F1 score of 0.3156. The RF model was trained using 100 estimators, whereas we considered the hyperparameters $C = 0.1, penalty = L2$ for training the model.

In the fourth experiment, the LaBSE model was used to transform the input text into embeddings. This model is trained and optimized for bilingual sentence pairs. The performance scores of different classifiers used in this experiment are shown in Table 5. Here, both SVM and RF showed the best accuracy with a score of 74.10%, whereas LR achieved the best F1 score of 0.3353. The SVM, RF and LR were trained using the hyperparameters $C = 1, gamma = 1, kernel = RBF$, 50 estimators and $C = 0.1, penalty = L2$, respectively.

In the fifth experiment, we utilized IndicBERT (Kakwani et al., 2020), a multilingual model pre-trained on 12 major Indian languages. The result of this experiment is shown in Table 6. It is observed that RF obtained an accuracy of 74.40%, and SVM and LR scored the highest F1 score of 0.2786. RF model consisted of 50 estimators, whereas SVM and LR models were built using the hyperparameters $C = 0.1, gamma = 1, kernel = Linear$ and $C = 0.1, penalty = L2$, respectively.

Among all the classifiers, LR achieved the highest F1 score with four feature embeddings, and SVM demonstrated the best performance with Malayalam BERT, with a score of 0.3392. The best score attained by LR was 0.3393 LaBSE embeddings. LR exhibited comparable performance with an F1 score of 0.3052 with Malayalam BERT embeddings.

6 Conclusion

This paper proposes a new dataset to categorize fake news in Malayalam into different fake categories based on the degree of falseness. To the best of our knowledge, this is the first dataset curated for fake news classification in Malayalam. In addition, we developed baseline models for identifying the fake category of false news in this work using various multilingual BERT models and machine learning classifiers. Among all the models, the logistic regression model trained over LaBSE features was the best, with an F1 score of 0.3393. The high imbalance in the training data significantly affected the model's performance.

The dataset exhibits a significant imbalance, potentially resulting in model biases favouring the majority class. Potential solutions to this problem include implementing cost-sensitive learning and oversampling techniques; these represent the future trajectories of this research.

Acknowledgements

The author Bharathi Raja Chakravarthi was supported in part by a research grant from Science Foundation Ireland (SFI) under Grant Number SFI/12/RC/2289_P2(Insight_2).

References

Hadeer Ahmed, Issa Traore, and Sherif Saad. 2018. Detecting opinion spams and fake news using text classification. *SECURITY AND PRIVACY*, 1(1):e9.

Nihel Fatima Baarir and Abdelhamid Djeffal. 2021. Fake news detection using machine learning. In *2020 2nd International Workshop on Human-Centric Smart Environments for Health and Well-being (IHSH)*, pages 125–130.

Abhinaba Bala and Parameswari Krishnamurthy. 2023. AbhiPaw@ DravidianLangTech: Fake news detection in Dravidian languages using multilingual BERT. In *Proceedings of the Third Workshop on Speech and Language Technologies for Dravidian Languages*, pages 235–238, Varna, Bulgaria. INCOMA Ltd., Shoumen, Bulgaria.

Varsha Balaji, Shahul Hameed T, and Bharathi B. 2023. NLP_SSN_CSE@DravidianLangTech: Fake news detection in Dravidian languages using transformer models. In *Proceedings of the Third Workshop on Speech and Language Technologies for Dravidian Languages*, pages 133–139, Varna, Bulgaria. INCOMA Ltd., Shoumen, Bulgaria.

Murari Choudhary, Shashank Jha, Deepika Saxena, and Ashutosh Singh. 2021. A review of fake news detection methods using machine learning.

Sharal Coelho, Asha Hegde, Kavya G, and Hosahalli Lakshmaiah Shashirekha. 2023. MUCS@DravidianLangTech2023: Malayalam fake news detection using machine learning approach. In *Proceedings of the Third Workshop on Speech and Language Technologies for Dravidian Languages*, pages 288–292, Varna, Bulgaria. INCOMA Ltd., Shoumen, Bulgaria.

Arkadipta De, Dibyanayan Bandyopadhyay, Baban Gain, and Asif Ekbal. 2022. A transformer-based approach to multilingual fake news detection in low-resource languages. *ACM Transactions on Asian and Low-Resource Language Information Processing*, 21:1–20.

Jacob Devlin, Ming-Wei Chang, Kenton Lee, and Kristina Toutanova. 2018. BERT: pre-training of deep bidirectional transformers for language understanding. *CoRR*, abs/1810.04805.

Anjali Jain, Avinash Shakya, Harsh Khatter, and Amit Gupta. 2019. A smart system for fake news detection using machine learning. pages 1–4.

Raviraj Joshi. 2022. L3Cube-HindBERT and DevBERT: Pre-Trained BERT Transformer models for Devanagari based Hindi and Marathi languages. *arXiv preprint arXiv:2211.11418*.

Divyanshu Kakwani, Anoop Kunchukuttan, Satish Golla, Gokul N.C., Avik Bhattacharyya, Mitesh M. Khapra, and Pratyush Kumar. 2020. IndicNLPSuite: Monolingual Corpora, Evaluation Benchmarks and Pre-trained Multilingual Language Models for Indian Languages. In *Findings of EMNLP*.

Simran Khanuja, Diksha Bansal, Sarvesh Mehtani, Savya Khosla, Atreyee Dey, Balaji Gopalan, Dilip Kumar Margam, Pooja Aggarwal, Rajiv Teja Nagipogu, Shachi Dave, Shruti Gupta, Subhash Chandra Bose Gali, Vish Subramanian, and Partha Talukdar. 2021. MuRIL: Multilingual Representations for Indian Languages.

Jayashree Nair, S S Akhil, and V Harisankar. 2022. Fake news detection model for regional language. In *2022 IEEE 7th International conference for Convergence in Technology (I2CT)*, pages 1–7.

Ray Oshikawa, Jing Qian, and William Yang Wang. 2020. A survey on natural language processing for fake news detection.

B Premjith, KP Soman, M Anand Kumar, and D Jyothi Ratnam. 2019. Embedding linguistic features in word embedding for preposition sense disambiguation in English—Malayalam machine translation context. *Recent advances in computational intelligence*, pages 341–370.

Eduri Raja, Badal Soni, and Sami Kumar Borgohain. 2023a. nlpt malayalm@DravidianLangTech : Fake news detection in Malayalam using optimized XLM-RoBERTa model. In *Proceedings of the Third Workshop on Speech and Language Technologies for Dravidian Languages*, pages 186–191, Varna, Bulgaria. INCOMA Ltd., Shoumen, Bulgaria.

Eduri Raja, Badal Soni, and Samir Kumar Borgohain. 2023b. Fake news detection in Dravidian languages using transfer learning with adaptive finetuning. *Engineering Applications of Artificial Intelligence*, 126:106877.

Eduri Raja, Badal Soni, Candy Lalrempuii, and Samir Kumar Borgohain. 2024. An adaptive cyclical learning rate based hybrid model for Dravidian fake news detection. *Expert Systems with Applications*, 241:122768.

Aswini Thota, Priyanka Tilak, Simrat Ahluwalia, and Nibrat Lohia. 2018. Fake News Detection: A Deep Learning Approach. *SMU Data Science Review*, 1(3):10.

Social Media Fake News Classification Using Machine Learning Algorithm

Girma Yohannis Bade, Olga Kolesnikova , Grigori Sidorov,
José Luis Oropeza
Instituto Politécnico Nacional (IPN), Centro de Investigación en Computación (CIC),
Mexico City, Mexico
Correspondence : `girme2005@gmail.com`

Abstract

The rise of social media has facilitated easier communication, information sharing, and current affairs updates. However, the prevalence of misleading and deceptive content, commonly referred to as fake news, poses a significant challenge. This paper focuses on the classification of fake news in Malayalam, a Dravidian language, utilizing natural language processing (NLP) techniques. To develop a model, we employed a random forest machine learning method on a dataset provided by a shared task(DravidianLangTech@EACL 2024)[1]. When evaluated by the separate test dataset, our developed model achieved a 0.71 macro F1 measure.

1 Introduction

The rise in usage of social media sites has made it easier for people to communicate with one another. Social media users can converse, share information, and keep up with current affairs. However, a lot of the current material that has surfaced on social media is misleading and, in certain situations, is an attempt to deceive users. This kind of stuff is frequently referred to as false news. Any incorrect or deceptive information that purports to be newsworthy is referred to as fake news (Subramanian et al., 2023; Yigezu et al., 2023e). Customers and retailers have both been impacted by fake reviews. Furthermore, in 2016, the issue of false news came to light, particularly in the wake of the previous US presidential election. Since both fake reviews and fake news involve producing and disseminating incorrect information or opinions, they are closely related phenomena (Ahmed et al., 2018).

The rapid expansion of internet news sources has made it exceedingly challenging to distinguish between fraudulent and true information (Bade, 2021; Yigezu et al., 2023d). Because of this, fake news is now widely spread and very difficult to evaluate and confirm. Discussing the subject case by case indeed presents a significant difficulty to both the public and the government (Yigezu et al., 2023b). For this reason, a system for fact-checking rumors and statements needs to be implemented, especially for those that receive thousands of views and likes before being disproved and disputed by reliable sources. Similarly, humans are incapable of identifying all of these false reports. Machine learning classifiers are therefore required to automatically identify these false news items (Ahmed et al., 2021). Even though a range of machine-learning methods have been employed to identify and categorize false information, these methods have limitations in terms of accuracy (Fayaz et al., 2022; Yigezu et al., 2023c). Several factors, including imbalanced datasets, ineffective parameter tuning, and bad feature selection, might be blamed for the low accuracy (Hakak et al., 2021).

Although numerous studies are in charge of taking fake news countermeasures in English, languages other than English are also taking advantage of natural language processing(NLP) to mitigate the growing challenge of their language aspect. In this regard, the Dravidian Language is gaining popularity in leveraging the NLP task including fake news classification, sentiment analysis, hate speech detection, and stress identification in general. In particular, this study focuses on the social media fake news classification in the Malayalam language which is one of the Dravidian languages. The golden standard dataset was offered to us by the task organizer as a shared task(DravidianLangTech@EACL 2024)(Subramanian et al., 2023). Via Codalab, we are given the datasets containing YouTube comments in the Malayalam language annotated for fake news detection. In this regard, we have used a random forest machine-learning model and developed a Malayalam language fake news classifier as intended in

[1] `https://codalab.lisn.upsaclay.fr/competitions/16055`

Proceedings of the Fourth Workshop on Speech, Vision, and Language Technologies for Dravidian Languages, pages 24–29
March 22, 2024

the shared task competition. The rest of the paper details the related works, system or methodology descriptions,the results generated, and the recommendations for future works.

2 Related Works

Several machine and deep learning algorithms have been used in different articles to detect and analyze bogus news on social media sites (Yigezu et al., 2023a). According to the article proposed in (Hakak et al., 2021), the ensemble classification had a higher accuracy in detecting fake news when compared to the state-of-the-art. Important features are collected from the fake news datasets by the suggested model, and these features are then classified using an ensemble model made up of three well-known machine learning models: Decision Tree, Random Forest, and Extra Tree Classifier.

A study (Kareem and Awan, 2019)was conducted to identify fake news in Pakistani media, as it is a challenging process to classify. The popular news website scrape was served as the source of the dataset for this investigation. 344 news stories that have been manually classified as True or Fake make up the generated corpus. It has employed seven distinct supervised Machine Learning (ML) classification methods for the result comparison, in addition to two feature extraction strategies (Term Frequency (TF) and Term Frequency-Inverse Document Frequency (TF-IDF). K-Nearest Neighbors (KNN) provided 70% accuracy, whereas logistic regression produced 69% accuracy, making it the highest-performing classifier.

To categorize and identify the bogus news on multiple social media sites, algorithms such as Naive Bayes, Support Vector Machines, Passive Aggressive Classifier, Random Forest, BERT, LSTM, and Logistic Regression were employed. The work is based on an ISOT dataset consisting of 44,898 news items that were collected from multiple sources and pre-processed using count vectorizer and TF-IDF. The SVM is deemed to be among the most accurate algorithms for spotting false information on social media (Kumar et al., 2023).

Deep learning's growth is greatly aided by its widespread use. Three types of neural network techniques: convolution filtering-based neural network approaches, sequential analysis-based neural network approaches, and attention mechanism-based neural network approaches can be distinguished from the model structure of the research work that now exist (Tash et al., 2023; Bade and Afaro, 2018). But nearly all of them were created with scenarios in a single language in mind, without taking into account mixed-lingual contexts. The article(Guo et al., 2023) proposed a unique false news detection model for the context of mixed languages through a multiscale transformer to completely capture the semantic information of the text, bridging this gap by extending the basic pretraining language processing model transformer into the multiscale format. Additionally, it improved accuracy in mixed language contexts by roughly 2%–10% as compared to baseline models that are frequently utilized.

The multi-modal transformer employing two-level visual characteristics (MTTV) was suggested as an alternative to text for the identification of false news(Wang et al., 2023). Firstly, news texts and photos are universally modeled as sequences that may be processed by a transformer. To enhance the use of news photographs, two-level visual features global feature and entity level feature are employed. Second, it creates a multi-modal transformer that expands the transformer paradigm for natural language processing, enabling complete interaction and semantic relationship capturing between multi-modal data. Furthermore, it suggested a scalable classifier to address the issue of class imbalance and enhance the classification balance of fine-grained false news detection. Comprehensive tests on two publicly available datasets show that our approach outperformed the state-of-the-art techniques by a significant margin.

Even though the majority of studies have been conducted on binary fake news classification tasks, the work (Shushkevich et al., 2023) addresses a more realistic scenario by assessing a corpus with unknown themes through multiclass classification, encompassing true, false, partially false, and other categories. Three BERT-based models: SBERT, RoBERTa, and mBERT are explored; artificial data generated by ChatGPT is used to improve results for class balance; and a two-step binary classification process is employed to improve outcomes. The testing results indicate that, while it is an optimal performance in comparison to past accomplishments, it still requires refinement to remain at the forefront of technology.

3 System Description

In this section, we offer thorough information regarding the dataset and the details of experimental tools. Moreover, it dives into the format of datasets, preprocessing, and experimental environmental tools to develop the proposed model.

3.1 Datasets

In the real world, the problems are always existing until the solutions are investigated. To investigate solutions for computational linguistic challenges, the availability of data is crucial (Bade, 2021; Bade and Afaro, 2018). The dataset for this particular task was provided on Codalab by the Shared_task (DravidianLangTech@EACL 2024) organizer (B et al., 2024). There are two subtasks provided to participate in this competition.Task_1 is to classify the given social media dataset that was prepared for this aim into fake or original and Task_2 is the Fake News Detection from Malayalam News(False, Half True, Mostly False, Partly False, and Mostly True). Among the offered tasks, we participated only in the first task(Task_1) based on our interests (Subramanian et al., 2023, 2024). The dataset is arranged in three different lists training, development, and test(without label) set. The training and development data sets are made available when we register for the competition on the Codalab and the test set was released when ten days left for the run submission deadline.

Table 1: The overview of dataset offer

No	Text	Label	Dataset	size
1	Masha Allah	Fake	Training	3257
2	à´¬à´¿à´œàµ	Original		
3	Well planned... China.	Fake	Development	815
4	à´ªà´°à´¨à´¾à´±à	Original		
5	Shame for entire Woman	—	Test	1019
6	à´ªàµà´°à´µà´¾à´¸à´¿	—		

The Table1 shows us three things:1) how the sample of the dataset and its class variable look like,2) how the code-mixed writing is taking place, and 3) how the test dataset is given without the class label. In the case of training and development datasets, the class variable or dependent variable is given with their features, however, in the case of test dates there is no class label given because it is expected that the model would predict its class label how it was in training data.

3.2 Preprocessing

Preprocessing is the process of preparing raw data for machine learning algorithms by cleaning, converting, and organizing the data and rendering it to the machine. It is the vital stage that fills in the gaps between raw data and useful insights because raw data is rarely in an ideal state (Bade and Seid, 2018). During the data preparation phase of machine learning tasks, there are typical or standard activities that we should use. The following are some among others.

Importing dependency libraries:- There are two libraries that we must always bring in. A library containing mathematical functions is called NumPy and the library used to import and manage the 'CSV' data sets is called Pandas.

Loading the data set:- In most cases, data sets are offered in a csv format. Tabular data is stored in plain text in a CSV file. In a file, every line represents a data record. To read a local CSV file as a data frame, the pandas library's (read_csv) function was utilized.

Handling Missing Data:- In real-world datasets, handling missing data is a prevalent difficulty. Preprocessing methods like imputation and the removal of missing data or null values ensure that the model is fed accurate and comprehensive data. For a variety of reasons, data may be missing, and it must be handled to prevent our machine-learning model from performing worse. In addition, we used "raw['category'].fillna(0, inplace=True)" to handle empty strings of class labels.

Data Cleaning:- is finding and fixing inaccuracies or flaws in the data.

Handling Outliers:- Anomalies that drastically depart from the average might cause distortions in the process of learning. Preprocessing techniques such as transformation or scaling lessen the negative effects of outliers on model performance.

Data Encoding:- Since machine learning algorithms usually operate on numerical data, it is necessary to properly encode our text inputs in numerical equivalent. To do so we have specifically used the TF-IDF text vectorization technique. It preserves the semantics and instance positions in addition to converting the provided text into a numeric representation. However, in the case of converting 'class label', we used the "to_numeric()" function known as "raw['category'] = pd.to_numeric(raw['category'], errors='coerce')"

3.3 Model Selection and Experimentation

The selected machine learning model for this study is a random forest. This is because several decision trees are combined in a random forest, an ensemble learning technique to produce predictions that are more reliable and accurate (Tonja et al., 2022). In a random forest, every decision tree is trained using a random subset of features and a random subset of the data (bootstrap samples). The diversity among the individual trees is increased and overfitting is lessened by this randomization (Yigezu et al., 2023b). During prediction, the ultimate result is established by combining all of the trees' predictions, either by average (for regression) or by majority voting (for classification). The capacity to manage complicated datasets, high-dimensional data, and non-linear interactions is a well-known feature of random forests. They are also frequently utilized in machine learning applications and are less prone to overfitting than a single decision tree.

Experimental setup:- This section discusses the details of the developmental tool and the dependency libraries we used. For this research, we used Jupyter Notebook3 which is the Integrated Development Environment(IDE) of Python. After the tool setup was finished, we imported the four basic dependency libraries known as pandas, TfidfVectorizer, RandomForest, Joblib. Among those, the first three(pandas, TfidfVectorizer, RandomForest) are found in the Sklearn module. Pandas is used to read CSV files from the local drive to a Python-run environment, TfidfVectorizer is for converting text data inputs into a numerical representation, and Random-Forest is the principal algorithm to train the input data based on the predefined class. Finally, joblib is a standalone module for saving the trained model for later use.

4 Result and Discussion

The Random Forest based developed model classified the test dataset into two classes as they present in training data.

Table 2: Class label test data overview of manually or by annotator classified and machine or our model classified classification distribution.

Class	Manually classified	**Machine classified**
Original	512	**628**
Fake	507	**391**
Total	1019	**1019**

From the Table 2 can understand that 116 instances of the class 'Fake' were incorrectly classified into the 'Original ' class category. Here 'manually classified' in column_2 refers to the answer key that has been released after the competition is over, whereas the 'machine classified' in column _3 refers to our model. The test output was sent to the organizers to test the performance of the model in macro F1 metrics. According to the result published, our model has achieved 0.71 macro F1. It is also a promising result to the other code mixed social media posts.

5 Conclusion

In this particular task, we have developed a classifier to classify social media posts into two binary classes, fake and original. The model has used the Random Forest algorithm method. The numeric features are extracted using TF-IDF techniques. The newly developed model has been evaluated with the new unseen test dataset and the results also promising for other code mixed languages.

6 Future work

Since social media posts that classify fake news are very critical, the jobs ought to be transferred to other various languages. Furthermore, by offering additional algorithms for the languages utilized here and expanding the number of dataset sizes, the performance of the suggested model in this study should be enhanced.

Acknowledgements

The work was done with partial support from the Mexican Government through the grant A1-S-47854 of CONACYT, Mexico, grants 20232138, 20231567, and 20232080 of the Secretaría de Investigación y Posgrado of the Instituto Politécnico Nacional, Mexico. The authors thank the CONACYT for the computing resources brought to them through the Plataforma de Aprendizaje Profundo para Tecnologías del Lenguaje of the Laboratorio de Supercómputo of the INAOE, Mexico and acknowledge the support of Microsoft through the Microsoft Latin America PhD Award.

Limitation and Ethics Statement

Finding words outside of one's lexicon or linguistic occurrences that were not taken into consideration during preprocessing are limitations. Code-mixing can bring linguistic variances that the current language processing algorithms may not be able to handle well enough, which could result in incorrect classifications. Future studies could improve the model's performance and generalization capacities by addressing these linguistic issues. Notably, out of all the participating systems, our method achieved the 12th rank in the shared job. Our model performs well in classifying Fake News comments in code-mixed text, even in the face of competition from other participants and obstacles in the competition. Furthermore, our work obeyed the computational ethics[2].

References

Alim Al Ayub Ahmed, Ayman Aljabouh, Praveen Kumar Donepudi, and Myung Suh Choi. 2021. Detecting Fake News using Machine Learning: A systematic literature review. *arXiv preprint arXiv:2102.04458*.

Hadeer Ahmed, Issa Traore, and Sherif Saad. 2018. Detecting opinion spams and fake news using text classification. *Security and Privacy*, 1(1):e9.

Premjth B, Bharathi Raja, Prasanna Kumar Kumaresan, Saranya Rajiakodi, Sai Prashanth Karnati, Sai Rishith Reddy Mangamuru, and Janakiram Chandu. 2024. Findings of the Shared Task on Hate and Offensive Language Detection in Telugu Codemixed Text (HOLD-Telugu). In *Proceedings of the Fourth Workshop on Speech, Vision, and Language Technologies for Dravidian Languages*, Malta. European Chapter of the Association for Computational Linguistics.

Girma Yohannis Bade. 2021. Natural Language Processing and Its Challenges on Omotic Language Group of Ethiopia. *Journal of Computer Science Research*, 3(4):26–30.

Girma Yohannis Bade and Akalu Assefa Afaro. 2018. Object Oriented Software Development for Artificial Intelligence. *American Journal of Software Engineering and Applications*, 7(2):22–24.

Girma Yohannis Bade and Hussien Seid. 2018. Development of Longest-Match Based Stemmer for Texts of Wolaita Language. *vol*, 4:79–83.

Muhammad Fayaz, Atif Khan, Muhammad Bilal, and Sana Ullah Khan. 2022. Machine learning for fake news classification with optimal feature selection. *Soft Computing*, 26(16):7763–7771.

Zhiwei Guo, Qin Zhang, Feng Ding, Xiaogang Zhu, and Keping Yu. 2023. A Novel Fake News Detection Model for Context of Mixed Languages Through Multiscale Transformer. *IEEE Transactions on Computational Social Systems*, pages 1–11.

Saqib Hakak, Mamoun Alazab, Suleman Khan, Thippa Reddy Gadekallu, Praveen Kumar Reddy Maddikunta, and Wazir Zada Khan. 2021. An ensemble machine learning approach through effective feature extraction to classify fake news. *Future Generation Computer Systems*, 117:47–58.

Irfan Kareem and Shahid Mahmood Awan. 2019. Pakistani Media Fake News Classification using Machine Learning Classifiers. In *2019 International Conference on Innovative Computing (ICIC)*, pages 1–6.

Ashish Kumar, M Izharul Hasan Ansari, and Kshatrapal Singh. 2023. A Fake News Classification and Identification Model Based on Machine Learning Approach. In *Information and Communication Technology for Competitive Strategies (ICTCS 2022) Intelligent Strategies for ICT*, pages 473–484. Springer.

Elena Shushkevich, Mikhail Alexandrov, and John Cardiff. 2023. Improving Multiclass Classification of Fake News Using BERT-Based Models and ChatGPT-Augmented Data. *Inventions*, 8(5):112.

Malliga Subramanian, Bharathi Raja Chakravarthi, Kogilavani Shanmugavadivel, Santhiya Pandiyan, Prasanna Kumar Kumaresan, Balasubramanian Palani, Premjith B, Sandhiya Raja, Vanaja, Mithunajha S, Devika K, Hariprasath S.B, Haripriya B, and Vigneshwar E. 2024. Overview of the Second Shared Task on Fake News Detection in Dravidian Languages. In *Proceedings of the Fourth Workshop on Speech, Vision, and Language Technologies for Dravidian Languages*, Malta. European Chapter of the Association for Computational Linguistics.

Malliga Subramanian, Bharathi Raja Chakravarthi, Kogilavani Shanmugavadivel, Santhiya Pandiyan, Prasanna Kumar Kumaresan, Balasubramanian Palani, Muskaan Singh, Sandhiya Raja, Vanaja, and Mithunajha S. 2023. Overview of the Shared Task on Fake News Detection from Social Media Text. In *Proceedings of the Third Workshop on Speech and Language Technologies for Dravidian Languages*, Varna, Bulgaria. Recent Advances in Natural Language Processing.

Moein Tash, Jesus Armenta-Segura, Zahra Ahani, Olga Kolesnikova, Grigori Sidorov, and Alexander Gelbukh. 2023. LIDOMA@ DravidianLangTech: Convolutional Neural Networks for Studying Correlation Between Lexical Features and Sentiment Polarity in Tamil and Tulu Languages. In *Proceedings of the Third Workshop on Speech and Language Technologies for Dravidian Languages*, pages 180–185.

Atnafu Lambebo Tonja, Mesay Gemeda Yigezu, Olga Kolesnikova, Moein Shahiki Tash, Grigori Sidorov, and Alexander Gelbuk. 2022. Transformer-based model for word level language identification in code-mixed kannada-english texts. *arXiv preprint arXiv:2211.14459*.

[2] https://www.aclweb.org/portal/content/acl-code-ethics

Bin Wang, Yong Feng, Xian-cai Xiong, Yong-heng Wang, and Bao-hua Qiang. 2023. Multi-modal transformer using two-level visual features for fake news detection. *Applied Intelligence*, 53(9):10429–10443.

Mesay Gemeda Yigezu, Girma Yohannis Bade, Olga Kolesnikova, Grigori Sidorov, and Alexander Gelbukh. 2023a. Multilingual Hope Speech Detection using Machine Learning.

Mesay Gemeda Yigezu, Selam Kanta, Olga Kolesnikova, Grigori Sidorov, and Alexander Gelbukh. 2023b. Habesha@ DravidianLangTech: Abusive Comment Detection using Deep Learning Approach. In *Proceedings of the Third Workshop on Speech and Language Technologies for Dravidian Languages*, pages 244–249.

Mesay Gemeda Yigezu, Tadesse Kebede, Olga Kolesnikova, Grigori Sidorov, and Alexander Gelbukh. 2023c. Habesha@ DravidianLangTech: Utilizing Deep and Transfer Learning Approaches for Sentiment Analysis. In *Proceedings of the Third Workshop on Speech and Language Technologies for Dravidian Languages*, pages 239–243.

Mesay Gemeda Yigezu, Olga Kolesnikova, Grigori Sidorov, and Alexander Gelbukh. 2023d. Transformer-Based Hate Speech Detection for Multi-Class and Multi-Label Classification.

Mesay Gemeda Yigezu, Moges Ahmed Mehamed, Olga Kolesnikova, Tadesse Kebede Guge, Alexander Gelbukh, and Grigori Sidorov. 2023e. Evaluating the Effectiveness of Hybrid Features in Fake News Detection on Social Media. In *2023 International Conference on Information and Communication Technology for Development for Africa (ICT4DA)*, pages 171–175. IEEE.

Exploring the impact of noise in low-resource ASR for Tamil

Vigneshwar Lakshminarayanan
Walmart Global Tech
vicky18.kb@gmail.com

Emily Prud'hommeaux
Boston College
prudhome@bc.edu

Abstract

The use of deep learning algorithms has resulted in significant progress in automatic speech recognition (ASR). Robust high-accuracy deep neural ASR models typically require thousands or tens of thousands of hours of speech data, but even the strongest models can fail under noisy conditions. Unsurprisingly, the impact of noise on accuracy is more dramatic in low-resource settings. In this paper, we investigate the impact of noise on ASR in a low-resource setting. We explore novel methods for developing noise-robust ASR models using a small dataset for Tamil, a widely-spoken but under-resourced Dravidian language. We add various noises to the audio data to determine the impact of different kinds of noise (e.g., punctuated vs. continuous, mechanical vs natural). We also explore whether different data augmentation methods are better suited to handling different types of noise. Our results show that all noises, regardless of the type, had an impact on ASR performance, and that upgrading the architecture alone could not fully mitigate the impact of noise. In our experiments, SpecAugment, a common data augmentation method for end-to-end neural ASR, was not as helpful as raw data augmentation, in which noise is explicitly added to the training data. Raw data augmentation enhances ASR performance on both clean data and noise-mixed data.

1 Introduction

Automatic Speech Recognition (ASR) technology is widely used in many modern applications for high-resource languages, such as dictation and personal assistants like Amazon Alexa and Apple's Siri (Yoshioka et al., 2012). The success of ASR for these applications is due largely to the emergence of deep learning architectures, improvements in computing hardware, and the large amounts of data available for languages like English and Mandarin (Ruan et al., 2018). The performance of even high-accuracy ASR models, however, remains fragile in the presence of external noise. ASR accuracy degrades even further in low-resource settings.

The motivation for this paper is to research the impact of several types of noise (e.g., continuous vs. punctuated, mechanical vs. natural) on ASR performance in a low-resource setting for the Dravidian language, Tamil. We explore a range of ASR architectures, including traditional GMM-HMM (Reynolds, 2009), SGMM, (Povey et al., 2010), and a hybrid DNN model (Veselý et al., 2013). Additionally, we evaluate whether different data augmentation approaches, such as raw audio augmentation and spectral augmentation (SpecAugment) (Park et al., 2019), are particularly well suited to different types of noise. We explore these questions using a low-resource dataset for Tamil provided by SpeechOcean.com and Microsoft for a low-resource ASR challenge in Interspeech 2018 (Srivastava et al., 2018). We observe that all types of noises, regardless of the acoustic model architecture, degrade ASR performance. Although not entirely surprising, we also find that raw audio augmentation outperforms the popular SpecAugment (Park et al., 2019) data augmentation method on clean data as well as noise-mixed data.

2 Previous Work

There is some prior work on using noise-mixed data to make ASR more robust to noise and other external conditions, but most of this work focuses on high-resource languages. Pervaiz et al. (2020) provided a comparative study on various acoustic and deep learning models, creating robust models in a noisy environment. The models were trained on noise-augmented training data and tested on both clean and noisy data. Hu et al. (2021) proposed a noise-robust speech recognition system called Interactive Feature Fusion Fetwork (IFF-Net) to learn the missing latent information by combin-

Proceedings of the Fourth Workshop on Speech, Vision, and Language Technologies for Dravidian Languages, pages 30–34
March 22, 2024 ©2024 Association for Computational Linguistics

ing the enhanced features and the original noisy features into a fused representation. This system achieved better results on the RATS Channel-A corpus. Shrawankar and Thakare (2013) investigated challenges due to changes in environmental conditions and speaker characteristics and proposed a method to increase the robustness of the ASR systems using speech enhancement techniques like spectral normalization and spectral subtraction. Giurgiu and Kabir (2011) explained how energy normalization and speech re-synthesis can improve the performance of ASR systems by recognizing speech signals in high-noisy conditions (negative SNR). Kinoshita et al. (2020) investigated whether the usage of single-channel time-domain neural networks can help in the reduction of noise and thereby improve the performance. Gupta et al. (2016) proposed a Back-propagation Artificial Neural Network with feature compression using MFCCs yielding improved performance with low signal-to-noise ratios.

3 Data

The data used for the approach is a low-resource Tamil language dataset, provided by SpeechOcean.com and Microsoft for a low-resource ASR challenge for Indian languages at Interspeech 2018 (Srivastava et al., 2018). The dataset consists of read speech and conversations that have been split into utterances and transcribed. The dataset contains a total of 50 hours of recorded speech data in a clean noise-free environment. The dataset is partitioned into 40 hours of speech data for training, 5 hours for testing, and 5 hours for development. We do not use the dev set in our work. All the audio files are 16-bit mono audio sampled at 16kHz. A total of 1900 speakers are included in the dataset. Utterances range in length from 3000ms to 10000ms. There are a total of 42,212 unique utterances in the dataset.

4 Methodology

We explore three different ASR architectures available with the Kaldi speech recognition toolkit (Povey et al., 2011). We note that none of these can be considered state-of-the-art. However, prior work has shown that the Kaldi hybrid DNN is competitive with fine-tuning from multilingual end-to-end models using wav2vec XLSR (Baevski et al., 2020) and Whisper (Radford et al., 2022) in low-resource settings (Jimerson et al., 2023).

GMM-HMM Acoustic Model The Gaussian Mixture Model (GMM) is used to estimate the probability density function used in statistical classification systems (Reynolds, 2009). GMMs are commonly used in statistical ASR to estimate likelihoods of phones (speech sounds) given their acoustic features (typically MFCCs, Mel-frequency cepstral coefficients). Combined with Hidden Markoc Models (HMMs), GMMs are used to estimate the density and maximize the likelihood of the distribution of the speech sounds.

Subspace GMM Acoustic Model A subspace GMM is a type of acoustic model where all the phoneme states use a common Gaussian Mixture Model structure (Povey et al., 2010). The SGMM model is trained by clustering the Gaussians from the GMM-HMM model using the Universal Background Model (UBM). The UBM model is a speaker-independent high order GMM model(Povey et al., 2008). The SGMM models are trained using the UBM model with the state probability distribution functions identical. The final step of the training process is to use the EM algorithm to train the SGMM model using the alignments from the GMM-HMM and also from the SGMM model as well (Povey et al., 2010).

Hybrid Deep Neural Network Acoustic Model As noted above, more recent research has turned from statistical ASR to Deep Neural Networks (DNN). Here we use a relatively simple fully-connected feed-forward DNN using "Karel's implementation" (Veselý et al., 2013) within the Kaldi toolkit. (Povey et al., 2011). The DNN model consists of 6 hidden layers where each hidden layer has 2048 nodes (Cosi, 2015). The DNN model is trained using the features extracted in the GMM-HMM acoustic model described above, yielding a hybrid, rather than end-to-end, architecture.

4.1 Data Augmentation

Data augmentation is the process of including additional data in the ASR training data set with the goal of improving performance by increasing and diversifying the training data. Usually, the added data is created synthetically – either by modifying the existing training data in some way or by generating new data through speech synthesis. Here we focus on modifying the existing data through raw audio augmentation and through spectral augmentation.

Model	Clean WER	Continuous Natural		Punctuated Natural		Continuous Mechanical		Punctuated Mechanical	
		Party	*Restaurant*	*Dog*	*Cat*	*Tap*	*Dishes*	*Truck Horn*	*Door Slam*
GMM-HMM	44.66	66.23	53.20	52.20	48.0	61.2	55.1	50.52	50.21
SGMM	36.15	66.05	47.75	45.19	41.26	54.4	48.18	45.24	44.94
DNN	32.58	56.88	41.18	39.91	35.91	47.18	41.54	39.44	39.12

Table 1: Results for test data mixed with the eight noises using ASR models trained on unaugmented training data.

Augmentation Noise	Model	Clean WER	Continuous Natural		Punctuated Natural		Continuous Mechanical		Punctuated Mechanical	
			Party	*Restaurant*	*Dog*	*Cat*	*Tap*	*Dishes*	*Horn*	*Door Slam*
None	DNN	32.58	56.88	41.18	39.81	35.91	47.18	41.54	39.44	39.12
	SGMM	36.15	66.05	47.75	45.19	41.26	54.4	48.18	45.23	44.94
Tap and Dishes	DNN	31.88	52.84	37.81	38.83	35.09	38.03	36.21	38.16	38.27
	SGMM	36.16	63.42	45.87	44.34	41.02	48.81	44.23	44.38	42.87
Horn and Door	**DNN**	31.47	55.79	39.91	38.83	33.23	35.88	39.17	36.06	35.88
	SGMM	35.19	63.47	46.15	44.13	40.9	52.88	46.67	40.97	40.2
Party and Restaurant	**DNN**	31.85	46.16	35.18	37.35	33.87	38.41	36.91	35.26	38.41
	SGMM	35.84	57.27	41.7	43.1	39.35	50.71	44.48	41.18	44.03
Dog and Cat	**DNN**	31.72	54.85	38.97	34.26	32.07	38.11	39.83	38.24	38.11
	SGMM	35.49	64.0	45.73	38.25	36.59	53.18	46.8	43.89	42.25
SpecAug	**DNN**	35.75	58.86	45.03	46.27	39.53	50.63	43.97	44.81	42.74
	SGMM	43.06	68.56	54.27	51.68	47.11	64.62	54.52	52.32	51.31

Table 2: Results for test data mixed with the eight noises (columns) using ASR models trained on data augmented with the eight different noises (rows), using the two strongest architectures, DNN and SGMM.

4.1.1 Spectral Augmentation

In Spectral Augmentation (SpecAugment) (Park et al., 2019) random sections of the spectral representation of a speech sample are set to zero. It is performed using the log Mel spectrogram of the input speech data. SpecAugment is widely used because of its simplicity and effectiveness within neural end-to-end ASR frameworks. It does not require knowledge of the phonetic content of the speech signal, and because it is applied to a spectral representation and simply involves reducing to zero, it is computationally inexpensive. We note that SpecAugment was designed for end-to-end neural ASR rather than the statistical and hybrid architectures we explore in this paper, so its performance in our models may not be ideal.

4.1.2 Raw Augmentation

Raw augmentation involves directly modifying the raw audio signal. Here, in order to investigate the differential impact of noise, we create a new version of the existing training data by mixing various noise samples (e.g., faucet running, cocktail party chatter, dog barking) into the existing audio. We refer to the resulting datasets as the noise-mixed augmented training sets. A small set of noises, again 16-bit mono sound files samples at 16kHz, were selected from an existing noise dataset. We experimented with two dimensions of noise: mechanical vs. natural, and punctuated vs. continuous. The categorization across these dimensions of the eight sounds used is shown in Table 3. Each sound was decreased by 20dB and then superimposed on the existing data.

	Continuous	**Punctuated**
Mechanical	Tap running Washing dishes	Truck horn Door slam
Natural	Restaurant Party chatter	Dog bark Cat meow

Table 3: The eight sounds used in the project, categorized in the two dimensions: continuous vs. punctuated, and mechanical vs. natural.

For each speech file (utterance) in the test set, there are 9 versions: one clean (i.e., the original data), and one with each of the eight specified noises. The unaugmented training set consists solely of the original training data. There are 4 raw audio augmented (noise-mixed) training sets, one for each of the four categories shown in Table 3. Each of these four training sets consists of one clean copy of each training utterance, one copy of that utterance with one of the relevant noises in that category (e.g., one mechanical continuous noise, tap running) superimposed, and one copy with the other relevant noise in that category (e.g., the other mechanical continuous noise, dish washing) superimposed. Finally, the sixth training set, for exploring SpecAugment, consists of a clean copy of each utterance and a copy that has been passed through SpecAugment with the parameters $F = 30, T = 40, m_T = m_F = 2$.

4.2 Evaluation Metric

We use the standard ASR evaluation metric, Word Error Rate (WER), to assess the performance of the ASR models under different training and testing conditions. WER is calculated as the number of insertions, deletions, and substitutions in the hypothesized ASR output relative to a reference transcript divided by the number of words in the reference transcript. A lower WER indicates higher ASR accuracy.

5 Results

The baseline model was trained using the 40 hours of unaugmented training data and tested using the five hours of test data with no modification or augmentation of the test or train data. In the **Clean WER** column in Table 4, we see the baseline performance for the top-performing architectures discussed above: GMM-HMM, SGMM, and DNN, all trained with the Kaldi ASR toolkit (Povey et al., 2011). The remaining columns of that table show the performance of these models, trained on unaugmented data, on test data with the 8 noises inserted.

We see that, not unsurprisingly, the DNN architecture produces the best (lowest) WER, with the GMM-HMM acoustic model having the weakest performance. The results on test data mixed with the eight noises show that adding noises degrades ASR performance regardless of architecture and sound type, sometimes very dramatically. The cat meowing has the smallest impact of the 8 noises, while party chatter has the largest.

Table 2 shows that the impact of noise can be reduced by augmenting the training data via noise mixing, as desribed above. Every raw audio augmentation approach reduces WER, even if the noise type differs on one or both dimensions. It appears that adding any noise at all to the training data will yield improvements in WER, regardless of the architecture used. Raw audio data augmentation consistently outperforms the widely used SpecAugment augmentation technique, but we note that SpecAugment is intended to be used with neural end-to-end ASR architectures.

6 Conclusion

The goal of this research is to investigate the impact of noise on Automatic Speech Recognition models using a low-resource Tamil language dataset. We investigated the impact of noise by mixing several kinds of noises into the testing data. We evaluated the performance on the baseline model trained exclusively on the original unaugmented data. We discovered that all noises, regardless of whether they were mechanical or natural, continuous or punctuated, degraded ASR performance, and that upgrading the architecture alone was unable to fully mitigate the impact of noise.

To reduce the impact of noise in ASR models, we augmented the training data by superimposing noises from each of the four categories onto the training data. We also employed the popular spectral augmentation technique, SpecAugment to create another augmented training dataset. We discovered that raw data augmentation improves WER, regardless of the combination of noises in the training and test sets. We also found that targeted raw augmentation improves ASR performance: adding noise to the training data that shares one or more characteristics with the noise in the test data yields larger improvements.

Our methods outperform SpecAugment, although we recognize that SpecAugment is designed for end-to-end neural ASR architectures rather than statistical or hybrid architectures like those explored here. In our future work, we plan to investigate these augmentation methods with an end-to-end architectures, with a particular focus on approaches that involve fine-tuning multilingual models to low resource datasets, including wav2vec XLSR (Baevski et al., 2020) and Whisper (Radford et al., 2022).

References

Alexei Baevski, Yuhao Zhou, Abdelrahman Mohamed, and Michael Auli. 2020. wav2vec 2.0: A framework for self-supervised learning of speech representations. In *Advances in Neural Information Processing Systems*, volume 33, pages 12449–12460.

Piero Cosi. 2015. A kaldi-dnn-based asr system for italian. pages 1–5.

Mircea Giurgiu and Ahsanul Kabir. 2011. Improving automatic speech recognition in noise by energy normalization and signal resynthesis. In *2011 IEEE 7th International Conference on Intelligent Computer Communication and Processing*, pages 311–314.

Santosh Gupta, Kishor M. Bhurchandi, and Avinash G. Keskar. 2016. An efficient noise-robust automatic speech recognition system using artificial neural networks. In *2016 International Conference on Communication and Signal Processing (ICCSP)*, pages 1873–1877.

Yuchen Hu, Nana Hou, Chen Chen, and Eng Siong Chng. 2021. Interactive feature fusion for end-to-end noise-robust speech recognition. *arXiv preprint arXiv:2110.05267*.

Robert Jimerson, Zoey Liu, and Emily Prud'hommeaux. 2023. An (unhelpful) guide to selecting the best asr architecture for your under-resourced language. In *Proceedings of the 61st Annual Meeting of the Association for Computational Linguistics (ACL)*, pages 1008–1016.

Keisuke Kinoshita, Tsubasa Ochiai, Marc Delcroix, and Tomohiro Nakatani. 2020. Improving noise robust automatic speech recognition with single-channel time-domain enhancement network. In *ICASSP 2020 - 2020 IEEE International Conference on Acoustics, Speech and Signal Processing (ICASSP)*, pages 7009–7013.

Daniel S. Park, William Chan, Yu Zhang, Chung-Cheng Chiu, Barret Zoph, Ekin Dogus Cubuk, and Quoc V. Le. 2019. Specaugment: A simple data augmentation method for automatic speech recognition. In *INTERSPEECH*.

Ayesha Pervaiz, Fawad Hussain, Humayun Israr, Muhammad Ali Tahir, Fawad Riasat Raja, Naveed Khan Baloch, Farruh Ishmanov, and Yousaf Bin Zikria. 2020. Incorporating noise robustness in speech command recognition by noise augmentation of training data. *Sensors (Basel, Switzerland)*, 20.

Daniel Povey, Lukšš Burget, Mohit Agarwal, Pinar Akyazi, Kai Feng, Arnab Ghoshal, Ondřej Glembek, Nagendra Kumar Goel, Martin Karafiát, Ariya Rastrow, Richard C. Rose, Petr Schwarz, and Samuel Thomas. 2010. Subspace gaussian mixture models for speech recognition. In *2010 IEEE International Conference on Acoustics, Speech and Signal Processing*, pages 4330–4333.

Daniel Povey, Stephen M. Chu, and Balakrishnan Varadarajan. 2008. Universal background model based speech recognition. In *2008 IEEE International Conference on Acoustics, Speech and Signal Processing*, pages 4561–4564.

Daniel Povey, Arnab Ghoshal, Gilles Boulianne, Lukas Burget, Ondrej Glembek, Nagendra Goel, Mirko Hannemann, Petr Motlicek, Yanmin Qian, Petr Schwarz, et al. 2011. The kaldi speech recognition toolkit. In *IEEE 2011 workshop on automatic speech recognition and understanding*, CONF. IEEE Signal Processing Society.

Alec Radford, Jong Wook Kim, Tao Xu, Greg Brockman, Christine McLeavey, and Ilya Sutskever. 2022. Robust speech recognition via large-scale weak supervision. *arXiv preprint arXiv:2212.04356*.

Douglas A. Reynolds. 2009. Gaussian mixture models. In *Encyclopedia of Biometrics*.

Sherry Ruan, Jacob O Wobbrock, Kenny Liou, Andrew Ng, and James A Landay. 2018. Comparing speech and keyboard text entry for short messages in two languages on touchscreen phones. *Proceedings of the ACM on Interactive, Mobile, Wearable and Ubiquitous Technologies*, 1(4):1–23.

Urmila Shrawankar and Vilas M. Thakare. 2013. Adverse conditions and ASR techniques for robust speech user interface. *CoRR*, abs/1303.5515.

Brij Mohan Lal Srivastava, Sunayana Sitaram, Rupesh Kumar Mehta, Krishna Doss Mohan, Pallavi Matani, Sandeepkumar Satpal, Kalika Bali, Radhakrishnan Srikanth, and Niranjan Nayak. 2018. Interspeech 2018 Low Resource Automatic Speech Recognition Challenge for Indian Languages. *Proc. 6th Workshop on Spoken Language Technologies for Under-Resourced Languages (SLTU 2018)*, pages 11–14.

Karel Veselý, A. Ghoshal, Lukas Burget, and Daniel Povey. 2013. Sequence-discriminative training of deep neural networks. *Proceedings of the Annual Conference of the International Speech Communication Association, INTERSPEECH*, pages 2345–2349.

Takuya Yoshioka, Armin Sehr, Marc Delcroix, Keisuke Kinoshita, Roland Maas, Tomohiro Nakatani, and Walter Kellermann. 2012. Making machines understand us in reverberant rooms: Robustness against reverberation for automatic speech recognition. *IEEE Signal Processing Magazine*, 29(6):114–126.

SetFit: A Robust Approach for Offensive Content Detection in Tamil-English Code-Mixed Conversations Using Sentence Transfer Fine-tuning

Kathiravan Pannerselvam[1]**,Saranya Rajiakodi**[1]**, Sajeetha Thavareesan**[2]**,**
Sathiyaraj Thangasamy[3]**, Kishore Kumar Ponnusamy**[4]

[1]Department of Computer Science, Central University of Tamil Nadu, India.
[2]Eastern University, Sri Lanka.
[3]Sri Krishna Adithya College of Arts and Science, India.
[4]Digital University of Kerala, India.

Abstract

Code-mixed languages are increasingly prevalent on social media and online platforms, presenting significant challenges in offensive content detection for natural language processing (NLP) systems. Our study explores how effectively the Sentence Transfer Fine-tuning (SetFit) method, combined with logistic regression, detects offensive content in a Tamil-English code-mixed dataset. We compare our model's performance with five other NLP models: Multilingual BERT (mBERT), LSTM, BERT, IndicBERT, and Language-agnostic BERT Sentence Embeddings (LaBSE). Our model, SetFit, outperforms these models in accuracy, achieving an impressive 89.72%, significantly higher than other models. These results suggest the sentence transformer model's substantial potential for detecting offensive content in code-mixed languages. Our study provides valuable insights into the sentence transformer model's ability to identify various types of offensive material in Tamil-English online conversations, paving the way for more advanced NLP systems tailored to code-mixed languages.

Keywords

Hate speech, SetFit, Natural language processing, Offensive detection, Code-mixed languages, Tamil-English dataset

1 Introduction

Text classification is a part of Information Extraction (IE), an emerging area of research and application that explores how to discover knowledge (information) from a vast amount of text (Ek et al., 2011). So many data resources are available on the internet, like social media, e-commerce sites, blogs, news portals, personal websites, and others, where

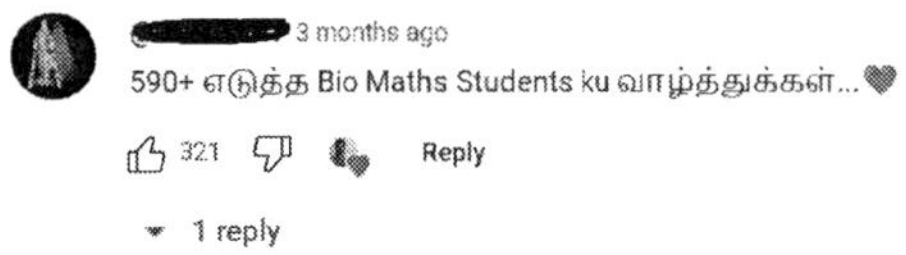

Figure 1: Example Tamil-English code-mixed youtube comment

people share their thoughts and opinions in their native language (Kathiravan and Haridoss, 2018). Code-mixed language is a phenomenon in which speakers interchange two or more languages or language varieties within a single conversation or text. It is common in multilingual societies, particularly in urban areas where people with diverse linguistic backgrounds interact regularly (Ravikiran and Annamalai, 2021) (Singh et al., 2018). Code-mixing is prevalent in many parts of the world, including India, Africa, and the Americas. Fig. 1 is an example YouTube comment with Tamil-English code-mixed languages. In code-mixed language, speakers often borrow words or phrases from one language and incorporate them into another, resulting in a hybrid language combining multiple languages' grammatical structures and vocabulary (Pannerselvam et al., 2023). The prevalence of code-mixed language in social media and online platforms has posed significant challenges for NLP systems. Traditional NLP models are designed to work with monolingual texts and struggle with the complexity of code-mixed language. Consequently, there is an increasing demand for developing NLP systems that can effectively process code-mixed language, especially in identifying offensive language (Li, 2021).

Detecting offensive content in code-mixed lan-

Proceedings of the Fourth Workshop on Speech, Vision, and Language Technologies for Dravidian Languages, pages 35–42
March 22, 2024 ©2024 Association for Computational Linguistics

guage is challenging due to the linguistic complexity of code-mixed language and the nuances of language use (Chakravarthi, 2023),(Kumaresan et al., 2023). Offensive language in code-mixed language can involve gender-based language, stereotypes, derogatory terms, and hate speech (Kumaresan et al., 2022). Developing NLP systems that effectively detect offensive language in a code-mixed language is crucial for promoting safe and inclusive online spaces (Ahluwalia et al., 2018),(Alowibdi et al., 2014). This study focuses on detecting offensives in a code-mixed Tamil-English dataset using Sentence Transformer Fine-Tune (SetFit). It is a substitute for few-shot text classification and involves fine-tuning a Sentence Transformer using task-specific data. This approach can be effortlessly implemented using the sentence-transformers library.

The main objective of this research is to evaluate the performance of the SetFit model and compare it with other NLP models in offensive content detection within code-mixed Tamil-English language data on social media and online platforms. The study aims to provide insights into the effectiveness of SetFit in identifying offensive content and its potential applicability in enhancing the robustness of NLP systems for code-mixed languages.

The following research questions are conceived from the above-mentioned objective of this research work.

RQ1 How does the performance of SetFit compare to LSTM, BERT, multilingual BERT (mBERT), IndicBERT, and LaBSE in the task of offensive content detection within a code-mixed Tamil-English dataset?

RQ2 To what extent does the performance of SetFit vary when detecting different types of offensive content (e.g., Offensive targetedilnsult group, Offensive untargeted, Not offensive, Not Tamil, Offensive targeted insult individual, Offensive targeted insult others) within code-mixed Tamil-English online discourses?

RQ3 How does the performance of the NLP models (SetFit, mBERT, LSTM, BERT, IndicBERT, LaBSE) differ in terms of precision, recall, and F1-score when identifying offensive content in the code-mixed Tamil-English dataset?
The findings from our research can be beneficial for developing NLP models that are more effective in detecting various offensives in code-mixed languages, which can help mitigate the harmful effects of such language on online platforms. The findings can benefit further research and practitioners developing NLP applications for social media and online platforms.

Additionally, developing NLP models capable of detecting various offensives in code-mixed languages can help mitigate the harmful effects of such language in online platforms, promote safer and more inclusive online spaces, and contribute to building a more equitable and inclusive society.

2 Related works

In this related work section, we review the existing literature on this topic, focusing on studies explicitly addressing the problem of various offensive language detection in code-mixed text. We also discuss the existing approaches to code-mixed text classification, including language-specific and language-agnostic models, and highlight the strengths and weaknesses of each approach.

Offensive language identification is a task that has been receiving considerable attention in recent years. However, identifying offensive spans in long sentences has been a challenging problem, especially for context-dependent ones. To address this issue, a study (Ravikiran and Annamalai, 2021) evaluated several models, including Bi-LSTM CRF, MuRIL, and LIME. The rationale extraction-based approach involving a combination of MuRIL and LIME performed significantly better than the other models. However, the Bi-LSTM CRF model was sensitive toward shorter sentences and performed worse than the random baseline. Extracting offensive spans for long sentences was also found to be complicated. In the future, the researchers plan to re-do the offensive span identification task, where participants will be required to identify offensive spans while simultaneously classifying different types of offensiveness. The researchers also plan to release this study's baseline models and datasets to encourage further research.

Kalaivani et al. (2021) (Kalaivani et al., 2021) propose a model called TOLD (Tamil Offensive Language Detection) that detects offensive language in code-mixed social media comments written in Tamil and English. The study uses Multilingual BERT (mBERT) with feature-based selection to generate contextualized word embeddings and selects relevant features using the chi-square test. The proposed TOLD model outperforms the accuracy, precision, recall, and F1 score of existing models. The study also analyzes the importance of various features and finds that character-based features and part-of-speech tags are highly effective in detecting offensive language. The study demonstrates the effectiveness of using mBERT with feature-based selection in identifying and moderating offensive language in social media platforms, promoting a safer and more inclusive online environment.

Ravikiran and Annamalai (2021) (Ravikiran and Annamalai, 2021) present a new dataset called DOSA (Dravidian Code-mixed Offensive Span Identification Dataset) for identifying the offensive language in code-mixed social media comments in four Dravidian languages: Tamil, Telugu, Kannada, and Malayalam. The authors collected and annotated the dataset with offensive spans, the smallest text segment containing an offensive word or phrase. The dataset contains 7,500 comments and 15,547 offensive spans, and multiple annotators did the annotations to ensure high inter-annotator agreement. The paper also provides baseline experiments on the dataset using various models and shows the effectiveness of the dataset in identifying offensive language in code-mixed comments in Dravidian languages.

Chakravarthi et al. (2021) (Chakravarthi et al., 2021) present a study on sentiment analysis of code-mixed text in four Dravidian languages: Tamil, Telugu, Kannada, and Malayalam. The authors collected a dataset of code-mixed social media comments and used various preprocessing techniques to prepare the data for sentiment analysis. They then used various machine and deep learning models to perform sentiment analysis and evaluated the performance using various metrics. The results showed that deep learning models such as LSTM and GRU outperformed traditional machine learning models in sentiment analysis of code-mixed text in Dravidian languages. The study provides insights into the challenges and opportunities in sentiment analysis of code-mixed text in Dravidian languages. It can help develop practical tools for sentiment analysis in these languages.

Rajalakshmi et al. (2021) (Rajalakshmi et al., 2021) present an approach for offensive language identification in code-mixed Tamil using a transformer-based model. The authors describe

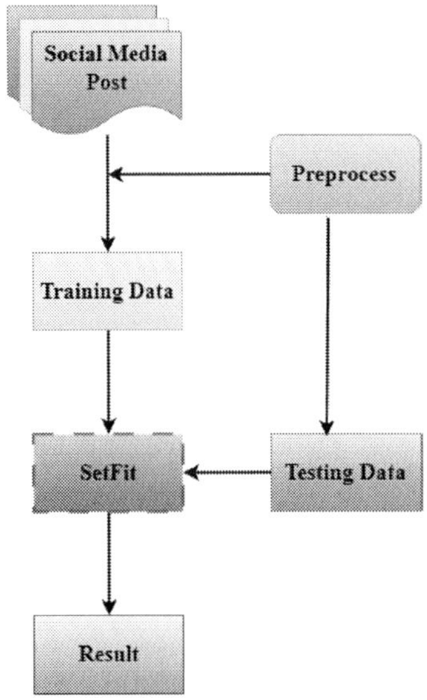

Figure 2: General architecture of proposed model

their participation in the DLRG shared task at the Dravidian Language Technologies Workshop 2021, which aimed to develop models for identifying the offensive language in code-mixed social media comments. The authors used a transformer-based model called RoBERTa and fine-tuned it on the provided dataset. They also used data augmentation techniques to improve the performance of the model. The results showed that their approach achieved high accuracy in identifying the offensive language in code-mixed Tamil, outperforming the baseline models provided by the shared task. The study demonstrates the effectiveness of transformer-based models for offensive language identification in code-mixed Tamil and provides insights into developing models for similar tasks in other Dravidian languages.

3 Proposed Methodology:

In this section, we described the experimental setup for our experimental work on classifying different types of offensive content in code-mixed text data in Tamil and English (Chakravarthi et al., 2021). Figure 2 illustrates the workflow of the general architecture of the offensive language detection framework.

3.1 Dataset

The benchmark dataset (Chakravarthi et al., 2022) contains a manually annotated dataset for sentiment analysis and offensive language identification in social media comments of three under-resourced Dravidian languages - Tamil, Kannada, and Malayalam-consisting of over 60,000 YouTube comments. The dataset contained various types of code-mixing and was annotated by volunteer annotators with high inter-annotator agreement. The authors also conducted baseline experiments using machine learning methods to establish benchmarks on the dataset.

We randomly selected 35139 code-mixed comments from the dataset mentioned above. Table 1 and Figure 3 illustrate the description of the dataset. Below are sample offensive YouTube comments along with their corresponding labels.

- **Offensive Targeted Insult Group**
  Dey dey deyyy,, loosu pasangala,, munna pinna jayalalitha amma va pathrukingal-ada gambeeramna ennanu avanga kannula tha paakanum,, amma oda history ah ithu,, soniya gandhi mari iruku chaiiii,,, avanga bio edukanumna a-z pathutu vanthu edungadaa,, dummy akkaathinga

- **Offensive Untargeted**
  Intha maari comments ku like kekuravangala india va vittu veliya annupanum.

- **Not offensive**
  Ellam okay than....but antha ponnu aasa pattu love panni avanaiye kola panna thappu illaya...yosinga...........

- **Not Tamil**
  Abe sale ye toh tatti hai

- **Offensive Targeted Insult Individual**
  Pa Ranjith paru Da unaku sc St quote job government job quarters ellam cancel pannanum

- **Offensive Targeted Insult Other**
  Iron man fans dis like podunga intha vidio kku

3.1.1 Preprocess and Data preparation

We preprocessed the data by removing stopwords, punctuations, and URLs and converted the text to lowercase. We then split the dataset into training and test sets in a 70:30 ratio, and we used various models such as LSTM, mBERT, BERT, IndicBERT, SetFit, and LaBSE.Finally, the accuracy of these models was on the test dataset.

Table 1: Dataset description.

Label	# of Posts
Not offensive	25,425
Not Tamil	1,454
Offensive Targeted Insult group	2,557
Offensive Targeted Insult Individual	2,343
Offensive Targeted Insult Other	454
Offensive Untargeted	2,906
Total	**35,139**

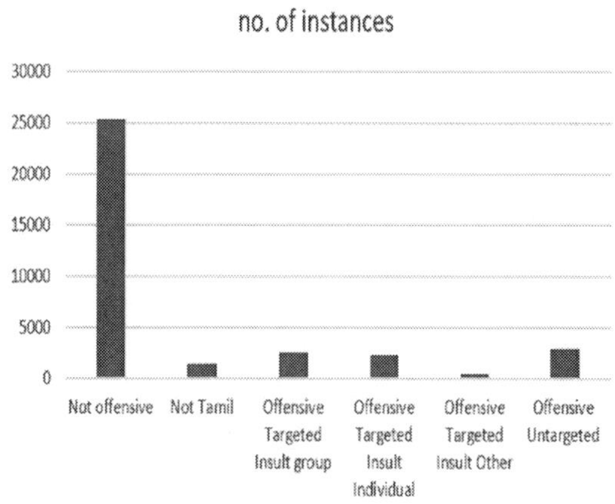

Figure 3: Dataset distribution among various class

3.2 Model

3.2.1 Sentence Transformer Fine-tuning (SetFit)

The Sentence Transformer (ST) method, widely utilized in semantic search, similarity, and clustering of words, encodes sentences into unique vector representations based on semantic content. This encoding process involves adapting a transformer model within a Siamese architecture, as detailed by (Reimers and Gurevych, 2019), (Wasserblat, 2021). The training process actively minimizes the distance between vectors of semantically similar sentences and maximizes it for those that are semantically distant through contrastive training. The performance of Sentence Transformers (ST) excels beyond other embedding representations, yet it does not match the classification capabilities of cross-encoders such as BERT (Reimers and Gurevych, 2019).

The initial stage of the training process involves selecting a sentence-transformers (ST) model from the model hub. Subsequent steps include configuring the training class, populating the training data loader, and fine-tuning. The training dataset consists of positive and negative sentence pairs to

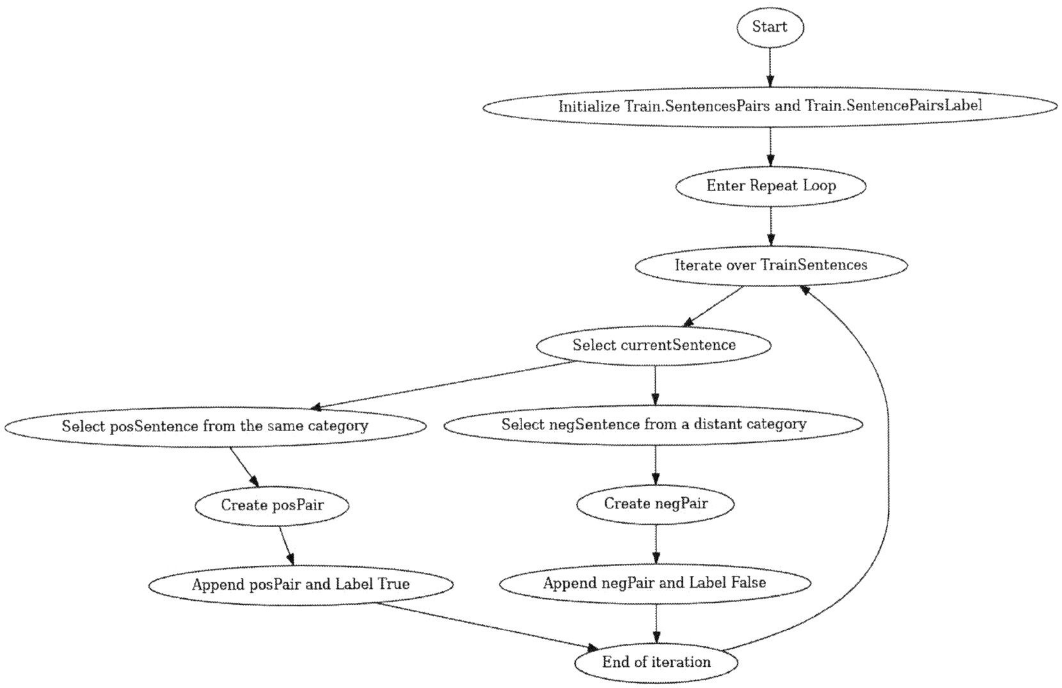

Figure 4: sentence pair selection of SetFit model

effectively address the limited labeled training data in the few-shot scenario. Positive pairs involve two sentences randomly selected from the same class, while antagonistic pairs comprise two sentences randomly chosen from different classes. Each iteration involving sentence pairs generates 2xN training pairs, where N represents the total number of training samples per task—illustrated in Figure 4.

These generated sentence pairs are employed for fine-tuning the ST model. Upon completion of the fine-tuning step, an adapted ST model is generated. The training data sentences are then encoded using the adapted ST, and the encoded data is used to train a Logistic Regression (LR) model for simplicity. Each test sentence undergoes encoding with the adapted ST in the inference phase, and the LR model predicts its category.

The proposed model is compared with the following state-of-the-art algorithms.

Long Short-Term Memory (LSTM) is an improved version of Recurrent Neural Network (RNN) architecture widely used in natural language processing and time-series prediction tasks. It is designed to address the vanishing gradient problem in standard RNNs by introducing memory cells that can selectively forget or retain information from the previous time steps. The LSTM network consists of three gates: the input gate, output gate, and forget gate, which controls the flow of information in and out of the memory cells (Zhang et al., 2018),(Kathiravan and Saranya, 2021). In this experimental work, we used the configuration for the LSTM model to include 100 hidden units, a dropout rate of 0.2, and a recurrent dropout rate of 0.2. The output layer consisted of 6 units, and the activation function used was softmax.

Bidirectional Encoder Representations from Transformers (BERT) is a pre-trained language model developed by Google, based on the Transformer architecture, and is trained on large amounts of text data to learn contextualized word embeddings. BERT is unique because it can learn bidirectional context by looking at the entire sentence, unlike other language models that only look at the previous or next word in the sequence (Alsharef et al., 2022),(Fan et al., 2021),(Li et al., 2022). The pre-trained model can be fine-tuned on a specific task with more minor task-specific data, making it useful for practical applications. We utilized CSE CUDA and trained the model for three epochs. CSE CUDA is a parallel computing platform that enables Graphics Processing Units (GPUs) to accelerate the training of deep learning models, significantly speeding up the training process. The choice of 3 epochs was based on experimentation with the dataset and the model architecture.

Multilingual BERT is a variant of the BERT model pre-trained in multiple languages. Google developed it and trained on massive text data in 104 languages. The goal of mBERT is to learn a shared representation for all languages, enabling the model to perform well on various NLP tasks for different languages without requiring language-specific training data. The model is fine-tuned on a specific task using task-specific data in the target language, and it has been shown to achieve state-of-the-art performance on various cross-lingual benchmarks. mBERT is a useful tool for multilingual applications, as it eliminates the need for separate training models for each language, saving time and resources (Kalaivani et al., 2021).

IndicBERT is a language model using the BERT architecture designed for Indian languages (Rajalakshmi et al., 2021). It is trained on large amounts of various Indian language text data. Researchers at IIT Bombay developed IndicBERT, which has shown promising results in various Indian language benchmarks. It is an open-source project. So, anybody can incorporate state-of-the-art language models into their projects (Kohli et al., 2021).

Language-agnostic BERT Sentence Embedding (LaBSE) is a multilingual language model based on the BERT architecture, trained on a large amount of text data from over 100 languages (Feng et al., 2020). It generates high-quality sentence embeddings for text in any language, making it useful for cross-lingual natural language processing tasks such as classification and machine translation. Developed by Google, LaBSE has shown state-of-the-art performance on benchmark datasets and is an open-source project for developers and researchers working with multilingual text data.

In the next section, we presented the results and analysis of our experiments on sentiment analysis in code-mixed social media comments in Tamil and English.

4 Results and Discussion

In this experimental work, we proposed Sentence Transfer Fine-tuning (SetFit) to detect offensive content in code-mixed languages. It achieved an impressive 89% accuracy on the test set, surpassing other models like LSTM, BERT, mBERT, IndicBERT, and LaBSE, which recorded accuracies of 76.3%, 78%, 86%, 80%, and 84.5% respectively. Figure 5 and Table 2 depict the detailed evaluation metrics used in our experiment. SetFit's remarkable effectiveness across these metrics, as discussed in Research Questions 1 and 3 (RQ1 and RQ3), showcases its capability to enhance offensive content detection in code-mixed languages.

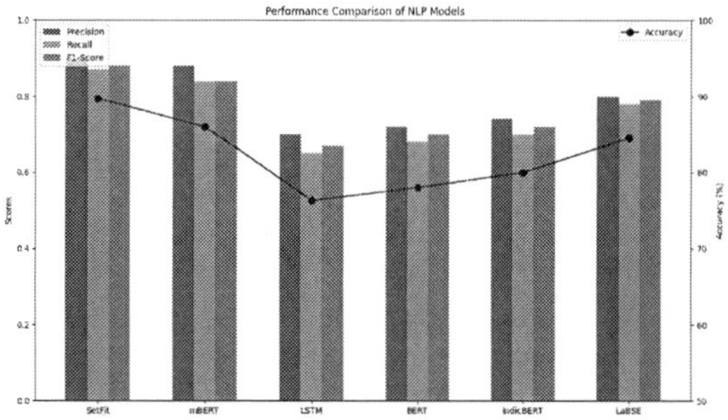

Figure 5: Accuracy of various classifiers

While a thorough analysis of SetFit's varied performance in identifying different kinds of offensive content is pending, its overall efficiency solidifies its position as a promising approach for improving NLP systems in code-mixed language contexts, aligning with the objectives outlined in Research Question 2 (RQ2).

Further analysis conducted to examine the impact of dataset size on model efficacy revealed that SetFit maintained consistent performance when the dataset size was increased from 10k to 35k samples. This finding suggests that SetFit is adept at handling larger datasets effectively.

These results endorse SetFit as a highly effective method for classifying various forms of offensive code-mixed text. The high accuracy achieved by SetFit likely stems from its ability to capture the complex linguistic patterns within the dataset effectively. Moreover, our findings stress the importance of employing large datasets for training models in this specialized area.

5 Conclusion

In conclusion, our experimental work, which introduced the Sentence Transfer Fine-tuning (SetFit) approach, marks a significant advancement in Natural Language Processing (NLP), particularly in code-mixed languages. The primary objective of our research was to enhance the detection of offensive content in such languages, a challenge that has grown increasingly relevant in today's digital communication landscape. Additionally, our analysis

Table 2: Evaluation metrics of various classifiers.

Model	Precision	Recall	F1-score	Accuracy
SetFit	0.90	0.87	0.88	0.89
mBERT	0.88	0.84	0.84	0.86
LSTM	0.70	0.65	0.67	0.76
BERT	0.72	0.68	0.70	0.78
indicBERT	0.74	0.70	0.72	0.80
LaBSE	0.80	0.78	0.79	0.84

of the impact of dataset size on model performance revealed a key strength of SetFit: its ability to maintain stable performance with the increase in dataset size from 10k to 35k samples. This robustness in handling larger datasets is crucial, especially in code-mixed language processing, where data variability is high. SetFit's high accuracy is attributed to its advanced capability to capture the complex linguistic patterns inherent in the dataset. This highlights the importance of using comprehensive and large datasets in training models for this domain.

Our research indicates that SetFit is a highly effective and reliable method for classifying different types of offensive content in code-mixed text. Its performance provides a new benchmark in the field and opens avenues for future research and development in creating more sophisticated and nuanced NLP systems for multilingual and culturally diverse digital communications.

References

Resham Ahluwalia, Himani Soni, Edward Callow, Anderson Nascimento, and Martine De Cock. 2018. Detecting hate speech against women in english tweets. *EVALITA Evaluation of NLP and Speech Tools for Italian*, 12:194.

Jalal S Alowibdi, Ugo A Buy, S Yu Philip, and Leon Stenneth. 2014. Detecting deception in online social networks. In *2014 IEEE/ACM International Conference on Advances in Social Networks Analysis and Mining (ASONAM 2014)*, pages 383–390. IEEE.

Ahmad Alsharef, Karan Aggarwal, Deepika Koundal, Hashem Alyami, Darine Ameyed, et al. 2022. An automated toxicity classification on social media using lstm and word embedding. *Computational Intelligence and Neuroscience*, 2022.

Bharathi Raja Chakravarthi. 2023. Detection of homophobia and transphobia in youtube comments. *International Journal of Data Science and Analytics*, pages 1–20.

Bharathi Raja Chakravarthi, Ruba Priyadharshini, Vigneshwaran Muralidaran, Navya Jose, Shardul Suryawanshi, Elizabeth Sherly, and John P. McCrae. 2022. Dravidiancodemix: sentiment analysis and offensive language identification dataset for dravidian languages in code-mixed text. *Language Resources and Evaluation*.

Bharathi Raja Chakravarthi, Ruba Priyadharshini, Sajeetha Thavareesan, Dhivya Chinnappa, Durairaj Thenmozhi, Elizabeth Sherly, John P McCrae, Adeep Hande, Rahul Ponnusamy, Shubhanker Banerjee, et al. 2021. Findings of the sentiment analysis of dravidian languages in code-mixed text. *arXiv preprint arXiv:2111.09811*.

Tobias Ek, Camilla Kirkegaard, Håkan Jonsson, and Pierre Nugues. 2011. Named entity recognition for short text messages. *Procedia-Social and Behavioral Sciences*, 27:178–187.

Hong Fan, Wu Du, Abdelghani Dahou, Ahmed A Ewees, Dalia Yousri, Mohamed Abd Elaziz, Ammar H Elsheikh, Laith Abualigah, and Mohammed AA Al-qaness. 2021. Social media toxicity classification using deep learning: real-world application uk brexit. *Electronics*, 10(11):1332.

Fangxiaoyu Feng, Yinfei Yang, Daniel Cer, Naveen Arivazhagan, and Wei Wang. 2020. Language-agnostic bert sentence embedding. *arXiv preprint arXiv:2007.01852*.

Adaikkan Kalaivani, Durairaj Thenmozhi, and Chandrabose Aravindan. 2021. Told: Tamil offensive language detection in code-mixed social media comments using mbert with features based selection.

P Kathiravan and N Haridoss. 2018. Preprocessing for mining the textual data-a review. *International Journal of Scientific Research in Computer Science Applications and Management Studies IJSRCSAMS*, 7(5).

Panner Selvam Kathiravan and Rajiakodi Saranya. 2021. Named entity recognition (ner) for social media tamil posts using deep learning with singular value decomposition. Technical report, EasyChair.

Guneet Kohli, Prabsimran Kaur, and Jatin Bedi. 2021. Arguably at comma@ icon: Detection of multilingual aggressive, gender biased, and communally charged tweets using ensemble and fine-tuned indicbert. In *Proceedings of the 18th International Conference on*

Natural Language Processing: Shared Task on Multilingual Gender Biased and Communal Language Identification, pages 46–52.

Prasanna Kumar Kumaresan, Rahul Ponnusamy, Ruba Priyadharshini, Paul Buitelaar, and Bharathi Raja Chakravarthi. 2023. Homophobia and transphobia detection for low-resourced languages in social media comments. *Natural Language Processing Journal*, 5:100041.

Prasanna Kumar Kumaresan, Rahul Ponnusamy, Elizabeth Sherly, Sangeetha Sivanesan, and Bharathi Raja Chakravarthi. 2022. Transformer based hope speech comment classification in code-mixed text. In *International Conference on Speech and Language Technologies for Low-resource Languages*, pages 120–137. Springer.

Hui Li, Lin Yu, Jie Zhang, and Ming Lyu. 2022. Fusion deep learning and machine learning for heterogeneous military entity recognition. *Wireless Communications and Mobile Computing*, 2022:1–11.

Zichao Li. 2021. Codewithzichao@ dravidianlangtech-eacl2021: Exploring multilingual transformers for offensive language identification on code mixing text. In *Proceedings of the first workshop on speech and language technologies for dravidian languages*, pages 164–168.

Kathiravan Pannerselvam, Saranya Rajiakodi, Rahul Ponnusamy, and Sajeetha Thavareesan. 2023. CSS-CUTN@DravidianLangTech:abusive comments detection in Tamil and Telugu. In *Proceedings of the Third Workshop on Speech and Language Technologies for Dravidian Languages*, pages 306–312, Varna, Bulgaria. INCOMA Ltd., Shoumen, Bulgaria.

Ratnavel Rajalakshmi, Yashwant Reddy, and Lokesh Kumar. 2021. Dlrg@ dravidianlangtech-eacl2021: Transformer based approachfor offensive language identification on code-mixed tamil. In *Proceedings of the First Workshop on Speech and Language Technologies for Dravidian Languages*, pages 357–362.

Manikandan Ravikiran and Subbiah Annamalai. 2021. Dosa: Dravidian code-mixed offensive span identification dataset. In *Proceedings of the First Workshop on Speech and Language Technologies for Dravidian Languages*, pages 10–17.

Nils Reimers and Iryna Gurevych. 2019. Sentence-bert: Sentence embeddings using siamese bert-networks. *arXiv preprint arXiv:1908.10084*.

Vinay Singh, Deepanshu Vijay, Syed Sarfaraz Akhtar, and Manish Shrivastava. 2018. Named entity recognition for hindi-english code-mixed social media text. In *Proceedings of the seventh named entities workshop*, pages 27–35.

Moshe Wasserblat. 2021. Sentence transformer finetuning (setfit) outperforms gpt-3 on few-shot text classification while. Accessed: 2021-12-14.

Ling Zhang, Magie Hall, and Dhundy Bastola. 2018. Utilizing twitter data for analysis of chemotherapy. *International journal of medical informatics*, 120:92–100.

Findings of the First Shared Task on Offensive Span Identification from Code-Mixed Kannada-English Comments

Manikandan Ravikiran [†,*] **Ratnavel Rajalakshmi** [⊕] **Bharathi Raja Chakravarthi** [‡]
Anand Kumar Madasamy [⋆], **Sajeetha Thavareesan** [⊖]
[†] Georgia Institute of Technology, Atlanta, Georgia
[⊕] Vellore Institute of Technology, Chennai, India
[⋆] National Institute of Technology Karnataka Surathkal, India
[‡] School of Computer Science, Univeristy of Galway, Ireland
[⊖] Eastern University, Srilanka
mravikiran3@gatech.edu
bharathi.raja@insight-centre.org

Abstract

Effectively managing offensive content is crucial on social media platforms to encourage positive online interactions. However, addressing offensive contents in code-mixed Dravidian languages faces challenges, as current moderation methods focus on flagging entire comments rather than pinpointing specific offensive segments. This limitation stems from a lack of annotated data and accessible systems designed to identify offensive language sections. To address this, our shared task presents a dataset comprising Kannada-English code-mixed social comments, encompassing offensive comments. This paper outlines the dataset, the utilized algorithms, and the results obtained by systems participating in this shared task.

1 Introduction

Addressing offensive content holds immense importance for various parties engaged in content moderation, such as social media companies and individuals (Subramanian et al., 2022; Chinnaudayar Navaneethakrishnan et al., 2023). Typically, moderation methods involve either human moderators reviewing content to flag offensive material or the use of semi-automated and automated tools employing basic algorithms and predefined block lists (Jhaver et al., 2018). Despite the appearance of content moderation as a straightforward decision between allowing or removing content, this process is complex (Swaminathan et al., 2022). This complexity is amplified on social media platforms due to the overwhelming volume of content, making it challenging for human moderators (Kumaresan et al., 2022; Chakravarthi, 2022b,a). With the continuous rise in offensive social media content, particularly offensive comments and statements, there's a preference for semi-automated and fully automated content moderation approaches (Ravikiran et al., 2022; Chakravarthi, 2023; Chakravarthi et al., 2023a).

Kannada, an ancient Dravidian language, holds a significant historical legacy (Narasimhacharya, 1990). Predominantly spoken in the Indian state of Karnataka, Kannada serves as the official language in the state, carrying cultural significance that extends beyond regional boundaries (TNN, 2010). With the emergence of digital communication platforms, code-switching has also found its way into Kannada discourse, especially in informal online exchanges. This blending of languages and linguistic variations within social media has led to the integration of code-switched content in discussions, including offensive content, impacting the nature of online conversations in Kannada-speaking communities.

Despite recent advancements in natural language processing (NLP), addressing offensive code-mixed content in Dravidian languages, including Kannada, remains challenging due to limitations in available data and tools (Sitaram et al., 2019). However, there has been a noticeable surge in research focused on offensive code-mixed texts in Dravidian languages (Chakravarthi, 2020;

[*] Work done during graduate school

Proceedings of the Fourth Workshop on Speech, Vision, and Language Technologies for Dravidian Languages, pages 43–48
March 22, 2024

Chakravarthi et al., 2023a,b), although few of these studies concentrate on pinpointing the specific segments within a comment that render it offensive (Ravikiran and Annamalai, 2021; Ravikiran et al., 2022). Identifying these specific segments could significantly aid content moderators and semi-automated tools that prioritize the detection and categorization of offensive content. The existing body of research on identifying offensive spans primarily stems from the works of Ravikiran and Annamalai (2021). Post this there are multiple iterations of shared tasks focusing on offensive span identification in Tamil Ravikiran and Annamalai (2021); LekshmiAmmal et al. (2022); Rajalakshmi et al. (2022); Ravikiran et al. (2023). However to date there are no works in code-mixed Kannada language. To address this gap, we introduced the first phase of code-mixed social media text in Kannada, encompassing offensive segments. We invited participants to develop and submit systems under two distinct settings for this collaborative task. Our CodaLab website[1] will remain open to encourage further research in this domain.

2 Task Description

Our task of offensive span identification required participants to identify offensive spans i.e, character offsets that were responsible for the offensive of the comments, when identifying such spans was possible. To this end, we created two subtasks each of which are as described.

2.1 Subtask 1: Supervised Offensive Span Identification

With provided comments and labeled offensive spans used for training, the systems were tasked with detecting these offensive segments within the comments in the test dataset. This challenge could be addressed through supervised sequence labeling, involving training on the given posts that contain verified offensive spans. Alternatively, it could be tackled as rationale extraction by employing classifiers trained on other datasets of posts manually marked for offensive content classification, even in the absence of specific span annotations.

3 Dataset

For this shared task, we build on top of the dataset from earlier work of Ravikiran and Annamalai (2021), which originally released 1801 code-mixed Kannada-English comments with 1641 offensive spans. We released this dataset to the participants during training phase for model development. No additional data were released for development/validation purposes. Meanwhile for testing we extended introduced new additional annotated comments. To this end, the dataset of Hande et al. (2021) was used. From this we selected 444 comments for testing purpose. The test data had multiple instances where the offensive parts were completely not present. Such comments would help in identification of model biases in predciting spans if any.

Building on prior investigations (Ravikiran et al., 2023), we established span-level annotations for this fresh selection of 444 test comments. Employing the same procedures and guidelines for annotation, including measures to maintain anonymity, we introduced a explanation regarding offensive contents in the data, offering the option to abstain from the annotation process if deemed necessary. To ensure precision, each annotation underwent scrutiny by one or more annotation verifiers before amalgamating them through hard voting to form a standardized gold test set. Overall, concerning the 444 comments, we achieved a Cohen's Kappa inter-annotator agreement of 0.61.

4 Competition Phases

4.1 Training Phase

In the training phase, the train split with 1801 comments, and their annotated spans were released for model development. Participants were given training data and offensive spans. Participants were also emphasized on cross-validation by creating their splits for preliminary evaluations or hyperparameter tuning. In total, 45 participants registered for the task and downloaded the dataset.

4.2 Testing Phase

Test set comments without any span annotation were released in the testing phase. Each participating team was asked to submit their generated span predictions for evaluation. Predictions are submitted via Google form, which was used to evaluate the systems. Though CodaLab supports evaluation inherently, we used google form due to its simplicity. Finally, we assessed the submitted spans of the test set and were scored using character-based F1.

[1] https://codalab.lisn.upsaclay.fr/competitions/16090

5 System Descriptions

Overall we received only a total of 14 submissions from 7 teams All these were only for subtask 1. No submissions were made for subtask 2.

5.1 The SELAM Submission

Selam Submission used large language models composing one of the BERT or RoBERTA models. The methods showed the best result of 81.18% in F1.

5.2 The MIT_KEC_NLP Submission

MIT_KEC_NLP submission preprocessed data using custom stop word removal. These processed sentences are used converted to form TF-IDF which were used to train ensemble of multiple models. These final ensemble showed the result of 61.05% in F1.

5.3 The BYTESIZED_LLM Submission

BYTESIZED_LLM team utilized embeddings generated from a large open dataset, encompassing 100,000 comments. Following this Bi-LSTM model was trained to predict token level labels on test set. The final F1 obtained was 33.02%.

5.4 The CUET_RUN2 Submission

CUET_RUN2 used text preprocessing involving punctuation removal without any addition of more training data. This prepared data was was used for BERT finetuning with supervised method with L3-cube Kannada model to achieve result of 31.84% in F1.

5.5 The DLRG_3 Submission

DLRG_3 used a Bi-LSTM architecture with results of 21.92% in F1.

5.6 The MLG Submission

MLG team used an inception layer based CNN with kernel sizes 3, 5, 7, 9 and 11 with prediction of character level offensiveness probability. The output span is created by taking all the characters with higher probability of being offensive and multiplying with a mask to ensure that output does not exceeds the original sentence length. Finally the result obtained was 23.65% in F1.

5.7 The TEAMKUBOK Submission

TEAMKUBOK employed preprocessing with changing character level spans to word level spans. They fine tuned four pretrained language models and their predictions were averaged for the first occurrence of the offensive span of all the models and the last occurrence of the offensive span of all the models. Between these spans are returned as final output. The final result obtained was 12.94% in F1.

6 Evaluation

This section focuses on the evaluation framework of the task. First, the official measure that was used to evaluate the participating systems is described. Then, we discuss benchmarking of overall results. Finally we present remark on the approaches used and the analysis of the results from these submitted systems.

In line with work of Pavlopoulos et al. (2021) each system was evaluated F1 score computed on character offset. For each system, we computed the F1 score per comments, between the predicted and the ground truth character offsets. Following this we calculated macro-average score over all the 444 test comments. If in case both ground truth and predicted character offsets were empty we assigned a F1 of 1 other wise 0 and vice versa.

The overall results of benchmarked systems are as shown in Table 1.

Table 1: Official rank and F1 score (%) of the 3 participating teams that submitted systems. The baselines benchmarks are also shown.

TEAM NAME	F1	RANK
SELAM	81.18	1
MIT_KEC_NLP	61.05	2
BYTESIZED LLM	33.02	3
CUET_RUN2	31.84	4
MLG	23.65	5
DLRG_3	21.92	6
TEAMKUBOK	12.94	7

Overall, the shared task showed higher level engagement compared to earlier iterations with members beyond Indian subcontinent showing interest in in obtaining datasets, and seeking potential baseline codes for the project. Infact many of the participants wanted earlier submission window open and have multiple runs to be submitted. To this end, we allowed maximum of three submission runs and selected the best. Moreover we received total of 12 different runs with variety of results and many interest unexplored approaches. Table 1 shows the scores and ranks of two teams that made their submission. SELAM (section 5.1) was ranked first, followed by the rest of the teams with lowest result of 12.94% by TEAMKUBOK (section 5.7) using ensemble of four language models. There is a large gap between the methods especially in top three after which we find the results to spread within 35% F1.

Throughout this shared task we can see the trend to shift more towards language specific pretrained language models. Especially top three systems all employ language models. Meanwhile explainable AI method finds its place inside the rank list with ensemble of simple classifiers. At the same team few teams employed significant preprocessing indeed leading to improvement in results. Besides, we also see that Bi-LSTM methods are still there in the overall list.

6.1 Analysis

Table 1 illustrates the comprehensive outcomes, showcasing the peak achievement of 81.18% by Team SELAM. The subsequent best performance, standing at approximately 61.05%, is notably trailing by roughly 20% from MIT_KEC_NLP, while BYTESIZED LLM lags further behind by a significant margin of 50% in F1 scores. Subsequently, the remaining five systems display closely competitive results. A noticeable trend among the lower-ranking four models reveals a tendency to overestimate (bias) the presence of offensive spans, primarily due to limited generalization. Furthermore, ensemble language models, particularly TEAMKUBOK, exhibit a stark overfitting issue, displaying an F1 score of 12.94%. Notably, we find that in the test set, deliberate inclusion of non-offensive samples aimed to distinctly benchmark the models' performances, has impacted the scores of several models.

7 Conclusion

In this research, we initiated a first shared task focused on identifying offensive spans within code-mixed Kannada-English text. Unlike our previous attempt, we worked with 2k+ social media comments that were annotated to pinpoint offensive sections. Among 45 registered participants, 7 teams submitted their systems. We detailed their approaches in our study and discussed their respective outcomes. Notably, a strategy that employed pretrained language models and explainable AI have shown the best results. Conversely, the LSTM model performed notably worse particularly displaying sensitivity to offensiveness. We've made the data and related information publicly accessible to support future investigations. Looking ahead, our plan involves revisiting the identification of offensive spans within a multitask framework, encompassing various forms of offensiveness alongside the identification of offensive language spans for kannada.

Ethics Statement

In this paper, we discuss the shared task organized around identifying offensive spans in Kannada-English text. To achieve this, we've introduced a novel dataset tailored for both model refinement and diagnostic purposes. Notably, our data collection process didn't involve human participants, eliminating the need for ethical board approval. All datasets utilized in this study are accessible under licenses permitting sharing and redistribution. Our aim is to encourage the development of NLP systems using these datasets, fostering a deeper understanding of offensive spans. This, in turn, could significantly enhance the identification of offensive language across various platforms, carrying considerable societal implications. When appropriately used, these models and datasets hold promise for elevating the quality of discussions on social media channels. However, it's crucial to acknowledge potential biases in the models and the datasets themselves. Our analysis might lean in certain directions due relatively small dataset so used for evaluation. To counteract this to some degree, we have considered offensive content aimed at underrepresented communities, aiming to minimize potential biases and negative repercussions.

Acknowledgements

We thank our anonymous reviewers for their valuable feedback. Any opinions, findings, and conclusion or recommendations expressed in this material are those of the authors only and does not reflect the view of their employing organization or graduate schools. The shared task was result of series projects done during CS7646-ML4T (Fall 2020), CS6460-Edtech Foundations (Spring 2020) and CS7643-Deep learning (Spring 2022) at Georgia Institute of Technology by Manikandan Ravikiran. Bharathi Raja Chakravarthi were supported in part by a research grant from Science Foundation Ireland (SFI) under Grant Number SFI/12/RC/2289_P2 (Insight_2).

References

Bharathi Raja Chakravarthi. 2020. HopeEDI: A multilingual hope speech detection dataset for equality, diversity, and inclusion. In *Proceedings of the Third Workshop on Computational Modeling of People's Opinions, Personality, and Emotion's in Social Media*, pages 41–53, Barcelona, Spain (Online). Association for Computational Linguistics.

Bharathi Raja Chakravarthi. 2022a. Hope speech detection in youtube comments. *Social Network Analysis and Mining*, 12(1):75.

Bharathi Raja Chakravarthi. 2022b. Multilingual hope speech detection in english and dravidian languages. *International Journal of Data Science and Analytics*, 14(4):389–406.

Bharathi Raja Chakravarthi. 2023. Detection of homophobia and transphobia in youtube comments. *International Journal of Data Science and Analytics*, pages 1–20.

Bharathi Raja Chakravarthi, Manoj Balaji Jagadeeshan, Vasanth Palanikumar, and Ruba Priyadharshini. 2023a. Offensive language identification in dravidian languages using mpnet and cnn. *International Journal of Information Management Data Insights*, 3(1):100151.

Bharathi Raja Chakravarthi, Ruba Priyadharshini, Shubanker Banerjee, Manoj Balaji Jagadeeshan, Prasanna Kumar Kumaresan, Rahul Ponnusamy, Sean Benhur, and John Philip McCrae. 2023b. Detecting abusive comments at a fine-grained level in a low-resource language. *Natural Language Processing Journal*, 3:100006.

Subalalitha Chinnaudayar Navaneethakrishnan, Bharathi Raja Chakravarthi, Kogilavani Shanmugavadivel, Malliga Subramanian, Prasanna Kumar Kumaresan, Bharathi, Lavanya Sambath Kumar, and Rahul Ponnusamy. 2023. Findings of shared task on sentiment analysis and homophobia detection of youtube comments in code-mixed dravidian languages. In *Proceedings of the 14th Annual Meeting of the Forum for Information Retrieval Evaluation*, FIRE '22, page 18–21, New York, NY, USA. Association for Computing Machinery.

Adeep Hande, Ruba Priyadharshini, Anbukkarasi Sampath, Kingston Pal Thamburaj, Prabakaran Chandran, and Bharathi Raja Chakravarthi. 2021. Hope speech detection in under-resourced kannada language. *ArXiv*, abs/2108.04616.

Shagun Jhaver, Sucheta Ghoshal, Amy S. Bruckman, and Eric Gilbert. 2018. Online harassment and content moderation: The case of blocklists. *ACM Trans. Comput. Hum. Interact.*, 25(2):12:1–12:33.

Prasanna Kumar Kumaresan, Rahul Ponnusamy, Elizabeth Sherly, Sangeetha Sivanesan, and Bharathi Raja Chakravarthi. 2022. Transformer based hope speech comment classification in code-mixed text. In *International Conference on Speech and Language Technologies for Low-resource Languages*, pages 120–137. Springer.

Hariharan LekshmiAmmal, Manikandan Ravikiran, and Anand Kumar Madasamy. 2022. NITK-IT_NLP@TamilNLP-ACL2022: Transformer based model for toxic span identification in Tamil. In *Proceedings of the Second Workshop on Speech and Language Technologies for Dravidian Languages*, pages 75–78, Dublin, Ireland. Association for Computational Linguistics.

Ramanujapuram Narasimhacharya. 1990. History of kannada language (readership lectures).

John Pavlopoulos, Léo Laugier, Jeffrey Sorensen, and Ion Androutsopoulos. 2021. Semeval-2021 task 5: Toxic spans detection (to appear). In *Proceedings of the 15th International Workshop on Semantic Evaluation*.

Ratnavel Rajalakshmi, Mohit More, Bhamatipati Shrikriti, Gitansh Saharan, Hanchate Samyuktha, and Sayantan Nandy. 2022. DLRG@TamilNLP-ACL2022: Offensive span identification in Tamil usingBiLSTM-CRF approach. In *Proceedings of the Second Workshop on Speech and Language Technologies for Dravidian Languages*, pages 248–253, Dublin, Ireland. Association for Computational Linguistics.

Manikandan Ravikiran and Subbiah Annamalai. 2021. DOSA: Dravidian code-mixed offensive span identification dataset. In *Proceedings of the First Workshop on Speech and Language Technologies for Dravidian Languages*, pages 10–17, Kyiv. Association for Computational Linguistics.

Manikandan Ravikiran, Bharathi Raja Chakravarthi, Anand Kumar Madasamy, Sangeetha S, Ratnavel Rajalakshmi, Sajeetha Thavareesan, Rahul Ponnusamy, and Shankar Mahadevan. 2022. Findings of the shared task on offensive span identification fromCode-mixed Tamil-English comments. In *Proceedings of the Second Workshop on Speech and Language Technologies for Dravidian Languages*, pages 261–270, Dublin, Ireland. Association for Computational Linguistics.

Manikandan Ravikiran, Ananth Ganesh, Anand Kumar M, R Rajalakshmi, and Bharathi Raja Chakravarthi. 2023. Findings of the second shared task on offensive span identification from code-mixed Tamil-English comments. In *Proceedings of the Third Workshop on Speech and Language Technologies for Dravidian Languages*, pages 52–58, Varna, Bulgaria. INCOMA Ltd., Shoumen, Bulgaria.

Sunayana Sitaram, Khyathi Raghavi Chandu, Sai Krishna Rallabandi, and A. Black. 2019. A survey of code-switched speech and language processing. *ArXiv*, abs/1904.00784.

Malliga Subramanian, Rahul Ponnusamy, Sean Benhur, Kogilavani Shanmugavadivel, Adhithiya Ganesan, Deepti Ravi, Gowtham Krishnan Shanmugasundaram, Ruba Priyadharshini, and Bharathi Raja Chakravarthi. 2022. Offensive language detection in tamil youtube comments by adapters and cross-domain knowledge transfer. *Computer Speech & Language*, 76:101404.

Krithika Swaminathan, Bharathi B, Gayathri G L, and Hrishik Sampath. 2022. SSNCSE_NLP@LT-EDI-ACL2022: Homophobia/transphobia detection in multiple languages using SVM classifiers and BERT-based transformers. In *Proceedings of the Second Workshop on Language Technology for Equality, Diversity and Inclusion*, pages 239–244, Dublin, Ireland. Association for Computational Linguistics.

TNN. 2010. Indiaspeak: English is our 2nd language: India news - times of india. TOI.

Findings of the Shared Task on Hate and Offensive Language Detection in Telugu Codemixed Text (HOLD-Telugu)@DravidianLangTech 2024

Premjith B[1], **Bharathi Raja Chakravarthi** [2], **Prasanna Kumar Kumaresan**[3], **Saranya Rajiakodi**[4], **Sai Prashanth Karnati**[1], **Sai Rishith Reddy Mangamuru**[1], **Chandu Janakiram**[1]

[1]Amrita School of Artificial Intelligence, Coimbatore, Amrita Vishwa Vidyapeetham, India
[2]School of Computer Science, University of Galway, Ireland
[3]Data Science Institute, University of Galway, Ireland
[4]Central University of Tamil Nadu, India

Abstract

This paper examines the submissions of various participating teams to the task on Hate and Offensive Language Detection in Telugu Codemixed Text (HOLD-Telugu) organized as part of DravidianLangTech 2024. In order to identify the contents containing harmful information in Telugu codemixed social media text, the shared task pushes researchers and academicians to build models. The dataset for the task was created by gathering YouTube comments and annotated manually. A total of 23 teams participated and submitted their results to the shared task. The rank list was created by assessing the submitted results using the macro F1-score.

1 Introduction

In the present technological era, detecting hate comments on social media has become a crucial and challenging task (Chakravarthi et al., 2023b; Priyadharshini et al., 2022; Prasanth et al., 2022). The growth of internet platforms made it easier for people to disseminate information, including offensive and violent postings and comments. Consequently, it is now crucial to address and mitigate hazardous content in order to automatically maintain online platforms clean (Chakravarthi et al., 2022a,b, 2023b; Chakravarthi, 2023). This is a challenging endeavour because of the complexity of the languages and codemix nature of the contents. However, recently, sophisticated machine learning algorithms and methods were presented to automatically detect and flag offensive remarks, ranging from threats and harassment to hate speech and cyberbullying (Premjith et al., 2023). These technologies analyze the post content and context for hate language. In a codemixed Dravidian language, it is much harder to find hateful words because the text is codemixed and has linguistic properties like morphological richness and agglutinative characteristics (Premjith et al., 2018). Furthermore, sizable datasets of tagged offensive content are needed to train and optimize the AI-based models and make them capable of identifying trends and differentiating between benign and harmful texts (Premjith et al., 2023).

The shared task on hate and offensive language detection in Telugu codemixed text intends to detect hate and offensive content in social media posts and comments written using codemixed Telugu data. The shared task was conceived as a binary class problem, where the dataset has two labels for each data - hate and non-hate. This paper discusses the task in detail and the models submitted to task by the participants.

2 Related Works

(Chakravarthi et al., 2023b) presents a compilation of four datasets extracted from YouTube, which comprise abusive remarks in Tamil and codemixed Tamil-English. Polarity has been ascribed to each dataset's annotations at the comment level. In order to establish baselines for these datasets, the authors conducted experiments utilizing various machine learning classifiers. They subsequently presented their results in F1-score, precision, and recall. In (Chakravarthi et al., 2020), the authors discussed the shared task on offensive language detection in codemixed Dravidian languages conducted as part of the HASOC shared task. (Kumaresan et al., 2021) discuss the overview of the shared task conducted for detecting hate and offensive language detection in Dravidian languages as part of HASCO-FIRE.

(Chakravarthi et al., 2023a) proposed a fusion of multilingual MPNet and CNN for classifying offensive content in social posts written in codemixed Dravidian languages such as Kannada, Malayalam and Tamil. (Subramanian et al., 2022) employed transformer-based and conventional machine learning models to categorize the codemixed text into

Proceedings of the Fourth Workshop on Speech, Vision, and Language Technologies for Dravidian Languages, pages 49–55
March 22, 2024

offensive and non-offensive categories. Moreover, the authors utilized an adapter-based approach to fine-tune the pre-trained transformer models. (Vadakkekara Suresh et al., 2021) discusses a meta-learning approach for detecting offensive content in Dravidian language codemixed text.

(Chakravarthi et al., 2022c) introduced a codemixed dataset for sentiment analysis and offensive language identification in Dravidian languages. The dataset was prepared in codemixed Kannada, Malayalam and Tamil.

3 Task Description

We used the CodaLab platform to conduct the task [1]. The task aims to develop models to identify hate and offensive language content in Telugu-English codemixed social media comments. The hateful remarks on YouTube were gathered to create the dataset. Finding the videos where the hate comments could be found was the first challenge. When generating the dataset, consideration was given to comments containing both Telugu and English words written in their respective scripts and comments that wrote Telugu characters using Latin scripts. According to YouTube's rules [2], we annotated the comments into hate and non-hate categories. Slang was taken into account when annotating the Telugu remarks with additional care. Furthermore, an additional obstacle was presented by the existence of spam content, which was extraneous to the dataset due to its lack of contextual information. Those remarks were disregarded with respect to the intended dataset. The effective analysis and categorization of YouTube comments may present a challenge due to the prevalence of incorrect syntax, typographical errors, and non-standard language usage in social media posts and comments. Before annotating the text, these remarks were reviewed to ensure that the annotators understood the context properly. The annotators were native Telugu speakers with strong academic credentials and fluency in English. In conclusion, the dataset comprised 4,500 annotated comments, of which 4,000 were training data and 500 were test data. Some statistics about the dataset is given in Table 1.

The test data contained 250 hate and non-hate data, while the training dataset contained 1,939 hate and 2,061 non-hate comments. There is not

Table 1: Statistics of the dataset

Statistics	Value
Total no.of words	43,432
No.of tokens	18,600
Maximum sentence length	71
Average sentence length	9.65

a significant issue with class imbalance based on the distribution of data points in each class. Table 2 provides the train-test split of the dataset as well as the quantity of data points in each class.

Table 2: Distribution of training and test datasets used for the shared task on abusive language detection in Telugu-English

Category	Train	Test
Hate	1,939	250
Non-hate	2,061	250
Total	4,000	250

Sixty-nine teams signed up for the competition. Only twenty-five teams, though, turned in their predictions for the test set. Each team was allowed to submit up to three runs, and the run with the best performance score was considered for creating the rank list, which is displayed in Table 3. The rank list was created, and the performance of the supplied findings was assessed using the macro F1-score.

4 System Description

This section discusses the models submitted to the shared task.

4.1 Sandalphon

This team used a fine-tuned Telugu-BERT model (Joshi, 2022) for implementation. The authors used a transliteration-based augmentation technique. A transliteration model was utilized for transliterating all the texts to the Telegu script, and another model to transliterate all the texts to Romanized script. This team scored the highest F1 score of 0.7711 in the shared task and shared first place.

4.2 Selam

This team shared first place with team Sandalphon. The submitted models were based on Convolutional Neural Network (CNN) and logistic regression for the classification.

[1] https://codalab.lisn.upsaclay.fr/competitions/16095
[2] http://tinyurl.com/ys56hrr5

Table 3: Rank list for the Telugu-English subtask

Team Name	macro F1	Rank
Sandalphon (Tabassum et al., 2024)	0.7711	1
Selam (Kanta et al., 2024)	0.7711	1
Kubapok	0.7431	3
DLRG1	0.7101	4
DLRG (Rajalakshmi et al., 2024)	0.7041	5
CUET_Binary_Hackers (Farsi et al., 2024)	0.7013	6
CUET_OpenNLP_HOLD	0.6878	7
Zavira (Ahani et al., 2024)	0.6819	8
IIITDWD-zk (Shaik et al., 2024)	0.6739	9
lemlem - Moein Tash	0.6708	10
Mizan	0.6616	11
byteSizedLLM	0.6609	12
pinealai	0.6575	13
IIITDWD_SVC (Sai et al., 2024)	0.6565	14
MUCS (KK et al., 2024)	0.6501	15
Lemlem-eyob	0.6498	16
Tewodros (Achamaleh et al., 2024)	0.6498	16
Fida (Ullah et al., 2024)	0.6369	18
Lidoma (Zamir et al., 2024)	0.6151	19
MasonTigers - Dhiman Goswami	0.5621	20
Habesha	0.5284	21
MasonTigers - AL Nahian Bin Emran	0.4959	22
CUET_DASH	0.4956	23
Fango	0.4921	24
Tayyab	0.4653	25

4.3 Kubapok

This team trained the transfer model for text classification. The model was trained with the following hyperparameters: warmup_ratio=0.1 and num_epochs=30. The team selected the best epoch checkpoint based on the F1 score computed over the development set to fix the model. The final score was fixed by taking the average of the five models' probabilities. The threshold was set at 0.5; class 0 was selected when the score fell below 0.5, and class 1 for data with a score greater than 0.5.

4.4 DLRG1

The team employed a Bi-LSTM (Bidirectional Long Short-Term Memory) to process sequential data by considering past and future contexts. They used stacked ensembles to combine predictions from multiple models to improve accuracy, leveraging the strength of diverse model architectures. A custom stacking model was employed by combining diverse classifiers, swiftly pinpointing hate speech with heightened accuracy, ensuring a safer and more inclusive online environment in Telugu-speaking communities.

4.5 DLRG

The team initially performed transliteration using the ai4bharat library's XlitEngine (Madhani et al., 2022) for Hate and Offensive Language Detection in Telugu Codemixed Text. The text was transliterated to enhance uniformity and facilitate subsequent processing. Following transliteration, two detection methods were implemented. Firstly, logistic regression with TF-IDF features was employed. Secondly, a single-cell Bi-GRU model was built. The model architecture included an embedding layer, two bidirectional GRU layers, and dense layers with ReLU activations. Training of the models included the hyperparameters such as binary cross-entropy loss and the Adam optimizer (Kingma and Ba, 2014). The combined approach leverages transliteration for text normalization and employs diverse models to capture linguistic nuances and sequential patterns in the Telugu Codemixed Text.

4.6 CUET_Binary_Hackers

The team used the pre-trained BERT large models such as MuRIL (Khanuja et al., 2021), indicBERT (Kakwani et al., 2020) and mBERT (Devlin et al., 2018) by fine-tuning the learning rates and batch size. Out of all the BERT models tried, the team's submission focuses on a fine-tuned indicBERT model, which gives better accuracy with a good F1 score.

4.7 CUET_OpenNLP_HOLD

This team used a transformer-based approach. The team fine-tuned XLM-R-base with the given training data.

4.8 Zavira

This team used a BI-LSTM network for classification.

4.9 IIITDWD-zk

The team utilized large language models such as Zephyr-7b-beta (Tunstall et al., 2023) and OpenChat-3.5 (Wang et al., 2023). In the second work, the team used an LSTM model to understand the context of the comments.

4.10 lemlem - Moein Tash

This team used Support Vector Machine (SVM), Simple Recurrent Neural Network (RNN) and Logistic Regression for the classification.

4.11 Mizan

This team used Simple Recurrent Neural Network (RNN) and Logistic Regression for the classification.

4.12 byteSizedLLM

They utilized embeddings generated from a subset of AI4Bharat's data (Kakwani et al., 2020), encompassing 100,000 randomized lines. These embeddings were created using our custom-built subword tokenizers for Telugu (with a size of 7.6 MB) and Tamil (with 1.3 MB) languages. The team employed a Bi-LSTM classifier to perform classification tasks.

4.13 pinealai

The team opted for fasttext (Bojanowski et al., 2017) and SVM for building the model. They applied GridSearch for the SVM model to know the best parameters for the model without overfitting the dataset. They also shuffled the dataset before any preprocessing to ensure that each observation was random.

4.14 IIITDWD_SVC

This team used the transliteration method to bring the text into the Telugu format ultimately and then used the translation model to translate the Telugu sentences into the English format and then trained with different models such as BERT model (cased), hate BERT and used that translated text and saved the model in h5 file and then used that model to predict the labels for the test dataset.

4.15 MUCS

The team used three models - Transfer learning with BERT model (Mathew et al., 2020), an ensemble of classifiers trained with Rchar and word-level TF-IDF features and a logistic regression classifier trained with word, subword and rchar concatenated features.

4.16 Tewodros

This team used Naive Bayes, Simple Recurrent Neural Network (RNN) and Logistic Regression for the classification.

4.17 Fida

The team used multimodels like BERT (Devlin et al., 2018), roBERTa (Liu et al., 2019) and DistilBERT (Sanh et al., 2019) for classification.

4.18 Lidoma

The team used BERT models (Devlin et al., 2018) for classification.

4.19 MasonTigers

They used XLM-R model (Conneau et al., 2019) for classification.

4.20 Habesha

The team used character-based RNN and distilBERT models.

4.21 CUET_DASH

The submission employs a multi-faceted approach using three distinct models for hate and offensive language detection in Telugu codemixed text. Logistic Regression was applied with feature extraction, incorporating n-grams and syntactic features for simplicity and interpretability. Telugu BERT enhances contextual understanding through fine-tuning on task-specific data, leveraging deep contextual embeddings..

4.22 Fango

They used Logistic regression with encoder-decoder method and SVM with encoder-decoder models were used.

4.23 Tayyab

They used BERT models for classification.

The majority of the teams used BERT-based models for feature extraction. Vairants of the BERT such as Telugu-BERT (Joshi, 2022), indicBERT (Kakwani et al., 2020), hate-BERT

(Mathew et al., 2020), and other multilingual BERT models achieved significant performance in classifiying a Telugu codemixed comment into hate and non-hate. Teams also used BERT classifier in addition to BERT embeddings for classification. There were submissions based on LSTMs and Bi-LSTMs. However, the performance of those models were not at par with the performance of the transformer models.

5 Conclusion

This paper discussed the findings of the shared task on Hate and Offensive Language Detection in Telugu Codemixed Text (HOLD-Telugu) conducted as part of the Fourth Workshop on Speech, Vision, and Language Technologies for Dravidian Languages (DravidianLangTech-2024) at EACL 2024. The datasets used for the competition were collected from YouTube comments and annotated with experts' help in compliance with YouTube's regulations. There were twenty-five submissions for this task. Most teams used multilingual BERT-based pre-trained models to transform the input text into the feature vector. The other submissions consisted of models using TF-IDF features and machine learning classifiers. We used macro F1-score to compute the classification performance and prepared the rank list accordingly.

Acknowledgements

This work was conducted with the financial support of the Science Foundation Ireland Centre for Research Training in Artificial Intelligence under Grant No. 18/CRT/6223, supported in part by a research grant from Science Foundation Ireland (SFI) under Grant Number SFI/12/RC/2289_P2(Insight_2).

References

Tewodros Achamaleh, Lemlem Eyob Kawo, Ildar Batyrshin, and Grigori Sidorov. 2024. Tewodros@DravidianLangTech 2024: Hate Speech Recognition in Telugu Codemixed Text. In *Proceedings of the Fourth Workshop on Speech, Vision, and Language Technologies for Dravidian Languages*, Malta. European Chapter of the Association for Computational Linguistics,.

Z Ahani, M. Shahiki Tash, M.T Zamir, I Gelbukh, and A Gelbukh. 2024. Zavira@DravidianLangTech 2024:Telugu hate speech detection using LSTM. In *Proceedings of the Fourth Workshop on Speech, Vision, and Language Technologies for Dravidian Languages*, Malta. European Chapter of the Association for Computational Linguistics,.

Piotr Bojanowski, Edouard Grave, Armand Joulin, and Tomas Mikolov. 2017. Enriching word vectors with subword information. *Transactions of the association for computational linguistics*, 5:135–146.

Bharathi Raja Chakravarthi. 2023. Detection of homophobia and transphobia in Youtube comments. *International Journal of Data Science and Analytics*, pages 1–20.

Bharathi Raja Chakravarthi, Adeep Hande, Rahul Ponnusamy, Prasanna Kumar Kumaresan, and Ruba Priyadharshini. 2022a. How can we detect Homophobia and Transphobia? Experiments in a multilingual code-mixed setting for social media governance. *International Journal of Information Management Data Insights*, 2(2):100119.

Bharathi Raja Chakravarthi, Manoj Balaji Jagadeeshan, Vasanth Palanikumar, and Ruba Priyadharshini. 2023a. Offensive language identification in Dravidian languages using MPNet and CNN. *International Journal of Information Management Data Insights*, 3(1):100151.

Bharathi Raja Chakravarthi, Anand Kumar M, John P McCrae, B Premjith, KP Soman, and Thomas Mandl. 2020. Overview of the track on Hasoc-Offensive Language Identification-DravidianCodeMix. In *FIRE (Working notes)*, pages 112–120.

Bharathi Raja Chakravarthi, Ruba Priyadharshini, Shubanker Banerjee, Manoj Balaji Jagadeeshan, Prasanna Kumar Kumaresan, Rahul Ponnusamy, Sean Benhur, and John Philip McCrae. 2023b. Detecting abusive comments at a fine-grained level in a low-resource language. *Natural Language Processing Journal*, 3:100006.

Bharathi Raja Chakravarthi, Ruba Priyadharshini, Thenmozhi Durairaj, John McCrae, Paul Buitelaar, Prasanna Kumaresan, and Rahul Ponnusamy. 2022b. Overview of the Shared Task on Homophobia and Transphobia Detection in Social Media Comments. In *Proceedings of the Second Workshop on Language Technology for Equality, Diversity and Inclusion*, pages 369–377, Dublin, Ireland. Association for Computational Linguistics.

Bharathi Raja Chakravarthi, Ruba Priyadharshini, Vigneshwaran Muralidaran, Navya Jose, Shardul Suryawanshi, Elizabeth Sherly, and John P McCrae. 2022c. DravidianCodeMix: sentiment analysis and offensive language identification dataset for Dravidian languages in code-mixed text. *Language Resources and Evaluation*, 56(3):765–806.

Alexis Conneau, Kartikay Khandelwal, Naman Goyal, Vishrav Chaudhary, Guillaume Wenzek, Francisco Guzmán, Edouard Grave, Myle Ott, Luke Zettlemoyer, and Veselin Stoyanov. 2019. Unsupervised Cross-lingual Representation Learning at Scale. *arXiv preprint arXiv:1911.02116*.

Jacob Devlin, Ming-Wei Chang, Kenton Lee, and Kristina Toutanova. 2018. BERT: pre-training of deep bidirectional transformers for language understanding. *CoRR*, abs/1810.04805.

Salman Farsi, Asrarul Hoque Eusha, Jawad Hossain, Shawly Ahsan, Avishek Das, and Mohammed Moshiul Hoque. 2024. CUET_Binary_Hackers@DravidianLangTech 2024: Hate and Offensive Language Detection in Telugu Code-Mixed Text Using Sentence Similarity BERT. In *Proceedings of the Fourth Workshop on Speech, Vision, and Language Technologies for Dravidian Languages*, Malta. European Chapter of the Association for Computational Linguistics,.

Raviraj Joshi. 2022. L3Cube-HindBERT and DevBERT: Pre-Trained Bert Transformer models for Devanagari based Hindi and Marathi Languages. *arXiv preprint arXiv:2211.11418*.

Divyanshu Kakwani, Anoop Kunchukuttan, Satish Golla, Gokul N.C., Avik Bhattacharyya, Mitesh M. Khapra, and Pratyush Kumar. 2020. IndicNLPSuite: Monolingual Corpora, Evaluation Benchmarks and Pre-trained Multilingual Language Models for Indian Languages. In *Findings of EMNLP*.

Selam Abitte Kanta, Grigori Sidorov, and Alexander Grigori. 2024. Selam@DravidianLangTech 2024:Identifying Hate Speech and Offensive Language. In *Proceedings of the Fourth Workshop on Speech, Vision, and Language Technologies for Dravidian Languages*, Malta. European Chapter of the Association for Computational Linguistics,.

Simran Khanuja, Diksha Bansal, Sarvesh Mehtani, Savya Khosla, Atreyee Dey, Balaji Gopalan, Dilip Kumar Margam, Pooja Aggarwal, Rajiv Teja Nagipogu, Shachi Dave, et al. 2021. MuRIL: Multilingual Representations for Indian Languages. *arXiv preprint arXiv:2103.10730*.

Diederik P Kingma and Jimmy Ba. 2014. Adam: A method for stochastic optimization. *arXiv preprint arXiv:1412.6980*.

Manavi KK, Sonali, Gauthamraj, Kavya G, Asha Hegde, and H L Shashirekha. 2024. MUCS@DravidianLangTech-2024: Role of Learning Approaches in Strengthening Hate-Alert Systems for code-mixed text. In *Proceedings of the Fourth Workshop on Speech, Vision, and Language Technologies for Dravidian Languages*, Malta. European Chapter of the Association for Computational Linguistics,.

Prasanna Kumar Kumaresan, Premjith, Ratnasingam Sakuntharaj, Sajeetha Thavareesan, Subalalitha Navaneethakrishnan, Anand Kumar Madasamy, Bharathi Raja Chakravarthi, and John P McCrae. 2021. Findings of shared task on offensive language identification in Tamil and Malayalam. In *Proceedings of the 13th Annual Meeting of the Forum for Information Retrieval Evaluation*, pages 16–18.

Yinhan Liu, Myle Ott, Naman Goyal, Jingfei Du, Mandar Joshi, Danqi Chen, Omer Levy, Mike Lewis, Luke Zettlemoyer, and Veselin Stoyanov. 2019. RoBERTa: A robustly optimized bert pretraining approach. *arXiv preprint arXiv:1907.11692*.

Yash Madhani, Sushane Parthan, Priyanka A. Bedekar, Ruchi Khapra, Vivek Seshadri, Anoop Kunchukuttan, Pratyush Kumar, and Mitesh M. Khapra. 2022. Aksharantar: Towards building open transliteration tools for the next billion users. *ArXiv*, abs/2205.03018.

Binny Mathew, Punyajoy Saha, Seid Muhie Yimam, Chris Biemann, Pawan Goyal, and Animesh Mukherjee. 2020. HateXplain: A Benchmark Dataset for Explainable Hate Speech Detection. *arXiv preprint arXiv:2012.10289*.

SN Prasanth, R Aswin Raj, P Adhithan, B Premjith, and Soman Kp. 2022. CEN-Tamil@ DravidianLangTech-ACL2022: Abusive comment detection in Tamil using TF-IDF and random kitchen sink algorithm. In *Proceedings of the Second Workshop on Speech and Language Technologies for Dravidian Languages*, pages 70–74.

B Premjith, KP Soman, and M Anand Kumar. 2018. A deep learning approach for Malayalam morphological analysis at character level. *Procedia computer science*, 132:47–54.

B Premjith, V Sowmya, Bharathi Raja Chakravarthi, Rajeswari Natarajan, K Nandhini, Abirami Murugappan, B Bharathi, M Kaushik, Prasanth Sn, et al. 2023. Findings of the shared task on multimodal abusive language detection and sentiment analysis in Tamil and Malayalam. In *Proceedings of the Third Workshop on Speech and Language Technologies for Dravidian Languages*, pages 72–79.

Ruba Priyadharshini, Bharathi Raja Chakravarthi, Subalalitha Chinnaudayar Navaneethakrishnan, Thenmozhi Durairaj, Malliga Subramanian, Kogilavani Shanmugavadivel, Siddhanth U Hegde, and Prasanna Kumar Kumaresan. 2022. Findings of the shared task on Abusive Comment Detection in Tamil. In *Proceedings of the Second Workshop on Speech and Language Technologies for Dravidian Languages. Association for Computational Linguistics*.

Ratnavel Rajalakshmi, Saptharishee M, Hareesh Teja S, Gabriel Joshua R, and Varsini SR. 2024. DLRG@DravidianLangTech2024:Combating Hate Speech in Telugu Code-mixed Text on Social Media. In *Proceedings of the Fourth Workshop on Speech, Vision, and Language Technologies for Dravidian Languages*, Malta. European Chapter of the Association for Computational Linguistics,.

Chava Srinivasa Sai, Rangoori Vinay Kumar, Sunil Saumya, and Shankar Biradar. 2024. IIITDWD_svc@DravidianLangTech-2024: Breaking Language Barriers; Hate Speech Detection in Telugu-English Code-Mixed Text. In *Proceedings* of the Fourth Workshop on Speech, Vision, and Language Technologies for Dravidian Languages, Malta. European Chapter of the Association for Computational Linguistics,.

Victor Sanh, Lysandre Debut, Julien Chaumond, and Thomas Wolf. 2019. DistilBERT, a distilled version of BERT: smaller, faster, cheaper and lighter. *arXiv preprint arXiv:1910.01108*.

Zuhair Hasan Shaik, Sai Kartheek Reddy Kasu, Sunil Saumya, and Shankar Biradar. 2024. IIITDWD-zk@DravidianLangTech-2024: Leveraging the Power of Language Models for Hate Speech Detection in Telugu-English Code-Mixed Text. In *Proceedings of the Fourth Workshop on Speech, Vision, and Language Technologies for Dravidian Languages*, Malta. European Chapter of the Association for Computational Linguistics,.

Malliga Subramanian, Rahul Ponnusamy, Sean Benhur, Kogilavani Shanmugavadivel, Adhithiya Ganesan, Deepti Ravi, Gowtham Krishnan Shanmugasundaram, Ruba Priyadharshini, and Bharathi Raja Chakravarthi. 2022. Offensive language detection in Tamil YouTube comments by adapters and cross-domain knowledge transfer. *Computer Speech & Language*, 76:101404.

Nafisa Tabassum, Mosabbir Hossain Khan, Shawly Ahsan, Jawad Hossain, and Mohammed Moshiul Hoque. 2024. Sandalphon@DravidianLangTech-EACL2024: Hate and Offensive Language Detection in Telugu Code-mixed Text using Transliteration-Augmentation. In *Proceedings of the Fourth Workshop on Speech, Vision, and Language Technologies for Dravidian Languages*, Malta. European Chapter of the Association for Computational Linguistics,.

Lewis Tunstall, Edward Beeching, Nathan Lambert, Nazneen Rajani, Kashif Rasul, Younes Belkada, Shengyi Huang, Leandro von Werra, Clémentine Fourrier, Nathan Habib, et al. 2023. Zephyr: Direct Distillation of LM Alignment. *arXiv preprint arXiv:2310.16944*.

Fida Ullah, Muhammad Tayyab Zamir, Muhammad Arif, M Ahmad, E Felipe-Riveron, and A Gelbukh. 2024. Fida@DravidianLangTech 2024: A Novel Approach to Hate Speech Detection Using Distilbert-base-multilingual-cased. In *Proceedings of the Fourth Workshop on Speech, Vision, and Language Technologies for Dravidian Languages*, Malta. European Chapter of the Association for Computational Linguistics,.

Gautham Vadakkekara Suresh, Bharathi Raja Chakravarthi, and John Philip McCrae. 2021. Meta-learning for offensive language detection in code-mixed texts. In *Proceedings of the 13th Annual Meeting of the Forum for Information Retrieval Evaluation*, pages 58–66.

Guan Wang, Sijie Cheng, Xianyuan Zhan, Xiangang Li, Sen Song, and Yang Liu. 2023. Openchat: Advancing open-source language models with mixed-quality data. *arXiv preprint arXiv:2309.11235*.

M.T Zamir, M.S Tash, Z Ahani, A Gelbukh, and G Sidorov. 2024. Lidoma@DravidianLangTech 2024: Identifying Hate Speech in Telugu Code-Mixed Texts: A BERT Multilingual Approach. In *Proceedings of the Fourth Workshop on Speech, Vision, and Language Technologies for Dravidian Languages*, Malta. European Chapter of the Association for Computational Linguistics,.

Findings of the Shared Task on Multimodal Social Media Data Analysis in Dravidian Languages (MSMDA-DL)@DravidianLangTech 2024

Premjith B[1], Jyothish Lal G[1], Sowmya V[1], Bharathi Raja Chakravarthi [2], K Nandhini[3] Rajeswari Natarajan [4], Abirami Murugappan[5], Bharathi B[6], Saranya Rajiakodi[7] Rahul Ponnusamy[2], Jayanth Mohan[1], Mekapati Spandana Reddy[1]

Amrita School of Artificial Intelligence, Coimbatore, Amrita Vishwa Vidyapeetham, India
[2]School of Computer Science, University of Galway, Ireland
[3]School of Mathematics and Computer Sciences, Central University of Tamil Nadu, India
[4]SASTRA University, India [5]Department of Information Science and Technology, Anna University, India [6]SSN College of Engineering, Tamil Nadu, India
[7]Central University of Tamil Nadu, India

Abstract

This paper presents the findings of the shared task on multimodal sentiment analysis, abusive language detection and hate speech detection in Dravidian languages. Through this shared task, researchers worldwide can submit models for three crucial social media data analysis challenges in Dravidian languages: sentiment analysis, abusive language detection, and hate speech detection. The aim is to build models for deriving fine-grained sentiment analysis from multimodal data in Tamil and Malayalam, identifying abusive and hate content from multimodal data in Tamil. Three modalities make up the multimodal data: text, audio, and video. YouTube videos were gathered to create the datasets for the tasks. Thirty-nine teams took part in the competition. However, only two teams, though, turned in their findings. The macro F1-score was used to assess the submissions.

1 Introduction

Analyzing insights from social media data with several modalities—text, audio, and video—is known as multimodal social media data. Text data from sources like Facebook posts, YouTube comments, and tweets make up conventional social media data. The primary goal of social media data analysis is to extract useful information from text data. However, a study published in (Chakravarthi et al., 2021) considers the variety of content posted on social media sites. Multiple modalities in the data can be analyzed to provide a more thorough knowledge of user behaviour, attitudes, and trends. It is possible to think of the features retrieved from audio and video data as extra information that improves the text features of the input data. Pitch, tone, and the video's facial expressions can all be used to fine-tune the elements used to identify various viewpoints and expressions more accurately. To analyze and identify various data categories, multimodal social media data analysis integrates methods from several fields, such as computer vision (CV), speech processing, and natural language processing (NLP).

The Multimodal Social Media Data Analysis in Dravidian Languages (MSMDA-DL) at the Fourth Workshop on Speech, Vision, and Language Technologies for Dravidian Languages (DravidianLangTech-2024) at EACL 2024 has three tasks: multimodal sentiment analysis in Tamil and Malayalam; multimodal detect abusive language in Tamil; and multimodal detect hate speech in Tamil. The primary goal of the shared task is to motivate researchers and academicians worldwide to join and submit their methods and findings to help research in languages with limited resources, such as Tamil and Malayalam.

The shared task on Multimodal Social Media Data Analysis in Dravidian Languages (MSMDA-DL) is summarized in this work. Additionally, the results of the submitted models for the three subtasks are discussed in this study. The shared task was hosted on the CodaLab [1]. All enrolled participants received access to training and validation data to construct their models. The test data without labels were later shared to use the developed models to forecast the future. Thirty-nine teams signed up for the two subtasks. Only two teams, though, turned in their findings.

2 Literature Review

Users on many social media sites write messages and comments in their native tongue and codemixed languages. As a result, machine learning models developed using monolingual datasets are inappropriate for classifying abusive language or deciphering the emotions present in languages with mixed coding. However, scientists are making strides toward creating systems with codemixed

[1]https://codalab.lisn.upsaclay.fr/competitions/16093

Proceedings of the Fourth Workshop on Speech, Vision, and Language Technologies for Dravidian Languages, pages 56–61
March 22, 2024 ©2024 Association for Computational Linguistics

datasets. One major problem is, as mentioned above, the process of gathering and annotating data.

2.1 Datasets

To detect hate speech and offensive content, (Chakravarthi et al., 2020b,a; Hande et al., 2021a; Mandl et al., 2020) provided a few Dravidian language datasets. The datasets (Saumya et al., 2021; Yasaswini et al., 2021; Hande et al., 2021b; Kedia and Nandy, 2021; Renjit and Idicula, 2020; Chakravarthi et al., 2022) have been used to suggest several models. For emotion analysis and offensive language detection tasks, the authors (Chakravarthi et al., 2022) created datasets using the YouTube comments of three Dravidian languages: Malayalam–English (20,000), Tamil–English (44,000), and Kannada–English (7000).

2.2 Models

An ensemble of multilingual BERT models was used by the authors (Singh and Bhattacharyya, 2020) to identify objectionable content and hate speech in Dravidian languages. For tasks including detecting hate speech and offensive content, they received an F-score of 0.95. In Malayalam comments on YouTube (mixing code and script). F-scores 0.86 and 0.72 were obtained for hate speech and offensive content detection tasks for YouTube or Twitter datasets in Malayalam (codemixed: Tanglish and Manglish). The obtained weighted average F1-score was 0.89. To identify offensive language, transformer-based models and machine learning were employed by (Dave et al., 2021). The authors used pre-trained word embedding and character n-gram to represent the sentences. For Tamil and Malayalam, the F1 scores were 0.71 and 0.95 respectively. Transformer-based models, including BERT, RoBERTa, and MuRiL, have been employed by (Li, 2021; Dowlagar and Mamidi, 2021; Zhao and Tao, 2021; Chen and Kong, 2021; Dave et al., 2021) for the job of identifying offensive languages for Dravidian languages. Text-based datasets and models are available for sentiment analysis, abusive language detection, and hate speech detection in Dravidian languages. However, multimodal dataset research still needs to be improved.

3 Description of the subtasks

The three subtasks - multimodal sentiment analysis in Tamil and Malayalam, multimodal abusive language identification in Tamil and multimodal hate speech detection in Tamil - as well as the dataset utilized, are covered in this section. There are two tasks in the "Multimodal Sentiment Analysis in Tamil and Malayalam" subtask: one in Tamil and one in Malayalam. Both tasks are modelled as a multiclass classification task with. The subtask "Multimodal abusive language detection in Tamil" is a binary class classification task, whereas the third task, "multimodal hate speech detection in Tamil", is a multiclass classification task. All of the tasks mentioned above included text, audio, and video data, and participants could use any combination of modalities to create their models.

Table 1: Details of the dataset used for the shared task on multimodal Sentiment Analysis in Tamil and Malayalam

Dataset	Tamil	Malayalam
Training	44	50
Validation	10	10
Test	10	10

3.1 Multimodal Sentiment Analysis in Tamil and Malayalam

This is the third edition of this subtask (Premjith et al., 2023), (Premjith et al., 2022). There are two sections in this subtask: one for Tamil and another for Malayalam (Chakravarthi et al., 2021). We considered YouTube to gather data for this work. We gave the participants test, validation, and training data. Data for training and validation were made available simultaneously, and unlabeled test data was provided during the testing stage. The data points were annotated with five labels in both languages: Highly Positive, Positive, Neutral, Negative, and Highly Negative.

The 64 data samples in the Tamil data were divided into training, validation, and test data in a 22:5:5 ratio. There were 70 data samples in the Malayalam corpus, of which 50 were used for training and 10 for each validation and testing. The divide is explained in depth in Table 2, which 2 shows the class-wise distribution of the data points in both languages. The class-wise distribution of the data points utilized in the training, validation, and test datasets is provided in the Tables 3 and 4. It is clear from the dataset specifics that there is an issue with high-class imbalance. There are substantially more data points in the positive category.

Table 2: Class-wise distribution of the dataset used for the shared task on multimodal Sentiment Analysis in Tamil and Malayalam

Category	Tamil	Malayalam
Highly Positive	8	9
Positive	38	39
Neutral	8	8
Negative	5	12
Highly Negative	5	2
Total	64	70

Table 3: Distribution of training, validation, and test datasets used for the shared task on multimodal Sentiment Analysis in Tamil

Category	Train	Validation	Test
Highly Positive	5	3	1
Positive	29	4	5
Neutral	4	2	2
Negative	3	1	1
Highly Negative	3	0	1
Total	44	10	10

Table 4: Distribution of training, validation, and test datasets used for the shared task on multimodal Sentiment Analysis in Malayalam

Category	Train	Validation	Test
Highly Positive	5	2	2
Positive	31	5	3
Neutral	5	1	2
Negative	8	2	2
Highly Negative	1	0	1
Total	50	10	10

Table 5: Details of the dataset used for the shared task on multimodal abusive language detection in Tamil

Dataset	Abusive	Non-abusive
Training	38	32
Test	9	9

3.2 Multimodal Abusive Language Detection in Tamil

This is the second edition of this task (Premjith et al., 2023). We supplied test and training data for this competition. Seventy YouTube videos, both abusive and non-abusive, comprise the training data. The dataset collection process is similar to that of the sentiment analysis task. Following that, 88 films were classified as abusive or non-abusive using the assistance of qualified native speakers (Ashraf et al., 2021).

The dataset was split into test and training subsets. Eighteen videos were in the test dataset, and seventy in the training dataset. Both datasets contain text and audio data in addition to videos. There are 38 videos in the abusive category and 32 in the non-abusive category in the training dataset. The quantity of data points in every class indicates a little issue with class imbalance. There are nine abusive and nine non-abusive videos in the set of 18 test videos. We sent the test data without labels for the competition's testing phase. However, following the competition's conclusion, we made the test data with labels available. Table 5 details the training and testing data.

3.3 Multimodal Hate Speech Detection in Tamil

The hate speech detection task is a multiclass classification problem, where the data points are labelled into four categories: caste, offensive, racist, and sexist. The training data comprised 40 samples, whereas the test data comprised 12. The class-wise distribution of data in both train and test data is shown in Tables 6 and 7.

4 System Description

We received two submissions; only one team participated in all three tasks. Each team could submit up to three runs. The run with the highest macro F1 score was considered when creating the rank list. Below are the system descriptions that were submitted for the shared tasks.

Table 6: Details of the training dataset used for the shared task on multimodal hate speech detection in Tamil

Class	# Data points
Caste	12
Offensive	13
Racist	12
Sexist	3
Total	40

Table 7: Details of the test dataset used for the shared task on multimodal hate speech detection in Tamil

Class	# Data points
Caste	3
Offensive	4
Racist	4
Sexist	1
Total	12

Table 8: Ranklist for the shared task on multimodal sentiment analysis in Tamil

Team	Macro F1	Rank
Wit Hub	0.2444	1

Table 9: Ranklist for the shared task on multimodal abusive language detection in Tamil

Team	Macro F1	Rank
Binary_Beasts	0.7143	1
Wit Hub	0.4156	2

Table 10: Ranklist for the shared task on multimodal hate speech detection in Tamil

Team	Macro F1	Rank
Wit Hub	0.2881	1

4.1 Binary_Beasts

The team (Rahman et al., 2024) participated only in abusive language detection. The team used ConvLSTM for the video dataset, and for the audio dataset, they used BiLSTM and multinomial naive Bayes for the text dataset. They did not use any external data to build the model. This team developed three models. From these models, they counted the majority-based result for the final output.

4.2 Wit Hub

The team (HS et al., 2024) used three different models for each subtask. They considered only text data for the analysis. For the sentiment analysis task, the team used LSTM, K-means, KNN and logistic regression models for classification. TF-IDF features and Multinomial Naive Bayes classifier were used to train the model for categorising data into abusive and non-abusive categories. In contrast, TF-IDF and random forest feature-classifier combination were considered for the hate speech identification task. This team did not use any external data to train the model.

The rank lists for multimodal sentiment analysis in Tamil, multimodal abusive language detection in Tamil, and multimodal hate speech detection in Tamil are shown in Tables 8, 9 and 10, respectively.

Among the submitted models, only Binary_Beats used three modalities to develop their model. The ConvLSTM model used by this team captures the features from the image frames and the LSTM can model the sequentiality of the image frames, which is an interesting approach. They considered LSTM for capturing the sequential properties of other modalities. The second team, Wit Hub relied on text data and extracted TF-IDF features for classification. From the results, it is evident that TF-IDF features are not good enough to classify the data into different categories for the data used in this shared task.

5 Conclusion

The results of the shared task on Multimodal Social Media Data Analysis in Dravidian Languages (MSMDA-DL) are presented in this study. The task dataset was made up of transcripts and audio that went along with videos that were gathered from YouTube. Thirty-nine people signed up for each of the three subtasks. Nevertheless, only two teams turned in their predictions for the test data that the participants were given. To create the rank list and evaluate the performance of the submitted forecasts, we employed the macro F1-score.

6 Acknowledgement

This work was conducted with the financial support of the Science Foundation Ireland Centre for Research Training in Artificial Intelligence under Grant No. 18/CRT/6223, supported in part by a research grant from Science Foundation Ireland (SFI) under Grant Number SFI/12/RC/2289_P2(Insight_2).

References

Noman Ashraf, Arkaitz Zubiaga, and Alexander Gelbukh. 2021. Abusive language detection in YouTube comments leveraging replies as conversational context. *PeerJ Computer Science*, 7:e742.

Bharathi Raja Chakravarthi, Anand Kumar M, John P McCrae, B Premjith, KP Soman, and Thomas Mandl. 2020a. Overview of the track on HASOC-Offensive Language Identification-DravidianCodeMix. In *FIRE (Working notes)*, pages 112–120.

Bharathi Raja Chakravarthi, Vigneshwaran Muralidaran, Ruba Priyadharshini, and John P McCrae. 2020b. Corpus creation for sentiment analysis in code-mixed Tamil-English text. *arXiv preprint arXiv:2006.00206*.

Bharathi Raja Chakravarthi, Ruba Priyadharshini, Vigneshwaran Muralidaran, Navya Jose, Shardul Suryawanshi, Elizabeth Sherly, and John P McCrae. 2022. DravidianCodeMix: sentiment analysis and offensive language identification dataset for Dravidian languages in code-mixed text. *Language Resources and Evaluation*, 56(3):765–806.

Bharathi Raja Chakravarthi, KP Soman, Rahul Ponnusamy, Prasanna Kumar Kumaresan, Kingston Pal Thamburaj, John P McCrae, et al. 2021. Dravidianmultimodality: A dataset for multi-modal sentiment analysis in tamil and malayalam. *arXiv preprint arXiv:2106.04853*.

Shi Chen and Bing Kong. 2021. cs@ dravidianlangtech-eacl2021: Offensive language identification based on multilingual BERT model. In *Proceedings of the First Workshop on Speech and Language Technologies for Dravidian Languages*, pages 230–235.

Bhargav Dave, Shripad Bhat, and Prasenjit Majumder. 2021. IRNLP_DAIICT@DravidianLangTech-EACL2021:Offensive Language identification in Dravidian Languages using TF-IDF Char N-grams and MuRIL. In *Proceedings of the First Workshop on Speech and Language Technologies for Dravidian Languages*, pages 266–269.

Suman Dowlagar and Radhika Mamidi. 2021. OFFLangOne@DravidianLangTech-EACL2021: Transformers with the class balanced loss for offensive language identification in Dravidian code-mixed text. In *Proceedings of the first workshop on speech and language technologies for dravidian languages*, pages 154–159.

Adeep Hande, Siddhanth U Hegde, Ruba Priyadharshini, Rahul Ponnusamy, Prasanna Kumar Kumaresan, Sajeetha Thavareesan, and Bharathi Raja Chakravarthi. 2021a. Benchmarking multi-task learning for sentiment analysis and offensive language identification in under-resourced Dravidian languages. *arXiv preprint arXiv:2108.03867*.

Adeep Hande, Karthik Puranik, Konthala Yasaswini, Ruba Priyadharshini, Sajeetha Thavareesan, Anbukkarasi Sampath, Kogilavani Shanmugavadivel, Durairaj Thenmozhi, and Bharathi Raja Chakravarthi. 2021b. Offensive language identification in low-resourced code-mixed Dravidian languages using pseudo-labeling. *arXiv preprint arXiv:2108.12177*.

Anierudh HS, Abhishek R, Ashwin V Sundar, Amrit Krishnan, and Bharathi B. 2024. Wit Hub@DravidianLangTech-2024:Multimodal Social Media Data Analysis in Dravidian Languages using Machine Learning Models. In *Proceedings of the Fourth Workshop on Speech, Vision, and Language Technologies for Dravidian Languages*, Malta. European Chapter of the Association for Computational Linguistics.

Kushal Kedia and Abhilash Nandy. 2021. indicnlp@ kgp at DravidianLangTech-EACL2021: Offensive language identification in Dravidian languages. *arXiv preprint arXiv:2102.07150*.

Zichao Li. 2021. Codewithzichao@ dravidianlangtech-eacl2021: Exploring multilingual transformers for offensive language identification on code mixing text. In *Proceedings of the First Workshop on Speech and Language Technologies for Dravidian Languages*, pages 164–168.

Thomas Mandl, Sandip Modha, Anand Kumar M, and Bharathi Raja Chakravarthi. 2020. Overview of the HASOC track at FIRE 2020: Hate speech and offensive language identification in Tamil, Malayalam, Hindi, English and German. In *Forum for information retrieval evaluation*, pages 29–32.

B Premjith, Bharathi Raja Chakravarthi, Malliga Subramanian, B Bharathi, Soman Kp, V Dhanalakshmi, K Sreelakshmi, Arunaggiri Pandian, and Prasanna Kumaresan. 2022. Findings of the shared task on multimodal sentiment analysis and troll meme classification in Dravidian languages. In *Proceedings of the Second Workshop on Speech and Language Technologies for Dravidian Languages*, pages 254–260.

B Premjith, V Sowmya, Bharathi Raja Chakravarthi, Rajeswari Natarajan, K Nandhini, Abirami Murugappan, B Bharathi, M Kaushik, Prasanth Sn, et al.

2023. Findings of the shared task on multimodal abusive language detection and sentiment analysis in Tamil and Malayalam. In *Proceedings of the Third Workshop on Speech and Language Technologies for Dravidian Languages*, pages 72–79.

Md. Tanvir Rahman, Abu Bakkar Siddique Raihan, Tanzim Rahman, Shawly Ahsan, Jawad Hossain, Avishek Das, and Mohammed Moshiul Hoque. 2024. Binary_Beasts@DravidianLangTech@EACL 2024: Multimodal Abusive Language Detection in Tamil based on Integrated Approach of Machine Learning and Deep Learning Techniques. In *Proceedings of the Fourth Workshop on Speech, Vision, and Language Technologies for Dravidian Languages*, Malta. European Chapter of the Association for Computational Linguistics.

Sara Renjit and Sumam Mary Idicula. 2020. CUSATNLP@HASOC-Dravidian-CodeMix-FIRE2020:Identifying Offensive Language from Manglish Tweets. *arXiv preprint arXiv:2010.08756*.

Sunil Saumya, Abhinav Kumar, and Jyoti Prakash Singh. 2021. Offensive language identification in Dravidian code mixed social media text. In *Proceedings of the first workshop on speech and language technologies for Dravidian languages*, pages 36–45.

Pankaj Singh and Pushpak Bhattacharyya. 2020. CFILT IIT Bombay@ HASOC-Dravidian-Codemix FIRE 2020: Assisting ensemble of transformers with random transliteration. In *FIRE (Working Notes)*, pages 411–416.

Konthala Yasaswini, Karthik Puranik, Adeep Hande, Ruba Priyadharshini, Sajeetha Thavareesan, and Bharathi Raja Chakravarthi. 2021. IIITT@DravidianLangTech-EACL2021: Transfer learning for offensive language detection in Dravidian languages. In *Proceedings of the First Workshop on Speech and Language Technologies for Dravidian Languages*, pages 187–194.

Yingjia Zhao and Xin Tao. 2021. ZYJ123@DravidianLangTech-EACL2021: Offensive language identification based on XLM-RoBERTa with DPCNN. In *Proceedings of the first workshop on speech and language technologies for Dravidian languages*, pages 216–221.

Overview of Second Shared Task on Sentiment Analysis in Code-mixed Tamil and Tulu

Lavanya Sambath Kumar[1] **, Asha Hegde**[2] **, Bharathi Raja Chakravarthi**[3]**,**
Hosahalli Lakshmaiah Shashirekha[2]**, Rajeshwari Natarajan**[4]**,**
Sajeetha Thavareesan[5]**, Ratnasingam Sakuntharaj**[5]**, Durairaj Thenmozhi**[6]**,**
Prasanna Kumar Kumaresan[7]**, Charumathi Rajakumar**[8]
[1] Anna University, Tamil Nadu, India, [2] Mangalore University, Mangalore, India
[3] School of Computer Science, University of Galway, Ireland
[4] SASTRA University, Tamil Nadu, India, [5] Eastern University, Sri Lanka
[6] Sri Sivasubramaniya Nadar College of Engineering, Chennai, India
[7] Data Science Institute, University of Galway, Ireland
[8] The American College, Madurai, Tamil Nadu, India
bharathiraja.akr@gmail.com

Abstract

Sentiment Analysis (SA) in Dravidian code-mixed text is a hot research area right now. In this regard, the "Second Shared Task on SA in Code-mixed Tamil and Tulu" at Dravidian-LangTech (EACL-2024) is organized. Two tasks namely SA in Tamil-English and Tulu-English code-mixed data, make up this shared assignment. In total, 64 teams registered for the shared task, out of which 19 and 17 systems were received for Tamil and Tulu, respectively. The performance of the systems submitted by the participants was evaluated based on the macro F1-score. The best method obtained macro F1-scores of 0.260 and 0.584 for code-mixed Tamil and Tulu texts, respectively.

1 Introduction

Sentiment Analysis (SA) employs machine learning and artificial intelligence techniques to extract and classify the sentiments and emotions about a person (Raj et al., 2024), service, event or a topic that individuals may be hiding behind a text. SA finds its applications in a wide range of fields, such as e-commerce, healthcare, banking, politics, and others. SA is challenging as sentiments vary based on context, emojis and usage of irony and sarcasm in casual conversations (Hegde et al., 2023b). Digital revolution paved the way for the native speakers of Dravidian languages to express their opinion in social media platforms which has lead to a great deal of attention for SA in Dravidian languages (Chakravarthi et al., 2020c). It is challenging due to language complexity and availability of low resources. Code-mixing adds much more complexity in analysing the sentiments as people have the tendency of using non-native scripts in place various historically used scripts (Chakravarthi et al., 2021b; Hegde and Shashirekha, 2022). In such cases, SA models trained on monolingual data may not suit for code-mixed data because of complex linguistic patterns (Chakravarthi et al., 2022, 2021a).

Tamil- holds the distinction of being one of India's oldest surviving classical languages (Vasantharajan et al., 2022; Hegde et al., 2022b). Recognized as a scheduled language under the Indian constitution, it serves as the official language in Tamil Nadu and Puducherry. Beyond India, Tamil is acknowledged as a national language in both Singapore and Sri Lanka. With a significant presence, it is spoken by a sizable minority in additional south Indian states, including Kerala, Karnataka, Andhra Pradesh, Telangana, and the Union Territory of Andaman and Nicobar Islands (Bharathi et al., 2023). The archaeological evidence of the first Tamil script, dating back to 580 BCE, was discovered on pottery in the Keezhadi, Sivagangai, and Madurai districts of Tamil Nadu by the Tamil Nadu State Department of Archaeology and the Archaeological Survey of India (Sivanantham and Seran, 2019).

Tulu - is a prominent Dravidian language, spoken by around 2.5 million people, primarily in the Dakshina Kannada and Udupi districts of Karnataka, along with certain areas in Kasaragod, Kerala. The language preserves key features of ancient Dravidian languages, offering a glimpse into linguistic traditions while also introducing unique innovations not observed in other Dravidian languages (Padmanabha Kekunnaya). Tulu stands as a testament to the linguistic diversity and rich cultural tapestry present in the Indian subcontinent (Antony et al., 2012; Hegde et al., 2022c).

Proceedings of the Fourth Workshop on Speech, Vision, and Language Technologies for Dravidian Languages, pages 62–70
March 22, 2024

Team name	Run name	Precision	Recall	Macro F1-score	Rank
MUCS (B et al., 2024)	Run2	0.291	0.279	0.260	1
CUETSentimentSillies (Tripty et al., 2024)	Run1	0.288	0.270	0.258	2
CUET_Binary_Hackers (Eusha et al., 2024)	Run3	0.279	0.268	0.227	3
CEN-Amrita	Run1	0.250	0.259	0.220	4
Transformers (Singhal and Bedi, 2024)	Run1	0.245	0.279	0.212	5
KEC_DL_KSK	Run3	0.278	0.263	0.197	6
Habesha	Run2	0.299	0.253	0.171	7
KEC_AI_CODE_MAKER (Shanmugavadivel et al., 2024a)	Run1	0.284	0.258	0.170	8
bytesizedllm	Run1	0.277	0.245	0.157	9
kubapok	Run2	0.144	0.131	0.122	10
wordwizards (Balaji et al., 2024)	Run1	0.213	0.243	0.074	11
Fango	Run1	0.075	0.162	0.060	12
InnovationEngineers (Shanmugavadivel et al., 2024b)	Run1	0.102	0.165	0.035	13

Table 1: Rank list based on macro average F1 score for code-mixed Tamil text

2 Task Description

Tamil and Tulu are low-resource Dravidian languages, where limited resources are available specifically for SA. The primary objective of the proposed shared task[1] is to find the sentiment polarity in gold standard code-mixed Tamil-English (Chakravarthi et al., 2020b) and Tulu-Kannada-English (Hegde et al., 2022a) datasets. These code-mixed datasets consist of posts and comments gathered from YouTube comments. Class imbalance issues are also present in this dataset, which represents a real-world situation (Hegde et al., 2023a). The secondary objective is to support studies that will shed light on the expression of sentiment in code-mixed scenarios. This task involves classifying polarity of YouTube comments into four categories: positive, negative, neutral, or mixed emotions.

3 Dataset

Due to the widespread expansion of digital content on social media platforms like YouTube, Twitter, and Instagram, there has been a substantial increase in SA of social media text in even low-resource languages, including Kannada, Tamil, Telugu, and Malayalam (Hande et al., 2020; Chakravarthi et al., 2020a). Despite the development of numerous SA models, the evolving nature of user-generated content, which is becoming more diverse and creative, underscores the need for more efficient tools (Hegde et al., 2023c; Rachana et al., 2023). Focusing on YouTube comments for SA, two gold standard corpora: i) Tamil-English and ii) Tulu-Kannada-English are made available to the research community through this shared task. The corpora, acting as a crucial repository, offer substantial support for researchers and practitioners engaged in SA within multilingual contexts. Specifically, they enable the development and evaluation of models adept at processing code-mixed data present in Tamil and Tulu texts derived from YouTube comments. The statistics of these corpora are given in Table 2.

[1] https://codalab.lisn.upsaclay.fr/competitions/16088

4 Related work

Recent advancements in SA on social media have witnessed notable progress, particularly in the realm of the internet (Wankhade et al., 2022). These studies have extended their focus to encompass not only high-resource languages but also low-resource languages, reflecting a growing recognition of the importance of linguistic diversity in understanding and analyzing user sentiments across various social media platforms (Chakravarthi et al., 2022; Priyadharshini et al., 2021). This inclusive approach enhances the applicability and effectiveness of sentiment analysis techniques in capturing the nuances of expression in a wide array of languages. With this view, Chakravarthi et al. (2020c) and B et al. (2022) organized shared tasks in code-mixed Dravidian languages to promote SA under low-resource scenarios.

SR et al. (2022) presented kernel-based extreme learning for SA in code-mixed Dravidian languages (Tamil, Kannada, and Malayalam). Their focus was

Label	Train Set		Development Set		Test set	
	Tamil	Tulu	Tamil	Tulu	Tamil	Tulu
Positive	20,070	3,118	2,257	369	73	248
Neutral	5,628	1,719	611	202	137	140
Mixed Feeling	4,020	974	480	120	101	70
Negative	4,271	646	438	90	338	43

Table 2: Class-wise distribution of code-mixed Tamil and Tulu texts

more on handling data imbalance issues and extracting more relevant features employing feature selection techniques. A Deep Learning (DL) technique for SA on code-mixed Malayalam text using Hierarchical Attention Network (HAN) model was proposed by Pillai and Arun (2024). ALBERT[2] tokenization was executed and key features specifically Term Frequency-Inverse Document Frequency (TF-IDF) based and n-grams features were extracted in the feature extraction step. Feature fusion was applied to the retrieved features using HAN and Shannon entropy. Finally, sentiment in the comments was categorized into positive or negative class. They concluded that the Feature fusion+HAN technique achieved better results for Malayalam code-mixed data. SA on Tamil code-mixed data using a variety of cutting-edge learning and hybrid deep learning algorithms was implemented by Shanmugavadivel et al. (2022). Various pre-processing procedures, such as emojis removal, repeated characters removal, punctuation, symbols, and number removal were employed to clean the data set. TF-IDF technique was used for feature extraction. The authors made a claim stating that the creation of hybrid DL models by merging Convolutional Neural Network (CNN) + Long Short Term Memory (LSTM), LSTM+CNN, CNN+Bidirectional LSTM (BiLSTM), and BiLSTM+CNN makes their study effort novel. It was found that the hybrid DL model CNN+BiLSTM was effective at SA on data with mixed Tamil and English codes.

Late-off transformer models have gained tremendous attention from the scholarly community, specifically for SA in Dravidian languages (Elankath and Ramamirtham, 2023). The existing research on SA in code-mixed Dravidian languages has identified key trends and emphasized the need for further exploration (Saini and Roy, 2023). While some studies have utilized good-quality datasets and models, the literature underscores the substantial gaps that persist in understanding hidden sentiments within these languages (Hande et al., 2022). Despite the progress made, a significant research opportunity exists to delve deeper into the complexities of sentiment analysis in code-mixed Dravidian languages and contribute to the advancement of this field.

5 Methodology

We received a total of 19 submissions for Tamil and 17 submissions for Tulu. The systems were evaluated based on macro average F1 scores and rank lists were prepared. Table 1 and Table 3 show the rank lists of code-mixed Tamil and Tulu texts respectively. We briefly describe below the methodologies used by the top five teams.

- MUCS (B et al., 2024): The authors implemented SVM and an ensemble of three Machine Learning (ML) classifiers (Support Vector Model (SVM), Random Forest (RF), and k Nearest Neighbors (kNN)) for SA in code-mixed Tamil and Tulu text. They also employed Gridsearch algorithm to get the optimal hyperparameters of the classifiers. Their proposed model obtained macro F1 scores of 0.260 and 0.584 for code-mixed Tamil and Tulu texts securing 1st and 2nd ranks in the shared task.

- CUET_Binary_Hackers (Eusha et al., 2024): The authors fine-tuned indicbert[3] (Kakwani et al., 2020) and indic-sentence-bert-nli[4] (Deode et al., 2023) models for Tamil language and bert-base-multilingual-cased[5] (Devlin et al., 2018) (mBERT) model for Tulu language. In addition, they ensembled ML classifiers with majority voting for SA in Tamil

[2]https://huggingface.co/docs/transformers/en/model_doc/albert

[3]https://huggingface.co/ai4bharat/indic-bert

[4]https://huggingface.co/l3cube-pune/indic-sentence-bert-nli

[5]https://huggingface.co/bert-base-multilingual-cased

Team name	Run name	Precision	Recall	Macro F1-score	Rank
CUET_Binary_Hackers (Eusha et al., 2024)	Run1	0.590	0.580	0.584	1
kubapok	Run1	0.617	0.57	0.584	1
MUCS (B et al., 2024)	Run2	0.548	0.554	0.550	2
Habesha	Run1	0.502	0.531	0.504	3
CEN-Amrita	Run1	0.488	0.489	0.477	4
CUETSentimentSillies (Tripty et al., 2024)	Run1	0.512	0.468	0.468	5
KEC_DL_KSK	Run2	0.485	0.446	0.443	6
Fango	Run1	0.316	0.404	0.344	7
wordwizards_tulu (Balaji et al., 2024)	Run1	0.296	0.270	0.251	8
Transformers (Singhal and Bedi, 2024)	Run1	0.222	0.251	0.221	9

Table 3: Rank list based on macro average F1 score for code-mixed Tulu text

and Tulu languages. Their proposed ensemble model obtained a macro F1 score of 0.227 securing 3rd rank in the shared task for Tamil language. Further, their fine-tuned mBERT model obtained a macro F1 score of 0.584 securing 1st rank in the shared task for Tulu language.

- CUETSentimentSillies (Tripty et al., 2024): The authors have resampled the Tamil dataset before pre-processing and fine-tuned xlm-roberta-base-language-detection[6] - a pre-trained model to fins SA in code-mixed Tamil text (Conneau et al., 2019). Whereas, for Tulu, they fine-tuned bert-base-multilingual-uncased-sentiment[7] model for SA in code-mixed Tulu text. Their proposed models obtained macro F1 scores of 0.258 and 0.468 securing 2nd and 5th ranks in the shared task for code-mixed Tamil and Tulu texts respectively.

- CEN-Amrita: The team employs a combination of CNN in feature extraction and BiLSTM layers to capture contextual information for SA in Tamil and Tulu languages. Their proposed model obtained macro F1 scores of 0.220 and 0.477 for Tamil and Tulu languages respectively securing 4th rank in the shared task for both the languages.

- kubapok: The authors fine-tuned five BERT variants: twhin-bert-large[8] (Zhang et al., 2023), muril-base-cased[9] (MuRIL) (Khanuja et al., 2021), mDeBERTa V3 base[10] (He et al., 2021), xlm-roberta-large[11] (Conneau et al., 2019), and xlm-roberta-large for SA in code-mixed Tamil and Tulu texts. They averaged all the probabilities of the five models while taking considering the prediction. Their proposed methodology achieved macro F1 scores of 0.122 and 0.584 securing 10th and 1st ranks in the shared task for code-mixed Tamil and Tulu texts respectively.

- Transformers (Singhal and Bedi, 2024): The authors have carried out minority undersampling for both the datasets as the provided Tamil and Tulu datasets are imbalanced. They separately fine-tuned XLM Roberta (Conneau et al., 2019) for Tamil and Tulu languages. Their proposed models obtained the macro F1 scores of 0.212 and 0.221 securing 5th and 9th ranks in the shared task for code-mixed Tamil and Tulu texts respectively.

- Habesha: The team employs two distinct models: i) Run1 - a model based on transformers for embedding, coupled with DL techniques for the purpose of classification and ii) Run 2 - a fine-tuned DistilBERT[12] (Sanh et al., 2019) model for SA in Tamil and Tulu languages. Run 2 obtained macro F1 score of 0.171 for code-mixed Tamil text. Further, Run 1 obtained a macro F1 score of 0.504 for code-

[6]https://huggingface.co/papluca/xlm-roberta-base-language-detection
[7]https://huggingface.co/nlptown/bert-base-multilingual-uncased-sentiment
[8]https://huggingface.co/Twitter/twhin-bert-large
[9]https://huggingface.co/google/muril-base-cased
[10]https://huggingface.co/microsoft/mdeberta-v3-base
[11]https://huggingface.co/FacebookAI/xlm-roberta-large
[12]https://huggingface.co/docs/transformers/en/model_doc/distilbert

mixed Tulu text. This team secured 7th and 5th ranks in the shared task for Tamil and Tulu languages.

6 Evaluation

The sentiment class distribution is imbalanced in datasets, particularly in the Tamil code-mixed dataset, where the majority of comments are categorized as Positive sentiment (20,070). Addressing this imbalance is crucial for developing a robust SA model that can effectively capture nuanced patterns across different sentiment classes. Similarly, the Tulu code-mixed dataset has class imbalance with Positive (3,118) and Neutral (1,719) being the majority classes. In addressing class imbalance, the utilization of the macro F1 score serves as a robust metric for ranking systems. This approach is beneficial when evaluating models trained on imbalanced datasets, as it offers a balanced assessment of performance across all classes, irrespective of their distribution. Unlike accuracy, which can be misleading in imbalanced scenarios where a model may excel by predominantly predicting the majority class, the macro F1 score assigns equal importance to each class. This makes it a reliable metric for evaluating model performance in situations characterized by class imbalances, as it takes into account both precision and recall for each class. The computation of the macro F1 score involves averaging the F1 scores of individual classes in a multi-class classification problem, providing a comprehensive and fair evaluation of the model's effectiveness. To facilitate this calculation, we leveraged the classification report tool from Scikit-learn[13], which provided comprehensive metrics and insights for evaluating the performance of the systems.

7 Results and Discussion

There are 64 participants in the SA shared task, which focused on two languages: code-mixed Tamil and Tulu text. Among them, 19 for Tamil and 17 teams for Tulu actively engaged in the challenge, submitting their systems for Tamil and Tulu language tracks. The resulting rank lists, depicted in Tables 1 and 3 for Tamil and Tulu languages respectively, outline the performance of these systems. Notably, a majority of the submissions were adept at handling SA for both languages concurrently. This section unveils the top-ranked outcomes for both languages, emphasizing macro F1 scores as the evaluation metric. The rankings signify the systems' proficiency on the dataset, with higher positions denoting superior macro F1 scores across all classes, thereby providing a comprehensive assessment of their performance.

Teams that participated in the SA shared task have frequently employed transformer models such as XLM-RoBERTa, mBERT, DeBERTa-Large[14], MuRIL, and IndicBERT[15], despite these models not being originally pre-trained on code-mixed text. The application of these linguistic representations has been diverse, with teams exploring a variety of ML models, including SVM, kNN, Multi Layer Perceptron, Linear Support Vector Classifier, and RF. Furthermore, DL models such as CNN and BiLSTM have been extensively experimented with. To effectively address the challenges associated with processing code-mixed text, these models are combined with TF-IDF of word and character n-grams, showcasing a holistic approach to SA on multilingual and code-mixed data. One team (MUCS (B et al., 2024)) in the SA shared task has distinguished itself by employing a grid-search algorithm to meticulously determine optimal hyperparameter values for their ML algorithms. Going beyond individual models, this team has implemented a sophisticated ensemble approach, utilizing majority voting across three distinct ML classifiers. This ensemble strategy, combined with the fine-tuned hyperparameter values, underscores the team's commitment to maximizing performance and robustly addressing the challenges of SA in code-mixed text.

Participants in the SA shared task faced challenges when working with code-mixed text, particularly due to the inclusion of non-native scripts in the corpus. In response, they addressed this issue by acquiring pre-trained models from libraries and fine-tuning them to better suit their corpora. Notably, the limited availability of resources for Tulu code-mixed text, in contrast to Tamil, prompted participants to take proactive measures, including resource generation and training pre-trained models from scratch. Acknowledging the data imbalance within the dataset, participants strategically employed the undersampling technique to effectively mitigate the imbalance and enhance the per-

[13]https://scikit-learn.org/stable/modules/generated/sklearn.metrics.f1_score.html

[14]https://huggingface.co/microsoft/deberta-large

[15]https://huggingface.co/ai4bharat/IndicBERTv2-MLM-only

formance of their SA models. Despite earnest efforts, both BiLSTM models and traditional ML algorithms fell short of delivering satisfactory results when compared to the performance of transformer-based models. Notably, among the diverse models tested, mBERT and other transformer-based architectures demonstrated the most promising and superior performance. Further, Gridsearch algorithm was found to be more beneficial in obtaining better performance.

The participated teams in the competition have highlighted a concerning trend of persistently low F1 scores, indicating a notable challenge in achieving robust SA. The likely reason for this issue is the significant data imbalance present in the provided datasets, a factor that has not been adequately addressed in the system descriptions provided by participating teams. Moreover, a predominant reliance on feature extraction and classifier construction methods by most participants, instead of incorporating feature selection techniques, may contribute to the suboptimal performance.

8 Conclusion

In presenting the results of the SA shared task on code-mixed Tamil and Tulu text, the dataset used was comprised of code-mixed instances sourced from social media, notably YouTube comments. A prevalent strategy among the participants involved the application of fine-tuning techniques to pre-train multilingual language models to address the SA challenge. By adopting this approach, participants were able to capitalize on the pre-existing knowledge embedded in the multilingual models while tailoring them to the context of given code-mixed Dravidian languages. This method proved effective in leveraging the strengths of pre-trained models for improved SA performance in the specific domain of social media discourse.

The top-performing systems in the shared tasks demonstrated success through the incorporation of Gridsearch algorithm, voting classifiers, and fine-tuned pre-trained models. Despite their achievements, the results underscore the existing potential for further enhancement in SA across Tamil and Tulu languages. The increased participation and improved performance of the systems signal a growing interest in the field of Dravidian Natural Language Processing (NLP) and indicate a positive trend toward advancing research within this domain. The ongoing efforts and achievements in the shared tasks suggest a promising trajectory for continued development and refinement of SA techniques for these languages.

Acknowledgement

This work was conducted with the financial support of the Science Foundation Ireland Centre for Research Training in Artificial Intelligence under Grant No. 18/CRT/6223, supported in part by a research grant from Science Foundation Ireland (SFI) under Grant Number SFI/12/RC/2289_P2(Insight_2).

References

PJ Antony, Hemant B Raj, BS Sahana, Dimple Sonal Alvares, and Aishwarya Raj. 2012. Morphological Analyzer and Generator for Tulu Language: A Novel Approach. In *Proceedings of the International Conference on Advances in Computing, Communications and Informatics*, pages 828–834.

Prathvi B, Manavi K K, Subrahmanya, Asha Hegde, Kavya G, and H L Shashirekha. 2024. MUCS@DravidianLangTech-2024: A Grid Search Approach to Explore Sentiment Analysis in Code-mixed Tamil and Tulu . In *Proceedings of the Fourth Workshop on Speech, Vision, and Language Technologies for Dravidian Languages*, Malta. European Chapter of the Association for Computational Linguistics.

Premjith B, Bharathi Raja Chakravarthi, Malliga Subramanian, Bharathi B, Soman Kp, Dhanalakshmi V, Sreelakshmi K, Arunaggiri Pandian, and Prasanna Kumaresan. 2022. Findings of the Shared Task on Multimodal Sentiment Analysis and Troll Meme Classification in Dravidian Languages. In *Proceedings of the Second Workshop on Speech and Language Technologies for Dravidian Languages*, pages 254–260, Dublin, Ireland. Association for Computational Linguistics.

Shreedevi Seluka Balaji, Akshatha Anbalagan, Niranjana A, Priyadharshini T, and Durairaj Thenmozhi. 2024. WordWizards@DravidianLangTech 2024: Sentiment Analysis in Tamil and Tulu using Sentence Embedding. In *Proceedings of the Fourth Workshop on Speech, Vision, and Language Technologies for Dravidian Languages*, Malta. European Chapter of the Association for Computational Linguistics.

B Bharathi, Bharathi Raja Chakravarthi, Subalalitha Cn, Sripriya Natarajan, Rajeswari Natarajan, S Suhasini, and Swetha Valli. 2023. Overview of the Second Shared Task on Tpeech Recognition for Vulnerable Individuals in Tamil. In *Proceedings of the Third Workshop on Language Technology for Equality, Diversity and Inclusion*, pages 31–37.

Bharathi Raja Chakravarthi, Navya Jose, Shardul Suryawanshi, Elizabeth Sherly, and John P McCrae. 2020a. A Sentiment Analysis Dataset for Code-mixed Malayalam-English. *arXiv preprint arXiv:2006.00210*.

Bharathi Raja Chakravarthi, Vigneshwaran Muralidaran, Ruba Priyadharshini, and John P McCrae. 2020b. Corpus creation for sentiment analysis in code-mixed Tamil-English text. In *Proceedings of the 1st Joint Workshop on Spoken Language Technologies for Under-resourced languages (SLTU) and Collaboration and Computing for Under-Resourced Languages (CCURL)*.

Bharathi Raja Chakravarthi, Ruba Priyadharshini, Vigneshwaran Muralidaran, Navya Jose, Shardul Suryawanshi, Elizabeth Sherly, and John P McCrae. 2022. Dravidiancodemix: Sentiment Analysis and Offensive Language Identification Dataset for Dravidian Languages in Code-mixed Text. In *Language Resources and Evaluation*, volume 56, pages 765–806. Springer.

Bharathi Raja Chakravarthi, Ruba Priyadharshini, Vigneshwaran Muralidaran, Shardul Suryawanshi, Navya Jose, Elizabeth Sherly, and John P McCrae. 2020c. Overview of the Track on Sentiment Analysis for Dravidian Languages in Code-mixed Text. In *Forum for information retrieval evaluation*, pages 21–24.

Bharathi Raja Chakravarthi, Ruba Priyadharshini, Sajeetha Thavareesan, Dhivya Chinnappa, Durairaj Thenmozhi, Elizabeth Sherly, John P. McCrae, Adeep Hande, Rahul Ponnusamy, Shubhanker Banerjee, and Charangan Vasantharajan. 2021a. Findings of the Sentiment Analysis of Dravidian Languages in Code-Mixed Text. In *CEUR Workshop Proceedings*.

BR Chakravarthi, PK Kumaresan, R Sakuntharaj, AK Madasamy, S Thavareesan, S Chinnaudayar Navaneethakrishnan, and T Mandl. 2021b. Overview of the HASOC-DravidianCodeMix shared task on offensive language detection in Tamil and Malayalam. In *Working Notes of FIRE 2021-Forum for Information Retrieval Evaluation*. CEUR.

Alexis Conneau, Kartikay Khandelwal, Naman Goyal, Vishrav Chaudhary, Guillaume Wenzek, Francisco Guzmán, Edouard Grave, Myle Ott, Luke Zettlemoyer, and Veselin Stoyanov. 2019. Unsupervised Cross-lingual Representation Learning at Scale. *CoRR*, abs/1911.02116.

Samruddhi Deode, Janhavi Gadre, Aditi Kajale, Ananya Joshi, and Raviraj Joshi. 2023. L3Cube-IndicSBERT: A Simple Approach for Learning Cross-lingual Sentence Representations using Multilingual BERT. *arXiv preprint arXiv:2304.11434*.

Jacob Devlin, Ming-Wei Chang, Kenton Lee, and Kristina Toutanova. 2018. BERT: Pre-training of Deep Bidirectional Transformers for Language Understanding. *CoRR*, abs/1810.04805.

Syam Mohan Elankath and Sunitha Ramamirtham. 2023. Sentiment Analysis of Malayalam Tweets using Bidirectional Encoder Representations from Transformers: A Study. *Indonesian Journal of Electrical Engineering and Computer Science*, 29(3):1817–1826.

Asrarul Hoque Eusha, Salman Farsi, Ariful Islam, Avishek Das, Jawad Hossain, Shawly Ahsan, and Mohammed Moshiul Hoque. 2024. CUET_Binary_Hackers@DravidianLangTech-EACL 2024: Sentiment Analysis using Transformer-Based Models in Code-Mixed and Transliterated Tamil and Tulu. In *Proceedings of the Fourth Workshop on Speech, Vision, and Language Technologies for Dravidian Languages*, Malta. European Chapter of the Association for Computational Linguistics.

Adeep Hande, Siddhanth U Hegde, and Bharathi Raja Chakravarthi. 2022. Multi-task learning in under-resourced Dravidian Languages. *Journal of Data, Information and Management*, 4(2):137–165.

Adeep Hande, Ruba Priyadharshini, and Bharathi Raja Chakravarthi. 2020. KanCMD: Kannada CodeMixed dataset for Sentiment Analysis and Offensive Language Letection. In *Proceedings of the Third Workshop on Computational Modeling of People's Opinions, Personality, and Emotion's in Social Media*, pages 54–63.

Pengcheng He, Jianfeng Gao, and Weizhu Chen. 2021. DeBERTaV3: Improving DeBERTa using ELECTRA-Style Pre-Training with Gradient-Disentangled Embedding Sharing.

Asha Hegde, Mudoor Devadas Anusha, Sharal Coelho, Hosahalli Lakshmaiah Shashirekha, and Bharathi Raja Chakravarthi. 2022a. Corpus Creation for Sentiment Analysis in Code-Mixed Tulu Text. In *Proceedings of the 1st Annual Meeting of the ELRA/ISCA Special Interest Group on Under-Resourced Languages*, pages 33–40.

Asha Hegde, Shubhanker Banerjee, Bharathi Raja Chakravarthi, Ruba Priyadharshini, Hosahalli Shashirekha, John Philip McCrae, et al. 2022b. Overview of the Shared Task on Machine Translation in Dravidian Languages. In *Proceedings of the second workshop on speech and language technologies for Dravidian languages*, pages 271–278.

Asha Hegde, Bharathi Raja Chakravarthi, Hosahalli Lakshmaiah Shashirekha, Rahul Ponnusamy, Subalalitha Chinnaudayar Navaneethakrishnan, Lavanya Sambath Kumar, Durairaj Thenmozhi, Martha Karunakar, Shreya Sriram, and Sarah Aymen. 2023a. Findings of the Shared Task on Sentiment Analysis in Tamil and Tulu Code-Mixed Text. In *Third Workshop on Speech and Language Technologies for Dravidian Languages*, pages 64–71.

Asha Hegde, Bharathi Raja Chakravarthi, Hosahalli Lakshmaiah Shashirekha, Rahul Ponnusamy, Subalalitha Cn, SK Lavanya, Durairaj Thenmozhi, Martha

Karunakar, Shreya Shreeram, and Sarah Aymen. 2023b. Findings of the Shared task on Sentiment Analysis in Tamil and Tulu Code-mixed Text. In *Proceedings of the Third Workshop on Speech and Language Technologies for Dravidian Languages*, pages 64–71.

Asha Hegde, G Kavya, Sharal Coelho, Pooja Lamani, and Hosahalli Lakshmaiah Shashirekha. 2023c. MUNLP@ DravidianLangTech2023: Learning Approaches for Sentiment Analysis in Code-mixed Tamil and Tulu Text. In *Proceedings of the Third Workshop on Speech and Language Technologies for Dravidian Languages*, pages 275–281.

Asha Hegde and Hosahalli Lakshmaiah Shashirekha. 2022. Leveraging Dynamic Meta Embedding for Sentiment Analysis and Detection of Homophobic. *Transphobic Content in Code-mixed Dravidian Languages*.

Asha Hegde, Hosahalli Lakshmaiah Shashirekha, Anand Kumar Madasamy, and Bharathi Raja Chakravarthi. 2022c. A Study of Machine Translation Models for Kannada-Tulu. In *Congress on Intelligent Systems*, pages 145–161. Springer.

Divyanshu Kakwani, Anoop Kunchukuttan, Satish Golla, Gokul N.C., Avik Bhattacharyya, Mitesh M. Khapra, and Pratyush Kumar. 2020. IndicNLPSuite: Monolingual Corpora, Evaluation Benchmarks and Pre-trained Multilingual Language Models for Indian Languages. In *Findings of EMNLP*.

Simran Khanuja, Diksha Bansal, Sarvesh Mehtani, Savya Khosla, Atreyee Dey, Balaji Gopalan, Dilip Kumar Margam, Pooja Aggarwal, Rajiv Teja Nagipogu, Shachi Dave, Shruti Gupta, Subhash Chandra Bose Gali, Vish Subramanian, and Partha Talukdar. 2021. MuRIL: Multilingual Representations for Indian Languages.

K Padmanabha Kekunnaya. A comparative study of Tulu dialects.

Aditya R Pillai and Biri Arun. 2024. A Feature Fusion and Detection Approach using Deep Learning for Sentimental Analysis and Offensive Text Detection from Code-mix Malayalam Language. *Biomedical Signal Processing and Control*, 89:105763.

Ruba Priyadharshini, Bharathi Raja Chakravarthi, Sajeetha Thavareesan, Dhivya Chinnappa, Durairaj Thenmozhi, and Rahul Ponnusamy. 2021. Overview of the DravidianCodeMix 2021 Shared Task on Sentiment Detection in Tamil, Malayalam, and Kannada. In *Proceedings of the 13th Annual Meeting of the Forum for Information Retrieval Evaluation*, pages 4–6.

K Rachana, M Prajnashree, Asha Hegde, and HL Shashirekha. 2023. MUCS@ DravidianLangTech2023: Sentiment Analysis in Code-mixed Tamil and Tulu Texts using fastText. In *Proceedings of the Third Workshop on Speech and Language Technologies for Dravidian Languages*, pages 258–265.

Vivek Suresh Raj, Subalalitha Chinnaudayar Navaneethakrishnan, Lavanya S.K, Frank Glavin, and Bharathi Raja Chakravarthi. 2024. ConBERT-RL: A Policy-driven Deep Reinforcement Learning Based Approach for Detecting Homophobia and Transphobia in Low-resource Languages. *Natural Language Processing Journal*, 6:100040.

Jatinderkumar R Saini and Saikat Roy. 2023. Preparation of Rich Lists of Research Gaps in the Specific Sentiment Analysis Tasks of Code-mixed Indian Languages. *SN Computer Science*, 5(1):117.

Victor Sanh, Lysandre Debut, Julien Chaumond, and Thomas Wolf. 2019. DistilBERT, A Distilled Version of BERT: Smaller, Faster, Cheaper and Lighter. In *NeurIPS* $EMC^2 Workshop$.

Kogilavani Shanmugavadivel, Sowbharanika Janani J S, Navbila K, and Malliga Subramanian. 2024a. Code Maker@DravidianLangTech-EACL 2024: Sentiment Analysis in Code-Mixed Tamil using Machine Learning Techniques. In *Proceedings of the Fourth Workshop on Speech, Vision, and Language Technologies for Dravidian Languages*, Malta. European Chapter of the Association for Computational Linguistics.

Kogilavani Shanmugavadivel, Sai Haritha Sampath, Pramod Nandhakumar, Prasath Mahalingam, Malliga Subramanian, Prasanna Kumar Kumaresan, and Ruba Priyadharshini. 2022. An Analysis of Machine Learning Models for Sentiment Analysis of Tamil Code-mixed Data. *Computer Speech Language*, 76:101407.

Kogilavani Shanmugavadivel, Malliga Subramanian, Palanimurugan V, and Pavul chinnappan D. 2024b. InnovationEngineers@DravidianLangTech-EACL 2024: Sentimental Analysis of YouTube Comments in Tamil by using Machine Learning. In *Proceedings of the Fourth Workshop on Speech, Vision, and Language Technologies for Dravidian Languages*, Malta. European Chapter of the Association for Computational Linguistics.

Kriti Singhal and Jatin Bedi. 2024. Transformers@DravidianLangTech-EACL2024: Sentiment Analysis of Code-Mixed Tamil Using RoBERTa. In *Proceedings of the Fourth Workshop on Speech, Vision, and Language Technologies for Dravidian Languages*, Malta. European Chapter of the Association for Computational Linguistics.

R Sivanantham and M Seran. 2019. Keeladi: An Urban Settlement of Sangam Age on the Banks of River Vaigai. In *India: Department of Archaeology, Government of Tamil Nadu, Chennai*.

Mithun Kumar SR, Lov Kumar, and Aruna Malapati. 2022. Sentiment Analysis on Code-Switched Dravidian Languages with Kernel Based Extreme Learning Machines. In *Proceedings of the Second Workshop on Speech and Language Technologies for Dravidian Languages*, pages 184–190.

Zannatul Fardaush Tripty, Md. Arian Al Nafis, Antu Chowdhury, Jawad Hossain, Shawly Ahsan, Avishek Das, and Mohammed Moshiul Hoque. 2024. CUETSentimentSillies@DravidianLangTech-EACL2024: Transformer-based Approach for Sentiment Analysis in Tamil and Tulu Code-Mixed Texts . In *Proceedings of the Fourth Workshop on Speech, Vision, and Language Technologies for Dravidian Languages*, Malta. European Chapter of the Association for Computational Linguistics.

Charangan Vasantharajan, Ruba Priyadharshini, Prasanna Kumar Kumarasen, Rahul Ponnusamy, Sathiyaraj Thangasamy, Sean Benhur, Thenmozhi Durairaj, Kanchana Sivanraju, Anbukkarasi Sampath, and Bharathi Raja Chakravarthi. 2022. TamilEmo: Fine-grained Emotion Detection Dataset for Tamil. In *International Conference on Speech and Language Technologies for Low-resource Languages*, pages 35–50. Springer.

Mayur Wankhade, Annavarapu Chandra Sekhara Rao, and Chaitanya Kulkarni. 2022. A Survey on Sentiment Analysis Methods, Applications, and Challenges. *Artificial Intelligence Review*, 55(7):5731–5780.

Xinyang Zhang, Yury Malkov, Omar Florez, Serim Park, Brian McWilliams, Jiawei Han, and Ahmed El-Kishky. 2023. TwHIN-BERT: A Socially-enriched Pre-trained Language Model for Multilingual Tweet Representations at Twitter. In *Proceedings of the 29th ACM SIGKDD conference on knowledge discovery and data mining*, pages 5597–5607.

Overview of the Second Shared Task on Fake News Detection in Dravidian Languages: DravidianLangTech@EACL 2024

Malliga Subramanian[1], **Bharathi Raja Chakravarthi**[2], **Kogilavani Shanmugavadivel**[1], **Santhiya Pandiyan**[1], **Prasanna Kumar Kumaresan**[3], **Balasubramanian Palani**[4], **Premjith B**[5], **Vanaja**[1], **Mithunajha S**[1], **Devika K**[5] **Hariprasath S.B**[5], **Haripriya B**[5], **Vigneshwar E**[5]

[1] Kongu Engineering College, Tamil Nadu, India.
[2] School of Computer Science, University of Galway, Ireland.
[3] Data Science Institute, University of Galway, Ireland.
[4] National Institute of Technology, Tamil Nadu, India.
[5] Amrita School of Artificial Intelligence, Amrita Vishwa Vidyapeetham, Coimbatore, Amrita Vishwa Vidyapeetham, India.

Abstract

The rise of online social media has revolutionized communication, offering users a convenient way to share information and stay updated on current events. However, this surge in connectivity has also led to the proliferation of misinformation, commonly known as fake news. This misleading content, often disguised as legitimate news, poses a significant challenge as it can distort public perception and erode trust in reliable sources. This shared task consists of two subtasks such as task 1 and task 2. Task 1 aims to classify a given social media text into original or fake. The goal of the FakeDetect-Malayalam task2 is to encourage participants to develop effective models capable of accurately detecting and classifying fake news articles in the Malayalam language into different categories like False, Half True, Mostly False, Partly False, and Mostly True. For this shared task, 33 participants submitted their results.

1 Introduction

The Second Shared Task on Fake News Detection in Dravidian Languages, held at DravidianLangTech@EACL 2024[1], is a significant initiative in the field of natural language processing (NLP) and computational linguistics. This research article provides an overview of this event, which focuses on developing and evaluating techniques for identifying fake news specifically in the Dravidian language family. The task aims to address the growing challenge of misinformation in online content by leveraging the linguistic characteristics unique to Dravidian languages. By highlighting the importance of language-specific approaches to fake news detection, this work contributes to advancing the capabilities of NLP models in combating misinformation across diverse linguistic contexts. Fake News Detection (FND) can be categorized as either monolingual or multilingual. Monolingual FND focuses on detecting fake news in a single language, while multilingual FND involves identifying deceptive content that may involve code-mixing or code-switching across two or more languages. Detecting fake news in low-resource languages poses challenges due to limited language resources such as annotated datasets, language models, and pre-trained embeddings. Nevertheless, there are strategies to enhance fake news detection in these languages, including the collection and annotation of data, utilization of cross-lingual models, implementation of transfer learning, and the development of domain-specific models. In the study conducted by Raja et al. (2023), they employed two pre-trained transformer models namely mBERT and XLM-R to assess the feasibility of transfer learning from high-resource languages to low-resource languages in the context of fake news detection within Dravidian languages.

2 Related Work

The authors (Palani and Elango, 2023) utilize contextual word embedding using pre-trained language models like BERT and RoBERTa, and deep learning-based models to identify fake news in Dravidian languages. The authors Chakravarthi et al. (2022) introduced the DL-based FND system, which uses FFN and RoBERTa to identify fake news and extract contextually dependent features, respectively. A Deep learning-based hope speech detection model in which the contextual link between words is captured through word embedding using T5-sentence and Indic-BERT was

[1] https://codalab.lisn.upsaclay.fr/competitions/16055

Proceedings of the Fourth Workshop on Speech, Vision, and Language Technologies for Dravidian Languages, pages 71–78
March 22, 2024

developed by Chakravarthi (2022). In order to identify the hope speech comments, the contextual elements are fed as input to the CNN model according to Subramanian et al. (2022). The performance of the suggested model is assessed using the HopeEDI multilingual dataset, which is presented in the shared task 2021 (Chakravarthi, 2020).

A multichannel CNN can be used to teach the model a variety of features from multiple perspectives. According to Shanmugavadivel et al. (2022), the model's several channels each extract features from the same input in a different way, resulting in a more accurate representation. A two-stage hope detection approach was proposed by Chinnappa (2021). In this approach, the language detector determines the model's language, and the hope detector categorizes the text as either hope speech, non-hope speech, or not lang. The authors Ahmad et al. (2020) used textual features in conjunction with machine learning-based ensemble algorithms to differentiate between authentic and fraudulent news.

3 Task Description

Task 1: The goal of this task is to classify a given social media text into original or fake. The data sources are various social media platforms such as Twitter, Facebook, etc. Given a social media post, the objective of the shared task is to classify it into either fake or original news. For example, the following two posts belong to fake and original categories, respectively. This is a comment/post-level classification task. Given a YouTube comment, the systems submitted by the participants should classify it into original or fake news. To download the data and participate, go to the Participate tab.

Task 2: The Fake News Detection from Malayalam News (FakeDetect-Malayalam) shared task provides a platform for researchers to address the pressing challenge of identifying and flagging fake news within the realm of Malayalam-language news articles. In an age of information overload, accurate detection of misinformation is crucial for fostering trustworthy communication. The core objective of the FakeDetect-Malayalam shared task is to encourage participants to develop effective models capable of accurately detecting and classifying fake news articles in the Malayalam language into different categories. Here, we considered five fake categories - False, Half True, Mostly False, Partly False, and Mostly True.

4 Dataset

The dataset described in the provided Table 1 pertains to the Second Shared Task on Fake News Detection in Dravidian Languages, conducted at DravidianLangTech@EACL 2024, focusing on two distinct tasks. For Task A, the objective is to classify news items into 'Fake' and 'Original' categories. The dataset for this task comprises 1,599 training instances for 'Fake' and 1,658 for 'Original', with respective testing sets of 507 and 512 instances, and development sets of 406 and 409 instances. Task B is more granular, aiming to categorize news into 'Half True', 'False', 'Partly False', and 'Mostly False'. The numbers of training samples for these categories are 145, 1,251, 44, and 242, respectively. The test set includes 24 instances for 'Half True', 149 for 'False', 14 for 'Partly False', and 63 for 'Mostly False'. The dataset does not include development sets for Task B. This carefully curated dataset is instrumental for researchers in the field of computational linguistics, particularly for those focusing on the development of automated fake news detection systems within the scope of Dravidian languages, which are less commonly addressed in computational research.

Task	Classes	Train	Test	Dev
Task A	Fake	1,599	507	406
	Original	1,658	512	409
Task B	Half True	145	24	-
	False	1,251	149	-
	Partly False	44	14	-
	Mostly False	242	63	-

Table 1: Dataset statistics for Malayalam

5 Participants Methodology

5.1 Task A

- The team **"CUETDUO"** (Rahman et al., 2024) employed a state-of-the-art text classification approach using a pre-trained Malayalam BERT model (Joshi, 2022). The method involved fine-tuning the BERT model on a labeled dataset consisting of Malayalam text samples with corresponding Fake labels. This approach achieved an F1 score of 0.88.

- **"Punny_Punctuators"** (Tabassum et al., 2024) team has used BERT (Devlin et al., 2018) and XLMRoBERTa Base (Conneau et al., 2019) for task A and obtained an F1 score of 0.87.

- The team called **"TechWhiz"**(M et al., 2024) used transformer models to classify the fake news. This team achieved a score of 0.86.

- The team **"CUET_Binary_Hackers"** (Farsi et al., 2024) team employed many BERT models, including indicBert (Kakwani et al., 2020), mBert, specifically MuRIL (Khanuja et al., 2021), and other multilingual BERT models. Out of all the models considered, the team specifically focused on a fine-tuned MuRIL BERT model for the submission and demonstrated an F1 score of 0.86.

- In an attempt by the team **"CUET_NLP_GoodFellows"** (Osama et al., 2024), they have used transformer-based approaches such as XLM-R and mBERT for task 1. And, this attempt produced an F1 score of 0.85.

- The team **"CUETSentimentSillies"** (Fardaush Tripty et al., 2024) did some preprocessing like emoji removal, punctuation removal, English stopwords removal, url removing, and lowercasing. This team also found some most frequent words removed them from the dataset and finetuned the m-bert transformer using huggingFace trainer API. 0.84 is the F1 score from this work.

- The team **"Habesha"** used transformer-based DistilBERT (Sanh et al., 2019) and a combination of deep learning and transformers. This team used the character-based deep learning approach GRU and achieved an F1-Score of 0.82.

- **"KEC_DL_KSK"** team has applied sampling techniques like SMOTE and Random Oversampler to overcome the class imbalance problem. This work tried different word embedding techniques like TFIDF, Word2Vec, Doc2Vec, BERT, and FastText. Machine learning algorithms like Random Forest, SVM, Logistic Regression, Naive Bayes, and Deep Learning models like LSTM, BiLSTM, GRU, BIGRU, and Pre-trained Model BERT for model building and classification have been used in this work.

- The team **"MUCS"** has trained LSVC with word+RcharML, Syllable+ensemble, and TL BERT model and produced 0.84 as F1-Score.

- The team **"Quartet_FakeNews"** implemented the Multinomial Naive Bayes model which leverages advanced text preprocessing techniques and the TF-IDF representation of text data to classify news articles as either fake or not. The Naive Bayes algorithm's assumption of conditional independence among features given the class label makes it a suitable choice for text classification tasks, and the model's performance is thoroughly evaluated to ensure its effectiveness in the context of fake news detection.

- In an attempt by the team **"SCOPE"**, the participant implemented the following steps. Firstly, the text or news data was tokenized, which typically involves breaking down the text into individual words or tokens. Subsequently, four machine learning algorithms—Support Vector Machine (SVM), Naive Bayes, Random Forest, and Logistic Regression—were employed. These algorithms were used for classification tasks, such as sentiment analysis or topic categorization. Each algorithm has its strengths and characteristics, and its performance was evaluated to determine which one yielded the best results for the given task.

- The teams **"Tayyab"** (Zamir et al., 2024) and **"TechWhiz"** (M et al., 2024) have implemented CNN and transformer-based models respectively.

- The team **"WordWizard"** (Anbalagan et al., 2024), Support Vector Machines (SVM), and Naive Bayes models were used. These approaches leveraged features extracted from textual content with Bag-of-Words representations and word embeddings. Comparative analysis with baseline models revealed the superiority of the SVM and Naive Bayes ensemble, achieving competitive accuracy, precision, recall, and F1-score metrics. The model used for the submission of task 1 is Support Vector Machine. TF-IDF has been used to vectorize the given text based on the relevancy of the word. For the second task, the predictions given by the Naive Bayes Model have been submitted.

5.2 Task B

A total of twelve teams submitted their models' predictions for problem 2. Each team had the opportunity to submit a maximum of three runs. This section provides a concise overview of the methods employed by the participants to address the issue of classifying fake news in Malayalam.

- **CUET_Binary_Hackers**: The team CUET_Binary_Hackers (Farsi et al., 2024) team employed many BERT models, including indicBert, mBert, MuRIL, and other multilingual BERT models. Out of all the models considered, the team specifically concentrated on a fine-tuned MuRIL BERT model for the submission, which demonstrated superior accuracy and F1 score performance. Throughout the fine-tuning process, the team made modifications and conducted trials with various hyperparameters, including learning rates, batch size, and optimization strategies, to enhance performance.

- **CUETSentimentSilles**: The data was cleaned by excluding punctuation, URLs, emojis, digits, and the most commonly utilized words from the corpus (Fardaush Tripty et al., 2024). Due to the significant corpus imbalance, the authors employed a data augmentation strategy to achieve class balance. The team fine-tuned the Malayalam BERT transformer to construct the models for task 2.

- **Quartet**: The model developed by the team Quartet for this task is constructed via a Multinomial Naive Bayes classifier, and its effectiveness is improved by employing a TfidfVectorizer to transform text data into a numerical representation suited for machine learning. The model development process commences with the application of a sequence of text preparation procedures. The process involves eliminating numerical values and special characters and lemmatizing words using the WordNet lemmatizer. The optimal model, identified through a previous grid search conducted with GridSearchCV, is subsequently employed on the complete training dataset. The model comprises a TfidfVectorizer that utilizes a predefined n-gram range and a Multinomial Naive Bayes classifier that incorporates an ideal alpha parameter. After being trained, the model is then utilized to generate predictions on the test set, generating numerical labels for each news article. In order to simplify the interpretation and reporting process, a mapping dictionary is used to transform the numerical predictions into their appropriate textual labels. This mapping encompasses the five categories of the task.

- **byteSizedLLM**: The team employed embeddings derived from a subset of AI4Bharat's data, comprising 100,000 randomly selected lines (Kodali and Manukonda, 2024). The embeddings were generated using custom-built subword tokenizers for Telugu (7.6 MB) and Tamil (1.3 MB) languages. A Bidirectional Long Short-Term Memory (BiLSTM) classifier was used for classification tasks. The model underwent training using datasets annotated with labels, which were later used to deduce test set outcomes. A customized subword tokenizer was employed on a limited dataset with BiLSTM models, which exhibit exceptional speed and have a small memory footprint (less than 8 MB).

- **KEC_DL_KSK**: The team utilized sampling techniques such as SMOTE and Random Oversampler to address the issue of class imbalance. Various word embedding algorithms were employed, including TFIDF, Word2Vec, Doc2Vec, BERT, and FastText. The team employed various machine learning methods, including Random Forest, Support Vector Machine (SVM), Logistic Regression, and Naive Bayes, as well as deep learning models such as Long Short-Term Memory (LSTM), Bidirectional LSTM (BiLSTM), Gated Recurrent Unit (GRU), Bidirectional GRU (BIGRU), and a pre-trained BERT model, to construct the classifier.

- **WordWizard**: The team introduced a methodology for classifying fake news using the Naive Bayes model (Anbalagan et al., 2024). The proposed approach utilizes features derived from textual content by merging embeddings from the LaBSE model with TF-IDF features. Data preprocessing is a compelling component of the system. The dataset was cleaned to exclude commonly used Malayalam stop-words, ensuring that only the most relevant terms are retained. Additional preprocessing techniques, such as stemming and lemmatization, were employed. Compared with baseline models, the Naive Bayes model demonstrates superiority by obtaining competitive accuracy, precision, recall, and F1-score metrics.

- **Habesha**: The team employed character-based Recurrent Neural Network (RNN), Gated Recurrent Unit (GRU), and DistilBERT models to build the classifier.

- **SCOPE**: The team employed a series of sequential steps. Initially, the input text data underwent tokenization. Following that, four machine learning techniques, namely Support Vector Machine (SVM), Naive Bayes, Random Forest, and Logistic Regression, were utilized for classification.

- **Tayyab**: This team used Convolution Neural Networks (CNN) for classification (Zamir et al., 2024).

- **MUCS**: The team employed a linear support vector machine classifier trained using word-level TF-IDF features. An oversampling strategy was utilized to address the class imbalance issue in the data. Subsequently, a logistic regression classifier was employed for classification. A collection of Siamese networks was also considered for constructing the classifier.

- **Punny_Punctuators**: The team employed a multilingual BERT-cased model and a CNN for categorization. The class imbalance problem was handled by implementing a data augmentation technique known as back translation (Tabassum et al., 2024).

- **TechWhiz**: The team used transformer models to classify the fake news (M et al., 2024).

6 Results

The rank list for Task A and Task B with Macro F1-Score is shown in Table 2 and Table 3. The models proposed by the participant teams are evaluated using the macro F1-Score metric. The evaluation results of task A are presented in Table 2 which represents the macro F1-score of each team rank-wise. 18 teams are participating in Task A and submitted their runs.

From the submissions, it is interpreted that transformer-based models outperform machine learning and deep learning models with better F1-Score. A few methods based on RNN and CNN gave slightly lesser F1-Score than transformer models. Following the RNNs and CNNs, the machine learning models such as SVM, Naive Bayes, Random Forest, and Logistic Regression gave F1-Score ranging from 0.80 to 0.71

7 Conclusion

This paper presents an overview of the Second Shared Task on Fake News Detection in Dravidian Languages - DravidianLangTech@EACL 2024. The task attracted participation from eighteen teams for Task A and Twelve teams for Task B. They employed methods varied among the teams, ranging from traditional TF-IDF vectorizers with machine learning to contemporary pre-trained transformer models for data representation. Upon analyzing the methodologies, a consistent trend emerged: transformer-based approaches consistently outperformed other techniques, as evidenced by evaluation metrics like classification accuracy and confusion matrices. This underscores the effectiveness of transformer models in capturing the performance of fake news detection. To sum up, the paper summarizes the DravidianLangTech@EACL 2024 fake news detection shared task for Malayalam, emphasizing diverse strategies and highlighting the prevalence of transformer-based methods for enhanced performance.

Acknowledgements

This work was conducted with the financial support of the Science Foundation Ireland Centre for Research Training in Artificial Intelligence under Grant No. 18/CRT/6223, supported in part by a research grant from Science Foundation Ireland (SFI) under Grant Number SFI/12/RC/2289_P2(Insight_2).

References

Iftikhar Ahmad, Muhammad Yousaf, Suhail Yousaf, and Muhammad Ovais Ahmad. 2020. Fake news detection using machine learning ensemble methods. *Complexity*, 2020:1–11.

S. No.	Team Name	Run	Macro F1-Score	Rank
1	CUET_DUO (Rahman et al., 2024)	1	0.88	1
2	Punny_Punctuators (Tabassum et al., 2024)	1, 2 & 3	0.87	2
3	TechWhiz (M et al., 2024)	xlmr	0.86	3
4	CUET_Binary_Hackers (Farsi et al., 2024)	1 & 2	0.86	3
5	CUET_NLP_GoodFellows (Osama et al., 2024)	1	0.85	4
6	CUETSentimentSilles (Fardaush Tripty et al., 2024)	1	0.84	5
7	DLRG	1	0.84	5
8	MUCS	2 & 3	0.84	5
9	CUET_DASH	3	0.83	6
10	Habesha	1	0.82	7
11	KEC_TECH	1	0.82	7
12	Quartet_FakeNews	1	0.81	8
13	KEC_HAWKS (Subramanian et al., 2024)	2	0.80	9
14	KEC_DL_KSK	2	0.79	10
15	SCOPE	1	0.78	11
16	Tayyab (Zamir et al., 2024)	1	0.78	11
17	WordWizard (Anbalagan et al., 2024)	1	0.78	11
18	Fango	1	0.71	12

Table 2: Rank list for the Task A

S. No.	Team	Run	macro F1 score	Rank
1	CUET_Binary_Hackers (Farsi et al., 2024)	1	0.5191	1
2	CUETSentimentSilles (Fardaush Tripty et al., 2024)	1	0.4964	2
3	Quartet	1	0.4868	3
4	byteSizedLLM (Kodali and Manukonda, 2024)	1	0.4797	4
5	KEC_DL_KSK	2	0.4763	5
6	WordWizard (Anbalagan et al., 2024)	1	0.3517	6
7	Habesha	1	0.3153	7
8	SCOPE	1	0.3039	8
9	Tayyab (Zamir et al., 2024)	1	0.2393	9
10	MUCS	1	0.1867	10
11	Punny_Punctuators (Tabassum et al., 2024)	3	0.1747	11
12	TechWhiz (M et al., 2024)	2	0.1733	12

Table 3: Rank list for the Task B

Akshatha Anbalagan, Priyadharshini T, Niranjana A, Shreedevi Seluka Balaji, and Durairaj Thenmozhi. 2024. Wordwizarddravidianlangtech@eacl 2024-fake news detection in dravidian languages. In *Proceedings of the Fourth Workshop on Speech, Vision, and Language Technologies for Dravidian Languages*, Malta. European Chapter of the Association for Computational Linguistics.

Bharathi Raja Chakravarthi. 2020. Hopeedi: A multilingual hope speech detection dataset for equality, diversity, and inclusion. In *Proceedings of the Third Workshop on Computational Modeling of People's Opinions, Personality, and Emotion's in Social Media*, pages 41–53.

Bharathi Raja Chakravarthi. 2022. Hope speech detection in youtube comments. *Social Network Analysis and Mining*, 12(1):75.

Bharathi Raja Chakravarthi, Vigneshwaran Muralidaran, Ruba Priyadharshini, Subalalitha Cn, John Philip McCrae, Miguel Ángel García, Salud María Jiménez-Zafra, Rafael Valencia-García, Prasanna Kumaresan, Rahul Ponnusamy, et al. 2022. Overview of the shared task on hope speech detection for equality, diversity, and inclusion. In *Proceedings of the second workshop on language technology for equality, diversity and inclusion*, pages 378–388.

Dhivya Chinnappa. 2021. dhivya-hope-detection@ lt-edi-eacl2021: multilingual hope speech detection for code-mixed and transliterated texts. In *Proceedings of the First Workshop on Language Technology for Equality, Diversity and Inclusion*, pages 73–78.

Alexis Conneau, Kartikay Khandelwal, Naman Goyal, Vishrav Chaudhary, Guillaume Wenzek, Francisco Guzmán, Edouard Grave, Myle Ott, Luke Zettlemoyer, and Veselin Stoyanov. 2019. Unsupervised cross-lingual representation learning at scale. *CoRR*, abs/1911.02116.

Jacob Devlin, Ming-Wei Chang, Kenton Lee, and Kristina Toutanova. 2018. BERT: pre-training of deep bidirectional transformers for language understanding. *CoRR*, abs/1810.04805.

Zannatul Fardaush Tripty, Md. Arian Al Nafis, Antu Chowdhury, Jawad Hossain, Shawly Ahsan, and Mohammed Moshiul Hoque. 2024. Cuetsentimentsillies@dravidianlangtech-eacl2024: Transformer-based approach for detecting and categorizing fake news in malayalam language. In *Proceedings of the Fourth Workshop on Speech, Vision, and Language Technologies for Dravidian Languages*, Malta. European Chapter of the Association for Computational Linguistics.

Salman Farsi, Asrarul Hoque Eusha, Ariful Islam, Hasan Mesbaul Ali Taher, Jawad Hossain, Shawly Ahsan, and Mohammed Moshiul Hoque. 2024. Cuet_binary_hackers@dravidianlangtech 2024: Malayalam fake news detection by fine-tuned muril bert. In *Proceedings of the Fourth Workshop on Speech, Vision, and Language Technologies for Dravidian Languages*, Malta. European Chapter of the Association for Computational Linguistics.

Raviraj Joshi. 2022. L3cube-hindbert and devbert: Pre-trained bert transformer models for devanagari based hindi and marathi languages. *arXiv preprint arXiv:2211.11418*.

Divyanshu Kakwani, Anoop Kunchukuttan, Satish Golla, Gokul N.C., Avik Bhattacharyya, Mitesh M. Khapra, and Pratyush Kumar. 2020. IndicNLPSuite: Monolingual Corpora, Evaluation Benchmarks and Pre-trained Multilingual Language Models for Indian Languages. In *Findings of EMNLP*.

Simran Khanuja, Diksha Bansal, Sarvesh Mehtani, Savya Khosla, Atreyee Dey, Balaji Gopalan, Dilip Kumar Margam, Pooja Aggarwal, Rajiv Teja Nagipogu, Shachi Dave, Shruti Gupta, Subhash Chandra Bose Gali, Vish Subramanian, and Partha Talukdar. 2021. Muril: Multilingual representations for indian languages.

Rohith Gowtham Kodali and Durga Prasad Manukonda. 2024. bytesizedllm@dravidianlangtech 2024: Fake news detection in dravidian languages - unleashing the power of custom subword tokenization with subword2vec and bilstm. In *Proceedings of the Fourth Workshop on Speech, Vision, and Language Technologies for Dravidian Languages*, Malta. European Chapter of the Association for Computational Linguistics.

Madhumitha M, Kunguma Akshatra M, Tejashri J, and C Jerin Mahibha. 2024. Techwhiz@eacl 2024: Fake news detection using deep learning models. In *Proceedings of the Fourth Workshop on Speech, Vision, and Language Technologies for Dravidian Languages*, Malta. European Chapter of the Association for Computational Linguistics.

Md Osama, Kawsar Ahmed, Hasan Mesbaul Ali Taher, Jawad Hossain, Shawly Ahsan, and Mohammed Moshiul Hoque. 2024. Cuet_nlp_goodfellows@dravidianlangtech 2024: A transformer-based approach for detecting fake news in dravidian languages. In *Proceedings of the Fourth Workshop on Speech, Vision, and Language Technologies for Dravidian Languages*, Malta. European Chapter of the Association for Computational Linguistics.

Balasubramanian Palani and Sivasankar Elango. 2023. Bbc-fnd: An ensemble of deep learning framework for textual fake news detection. *Computers and Electrical Engineering*, 110:108866.

Tanzim Rahman, Abu Bakkar Siddique Raihan, Md. Tanvir Rahman, Jawad Hossain, Shawly Ahsan, Avishek Das, and Mohammed Moshiul Hoque. 2024. Cuet_duo@dravidianlangtech 2024: Fake news classification using malayalam-bert. In *Proceedings of the Fourth Workshop on Speech, Vision, and Language Technologies for Dravidian Languages*, Malta. European Chapter of the Association for Computational Linguistics.

Eduri Raja, Badal Soni, and Samir Kumar Borgohain. 2023. Fake news detection in dravidian languages using transfer learning with adaptive finetuning. *Engineering Applications of Artificial Intelligence*, 126:106877.

Victor Sanh, Lysandre Debut, Julien Chaumond, and Thomas Wolf. 2019. Distilbert, a distilled version of bert: smaller, faster, cheaper and lighter. *ArXiv*, abs/1910.01108.

Kogilavani Shanmugavadivel, Sai Haritha Sampath, Pramod Nandhakumar, Prasath Mahalingam, Malliga Subramanian, Prasanna Kumar Kumaresan, and Ruba Priyadharshini. 2022. An analysis of machine learning models for sentiment analysis of tamil code-mixed data. *Computer Speech & Language*, 76:101407.

Malliga Subramanian, Ramya Chinnasamy, Prasanna Kumar Kumaresan, Vasanth Palanikumar, Madhoora Mohan, and Kogilavani Shanmugavadivel. 2022. Development of multi-lingual models for detecting hope speech texts from social media comments. In *International Conference on Speech and Language Technologies for Low-resource Languages*, pages 209–219. Springer.

Malliga Subramanian, Jayanth J R, Muthu Karuppan P, KeerthiBala A T, and Kogilavani Shanmugavadivel. 2024. Kec hawks@dravidianlangtech-2024 : Detecting malayalam fake news using machine learning models. In *Proceedings of the Fourth Workshop on Speech, Vision, and Language Technologies for Dravidian Languages*, Malta. European Chapter of the Association for Computational Linguistics.

Nafisa Tabassum, Sumaiya Rahman Aodhora, Rowshon Akter, Jawad Hossain, Shawly Ahsan, and Mohammed Moshiul Hoque. 2024. Punny_punctuators@dravidianlangtech-eacl2024: Transformer-based approach for detection and classification of fake news in malayalam social media text. In *Proceedings of the Fourth Workshop on Speech, Vision, and Language Technologies for Dravidian Languages*, Malta. European Chapter of the Association for Computational Linguistics.

M. T. Zamir, M. S Tash, Z. Ahani, A. Gelbukh, and G. Sidorov. 2024. Tayyab@dravidianlangtech 2024:detecting fake news in malayalam lstm approach and challenges. In *Proceedings of the Fourth Workshop on Speech, Vision, and Language Technologies for Dravidian Languages*, Malta. European Chapter of the Association for Computational Linguistics.

byteSizedLLM@DravidianLangTech 2024: Fake News Detection in Dravidian Languages - Unleashing the Power of Custom Subword Tokenization with Subword2Vec and BiLSTM

Rohith Gowtham Kodali
ASRlytics
Hyderabad, India
`rohitkodali@gmail.com`

Durga Prasad Manukonda
ASRlytics
Hyderabad, India
`mdp0999@gmail.com`

Abstract

This paper focuses on detecting fake news in resource-constrained languages, particularly Malayalam. We present a novel framework combining subword tokenization, Sanskrit-transliterated Subword2vec embeddings, and a powerful Bidirectional Long Short-Term Memory (BiLSTM) architecture. Despite using only monolingual Malayalam data, our model excelled in the FakeDetect-Malayalam challenge, ranking 4th. The innovative subword tokenizer achieves a remarkable 200x compression ratio, highlighting its efficiency in minimizing model size without compromising accuracy. Our work facilitates resource-efficient deployment in diverse linguistic landscapes and sparks discussion on the potential of multilingual data augmentation. This research provides a promising avenue for mitigating linguistic challenges in the NLP-driven battle against deceptive content.

1 Introduction

The surge in online social media platforms has transformed communication dynamics, facilitating seamless information exchange, dialogue, and real-time awareness of current events. However, this unprecedented connectivity has also given rise to a worrisome proliferation of misinformation, commonly known as fake news (Subramanian et al., 2023).

In response to this escalating issue, we introduce the Fake News Detection in Dravidian Languages challenge—DravidianLangTech@EACL 2024[1]. This initiative addresses the critical need for robust fake news detection mechanisms, particularly in Dravidian languages. The challenge focuses on developing effective models capable of distinguishing between authentic and fake content across various social media platforms, such as Twitter and Facebook.

Task 2, the FakeDetect-Malayalam shared task, is a crucial platform for researchers addressing the challenge of identifying fake news within Malayalam-language articles. In an era of information overload, precise detection of misinformation is vital for trustworthy communication. The task's primary goal is to motivate participants to develop effective models for accurately classifying fake news into categories like False, Half True, Mostly False, Partly False, and Mostly True. This research paper, inspired by the task, explores innovative approaches for fake news detection in Dravidian languages, focusing on Malayalam, aiming to contribute novel insights and methodologies to advance the state of the art.

Our study focuses on Fake News Detection in South Indian social media, introducing an innovative approach featuring a custom-designed tokenizer and a Bidirectional Long Short-Term Memory (BiLSTM) architecture. A key innovation is our tokenizer, which reduces model sizes, improves efficiency, and addresses challenges related to real-time deployment, enhancing the practicality of deploying detection systems in dynamic online environments.

The implementation of BiLSTM, coupled with our specialized tokenizer, exhibits significant enhancements in fake news detection accuracy, demonstrating heightened sensitivity to linguistic nuances. The use of compact models effectively addresses inference challenges, ensuring swift real-time detection and practical deployment. Our work establishes a framework for Fake News Detection, providing valuable insights into model size, inference speed, and the challenges of real-time deployment in countering online misinformation within Dravidian languages.

This paper explains our approach, technical improvements, and findings, thoroughly investigating the detection of fake news in Dravidian languages. Our goal is to contribute not only to addressing the

[1] `https://codalab.lisn.upsaclay.fr/competitions/16055`

Proceedings of the Fourth Workshop on Speech, Vision, and Language Technologies for Dravidian Languages, pages 79–84
March 22, 2024 ©2024 Association for Computational Linguistics

challenges of fake news in Malayalam but also to enhancing our understanding of effective detection methods suitable for various linguistic contexts.

2 Related Work

The growing concern over disinformation and propaganda has led to increased research on fake news detection. In recent works, Raja et al. (2023) focused on detecting fake news in Dravidian languages using transfer learning with adaptive fine-tuning, emphasizing different techniques with Transformer-based models. Keya et al. (2022) employed a pretrained BERT model with data augmentation, comparing their results with twelve different models. Goldani et al. (2021) utilized capsule networks with varied architectures and n-gram levels for feature extraction. In the context of languages other than English, studies like Gereme et al. (2021) and Saghayan et al. (2021) explored fake news detection in Amharic and Persian, respectively. Chu et al. (2021) investigated the ability to generalize fake news detection models across languages, finding the BERT model effective. Faustini and Covões (2020) covered multiple languages, including Slavic, Latin, and German, emphasizing the need for fake news identification in resource-poor languages like Dravidian languages. Additionally, Vijjali et al. (2020) addressing COVID-19 fake news and proposing a two-stage automated pipeline employs BERT and ALBERT models for efficient verification. Notably, many studies primarily focus on English and other major languages, highlighting the potential for advancements in resource-poor languages.

3 Dataset

3.1 Embedding Malayalam Dataset

We employed a substantial corpus extracted from the AI4Bharath Malayalam dataset[2], comprising the initial 11,512,628 lines of a 1GB text corpus. This dataset serves as a rich source of diverse linguistic content, fostering the development of robust embeddings for our research endeavors. The dataset exhibits linguistic variety and covers a spectrum of topics relevant to the scope of our research.

3.2 Fake news DravidianLangTech@EACL 2024 Malayalam dataset

The dataset utilized in this challenge is derived from the corpus provided by the workshop organizers (Subramanian et al., 2024). For Task 2, the dataset is divided into 1,669 training samples, 250 development samples, and 250 test samples. This division enables a balanced approach to model training, validation, and evaluation, specifically addressing Task 2's requirements.

4 Methodology

This section unveils the intricate details of our innovative architecture, which seamlessly integrates two crucial components: a dynamic Subword Embeddings module and a robust BiLSTM Tagger module. We embark on a journey through the art of data preprocessing, the finesse of subword tokenization, the mastery of embedding training, and ultimately, the orchestration of our advanced classifier.

4.1 Preprocessing and Tokenization

This section outlines the data preprocessing and tokenization procedures employed for the Shared Task on Homophobia/Transphobia Detection in social media comments, aiming to prepare the data for effective model training and enhance the performance of the homophobia/transphobia detection system.

Our comprehensive preprocessing involved normalization, cleaning (eliminating noise such as URLs and hashtags), and transliteration using the `indic_transliteration` library[3]. This ensured uniform processing across the dataset.

In the dataset, we identified 6,161,116 unique words and 19,155 distinct subword units. After establishing a minimum frequency for embedding training, 14,190 subword units were finalized, showcasing the linguistic diversity within the AI4Bharath text. Utilizing a meticulous preprocessing pipeline and transliterator, we applied subword tokenization to enhance the granularity of linguistic representation, paving the way for a more nuanced embedding model.

4.1.1 Subword Tokenization Details

Our subword tokenizer (VowelToken), utilizes universal linguistic principles derived from vowel boundaries, ensuring accurate segmentation across diverse languages.

Engineered with a rule-based design, VowelToken focuses on consistent vowel boundary patterns

[2]https://github.com/AI4Bharat/indicnlp_corpus

[3]https://github.com/indic-transliteration/indic_transliteration_py

observed in multiple languages, facilitating accurate identification and segmentation of compound words. This design enhances precision in subword tokenization across languages.

4.2 Subword Embeddings Module

The subword embeddings (Subword2Vec) module is responsible for obtaining subword embeddings using the Word2Vec method by Mikolov et al. (2013) from a given corpus. It operates as follows:

The module's initialization involves specifying critical parameters, starting with the vocabulary size (V) that sets the upper limit for subword consideration. Additionally, the minimum frequency parameter (f_{min}) serves as the threshold for subword inclusion based on frequency. The embedding dimension ($d_{subword}$), characterizing the dimensionality of subword embeddings, is also defined. These parameters collectively configure the module during the initialization process, a pivotal aspect of our research.

Subword counts are collected from the corpus to construct a subword vocabulary (S). The subword splitting process is executed based on vowels, excluding subwords with counts below f_{min}. This process is mathematically expressed as:

S = {s | $sisasubword, count(s) \geq f_{min}, |S| \leq V\}$

$= \{s \in \mathcal{W} \mid count(s) \geq f_{min}, |S| \leq V\}$

The subword splitting process involves dividing the input word into subwords based on vowel boundaries. Consonant prefixes and suffixes are included in the subwords when applicable, and special tokens "_" (start of subword) are added to the first letter. Subword embeddings ($E_{subword}$) are initialized as a random matrix with dimensions ($|S|$, $d_{subword}$).

The training phase employs Stochastic Gradient Descent (SGD) (Tian et al., 2023) to train subword embeddings. The objective is to minimize the Mean Squared Error (MSE) loss (L) between subword pairs. The SGD update is expressed as:

$$E_{subword}^{(t+1)} = E_{subword}^{(t)} - \eta \nabla L(E_{subword}^{(t)})$$

Here, t represents the training iteration, η is the learning rate, and ∇L is the gradient of the loss function. Training subword embeddings is a crucial step in refining the model's representation of subword relationships.

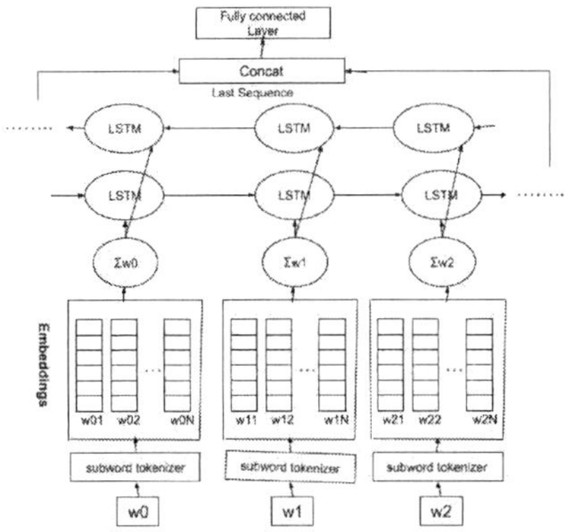

Figure 1: The unfolded architecture of BiLSTM classifier with three 3 word example sample.

4.3 BiLSTM Classifier

The BiLSTM architecture, inspired by Ghosh et al. (2020), plays a crucial role in the fake news classification task. It consists of two essential components: a subword embedding layer and a bi-directional LSTM layer.

The Sub-Word Embedding Layer operates on an input word sequence $x = [w_1, w_2, ..., w_n]$ utilizing a subword embedding function. Each word w_i is mapped to its corresponding subword embeddings, denoted as $w_{i1}, w_{i2}, ..., w_{in}$, where n represents the number of subwords for the i-th word. The final word embedding for w_i, denoted as $\mathbf{e}_i$, is obtained by summing the embeddings of its constituent subwords:

$$\mathbf{e}_i = w_{i1} + w_{i2} + \ldots + w_{in}$$

The output of this layer is a tensor X_{embed} of dimensions $1 \times n \times d_{embed}$, where d_{embed} signifies the size of each word embedding.

$$X_{embed} = [\mathbf{e}_1, \mathbf{e}_2, ..., \mathbf{e}_n]$$

Here, $\mathbf{e}_i$ represents the word embedding for the i-th word in the sequence, and n is the length of the sequence.

The subsequent Bi-directional LSTM Layer engages with the embedded sequence X_{embed} to adeptly capture contextual information. Configured with an input size of 100 (matching the embedding size) and a hidden size of 128, the bidirectional LSTM ensures the seamless flow of information both in forward and backward directions. The resulting output, denoted as $blstm\_out$, manifests as a tensor of shape $1 \times n \times 256$.

	Precision	Recall	F1-Score	Support
HALF TRUE	0.68	0.88	0.77	149
MOSTLY FALSE	0.47	0.29	0.36	24
FALSE	0.67	0.35	0.46	63
PARTLY FALSE	0.40	0.29	0.33	14
MOSTLY TRUE	0.0	0.0	0.0	0
Macro Avg	0.55	0.45	0.48	250
Weighted Avg	0.64	0.66	0.63	250
Accuracy			0.66	250

Table 1: Classification Report of the Task2 test set

In essence, the model navigates the input sequence through an embedding layer, harnesses the bidirectional LSTM layer to adeptly capture contextual nuances, and formulates predictions utilizing a streamlined process. The forward pass of the model can be succinctly expressed in mathematical terms as follows:

$$h_i^{(f)}, h_i^{(b)} = BiLSTM(e_{1:i}, e_{i:n}), \quad \forall i \in \{1, ..., n\}$$

$$y = Wh_n^{(f)} + b$$

Here, $h_i^{(f)}$ and $h_i^{(b)}$ represent the forward and backward hidden states at position i, respectively. The BiLSTM function operates on subword embeddings $e_{1:i}$ and $e_{i:n}$ for each i in the sequence. The final prediction y is obtained by a linear transformation with weights matrix W and bias b.

Figure 1 depicts the unfolded architecture of the BiLSTM Classifier module, illustrating a three-word example sample. This design seamlessly integrates subword embeddings with a BiLSTM-based approach, yielding promising results across diverse natural language processing applications. It underscores the model's adaptability and potential in a wide array of contexts.

5 Experimental Setup

Our experimental setup aims to showcase the effectiveness of our proposed approach for fake news detection in Dravidian languages, with a specific focus on Malayalam. Utilizing the custom subword tokenizer "VowelToken," which considers vowel boundaries for efficient tokenization, and Subword2Vec for generating 100-dimensional subword embeddings, we meticulously trained the embeddings on a 1GB monolingual Malayalam text corpus. A Sanskrit transliterator was employed to aid the training process. Despite limiting the training to a single epoch, exceptional results were achieved, with a perplexity of 1.07 on a 10MB development dataset, highlighting the effectiveness of our approach. The final 100-dimensional embedding size after training was 5.92MB, striking a balance between efficiency and accuracy.

To assess the effectiveness of the subword embeddings, we seamlessly incorporated them into our BiLSTM-based model architecture. The ClassificationModel comprises a Sub-Word Embedding Layer, a Bi-directional LSTM Layer, and a Linear Classification Layer, leveraging subword embeddings obtained from VowelToken. The BiLSTM layer is configured with an input size of 100 and a hidden size of 128. Moreover, the model employs the Adam optimizer with a learning rate of 0.001 throughout the training process.

Our model underwent rigorous training on Task 2, the Multi-Class Classifier, to comprehensively assess its performance. This experiment aimed to demonstrate the robustness of our custom subword tokenizer and explore the contribution of subword embeddings within the BiLSTM-based classification model to fake news detection in the context of Dravidian languages, especially Malayalam. Evaluation metrics, including recall, precision, F1 score, and accuracy, were used to measure the model's effectiveness.

6 Experimental results and discussions

Motivated by the challenges of obtaining large multilingual datasets, we intentionally trained our subword embeddings on a limited 1GB monolingual text corpus. Despite this constraint, the embeddings exhibited competitive performance, achieving remarkable accuracy on unseen data.

The classification report (see Table 1) provides a detailed analysis of the model's performance on each category within Task 2. The F1-Scores for each category vary, with "HALF TRUE" achieving the highest at 0.77, indicating strong precision and recall. Categories like "MOSTLY FALSE" and "PARTLY FALSE" have lower F1-Scores, suggesting challenges in correctly classifying instances in these categories.

The overall accuracy of 0.66 showcases the model's competence in classifying news articles into various categories. It is essential to note that the model achieves a reasonable performance, considering the complexity of the task and the limited size of the model (6.87MB), ensuring efficient deployment with approximately 10X faster inference compared to Large Language Models (LLMs).

Team	F1-Score (macro)
CUET_Binary_Hackers	0.5191
CUETSentimentSilles	0.4964
Quartet	0.4868
byteSizedLLM	0.4797
KEC_DL_KSK	0.4763

Table 2: Top 5 results in Fake News Detection - Task 2

It's noteworthy that acquiring training data for embedding training from social media poses a significant challenge. Despite these difficulties and limited data embeddings, our model still achieves top-notch performance, as demonstrated by our ByteSizedLLM team securing the 4th rank overall in the Task 2 competition (see Table 2). This highlights the crucial role of diverse and contextually relevant training data in achieving superior results.

The effectiveness of our subword tokenization is evident in low perplexity after just one epoch, showcasing the model's potential. Unlocking its full capabilities involves leveraging more extensive training data for heightened accuracy and generalization. While expanding the dataset may increase subword tokens, the model size is expected to remain manageable due to the saturation of subword tokens within the initial 1GB of text.

7 Conclusion and future work

Our innovative fake news detection approach for Dravidian languages leverages VowelToken, a custom subword tokenizer capturing vowel nuances within Dravidian languages. This granular understanding improves subword embedding generation, enhancing model performance. The BiLSTM architecture coupled with custom subword embeddings demonstrates efficient information extraction and classification, achieving promising results despite limited training data. The model's compactness facilitates implementation, further contributing to real-world applicability. Future work will explore larger social media and multilingual datasets and investigate advanced embedding techniques like contextualized embeddings, aiming to further improve the model's performance and unlock its full potential in diverse Dravidian language contexts.

References

Samuel Kai Wah Chu, Runbin Xie, and Yanshu Wang. 2021. Cross-language fake news detection. *Data and Information Management*, 5(1):100–109.

Pedro Henrique Arruda Faustini and Thiago Ferreira Covões. 2020. Fake news detection in multiple platforms and languages. *Expert Systems with Applications*, 158:113503.

Fantahun Gereme, William Zhu, Tewodros Ayall, and Dagmawi Alemu. 2021. Combating fake news in "low-resource" languages: Amharic fake news detection accompanied by resource crafting. *Information*, 12(1).

Koyel Ghosh, Dr. Apurbalal Senapati, and Dr. Ranjan Maity. 2020. Technical domain identification using word2vec and BiLSTM. In *Proceedings of the 17th International Conference on Natural Language Processing (ICON): TechDOfication 2020 Shared Task*, pages 21–26, Patna, India. NLP Association of India (NLPAI).

Mohammad Hadi Goldani, Saeedeh Momtazi, and Reza Safabakhsh. 2021. Detecting fake news with capsule neural networks. *Applied Soft Computing*, 101:106991.

Ashfia Jannat Keya, Md. Anwar Hussen Wadud, M. F. Mridha, Mohammed Alatiyyah, and Md. Abdul Hamid. 2022. Augfake-bert: Handling imbalance through augmentation of fake news using bert to enhance the performance of fake news classification. *Applied Sciences*, 12(17).

Tomas Mikolov, Kai Chen, Greg Corrado, and Jeffrey Dean. 2013. Efficient estimation of word representations in vector space.

Eduri Raja, Badal Soni, and Samir Kumar Borgohain. 2023. Fake news detection in dravidian languages using transfer learning with adaptive finetuning. *Engineering Applications of Artificial Intelligence*, 126:106877.

Masood Hamed Saghayan, Seyedeh Fatemeh Ebrahimi, and Mohammad Bahrani. 2021. Exploring the impact of machine translation on fake news detection: A case study on persian tweets about covid-19. In *2021 29th Iranian Conference on Electrical Engineering (ICEE)*, pages 540–544.

Malliga Subramanian, Bharathi Raja Chakravarthi, Kogilavani Shanmugavadivel, Santhiya Pandiyan, Prasanna Kumar Kumaresan, Balasubramanian Palani, Premjith B, Sandhiya Raja, Vanaja, Mithunajha S, Devika K, Hariprasath S.B, Haripriya B, and Vigneshwar E. 2024. Overview of the Second Shared Task on Fake News Detection in Dravidian Languages. In *Proceedings of the Fourth Workshop on Speech, Vision, and Language Technologies for Dravidian Languages*, Malta. European Chapter of the Association for Computational Linguistics.

Malliga Subramanian, Bharathi Raja Chakravarthi, Kogilavani Shanmugavadivel, Santhiya Pandiyan, Prasanna Kumar Kumaresan, Balasubramanian Palani, Muskaan Singh, Sandhiya Raja, Vanaja, and Mithunajha S. 2023. Overview of the shared task on fake news detection from social media text. In *Proceedings of the Third Workshop on Speech and Language Technologies for Dravidian Languages*, Varna, Bulgaria. Recent Advances in Natural Language Processing.

Yingjie Tian, Yuqi Zhang, and Haibin Zhang. 2023. Recent advances in stochastic gradient descent in deep learning. *Mathematics*, 11(3).

Rutvik Vijjali, Prathyush Potluri, Siddharth Kumar, and Sundeep Teki. 2020. Two stage transformer model for covid-19 fake news detection and fact checking.

Fida @DravidianLangTech 2024: A Novel Approach to Hate Speech Detection Using Distilbert-base-multilingual-cased

Fida Ullah, Muhammad Tayyab Zamir, Muhammad Arif, M.Ahmad, E Felipe-Riveron, A. Gelbukh
Instituto Politécnico Nacional (IPN), Centro de Investigación en Computación (CIC)
Corresponding: fullah-2022@cic.ipn.mx

Abstract

In the contemporary digital landscape, social media has emerged as a prominent means of communication and information dissemination, offering a rapid outreach to a broad audience compared to traditional communication methods. Unfortunately, the escalating prevalence of abusive language and hate speech on these platforms has become a pressing issue. Detecting and addressing such content on the Internet has garnered considerable attention due to the significant impact it has on individuals. The advent of deep learning has facilitated the use of pre-trained deep neural network models for text classification tasks. While these models demonstrate high performance, some exhibit a substantial number of parameters. In the DravidianLangTech@EACL 2024 task, we opted for the Distilbert-base-multilingual-cased model, an enhancement of the BERT model that effectively reduces the number of parameters without compromising performance. This model was selected based on its exceptional results in the task. Our system achieved a commendable macro F1 score of 0.6369, securing the 18th position among the 27 participating teams.

1 Introduction

In recent times, the exponential growth of Internet technology has led to a surge in the user base, accompanied by the emergence of various social platforms. These platforms provide a space for netizens to freely express their opinions, often leveraging anonymous features. Consequently, this freedom has led to an increase in hate speech (Shahiki-Tash et al., 2023a; Yigezu et al., 2023a) and offensive content on the Internet. Addressing this issue is crucial, as it not only causes distress but also poses severe risks, including mental health concerns and potential instances of suicide. Given the enormous volume of comments generated daily on the Internet, manual moderation is impractical. Therefore, the integration of artificial intelligence methods becomes imperative. However, identifying hate speech and offensive content poses several challenges. Firstly, social media posts encompass multiple languages and diverse writing styles. The presence of irregular writing and the evolution of new Internet expressions further complicate the detection task. Additionally, some comments may not overtly contain derogatory language but instead employ implicit or ironic attacks, adding another layer of complexity.

Furthermore, the absence of a clear standard for the definition of hate speech contributes to the intricacy of the task. Model performance is highly contingent on the training dataset, influenced by the annotator's perspectives to a considerable extent. In response to these challenges, the NLP community has introduced various tasks focused on hate speech identification, including the Dravidianlangtech-eacl2021 shared task (Saha et al., 2021; Priyadharshini et al., 2023b; Yigezu et al., 2023b). This particular task is dedicated to identifying hate speech and offensive content in both Telugu and English languages.In the realm of NLP, numerous tasks such as identifying hope speech (Shahiki-Tash et al., 2023b), sentiment analysis (Tash et al., 2023), and detecting hate speech utilize various models like deep learning (Yigezu et al., 2022), transformers (Tonja et al., 2022), and traditional machine learning (Tash et al., 2022).

In this paper, our focus is on hate speech using the pre-trained model Distilbert-base-multilingual-cased (Ghosh and Senapati, 2022; Yigezu et al., 2023c), which builds upon the BERT model (Renjit and Idicula, 2020; Yigezu et al., 2023d), by significantly reducing the number of parameters, consequently enhancing training speed. The structure of this article encompasses an exploration of related research on hate speech and offensive speech recognition (Section 2), an explanation of the model used in the task (Section 3), an elucidation of the exper-

Proceedings of the Fourth Workshop on Speech, Vision, and Language Technologies for Dravidian Languages, pages 85–90
March 22, 2024 ©2024 Association for Computational Linguistics

imental procedure (Section 4), a presentation of the experimental results and their analysis (Section 5), and a comprehensive summary of this work (Section 6).

2 Related work

Numerous research endeavors have sought to identify and address abusive comments across various languages; however, there is a noticeable research gap in the domain of low-resource languages. (Priyadharshini et al., 2023b, 2022) and addressed this gap by conducting a shared task at ACL 2022, focusing on detecting categories of abusive comments on social media. Their study encompassed comments in Tamil and a code-mixed language featuring both Tamil and English scripts (Akhter et al., 2021) contributed a comprehensive investigation into abusive language detection, specifically in Urdu and Roman Urdu comments. Employing a diverse set of machine learning and deep learning models, the author evaluated the performance of five ML models (Naive Bayes, Support Vector Machine, Instance-Based Learning, Logistic Regression, and JRip) and four DL models (CNN, LSTM, BLSTM, and Convolutional LSTM) across two datasets— one comprising tens of thousands of Roman Urdu comments and another with over two thousand comments in Urdu. The CNN exhibited notable superiority, achieving accuracy rates of 96.2% for Urdu and 91.4% for Roman Urdu, establishing itself as the most adept model in identifying abusive language in these linguistic contexts. Some researchers have explored multiple methods independently to determine the most effective model rajalakshmi2022dlrg employed three methodologies—Machine Learning, Deep Learning, and Transformer-based modeling. For Machine Learning, eight algorithms were implemented, with Random Forest yielding the best results for the Tamil-English dataset. In Deep Learning, Bi-Directional LSTM outperformed other models, especially with pre-trained word embeddings. In Transformer-based modeling, IndicBERT and mBERT with fine-tuning were employed, with mBERT delivering the most favorable results. (Eshan and Hasan, 2017) delved into machine learning algorithms for Bengali abusive text detection, revealing that SVM with a Linear kernel performed optimally using trigram TfidfVectorizer features. (Djuric et al., 2015)proposed a binary classification model for hate speech detection, utilizing advanced deep learning techniques such as continuous bag-of-words (CBOW) and paragraph2vec to represent text in a low-dimensional vector space, achieving an AUC value of 0.80. (Kedia and Nandy, 2021) developed an offensive content classification model for Dravidian code-mixed languages (Tamil, Malayalam, and Kannada) using transformer-based models—BERT and RoBERTa. Renjit and Idicula (2020) employed word embedding for the Manglish dataset, achieving a weighted F1-score of 0.53 and 0.48 using Keras Embedding and Doc2Vec approaches for sentence representation, respectively. (Burnap and Williams, 2015) focused on hate speech detection by extracting uni-to-five-gram features from a dataset of 450,000 tweets. Using ensemble learning, logistic regression, and SVM classification techniques, they predicted hate speech with an accuracy of 89% using the ensemble learning model.

3 Methodology

The methodology employed in this study leverages the Distilbert-base-multilingual-cased model (Sanh et al., 2019), a pre-trained transformer-based language model, to address the research objectives. The model, developed by Hugging Face, has been fine-tuned for multilingual understanding and exhibits capabilities across various languages. To train and evaluate the Distilbert-base-multilingual-cased model a diverse and representative dataset encompassing multiple languages is gathered. This dataset spans domains relevant to the research focus. The collected data undergoes preprocessing to ensure uniformity and compatibility with the model's requirements. This step involves tokenization, stemming, and the removal of irrelevant information to enhance the model's efficiency. The Distilbert-base-multilingual-cased model is configured with specific parameters to align with the research objectives. This includes setting appropriate learning rates, batch sizes, and training epochs for optimal performance. The pre-trained Distilbert-base-multilingual-cased model is fine-tuned on the task-specific dataset as seen in figure 1.

This involves updating the model's weights based on the unique characteristics of the dataset and the objectives of the research. Fine-tuning enhances the model's ability to grasp nuances within the target domain. To assess the generalizability of the model, a cross-validation strategy is employed. The dataset is partitioned into training, validation,

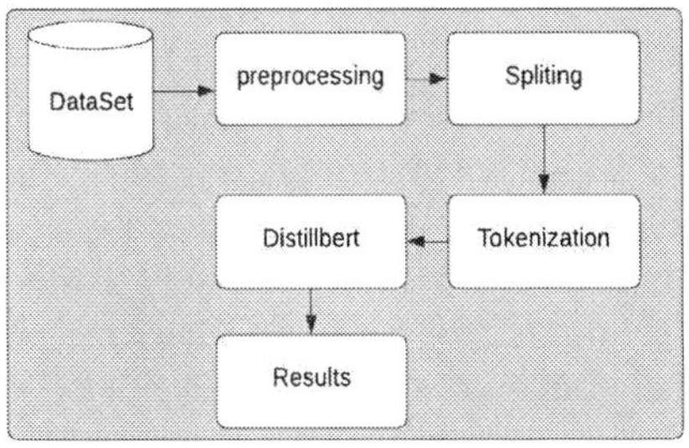

Figure 1: workflow our proposed method

and test sets, ensuring that the model is rigorously evaluated on diverse samples. This step aids in mitigating over-fitting and enhances the robustness of the model. The model's performance is evaluated using appropriate metrics tailored to the research task. Common metrics such as precision, recall, and F1 score are computed to quantify the model's effectiveness in capturing patterns and making accurate predictions. The outcomes of the experiments are analyzed comprehensively to draw meaningful conclusions. This involves an in-depth examination of the model's predictions, identification of potential challenges, and exploration of areas for improvement. Throughout the implementation of the Distilbert-base-multilingual-cased model, ethical considerations are prioritized. Data privacy and confidentiality are ensured, and the research adheres to established guidelines for responsible AI usage.

3.1 Data Description

The Shared Task on Hate and Offensive Language Detection in Telugu Codemixed Text (HOLD-Telugu) hosted by DravidianLangTech@EACL 2024, as proposed by (B et al., 2024; Priyadharshini et al., 2023a) addresses the challenge of mitigating offensive content within social media through a post-classification approach. This task seeks to advance methodologies and language models specifically tailored for code-mixed data in languages with limited linguistic resources. It recognizes the inadequacy of models trained on monolingual data in capturing the intricate semantics inherent in code-mixed datasets. The task at hand involves hate speech classification within a dataset consisting of 4000 sentences expressed in both native Telugu script and Romanized Telugu. The training dataset encompasses 2061 sentences labeled as non-hate and 1939 as hate. Furthermore, a test dataset comprising 500 sentences is provided, devoid of labeled categories. The primary objective is to employ machine learning models to predict whether these 500 test sentences can be classified into hate speech or non-hate categories. This classification is to be based on the discernment of patterns learned from the labeled training data. Figure 2 illustrating the distribution of Hate and Non-Hate labels.

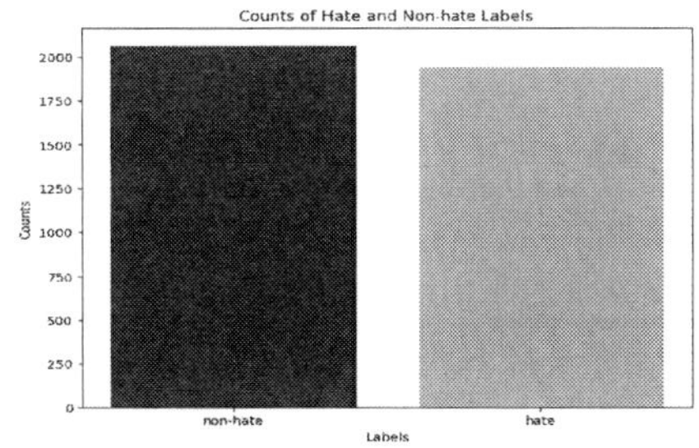

Figure 2: Value counts for hate and non hate comments in training dataset

3.2 Data Preprocessing

Upon reception from the organizer (B et al., 2024), the received data was partitioned into two distinct segments: the training set and the testing set. However, prior to deploying this data for training purposes, it is imperative to undergo a pre-processing phase. The current state of the data renders it unsuitable for effective model training, necessitating a transformation into a structured and intelligible format compatible with the requisites of the training process. An essential facet of pre-processing involves the removal of extraneous elements inherent in the data. Such elements encompass hyperlinks, HTML tags, numeric values, and symbols, which possess the potential to impede the training process or introduce noise into the dataset. The elimination of these undesirable components serves to enhance the cleanliness and focus of the data, thereby empowering the model to discern patterns and relationships within the textual content more effectively. Upon the successful removal of these extraneous elements, the data becomes more amenable to model training. Pre-processing, in this context, facilitates a concentrated focus on pertinent linguistic features and patterns within the text, thereby augmenting the model's capacity for generalization and accurate predictions or classifications. These pre-processing steps are instrumental in optimizing the dataset for subsequent model training, ultimately contributing to enhanced accuracy and meaningful outcomes in subsequent analytical pursuits or practical applications.

4 Result

The performance parameter used to assess the detection model's overall efficacy is the macro average F1-score. It is computed by taking the average of all classes after determining the F1-score for each class separately. The macro average F1-score assigns equal weight to each class by computing the average after considering each class's performance individually, regardless of class size or imbalance. In Telugu, we obtained a macro F1-score of 0.6369. securing the 18th position among the 27 participating teams. For a comprehensive summary of the outcomes attained by all competing teams, as outlined in Table 1, offering a detailed overview of the performance metrics and points garnered by each participant in the competition.

Table 1 Result of all participants in Telugu hate speech

Team	Run	F1-score	Rank
Sandalphon	1	0.7711	1
Selam	2	0.7711	1
Kubapok	1	0.7431	3
DLRG1	1	0.7101	4
DLRG	1	0.7041	5
CUET_Binary	2	0.7013	6
CUET_OpenNLP	1	0.6878	7
Zavira	1	0.6819	8
IIITDWD-zk_lstm	2	0.6739	9
lemlem	1	0.6708	10
Mizan	1	0.6616	11
byteSizedLLM	1	0.6609	12
pinealai	1	0.6575	13
IIITDWD_SVC	2	0.6565	14
MUCS	3	0.6501	15
Lemlem-eyob	2	0.6498	16
Tewodros	2	0.6498	16
Fida	2	0.6369	18
Lidoma	1	0.6151	19
MasonTigers	1	0.5621	29
Habesha	1	0.5284	21
MasonTigers	1	0.4959	22
CUET_DASH	3	0.4956	23
Fango	1	0.4921	24
Tayyab	1	0.4653	25

5 Error analysis

The distilbert model excels in detecting hate speech, boasting high accuracy with a notable true positive count. However, challenges arise with false positives, even in balanced datasets. This necessitates careful analysis, urging strategic adjustments like fine-tuning parameters to enhance overall efficiency. Ongoing evaluations on validation and test sets are vital for adapting the model and ensuring reliable performance.

6 Limitations

The utilization of pre-trained transformers, specifically multilingual distilbert, presents a significant consideration in our endeavors to detect hate speech. While leveraging these pre-trained models can enhance our comprehension of textual data, their effectiveness may be limited by the specificity of the pre-training corpus. This potential limitation could result in a mismatch with the unique characteristics of hate speech, underscoring the necessity for meticulous fine-tuning to ensure optimal performance. Moreover, the inherent linguistic complexities of Telugu Codemixed Text may pose challenges impacting the model's ability to discern subtle patterns. Consequently, further investigation and refinement are warranted to address these challenges and enhance the model's accuracy in fake news detection for Telugu Codemixed Text.

7 Conclusion

Hate and offensive posts on social media can put the victim in hazardous circumstances and increase their risk of mental health issues like depression, insomnia, and in extreme cases, suicide. As a result, identifying such hateful and harmful social media information is crucial for jobs involving natural language processing. Our work presents an improved Distilbert-base-multilingual-cased model for identifying hateful and abusive tweets from Telugu text. For Telugu language tweets, the suggested fine-tuned Distilbert-base-multilingual-cased model achieved 0.6369% accuracy. The role of embedding with an improved BERT model for higher classification performance may be investigated in subsequent work.

Acknowledgments

The work was done with partial support from the Mexican Government through the grant A1-S-47854 of CONACYT, Mexico, grants 20241816,

20241819, and 20240951 of the Secretaría de Investigación y Posgrado of the Instituto Politécnico Nacional, Mexico. The authors thank the CONACYT for the computing resources brought to them through the Plataforma de Aprendizaje Profundo para Tecnologías del Lenguaje of the Laboratorio de Supercómputo of the INAOE, Mexico and acknowledge the support of Microsoft through the Microsoft Latin America PhD Award.

References

Muhammad Pervez Akhter, Zheng Jiangbin, Irfan Raza Naqvi, Mohammed AbdelMajeed, and Tehseen Zia. 2021. Abusive language detection from social media comments using conventional machine learning and deep learning approaches. *Multimedia Systems*, pages 1–16.

Premjth B, Bharathi Raja, Prasanna Kumar Kumaresan, Saranya Rajiakodi, Sai Prashanth Karnati, Sai Rishith Reddy Mangamuru, and Janakiram Chandu. 2024. Findings of the shared task on hate and offensive language detection in telugu codemixed text (hold-telugu). In *Proceedings of the Fourth Workshop on Speech, Vision, and Language Technologies for Dravidian Languages*, Malta. European Chapter of the Association for Computational Linguistics.

Pete Burnap and Matthew L Williams. 2015. Cyber hate speech on twitter: An application of machine classification and statistical modeling for policy and decision making. *Policy & internet*, 7(2):223–242.

Nemanja Djuric, Jing Zhou, Robin Morris, Mihajlo Grbovic, Vladan Radosavljevic, and Narayan Bhamidipati. 2015. Hate speech detection with comment embeddings. In *Proceedings of the 24th international conference on world wide web*, pages 29–30.

Shahnoor C Eshan and Mohammad S Hasan. 2017. An application of machine learning to detect abusive bengali text. In *2017 20th International Conference of Computer and Information Technology (ICCIT)*, pages 1–6. IEEE.

Koyel Ghosh and Apurbalal Senapati. 2022. Hate speech detection: a comparison of mono and multilingual transformer model with cross-language evaluation. In *Proceedings of the 36th Pacific Asia Conference on Language, Information and Computation*, pages 853–865.

Kushal Kedia and Abhilash Nandy. 2021. indicnlp@ kgp at dravidianlangtech-eacl2021: Offensive language identification in dravidian languages. *arXiv preprint arXiv:2102.07150*.

Bharathi Raja andS Malliga andCN SUBALALITHA Priyadharshini, Ruba andChakravarthi, Premjith and-Murugappan Abirami S V, Kogilavani andB, and Prasanna Kumar Kumaresan. 2023a. Overview of shared-task on abusive comment detection in tamil and telugu. In *Proceedings of the Third Workshop on Speech and Language Technologies for Dravidian Languages*, Varna, Bulgaria. Recent Advances in Natural Language Processing.

Ruba Priyadharshini, Bharathi Raja Chakravarthi, Subalalitha Cn, Thenmozhi Durairaj, Malliga Subramanian, Kogilavani Shanmugavadivel, Siddhanth U Hegde, and Prasanna Kumaresan. 2022. Overview of abusive comment detection in tamil-acl 2022. In *Proceedings of the Second Workshop on Speech and Language Technologies for Dravidian Languages*, pages 292–298.

Ruba Priyadharshini, Bharathi Raja Chakravarthi, S Malliga, Subalalitha Cn, SV Kogilavani, B Premjith, Abirami Murugappan, and Prasanna Kumar Kumaresan. 2023b. Overview of shared-task on abusive comment detection in tamil and telugu. In *Proceedings of the Third Workshop on Speech and Language Technologies for Dravidian Languages*, pages 80–87.

Sara Renjit and Sumam Mary Idicula. 2020. Cusatnlp@ hasoc-dravidian-codemix-fire2020: identifying offensive language from manglishtweets. *arXiv preprint arXiv:2010.08756*.

Debjoy Saha, Naman Paharia, Debajit Chakraborty, Punyajoy Saha, and Animesh Mukherjee. 2021. Hate-alert@ dravidianlangtech-eacl2021: Ensembling strategies for transformer-based offensive language detection. *arXiv preprint arXiv:2102.10084*.

Victor Sanh, Lysandre Debut, Julien Chaumond, and Thomas Wolf. 2019. Distilbert, a distilled version of bert: smaller, faster, cheaper and lighter. *arXiv preprint arXiv:1910.01108*.

Moein Shahiki-Tash, Jesús Armenta-Segura, Zahra Ahani, Olga Kolesnikova, Grigori Sidorov, and Alexander Gelbukh. 2023a. Lidoma at homomex2023@ iberlef: Hate speech detection towards the mexican spanish-speaking lgbt+ population. the importance of preprocessing before using bert-based models. In *Proceedings of the Iberian Languages Evaluation Forum (IberLEF 2023)*.

Moein Shahiki-Tash, Jesús Armenta-Segura, Olga Kolesnikova, Grigori Sidorov, and Alexander Gelbukh. 2023b. Lidoma at hope2023iberlef: Hope speech detection using lexical features and convolutional neural networks. In *Proceedings of the Iberian Languages Evaluation Forum (IberLEF 2023), co-located with the 39th Conference of the Spanish Society for Natural Language Processing (SEPLN 2023), CEUR-WS. org*.

M Shahiki Tash, Z Ahani, Al Tonja, M Gemeda, N Hussain, and O Kolesnikova. 2022. Word level language identification in code-mixed kannada-english texts using traditional machine learning algorithms. In *Proceedings of the 19th International Conference on Natural Language Processing (ICON): Shared*

Task on Word Level Language Identification in Code-mixed Kannada-English Texts, pages 25–28.

Moein Tash, Jesus Armenta-Segura, Zahra Ahani, Olga Kolesnikova, Grigori Sidorov, and Alexander Gelbukh. 2023. Lidoma@ dravidianlangtech: Convolutional neural networks for studying correlation between lexical features and sentiment polarity in tamil and tulu languages. In *Proceedings of the Third Workshop on Speech and Language Technologies for Dravidian Languages*, pages 180–185.

Atnafu Lambebo Tonja, Mesay Gemeda Yigezu, Olga Kolesnikova, Moein Shahiki Tash, Grigori Sidorov, and Alexander Gelbuk. 2022. Transformer-based model for word level language identification in code-mixed kannada-english texts. *arXiv preprint arXiv:2211.14459*.

Mesay Gemeda Yigezu, Girma Yohannis Bade, Olga Kolesnikova, Grigori Sidorov, and Alexander Gelbukh. 2023a. Multilingual hope speech detection using machine learning.

Mesay Gemeda Yigezu, Tadesse Kebede, Olga Kolesnikova, Grigori Sidorov, and Alexander Gelbukh. 2023b. Habesha@ dravidianlangtech: Utilizing deep and transfer learning approaches for sentiment analysis. In *Proceedings of the Third Workshop on Speech and Language Technologies for Dravidian Languages*, pages 239–243.

Mesay Gemeda Yigezu, Olga Kolesnikova, Grigori Sidorov, and Alexander Gelbukh. 2023c. Transformer-based hate speech detection for multi-class and multi-label classification.

Mesay Gemeda Yigezu, Moges Ahmed Mehamed, Olga Kolesnikova, Tadesse Kebede Guge, Alexander Gelbukh, and Grigori Sidorov. 2023d. Evaluating the effectiveness of hybrid features in fake news detection on social media. In *2023 International Conference on Information and Communication Technology for Development for Africa (ICT4DA)*, pages 171–175. IEEE.

Mesay Gemeda Yigezu, Atnafu Lambebo Tonja, Olga Kolesnikova, Moein Shahiki Tash, Grigori Sidorov, and Alexander Gelbukh. 2022. Word level language identification in code-mixed kannada-english texts using deep learning approach. In *Proceedings of the 19th International Conference on Natural Language Processing (ICON): Shared Task on Word Level Language Identification in Code-mixed Kannada-English Texts*, pages 29–33.

Selam@DravidianLangTech 2024:Identifying Hate Speech and Offensive Language

Selam Abitte Kanta, Grigori Sidorov and **Alexander Gelbukh**
Instituto Politécnico Nacional (IPN),
Centro de Investigación en Computación (CIC), Mexico City, Mexico
Corresponding: selaminadady300@gmail.com

Abstract

Social media has transformed into a powerful tool for sharing information while upholding the principle of free expression. However, this open platform has given rise to significant issues like hate speech, cyberbullying, aggression, and offensive language, negatively impacting societal well-being. These problems can even lead to severe consequences such as suicidal thoughts, affecting the mental health of the victims. Our primary goal is to develop an automated system for the rapid detection of offensive content on social media, facilitating timely interventions and moderation. This research employs various machine learning classifiers, utilizing character N-gram TF-IDF features. Additionally, we introduce SVM, RL, and Convolutional Neural Network (CNN) models specifically designed for hate speech detection. SVM utilizes character N-gram TF-IDF features, while CNN employs word embedding features. Through extensive experiments, we achieved optimal results, with a weighted F1-score of 0.77 in identifying hate speech and offensive language.

1 Introduction

In the digital age, social media plays an important role in online communication, allowing users to create and share material while also giving accessible means to express their views and thoughts on anything at any time (Edosomwan et al., 2011). However, with the advent of social media, platforms such as YouTube, Facebook, and Twitter not only aided in information sharing and networking, but they also became a place where people were targeted, defamed, and marginalized based solely on their physical appearance, religion, or sexual orientation(Keipi et al., 2016) Social media platforms have become more integrated with this digital era and have impacted various people's perceptions of networking and socializing(Tonja et al., 2022b).

Not only human beings, the hate content can corrupt the chatbots as well. Microscoft's chatbot 'Tay' which was developed to engage people through casual and playful conversation started using filthy language, which it learned from the conversation with people. The chatbot was unable to understand and avoid the hate content. So the detection of hate speech in tweets and social media sites has important applications in Chatbot building, content recommendation, sentiment analysis, etc.

India being a diverse country in terms of its culture and language has a huge population using code-mixed language in social media. Around 44% of the Indian population speak Hindi. So the usage of Hindi-English code-mixed language is very high on Twitter and Facebook. It is mainly seen among bilingual and multilingual communities. Code-mixing is the usage of certain words, phrases, or morphemes of one language in other languages.

This influence allowed different users to communicate via various social media platforms using a mix of texts. NLP technology has advanced rapidly in many applications, including machine translation(Tonja et al., 2022a),(Tash et al., 2022) Although considerable progress has been achieved in identifying offensive English language and hate speech, most research has mostly concentrated on identifying the abusive and offensive language in monolingual settings. This subject still appears to be at a very early stage of research for under resourced languages such as Tamil, Malayalam, and Kannada, which lack tools and datasets (Chakravarthi et al., 2020), (Yigezu et al., 2023d).

The task at hand involves identifying hate or offensive content in Telugu code-mixed text, with annotations made at the comment or post level. Given the complexity of language mixing in the Telugu context, where expressions may span multiple sentences, a tailored approach is crucial. In response, we deploy a Convolutional Neural Network (CNN)

Proceedings of the Fourth Workshop on Speech, Vision, and Language Technologies for Dravidian Languages, pages 91–95
March 22, 2024 ©2024 Association for Computational Linguistics

(Yigezu et al., 2023c,a)to enhance the effectiveness of detection methods. This research not only contributes to hate speech detection but also addresses the specific challenges posed by code-mixed expressions in Telugu. The subsequent sections delve into the deployment of CNN in our methodology, present experimental results, and discuss the implications of our approach.

2 Related Work

Currently, solving NLP problems in code-mixed data is getting attention from many researchers.

Social platforms are inundated with hate speech and offensive content, necessitating swift filtration (Yigezu et al., 2023e,b). However, manual filtering is nearly impossible due to the immense volume of incoming posts. This issue has garnered significant attention from the research community. Numerous studies have focused on predicting offensive and hate speech posts on social platforms, encompassing various languages. However, a majority of these studies have predominantly utilized English languages. languages

Detecting offensive content in social media comments is not a novel concept for the English language(Mandl et al., 2021). Several systems have also been developed for languages other than English, such as Hindi, Germany (Rajalakshmi et al., 2022),(Rajalakshmi and Reddy, 2019). However, there is limited research focused on identifying offensive content in low-resource Dravidian languages such as Tamil, Malayalam, and Kannada (Garain et al., 2021). The study proposes a method for identifying offensive language in code-mixed Kannada-English, Malayalam-English, and Tamil-English language pairs sourced from social media.(Ojo et al., 2023) The authors advocate for a multi-label classification approach, leveraging an ensemble of IndicBERT and generic BERT models, to recognize and mitigate offensive content on social media platforms.(Yigezu et al., 2022),(Yigezu et al., 2021) Addressing a multi-label classification challenge with various sub-categories, the system employs tokenization of the data before model training.

The calculation of class-wise confidence scores, subsequently combined into an output vector, facilitates effective classification. Across the Malayalam–English, Tamil-English, and Kannada-English datasets, the achieved F1 scores are 0.54, 0.72, and 0.66, respectively. This research task is outlined in the study conducted by(Kedia and Nandy, 2021). Introduced is a potent multiclass abusive detection model, showcasing an impressive accuracy and F1-score of 0.99 on a well-balanced dataset. The model detected abusive comments within Tamil and Telugu English code-mixed text, and employed the TF-IDF technique in conjunction with SVM, as demonstrated by (Balakrishnan et al., 2023).

3 Datasets

The dataset employed in this research is sourced from the Hate and Offensive Language Detection in Telugu Code-mixed Text (HOLD-Telugu) dataset provided by Dravidian-LangTech@EACL(Balakrishnan et al., 2023) The data look below in 1 The data set contains Telugu-English code-mixed language comments, along with the labels and text IDs. The labels indicate whether the comment is offensive language or hate speech Since there were only 2 category comments in the training set and no such labeled comments found in the test set, we have discarded those hate or offensive labeled samples from our corpus. Hence, we have viewed this as a binary classification In this dataset, we have a total of 6930 Telugu tweet comments, of which tried 5355. The remaining 1575 samples were part of the testing set we have tried to find a suitable representation for Telugu language text data and also studied the effect of stemming and stop word removal by applying various methods. The details of the proposed methodology are presented in the following sections.

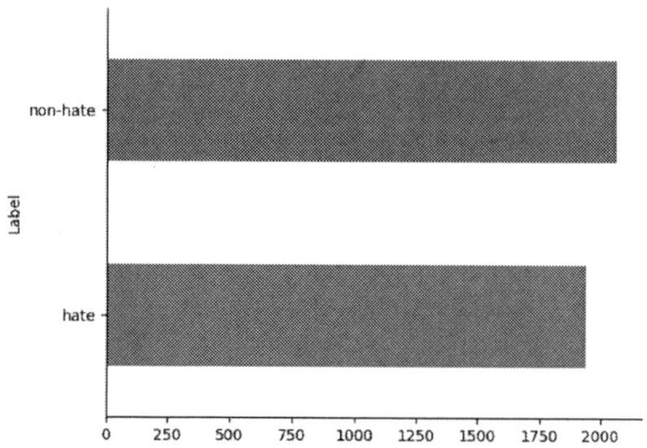

Figure 1: Categorical distributions

4 Methodology

The described methodology is extensively detailed in this section. Figure 2 illustrates the comprehensive flowchart outlining the process of identifying hate speech and offensive tweets. The section commences with an overview of the dataset,1 followed by an in-depth exploration of the proposed models. We used the DravidianLangTech dataset to carry out our experimentations. Each comment in the dataset is labeled as offensive (Hate) or not offensive (NOT hate). We experimented with different conventional classifiers such as (i) Support Vector Machine (SVM), (ii) Naïve Bayes (NB), (iii) Random Forest (RF), and (iv) Convolutional Neural Network (CNN.

We employed character N-gram TF-IDF features in conventional machine learning classifiers and the DNN model. In the case of CNN, we used a 100-dimensional word embedding vector to represent each word of the tweet. In our case, we fixed the maximum word length for comments to 10000 words. As in our dataset, we found most of the comments were less than 100 words, due to this we chose the maximum length of 1000 words for the experiments. It means we curtailed the words of the comments that have more than 42 words and padded for the comments that have less than 100 words. It means a comments matrix with a (42 × 100) dimension is passed through the CNN network to extract features from the comments to classify them into hate and NOT hate classes. A convolutional neural network is a multi-layered neural network with a unique design that is used to recognize complex data features.

We implemented one layered convolutional neural network with 128 filters of 3-gram to extract features from the text and then this feature is passed through the Max Pooling operation and the activation function to get the feature map and this feature map is then used by the dense layer to classify tweets into hate and not-hate classes.

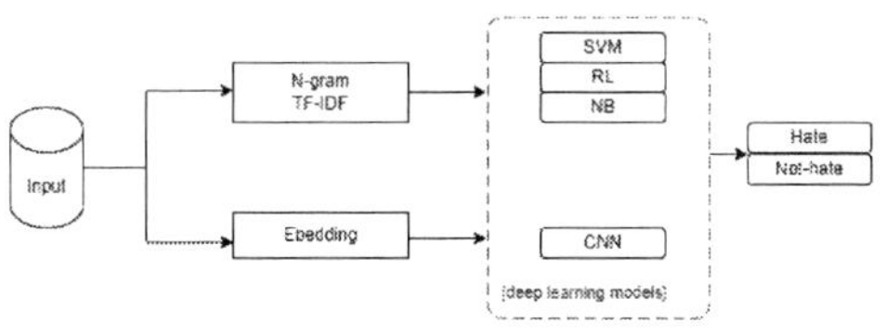

Figure 2: Proposed model architecture

4.1 Conclusion

Our Task focused on evaluating the effectiveness of diverse machine learning models in the identification of hate speech and offensive/non-offensive

Model	**Hate**	**Not-hate**
CNN	0.76	0.78
SVM	0.74	0.75
NB	0.68	0.76
RF	0.7	0.73

Table 1: F1 Score in each model

content in comments. We conducted a comparative analysis, assessing Support Vector Machine (SVM), Naive Bayes, Random Forest, and Convolutional Neural Network (CNN) models. The performance evaluation relied on the weighted F1 score, a pivotal metric that considers both precision and recall. show in figure 3 The results underscored the exceptional success of the CNN model, achieving a weighted F1 score of 0.7711.

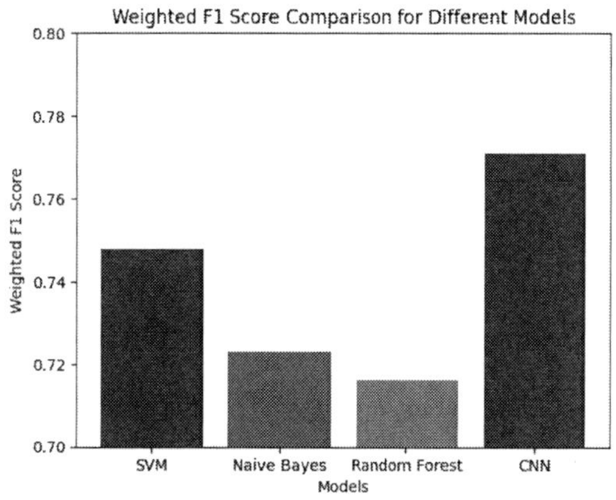

Figure 3: F1- Score Weighted

This emphasizes CNN's ability to effectively balance accurate identification of offensive or non-offensive content while minimizing false positives and negatives. Although SVM, Naive Bayes, and Random Forest demonstrated commendable performances, the superior performance of the CNN model highlights the significance of deploying deep learning techniques for intricate tasks such as identifying hate and offensive speech. The visual representation through the bar graph further emphasized the comparative performance, with the CNN model standing out due to its higher weighted F1 score. Looking ahead, the integration of machine learning and deep learning models, alongside ongoing parameter tuning for the CNN-based model, presents promising avenues for enhancing the efficiency of hate speech identification in comments.

Acknowledgments

The work was done with partial support from the Mexican Government through the grant A1-S-47854 of CONACYT, Mexico, grants 20241816, 20241819, and 20240951 of the Secretaría de Investigación y Posgrado of the Instituto Politécnico Nacional, Mexico. The authors thank the CONACYT for the computing resources brought to them through the Plataforma de Aprendizaje Profundo para Tecnologías del Lenguaje of the Laboratorio de Supercómputo of the INAOE, Mexico and acknowledge the support of Microsoft through the Microsoft Latin America PhD Award.

References

Vimala Balakrishnan, Vithyatheri Govindan, and Kumanan N Govaichelvan. 2023. Tamil offensive language detection: Supervised versus unsupervised learning approaches. *ACM Transactions on Asian and Low-Resource Language Information Processing*, 22(4):1–14.

Bharathi Raja Chakravarthi, Navya Jose, Shardul Suryawanshi, Elizabeth Sherly, and John P McCrae. 2020. A sentiment analysis dataset for code-mixed malayalam-english. *arXiv preprint arXiv:2006.00210*.

Simeon Edosomwan, Sitalaskshmi Kalangot Prakasan, Doriane Kouame, Jonelle Watson, and Tom Seymour. 2011. The history of social media and its impact on business. *Journal of Applied Management and entrepreneurship*, 16(3):79.

Avishek Garain, Atanu Mandal, and Sudip Kumar Naskar. 2021. Junlp@ dravidianlangtech-eacl2021: Offensive language identification in dravidian langauges. In *Proceedings of the First Workshop on Speech and Language Technologies for Dravidian Languages*, pages 319–322.

Kushal Kedia and Abhilash Nandy. 2021. indicnlp@ kgp at dravidianlangtech-eacl2021: Offensive language identification in dravidian languages. *arXiv preprint arXiv:2102.07150*.

Teo Keipi, Matti Näsi, Atte Oksanen, and Pekka Räsänen. 2016. *Online hate and harmful content: Cross-national perspectives*. Taylor & Francis.

Thomas Mandl, Sandip Modha, Gautam Kishore Shahi, Hiren Madhu, Shrey Satapara, Prasenjit Majumder, Johannes Schäfer, Tharindu Ranasinghe, Marcos Zampieri, Durgesh Nandini, et al. 2021. Overview of the hasoc subtrack at fire 2021: Hate speech and offensive content identification in english and indo-aryan languages. *arXiv preprint arXiv:2112.09301*.

Olumide Ebenezer Ojo, Olaronke Oluwayemisi Adebanji, Hiram Calvo, Alexander Gelbukh, Anna Feldman, and Grigori Sidorov. 2023. Hate and offensive content identification in indo-aryan languages using transformer-based models.

R Rajalakshmi and B Yashwant Reddy. 2019. Dlrg@ hasoc 2019: An enhanced ensemble classifier for hate and offensive content identification. In *FIRE (Working Notes)*, pages 370–379.

Ratnavel Rajalakshmi, Ankita Duraphe, and Antonette Shibani. 2022. DLRG@DravidianLangTech-ACL2022: Abusive comment detection in Tamil using multilingual transformer models. In *Proceedings of the Second Workshop on Speech and Language Technologies for Dravidian Languages*, pages 207–213, Dublin, Ireland. Association for Computational Linguistics.

M Shahiki Tash, Z Ahani, Al Tonja, M Gemeda, N Hussain, and O Kolesnikova. 2022. Word level language identification in code-mixed kannada-english texts using traditional machine learning algorithms. In *Proceedings of the 19th International Conference on Natural Language Processing (ICON): Shared Task on Word Level Language Identification in Code-mixed Kannada-English Texts*, pages 25–28.

Atnafu Lambebo Tonja, Olga Kolesnikova, Muhammad Arif, Alexander Gelbukh, and Grigori Sidorov. 2022a. Improving neural machine translation for low resource languages using mixed training: The case of ethiopian languages. In *Mexican International Conference on Artificial Intelligence*, pages 30–40. Springer.

Atnafu Lambebo Tonja, Olumide Ebenezer Ojo, Mohammed Arif Khan, Abdul Gafar Manuel Meque, Olga Kolesnikova, Grigori Sidorov, and Alexander Gelbukh. 2022b. Cic nlp at smm4h 2022: a bert-based approach for classification of social media forum posts. In *Proceedings of The Seventh Workshop on Social Media Mining for Health Applications, Workshop & Shared Task*, pages 58–61.

Mesay Gemeda Yigezu, Girma Yohannis Bade, Olga Kolesnikova, Grigori Sidorov, and Alexander Gelbukh. 2023a. Multilingual hope speech detection using machine learning.

Mesay Gemeda Yigezu, Selam Kanta, Olga Kolesnikova, Grigori Sidorov, and Alexander Gelbukh. 2023b. Habesha@ dravidianlangtech: Abusive comment detection using deep learning approach. In *Proceedings of the Third Workshop on Speech and Language Technologies for Dravidian Languages*, pages 244–249.

Mesay Gemeda Yigezu, Tadesse Kebede, Olga Kolesnikova, Grigori Sidorov, and Alexander Gelbukh. 2023c. Habesha@ dravidianlangtech: Utilizing deep and transfer learning approaches for sentiment analysis. In *Proceedings of the Third Workshop on Speech and Language Technologies for Dravidian Languages*, pages 239–243.

Mesay Gemeda Yigezu, Olga Kolesnikova, Grigori Sidorov, and Alexander Gelbukh. 2023d. Transformer-based hate speech detection for multi-class and multi-label classification.

Mesay Gemeda Yigezu, Moges Ahmed Mehamed, Olga Kolesnikova, Tadesse Kebede Guge, Alexander Gelbukh, and Grigori Sidorov. 2023e. Evaluating the effectiveness of hybrid features in fake news detection on social media. In *2023 International Conference on Information and Communication Technology for Development for Africa (ICT4DA)*, pages 171–175. IEEE.

Mesay Gemeda Yigezu, Atnafu Lambebo Tonja, Olga Kolesnikova, Moein Shahiki Tash, Grigori Sidorov, and Alexander Gelbukh. 2022. Word level language identification in code-mixed kannada-english texts using deep learning approach. In *Proceedings of the 19th International Conference on Natural Language Processing (ICON): Shared Task on Word Level Language Identification in Code-mixed Kannada-English Texts*, pages 29–33.

Mesay Gemeda Yigezu, Michael Melese Woldeyohannis, and Atnafu Lambebo Tonja. 2021. Multilingual neural machine translation for low resourced languages: Ometo-english. In *2021 International Conference on Information and Communication Technology for Development for Africa (ICT4DA)*, pages 89–94. IEEE.

Tewodros@DravidianLangTech 2024: Hate Speech Recognition in Telugu Codemixed Text

Tewodros Achamaleh[2],Lemlem Eyob Kawo [1], Ildar Batyrshin[1], and Grigori Sidorov[1]
[1]Instituto Politécnico Nacional (IPN), Centro de Investigación en Computación (CIC), Mexico City, Mexico
[2]Rift Valley University (RVU), Department of Technology and Engineering, Addis Ababa, Ethiopia

Abstract

This study goes into our team's active participation in the Hate and Offensive LanguageDetection in Telugu Codemixed Text (HOLDTelugu) shared task, which is an essential component of the DravidianLangTech@EACL 2024 workshop. The ultimate goal of this collaborative work is to push the bounds of hatespeech recognition, especially tackling the issues given by codemixed text in Telugu, where English blends smoothly. Our inquiry offers a complete evaluation of the task's aims, the technique used, and the precise achievements obtained by our team, providing a full insight into our contributions to this crucial linguistic and technical undertaking.

1 Introduction

The prevalence of hate speech and provocative language in online interactions has raised serious concerns about their negative impact on people and society. With its unequal reach and simplicity of use, social media has become a breeding ground for the spread of such toxic information. While considerable strides have been made in identifying hate speech in English, the issue remains largely unexplored for Dravidian languages such as Telugu.

Telugu, which is spoken by almost 80 million people in India, is a sophisticated language that incorporates words and phrases from other languages, mostly English. This linguistic feature creates additional challenges for effectively detecting hate speech in Telugu literature. Recognizing the need to bridge this knowledge gap and support innovation in Telugu hate speech detection, the DravidianLangTech@EACL 2024 workshop included the Shared task on Hate and Offensive Language Detection in Telugu Codemixed Text (HOLD-Telugu).The collaborative effort aims to bring together diverse experts in order to create effective methods for detecting hate and abuse terms in Telugu codemixed text.

2 Related Work

While hate speech identification in English has gained significant study interest, the topic for Dravidian languages like Telugu remains relatively new and unexplored. However, in the past year, tasks such as sentiment analysis have been done on the Tulu-English code-mixing language dataset (Tash et al., 2023), and the following earlier research gives vital facts and insights linked to the HOLD-Telugu joint task:

In the work of (Priyadharshini et al., 2022), the authors attempt to present an overview of detecting abusive comments and hope speech involving homophobia, misandry, counter-speech, misogyny, xenophobia, and transphobia using data in Tamil and Tamil-English code-mixed languages. along with dataset details and participant findings.

In (Pavlopoulos et al., 2019), the authors provide the evaluation of two powerful baselines for offensive language identification (Perspective) and categorization (BERT). Their experiment shows that Perspective outperformed BERT in detecting toxicity, whereas BERT outperformed Perspective in categorizing the offensive type. In the SEMEVAL-2019 OFFENSEVAL competition, Perspective ranked 12th in detecting an offensive post, while BERT ranked 11th in categorizing it.

In (Chakravarthi et al., 2022), the authors constructed a multilingual, manually annotated dataset and experimented with machine learning and deep learning algorithms. The dataset contains around 60,000 YouTube comments, including approximately 44,000 comments in Tamil-English, 7000 comments in Kannada-English, and 20,000 comments in Malayalam-English. They make it publicly available on GitHub and Zenodo.

The authors in (Ayele et al., 2022b) build a dataset of 5,267 tweets, and machine learning methods LR and SVM achieve an F1 score of 0.49, whereas NB achieves an F1 value of 0.46. The

Proceedings of the Fourth Workshop on Speech, Vision, and Language Technologies for Dravidian Languages, pages 96–100
March 22, 2024 ©2024 Association for Computational Linguistics

deep learning algorithms (LSTM, BiLSTM, and CNN) achieve an equal F1 score of 0.44, the lowest of all models. Am-FLAIR and Am-RoBERTa, two contextual embedding models, attain F1 scores of 0.48 and 0.50, respectively.

The authors in (Shahiki-Tash et al., 2023) conducted experiments using transformer architectures and BERT-based models, present hate speech detection toward the Mexican Spanish-speaking LGBT+ population, and achieve results with a Macro F1 score of 0.73.

The authors in (Shahiki-Tash et al., 2023) presented a word-based tokenization approach to train a convolutional Neural network (CNN).

In (Yigezu et al., 2023), To examine language patterns, the authors use deep learning models such as Long Short-Term Memory (LSTM) and Recurrent Neural Networks (RNNs). The LSTM model, which is a form of RNN, is used to comprehend the context by capturing long-term relationships and detailed patterns in input sequences.

The authors in (Ayele et al., 2022a) examine the primary concerns associated with crowdsourcing annotation for the collection of Amharic hate speech data using Yandex Toloka.An estimated 1,000 tweets are annotated annually, or 5,400 in total. Classification models based on deep learning were developed utilizing LSTM and BiLSTM. Both models achieved an F1-score of 0.44.

3 Methodology

Various machine learning algorithms, including classical methods and deep learning techniques, can be used. Neural networks and deep learning are among the most helpful AI approaches that have been developed (Ahani et al., 2024). RNN is often used as a building block in modern neural networks to detect hate speech (Yigezu et al., 2022). Our team deployed a task of automatic hate and offensive language detection in Telugu codemixed text using a deep learning-based simple neural network (Simple RNN) model.

This design was chosen for its efficacy in capturing temporal dependencies within text data vital for understanding the sequential nature of language, and their ability to model short-term dependencies is useful for applications such as hate speech and offensive language detection. They are computationally simple compared to advanced architectures like Long Short Term Memory (LSTM) or Gated Recurrent Unit (GRU), which allow faster training, especially on small datasets. The interpretability of simple RNNs is advantageous in applications requiring a transparent decision-making process, such as hate speech detection.

The model is trained on a training and validation dataset and evaluated on the test set. We perform pre-processing procedures, including tokenization and padding, removing punctuation marks, and filtering out stop words, to turn the text data into a format appropriate for neural network computation. The general methodology pipeline is shown in Figure 2

3.1 Dataset Analysis

The main point of our research resides in the HOLD-Telugu dataset which is collected from social media (Priyadharshini et al., 2022), carefully curated with 4000 items of Telugu codemixed text. Each entry is extensively annotated for hate or non-hate content, capturing varied linguistic phrases and cultural nuances. Code-Mix is used in nearly all social media networks where individuals speak many languages. The use of code-mixed data in natural language processing (NLP) research is receiving a lot of interest right now (Tash et al., 2022).

Due to the expansion and significance of social media in communication, hate speech detection of social media code-mixed text has been an attractive subject of study in recent years (Tonja et al., 2022). Our investigation delves into the nature of the dataset, analyzing the distribution of hate vs. non-hate samples, the intricacies of codemixing patterns, and the possible issues these aspects represent for hate speech recognition programs. We show the Distribution of Data in Figure 1

3.2 Shared Task Description

The HOLD-Telugu shared task supplied users with a rich dataset of Telugu code-mixed text(Priyadharshini et al., 2023; Premjth et al.,2024"), painstakingly annotated for hate and offensive content. This dataset includes different online sources, including social networking platforms, discussion forums, and news websites. Participants were tasked with constructing models capable of reliably detecting whether a particular comment contained hate or derogatory language. The performance of the suggested models was evaluated using the macro-F1 score, a balanced metric that combines both precision and recall across both classes,ensuring a full and trustworthy assessment.

3.3 Model Architecture

We painstakingly study the model architecture, uncovering the rationale behind each design decision. The embedding layer transforms the discrete word tokens into dense vectors, capturing semantic links between words. The simple RNN layer then analyzes these vectors sequentially, allowing the model to learn from the context and sequence of the words. Dropout regularization is employed to prevent overfitting and increase model generalization. Finally, a thick layer with softmax activation classifies each input as hate or non-hate content. We show the parameters we use in Table 1:

Table 1: parameter Setting

Parameters	Values
embed_units	64
hidden_units	128
dropout	0.5
optimizer	adam
batch_size	64
loss	categorical_crossentropy
epoch	5
activation	SoftMax
restore best weights	TRUE
SimpleRNN layer	early stop
callbacks	32 units

3.4 Experimental setup

Our model attained a test accuracy of 64.9 %, assessed using the macro-F1 score as stated by the shared task. Each entry is extensively annotated for hate or non-hate content and further divided into 70% training, 15% testing, and 15% validation sets. We deconstruct the results, assessing the performance on several types of hate speech and exploring the effects of codemixing on model effectiveness. We identify areas for improvement and discuss critical lessons learned during the trial process.

3.5 Predictions on Unseen Data

To highlight the real-world applicability of our model, we apply it to a separate test dataset, proving its capacity to generalize to previously unseen data. The anticipated categories are saved in a conveniently accessible format, enabling additional research and review.

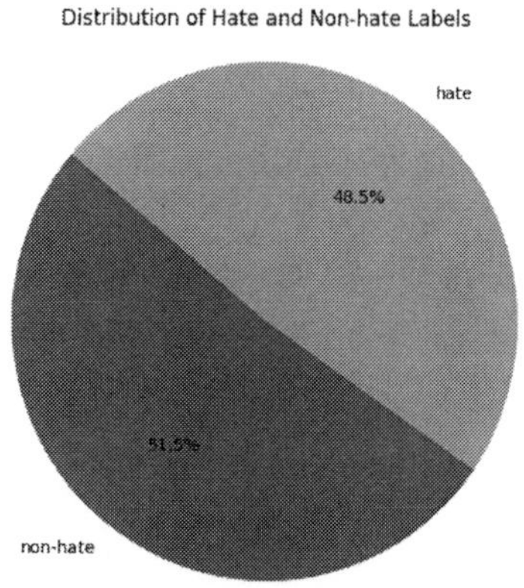

Figure 1: Distribution of Data

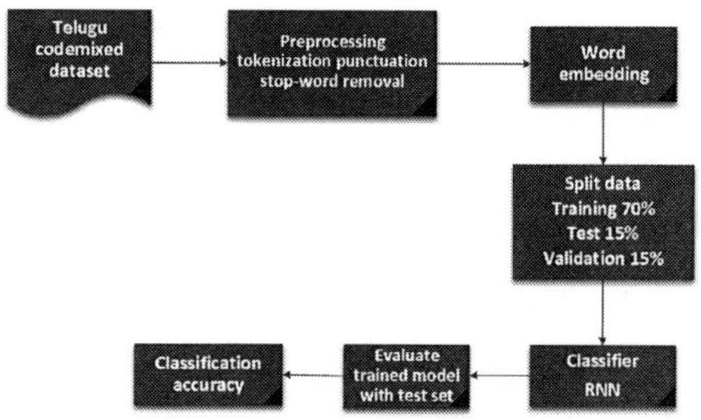

Figure 2: Steps for task evaluations

4 Discussion

While our model achieved promising results, we acknowledge the limits inherent in the simple RNN design and the issues provided by codemixing. In future work, we will have a plan to address potential routes for development, including studying more complicated neural networks,adding additional variables like sentiment analysis, and leveraging larger and more diverse datasets.

5 Conclusion

The HOLD-Telugu collaborative initiative effectively addressed the critical problem of identifying hate speech in Telugu code-mixed text. The shared employment enabled significant discoveries in this under-researched subject by bringing together divergent researchers and promoting teamwork. The large and diverse dataset, high-quality submissions, and intelligent analysis have paved the way for the continuing development of powerful hate speech detection algorithms for Telugu code-mixed text.

The successes of collaborative work go beyond technical advancements. The HOLD-Telugu work helps to a more inclusive and healthier online environment for Telugu communities by reducing the prevalence of toxic language. The shared task resources and results enable researchers and developers to continue this endeavor, resulting in better online interactions and protecting people from the negative consequences of hate speech.

Looking forward, the HOLD-Telugu collaboration lays the groundwork for future research on hate speech detection in Dravidian languages and code-mixed text. More research into sophisticated NLP methods, such as multilingual language models and fine-tuning procedures, has the potential to significantly improve the accuracy and general applicability of hate speech detection systems. Furthermore, the data from the shared job may be used to create tools and resources that enable people and organizations to reject hate speech and promote online safety.

The achievement of the HOLD-Telugu joint endeavor demonstrates the enormous potential of collaborative research in addressing difficult social issues. Research communities may positively contribute to the establishment of safer and more inclusive online environments for everybody by facilitating open data exchange, fostering diverse perspectives, and concentrating on practical applications.

6 Limitations

The problems faced while interacting with a Telugu language dataset originate from the lack of resources that hinder preprocessing techniques. The dynamics of spoken language create challenges in adaptability for models that were trained on historical data. Proper identification of relevant features for successful training is also a challenging task, especially when dealing with a language that has certain unique linguistic.

Acknowledgements

We extend our heartfelt gratitude to the organizers of the HOLD-Telugu shared task and the DravidianLangTech@EACL 2024 workshop for providing a useful forum for this joint study. We also recognize the contributions of the dataset producers and annotators, whose hard efforts made this research feasible.

The work was done with partial support from the Mexican Government through the grant A1-S-47854 of CONACYT, Mexico,grants 20241816, 20241819, and 20240951 of the Secretaría de Investigación y Posgrado of the Instituto Politécnico Nacional, Mexico. The authors thank the CONACYT for the computing resources brought to them through the Plataforma de Aprendizaje Profundo para Tecnologías del Lenguaje of the Laboratorio de Supercómputo of the INAOE, Mexico and acknowledge the support of Microsoft through the Microsoft Latin America PhD Award.

References

Zahra Ahani, Moein Shahiki Tash, Yoel Ledo Mezquita, and Jason Angel. 2024. Utilizing deep learning models for the identification of enhancers and super-enhancers based on genomic and epigenomic features. *arXiv preprint arXiv:2401.07470*.

Abinew Ali Ayele, Tadesse Destaw Belay, Seid Muhie Yimam, Skadi Dinter, Tesfa Tegegne Asfaw, and Chris Biemann. 2022a. Challenges of amharic hate speech data annotation using yandex toloka crowdsourcing platform. In *Proceedings of the The Sixth Widening NLP Workshop (WiNLP), Abu Dhabi, United Arab Emirates. Association for Computational Linguistics*.

Abinew Ali Ayele, Skadi Dinter, Tadesse Destaw Belay, Tesfa Tegegne Asfaw, Seid Muhie Yimam, and Chris Biemann. 2022b. The 5js in ethiopia: Amharic hate speech data annotation using toloka crowdsourcing platform. In *2022 International Conference on Information and Communication Technology for Development for Africa (ICT4DA)*, pages 114–120. IEEE.

Bharathi Raja Chakravarthi, Ruba Priyadharshini, Vigneshwaran Muralidaran, Navya Jose, Shardul Suryawanshi, Elizabeth Sherly, and John P McCrae. 2022. Dravidiancodemix: Sentiment analysis and offensive language identification dataset for dravidian languages in code-mixed text. *Language Resources and Evaluation*, 56(3):765–806.

John Pavlopoulos, Nithum Thain, Lucas Dixon, and Ion Androutsopoulos. 2019. Convai at semeval-2019 task 6: Offensive language identification and categorization with perspective and bert. In *Proceedings of the 13th international Workshop on Semantic Evaluation*, pages 571–576.

Ruba Priyadharshini, Bharathi Raja Chakravarthi, Subalalitha Cn, Thenmozhi Durairaj, Malliga Subramanian, Kogilavani Shanmugavadivel, Siddhanth U Hegde, and Prasanna Kumaresan. 2022. Overview of abusive comment detection in tamil-acl 2022. In *Proceedings of the Second Workshop on Speech and Language Technologies for Dravidian Languages*, pages 292–298.

Moein Shahiki-Tash, Jesús Armenta-Segura, Olga Kolesnikova, Grigori Sidorov, and Alexander Gelbukh. 2023. Lidoma at hope2023iberlef: Hope speech detection using lexical features and convolutional neural networks. In *Proceedings of the Iberian*

Languages Evaluation Forum (IberLEF 2023), co-located with the 39th Conference of the Spanish Society for Natural Language Processing (SEPLN 2023), CEUR-WS. org.

M Shahiki Tash, Z Ahani, Al Tonja, M Gemeda, N Hussain, and O Kolesnikova. 2022. Word level language identification in code-mixed kannada-english texts using traditional machine learning algorithms. In *Proceedings of the 19th International Conference on Natural Language Processing (ICON): Shared Task on Word Level Language Identification in Code-mixed Kannada-English Texts*, pages 25–28.

Moein Tash, Jesus Armenta-Segura, Zahra Ahani, Olga Kolesnikova, Grigori Sidorov, and Alexander Gelbukh. 2023. Lidoma@ dravidianlangtech: Convolutional neural networks for studying correlation between lexical features and sentiment polarity in tamil and tulu languages. In *Proceedings of the Third Workshop on Speech and Language Technologies for Dravidian Languages*, pages 180–185.

Atnafu Lambebo Tonja, Mesay Gemeda Yigezu, Olga Kolesnikova, Moein Shahiki Tash, Grigori Sidorov, and Alexander Gelbuk. 2022. Transformer-based model for word level language identification in code-mixed kannada-english texts. *arXiv preprint arXiv:2211.14459*.

Mesay Gemeda Yigezu, Selam Kanta, Olga Kolesnikova, Grigori Sidorov, and Alexander Gelbukh. 2023. Habesha@ dravidianlangtech: Abusive comment detection using deep learning approach. In *Proceedings of the Third Workshop on Speech and Language Technologies for Dravidian Languages*, pages 244–249.

Mesay Gemeda Yigezu, Atnafu Lambebo Tonja, Olga Kolesnikova, Moein Shahiki Tash, Grigori Sidorov, and Alexander Gelbukh. 2022. Word level language identification in code-mixed kannada-english texts using deep learning approach. In *Proceedings of the 19th International Conference on Natural Language Processing (ICON): Shared Task on Word Level Language Identification in Code-mixed Kannada-English Texts*, pages 29–33.

Lidoma@DravidianLangTech 2024: Identifying Hate Speech in Telugu Code-Mixed: A BERT Multilingual

Muhammad Tayyab Zamir, Moein Shahiki Tash, Zahra Ahani, Alexander Gelbukh, Girigori Sidorov
Instituto Politécnico Nacional (IPN), Centro de Investigación en Computación (CIC) Mexico
Corresponding: mzamir2023@cic.ipn.mx

Abstract

Over the past few years, research on hate speech and offensive content identification on social media has been ongoing. Since most people in the world are not native English speakers, unapproved messages are typically sent in code-mixed language. We accomplished collaborative work to identify the language of code-mixed text on social media in order to address the difficulties associated with it in the Telugu language scenario. Specifically, we participated in the shared task on the provided dataset by the DravidianLangTech Organizer for the purpose of identifying hate and non-hate content. The assignment is to classify each sentence in the provided text into two predetermined groups: hate or non-hate. We developed a model in Python and selected a BERT multilingual to do the given task. Using a train-development data set, we developed a model, which we then tested on test data sets. An average macro F1 score metric was used to measure the model's performance. For the task, the model reported an average macro F1 of 0.6151.

1 Introduction

India is a multilingual nation with a diverse linguistic past in South Asia. As the official and administrative language of the state of Andhra Pradesh in southern India, Telugu is one of the most widely spoken languages in the country. having 96 million or more Telugu speakers as native speakers(tel).

In addition to their native, local, or regional tongue, many in the region feel at ease utilizing English for daily communication. These multilingual people prefer to share their thoughts, opinions, and comments on social media sites in several scripts and/or languages, which makes code-mixing the norm on social media(Priyadharshini et al., 2023b; Chakravarthi et al., 2021; Priyadharshini et al., 2023a). The spread of hate speech(Yigezu et al., 2023b; Shahiki-Tash et al., 2023) and objectionable content has far-reaching effects, increasing tensions, encouraging discrimination, and widening societal divisions as social media and online platforms become an essential part of daily life in India. In light of the pressing need to address such content, this study attempts to manage the complexities of Telugu codemixed (B et al., 2024; Yigezu et al., 2022) language by utilizing sophisticated natural language processing (NLP) models, most notably BERT (Bidirectional Encoder Representations from Transformers) (Bade, 2021; Tonja et al., 2022). Sentiment analysis (Kanta and Sidorov, 2023; Tash et al., 2023; Bade and Afaro, 2018), a powerful tool in natural language processing, often focuses on discerning emotions conveyed in the text. When applied to hate speech, it plays a crucial role in understanding the underlying sentiment behind abusive language, shedding light on the detrimental impact of hateful expressions within the digital sphere.

The results of this work aim to establish a basic framework for continued attempts to prevent the spread of damaging content, provide platforms with efficient tools for moderation, and foster a more favorable and supportive online environment among the diverse range of languages found in India's digital space.

2 Related work

The identification of hate speech has grown in importance in the social media and internet communication era. Due to the increase in hate speech occurrences, academics are investigating many approaches to effectively address this problem, such as deep learning (Yigezu et al., 2023a; Ahani et al., 2024),

Proceedings of the Fourth Workshop on Speech, Vision, and Language Technologies for Dravidian Languages, pages 101–106
March 22, 2024 ©2024 Association for Computational Linguistics

transformer-based models, Convolutional Neural Network (Bade and Seid, 2018; sha), and machine learning (Tash et al., 2022).

Traditional machine learning techniques played a major role in the early stages of hate speech identification, laying the groundwork for later studies in the area. Davidson et al(Devlin et al., 2018) made a significant addition in 2017 by offering a data set and a number of features created especially for the detection of hate speech. This groundbreaking discovery launched a trajectory of developments in the field and signaled the beginning of systematic hate speech detection research.

A crucial element of conventional machine learning methodologies was the feature engineering process. Scholars employed attributes like n-grams, sentiment analysis, and lexical aspects to efficiently depict textual content. Sentiment analysis assessed the text's emotional tone, whereas N-grams in particular demonstrated how language is sequential. Lexical features, which include language patterns and vocabulary. Hate speech detection research was first driven by traditional machine learning techniques, which were crucial in laying the groundwork for further advancements and offering insightful information. The advent of more sophisticated strategies was spurred by these systems' limits in addressing language complexity and context, despite their promising outcomes.

Zhang et al (Zhang and LeCun, 2015) introduced a Convolutional Neural Network (CNN) model presenting a novel method for detecting hate speech. This model outperformed other approaches in terms of performance. Because hate speech frequently uses certain phrases, keywords, and linguistic clues, CNNs are particularly good at identifying local patterns within the text. In 2018 (Ribeiro et al., 2018) presented a hierarchical attention-based model This strategy focused on attention mechanisms and hierarchical representations in order to address the need to record nuanced hate speech (Mathew et al., 2021) . A more thorough examination of the substance of hate speech was made possible by the use of hierarchical attention models, which made it possible to examine data at the word and sentence levels.

A breakthrough in natural language processing, BERT (Bidirectional Encoder Representations from Transformers) was introduced by Devlin et al (Devlin et al., 2018) in 2019 . The novel aspect of BERT is its capacity to comprehend a word's context by taking the complete phrase into account. This contextual awareness is especially important in the complex and frequently subtle realm of hate speech. BERT can more precisely and thoroughly identify hate speech by collecting the entire context (Dowlagar and Mamidi, 2021) . The promise of BERT in the area of hate speech identification was immediately recognised by researchers. They efficiently used BERT's potent language understanding capabilities to discern between hateful and non-hateful information by honing it on hate speech data sets (Khanduja et al.). Modern outcomes in hate speech identification can be attributed to this adaptation.The Transformer family has grown ever since BERT was introduced.

3 Data set and Task description

The task at hand focuses on hate speech classification within a data set encompassing 4000 sentences expressed in Telugu, represented both in native script and Romanized forms. Within this data set, 2061 sentences are categorized as non-hate, while 1939 sentences are designated as hate in the training set[1].Moreover, an additional test data set containing 500 sentences is provided, lacking categorized labels. The primary goal of this task is to employ BERT multilingual model to discern patterns from the labeled training data in order to predict whether the 500 test sentences fall into the categories of hate speech or non-hate (Priyadharshini et al., 2023a; B et al., 2024).

This classification task presents a significant challenge in analyzing and identifying hate speech within Telugu text, considering the multilingual aspect involving both native script and Romanized forms. With a substantial dataset comprising labeled examples of hate and non-hate speech, machine learning models can be trained to recognize intricate patterns, linguistic nuances, and context-specific features associated with hate speech (Marreddy et al., 2022).

[1]https://codalab.lisn.upsaclay.fr/competitions/16095

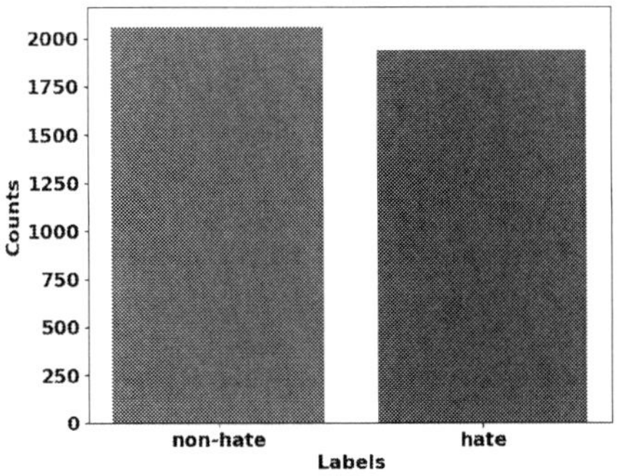

Figure 1: counts for hate and non in training data set

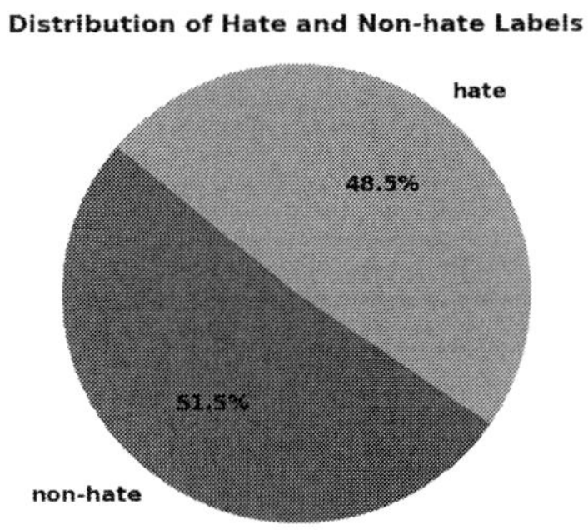

Figure 2: Percentage Distribution of Labels

4 Data preprocessing

During the preprocessing phase of our data, a series of crucial steps were undertaken to enhance the quality and applicability of the text data for hate speech identification and other Natural Language Processing (NLP) tasks. A key focus was placed on text preprocessing, involving the removal of special characters, numeric digits, and emoticons. Emojis, despite often expressing emotions or nonverbal cues, were eliminated from the text due to their limited contribution to semantic meaning in text analysis. Moreover, special characters and numerical digits were also omitted from the text corpus. These elements were considered as they could potentially complicate later processing stages and generally convey minimal linguistic information within NLP tasks. The primary objective behind this meticulous cleaning procedure was to streamline the text data, reducing noise and irrelevant features, while retaining a more refined and cohesive representation suitable for subsequent analysis or model development.

5 Training the Model

5.1 Model Description

In our hate and offensive language task, we utilized the BERT (Bidirectional Encoder Representations from Transformers) multilingual Transformer (Devlin et al., 2018), a sophisticated language model renowned for its contextual understanding of text across various languages. Through the adoption of this different model architecture, our approach involved comprehensive experimentation aimed at fully harnessing the capabilities of this advanced technology within our task domain. The overarching goal was to create a robust and precise system for detecting and categorizing hate speech accurately.

By leveraging the BERT multilingual Transformer model, our objective revolved around developing a highly capable system capable of recognizing and effectively classifying hate speech content. Through thorough exploration and experimentation with this model, our focus was on identifying the most optimal architecture and configurations that would yield superior performance in the identification and mitigation of hate and offensive content within textual data. This process involved fine-tuning the model parameters, experimenting with various training methodologies, and optimizing the model's ability to comprehend and categorize hate speech expressions, ultimately aiming for heightened accuracy and efficiency in the detection and classification process. The utilization of the BERT multilingual Transformer represented our concerted effort to leverage cutting-edge technology, exploring its potential to enhance the efficacy of hate speech identification systems through state-of-the-art natural language understanding and classification capabilities (Sohn and Lee, 2019).

5.2 Training the Model

5.2.1 Data Splitting

The data set is initially divided into a training set and a validation set and testing set, where in 70 percent of the labeled data is allocated for training the BERT multilingual model and 10 percent for validation. This substantial portion serves as the foundation for the model to learn and extract patterns, linguistic nuances, and hate speech indicators from the provided Telugu codemixed text. The model undergoes the training process using this data to adjust its parameters and optimize its understanding of hate speech expressions.

Simultaneously, a smaller subset, constituting 20 percent of the labeled data set, is set aside as the validation set. This portion is crucial for fine-tuning the model's performance and validating its effectiveness. The validation set assists in adjusting hyper parameters, evaluating the model's performance on unseen data, and preventing over fitting, ultimately enhancing the model's generalized. It provides a means to measure how well the model learns from the training data and how effectively it can predict hate speech occurrences in new, unseen instances of codemixed Telugu text.

Finally, the unlabeled test data, separate from the training and validation sets, serves as a means to assess the model's real-world performance. This data set, containing instances of Telugu codemixed text without labeled categories, enables the evaluation of how well the trained BERT multilingual model can generalize its learning and accurately.

5.2.2 Training Parameters for the Model

The training process of the BERT multilingual model involves several critical parameters aimed at optimizing its learning from the data set while ensuring computational efficiency and convergence stability. Primarily, the choice of 3 epochs for training iterations indicates that the entire labeled data set is iterated through the model 3 times.

The batch size, set at 32, determines the number of data samples processed simultaneously in each iteration during training. The learning rate, specified as 1e-5, governs the size of parameter updates during training. A lower learning rate typically facilitates more precise updates but might prolong the training process.

Additionally, determining the update size involves settings that regulate how the model's parameters are adjusted based on the calculated gradients during training. These settings aim to strike a balance between stability and efficiency during the model's learning process.

While these parameters have been set to strike a balance between computational efficiency and convergence stability, optimizing these settings might further enhance the model's performance in recognizing hate and offensive content. Fine-tuning parameters such as the learning rate, batch size, training epochs, or update size could potentially refine the model's accuracy.

6 Evaluation Metrics and Results

The F1-score, computed as the harmonic mean of precision and recall, provides a balanced assessment by considering both metrics. Achieving a macro F1-score of 0.6151 in our task indicates a moderate level of overall performance, suggesting a reasonable balance between precision and recall across multiple classes. This metric signifies the model's effectiveness in correctly identifying hate and offensive content in a multi-class classification scenario, highlighting its general capability in accurately categorizing various classes within the data set.

7 Error Analysis

The BERT multilingual model applied to Telugu hate speech exhibits notable accuracy, particularly in correctly identifying true positives. However, a significant challenge arises with false positives, misclassified instances even in a balanced dataset. This pattern necessitates thorough analysis and adjustments in the model's discriminatory capabilities. Comprehensive evaluations on validation and test sets are essential for assessing the model's adaptability. Proposed strategic modifications involve fine-tuning parameters and scrutinizing false positive occurrences to enhance overall accuracy and efficacy.

8 Limitations

Challenges in a Telugu language dataset include limited resources hindering preprocessing techniques. The dynamic nature of evolving fake news poses adaptability issues for models trained on historical data. Identifying relevant features for effective training is challenging, particularly in a language with unique linguistic characteristics not well-captured by standard NLP techniques.

9 Conclusion

Utilizing the BERT model, this study focuses on detecting Hate and Offensive Language within Telugu Codemixed Text, achieving a macro F1-score of 0.6151. It showcases the model's proficiency in identifying hate speech amidst the intricate linguistic composition of Telugu codemixed text. Despite this success, the research underscores the imperative for continual improvement in both model architecture and data set expansion to heighten the accuracy of hate speech detection. The study serves as a foundational milestone, laying the groundwork for future advancements. It sets a benchmark for the development of more sophisticated and sensitive systems crucial for accurately identifying and mitigating harmful information present in multilingual digital realms. This work not only validates the potential of the BERT model but also emphasizes the ongoing need for refinement and innovation in combating hate speech in diverse linguistic contexts.

10 Future work

The future work for this task involves enhancing the existing framework through various approaches. It includes refining model architectures tailored for codemixed languages, diversifying and augmenting data sets, fine-tuning model parameters, exploring multimodal approaches, ensuring cultural sensitivity, implementing real-time detection systems, and establishing standardized evaluation metrics. These efforts aim to develop more effective and culturally sensitive mechanisms for detecting hate speech in Telugu codemixed text, fostering safer and more inclusive digital spaces.

Ethics Statement

We affirm our commitment to ethical research practices and compliance with ACL guidelines in conducting and presenting our study. No ethical concerns or conflicts of interest arose during the course of this research.

Acknowledgments

The work was done with partial support from the Mexican Government through the grant A1-S-47854 of CONACYT, Mexico, grants 20242138, 20241567, and 20242080 of the Secretaría de Investigación y Posgrado of the Instituto Politécnico Nacional, Mexico. The authors thank the CONACYT for the computing resources brought to them through the Plataforma de Aprendizaje Profundo para Tecnologías del Lenguaje of the Laboratorio de Supercómputo of the INAOE, Mexico and acknowledge the support of Microsoft through the Microsoft Latin America PhD Award.

References

Telugu Language - Wikipedia. Accessed on: February 6, 2024.

Zahra Ahani, Moein Shahiki Tash, Yoel Ledo Mezquita, and Jason Angel. 2024. Utilizing deep learning models for the identification of enhancers and super-enhancers based on genomic and epigenomic features. *arXiv preprint arXiv:2401.07470.*

Premjth B, Bharathi Raja, Prasanna Kumar Kumaresan, Saranya Rajiakodi, Sai Prashanth Karnati, Sai Rishith Reddy Mangamuru, and Janakiram Chandu. 2024. "Findings of the Shared Task on Hate and Offensive Language Detection in Telugu Codemixed Text (HOLD-Telugu)". In *Proceedings of the Fourth Workshop on Speech, Vision, and Language Technologies for Dravidian Languages*, Malta. European Chapter of the Association for Computational Linguistics.

Girma Yohannis Bade. 2021. Natural Language Processing and Its Challenges on Omotic Language Group of Ethiopia. volume 3, pages 26–30.

Girma Yohannis Bade and Akalu Assefa Afaro. 2018. Object Oriented Software Development for Artificial Intelligence. volume 7, pages 22–24.

Girma Yohannis Bade and Hussien Seid. 2018. Development of Longest-Match Based Stemmer for Texts of Wolaita Language. *vol*, 4:79–83.

Bharathi Raja Chakravarthi, Ruba Priyadharshini, Navya Jose, Thomas Mandl, Prasanna Kumar Kumaresan, Rahul Ponnusamy, RL Hariharan, John Philip McCrae, Elizabeth Sherly, et al. 2021. Findings of the shared task on offensive language identification in Tamil, Malayalam, and Kannada. In *Proceedings of the first workshop on speech and language technologies for Dravidian languages*, pages 133–145.

Jacob Devlin, Ming-Wei Chang, Kenton Lee, and Kristina Toutanova. 2018. Bert: Pre-training of deep bidirectional transformers for language understanding. *arXiv preprint arXiv:1810.04805.*

Suman Dowlagar and Radhika Mamidi. 2021. Hasocone@ fire-hasoc2020: Using BERT and multilingual BERT models for hate speech detection. *arXiv preprint arXiv:2101.09007.*

Selam Kanta and Grigori Sidorov. 2023. Selam@ DravidianLangTech: Sentiment Analysis of Code-Mixed

Dravidian Texts using SVM Classification. In *Proceedings of the Third Workshop on Speech and Language Technologies for Dravidian Languages*, pages 176–179.

Namit Khanduja, Nishant Kumar, and Arun Chauhan. Unmasking Hate: Telugu Language Hate Speech Detection Using Transformers. *Available at SSRN 4642780.*

Mounika Marreddy, Subba Reddy Oota, Lakshmi Sireesha Vakada, Venkata Charan Chinni, and Radhika Mamidi. 2022. Am I a Resource-Poor Language? Data Sets, Embeddings, Models and Analysis for four different NLP Tasks in Telugu Language. *ACM Transactions on Asian and Low-Resource Language Information Processing*, 22(1):1–34.

Binny Mathew, Punyajoy Saha, Seid Muhie Yimam, Chris Biemann, Pawan Goyal, and Animesh Mukherjee. 2021. Hatexplain: A benchmark dataset for explainable hate speech detection. In *Proceedings of the AAAI conference on artificial intelligence*, volume 35, pages 14867–14875.

Bharathi Raja andS Malliga andCN SUBALALITHA Priyadharshini, Ruba andChakravarthi, Premjith and-Murugappan Abirami S V, Kogilavani andB, and Prasanna Kumar Kumaresan. 2023a. "Overview of Shared-task on Abusive Comment Detection in Tamil and Telugu". In *Proceedings of the Third Workshop on Speech and Language Technologies for Dravidian Languages*, Varna, Bulgaria. Recent Advances in Natural Language Processing.

Ruba Priyadharshini, Bharathi Raja Chakravarthi, S Malliga, Subalalitha Cn, SV Kogilavani, B Premjith, Abirami Murugappan, and Prasanna Kumar Kumaresan. 2023b. Overview of shared-task on abusive comment detection in tamil and telugu. In *Proceedings of the Third Workshop on Speech and Language Technologies for Dravidian Languages*, pages 80–87.

Ícaro JS Ribeiro, Rafael Pereira, Ivna V Freire, Bruno G de Oliveira, Cezar A Casotti, and Eduardo N Boery. 2018. Stress and quality of life among university students: A systematic literature review. *Health Professions Education*, 4(2):70–77.

Moein Shahiki-Tash, Jesús Armenta-Segura, Zahra Ahani, Olga Kolesnikova, Grigori Sidorov, and Alexander Gelbukh. 2023. Lidoma at homomex2023@ iberlef: Hate speech detection towards the mexican spanish-speaking lgbt+ population. the importance of preprocessing before using bert-based models. In *Proceedings of the Iberian Languages Evaluation Forum (IberLEF 2023).*

Hajung Sohn and Hyunju Lee. 2019. Mc-bert4hate: Hate speech detection using multi-channel bert for different languages and translations. In *2019 International Conference on Data Mining Workshops (ICDMW)*, pages 551–559. IEEE.

M Shahiki Tash, Z Ahani, Al Tonja, M Gemeda, N Hussain, and O Kolesnikova. 2022. Word Level Language Identification in Code-mixed Kannada-English Texts using traditional machine learning algorithms. In *Proceedings of the 19th International Conference on Natural Language Processing (ICON): Shared Task on Word Level Language Identification in Code-mixed Kannada-English Texts*, pages 25–28.

Moein Tash, Jesus Armenta-Segura, Zahra Ahani, Olga Kolesnikova, Grigori Sidorov, and Alexander Gelbukh. 2023. LIDOMA@ DravidianLangTech: Convolutional Neural Networks for Studying Correlation Between Lexical Features and Sentiment Polarity in Tamil and Tulu Languages. In *Proceedings of the Third Workshop on Speech and Language Technologies for Dravidian Languages*, pages 180–185.

Atnafu Lambebo Tonja, Mesay Gemeda Yigezu, Olga Kolesnikova, Moein Shahiki Tash, Grigori Sidorov, and Alexander Gelbuk. 2022. Transformer-based model for word level language identification in code-mixed kannada-english texts. *arXiv preprint arXiv:2211.14459.*

Mesay Gemeda Yigezu, Girma Yohannis Bade, Olga Kolesnikova, Grigori Sidorov, and Alexander Gelbukh. 2023a. Multilingual Hope Speech Detection using Machine Learning.

Mesay Gemeda Yigezu, Olga Kolesnikova, Grigori Sidorov, and Alexander Gelbukh. 2023b. Transformer-Based Hate Speech Detection for Multi-Class and Multi-Label Classification.

Mesay Gemeda Yigezu, Atnafu Lambebo Tonja, Olga Kolesnikova, Moein Shahiki Tash, Grigori Sidorov, and Alexander Gelbukh. 2022. Word Level Language Identification in Code-mixed Kannada-English Texts using Deep Learning Approach. In *Proceedings of the 19th International Conference on Natural Language Processing (ICON): Shared Task on Word Level Language Identification in Code-mixed Kannada-English Texts*, pages 29–33.

Xiang Zhang and Yann LeCun. 2015. Text understanding from scratch. *arXiv preprint arXiv:1502.01710.*

Zavira@DravidianLangTech 2024:Telugu hate speech detection using LSTM

Z. Ahani, M. Shahiki Tash, M. T. Zamir, I. Gelbukh and **A. Gelbukh**
Instituto Politécnico Nacional (IPN), Centro de Investigación en Computación (CIC)
Corresponding: `z.ahani2023@cic.ipn.mx`

Abstract

Hate speech is communication, often oral or written, that incites, stigmatizes, or incites violence or prejudice against individuals or groups based on characteristics such as race, religion, ethnicity, gender, sexual orientation, or other protected characteristics. This usually involves expressions of hostility, contempt, or prejudice and can have harmful social consequences. Among the broader social landscape, an important problem and challenge facing the medical community is related to the impact of people's verbal expression. These words have a significant and immediate effect on human behavior and psyche. Repeating such phrases can even lead to depression and social isolation. In an attempt to identify and classify these Telugu text samples in the social media domain, our research LSTM and the findings of this experiment are summarized in this paper, in which out of 27 participants, we obtained 8th place with an F1 score of 0.68.

1 Introduction

While hate speech (HS) legislation varies among different countries, it is generally conceptualized as encompassing expressions of hostility or derogation directed at an individual or a group based on attributes such as race, color, national origin, sex, disability, religion, or sexual orientation (Nockleby, 2000; Jahan and Oussalah, 2023).

On platforms such as Twitter, Facebook, and various other social media outlets, hateful comments manifest as expressions containing abusive language directed towards individuals (including cyber-bullying, politicians, celebrities, or products) or specific groups (such as countries, the LGBT community, religions, genders, organizations, etc) (Badjatiya et al., 2017)

Numerous intricate challenges are currently evident in applications related to speech, vision, and text, all aimed at enhancing accuracy. The pioneering work of (Badjatiya et al., 2017). In 2017 marks the initial exploration of neural architectures for detecting hate speech. The advancement of natural language processing (NLP) (Bade, 2021) technology has spurred considerable investigation into the automated detection of textual hate speech in recent years. Notable competitions such as SemEval-2019 (Zampieri et al., 2019) and 2020 (Zampieri et al., 2020), as well as GermEval-2018 (Wiegand et al., 2018), have organized diverse events aimed at seeking improved solutions for automated hate speech detection. In response, researchers have compiled extensive datasets from various sources, fostering significant progress in the field. Numerous studies have addressed hate speech in multiple non-English languages and online communities, prompting exploration and comparison of different processing pipelines. This includes the examination of feature sets and Machine Learning (ML) methods (Tash et al., 2022; Kanta and Sidorov, 2023), encompassing supervised, unsupervised, and semi-supervised approaches, as well as various classification algorithms such as Naive Bayes, Logistic Regression (LR), Convolutional Neural Network (CNN) (Tash et al., 2023; Shahiki-Tash et al., 2023b), Long Short-Term Memory (LSTM), BERT deep learning(Yigezu et al., 2022) architectures, among others. The pervasive issue of abusive language is both common and troubling. Offensive language takes many forms, depending on the target group and the specific target, such as hate speech, cyberbullying, adult content, trolling, abuse, racism, or profanity.

In recent advancements, transformer-based models (Tonja et al., 2022), such as BERT, have significantly impacted the detection and understanding of hate speech. Hate speech, a particularly alarming category of abusive language, involves the intentional intimidation of a target group or individual with the intent of causing harm, violence, or social disruption (Husain and Uzuner, 2021; Khan et al., 2022a)

Proceedings of the Fourth Workshop on Speech, Vision, and Language Technologies for Dravidian Languages, pages 107–112
March 22, 2024 ©2024 Association for Computational Linguistics

So there are subtle distinctions between different types of offensive language. The targeting of LGBT+ people with hate speech is a deep-rooted issue with far-reaching consequences, including the potential for substance abuse disorders (Shahiki-Tash et al., 2023a) and racism (Badjatiya et al., 2017). The rest of the paper is organized as follows: the related work and methodology are discussed in Section 2 and 3 respectively followed by results in Section 4.

2 Related work

Balouchzahi et al. address the ongoing challenge of hate speech (HS) by emphasizing the limitations of conventional identification and blocking methods. Thay advocate the development of systems that are capable of not only identifying but also profiling HS content contaminants. Using a vote classifier (VC) contributes to the hate speech broadcaster detection task organized by PAN 2021 (Bevendorff et al., 2021), which focuses on the profiles of HS broadcasters in English and Spanish on Twitter. The proposed model uses a combination of traditional character and word n-gram along with syntactic n-grams as features for classification. Using a support vector machine (SVM), logistic regression (LR) and random forest (RF) vote classifier, the models achieve commendable accuracies of 73% and 83% for English and Spanish, respectively.

In the BiCHAT (Khan et al., 2022a) research, an innovative deep learning(Ahani et al., 2024) model, combining BiLSTM with deep CNN and hierarchical attention, is employed to acquire tweet representations for the detection of hate speech. The proposed model undergoes a process of mining, training, and evaluation using three benchmark datasets from Twitter. These datasets include HD1, introduced by (Founta et al., 2018; Bade and Afaro, 2018), HD2, derived from the Kaggle [1] competition dataset, and HD3 with statistics presented in Table 1, provided by (Davidson et al., 2017; Bade and Seid, 2018). The F1-score outcomes (HD1=0.88, HD2=0.91, and HD3=0.75) demonstrate superior performance compared to the State-of-the-Art (SOTA) methods (Khan et al., 2022b; Roy et al., 2020; Ding et al., 2019).

In the publication (Badjatiya et al., 2017), an examination was conducted on 16,000 tweets employing three neural network models (CNN and BOWL, LSTM) and various methodologies, including GBDT, TF_IDF, and Random Embedding. The dataset originates from the (Waseem and Hovy, 2016). The study demonstrated that combining embeddings acquired from deep neural network models with gradient-boosted decision trees yields the highest accuracy values. Specifically, the combination of LSTM+Random Embedding+GBDT achieved an F1-score of 0.930.

In this study(Waseem and Hovy, 2016), the method is based on a dataset of 16,000 tweets collected by (Waseem and Hovy, 2016) and colleagues. This dataset, which includes a total of 136,052 tweets, was annotated by the researchers, and 16,914 tweets were specifically flagged. Of these, 3,383 tweets containing sexual content were identified, originating from 613 users. Additionally, 1,972 tweets were flagged for racist content and contributed by 9 users, while the remaining 11,559 tweets were deemed non-sexist or racist. The analysis of hate speech comments included a thorough review of the features used, with the aim of determining those that yielded the most effective detection performance. Notably, examination of the features influencing hate speech recognition in the dataset revealed that, despite potential variations in geographic distribution and word length, these factors did not consistently improve performance and rarely outperformed personality-level features. An exception to this trend can be seen with gender-related characteristics, as detailed in Table 2.

3 Methodology

in this section, we summarize the data set used in this task and the proposed methodology in detail. LSTM networks prove advantageous in binary text classification tasks, such as hate speech detection, due to their inherent ability to capture contextual dependencies and long-range dependencies in sequential data. Imbalanced datasets, on the other hand, might lead the model to be skewed towards the majority class, potentially hindering its performance in identifying instances of the minority class, such as hate speech, and affecting overall classification accuracy.

3.1 Dataset

The dataset, generously provided by Hold Telugu for the Telugu language, consists of two separate datasets for educational purposes. The first dataset contains 4000 tweets for training, while the second

[1] www.kaggle.com

Table 1: Statistics of the datasets

Datasets	Hate tweet	Normal tweet	Total
HD1 (Relatively balanced)	2615	5385	8000
HD2 (Unbalanced)	1421	10579	12000
HD3 (Unbalanced)	1430	4162	5592

Table 2: F1 achieved by using different features sets

	char n-grams	+gender	+gender +loc	word n-grams
F1	73.89	73.93	73.62	64.58

dataset contains 500 tweets for testing (B et al.; Priyadharshini et al., 2023)

Table 3: Data set samples

Tweets	Label
Adhi Show na lanjala kompana	Hate
Papam erry flower ayipoindu	Hate
Valla dhagara bochu vunttundi	Hate
West Godavari lo adii jarigindhi	Non-hate
Venakala unnonni adugu cheptadu	Non-hate
turning thisukuna vadihi	Non-hate

3.2 Embedding Layer

The model begins with an embedding layer, a fundamental component in natural language processing tasks. The 'Embedding' layer is responsible for converting the input text data into a dense vector representation. In this case, each word in the vocabulary is represented as a vector of 32 dimensions ("embedding_vector_length"). This vector representation allows the model to capture semantic relationships between words and enables better understanding of the textual data.

3.3 LSTM Layer

Following the embedding layer, the model incorporates an LSTM layer. LSTMs are a type of recurrent neural network (RNN) designed to address the vanishing gradient problem, making them effective for sequence modeling tasks. The LSTM layer with 100 units captures long-range dependencies and temporal patterns in the input sequences. The 'dropout' and 'recurrent_dropout' parameters are introduced to mitigate overfitting by randomly dropping connections during training.

3.4 Dense Layer and Sigmoid Activation

The LSTM layer is followed by a dense layer with a single output unit. This dense layer acts as a classifier for binary sentiment classification, with a sigmoid activation function applied to produce probabilities. The sigmoid activation function is well-suited for binary classification tasks as it squashes the output values between 0 and 1, representing the likelihood of the input belonging to the positive class (hate speech) or negative class (non-hate speech).

3.5 Model Loading and Compilation

The model is then loaded with pre-trained weights saved during training, specifically the weights that achieved the best performance on the validation set. This practice ensures that the model used for evaluation is the one that demonstrated the highest generalization ability during training.

The model is compiled using binary cross-entropy loss, which is suitable for binary classification problems, and the Adam optimizer, a popular choice for training neural networks. The evaluation metrics include loss and accuracy, providing insights into the model's performance on the test data.

3.6 Evaluation on Test Data

Finally, the model is evaluated on a separate test dataset ("X_test" and "y_test"). The "model.evaluate" method computes the loss and accuracy of the model on the test data, providing a quantitative measure of its generalization performance. The obtained accuracy is then printed as a percentage, offering a clear indication of how well the model is able to classify hate speech in unseen textual data.

In summary, this methodology section describes the architecture and training process of an LSTM-based hate speech detection model, emphasizing the role of embedding, LSTM, and dense layers in capturing intricate patterns in text data. The model's evaluation on a distinct test set ensures a robust assessment of its real-world performance.

4 Result

During the sharing task competition that focused on detecting hate and offensive language in Telugu mixed code text, our main goal was to determine the F1-score for the given data set. Using the previously trained LSTM model, we fed the entire test data into the model and obtained a prediction that yielded significant results. In a single performance evaluation, we scored an admirable 0.68%, placing 8th out of 27 participating teams. For an overview of the results achieved by all participating teams, please refer to Table 4, which provides a detailed insight into the performance metrics and points earned by each participant in the competition.

Table 4: Results of the participants in Telugu Hate speech

Team	Run	F1-score (macro)	Rank
Sandalphon	1	0.7711	1
Selam	2	0.7711	1
Kubapok	1	0.7431	3
DLRG1	1	0.7101	4
DLRG	1	0.7041	5
CUET_Binary	2	0.7013	6
CUET_OpenNLP	1	0.6878	7
Zavira	1	0.6819	8
IIITDWD-zk_lstm	2	0.6739	9
lemlem	1	0.6708	10
Mizan	1	0.6616	11
byteSizedLLM	1	0.6609	12
pinealai	1	0.6575	13
IIITDWD_SVC	2	0.6565	14
MUCS	3	0.6501	15
Lemlem-eyob	2	0.6498	16
Tewodros	2	0.6498	16
Fida	2	0.6369	18
Lidoma	1	0.6151	19
MasonTigers	1	0.5621	20
Habesha	1	0.5284	21
MasonTigers	1	0.4959	22
CUET_DASH	3	0.4956	23
Fango	1	0.4921	24
Tayyab	1	0.4653	25

5 limitations

1. The research grapples with a limitation arising from the exclusion of hyperparameter tuning in the experimental setup. Optimizing hyperparameter configurations is pivotal for refining the performance of machine learning models, and the absence of such optimization in our experiments may impact the overall efficacy of our approach.

2. Another constraint in our methodology arises from the absence of experiments specifically tailored to address the issue of imbalanced datasets. Tasks related to hate speech detection commonly face challenges with imbalances between the instances of different classes. Exploring strategies like oversampling, undersampling, or employing specialized algorithms for imbalanced datasets could be considered to enhance the model's capability in handling such distribution challenges.

6 Conclusion

Hate speech that incites violence or prejudice against individuals or groups based on different characteristics is an important challenge in contemporary society. The damaging effects of such expressions, including hostility and prejudice, go beyond immediate social consequences and can contribute to deep psychological effects such as depression and social isolation.

This research deals with the important issue of hate speech in the context of Telugu mixed code text on social media platforms. Using Natural Language Processing (NLP), specifically using short-term memory (LSTM) neural networks, we aimed to identify and classify hate speech in Telugu text samples. In a competitive environment of 27 participants, our LSTM-based model achieved eighth place with an F1 (large) score of 0.68

The significance of our research lies in the effective application of NLP techniques to combat hate speech in multilingual contexts, contributing valuable insights and solutions to a pervasive social problem. The balanced dataset, consisting of 4000 training tweets and 500 test tweets, provides a strong foundation for training and evaluating the model's performance.

Our findings underscore the potential of advanced technologies, such as deep learning models, in addressing complex social issues. The results of the competition presented in Table 4 show the relative performance of different teams and show the effectiveness of different approaches in detecting hate speech.

Ethics Statement

We affirm our commitment to ethical research practices and compliance with ACL guidelines in conducting and presenting our study. No ethical concerns or conflicts of interest arose during the course of this research.

Acknowledgments

The work was done with partial support from the Mexican Government through the grant A1-S-47854 of CONACYT, Mexico, grants 20241816, 20241819, and 20240951 of the Secretaría de Investigación y Posgrado of the Instituto Politécnico Nacional, Mexico. The authors thank the CONACYT for the computing resources brought to them through the Plataforma de Aprendizaje Profundo para Tecnologías del Lenguaje of the Laboratorio de Supercómputo of the INAOE, Mexico and acknowledge the support of Microsoft through the Microsoft Latin America PhD Award.

References

Zahra Ahani, Moein Shahiki Tash, Yoel Ledo Mezquita, and Jason Angel. 2024. Utilizing deep learning models for the identification of enhancers and super-enhancers based on genomic and epigenomic features. *arXiv preprint arXiv:2401.07470*.

Premjth B, Bharathi Raja, Prasanna Kumar Kumaresan, Saranya Rajiakodi, Sai Prashanth Karnati, Sai Rishith Reddy Mangamuru, and booktitle = Proceedings of the Fourth Workshop on Speech, Vision, and Language Technologies for Dravidian Languages month = March year = 2024 address = Malta publisher = European Chapter of the Association for Computational Linguistics Chandu, Janakiram". Findings of the shared task on hate and offensive language detection in telugu codemixed text (hold-telugu).

Girma Yohannis Bade. 2021. Natural language processing and its challenges on omotic language group of ethiopia. *Journal of Computer Science Research*, 3(4):26–30.

Girma Yohannis Bade and Akalu Assefa Afaro. 2018. Object oriented software development for artificial intelligence. *American Journal of Software Engineering and Applications*, 7(2):22–24.

Girma Yohannis Bade and Hussien Seid. 2018. Development of longest-match based stemmer for texts of wolaita language. *vol*, 4:79–83.

Pinkesh Badjatiya, Shashank Gupta, Manish Gupta, and Vasudeva Varma. 2017. Deep learning for hate speech detection in tweets. In *Proceedings of the 26th international conference on World Wide Web companion*, pages 759–760.

Fazlourrahman Balouchzahi, Hosahalli Lakshmaiah Shashirekha, and Grigori Sidorov. 2021. Hssd: Hate speech spreader detection using n-grams and voting classifier.

Janek Bevendorff, BERTa Chulvi, Gretel Liz De La Peña Sarracén, Mike Kestemont, Enrique Manjavacas, Ilia Markov, Maximilian Mayerl, Martin Potthast, Francisco Rangel, Paolo Rosso, et al. 2021. Overview of pan 2021: authorship verification, profiling hate speech spreaders on twitter, and style change detection. In *Experimental IR Meets Multilinguality, Multimodality, and Interaction: 12th International Conference of the CLEF Association, CLEF 2021, Virtual Event, September 21–24, 2021, Proceedings 12*, pages 419–431. Springer.

Thomas Davidson, Dana Warmsley, Michael Macy, and Ingmar Weber. 2017. Automated hate speech detection and the problem of offensive language. In *Proceedings of the international AAAI conference on web and social media*, volume 11, pages 512–515.

Yunxia Ding, Xiaobing Zhou, and Xuejie Zhang. 2019. Ynu_dyx at semeval-2019 task 5: A stacked bigru model based on capsule network in detection of hate. In *Proceedings of the 13th international workshop on semantic evaluation*, pages 535–539.

Antigoni Founta, Constantinos Djouvas, Despoina Chatzakou, Ilias Leontiadis, Jeremy Blackburn, Gianluca Stringhini, Athena Vakali, Michael Sirivianos, and Nicolas Kourtellis. 2018. Large scale crowdsourcing and characterization of twitter abusive behavior. In *Proceedings of the international AAAI conference on web and social media*, volume 12.

Fatemah Husain and Ozlem Uzuner. 2021. A survey of offensive language detection for the arabic language. *ACM Transactions on Asian and Low-Resource Language Information Processing (TALLIP)*, 20(1):1–44.

Md Saroar Jahan and Mourad Oussalah. 2023. A systematic review of hate speech automatic detection using natural language processing. *Neurocomputing*, page 126232.

Selam Kanta and Grigori Sidorov. 2023. Selam@ dravidianlangtech: Sentiment analysis of code-mixed dravidian texts using svm classification. In *Proceedings of the Third Workshop on Speech and Language Technologies for Dravidian Languages*, pages 176–179.

Shakir Khan, Mohd Fazil, Vineet Kumar Sejwal, Mohammed Ali Alshara, Reemiah Muneer Alotaibi, Ashraf Kamal, and Abdul Rauf Baig. 2022a. Bichat: Bilstm with deep cnn and hierarchical attention for hate speech detection. *Journal of King Saud University-Computer and Information Sciences*, 34(7):4335–4344.

Shakir Khan, Ashraf Kamal, Mohd Fazil, Mohammed Ali Alshara, Vineet Kumar Sejwal, Reemiah Muneer Alotaibi, Abdul Rauf Baig, and Salihah Alqahtani. 2022b. Hcovbi-caps: hate speech detection using convolutional and bi-directional gated recurrent unit with capsule network. *IEEE Access*, 10:7881–7894.

John T Nockleby. 2000. Hate speech. *Encyclopedia of the American constitution*, 3(2):1277–1279.

Bharathi Raja andS Malliga andCN SUBALALITHA Priyadharshini, Ruba andChakravarthi, Premjith and-Murugappan Abirami S V, Kogilavani andB, and Prasanna Kumar Kumaresan. 2023. Overview of shared-task on abusive comment detection in tamil and telugu. In *Proceedings of the Third Workshop on Speech and Language Technologies for Dravidian Languages*, Varna, Bulgaria. Recent Advances in Natural Language Processing.

Pradeep Kumar Roy, Asis Kumar Tripathy, Tapan Kumar Das, and Xiao-Zhi Gao. 2020. A framework for hate speech detection using deep convolutional neural network. *IEEE Access*, 8:204951–204962.

Moein Shahiki-Tash, Jesús Armenta-Segura, Zahra Ahani, Olga Kolesnikova, Grigori Sidorov, and Alexander Gelbukh. 2023a. Lidoma at homomex2023@ iberlef: Hate speech detection towards the mexican spanish-speaking lgbt+ population. the importance of preprocessing before using bert-based models. In *Proceedings of the Iberian Languages Evaluation Forum (IberLEF 2023)*.

Moein Shahiki-Tash, Jesús Armenta-Segura, Olga Kolesnikova, Grigori Sidorov, and Alexander Gelbukh. 2023b. Lidoma at hope2023iberlef: Hope speech detection using lexical features and convolutional neural networks. In *Proceedings of the Iberian Languages Evaluation Forum (IberLEF 2023), colocated with the 39th Conference of the Spanish Society for Natural Language Processing (SEPLN 2023), CEUR-WS. org*.

M Shahiki Tash, Z Ahani, Al Tonja, M Gemeda, N Hussain, and O Kolesnikova. 2022. Word level language identification in code-mixed kannada-english texts using traditional machine learning algorithms. In *Proceedings of the 19th International Conference on Natural Language Processing (ICON): Shared Task on Word Level Language Identification in Code-mixed Kannada-English Texts*, pages 25–28.

Moein Tash, Jesus Armenta-Segura, Zahra Ahani, Olga Kolesnikova, Grigori Sidorov, and Alexander Gelbukh. 2023. Lidoma@ dravidianlangtech: Convolutional neural networks for studying correlation between lexical features and sentiment polarity in tamil and tulu languages. In *Proceedings of the Third Workshop on Speech and Language Technologies for Dravidian Languages*, pages 180–185.

Atnafu Lambebo Tonja, Mesay Gemeda Yigezu, Olga Kolesnikova, Moein Shahiki Tash, Grigori Sidorov, and Alexander Gelbuk. 2022. Transformer-based model for word level language identification in code-mixed kannada-english texts. *arXiv preprint arXiv:2211.14459*.

Zeerak Waseem and Dirk Hovy. 2016. Hateful symbols or hateful people? predictive features for hate speech detection on twitter. In *Proceedings of the NAACL student research workshop*, pages 88–93.

Michael Wiegand, Melanie Siegel, and Josef Ruppenhofer. 2018. Overview of the germeval 2018 shared task on the identification of offensive language.

Mesay Gemeda Yigezu, Atnafu Lambebo Tonja, Olga Kolesnikova, Moein Shahiki Tash, Grigori Sidorov, and Alexander Gelbukh. 2022. Word level language identification in code-mixed kannada-english texts using deep learning approach. In *Proceedings of the 19th International Conference on Natural Language Processing (ICON): Shared Task on Word Level Language Identification in Code-mixed Kannada-English Texts*, pages 29–33.

Marcos Zampieri, Shervin Malmasi, Preslav Nakov, Sara Rosenthal, Noura Farra, and Ritesh Kumar. 2019. Semeval-2019 task 6: Identifying and categorizing offensive language in social media (offenseval). *arXiv preprint arXiv:1903.08983*.

Marcos Zampieri, Preslav Nakov, Sara Rosenthal, Pepa Atanasova, Georgi Karadzhov, Hamdy Mubarak, Leon Derczynski, Zeses Pitenis, and Çağrı Çöltekin. 2020. Semeval-2020 task 12: Multilingual offensive language identification in social media (offenseval 2020). *arXiv preprint arXiv:2006.07235*.

Tayyab@DravidianLangTech 2024:Detecting Fake News in Malayalam LSTM Approach and Challenges

M. T. Zamir[1], M. S Tash[2], Z. Ahani[3], A. Gelbukh[4] and G. Sidorov[5]
Instituto Politécnico Nacional (IPN), Centro de Investigación en Computación (CIC)
{[1]mzamir2023,[2]mshahikit2022,[3]z.ahani2023,[4]gelbukh,[5]sidorov}@cic.ipn.mx

Abstract

Global communication has been made easier by the emergence of online social media, but it has also made it easier for "fake news," or information that is misleading or false, to spread. Since this phenomenon presents a significant challenge, reliable detection techniques are required to discern between authentic and fraudulent content. The primary goal of this study is to identify fake news on social media platforms and in Malayalam-language articles by using LSTM (Long Short-Term Memory) model. This research explores this approach in tackling the DravidianLangTech@EACL 2024 tasks.[1]. Using LSTM networks to differentiate between real and fake content at the comment or post level, Task 1 focuses on classifying social media text. To precisely classify the authenticity of the content, LSTM models are employed, drawing on a variety of sources such as comments on YouTube. Task 2 is dubbed the FakeDetect-Malayalam challenge, wherein Malayalam-language articles with fake news are identified and categorized using LSTM models. In order to successfully navigate the challenges of identifying false information in regional languages, we use lstm model. This algoritms seek to accurately categorize the multiple classes written in Malayalam. In Task 1, the results are encouraging. LSTM models distinguish between orignal and fake social media content with an impressive macro F1 score of 0.78 when testing. The LSTM model's macro F1 score of 0.2393 indicates that Task 2 offers a more complex landscape. This emphasizes the persistent difficulties in LSTM-based fake news detection across various linguistic contexts and the difficulty of correctly classifying fake news within the context of the Malayalam language.

1 Introduction

Online social media has made communication easier on a global level, which allows people to seamlessly interact and share information with each other across the globe. In the realm of Natural Language Processing (NLP) (bad, 2021), diverse tasks hold significance, ranging from detecting hate speech(Shahiki-Tash et al., 2023a) and hopeful (Yigezu et al., 2023a; Shahiki-Tash et al., 2023b) sentiments (Tash et al., 2023) to language identification (Tash et al., 2022) and combatting fake news. Researchers leverage various models tailored to these tasks' intricacies. For hate speech detection (Yigezu et al., 2023b), models like Convolutional Neural Networks (CNNs), Recurrent Neural Networks (RNNs), traditional machine learning (Kanta and Sidorov, 2023), and Transformer-based (Tonja et al., 2022) architectures such as BERT and its variants have been instrumental. On the other hand, the spread of false information and fake news (yig, 2023) is a serious problem brought about by this increased connectivity. Significant doubts about the veracity and credibility of online content have been raised by the purposeful spread of inaccurate or misleading information through a variety of social media platforms. This trend has major ramifications for society cohesion, public confidence, and democratic discourse in addition to endangering the veracity of information.

The DravidianLangTech@EACL 2024 (Subramanian et al., 2024) task was created for this problem, with a specific focus on countering fake news in Dravidian languages. The goal of this innovative project is to use advanced technology, specifically LSTM (Long Short-Term Memory) models (Yigezu et al., 2022), to address the complex problems related to identifying and categorizing fake news(Fazlourrahman et al., 2022; Balouchzahi and Shashirekha, 2020). This initiative aims to achieve two main goals. Initially, Task 1 focuses on social media content classification, with a focus on distinguishing between accurate and false information. The challenge for participants is to create LSTM-based systems that can operate at the

[1]https://codalab.lisn.upsaclay.fr/competitions/16055

Proceedings of the Fourth Workshop on Speech, Vision, and Language Technologies for Dravidian Languages, pages 113–118
March 22, 2024 ©2024 Association for Computational Linguistics

comment or post level on social media sites like Facebook, YouTube, and Twitter and can distinguish between authentic content and fake content. Second, the goal of Task 2, also referred to as the FakeDetect-Malayalam challenge is to recognize and classify fake news in articles written in Malayalam. The task for participants is to create LSTM-based models that can effectively identify false information in Malayalam and categorize articles into groups such as Mostly True, False, Half True, Mostly False, and Partly False. The initiative aims to progress fake news detection, particularly in the context of Dravidian languages, through these tasks. The results and developments that come from this work will not only help create strong detection systems but also promote credibility, trustworthiness, and dependability in online content, forming a more genuine and informed digital environment.

2 Related Work

Trends in technology and extensive research have been made in the field of fake news detection in response to the spread of misinformation and fake news on online platforms in recent years. Various approaches, strategies, and methods have been investigated in a number of studies to address the widespread problem of fake news, which includes social media platforms and multilingual environments. One popular area of research has been identifying fake news on social media. By using neural networks to detect fake news on Twitter, (Shuaibo et al., 2022) invented the application of deep learning(Ahani et al., 2024) techniques (Zervopoulos et al., 2022).They showed how machine learning models can effectively separate false information from real content by focusing on feature extraction and classification in their study. Furthermore, Kumar et al. (2018) suggested a method for detecting fake news by analyzing the text of social media posts using natural language processing (NLP) techniques (Murugesan, 2019). Their research highlighted the value of sentiment analysis and linguistic characteristics in precisely detecting false information.

Moreover, studies have begun to focus on multilingual settings, recognizing the difficulties presented by false information in tongues other than English. Ruchansky et al. (2017) examined the transferability of models across languages in their investigation of cross-lingual fake news detection. (Ruchansky et al., 2017; Bade and Seid, 2018) Research on the identification of fake news in Dravidian languages is beginning to emerge. In their 2020 study, Vigneshwaran and Soman investigated the detection of fake news in Tamil-language news articles by using machine learning algorithms to categorize the authenticity of the (Huang, 2022). Their research highlighted how crucial Tamil-specific linguistic subtleties are to creating precise detection models.

Furthermore, the use of LSTM model has become more popular in the identification of fake news. Recurrent neural networks are effective at capturing temporal dependencies and contextual information in text; Ma et al. (2019) used LSTM networks to detect fake news in Chinese social media. (Zhang et al., 2018; Bade and Afaro, 2018) Furthermore, the focus has been directed to initiatives aimed at addressing the detection of fake news in languages like Malayalam. Kunnath and Jayaraman (2021) used machine learning models in conjunction with lexical and syntactic features to study the detection of fake news in Malayalam (Mirnalinee et al., 2022) . Their research demonstrated the importance of using language-specific strategies to effectively counteract misinformation.

In support of this research work, the DravidianLangTech@EACL 2024 initiative seeks to expand the reach of fake news detection to Dravidian languages. This initiative addresses a research gap by integrating the LSTM model concentrating on social media content and Malayalam-language articles. Overall, these studies present an overview of the DravidianLangTech@EACL 2024 initiative's pursuit of combating fake news within Dravidian languages by highlighting the various methodologies and approaches used in fake news detection across social media platform.

3 Task Description

This work aims to identify Fake News Detection in Dravidian Languages, as mentioned in the introduction . There are two sub-tasks in this work.

3.1 Task 1

This task requires binary classification of content, both in the native language and Roman, into two groups: Original and Fake. All participants must create systems that can reliably classify content authenticity into these two categories—Original and fake information—regardless of language.

3.2 Task 2

The purpose of Task 2, FakeDetect-Malayalam, is to identify fake news in Malayalam content. To accurately classify articles into False, Half True, Mostly False, Partly False, and Mostly True categories, participants develop language-specific models, highlighting the importance of precise identification within regional languages like Malayalam.

4 Methodology

Due to the complex nature of data for both tasks, it is quite obvious that the proposed model must have different aspects to precisely and accurately predict the fake and original content and similarly for multi-class classification for the second task.

4.1 Data sets

The data sets are obtained from (Subramanian et al., 2023) for both tasks, Task 1 involves training, validation, and test data sets and Task 2 has training and test data sets. Task 1 appears to involve binary classification to differentiate between original and fake content. Task 2 has multi-class classification having 5 classes False, Half True, Mostly False, Partly False, and Mostly True.Figure 1 shows the training samples and figure 2 shows the validation data samples for task1.Figure 3 shows the training data set labels for task2.

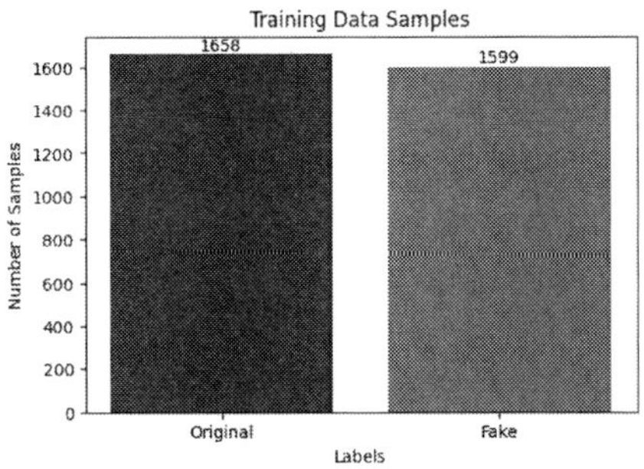

Figure 1: Validation Data Set samples

4.2 Data Preprocessing

Preprocessing includes removing HTML tags, numbers, and symbols (emojis included) from the data once it has been obtained for both tasks. These elements could add unnecessary noise to the data sets, which would impact the analysis. Removing them makes the corpus of texts cleaner, which makes natural language processing (NLP) jobs more accurate. In order for models to concentrate on relevant

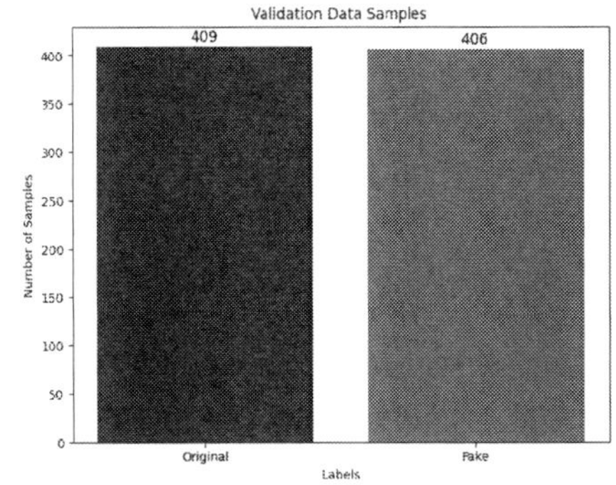

Figure 2: Validation Data Set samples

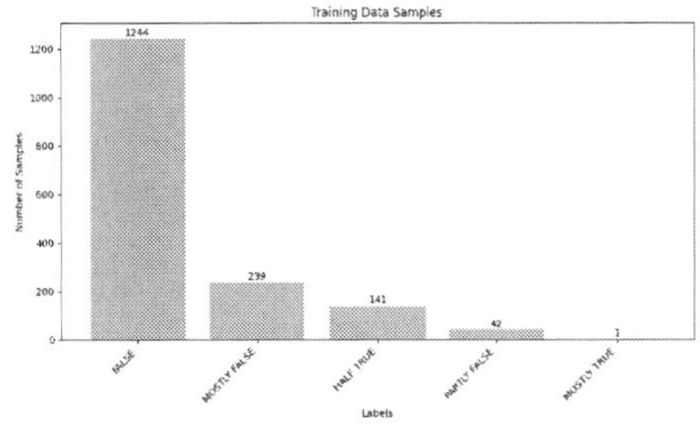

Figure 3: Training Data Set samples

language patterns and features for better performance and robustness in classification or analysis, this cleaning process is essential to improving the quality of data being used.

4.3 Model Evaluation

This ability of recurrent neural networks (RNNs) to preserve long-term dependencies makes Long Short-Term Memory (LSTM) networks particularly good at processing sequential data. Input, forget, and output gates are examples of gates that are incorporated into LSTMs to make learning from sequential data more efficient and to mitigate the disappearing or expanding gradient problems that are frequently seen in traditional RNNs.

Task 1 used an LSTM model with a post-RNN dropout layer for Real vs. Fake News Detection (Binary Classification). By controlling excessive learning from the training data and concentrating on identifying patterns within textual sequences, this design avoided overfitting. To prepare the data for the analysis of the LSTM model, the methodology included preliminary processes such as tokenization, sequence padding, and text preprocessing.

In Task 2, focused on Multi class Classification, the LSTM model was configured to handle multiple output categories, enabling the classification of news articles into various classes (e.g., True, false, partially true). Leveraging the LSTM's proficiency in understanding sequential data, similar prepossessing methods were applied, and the LSTM architecture was adapted to accommodate the multiple output classes.

Both tasks showcased the LSTM's efficacy as the primary architecture for text data processing. The LSTM's adeptness in capturing long-term dependencies and intricate patterns within sequences effectively fulfilled the objectives of differentiating between real and fake news in Task 1 and categorizing text into multiple classes in Task 2. The tailored preprocessing steps and LSTM configurations highlighted the versatility and success of LSTM networks in addressing various text classification challenges.

5 Results and Discussions

Different performance outcomes were found when our LSTM-based models were evaluated for both tasks. With an macro f1-score of 0.78, our model shown encouraging performance in Task 1, which focused on differentiating between Real and Fake News (Binary Classification). Due to the presence of dropout layers and proper pre processing, the model was able to identify unique patterns within textual sequences, which resulted in a balanced performance that showed notable results.

On the other hand, our LSTM model faced a more difficult environment in Task 2, which faced Multi class Classification. With an F1-score of 0.2393, the model encountered difficulties in accurately categorizing news articles into multiple classes.

6 Error Analysis

The LSTM model for Malayalam fake news detection demonstrates remarkable accuracy, particularly in true positive identification. However, a notable challenge arises with false positives, mislabeling instances as fake news even in a balanced dataset. This pattern warrants meticulous analysis and adjustment in the model's discriminatory capabilities. Comprehensive evaluations on validation and test sets are crucial for assessing the model's adaptability. Proposed strategic modifications involve fine-tuning parameters and scrutinizing false positive occurrences to enhance overall accuracy and efficacy.

7 Limitations

Utilizing the model LSTM in fake news detection offers improved textual comprehension, but effectiveness may be limited by corpus specificity. Fine-tuning is crucial to address potential mismatches with unique Malayalam fake news characteristics. The linguistic complexities of Malayalam may hinder the model's ability to discern subtle patterns, requiring further investigation and refinement.

8 Conclusion

In conclusion, Task 1 and Task 2 evaluation of our LSTM-based model highlights both achievements and weaknesses. Task 1 showed excellent performance, obtaining a noteworthy macro F1-score of 0.78 in binary classification, successfully differentiating Real News from Fake News. This success confirms the LSTM model's ability to identify distinct patterns in textual sequences and shows its ability to accurately classify binary data.

With an F1-score of 0.2393 Task 2, which involved Multi-class Classification, highlighted weaknesses. The model had difficulties correctly classifying content multiple classifications, indicating that it was not able to differentiate between different categories. This emphasizes that in order to increase multi-class classification skills, feature representation, data balance, or model refinement changes are required.

The differences in the tasks show the effectiveness of LSTMs in binary classification as well as the challenges that arise in multi class classification. Resolving these complexities requires concerted efforts, such as advanced feature engineering, possible data balancing techniques, or model improvements targeted at improving multi class classification. As we proceed, an iterative process that includes extensive testing, enhanced feature representations, and model optimizations is important.

9 Future work

In order to increase sequence understanding, future work will augment the text classification tasks using LSTM models by combining transformer-based architectures. Furthermore, using larger and large-scale data sets and advanced data balancing techniques to rectify class imbalances may improve the resilience of the model. In order to understand model decisions, more research will need to incorporate interpretability techniques. We will investigate how to enhance and customize models for particular applications by combining domain-specific embeddings with ensemble techniques and transfer learning from pre-trained models. The goal of this multimodal strategy is to improve LSTM models' adaptability and performance in text classification tasks, especially in multi-class settings.

Ethics Statement

We affirm our commitment to ethical research practices and compliance with ACL guidelines in conducting and presenting our study. No ethical concerns or conflicts of interest arose during the course of this research.

Acknowledgments

The work was done with partial support from the Mexican Government through the grant A1-S-47854 of CONACYT, Mexico, grants 20242138, 20241567, and 20242080 of the Secretaría de Investigación y Posgrado of the Instituto Politécnico Nacional, Mexico. The authors thank the CONACYT for the computing resources brought to them through the Plataforma de Aprendizaje Profundo para Tecnologías del Lenguaje of the Laboratorio de Supercómputo of the INAOE, Mexico and acknowledge the support of Microsoft through the Microsoft Latin America PhD Award.

References

2021. Natural Language Processing and Its Challenges on Omotic Language Group of Ethiopia, author=Bade, Girma Yohannis. *Journal of Computer Science Research*, 3(4):26–30.

2023. Evaluating the Effectiveness of Hybrid Features in Fake News Detection on Social Media, author=Yigezu, Mesay Gemeda and Mehamed, Moges Ahmed and Kolesnikova, Olga and Guge, Tadesse Kebede and Gelbukh, Alexander and Sidorov, Grigori. In *2023 International Conference on Information and Communication Technology for Development for Africa (ICT4DA)*, pages 171–175. IEEE.

Zahra Ahani, Moein Shahiki Tash, Yoel Ledo Mezquita, and Jason Angel. 2024. Utilizing deep learning models for the identification of enhancers and super-enhancers based on genomic and epigenomic features. *arXiv preprint arXiv:2401.07470*.

Girma Yohannis Bade and Akalu Assefa Afaro. 2018. Object Oriented Software Development for Artificial Intelligence. *American Journal of Software Engineering and Applications*, 7(2):22–24.

Girma Yohannis Bade and Hussien Seid. 2018. Development of Longest-Match Based Stemmer for Texts of Wolaita Language. *vol*, 4:79–83.

Fazlourrahman Balouchzahi and HL Shashirekha. 2020. Learning Models for Urdu Fake News Detection. In *FIRE (Working Notes)*, pages 474–479.

B Fazlourrahman, BK Aparna, and HL Shashirekha. 2022. Coffitt-covid-19 fake news detection using fine-tuned transfer learning approaches. In *Congress on Intelligent Systems: Proceedings of CIS 2021, Volume 2*, pages 879–890. Springer.

Xiaolei Huang. 2022. Easy adaptation to mitigate gender bias in multilingual text classification. In *Proceedings of the 2022 Conference of the North American Chapter of the Association for Computational Linguistics: Human Language Technologies*, pages 717–723, Seattle, United States. Association for Computational Linguistics.

Selam Kanta and Grigori Sidorov. 2023. Selam@ DravidianLangTech: Sentiment Analysis of Code-Mixed Dravidian Texts using SVM Classification. In *Proceedings of the Third Workshop on Speech and Language Technologies for Dravidian Languages*, pages 176–179.

TT Mirnalinee, Bhuvana Jayaraman, A Anirudh, R Jagadish, and A Karthik Raja. 2022. A Novel Dataset for Fake News Detection in Tamil Regional Language. In *International Conference on Speech and Language Technologies for Low-resource Languages*, pages 311–323. Springer.

Manoj Kumar Murugesan. 2019. *Comparative Analysis of Machine learning Algorithms using NLP Techniques in Automatic Detection of Fake News on Social Media Platforms*. Ph.D. thesis, Dublin, National College of Ireland.

Natali Ruchansky, Sungyong Seo, and Yan Liu. 2017. Csi: A hybrid deep model for fake news detection. pages 797–806.

Moein Shahiki-Tash, Jesús Armenta-Segura, Zahra Ahani, Olga Kolesnikova, Grigori Sidorov, and Alexander Gelbukh. 2023a. Lidoma at homomex2023@ iberlef: Hate speech detection towards the mexican spanish-speaking lgbt+ population. the importance of preprocessing before using bert-based models. In *Proceedings of the Iberian Languages Evaluation Forum (IberLEF 2023)*.

Moein Shahiki-Tash, Jesús Armenta-Segura, Olga Kolesnikova, Grigori Sidorov, and Alexander Gelbukh. 2023b. LIDOMA at HOPE2023IberLEF: Hope Speech Detection Using Lexical Features and Convolutional Neural Networks. In *Proceedings of the Iberian Languages Evaluation Forum (IberLEF 2023), co-located with the 39th Conference of the Spanish Society for Natural Language Processing (SEPLN 2023), CEUR-WS. org*.

Wang Shuaibo, Di Hui, Huang Hui, Lai Siyu, Ouchi Kazushige, Chen Yufeng, and Xu Jinan. 2022. Supervised contrastive learning for cross-lingual transfer learning. In *Proceedings of the 21st Chinese National Conference on Computational Linguistics*, pages 884–895, Nanchang, China. Chinese Information Processing Society of China.

Malliga Subramanian, Bharathi Raja Chakravarthi, Kogilavani Shanmugavadivel, Santhiya Pandiyan, Prasanna Kumar Kumaresan, Balasubramanian Palani, Premjith B, Sandhiya Raja, Vanaja, Mithunajha S, Devika K, Hariprasath S.B, Haripriya B, and Vigneshwar E. 2024. Overview of the Second Shared Task on Fake News Detection in Dravidian Languages. In *Proceedings of the Fourth Workshop on Speech, Vision, and Language Technologies for Dravidian Languages*, Malta.

Malliga Subramanian, Bharathi Raja Chakravarthi, Kogilavani Shanmugavadivel, Santhiya Pandiyan, Prasanna Kumar Kumaresan, Balasubramanian Palani, Muskaan Singh, Sandhiya Raja, Vanaja, and Mithunajha S. 2023. Overview of the Shared Task on Fake News Detection from Social Media Text. In *Proceedings of the Third Workshop on Speech and Language Technologies for Dravidian Languages*, Varna, Bulgaria. Recent Advances in Natural Language Processing.

M Shahiki Tash, Z Ahani, Al Tonja, M Gemeda, N Hussain, and O Kolesnikova. 2022. Word Level Language Identification in Code-mixed Kannada-English Texts using traditional machine learning algorithms. In *Proceedings of the 19th International Conference on Natural Language Processing (ICON): Shared Task on Word Level Language Identification in Code-mixed Kannada-English Texts*, pages 25–28.

Moein Tash, Jesus Armenta-Segura, Zahra Ahani, Olga Kolesnikova, Grigori Sidorov, and Alexander Gelbukh. 2023. LIDOMA@ DravidianLangTech: Convolutional Neural Networks for Studying Correlation Between Lexical Features and Sentiment Polarity in Tamil and Tulu Languages. In *Proceedings of the Third Workshop on Speech and Language Technologies for Dravidian Languages*, pages 180–185.

Atnafu Lambebo Tonja, Mesay Gemeda Yigezu, Olga Kolesnikova, Moein Shahiki Tash, Grigori Sidorov, and Alexander Gelbuk. 2022. Transformer-based model for word level language identification in code-mixed kannada-english texts. *arXiv preprint arXiv:2211.14459*.

Mesay Gemeda Yigezu, Girma Yohannis Bade, Olga Kolesnikova, Grigori Sidorov, and Alexander Gelbukh. 2023a. Multilingual Hope Speech Detection using Machine Learning.

Mesay Gemeda Yigezu, Olga Kolesnikova, Grigori Sidorov, and Alexander Gelbukh. 2023b. Transformer-Based Hate Speech Detection for Multi-Class and Multi-Label Classification.

Mesay Gemeda Yigezu, Atnafu Lambebo Tonja, Olga Kolesnikova, Moein Shahiki Tash, Grigori Sidorov, and Alexander Gelbukh. 2022. Word Level Language Identification in Code-mixed Kannada-English Texts using Deep Learning Approach. In *Proceedings of the 19th International Conference on Natural Language Processing (ICON): Shared Task on Word Level Language Identification in Code-mixed Kannada-English Texts*, pages 29–33.

Alexandros Zervopoulos, Aikaterini Georgia Alvanou, Konstantinos Bezas, Asterios Papamichail, Manolis Maragoudakis, and Katia Kermanidis. 2022. Deep learning for fake news detection on Twitter regarding the 2019 Hong Kong protests. *Neural Computing and Applications*, 34(2):969–982.

Jiawei Zhang, Limeng Cui, Yanjie Fu, and Fisher B Gouza. 2018. Fake news detection with deep diffusive network model. *arXiv preprint arXiv:1805.08751*.

IIITDWD_SVC@DravidianLangTech-2024: Breaking Language Barriers; Hate Speech Detection in Telugu-English Code-Mixed Text

Chava Srinivasa Sai[1] **Rangoori Vinay Kumar**[1] **Sunil Saumya**[1] and **Shankar Biradar**[1]
[1]Department of Data Science and Intelligent Systems,
Indian Institute of Information Technology, Dharwad, Karnatka, India
(srinivassaichava,vinaykumarrangoori33)@gmail.com
(shankar,sunil.saumya)@iiitdwd.ac.in

Abstract

Social media platforms have become increasingly popular and are utilized for a wide range of purposes, including product promotion, news sharing, accomplishment sharing, and much more. However, it is also employed for defamatory speech, intimidation, and the propagation of untruths about particular groups of people. Further, hateful and offensive posts spread quickly and often have a negative impact on people; it is important to identify and remove them from social media platforms as soon as possible. Over the past few years, research on hate speech detection and offensive content has grown in popularity. One of the many difficulties in identifying hate speech on social media platforms is the use of code-mixed language. The majority of people who use social media typically share their messages in languages with mixed codes, like Telugu–English. To encourage research in this direction, the organizers of *DravidianLangTech@EACL-2024* conducted a shared task to identify hateful content in Telugu-English code-mixed text. Our team participated in this shared task, employing three different models: Xlm-Roberta, BERT, and Hate-BERT. In particular, our BERT-based model secured the 14th rank in the competition with a macro F1 score of 0.65.

1 Introduction

In contemporary society, social media plays a pivotal role in the daily lives of many individuals. Text messages across various platforms hold considerable influence, both positively and negatively. On a positive note, social media serves as a global connector, fostering creativity, enhancing skills, and providing entertainment. Additionally, it facilitates the swift dissemination of breaking news. Conversely, the prevalence of hate speech and the dissemination of inaccurate information about individuals, groups, or societies represent undesirable phenomena. Social media platforms are regrettably exploited for expressing destructive views and eliciting negative emotions through hate and fraudulent communications.

In the present era, there is a high degree of trust in social media, so misinformation propagated by media outlets or influential figures is often accepted as true. Consequently, individuals disseminate false information using inappropriate language, with hashtags like *#HateSpeech* gaining prominence on platforms such as Twitter and YouTube, particularly during the emergencies like COVID-19 pandemic. Furthermore, some individuals erroneously believe that engaging in abusive language or hate speech can confer fame and notoriety. Social media platforms are actively striving to eradicate such negative textual content, recognizing the severe consequences it can have on individuals' lives.

While social media users are increasingly cognizant of the issue, exposure to hate news persists, even when the true story is known. Efforts to address this problem involve the development of machine learning and deep learning models capable of identifying hate speech in text data (Nozza, 2021). Given the language's global prevalence, numerous models have been trained on English data (Santosh and Aravind, 2019). However, it is imperative to acknowledge that hate speech extends beyond English, with regional languages being utilized for its propagation. Telugu, a Dravidian language spoken in Andhra Pradesh and Telangana, India, is one such language.

Motivated by this realization, *DravidianLangTech@EACL-2024* initiated a shared task for the classification of hate and non-hate speech detection in Tenglish (Telugu-English) code-mixed dataset (B et al., 2024). Our team participated in the shared task; we employed various techniques, including transliteration, and translation during preprocessing. In addition, we subsequently utilized three distinct models for embedding extraction,

Proceedings of the Fourth Workshop on Speech, Vision, and Language Technologies for Dravidian Languages, pages 119–123
March 22, 2024 ©2024 Association for Computational Linguistics

HateBERT, XLM-RoBERTa, and BERT, and secured 14th position with a F1-Score of 0.6565 for BERT-Based (cased) among all competing teams.

The article is structured as follows: Section 2 presents the background study. The details of the dataset and methodology are presented in Section 3, and finally, the results are discussed in Section 4. At last, in Section. 5 concluded and talked about Future research direction. We have written some Ethics in Section 6 for the work which had done.

2 Related work

The exploration of hate speech detection in Dravidian code-mixed text remains a relatively under explored topic, as most previous research has predominantly focused on high-resource languages such as English. However, recent attention from the research community has been directed towards hate speech detection in Dravidian code-mixed text data (Chakravarthi et al., 2020).

The gold standard corpus for detecting hate speech in three Dravidian languages: Tamil (Chakravarthi et al., 2020), Malayalam (Chakravarthi et al.), and Kannada (Hande et al., 2020) was developed by (Chakravarthi et al., 2020). This corpus was established as part of a shared task, stimulating active engagement from multiple teams. The majority of these teams concentrated on leveraging knowledge derived from pre-trained transformer models to address the challenges associated with low-resource languages. (Biradar et al., 2021; Fharook et al., 2022; Kavatagi et al., 2023) for instance, utilized a cross-lingual pre-trained model like Mbert in conjunction with Support Vector Machines (SVM) to identify hate speech in Tanglish and Manglish text. Furthermore, (Saumya et al., 2022) adopted an ensemble setup, combining machine learning (ML) and deep learning (DL) based models to effectively detect transphobic content in Tamil and Malayalam text. However, Telugu, being one of the major Dravidian languages widely spoken in Telangana and Andhra Pradesh, has been relatively less explored in this context. This marks the first attempt to identify hate content in Telugu-English code-mixed text.

3 Methodology

3.1 Task and Data

The *DravidianLangTech@EACL-2024* shared task has been a significant focus of our work. The organizers of this shared task have made available a comprehensive dataset consisting of 4000 and 500 comments in the train and test stages respectively. These comments were collected from Youtube, as stated by the organizers (B et al., 2024). The main objective of this task is to classify each Telugu-English code-mixed social media comment at the sentence level, determining whether it falls into the hate or non-hate categories. Our team actively participated in this task and achieved an impressive rank of 14th position. For more detailed information about this dataset, plese refer to Table 1

	Hate	Non-hate	Total
Train	1939	2061	4000
Test	250	250	500

Table 1: Data distribution

3.2 Data pre processing

Preprocessing raw data is essential in optimizing it for compatibility with machine learning models. Even a small adequate data preprocessing improves a model's efficiency significantly. The different kinds of data preprocessing methods we used as illustarted in Figure 1.

3.2.1 Transliteration

Transliteration is a process that does not alter the meaning of a sentence; instead, it modifies the words to facilitate pronunciation in the reader's native language (Deselaers et al., 2009). Our dataset comprises Telugu content presented in the English script. In this context, we employed a transliteration model designed to accurately convert the Tenglish (Telugu-English) script into the Telugu script. The IndicXlit [1] model was selected for this task; this model proficiently transliterates Tenglish into standard Telugu, enhancing comprehension and facilitating progress in subsequent stages of the project.

3.2.2 Translation

Following the transliteration process, we now possess high-quality Telugu text, which needs to be translated into English. This step is essential because the majority of the pre-trained models were trained on English datasets. Therefore, we have implemented a translation approach. We employed the "IndicTrans2"[2] model for translating the Tel-

[1]https://ai4bharat.iitm.ac.in/indicxlit-model/

[2]https://ai4bharat.iitm.ac.in/indic-trans2/

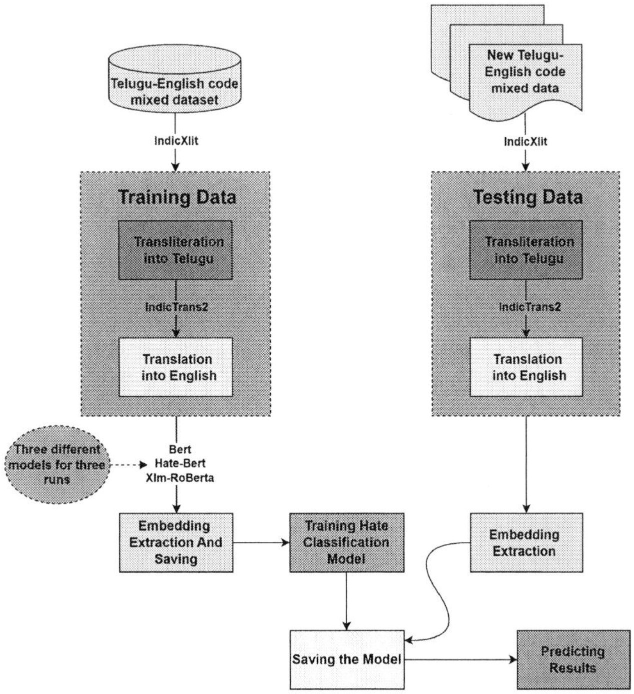

Figure 1: Flow diagram for the proposed work

ugu text into English. Table 2 illustrates the sample comments from translated text.

3.2.3 Tokenization

After translation , our training dataset is ready for tokenization , we loaded three different tokenizers for these models using the Hugging Face Transformers library[3]. We specifically used the AutoTokenizer class from that package to load the appropriate tokenizer for the chosen model architecture.

3.3 Feature Extraction

Tokenized text is subsequently employed for feature extraction. For this purpose, we deployed three encoder-based models with frozen weights: Bert, Hate-bert, and XLM-Roberta. The next step involves extracting embeddings using the mean-pooling approach, a widely adopted method in NLP applications that involve neural networks and word embedding. This method is employed to obtain a comprehensive representation by averaging embedding vectors along specific directions.

3.3.1 BERT

The BERT model, based on transformer architecture, has been widely adopted for its pretraining capabilities (Kenton and Toutanova, 2019). BERT is chosen in the proposed work due to its comprehensive language understanding capabilities. The embeddings from the CLS token are utilized in the proposed work to generate sentence-level representations. Specifically, 'bert-base-uncased' from the Hugging Face library[4] is employed to generate these sentence representations in the proposed work.

3.3.2 Xlm-RoBERTa

Xlm-RoBERTa is a widely-used RoBERTa model that supports multiple languages(English, Hindi etc.,). The model has been trained on a larger corpus comprising 100 different languages (Conneau et al., 2020). The present study utilizes the "xlm-roberta-base"[5] for comprehending cross-lingual representations.

3.3.3 Hate-BERT

It is a variant of the BERT model specifically designed for detecting abusive language in English text. This variant was derived through extensive training on the BERT uncased model, utilizing over one million posts that were banned in *Reddit* communities. Notably, this model has demonstrated superior performance compared to the original BERT

[3]https://huggingface.co/models

[4]https://huggingface.co/bert-base-uncased

[5]https://huggingface.co/xlm-roberta-base

Original comment	Translated text
Thappu chesina vaallaku vanike kaadu inka anni modalithavi . Enta kaalam students life tho aadukuntu crores earn chedtharu illegal ga.	It is not only a pity for the wrong doers, but also a first step towards them. How long will you play with the life of a student and play with him / her?
Kanipinche devudu CBN	The Seeing God CBN
Pavan Kalyan gari nayakatvam vardillali jai power star	Power Star Pawan Kalyan

Table 2: Sample comments for translated text

in understanding offensive language. The proposed method employs the "GroNLP/hateBERT"[6] model from Hugging Face to generate domain-specific representations.

3.4 Classifier

The generated features are subsequently passed through the final stage of our pipeline, which is the classifier for hate or non-hate class detection. This classifier remains consistent across all three models.

The proposed classifier is constructed using a simple feed-forward neural network with three layers: the input, hidden, and output layers. The size of the input layer is contingent upon the dimensions of the model embeddings. Proceeding to the hidden layer, it consists of a non-linear layer comprising 128 neurons and utilizes the Rectified Linear Unit (ReLU) activation function. This non-linear aspect allows the model to discern intricate patterns in the data, enhancing its capacity for producing more accurate predictions. A final sigmoid layer is incorporated to predict the output class. Subsequently, the model undergoes training for nine epochs employing the *Binary Cross-Entropy Loss* with the *Adam optimizer*.

4 Result and discussion

The proposed model was tested on three distinct embedding representations generated using pre-trained encoder-based models. The comparative results between these models are presented in Table 3. According to Table 3, the BERT and HateBERT-based models demonstrate a superior ability to comprehend the hate and non-hate nature of the text, achieving comparable results of F1-Score 0.6565 for BERT-Based (cased) on translated text data .

[6]https://huggingface.co/GroNLP/hateBERT

	Hate (F1)	Non Hate (F1)	Accuracy
HateBERT	**0.68**	**0.70**	**69**
BERT	**0.68**	**0.71**	**69**
XlmRoBERTa	0.64	0.64	64

Table 3: Comparative results

Team	F1 score	Rank
Sandalphon	0.7711	1
Selam	0.7711	2
Kubapok	0.7431	3
DLRG1	0.7101	4
IIITDWD_SVC	**0.6565**	**14**

Table 4: Leader board

In contrast, Xlm-RoBERTa slightly lags behind, likely due to the high-resource English text.

Our team presented the results of the best-performing model, BERT, in the competition. The organizers of the shared task evaluated model performance using the macro F1 score, and our team secured the 14th rank among the participating teams. Table 4 present the leaderboard, depicting the position of our team in the competition.

5 Conclusion and Future research direction

The study provides the working notes of the model presented during the DravidianLangTech-2024 shared task. The experimental findings suggest that the performance of the model can be enhanced by translating the original code-mixed text and leveraging the knowledge derived from monolingual pre-trained models. Additionally, this work can be extended to incorporate the fine-tuning of language models using domain-specific data.

6 Ethics

In our study on detecting hate speech in Telugu-English code-mixed text, ethical considerations have played a crucial role. We have been careful in using language models as we have openly shared our techniques, models, and findings. Our participation in the *DravidianLangTech@EACL-2024* shared task has also been conducted with ethical standards in mind, promoting collaboration and knowledge exchange within the research community. We are committed to responsible AI practices and continuously strive to reduce biases and ensure fair representation in hate speech detection.

References

Premjth B, Bharathi Raja, Prasanna Kumar Kumaresan, Saranya Rajiakodi, Sai Prashanth Karnati, Sai Rishith Reddy Mangamuru, and Janakiram Chandu. 2024. Findings of the shared task on hate and offensive language detection in telugu codemixed text (hold-telugu). In *Proceedings of the Fourth Workshop on Speech, Vision, and Language Technologies for Dravidian Languages*, Malta. European Chapter of the Association for Computational Linguistics.

Shankar Biradar, Sunil Saumya, and Arun Chauhan. 2021. mbert based model for identification of offensive content in south indian languages.

Bharathi Raja Chakravarthi, Navya Jose, Shardul Suryawanshi, Elizabeth Sherly, and John P McCrae. A sentiment analysis dataset for code-mixed malayalam-english. In *LREC 2020 Workshop Language Resources and Evaluation Conference 11–16 May 2020*, page 177.

Bharathi Raja Chakravarthi, Vigneshwaran Muralidaran, Ruba Priyadharshini, and John Philip McCrae. 2020. Corpus creation for sentiment analysis in code-mixed tamil-english text. In *Proceedings of the 1st Joint Workshop on Spoken Language Technologies for Under-resourced languages (SLTU) and Collaboration and Computing for Under-Resourced Languages (CCURL)*, pages 202–210.

Alexis Conneau, Kartikay Khandelwal, Naman Goyal, Vishrav Chaudhary, Guillaume Wenzek, Francisco Guzmán, Édouard Grave, Myle Ott, Luke Zettlemoyer, and Veselin Stoyanov. 2020. Unsupervised cross-lingual representation learning at scale. In *Proceedings of the 58th Annual Meeting of the Association for Computational Linguistics*, pages 8440–8451.

Thomas Deselaers, Saša Hasan, Oliver Bender, and Hermann Ney. 2009. A deep learning approach to machine transliteration. In *Proceedings of the Fourth Workshop on Statistical Machine Translation*, pages 233–241.

Shaik Fharook, Syed Sufyan Ahmed, Gurram Rithika, Sumith Sai Budde, Sunil Saumya, and Shankar Biradar. 2022. Are you a hero or a villain? a semantic role labelling approach for detecting harmful memes. In *Proceedings of the Workshop on Combating Online Hostile Posts in Regional Languages during Emergency Situations*, pages 19–23.

Adeep Hande, Ruba Priyadharshini, and Bharathi Raja Chakravarthi. 2020. Kancmd: Kannada codemixed dataset for sentiment analysis and offensive language detection. In *Proceedings of the Third Workshop on Computational Modeling of People's Opinions, Personality, and Emotion's in Social Media*, pages 54–63.

Sanjana M Kavatagi, Rashmi R Rachh, and Shankar S Biradar. 2023. Vtubgm@ lt-edi-2023: Hope speech identification using layered differential training of ulmfit. In *Proceedings of the Third Workshop on Language Technology for Equality, Diversity and Inclusion*, pages 209–213.

Jacob Devlin Ming-Wei Chang Kenton and Lee Kristina Toutanova. 2019. Bert: Pre-training of deep bidirectional transformers for language understanding. In *Proceedings of naacL-HLT*, volume 1, page 2.

Debora Nozza. 2021. Exposing the limits of zero-shot cross-lingual hate speech detection. In *Proceedings of the 59th Annual Meeting of the Association for Computational Linguistics and the 11th International Joint Conference on Natural Language Processing (Volume 2: Short Papers)*, pages 907–914.

TYSS Santosh and KVS Aravind. 2019. Hate speech detection in hindi-english code-mixed social media text. In *Proceedings of the ACM India joint international conference on data science and management of data*, pages 310–313.

Sunil Saumya, Vanshita Jha, and Shankar Biradar. 2022. Sentiment and homophobia detection on youtube using ensemble machine learning techniques. In *Working Notes of FIRE 2022-Forum for Information Retrieval Evaluation (Hybrid). CEUR.*

Beyond_Tech@DravidianLangTech2024 : Fake News Detection in Dravidian Languages Using Machine Learning

Kogilavani Shanmugavadivel[1], Malliga Subramanian[1], Sanjai R[1], Mohammed Sameer B[1], Motheeswaran K[1]

[1]Department of AI, Kongu Engineering College, Perundurai, Erode.
{kogilavani.sv, mallinishanth72}@gmail.com
{sanjair.22aid, mohammedsameerb.22aid}@kongu.edu
motheeswarank.22aid@kongu.edu

Abstract

In the digital age, identifying fake news is essential when fake information travels quickly via social media platforms. This project employs machine learning techniques, including Random Forest, Logistic Regression, and Decision Tree, to distinguish between real and fake news. With the rise of news consumption on social media, it becomes essential to authenticate information shared on platforms like YouTube comments. The research emphasizes the need to stop spreading harmful rumors and focuses on authenticating news articles. The proposed model utilizes machine learning and natural language processing, specifically Support Vector Machines, to aggregate and determine the authenticity of news. To address the challenges of detecting fake news in this paper, describe the Machine Learning (ML) models submitted to 'Fake News Detection in Dravidian Languages' at DravidianLangTech@EACL 2024 shared task. Four different models, namely: Naive Bayes, Support Vector Machine, Random forest, and Decision tree.

1 Introduction

People are increasingly choosing to search for and consume news from social media rather than traditional news sources as more and more of our lives are spent communicating online via social media platforms Albahr and Albahar (2020). Coelho et al. (2023) Fake news propagators have an opportunity to intentionally sway people's attitudes, beliefs, and trust by disseminating fake information. Rumors and false information typically travel quickly, harming specific relationships and social ties. Moreover, negative understanding, public scrutiny, and social distancing can also result in worry and emotional torment. Sharma et al. (2020) It is now necessary to relate to and filter out comparable false news automatically in order to lessen the harm and pain that fake news causes associations and communities. The internet and social media have made it much easier and more straightforward to obtain news information. It is true Gilda (2017) that there are a lot of websites that easily generate fake news. They usually use social media to boost their online presence and increase their impact. Dummy news websites pose as authoritative sources on topics (often political) in an attempt to sway public opinion. Jain et al. (2019) Fake information may be a global problem as well as a global task. Many experts think AI and machine literacy might potentially be used to address the problem of fake news. The paper is mainly concentrated on classifying whether a piece of news is fake or not.

In this paper, Problem and system description describes the dataset and how the dataset is preprocessed. The methodology uses classification algorithms to find the accuracy of models in classifying real and fake news in the given dataset and it also describes the algorithms. At last, the result gives the best model and its accuracy.

2 Literature Review

Ahmad and Lokeshkumar (2019) investigated text mining for the identification of false news. The dataset is initially preprocessed and relative algorithms are applied. Smitha and Bharath (2020) have taken data from many websites. The collected data are split into test and train and then the dataset is preprocessed, the preprocessed data are given to the ML algorithm after performing feature extraction.

The study Albahr and Albahar (2020) looks at random forests, Naive Bayes, and decision trees. The LIAR dataset, a popular dataset for identifying false news, was used for the experiment. To enhance the effectiveness of machine learning algorithms in identifying false news, They have employed NLP techniques. A variety of classification techniques, such as SVM, Bounded Decision Trees, Random Forests, Gradient Boosting, and Stochastic Gradient Descent, were employed byShaikh

Proceedings of the Fourth Workshop on Speech, Vision, and Language Technologies for Dravidian Languages, pages 124–128
March 22, 2024 ©2024 Association for Computational Linguistics

and Patil (2020). According to the Gilda (2017), TF-IDF of bi-grams fed into a Stochastic Gradient Descent model can identify non-credible sources with an accuracy of 77.2%.

Sharma et al. (2020) uses a machine learning classifier. After researching and using four distinct classifiers to train the model, They selected the most effective classifier for best model.

Jain et al. (2019) presented a method that combined SVM, and the Naive Bayes classifier. The three-part approach combines typical language preparation methods with machine learning calculations that split into controlled learning processes. In Coelho et al. (2023) they removed noise from the dataset containing Malayalam code-mixed data. They used ML models such as SVM and Random forest .Mandical et al. (2020) suggested to use hard voting with machine learning model as Multinomial Naive Bayes technique to detect bogus news in code-mixed Malayalam text.

Malliga et al. (2023) Shared task focused on categorizing social media posts in Malayalam using machine learning and transformer-based models. XLMRoBERTa-based model achieved exceptional performance with F1-score of 0.90.

3 Problem and System Description

Identifying and minimizing bogus news on social media is the aim of this collaborative effort on fake news identification.

3.1 Dataset Description

The shared task provides the dataset that is being utilized here. This project's main objective is to create machine learning-based model that can distinguish between authentic and bogus news.

Dataset	Original	Fake	Total
Training	1658	1,599	3,257
Testing	384	635	1,019

Table 1: Dataset Description

3.2 Preprocessing

The dataset consists of comments and their related labels such as fake and original. LabelEncoder is used to convert the categorical labels into numerical values as 0's and 1's.

4 Methodology

The methodology investigates a number of machine learning strategies and pre-processing techniques for the identification of fake news. The Naive Bayes classifier, SVM, Random Forest, and Decision Tree method are a few well-known classifiers that have been studied. The several steps taken while processing a text in order to classify it.

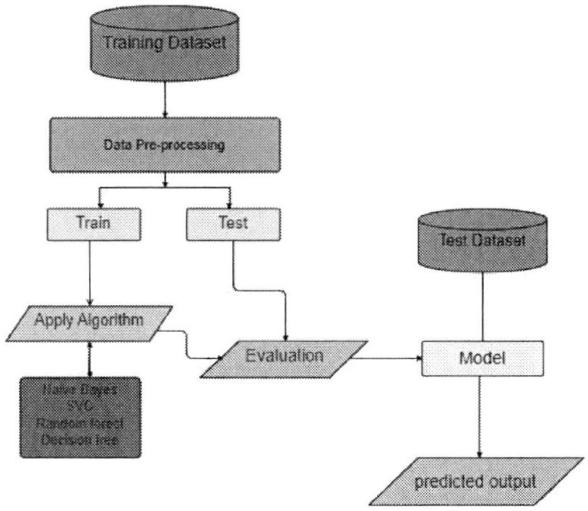

Figure 1: Processed workflow

4.1 Confusion Matrix

A confusion matrix serves as a tabular representation commonly employed to assess how well a classification model performs on a given set of test data with known true values. This matrix facilitates a visual depiction of the algorithm's performance, offering insights into its accuracy and error patterns.

Total		Predicted	
		Positive	Negative
Actual	True	TP	TN
	False	FP	FN

Figure 2: Confusion matrix

True Positive (TP) occurs when the model correctly identifies fake news as fake.
True Negative (TN) occurs when the model correctly classifies true news as true.

False Negative (FN) happens when the model mistakenly categorizes true news as fake.
False Positive (FP) happens when the model incorrectly labels fake news as true.

4.2 Naive Bayes classifier

Naive Bayes is a probabilistic algorithm that assumes features are independent for quick decision-making. It's often used in text classification and spam filtering, making predictions based on simple assumptions.

This can be stated as:

$$P(Y|X_1,X_{2,\dots}X_n) = \frac{P(X_1|Y)P(X_2|Y)\dots P(X_n|Y)}{P(X_1)P(X_2)\dots P(X_n)}$$

which can be further expressed as:

$$P(Y|X_1,X_{2,\dots}X_n) = \frac{P(Y)\prod_{i=1}^{n}P(X_i|Y)}{P(X_1)P(X_2)\dots P(X_n)}$$

where P(X—Y) is the likelihood that event X will occur given that event Y has already occurred.

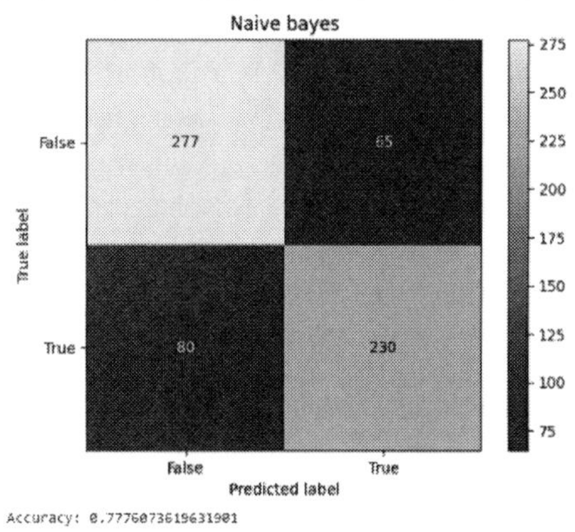

Figure 3: Confusion Matrix for Navie Bayes

	Precision	Recall	f1-score
Accuracy			0.78
Macro avg	0.78	0.78	0.78
Weighted avg	0.78	0.78	0.78

Table 2: Classification Report for Naive Bayes classifier

4.3 Support Vector Machine

SVM is an effective machine learning method for regression and classification that divides data classes into groups by finding the best hyperplane in high-dimensional space. support vectors are used to establish the decision boundary, SVM is resistant to overfitting. For big datasets, SVM can be computationally demanding despite its efficacy.

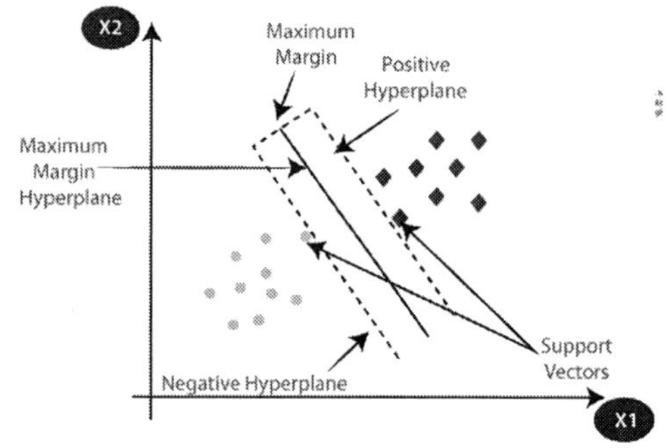

Figure 4: Support vector Machine Graph

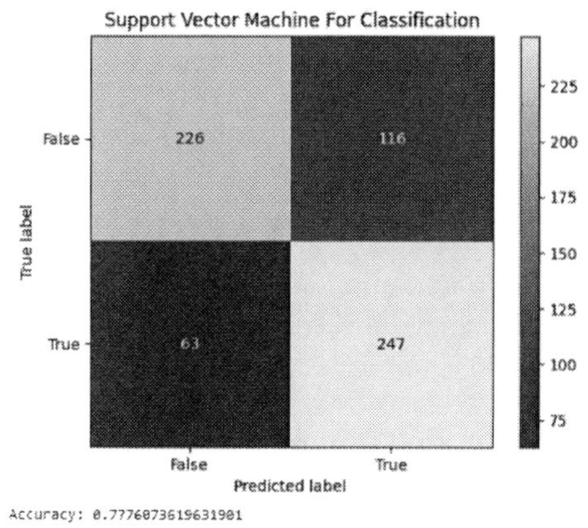

Figure 5: Confusion Matrix for SVM

	Precision	Recall	f1-score
Accuracy			0.73
Macro avg	0.73	0.73	0.73
Weighted avg	0.73	0.73	0.72

Table 3: Classification Report for SVM

4.4 Random Forest

Random Forest in machine learning is like a diverse group of decision-making experts collaborating on a complex problem. It constructs multiple decision trees, each with its perspective on the data.

Individually, these trees may have limitations, but collectively, they form a robust and versatile ensemble. The forest's strength lies in aggregating these diverse insights, reducing overfitting, and delivering a more accurate and reliable prediction, making it a go-to choice for various tasks, from classification to regression.

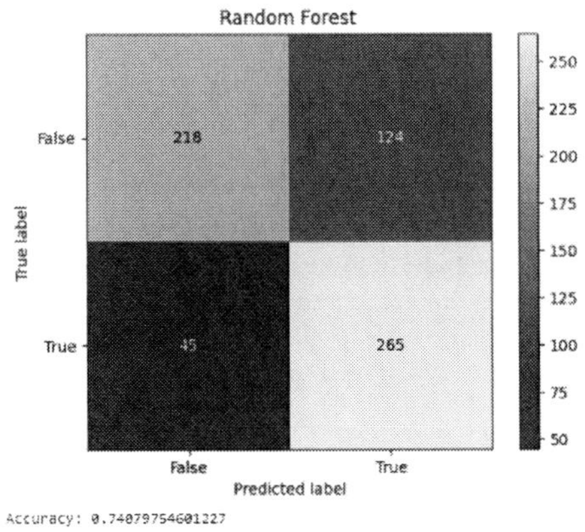

Figure 6: Confusion Matrix for Random Forest

	Precision	Recall	f1-score
Accuracy			0.74
Macro avg	0.76	0.75	0.74
Weighted avg	0.76	0.74	0.74

Table 4: Classification Report for Random Forest

4.5 Decision Tree

A decision tree, in supervised learning, structures attribute tests in a tree-like form for classification and regression. Nodes represent tests, branches show outcomes, and leaf nodes hold class labels. Attributes are chosen during training using metrics like entropy or Gini impurity for optimal information gain. The decision tree is recursively built, starting from the root node, until meeting stopping criteria like maximum depth. Impurity measures, such as Gini index or entropy, assess randomness, while pruning removes non-informative branches to prevent overfitting.

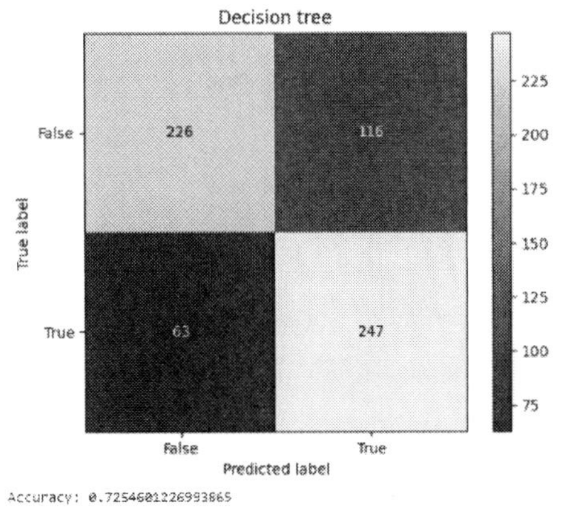

Figure 7: Confusion Matrix for Decision Tree

	Precision	Recall	f1-score
Accuracy			0.73
Macro avg	0.73	0.73	0.73
Weighted avg	0.73	0.73	0.72

Table 5: Classification Report for Decision Tree

5 Result

A good dataset is first used to train the model. Second, many performance metrics are used to evaluate performance. Lastly, headlines or articles are categorized using the best model—that is, the model with the highest accuracy. At 77.7%, Navie bayes and SVM proved to be the most effective model for static search.

6 Conclusion

Finally, it should be noted that when fake news spreads, it attempts to alter people's perceptions and attitudes about utilizing digital technologies. There are two possible outcomes when individuals fall for fake news: Initially, people begin to think that their preconceived notions about a given subject are accurate. Our fraudulent News Detection System was developed to stop this problem by evaluating user-submitted information and classifying it as real or fraudulent. Several machine learning and natural language processing (NLP) approaches must be used to do this.

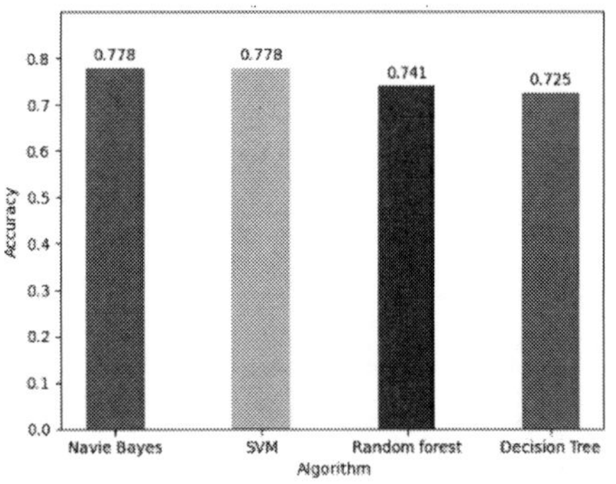

Classifier	Accuracy
Naive Bayes classifier	77.76
Support Vector Machine	77.76
Random Forest	74.07
Decision Tree	72.54

Table 6: algorithm and accuracy

References

Faraz Ahmad and R Lokeshkumar. 2019. A comparison of machine learning algorithms in fake news detection. *International Journal on Emerging Technologies*, 10(4):177–183.

Abdulaziz Albahr and Marwan Albahar. 2020. An empirical comparison of fake news detection using different machine learning algorithms. *International Journal of Advanced Computer Science and Applications*, 11(9).

Sharal Coelho, Asha Hegde, G Kavya, and Hosahalli Lakshmaiah Shashirekha. 2023. Mucs@ dravidianlangtech2023: Malayalam fake news detection using machine learning approach. In *Proceedings of the Third Workshop on Speech and Language Technologies for Dravidian Languages*, pages 288–292.

Shlok Gilda. 2017. Notice of violation of ieee publication principles: Evaluating machine learning algorithms for fake news detection. In *2017 IEEE 15th student conference on research and development (SCOReD)*, pages 110–115. IEEE.

Anjali Jain, Avinash Shakya, Harsh Khatter, and Amit Kumar Gupta. 2019. A smart system for fake news detection using machine learning. In *2019 International conference on issues and challenges in intelligent computing techniques (ICICT)*, volume 1, pages 1–4. IEEE.

S Malliga, Bharathi Raja Chakravarthi, SV Kogilavani, Santhiya Pandiyan, Prasanna Kumar Kumaresan, Balasubramanian Palani, and Muskaan Singh. 2023. Overview of the shared task on fake news detection from social media text. In *Proceedings of the Third Workshop on Speech and Language Technologies for Dravidian Languages*, pages 59–63.

Rahul R Mandical, N Mamatha, N Shivakumar, R Monica, and AN Krishna. 2020. Identification of fake news using machine learning. In *2020 IEEE International Conference on Electronics, Computing and Communication Technologies (CONECCT)*, pages 1–6. IEEE.

Jasmine Shaikh and Rupali Patil. 2020. Fake news detection using machine learning. In *2020 IEEE International Symposium on Sustainable Energy, Signal Processing and Cyber Security (iSSSC)*, pages 1–5. IEEE.

Uma Sharma, Sidarth Saran, and Shankar M Patil. 2020. Fake news detection using machine learning algorithms. *International Journal of Creative Research Thoughts (IJCRT)*, 8(6):509–518.

N Smitha and R Bharath. 2020. Performance comparison of machine learning classifiers for fake news detection. In *2020 Second international conference on inventive research in computing applications (ICIRCA)*, pages 696–700. IEEE.

Code_Maker@DravidianLangTech-EACL 2024: Sentiment Analysis in Code-Mixed Tamil using Machine Learning Techniques

Kogilavani Shanmugavadivel[1],**Sowbharanika Janani J S**[1], **Navbila K**[1], **Malliga Subramanian**[1]
Department of AI, Kongu Engineering College, Perundurai, Erode.
{kogilavani.sv}@gmail.com
{sowbharanikajananijs.22aid,navbilak.22aid}@kongu.edu
{mallinishanth72}@gmail.com

Abstract

The rising importance of sentiment analysis in online community research is addressed in our project, which focuses on the surge of code-mixed writing in multilingual social media. Targeting sentiments in texts combining Tamil and English, our supervised learning approach, particularly the Decision Tree algorithm, proves essential for effective sentiment classification. Notably, Decision Tree(accuracy: 0.99, macro average F1 score : 0.39), Random Forest exhibit high accuracy (accuracy: 0.99, macro average F1 score : 0.35), SVM (accuracy: 0.78, macro average F1 score : 0.68), Logistic Regression (accuracy: 0.75, macro average F1 score : 0.62), KNN (accuracy: 0.73, macro average F1 score : 0.26) also demonstrate commendable results. These findings showcase the project's efficacy, offering promise for linguistic research and technological advancements. Securing the 8th rank emphasizes its recognition in the field.[1]

1 Introduction

Sentiment analysis is an essential tool in the ever-changing world of social media for understanding the subtleties of user expressions. Sentiment analysis algorithms, which were previously designed for high-resource languages and single utterances, now confront additional difficulties in the age of multilingual societies and code-mixed writing. The expanding importance of sentiment analysis is discussed in this research, especially in light of the prevalence of code-mixed Tamil-English statements on social media platforms. The conventional supervised learning approaches, relying on annotated data, encounter limitations when applied to code-mixed languages. Notably, in this multilingual environment, lexical characteristics like word dictionaries and parts of speech labelling perform less than ideal. To tackle these problems, we concentrate our study on sentiment analysis in code-mixed Tamil-English. Using the Decision Tree technique, our strategy's key component offers a dependable way to classify emotions in this peculiar language fusion. This project not only showcases exceptional accuracy through detailed metrics like precision, recall, and F1-score but also introduces a substantial corpus for under-resourced code-mixed Tanglish. Marked by a high inter-annotator agreement, this dataset stands as a valuable resource for researchers exploring sentiment analysis and linguistic phenomena in code-mixed environments. Our project stands at the intersection of sentiment analysis, machine learning, and code-mixed language research. Its contributions extend beyond accurate sentiment classification, serving as a foundational resource for future investigations in the dynamic landscape of multilingual social media expressions.

Keywords: Sentiment analysis, Code-mixed writing, Decision tree algorithm, Machine learning, Tamil - English dataset

2 Literature Survey

A sentiment analysis of COVID-19 vaccine-related tweets on English-language Twitter is conducted in Liu and Liu (2021). They found that nearly 43 percent of the more than 2.6 million tweets they analysed were positive, 27 percent were neutral, and 30 percent were negative. Based on the research findings that these opinions varied by region and changed over time, health officials may adjust their efforts to educate people about vaccines. The study claims that sentiment analysis on Twitter can be utilised to learn more about the public's perceptions on vaccinations.

In social media especially, sentiment analysis of comments on photos or videos is crucial for decision-making. On social media, comments, however, are often multilingual and lack annotations for languages with low resource availability,

[1]S. K. et al. (2024)

Proceedings of the Fourth Workshop on Speech, Vision, and Language Technologies for Dravidian Languages, pages 129–133
March 22, 2024 ©2024 Association for Computational Linguistics

like Tamil 15,744 Tamil and English YouTube comment threads were code-switched, and sentiment analysis was done to establish a gold standard corpus. Results in F-Score, Precision, and Recall were obtained from Chakravarthi et al. (2020) with good inter-annotator agreement.

Raveendirarasa and Amalraj (2020) examines sentiment analysis of texts that move across codes on social networking sites such as Facebook. It suggests a method for applying natural language processing to recognise user behavioural patterns. Clustering-based pre-processing and hyperparameter optimisations are used by the system, which primarily targets Facebook users in Sri Lanka. The model's accuracy was 75 percent, and results for huge and uncommon words were enhanced by sub-word-level LSTM.

Within the field of Natural Language Processing, sentiment analysis (SA) examines user sentiments from internet reviews. It helps consumers comprehend and organise their travels, and search engines depend on it. Devika et al. (2016) focuses on four primary approaches to sentiment analysis: machine learning, semantic analysis, rule-based, and lexicon-based approaches.

In this study, Shanmugavadivel et al. (2022) uses transfer learning, hybrid deep learning, deep learning, and classic machine learning models to investigate the effects of pre-processing Tamil code-mixed data. The goal of the study is to eliminate from the data any emojis, punctuation, symbols, numerals, and repeated letters. With pre-processed Tamil code-mixed data, the hybrid deep learning model CNN+BiLSTM outperforms the others, with an accuracy of 0.66. The study evaluates these models' performance against the most advanced techniques, such as logistic regression, random forest, IndicBERT, multinomial Naive Bayes, and linear support vector classification. Future work should concentrate on multimodal data sets and context-based algorithms to improve the accuracy of sentiment analysis on social media data.

The dynamic field of sentiment analysis (SA) examines user opinions as they are conveyed in written language. It facilitates the gathering of input for manufacturers, governments, and companies. The limitations and future directions of research on implicit aspect extraction for SA have been evaluated in Ganganwar and Rajalakshmi (2019). Grammatical errors, double implicit problems, and semantic concept-centric aspect level sentiment analysis are some of the topics that should be the focus of future research.

Sentiment analysis is vital in the fast-paced world of the internet, especially on social media platforms like Twitter. A method for classifying customer evaluations as positive, negative, or neutral is presented in Rakshitha et al. (2021) utilising text blobs that are retrieved from Twitter APIs. This helps customers choose the best products more effectively, and it also allows businesses to modify as needed in response to customer input

Alshamsi et al. (2020) investigates sentiment analysis utilising many machine learning algorithms and a dataset of tweets. The research examined 16 scholarly works. In summary, the project excels in sentiment analysis, utilizing the Decision Tree algorithm with exceptional accuracy. The comprehensive classification report emphasizes crucial metrics, illuminating the model's robust performance. Beyond sentiment analysis, it stands as a pivotal resource for code-mixed research, marked by a high inter-annotator agreement, showcasing adaptability in exploring diverse linguistic phenomena in code-mixed Tanglish. While addressing concerns like overfitting, the project's strong foundation positions it as a commendable contribution to sentiment analysis in code-mixed languages. Exploration of alternative algorithms holds promise for further enhancement. Concerning text categorization and analysis on Twitter, assessing several classifiers for both balanced and unbalanced datasets. On balanced datasets, the ID3 and Naive Byes classifiers demonstrated greater accuracy levels; on unbalanced datasets, K-NN, Decision Tree, Random Forest, and Random Tree outperformed the others. The study emphasises how crucial it is to comprehend the data produced by social media platforms in order to enhance goods, services, and research.

Validating social media content requires sentiment analysis, especially when managing comments in multiple languages. Sripriya and Divya suggests a model that codes input data based on word frequency and applies a multiclass classification algorithm. The model receives an average weighted F1 score of 0.35 from the Dravidian Codemix dataset. Further learning techniques could enhance the functionality of the model.

Multilingual sentiment analysis is critical for recommendation systems, sentiment summarization, and opinion retrieval. Existing solutions include machine translation and bilingual dictionary methods. Thilagavathi and Krishnakumari (2016) employs supervised and unsupervised algorithms as well as Tamil language reviews that have been translated into English. The essay provides a product aspect ranking methodology for identifying essential characteristics from online consumer reviews, increasing usability, and influencing consumer opinions.[2]

3 Problem and System Description

The objective of the sentiment analysis project is to automatically analyse and categorize the sentiment expressed in a given text. The sentiment is classified into categories such as "Positive", "Negative", "Mixed feelings" or "Unknown State". The objective of the research is to use machine learning, namely the Decision Tree approach, to consistently predict the emotion of textual data.

4 Dataset Description

The training dataset comprises 33,989 code-mixed Tamil-English language samples encompassing a wide range of themes, with emotion labels such as Positive, Negative, Mixed Feelings, and Unknown State. X-train-tfdf matrix was created by TF-IDF vectorization of the text data. Achieving 99.97 percent accuracy on the training data, the Decision Tree classifier showed remarkable accuracy. The test dataset comprises 649 samples of code-mixed Tamil-English language. Each sample includes a text segment unseen during training, serving to assess the model's generalization to new data. The dataset includes predicted sentiment labels generated by the trained Decision Tree classifier, indicating the model's predictions for the sentiments expressed in the text segments.[3]

Dataset	No. of Comments
Train	33,989
Validation	3,786
Test	649

Table 1: Dataset Description

5 Predictions on Test Data

Text Segments: There are 649 text segments in the test sample that are code-mixed Tamil and English. Prediction Labels: The trained Decision Tree

[2]Chakravarthi et al. (2020)

[3](heg)

Text	Category
Vera level..Waiting for FDFS	Positive
Do or Die	Negative
it not vijay hair,setup paaa	Mixed feelings
598K left for 15M views	unknown state

Table 2: Text and Category examples

Class	Train	Dev
Positive	15,203	2,257
Negative	3,219	480
Mixed feelings	3,031	438
unknown state	4,242	611

Table 3: Class Description

Flow chart / Work flow

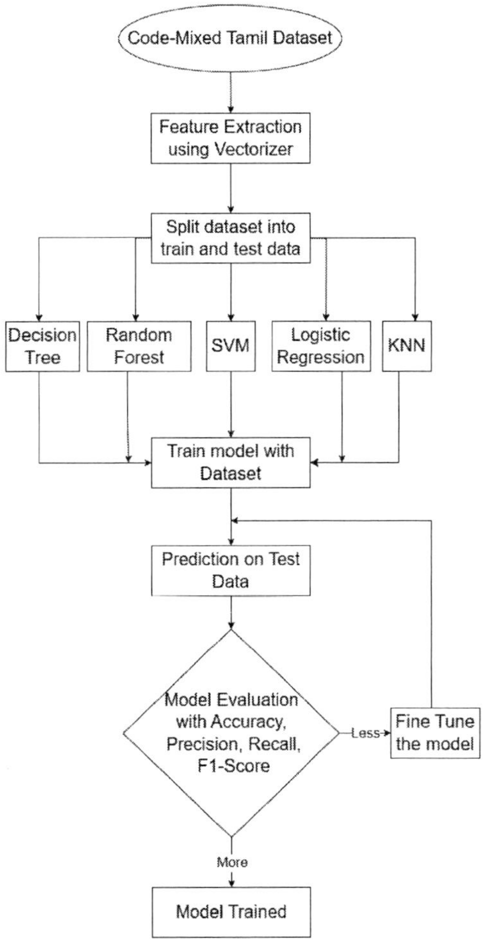

Figure 1: Proposed System Workflow

classifier was used to generate predicted sentiment labels, which classified each text segment into sentiments like Positive, Negative, Mixed Feelings, or

Unknown State. Model Generalisation: The test data predictions show how well the model can use learned patterns to interpret previously read text, providing insight into how well it functions with a range of natural language expressions. Evaluation: To evaluate the model's performance and accuracy on this new, independent dataset, the predicted sentiment labels can be compared with the ground truth labels, if available. Among the criteria considered are the accuracy and macro average F1 score of a model, which are two important markers of its efficiency. First off, the Decision Tree model has a macro average F1 score of 0.39 and an accuracy of 99.79 percent. Furthermore, with a 99.79 percent accuracy rate, the Random Forest model performs admirably. Its macro average F1 score, 0.35, is a little lower.The Support Vector Machine (SVM) is the next model, with a high macro average F1 score of 0.68 and an amazing accuracy of 78.55 percent.In comparison, the accuracy and macro average F1 score of Logistic Regression are 75.11 percent and 0.62, respectively. Ultimately, the macro average F1 score and accuracy of the K-Nearest Neighbours (KNN) model are 0.26 and 73.11 percent, respectively. The Decision Tree model outperforms the others with an impressive accuracy of 99.79 percent. This demonstrates a robust classification performance, setting it out as the top model in terms accuracy.[4]

6 Conclusion

Result:

Model	Accuracy	F1 Score
Decision Tree	0.99	0.39
Random Forest	0.99	0.35
SVM	0.78	0.68
Logistic Regression	0.75	0.62
KNN	0.73	0.26

Table 4: Accuracy and Macro average F1 Score

In summary, the project's standout feature lies in its adept utilization of the Decision Tree algorithm, showcasing exceptional accuracy in analyzing sentiments across a spectrum of classes. The comprehensive classification report deepens our understanding by emphasizing pivotal metrics like precision, recall, and macro average F1-score, illuminating the model's robust performance. Beyond its proficiency in sentiment analysis, the project serves as a pivotal resource for code-mixed research. The meticulously annotated dataset, marked by high inter-annotator agreement, lays a sturdy groundwork for prospective investigations. Its versatility extends into the exploration of diverse linguistic phenomena in code-mixed Tanglish, underscoring its adaptability and potential impact on linguistic research. While recognizing these strengths, it's imperative to address potential concerns like the risk of overfitting and challenges in generalizing to diverse contexts. These considerations pave the way for continual improvement. Nonetheless, the project's strong foundation, anchored by the Decision Tree algorithm and valuable resources, positions it as a commendable contribution to sentiment analysis in code-mixed languages. Exploring alternative algorithms promises to further elevate its already noteworthy capabilities.

[4]Hegde et al. (2022)

References

Findings of the shared task on sentiment analysis in tamil and tulu code-mixed text.

Arwa Alshamsi, Reem Bayari, and Said Salloum. 2020. Sentiment analysis in english texts. *Advances in Science, Technology and Engineering Systems Journal*, 5(6).

Bharathi Raja Chakravarthi, Vigneshwaran Muralidaran, Ruba Priyadharshini, and John Philip McCrae. 2020. Corpus creation for sentiment analysis in code-mixed Tamil-English text. In *Proceedings of the 1st Joint Workshop on Spoken Language Technologies for Under-resourced languages (SLTU) and Collaboration and Computing for Under-Resourced Languages (CCURL)*, pages 202–210, Marseille, France. European Language Resources association.

M.D. Devika, C. Sunitha, and Amal Ganesh. 2016. Sentiment analysis: A comparative study on different approaches. *Procedia Computer Science*, 87:44–49. Fourth International Conference on Recent Trends in Computer Science Engineering (ICRTCSE 2016).

Vaishali Ganganwar and R Rajalakshmi. 2019. Implicit aspect extraction for sentiment analysis: A survey of recent approaches. *Procedia Computer Science*, 165:485–491.

Asha Hegde, Mudoor Devadas Anusha, Sharal Coelho, Hosahalli Lakshmaiah Shashirekha, and Bharathi Raja Chakravarthi. 2022. Corpus creation for sentiment analysis in code-mixed Tulu text. In *Proceedings of the 1st Annual Meeting of the ELRA/ISCA Special Interest Group on Under-Resourced Languages*, pages 33–40, Marseille, France. European Language Resources Association.

Siru Liu and Jialin Liu. 2021. Public attitudes toward covid-19 vaccines on english-language twitter: A sentiment analysis. *Vaccine*, 39(39):5499–5505.

Kakuthota Rakshitha, H M Ramalingam, M Pavithra, H D Advi, and Maithri Hegde. 2021. Sentimental analysis of indian regional languages on social media. *Global Transitions Proceedings*, 2(2):414–420.

Vidyapiratha Raveendirarasa and C.R.J. Amalraj. 2020. Sentiment analysis of tamil-english code-switched text on social media using sub-word level lstm. In *2020 5th International Conference on Information Technology Research (ICITR)*, pages 1–5.

Lavanya S. K., Asha Hegde, Bharathi Raja Chakravarthi, Hosahalli Lakshmaiah Shashirekha, Rajeswari Natarajan, Sajeetha Thavareesan, Ratnasingam Sakuntharaj, Thenmozhi Durairaj, and Rajkumar Charmathi Kumaresan, Prasanna Kumar. 2024. Overview of Second Shared Task on Sentiment Analysis in Code-mixed Tamil and Tulu. In *Proceedings of the Fourth Workshop on Speech, Vision, and Language Technologies for Dravidian Languages*, Malta. European Chapter of the Association for Computational Linguistics.

Kogilavani Shanmugavadivel, Sai Haritha Sampath, Pramod Nandhakumar, Prasath Mahalingam, Malliga Subramanian, Prasanna Kumar Kumaresan, and Ruba Priyadharshini. 2022. An analysis of machine learning models for sentiment analysis of tamil code-mixed data. *Computer Speech Language*, 76:101407.

N Sripriya and S Divya. Sentiment analysis model for code-mixed tamil language.

R Thilagavathi and Kalyan Krishnakumari. 2016. Tamil english language sentiment analysis system. *International Journal of Engineering Research Technology (IJERT)*, 4:114–118.

IIITDWD-zk@DravidianLangTech-2024: Leveraging the Power of Language Models for Hate Speech Detection in Telugu-English Code-Mixed Text

Zuhair Hasan Shaik[1], **Sai Kartheek Reddy Kasu**[1], **Sunil Saumya**[1], and **Shankar Biradar**[1]
[1]Department of Data Science and Intelligent Systems,
Indian Institute of Information Technology Dharwad, Dharwad, Karnatka, India
(zuhashaik12, saikartheekreddykasu)@gmail.com
(sunil.saumya, shankar)@iiitdwd.ac.in

Abstract

Hateful online content is a growing concern, especially for young people. While social media platforms aim to connect us, they can also become breeding grounds for negativity and harmful language. This study tackles this issue by proposing a novel framework called HOLD-Z, specifically designed to detect hate and offensive comments in Telugu-English code-mixed social media content. HOLD-Z leverages a combination of approaches, including three powerful models: *LSTM* architecture, *Zypher*, and *openchat_3.5*. The study highlights the effectiveness of prompt engineering and Quantized Low-Rank Adaptation (QLoRA) in boosting performance. Notably, HOLD-Z secured the 9th place in the prestigious *HOLD-Telugu DravidianLangTech@EACL-2024* shared task, showcasing its potential for tackling the complexities of hate and offensive comment classification.

1 Introduction

In today's world, nearly everyone possesses a smartphone and easy internet access, making social media an integral part of daily life. Particularly among the youth, there is a keen interest in exploring the latest technologies and an active engagement on social media platforms to connect with diverse individuals and share thoughts. While this connectivity brings numerous positive aspects, such as information exchange and community building, it also introduces challenges. Some individuals exploit social media platforms, asserting their right to freedom of speech, but use it to share private or personal information about others. Moreover, certain users engage in trolling and spread hate on these platforms, revealing the darker side of technology. This misuse presents a significant challenge, especially considering the increasing number of children using the internet and social media, necessitating measures to protect them from harmful and hateful content.

Detecting hate speech online has become a critical but challenging task due to the vast amount of data that requires significant computing power. Furthermore, social media utilizes specific algorithms that identify repeated words in messages, subsequently placing them on the trending list. Unfortunately, this process may lead to the unintentional promotion of controversial content. This rapid spread raises the possibility that hate speech will reach a larger audience and inflict, hurt or offense on those who come across it. One solution to mitigate this issue is the development of machine learning and deep learning-based models capable of effectively detecting hate speech content (Nozza, 2021; Fharook et al.). However, the rising popularity of social media platforms and their expanding user bases have led to the dissemination of content in various languages, often taking the form of script-mixed expressions. Unfortunately, a significant proportion of existing methods are primarily trained to handle monolingual text (Nozza, 2021), neglecting the unique challenges posed by multilingual and code-mixed contexts. There has been only marginal effort directed towards addressing hate speech in low-resource code-mixed text (Biradar et al., 2021; Saumya et al., 2022). Moreover, considering the widespread usage of Dravidian languages across India, it is noteworthy that these languages remain largely unexplored in the context of hate speech detection.

To promote research in this direction, the organisers of *DravidianLangTech-2024*[1] created a shared task for hate speech detection in Telugu-English code-mixed text (B et al., 2024). Our team has participated in the task. We developed three different models, the openchat LLM which achieved a 79% Macro F1 on the validation data, while the Zephyr LLM reached an 80% Macro F1. Additionally, we implemented an LSTM architecture, which yielded

[1]https://sites.google.com/view/dravidianlangtech-2024/?pli=1

Proceedings of the Fourth Workshop on Speech, Vision, and Language Technologies for Dravidian Languages, pages 134–139

a 76% Macro F1 on the validation dataset. However, when applied to the test data, Zephyr achieved a 67.39% Macro F1, and the LSTM model achieved a 65.04% Macro F1.

The remainder of the article is organized as follows: Section 2 furnishes details about the proposed architecture. Subsequently, Section 3 presents the findings from the experiments. Lastly, Section 4 provides the conclusion and outlines future research directions.

2 Methodology

This section provides a comprehensive overview of the proposed HOLD-Z framework. Initially, a brief introduction to the problem statement and dataset is presented. Subsequently, the approaches employed to address this challenge are discussed.

2.1 Task and Data

The proposed work considers data from the *HOLD-Telugu DravidianLangTech@EACL 2024* shared task (Priyadharshini et al., 2023). The shared task organizers released the data in train and test, comprising 4,000 and 500 comments in each stage, respectively. Assuming our training dataset as $D = [s_1, s_2, ..., s_n]$ of length n, where s_1 represents sentence 1, s_2 represents sentence 2 and similarly s_n represents sentence n ($\leq$4000) in our dataset. According to the organizers, the dataset were collected from YouTube comments (B et al., 2024). The objective of the task involves sentence-level classification of each Telugu-English code-mixed social media comment into hate or no-hateful categories. The detailed specifications of the dataset are provided in Table 1.

	Hate	Non-hate	Total
Train	1,939	2,061	4,000
Test	250	250	500

Table 1: Data distribution

Code-mixing presents a unique challenge for our models. While translating directly to English might seem straightforward, it often misses the nuanced meaning. Take the Telugu-English sentence (example from training set) *Students tho adukovtam thappu*, which translates literally to *Playing games with students is wrong*. However, the intended meaning is far deeper: *Playing with students' lives is wrong*. This context-dependence makes accurate identification of hate and offensive comments in code-mixed text a complex task, pushing our models to truly understand the underlying intent.

2.2 Context focused

To understand context, *Model 1* utilizes context-aware embeddings and a multi-layered LSTM network. Embeddings capture contextual information, which is then fed into two bidirectional LSTMs followed by a standard LSTM for deeper context analysis and filtering. This forms the basis for the baseline score. The model architecture consists of an embedding layer, followed by two bidirectional LSTM layers and one standard LSTM layer, all connected to a single-neuron classifier with sigmoid activation for hate/non-hate prediction. Figure 1 showcases the complete pipeline.

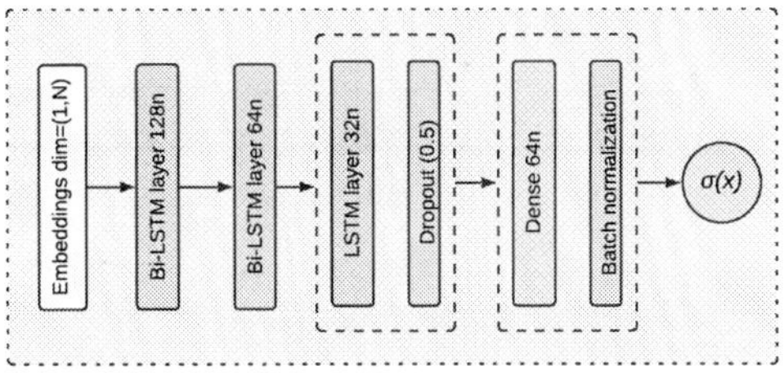

Figure 1: Model 1: Context focused LSTM Network.

We further explored alternative embedding approaches by replacing the initial layer (of *Model 1*) with pre-trained options like BERT(N=768) (Kenton and Toutanova, 2019), Hate-BERT (Tommaso-Caselli and JelenaMitrovic, 2021), mBERT(Kenton and Toutanova, 2019), and OpenAI's ada-embeddings-002 (N=1536) [2]. While the overall architecture remained unchanged, this experiment yielded notable gains in performance on the test data.

2.3 7B-LLMs cluster

Model 2 employs the capabilities of 7B LLMs, recognized for their proficiency in both Telugu and English. These models, with their advanced language processing abilities, can effectively capture the contextual intricacies of sentences, as outlined in the problem statement. Figure 2 presents an architectural overview of the *Model 2*. The implementation utilizes several prominent 7B LLMs, such as *"Llama-2-7b-chat-hf"*, *"Llama-2-13b-chat-hf"* (Touvron et al., 2023), *"Mistral-7B-Instruct-*

[2] https://arxiv.org/abs/2303.08774

v0.1" (Jiang et al., 2023), *"zephyr-7b-beta"* (Tunstall et al., 2023), and *"openchat_3.5"* (Wang et al., 2023).

2.3.1 Prompt engineering

Prompt engineering lies at the heart of successful LLM interaction. Figure 2 illustrates how each input (s_n) is crafted into a precise prompt. Let's dissect an example:

Input: "*Students tho adukovtam thappu*".
The processed prompt (for *Zephyr-7B-beta* LLM) looks something like this:

- System prompt: Defines the LLM's role and expected behavior within the interaction, guiding its response.

  <|*system*|> *You are an expert in sentiment analysis.*

- Hypothesis prompt: Presents a statement and requests the LLM to evaluate its truthfulness, promoting critical thinking.

  <|*hypothesis*|> *The sentence "Students tho adukovtam thappu" contains hateful or offensive content.*

- Assistant prompt: Provides an incomplete statement or scenario, inviting the LLM to complete it creatively, encouraging open-ended generation.

  <|*assistant*|>*The given hypothesis is..*

Each model leverages a specific prompt template for optimal performance. We demonstrate the *Zephyr-7B-beta* template for illustrative purposes. Through rigorous experimentation, we discovered that *openchat_3.5* achieves superior results with the *Zephyr* prompt. Notably, other LLMs utilize their own prompt templates.

2.3.2 Importance of Assistant prompt

The proposed LLM operates as a text completion model. Given an input sentence, it predicts the most likely next word (within its vocabulary) based on softmax probabilities. This predicted word is appended to the input, forming a new input for subsequent predictions. The process iterates until reaching the end-of-sequence (<eos>) token.

Leaving the assistant prompt (*(*<|*assistant*|>*The given hypothesis is..)*) incomplete leads the LLM to predict probabilities for all words in its vocabulary, with a bias towards terms like "True", "False", "right", "wrong", and so on. LLM selects the word with the highest probability as next word. However, we have now refined the output layer to solely consider two options: 0 (False hypothesis) or 1 (True hypothesis). This simplifies the LLM's learning process and facilitates a more definitive answer.

2.3.3 Fine Tuning with QLoRA

Given the constraints of catastrophic forgetting and computational limitations, we are unable to conduct the complete training of LLM's (7B's). Instead, we have chosen Quantized Low-Rank Adaptation (QLoRA). This approach involves quantizing the model during inference and subsequently applying LoRA. In LoRA, we freeze the model parameters and add an extra low-rank matrix next to the attention layer weights, instead of training all parameters. This significantly reduces training time and memory needs, while often leading to better performance compared to traditional fine-tuning techniques (Hu et al., 2021).In our case all models are inferred and trained in FP16 (Half-precision, float16). After extensive experiments we identified hyper parameters which worked for the proposed model are mentioned in Table 2. We also trained high-performing models in FP32 (float32), utilizing our substantial RAM and computing capabilities, with the support of 3×32G Nvidia V100 GPU's.

Hyper parameter	Value
Rank (LoRA config)	16
LoRA Alpha (LoRA config)	64
Dropout (LoRA config)	0.1, 0.2
Learning Rate	2×10^{-5}
Learning Rate Scheduler	Constant
adam_beta1	0.9
adam_beta2	0.999
adam_epsilon	1.000×10^{-8}
rms_norm_eps	1.000×10^{-5}

Table 2: Hyper parameters for Training 7B's

3 Results

In this section we give extensive study results conducted on different models and different approaches to the problem statement that involves context focused approach and 7 Billion-parameter models (7B's).

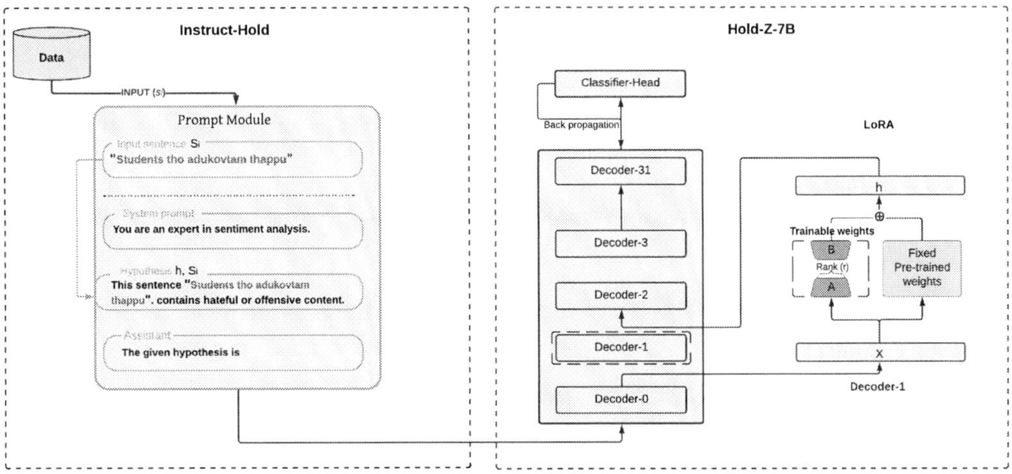

Figure 2: The overview of HOLD-Z framework

3.1 Context Focused approach

In Model 1, our exploration commenced with BERT variants serving as the baseline score. Subsequently, we delved into several cross-lingual pre-trained models to generate embeddings. The experimental findings are illustrated in Table 3. Notably, the Keras embedding layer outperformed all other models according to the results presented in Table 3.

Embedding model	Macro-F1
Keras	68.17
mBERT	60.13
XLM-Roberta	65.46
Telugu-BERT	63.94
Indic-BERT	58.11
OpenAI	64.83

Table 3: Macro-F1 scores with different embedding models

The performance of the Keras model can be attributed to the trainability of the Keras embedding layer. This feature enables the layer to autonomously comprehend and acquire optimal contextual representations for input sentences in code-mixed text. In contrast, the other models rely on pre-trained embeddings. This is the rationale behind our belief that Keras surpassed the performance of all other models.

3.2 7Bb's

In Model 2 (HOLD-Z) , we've conducted experiments with various models, exploring different hyperparameters, including *target_modules*. After examining LoRA configurations, we concluded that including all seven parameters in the *target_modules* along with optimal rank yielded better results. Further, we understand higher the value implies a greater number of trainable parameters and increased computational demands. To address this concern, we settled on the optimal community-consensus value of r=16, and to train all seven prameters in target_modules.
We observed minimal changes when altering dropouts beyond 0.3. Consequently, we focused on experimenting with dropout rates of 0.1 and 0.2, which ultimately led to the best outcomes as illustrated in Table 4 .

Model	D 0.1	D 0.2
Llama-2-7b-chat	43.52	64.95
Mistral-7B-Instruct-v0.1	72.39	72.98
Zephyr-7b-beta	73.98	73.79
openchat_3.5	72.80	74.62
Llama-2-13b-chat	**75.27**	71.94

Table 4: Macro-F1 of LLM's with Dropouts (D) in FP16 QLoRA

3.3 7B's on full precision

Training models with full precision takes a lot of time. Because of this, we set the configurations based on the best models to work around the computational limits. For instance, when we trained QLoRA using FP16, we achieved the best Macro F1 score of 75.27 with llama-2-13b-chat. We then use the same model configurations and train it in FP32 without quantization. Interestingly, the outcomes show a high similarity in model-to-model scores as illustrated in Figure 3.

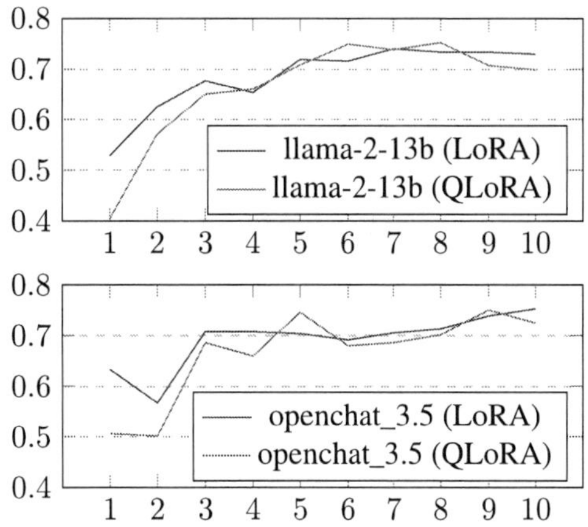

Figure 3: Macro-F1 scores with LoRA vs QLoRA for different LLM's and epochs.

The openchat_3.5 LLM outperformed numerous models and surpassed llama-70b-chat by 8 points in the lmsys-chatbot-arena [3], which is the reasoning behind considering openchat_3.5 in the proposed work. openchat_3.5 proved it self again by outperforming 13b model, and stood top of the board as illustrated in Table 5.

Model	Macro-F1
Llama-2-7b-chat	73.77 (D 0.2)
Mistral-7B-Instruct-v0.1	72.96 (D 0.2)
Zephyr-7b-beta	73.55 (D 0.2)
openchat_3.5	**75.28 (D 0.2)**
Llama-2-13b-chat	73.99 (D 0.1)

Table 5: Macro-F1 of LLM's with FP32 LoRA

4 Conclusion and Future work

In conclusion, our study introduced the HOLD-Z framework for Telugu-English code-mixed social media comments classification. Leveraging context-focused approaches and 7B LLMs, particularly openchat_3.5, proved its effectiveness. The exploration of prompt engineering and fine-tuning with QLoRA demonstrated promising results. The proposed work and model are added to Github[4] and HuggingFace[5] respectively. Future work involves refining model architectures, exploring additional embeddings, and addressing the evolving challenges of code-mixed text classification. The proposed work achieved 9th rank in the *HOLD-Telugu DravidianLangTech@EACL-2024* shared task signifies the potential for further advancements in this domain.

[3]https://huggingface.co/spaces/lmsys/chatbot-arena-leaderboard

[4]https://github.com/Zuhashaik/HOLD-Z

[5]https://huggingface.co/zuhashaik/HOLD-Z/tree/main

References

Premjth B, Bharathi Raja, Prasanna Kumar Kumaresan, Saranya Rajiakodi, Sai Prashanth Karnati, Sai Rishith Reddy Mangamuru, and Janakiram Chandu. 2024. "Findings of the Shared Task on Hate and Offensive Language Detection in Telugu Codemixed Text (HOLD-Telugu)". In *Proceedings of the Fourth Workshop on Speech, Vision, and Language Technologies for Dravidian Languages*, Malta. European Chapter of the Association for Computational Linguistics.

Shankar Biradar, Sunil Saumya, and Arun Chauhan. 2021. mBERT based model for identification of offensive content in south Indian languages.

Shaik Fharook, Syed Sufyan Ahmed, Gurram Rithika, Sumith Sai Budde, Sunil Saumya, and Shankar Biradar. Are you a hero or a villain? A semantic role labelling approach for detecting harmful memes.

Edward J Hu, Yelong Shen, Phillip Wallis, Zeyuan Allen-Zhu, Yuanzhi Li, Shean Wang, Lu Wang, and Weizhu Chen. 2021. Lora: Low-rank adaptation of large language models. *arXiv preprint arXiv:2106.09685*.

Albert Q Jiang, Alexandre Sablayrolles, Arthur Mensch, Chris Bamford, Devendra Singh Chaplot, Diego de las Casas, Florian Bressand, Gianna Lengyel, Guillaume Lample, Lucile Saulnier, et al. 2023. Mistral 7b. *arXiv preprint arXiv:2310.06825*.

Jacob Devlin Ming-Wei Chang Kenton and Lee Kristina Toutanova. 2019. Bert: Pre-training of deep bidirectional transformers for language understanding. In *Proceedings of naacL-HLT*, volume 1, page 2.

Debora Nozza. 2021. Exposing the limits of zero-shot cross-lingual hate speech detection. In *Proceedings of the 59th Annual Meeting of the Association for Computational Linguistics and the 11th International Joint Conference on Natural Language Processing (Volume 2: Short Papers)*, pages 907–914.

Ruba Priyadharshini, Bharathi Raja Chakravarthi, S Malliga, Subalalitha Cn, SV Kogilavani, B Premjith, Abirami Murugappan, and Prasanna Kumar Kumaresan. 2023. Overview of shared-task on abusive comment detection in Tamil and Telugu. In *Proceedings of the Third Workshop on Speech and Language Technologies for Dravidian Languages*, pages 80–87.

Sunil Saumya, Vanshita Jha, and Shankar Biradar. 2022. Sentiment and Homophobia Detection on YouTube using Ensemble Machine Learning Techniques. In *Working Notes of FIRE 2022-Forum for Information Retrieval Evaluation (Hybrid). CEUR*.

ValerioBasile TommasoCaselli and MichaelGranitzer JelenaMitrovic. 2021. HateBERT: Retraining BERT for Abusive Language Detection in English. *WOAH 2021*, page 17.

Hugo Touvron, Louis Martin, Kevin Stone, Peter Albert, Amjad Almahairi, Yasmine Babaei, Nikolay Bashlykov, Soumya Batra, Prajjwal Bhargava, Shruti Bhosale, et al. 2023. Llama 2: Open foundation and fine-tuned chat models. *arXiv preprint arXiv:2307.09288*.

Lewis Tunstall, Edward Beeching, Nathan Lambert, Nazneen Rajani, Kashif Rasul, Younes Belkada, Shengyi Huang, Leandro von Werra, Clémentine Fourrier, Nathan Habib, et al. 2023. Zephyr: Direct distillation of lm alignment. *arXiv preprint arXiv:2310.16944*.

Guan Wang, Sijie Cheng, Xianyuan Zhan, Xiangang Li, Sen Song, and Yang Liu. 2023. Openchat: Advancing open-source language models with mixed-quality data. *arXiv preprint arXiv:2309.11235*.

DLRG-DravidianLangTech@EACL2024 : Combating Hate Speech in Telugu Code-mixed Text on Social Media

Ratnavel Rajalakshmi, Saptharishee M, Hareesh Teja S, Gabriel Joshua R, and **Varsini SR**

School of Computer Science and Engineering
Vellore Institute of Technology, Chennai
Tamil Nadu, India
rajalakshmi.r@vit.ac.in

Abstract

Detecting hate speech in code-mixed language is vital for a secure online space, curbing harmful content, promoting inclusive communication, and safeguarding users from discrimination. Despite the linguistic complexities of code-mixed languages, this study explores diverse pre-processing methods. It finds that the Transliteration method excels in handling linguistic variations. The research comprehensively investigates machine learning and deep learning approaches, namely Logistic Regression and Bi-directional Gated Recurrent Unit (Bi-GRU) models. These models achieved F1 scores of 0.68 and 0.70, respectively, contributing to ongoing efforts to combat hate speech in code-mixed languages and offering valuable insights for future research in this critical domain.

1 Introduction

The surge in hateful speech online challenges maintaining respectful discourse. Hate speech, involving hostility or discrimination, has profound implications for social harmony. Digital platforms invest heavily in hate detection models to automate content flagging and removal, aiming to curb its spread. Addressing hate speech in Telugu code-mixed language is a growing concern due to the rapid adoption of digital platforms by the Indian population.

Automating hate speech detection is feasible for widely adopted languages like English, with ample models and labeled data. However, applying the same processes to niche languages like Telugu, Tamil, Malayalam, etc., remains unexplored due to complexities and nuances, making it a more expensive endeavor. The demand for automated hate speech detection in code-mix languages is underscored by the infeasibility of the conventional manual review approach for low-resourced languages in handling the vast amount of digital data.

In this study, two distinct models, the Bi-GRU and Logistic Regression, were carefully chosen to address the complexities of hate speech detection in code-mixed Telugu language. The Bi-GRU, a deep learning model, excels in capturing intricate contextual relationships, leveraging its ability to analyze sequences of data bidirectionally. This is particularly advantageous for understanding the nuanced linguistic structures present in code-mixed languages. On the other hand, Logistic Regression, a machine learning model, proves efficient in utilizing linguistic features, word embeddings, and statistical patterns. These models aims to harness the strengths of both paradigms, allowing for a comprehensive and nuanced approach to hate speech classification. These techniques reflects a thoughtful strategy to effectively tackle the multifaceted nature of hate speech detection in Telugu code-mixed languages in social media.

2 Related Works

Dealing with challenges in low-resource languages such as Dravidian languages involves addressing class imbalances as a major concern. These challenges were addressed by generating synthetic data through paraphrasing, utilizing the PEGASUS fine-tuned model, and employing backtranslation with the M2M100 neural machine translation model (Ganganwar and Rajalakshmi, 2023). A study on part-of-speech (POS) tagging for code-mixed English-Telugu social media text tackled challenges in combining elements from different languages. Classifiers like Linear SVMs, CRFs, and Multinomial Bayes, with varied feature combinations, were evaluated. CRF outperformed SVMs and Bayes classifiers in this context (Nelakuditi et al., 2018).

Hate speech and offensive content detection in Malayalam and Tamil code-mixed text used the

Proceedings of the Fourth Workshop on Speech, Vision, and Language Technologies for Dravidian Languages, pages 140–145
March 22, 2024 ©2024 Association for Computational Linguistics

HASOC-FIRE 2021 dataset. The MuRIL model achieved the best performance with a weighted F1-score of 0.636 for Tamil and 0.734 for Malayalam (Bhawal et al., 2022). Advanced multilingual Transformer models, adopting a unique fine-tuning approach with learning rate scheduling based on macro F1-scores (Ghosh Roy et al., 2021), have shown success in identifying hate speech. The mBERT-GRU framework for hate speech detection in multilingual societies outperforms monolingual and state-of-the-art methods (Singh et al., 2023).

The rise of hate speech on social media calls for automated detection using NLP models. Integrating convolutional and recurrent layers yields 77.16% accuracy in identifying hate speech (Shubhang et al., 2023). Multinomial Logistic Regression for hate speech on Twitter achieves an average precision of 80.02%, recall of 82%, and accuracy of 87.68% (Br Ginting et al., 2019). Hate speech detection in Bengali comments, with a dataset of 7,425 comments, successfully addresses challenges. The attention mechanism surpasses other algorithms with 77% accuracy (Das et al., 2021). The exploration of abusive comment detection within the Tamil+English dataset involved the utilization of Random Forest, resulting in a weighted average F1-score of 0.78 (Rajalakshmi et al., 2022).

The Random Forest Classifier exhibited a notable performance in the Hate Speech and Offensive Content Identification in Marathi and Hindi tweet datasets by achieving a macro F1 score of 75.19% and 73.12% (Rajalakshmi et al., 2021). Earlier study (Rajalakshmi, 2014) explored term weighting methods aimed at selecting pertinent URL features and assessing their influence on the effectiveness of URL classification, extending beyond the realm of text classification . In the domain of multilingual social media content, a novel relevance-based metric was introduced through the application of a statistics-based approach, facilitating the swift processing of multilingual queries (Rajalakshmi and Agrawal, 2017). As a progressive phase in social media data analysis, multimodal face emotion recognition on code-mixed Tamil memes was conducted by applying Convolutional Neural Network (CNN) with an efficiency of 0.3028 (Kannan et al., 2023). For sentiment analysis, various deep learning methods were applied (Sivakumar and Rajalakshmi, 2021, 2022). In Tamil hate and offensive content identification, the role of stemming and stop words were analysed in (Rajalakshmi et al., 2023)

3 Methodology

3.1 Data Overview

The dataset used in this study is a part of the shared task (B et al., 2024) in Codalab (`https://codalab.lisn.upsaclay.fr/competitions/16095`). The task given was to identify hate content in Telugu code-mixed text (Priyadharshini et al., 2023). The dataset has training and testing sets, comprising of 4000 and 500 entries respectively. The composition of data is shown in Table 1. The near-equal distribution of labels minimises sampling biases, enhancing the reliability of the subsequent analysis.

Data	Hate	Non-Hate
Training data	2,061	1,939
Testing Data	250	250

Table 1: Dataset Statistics

3.2 Data Pre-processing

Text pre-processing in Telugu code-mixed comments is crucial for enhancing model performance, addressing language variations, removing noise, and ensuring consistency for accurate analysis. The process begins with comment cleaning by removing unnecessary white spaces and lines. AI4Bharat Indic-Transliteration (Madhani, 2022) was employed for transliteration, converting text from one script to another without focusing on meaning of the translation. Transliteration aids hate speech identification in code-mixed Telugu on social media by converting mixed-script content to a uniform script. This process ensures consistent language representation, facilitating more effective and accurate detection of offensive language patterns. Post-transliteration, additional cleaning removes non-alphanumeric characters, and the text is converted to lowercase for uniformity. Tokenization using the Natural Language Toolkit (NLTK) follows standardized text processing. For machine learning models, Term Frequency-Inverse Document Frequency (TF-IDF) vectorizer extracts features, while deep learning models utilize tokenization and sequence padding to ensure consistent input sequence lengths.

3.3 Model Building

In this study, two different classification algorithms have been applied and the details are presented below.

3.3.1 Logistic Regression

Logistic regression is a common statistical classifier for binary classification tasks, utilizing a sigmoid function to transform the linear combination of input features. This mapping, ranging between 0 and 1, represents the probability of an instance belonging to the positive class. Default parameters, including L2 regularization (C = 1.0) to prevent over-fitting and the 'lbfgs' solver, were employed for hate speech classification. These defaults strike a balanced trade-off between model complexity and generalization, suitable for small to medium-sized datasets in logistic regression tasks.

The logistic regressor is represented as –

$$P(y = 1) = \frac{1}{1 + e^{-(w_1 x_1 + w_2 x_2 + \ldots + w_n x_n + c)}} \quad (1)$$

where $P(y = 1)$ is the probability of the instance belonging to the positive class, $x_1, \ldots, x_n$ are the input features, $w_1, \ldots, w_n$ are the weights assigned to each feature, and c is the bias.

3.3.2 Bidirectional Gated Recurrent Unit (Bi-GRU)

Bi-GRU, a variant of RNNs, uses gating mechanisms to control information flow. With two gates (update and reset) capturing contextual information bidirectionally, it enhances understanding of sequential dependencies. This bidirectional nature improves classification accuracy and overall performance by enabling the model to grasp nuanced relationships within the text.

The architecture of Double cell Bi-GRU model has an input layer which processes a 71-feature sequence vector, followed by an embedding layer. Two Bi-GRU layers with 128 and 64 neurons capture intricate patterns. Three dense layers use ReLU activation (64 and 32 neurons), and the final output layer employs sigmoid activation. The model uses the Adam optimizer with default settings, binary cross-entropy loss function, and trains for 5 epochs with a batch size of 32. This design ensures effective learning while maintaining computational efficiency in the Bi-GRU model.

4 Results and Discussion

Both proposed models for the classification task were studied and the results are discussed below. From Table 2, we can observe that Bi-GRU outperforms Logistic Regression in training accuracy (99.6% vs. 92.9%), indicating superior fitting to the training data. However, during testing, Bi-GRU's accuracy (69.4%) only slightly surpasses Logistic Regression (68.2%). Despite significantly lower training loss for Bi-GRU (0.014) compared to Logistic Regression (0.418), its testing loss (1.143) is higher than Logistic Regression (0.612), suggesting potential over-fitting. In summary, while Bi-GRU excels in training accuracy and loss, both models exhibit similar testing accuracy, with Logistic Regression demonstrating slightly better generalization performance.

Model	**Bi-GRU**	**Logistic Regression**
Training Accuracy	0.996	0.929
Testing Accuracy	0.694	0.682
Training Loss	0.014	0.418
Testing Loss	1.143	0.612

Table 2: Comparison of Performance

Class	**Precision**	**Recall**	**F1-Score**
Hate	0.68	0.70	0.69
Non-hate	0.69	0.67	0.68
Accuracy			0.68
Macro Avg	0.68	0.68	0.68
Weighted Avg	0.68	0.68	0.68

Table 3: Logistic Regression Classification Report

The classification report of models are shown in Table 3 and Table 4. The Bi-GRU model outperforms logistic regression. Logistic regression achieves balanced precision (0.68) and recall (0.70 for hate, 0.67 for non-hate) with F1-scores of 0.69 and 0.68, and contributing to an overall accuracy of 0.68. In comparison, Bi-GRU excels with precision (0.68 for hate, 0.71 for non-hate) and a high recall of 0.74 for hate. F1-scores for "Hate" and "Non-hate" are 0.71 and 0.68, respectively, culminating in an overall accuracy of 0.70, highlighting the model's performance across both classes.

Class	Precision	Recall	F1-Score
Hate	0.68	0.74	0.71
Non-hate	0.71	0.65	0.68
Accuracy			0.70
Macro Avg	0.70	0.70	0.70
Weighted Avg	0.70	0.70	0.70

Table 4: Bi-GRU Classification Performance

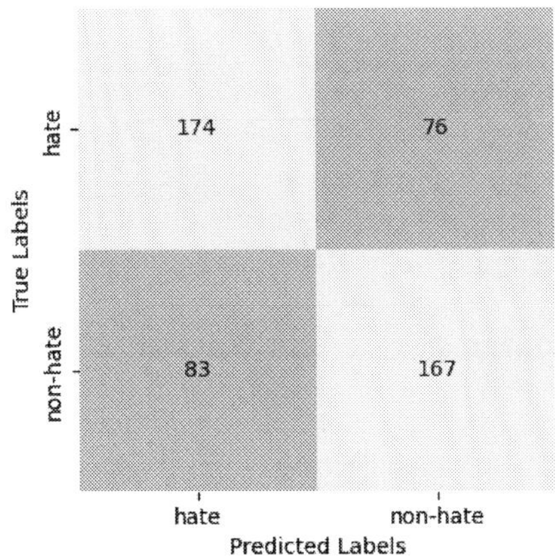

Figure 1: Logistic Regression Model - Confusion Matrix

The confusion matrix of Logistic regression and Bi-GRU are illustrated in Fig. 1 and Fig. 2. In Bi-GRU, 185 out of 250 hate comments were correctly classified, compared to 174 by Logistic Regression. For non-hate comments, Logistic Regression accurately classified 167, while bi-GRU correctly classified 163 out of 250. Although misclassifications are limited in both models, fine-tuning could further enhance performance.

A Receiver Operating Characteristic (ROC) plots visually showcase a binary classification model's ability to distinguish between classes across various threshold values. Fig. 3 and Fig. 4 depict the trade-off between sensitivity and specificity for logistic and Bi-GRU models. A curve closer to the top-left corner indicates superior discrimination compared to random chance (diagonal line). The Area Under the Curve (AUC) summarizes overall performance, and a higher AUC reflects better discrimination for both models in the hate speech detection task.

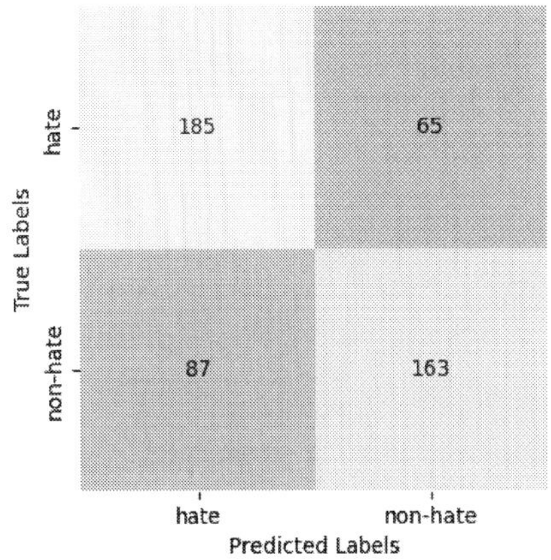

Figure 2: Bi-GRU Model - Confusion Matrix

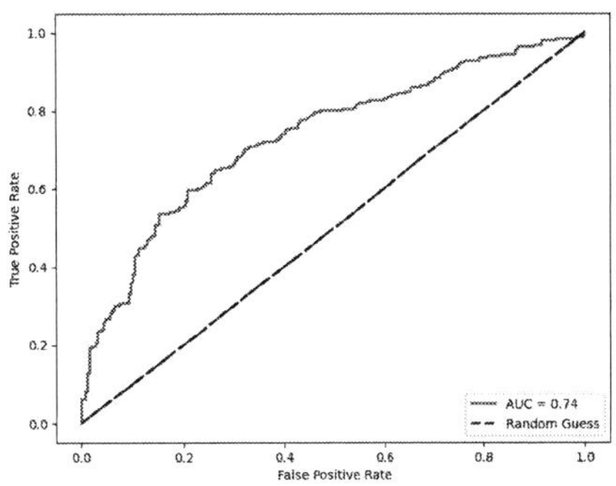

Figure 3: Logistic Regression - ROC Curve

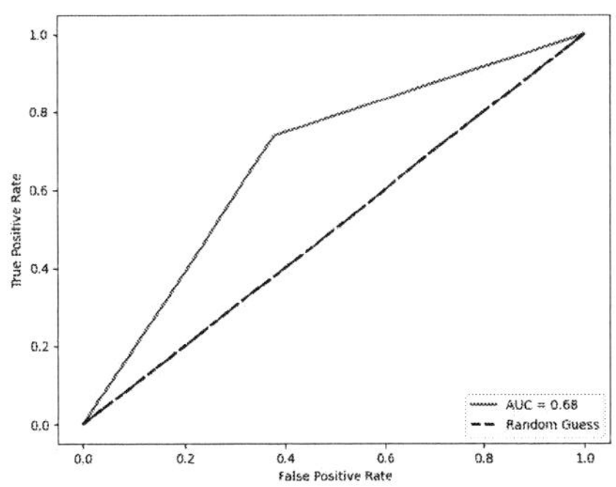

Figure 4: Bi-GRU - ROC Curve

Reduction in accuracy observed with incorporating regularization and dropout methods can be attributed to the dataset's limited size, leading to under-fitting. With a small dataset, regularization may hinder model complexity, exacerbating under-fitting issues. To enhance accuracy, the pragmatic approach involves adding more layers, compromising on simplicity but addressing the under-fitting challenge. The paper's suggestion of regularization methods aligns with the need for improved model generalization, yet the dataset's size necessitates a nuanced trade-off, favoring increased model complexity for enhanced performance on the limited training data.

Name	Score	Rank
Sandalphon	0.7711	1
Selam	0.7711	1
Kubapok	0.7431	3
DLRG1	0.7101	4
DLRG	0.7041	5
CUET_Binary_Hackers	0.7013	6
CUET_OpenNLP_HOLD	0.6878	7
Zavira	0.6819	8
IIITDWD-zk_lstm	0.6739	9
lemlem - Moein Tash	0.6708	10

Table 5: Ranklist of HOLD-Telugu

The outcomes of the Hate and Offensive Language Detection in Telugu code-mixed Text (HOLD-Telugu) Shared task of Codalab competition are presented in Table 5. Our proposed model achieved the 5th position, demonstrating exceptional performance attributed to its effective handling of code-mixed Telugu through transliteration. This critical step involved in mitigating variation in code-mixed text significantly contributed to the model's success. Furthermore, the employed methods, logistic regression along with word embedding, and Bi-GRU bidirectional sequence analysis, have proven to be effective in handling code-mixed Telugu language and accurately classifying them. Therefore, the ultimate goal of detecting and eliminating hate speech from social media, contributing to building a safe and inclusive digital society, has been achieved.

Future work involves expanding data collection across diverse platforms and regions to enhance dataset representativeness. Employing data augmentation techniques, such as oversampling and synthetic data generation, will address class imbalances. Implementing a data curation strategy is crucial to mitigate biases and ensure ethically sound models. Exploring alternative deep learning architectures aims to enhance overall model performance. Additionally, integration of the model into real-time systems on social media platforms will enable swift intervention against hate speech, contributing to a safer online environment.

5 Conclusion

Classifying code-mixed, low-resource Dravidian languages like Telugu in social media is challenging due to the availability of limited labeled data, diverse language variations, and informal expressions. Ambiguous language use and the absence of standardized resources make building effective models difficult, requiring tailored approaches for accurate sentiment and content analysis. Logistic regression and Bi-GRU for Telugu code-mix hate classification effectively capture complex patterns, enhancing contextual understanding for nuanced hate speech detection in Telugu code-mix. Refining fine-tuning and pre-processing techniques can further improve model efficacy.

Limitations

Despite the valuable insights provided by the dataset, its small size may limit the model's representation of online discourse, potentially impacting overall robustness. The presence of potential class imbalances within specific hate speech types could hinder accuracy, and inherent biases in the data based on social and cultural perspectives might result in unfair detection. The constrained model architecture may benefit from exploration of advanced approaches tailored for code-mixed languages. Transliteration errors introduced by IndicXlit-AI4Bharath further challenge the model's understanding of Telugu nuances. Additionally, relying solely on individual comments disregards surrounding context, affecting sarcasm and irony detection. This section underscores the need for continued research to address these limitations and advance the model's effectiveness in diverse linguistic and contextual scenarios.

Ethics Statement

This study on hate speech detection in code-mixed languages aligns with ACL's Ethics Policy, upholding principles of integrity and responsibility. We emphasize the significance of fostering a secure online environment and mitigating harmful content. Adhering to ethical considerations, we explore diverse pre-processing methods, identifying the Transliteration approach as effective in handling linguistic complexities. Our research delves into machine learning methods, presenting Logistic Regression and Bi-GRU models with F1 scores of 0.68 and 0.70. The ethical impact of our work is acknowledged, and we encourage further discourse on its societal implications. This statement, post-conclusion, reflects our commitment to transparency and responsible research, contributing to ethical standards in scientific inquiry.

References

Premjth B, Bharathi Raja, Prasanna Kumar Kumaresan, Saranya Rajiakodi, Sai Prashanth Karnati, Sai Rishith Reddy Mangamuru, and Janakiram Chandu. 2024. Findings of the shared task on Hate and Offensive Language Detection in Telugu code-mixed text (HOLD-Telugu).

Snehaan Bhawal, Pradeep Roy, and Abhinav Kumar. 2022. Hate speech and offensive language identification on multilingual code-mixed text using BERT.

P. S. Br Ginting, B. Irawan, and C. Setianingsih. 2019. Hate speech detection on twitter using multinomial logistic regression classification method. pages 105–111.

A. Das, A. Al Asif, A. Paul, and M. Hossain. 2021. Bangla hate speech detection on social media using attention-based recurrent neural network. *Journal of Intelligent Systems*, 30(1):578–591.

V. Ganganwar and R. Rajalakshmi. 2023. Employing synthetic data for addressing the class imbalance in aspect-based sentiment classification. *Journal of Information and Telecommunication*, pages 1–22.

S. Ghosh Roy, U. Narayan, T. Raha, Z. Abid, and V. Varma. 2021. Leveraging multilingual transformers for hate speech detection. *ArXiv*.

R. R. Kannan, M. Ravikiran, and R. Rajalakshmi. 2023. MMOD-Meme: A dataset for multimodal face emotion recognition on code-mixed Tamil memes. *Communications in Computer and Information Science*, pages 335–345.

Y. Madhani. 2022. Aksharantar: Open Indic-language transliteration datasets and models for the next billion users. *arXiv.org*.

K. Nelakuditi, D. S. Jitta, and R. Mamidi. 2018. Part-of-speech tagging for code-mixed english-telugu social media data. 9623:578–591.

Ruba Priyadharshini, Bharathi Raja Chakravarthi, Malliga S, SUBALALITHA CN, Kogilavani SV, Premjith B, Abirami Murugappan, and Prasanna Kumar Kumaresan. 2023. Overview of Shared-Task on Abusive Comment Detection in Tamil and Telugu.

R. Rajalakshmi. 2014. Supervised term weighting methods for URL classification. *Journal of Computer Science*, 10(10):1969–1976.

R. Rajalakshmi and R. Agrawal. 2017. Borrowing likeliness ranking based on relevance factor.

R. Rajalakshmi, A. Duraphe, and A. Shibani. 2022. DLRG@DravidianLangTech@2022: Abusive comment detection in Tamil using multilingual transformer models. In *Proceedings of the Second Workshop on Speech and Language Technologies for Dravidian Languages*.

R. Rajalakshmi, F. Mattins, S. Srivarshan, P. Reddy, and M. A. Kumar. 2021. Hate speech and offensive content identification in Hindi and Marathi language tweets using ensemble techniques. *Fire*.

R. Rajalakshmi, S. Selvaraj, F. M. R., P. Vasudevan, and A. K. M. 2023. Hottest: Hate and offensive content identification in tamil using transformers and enhanced stemming. *Computer Speech & Language*, 78:101464.

S. Shubhang, S. Kumar, U. Jindal, A. Kumar, and N. R. Roy. 2023. Identification of hate speech and offensive content using BI-GRU-LSTM-CNN Model. pages 536–541.

P. Singh, N. Singh, and S. Chand. 2023. mbert-gru multilingual deep learning framework for hate speech detection in social media. *Journal of Intelligent and Fuzzy Systems*, 44(5):8177–8192.

S. Sivakumar and R. Rajalakshmi. 2021. Self-attention based sentiment analysis with effective embedding techniques. *International Journal of Computer Applications in Technology*, 65(1):65.

S. Sivakumar and R. Rajalakshmi. 2022. Context-aware sentiment analysis with attention-enhanced features from bidirectional transformers. *Social Network Analysis and Mining*, 12(1).

MIT-KEC-NLP@DravidianLangTech-EACL 2024: Offensive Content Detection in Kannada and Kannada-English Mixed Text Using Deep Learning Techniques

Kogilavani Shanmugavadivel[1], **Sowbarnigaa K S**[1], **Mehal Sakthi M S**[1], **Subhadevi K**[1], **Malliga Subramanian**[1]
Department of AI, Kongu Engineering College, Perundurai, Erode.
{kogilavani.sv, mallinishanth72}@gmail.com
{sowbarnigaak, mehalsakthi}@gmail.com
{subhadevik.22aid}@kongu.edu

Abstract

This study presents a strong methodology for detecting offensive content in multilingual text, with a focus on Kannada and Kannada-English mixed comments. The first step in data preprocessing is to work with a dataset containing Kannada comments, which is backed by Google Translate for Kannada-English translation. Following tokenization and sequence labeling, BIO tags are assigned to indicate the existence and bounds of objectionable spans within the text. On annotated data, a Bidirectional LSTM neural network model is trained and BiLSTM model's macro F1 score is 61.0 in recognizing objectionable content. Data preparation, model architecture definition, and iterative training with Kannada and Kannada-English text are all part of the training process. In a fresh dataset, the trained model accurately predicts offensive spans, emphasizing comments in the aforementioned languages. Predictions that have been recorded and include offensive span indices are organized into a database.

Keywords: Offensive Content Detection, Deep Learning, Bidirectional Long Short-Term Memory(BiLSTM), Natural Language Processing(NLP), (B stands for Beginning, I for Inside, and O for Outside)BIO Tagging.

1 Introduction

The research focused on comments that were combined Kannada and English in order to investigate language processing processes for identifying unacceptable content in multilingual situations. In the first phase, which was called Data Preparation, a rich set of unacceptable spans in Kannada comments were chosen. Subsequently, the dataset was transformed and transliterated by Google Translate, facilitating an extensive examination of patterns in the usage of foul language.

During the labeling process, text was separated into tokens, such as words or subwords, using sequencing and tokenization. The offensive spans were classified as Beginning (B), Inside (I), or Outside (O) by the innovative BIO Tagging approach. This made it possible to assess the offensive context inside the language context more precisely.

A Bidirectional Long Short-Term Memory (BiLSTM) neural network was employed in this study to detect objectionable content in comments that were written in both Kannada and English. By addressing code-mixed text and distinct linguistic patterns, the natural language processing approach improved the detection of such information in a range of linguistic situations.

The research was focused on identifying incorrect information within mixed Kannada and Kannada-English comments, which contributed to the growing interest in Dravidian languages. It recognized the value of applying specialist techniques to successfully negotiate the nuances of diverse linguistic contexts. Using keywords and knowledge from earlier research, the goal was to make NLP applications more inclusive and culturally sensitive.

After training was finished, the computer confidently moved on to new datasets, tokenizing text and correctly identifying problematic spans. This step focused on the concept's adaptability and generalizability to different language situations. The model's work was arranged into a TSV file at the Export Results phase, signifying the conclusion of the ground-breaking inquiry. The offensive content that was discovered required more examination and in-depth analysis, which was made possible by these forecasts that included offensive span indices.

This study addresses the problem of multilingualism in natural language processing by providing a systematic way to find offensive gaps in comments. It combined state-of-the-art technology with a flow diagram that offered insights and strategies for overcoming language obstacles in order to lower language barriers and promote safety and inclusivity in the online environment.

Proceedings of the Fourth Workshop on Speech, Vision, and Language Technologies for Dravidian Languages, pages 146–150
March 22, 2024

2 Related Works

The multilingual analysis was development (Rajalakshmi et al., 2021) of a Transformer-based technique for identifying inappropriate language in code-mixed Tamil text. However, (Arivazhagan et al., 2020) concentrated on Named Entity Recognition (NER) in Tamil, demonstrating the variety of NLP applications in this language.Further, (Srinivasagan et al., 2014) translation explored sentiment analysis in Tamil using deep learning approaches.

Along with Tamil, there have been significant efforts done in Kannada language processing. Kannada text summarization challenges were the primary focus (Jk and Nn, 2015) , (R et al., 2019) concentrated on Kannada part-of-speech tagging, highlighting the diverse range of Kannada natural language processing (NLP) problems.

Morphological study and applications of Tamil text (Rekha et al., 2010). Additionally, in 2019 (B. et al., 2019) a deep learning-based machine translation system for the English language was developed for the Indian language (Amarappa and Sathyanarayana, 2015) a multinomial Naïve Bayes (MNB) classifier was used for the Kannada Named Entity Recognition and Classification (NERC). In 2019 (Shah and Bakrola, 2019) Indo-European Neural Machine Translation System. Moreover, using Tamil tweets, (Ramanathan et al., 2019) predicted the sentimental reviews of Tamil movies.

These initiatives shows the increasing interest in and need for Dravidian language-specific methodologies. For effective NLP applications, customized methods are needed due to the challenges inherent in these languages, such as code-mixed text and unique linguistic structures.

3 Problem and System Description

The dataset was shown in Table 1. The objective was to determine, given the supplied text, the range of spans that related to offending material. In the sample, the text "Tik tok Shata adds to offensiveness" matched a character offset between 8 and 13. As part of the shared effort on offensive span identification, the details of an offensive span annotation dataset were made available [1].

3.1 Dataset Description

One file had span annotations, while the other contained a shared task dataset that was open to the public. There were 444 unannotated cases in the testing dataset and 1800 offensive span samples in the training dataset.

Sample Text	Spans
Tik tok shata	[8,9,10,11,12,13]
Ade old same story	[0,1,2,3,4,5,6,7]
Bindu gowda lofer avlu	[12,13,14,15,16,17,18]
Eppa all fake	[5,6,7,8,9,10,11,12,13]

Table 1: Example of the dataset

4 Development Pipeline

The proposed system pipeline employed in this study was shown in Figure 1. Our pipeline consisted of four modules: (a) preparation of the data; (b) tokenization and sequence labeling; (c) training of the model; and (d) predictions on test data. After that, the predictions were exported and stored in a TSV file. This description was correct in every way.

4.1 Data Preparation Phase

Standardizing a group of unwanted spans in Kannada remarks was the main objective of the project's data preparation. Standardizing the offensive span annotations required pre-processing in order to give consistency for further analysis. The code sample demonstrated a practical technique for managing and enhancing the raw dataset, laying the groundwork for language normalization. With the use of language recognition and translation algorithms, the project attempted to give a consistent representation of text data, especially when converting Kannada comments into English. This stage was important because it laid the groundwork for an offensive span identification strategy that was both coherent and linguistically consistent. Making the dataset more appropriate for additional machine learning model training and evaluation was the ultimate goal.

4.2 Tokenization and Sequence Labeling

In order to assess Kannada comments with problematic spans during the Tokenization and Sequence Labeling step, the project employs a thorough technique. Two objectives are involved: first, tokenizc thc tcxt into meaningful units like as words or subwords; second, assign a BIO tag to each token designating where it falls within the offensive spans (B stands for Beginning, I for Inside,

[1](Ravikiran et al., 2022)

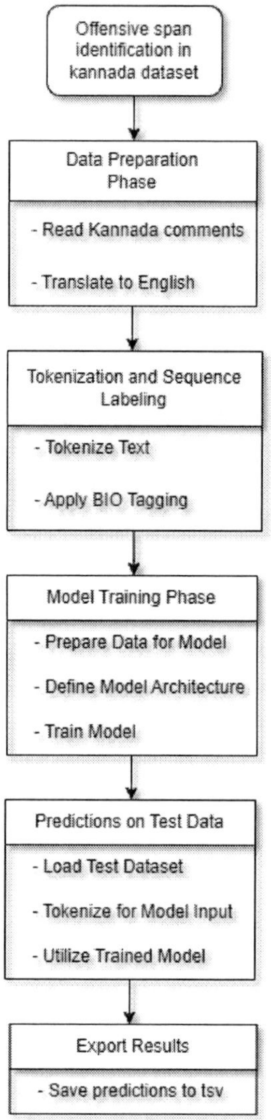

Figure 1: Proposed system pipeline

and O for Outside). This step involves creating a meticulously planned Python script that uses a bespoke function to carry out the BIO tagging strategy and the NLTK package for word tokenization. Using the dataset, the code functions flawlessly, guaranteeing that every token is categorized correctly based on how close it is to potentially dangerous text spans. This initial stage, which enables the creation of annotated papers, is essential for later phases.

4.3 Model Training phase

During the Model Training Phase, the project moves forward from the preliminary stages to the deployment of a Bidirectional Long Short-Term Memory (BiLSTM) neural network with the purpose of detecting offensive spans in Kannada comments. The main goal is to provide a numerical representation of the tokenized text data that can be fed into the model. Using a tokenizer, the textual content is transformed into numerical sequences. For model compatibility, the relevant BIO tags denoting offending span labels are one-hot encoded and encoded. The dataset is cleverly divided into training and testing subsets to facilitate in-depth model evaluation, guaranteeing strong performance on both known and unknown data. The definition of the neural network architecture, which has an embedding layer for word recognition, is crucial to this step.

The significance of this step in the research is that it marks the transition from data preparation to the application of sophisticated neural network architectures for offensive span recognition in Kannada literature. The careful coordination of the tokenizer makes sure that the model absorbs and comprehends the nuances of the language, and the encoding of BIO tags that follows establishes the basis for the neural network's ability to recognize and anticipate problematic spans. With the aid of the previously indicated iterative training technique that makes use of the BiLSTM architecture and fine-tuning parameters in Figure 2, the model is able to capture complex patterns in the Kannada comments dataset. The project's potential impact on multilingual content moderation is highlighted by its alignment with wider objectives and incorporation of deep learning and natural language processing technology.The adaptability of the model architecture makes it a flexible tool for resolving the problems caused by offensive language, enhancing the capacity to identify and reduce instances of hazardous content and promoting a safer online environment.

4.4 Predictions On Test Data

During the Predictions on Test Data phase, the study extends its offensive span identification capabilities to a fresh dataset of Kannada or Kannada-English statements. This step includes loading the test dataset, tokenizing the comments using the pre-established tokenizer, and padding the sequences to the maximum length allowed by the model. The trained BiLSTM model incorporates intricate patterns from the linguistic environment to provide offensive span predictions. In order to identify violating spans, the post-processing stage evaluates the model's predictions; the findings are then recorded in a new column within the test dataset. The project's flexibility in adjusting to new data is highlighted in this phase, showcasing its potential for reliable and sensitive problematic material identification in multilingual settings.

5 Results

The goal of the study was to create a technique for finding unacceptable stretches in multilingual literature by concentrating on mixed Kannada and English comments. Google Translate was used to train a Bidirectional LSTM neural network model for translation, tokenization, and sequence labeling on annotated data. Table 2 displays the BiLSTM model's macro F1 score of 61.0 and accuracy of 0.9759, demonstrating its capacity to identify problematic content. Next, using a Test dataset with an emphasis on multilingual comments, the algorithm predicted problematic spans.

```
Model: "model"
_________________________________________________________________
 Layer (type)                Output Shape              Param #
=================================================================
 input_1 (InputLayer)        [(None, 128)]             0

 embedding (Embedding)       (None, 128, 100)          500000

 dropout (Dropout)           (None, 128, 100)          0

 bidirectional (Bidirection  (None, 128, 256)          234496
 al)

 time_distributed (TimeDist  (None, 128, 3)            771
 ributed)

=================================================================
Total params: 735267 (2.80 MB)
Trainable params: 735267 (2.80 MB)
Non-trainable params: 0 (0.00 Byte)
_________________________________________________________________
```

Figure 2: BiLSTM Model Architecture

E	TL	TA	VL	VA
1	0.2144	94.18	0.0807	96.36
2	0.0763	96.36	0.0786	96.44
3	0.0705	96.73	0.0794	96.22
4	0.0651	97.20	0.0782	96.41
5	0.0594	97.59	0.0779	96.48

Table 2: BiLSTM Model Accuracy

Epoch (E)
Training Loss (TL)
Training Accuracy (TA)
Validation Loss (VL)
Validation Accuracy (VA)

6 Conclusion

A multilingual approach was employed in the study to pinpoint problematic spans in Kannada and Kannada-English literature. The Bidirectional LSTM model's macro F1 score of 61.0 was made possible by extensive pre-processing of the data. Because of its flexibility, the model was able to be used with new datasets to predict offensive spans in situations with a mixture of Kannada and English as well as pure Kannada. An important advancement in natural language processing was made by this work, which tackled the issue of culturally acceptable material filtering in online communication.

References

S. Amarappa and S. Sathyanarayana. 2015. Kannada named entity recognition and classification (nerc) based on multinomial naïve bayes (mnb) classifier. *International Journal on Natural Language Computing*, 4.

Naveen Arivazhagan, Colin Cherry, Wolfgang Macherey, and George Foster. 2020. Re-translation versus streaming for simultaneous translation. In *Proceedings of the 17th International Conference on Spoken Language Translation*, pages 220–227, Online. Association for Computational Linguistics.

Premjith B., M. Kumar, and Soman Kp. 2019. Neural machine translation system for english to indian language translation using mtil parallel corpus: Special issue on natural language processing. *Journal of Intelligent Systems*, 28.

Geetha Jk and Deepamala Nn. 2015. Kannada text summarization using latent semantic analysis. pages 1508–1512.

Swaroop R, Rakshit S, Shriram Hegde, and Sourabh U. 2019. Parts of speech tagging for kannada. pages 28–31.

Ratnavel Rajalakshmi, Yashwant Reddy, and Lokesh Kumar. 2021. DLRG@DravidianLangTech-EACL2021: Transformer based approachfor offensive language identification on code-mixed Tamil. In *Proceedings of the First Workshop on Speech and Language Technologies for Dravidian Languages*, pages 357–362, Kyiv. Association for Computational Linguistics.

Vallikannu Ramanathan, Meyyappan Thirunavukkarasu, and S.M. Thamarai. 2019. Predicting tamil movies sentimental reviews using tamil tweets. *Journal of Computer Science*, 15:1638–1647.

Manikandan Ravikiran, Bharathi Raja Chakravarthi, Anand Kumar Madasamy, Sangeetha Sivanesan, Ratnavel Rajalakshmi, Sajeetha Thavareesan, Rahul Ponnusamy, and Shankar Mahadevan. 2022. Findings of the shared task on Offensive Span Identification in code-mixed Tamil-English comments. In *Proceedings of the Second Workshop on Speech and Language Technologies for Dravidian Languages*. Association for Computational Linguistics.

R. Rekha, M. Kumar, V. Dhanalakshmi, Soman Kp, and Rajendran Sankaravelayuthan. 2010. A novel approach to morphological generator for tamil. pages 249–251.

Parth Shah and Vishvajit Bakrola. 2019. Neural machine translation system of indic languages - an attention based approach. pages 1–5.

K. Srinivasagan, S. Suganthi, and N. Jeyashenbagavalli. 2014. An automated system for tamil named entity recognition using hybrid approach. pages 435–439.

Transformers@DravidianLangTech-EACL2024: Sentiment Analysis of Code-Mixed Tamil Using RoBERTa

Kriti Singhal, Jatin Bedi
Computer Science and Engineering Department
Thapar Institute of Engineering and Technology
kritisinghal711@gmail.com, jatin.bedi@thapar.edu

Abstract

Sentiment analysis has been an active field of research for over 20 years and has gained immense popularity due to its applications in both academia and industry. Sentiment Analysis of code-mixed posts and comments on social media, especially in Dravidian languages, is gaining more and more traction. This paper describes the team Transformers' submission to the Sentiment Analysis in Tamil shared task organized by DravidianLangTech 2024 workshop at EACL 2024. A BERT-based architecture, RoBERTa was used for the shared task. The best macro average F1-score achieved was 0.212. We secured the 5th rank in the Sentiment Analysis shared task in Tamil.

1 Introduction

Sentiment analysis can be defined as the task of classifying text on the basis of the subjective ideas presented in it. The shared task[1] facilitated by DravidianLangTech aimed to identify the sentiment polarity of code-mixed dataset of comments and posts in Tamil-English from various social media platforms (S. K. et al., 2024).

With millions of people across the world gaining access to the internet, freedom of speech and expression now knows no borders. Posts and comments shared on social media platforms like Twitter and YouTube can be accessed by anyone, anywhere in the world, in just a few milliseconds (Shanmugavadivel et al., 2022). The amount of user-generated content available online has set new records. Many scholars have, hence, directed their efforts to identify the sentiments expressed in the content shared online (Yue et al., 2019).

Tamil holds the status of being one of the twenty-two scheduled languages recognized by the Constitution of India (Ghanghor et al., 2021b). Tamil is also is a part of the Dravidian languages' (Chakravarthi and Raja, 2020), dating back over 4500 years. However, Tamil remains under-resourced (Ghanghor et al., 2021a). Most of the resources available for Tamil are code-mixed in nature, i.e., the text comprises of different languages.

Recent advances in the field of Natural Language Processing (NLP) have helped overcome many of the challenges presented by long texts, under-resourced languages and code-mixed data. Some of these include Long Short Term Memory (Hochreiter and Schmidhuber, 1997) and Gated Recurrent Units (Chung et al., 2014). But transformers (Vaswani et al., 2017), have helped researchers reach new heights which was not possible earlier.

In this paper, we discuss our use of a transformer-based model, RoBERTa in the shared task of Sentiment Analysis in Tamil organized by DravidianLangTech at EACL 2024.

2 Related Work

In the past multiple researchers have proposed various approaches for sentiment analysis. Special efforts have been directed towards performing sentiment analysis on code-mixed and under-resourced languages such as Tamil.

Varsha et al. (2022) experimented with different tokenizers on various models, including Random Forest, Support Vector Machine, Adaboost, etc., on Tamil-English, Malayalam-English, and Kannada-English. They also tested how different feature extraction techniques, such as Count Vectorizer, TF-IDF, XLM feature extraction, etc., affected the performance of these models. They found that for Tamil-English data, the Count Vectorizer with the Random Forest model gave the best performance and achieved an F1-score of 0.61.

A 6-layer deep learning model was proposed by Ugursandi and Anand Kumar (2022). The first layer was an embedding layer, which used one-hot

[1] https://codalab.lisn.upsaclay.fr/competitions/16088

Proceedings of the Fourth Workshop on Speech, Vision, and Language Technologies for Dravidian Languages, pages 151–155
March 22, 2024 ©2024 Association for Computational Linguistics

Table 1: Dataset Distribution for Sentiment Analysis Task

Dataset	Label				Total
	Positive	unknown_state	Negative	Mixed_feelings	
Dev	2257	611	480	438	3768
Train	20070	5628	4271	4020	33989

encoding followed by a convolutional layer, which created a new vector over a specific geographic dimension. The third layer was a Max Pooling layer, which returned the maximum values for each feature in the vector returned by the convolutional layer. This was followed by a dropout layer to eliminate the contribution from some of the neurons in the subsequent dense layer.

Three Bidirectional Long Short Term Memory (Bi-LSTM) networks were concatenated together for feature extraction in the approach adopted by Mishra et al. (2021) for sentiment analysis in Dravidian languages. They found that on the Tamil dataset, the performance of the traditional machine learning classifiers was not at par with the deep learning approaches. A hybrid model of word2vec, random word embedding, and random char embeddings with three parallel BiLSTM models gave the best weighted F1 of 0.55.

Jada et al. (2021) used a soft voting approach from the results derived from various transformer models. They used multiple pre-trained models including MuRIL (Khanuja et al., 2021), mBERT (Devlin et al., 2019), DistilmBERT (Sanh et al., 2019) and XLM Roberta (Conneau et al., 2019). After obtaining the prediction from all the models, soft voting was performed by taking the weighted average for each class label and assigning the label with the highest probability. This approach achieved an F1 score of 0.626 on the Tamil text.

3 Dataset Description

The code-mixed Tamil dataset was provided by the organizers of the shared task (Chakravarthi et al., 2020; Hegde et al., 2022, 2023). The train and dev dataset comprised of three columns: id, text, and label. The test set comprised of only columns, i.e., id and text. The distributions of the dev and train datasets have been shown in the table 1.

The labels provided for the text were, 'Positive', 'unknown_state', 'Negative', and 'Mixed_feelings'. These labels were assigned to the text based on the polarity of sentiment expressed in the comment or post.

4 Methodology

Sentiment analysis is a text classification problem. This is one of the most important problems in NLP that researches are working on. Text classification can be described as a task where the given texts need to be categorized based upon context. Sentiment analysis makes use of the sentiment polarity to determine what is the sentiment expressed in a given piece of text.

After concatenating the dev and the train dataset, the procedure shown in 1 was used to fine-tune RoBERTA. Then the fine-tuned RoBERTa was used to classify the sentiment of an unseen text into one of the four possible classes, which are 'Positive', 'unknown_state', 'Negative', and 'Mixed_feelings', as represented in Figure 2.

4.1 Data Preprocessing

The data provided in the dataset had been collected from comments and posts on social media. Naturally, there was use of emojis, numbers, and other special characters. Emojis, numbers, and other special characters usually do not convey much about the sentiment and were hence removed from the text.

Table 1 shows the number of comments or posts for the various classes. It was observed that there was a data imbalance problem in the dataset, i.e., the number of samples for one class was much greater than the number of samples for another class. To tackle the issue of data imbalance, undersampling was performed on the data to randomly select samples from all the classes such that the number of samples for all the classes is same. Since 'Mixed_feelings' has the least number of samples, random sampling was performed on 'Positive', 'unknown_state', and 'Negative' to select samples such that the total number of samples from each class were equal. After performing undersampling, 4458 samples were present for each class in the dataset.

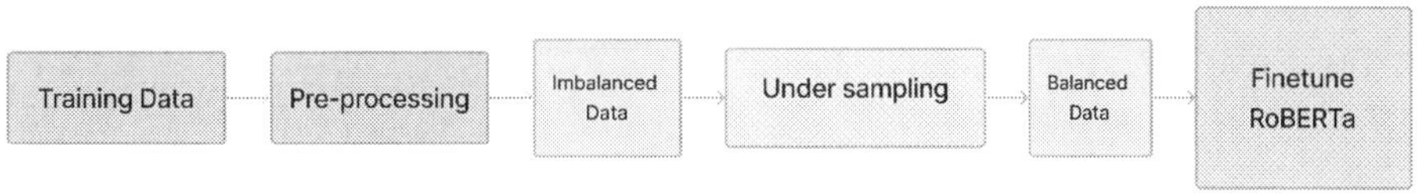

Figure 1: Proposed Methodology

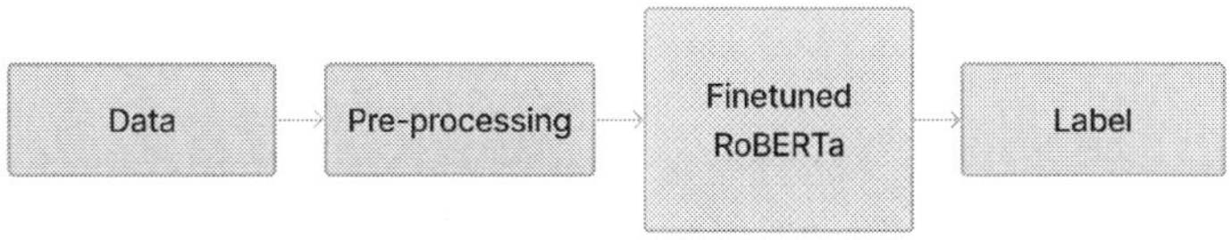

Figure 2: Label Generation for Unseen Data

4.2 Model Building

The XLM RoBERTa model is a transformer model trained using the unsupervised learning approach. It was based on the 2019 RoBERTa architecture by Facebook. This is a large multi-lingual language model that was trained on 2.5TB of data obtained from CommonCrawl after filtering. The model was trained for 100 different languages and then fine-tuned for various downstream tasks like sentiment analysis.

After preprocessing was completed, the text was tokenized using the XLM RoBERTA (Conneau et al., 2019) Tokenizer. The tokenized text was then used to fine-tune an XLM RoBERTA Large model, as shown in Figure 1.

After performing tokenization, the sentences were padded to the maximum length during the encoding procedure, where the maximum length was chosen as 512. Truncation was performed if the length exceeded the maximum limit of 512. The encoded sentences were then passed through the XLM Roberta Large to fine-tune the model. The performance of the model was tested from 5 to 40 epochs while performing hyperparameter tuning. Adam optimizer and cross entropy loss were chosen as the optimizer and the loss function, respectively. The highest performance was achieved at 20 epochs.

After the model was fine-tuned, the unseen or the test data was passed to the model to predict the labels as illustrated in Figure 2.

5 Results and Discussion

A transformer-based approach, XLM RoBERTa was discussed to perform sentiment analysis on code-mixed Tamil posts and comments.

The data imbalance issue was addressed by undersampling the majority class randomly. This was followed by text pre-processing to remove any special symbols, numbers, and emojis. The pre-processed text was used for fine-tuning various transformer based models for performing sentiment analysis.

At 20 epochs, the performance of the XLM RoBERTa model gave the highest F1 score compared to the other transformer-based models. The proposed methodology achieved an F1 score of 0.212.

6 Conclusion and Future Work

Sentiment analysis is the process of classifying text based on the subjective ideas it represents. The shared task by DravidianLangTech at EACL 2024 was focused on finding the sentiment of code-mixed dataset of comments and posts in Tamil-English on different social media platforms.

In this paper, we discussed our use of a BERT-based architecture, XML RoBERTa, in the Sentiment Analysis in Tamil shared task. We achieved a highest F1-score of 0.212 with the discussed approach.

Ensembling techniques using different multilingual transformers such as IndicBert and other deep learning-based techniques may help further improve the performance. Also, since Tamil is an under-resourced language, fine-tuning the model on different datasets may give better results.

References

Asoka Chakravarthi and Bharathi Raja. 2020. *Leveraging orthographic information to improve machine translation of under-resourced languages*. Ph.D. thesis, NUI Galway.

Bharathi Raja Chakravarthi, Vigneshwaran Muralidaran, Ruba Priyadharshini, and John Philip McCrae. 2020. Corpus creation for sentiment analysis in code-mixed Tamil-English text. In *Proceedings of the 1st Joint Workshop on Spoken Language Technologies for Under-resourced languages (SLTU) and Collaboration and Computing for Under-Resourced Languages (CCURL)*, pages 202–210, Marseille, France. European Language Resources association.

Junyoung Chung, Caglar Gulcehre, KyungHyun Cho, and Yoshua Bengio. 2014. Empirical evaluation of gated recurrent neural networks on sequence modeling. *arXiv preprint arXiv:1412.3555*.

Alexis Conneau, Kartikay Khandelwal, Naman Goyal, Vishrav Chaudhary, Guillaume Wenzek, Francisco Guzmán, Edouard Grave, Myle Ott, Luke Zettlemoyer, and Veselin Stoyanov. 2019. Unsupervised cross-lingual representation learning at scale. *arXiv preprint arXiv:1911.02116*.

Jacob Devlin, Ming-Wei Chang, Kenton Lee, and Kristina Toutanova. 2019. BERT: Pre-training of deep bidirectional transformers for language understanding. In *Proceedings of the 2019 Conference of the North American Chapter of the Association for Computational Linguistics: Human Language Technologies, Volume 1 (Long and Short Papers)*, pages 4171–4186, Minneapolis, Minnesota. Association for Computational Linguistics.

Nikhil Ghanghor, Parameswari Krishnamurthy, Sajeetha Thavareesan, Ruba Priyadharshini, and Bharathi Raja Chakravarthi. 2021a. IIITK@DravidianLangTech-EACL2021: Offensive language identification and meme classification in Tamil, Malayalam and Kannada. In *Proceedings of the First Workshop on Speech and Language Technologies for Dravidian Languages*, pages 222–229, Kyiv. Association for Computational Linguistics.

Nikhil Ghanghor, Rahul Ponnusamy, Prasanna Kumar Kumaresan, Ruba Priyadharshini, Sajeetha Thavareesan, and Bharathi Raja Chakravarthi. 2021b. IIITK@LT-EDI-EACL2021: Hope speech detection for equality, diversity, and inclusion in Tamil , Malayalam and English. In *Proceedings of the First Workshop on Language Technology for Equality, Diversity and Inclusion*, pages 197–203, Kyiv. Association for Computational Linguistics.

Asha Hegde, Mudoor Devadas Anusha, Sharal Coelho, Hosahalli Lakshmaiah Shashirekha, and Bharathi Raja Chakravarthi. 2022. Corpus creation for sentiment analysis in code-mixed Tulu text. In *Proceedings of the 1st Annual Meeting of the ELRA/ISCA Special Interest Group on Under-Resourced Languages*, pages 33–40, Marseille, France. European Language Resources Association.

Asha Hegde, Bharathi Raja Chakravarthi, Hosahalli Lakshmaiah Shashirekha, Rahul Ponnusamy, SUBALALITHA CN, Lavanya S K, Thenmozhi D, Martha Karunakar, Shreya Shreeram, and Sarah Aymen. 2023. Findings of the shared task on sentiment analysis in tamil and tulu code-mixed text. In *Proceedings of the Third Workshop on Speech and Language Technologies for Dravidian Languages*, Varna, Bulgaria. Recent Advances in Natural Language Processing.

Sepp Hochreiter and Jürgen Schmidhuber. 1997. Long short-term memory. *Neural computation*, 9(8):1735–1780.

Pawan Kalyan Jada, D Sashidhar Reddy, Konthala Yasaswini, Arunaggiri Pandian K, Prabakaran Chandran, Anbukkarasi Sampath, and Sathiyaraj Thangasamy. 2021. Transformer based sentiment analysis in dravidian languages. In *FIRE (Working Notes)*, pages 926–938.

Simran Khanuja, Diksha Bansal, Sarvesh Mehtani, Savya Khosla, Atreyee Dey, Balaji Gopalan, Dilip Kumar Margam, Pooja Aggarwal, Rajiv Teja Nagipogu, Shachi Dave, Shruti Gupta, Subhash Chandra Bose Gali, Vish Subramanian, and Partha Talukdar. 2021. Muril: Multilingual representations for indian languages.

Ankit Kumar Mishra, Sunil Saumya, and Abhinav Kumar. 2021. Sentiment analysis of dravidian-codemix language. In *Working Notes of FIRE 2021-Forum for Information Retrieval Evaluation (Online). CEUR.*

Lavanya S. K., Asha Hegde, Bharathi Raja Chakravarthi, Hosahalli Lakshmaiah Shashirekha, Rajeswari Natarajan, Sajeetha Thavareesan, Ratnasingam Sakuntharaj, Thenmozhi Durairaj, and Rajkumar Charmathi Kumaresan, Prasanna Kumar. 2024. Overview of Second Shared Task on Sentiment Analysis in Code-mixed Tamil and Tulu. In *Proceedings of the Fourth Workshop on Speech, Vision, and Language Technologies for Dravidian Languages*, Malta. European Chapter of the Association for Computational Linguistics.

Victor Sanh, Lysandre Debut, Julien Chaumond, and Thomas Wolf. 2019. Distilbert, a distilled version of bert: smaller, faster, cheaper and lighter. *arXiv preprint arXiv:1910.01108*.

Kogilavani Shanmugavadivel, Malliga Subramanian, Prasanna Kumar Kumaresan, Bharathi Raja Chakravarthi, B Bharathi, Subalalitha Chinnaudayar Navaneethakrishnan, Lavanya Sambath

Kumar, Thomas Mandl, Rahul Ponnusamy, Vasanth Palanikumar, et al. 2022. Overview of the shared task on sentiment analysis and homophobia detection of youtube comments in code-mixed dravidian languages.

Sushil Ugursandi and M Anand Kumar. 2022. Sentiment analysis and homophobia detection of youtube comments. In *Working Notes of FIRE 2022-Forum for Information Retrieval Evaluation (Hybrid). CEUR*.

Josephine Varsha, B Bharathi, and A Meenakshi. 2022. Sentiment analysis and homophobia detection of youtube comments in code-mixed dravidian languages using machine learning and transformer models. In *Working Notes of FIRE 2022-Forum for Information Retrieval Evaluation (Hybrid). CEUR*.

Ashish Vaswani, Noam Shazeer, Niki Parmar, Jakob Uszkoreit, Llion Jones, Aidan N Gomez, Łukasz Kaiser, and Illia Polosukhin. 2017. Attention is all you need. *Advances in neural information processing systems*, 30.

Lin Yue, Weitong Chen, Xue Li, Wanli Zuo, and Minghao Yin. 2019. A survey of sentiment analysis in social media. *Knowledge and Information Systems*, 60:617–663.

Habesha@DravidianLangTech 2024: Detecting Fake News Detection in Dravidian Languages using Deep Learning

Mesay Gemeda Yigezu, Olga Kolesnikova, Grigori Sidorov and **Alexander Gelbukh**
Instituto Politécnico Nacional (IPN),
Centro de Investigación en Computación (CIC), Mexico City, Mexico
Correspondence:mgemedak2022@cic.ipn.mx

Abstract

This research tackles the issue of fake news by utilizing the RNN-LSTM deep learning method with optimized hyperparameters identified through grid search. The model's performance in multi-label classification is hindered by unbalanced data, despite its success in binary classification. We achieved a score of 0.82 in the binary classification task, whereas in the multi-class task, the score was 0.32. We suggest incorporating data balancing techniques for researchers who aim to further this task, aiming to improve results in managing a variety of information.

1 Introduction

Getting updates about what's happening in the world is important for us. It helps us learn more about the different things going on. Many people like to watch the news or read the newspaper in the morning with a cup of tea to stay informed. Fake news is one of the most significant scourges in our digitally interconnected world. It is broadly defined as a subject encompassing news, data, reports, and information that is either wholly or partially false (Kong et al., 2020).

If the news is not true, it can confuse people and spread false information. Sometimes, fake news is used to create rumors or harm the reputation of political leaders. To tackle this issue, we've suggested a system to identify fake news. However, with the enormous amount of data on the internet and social media, it's challenging to manually check if each piece of news is fake or not (Yigezu et al., 2023e; Bade, 2021).

This pervasive phenomenon acts as a wildfire, influencing countless individuals daily. The reach of fake news is extensive and can pose a significant threat to a nation's security, economy, prosperity, and the well-being of its citizens. Unfortunately, many people may not be fully aware of how profoundly fake news can affect the matters that surround them, and they may lack the necessary skills to discern and handle such situations when they arise (Arif et al., 2022; Yigezu et al., 2023c; Bade and Afaro, 2018).

Fake news is crafted with the explicit intent of disseminating information under the guise of propaganda or a hoax, ultimately aimed at achieving financial or political gains (Yigezu et al., 2023d). This deceptive practice manipulates public opinion, steering it towards falsehoods and distortions. The creators of fake news strategically weave narratives designed to exploit vulnerabilities and biases, with the ultimate goal of influencing individuals and, in turn, shaping societal perceptions. This insidious tactic not only undermines the credibility of information but also poses a significant threat to the foundations of democracy and the well-being of communities. Recognizing the nefarious intentions behind fake news is essential for fostering a more discerning public and cultivating a media landscape rooted in truth and integrity (Yigezu et al., 2023b; Shahiki-Tash et al., 2023).

The organizers of a shared task organized this study, which consists of two tasks: identifying multiple labels in Malayalam news and classifying a given social media text as either original or fake (Subramanian et al., 2024).

The organization of this paper is as follows: In Section 2, we thoroughly examine several related research studies. Section 3 focuses on explaining the tasks we are considering, while Section 4 gives a detailed discussion of the chosen methodology and experiments carried out for the task. Section 5 is where we present results and have discussions about them. Lastly, in Section 6, we draw conclusions and discuss possible future trends in research within this field.

2 Related Works

Numerous researchers have delved into the study of fake news detection, employing a variety of ap-

Proceedings of the Fourth Workshop on Speech, Vision, and Language Technologies for Dravidian Languages, pages 156–161
March 22, 2024

proaches to unravel the complexities of understanding and categorizing fake news. Notably, these approaches encompass machine learning, deep learning, and transformer-based methodologies. Below, we explore a few notable studies that showcase the diversity of techniques employed:

In earlier studies, researchers leveraged on the traditional machine learning techniques (Reis et al., 2019; Shu et al., 2017; Yigezu et al., 2023a; Tash et al., 2022; Liu and Wu, 2018; Singh et al., 2018).

Ahmed et al. (2017) introduces a model for fake news detection utilizing n-gram analysis and machine learning methodologies. The study delves into an examination and comparison of two distinct feature extraction techniques and six varied machine classification methods. The experimental evaluation reveals optimal performance when employing Term Frequency-Inverted Document Frequency (TF-IDF) as the feature extraction technique and Linear Support Vector Machine (LSVM) as the classifier, achieving an impressive accuracy rate of 92%.

Granik and Mesyura (2017) employed a straightforward method for fake news detection, utilizing a naive Bayes classifier. This approach was translated into a software system and evaluated against a dataset comprising Facebook news posts. The achieved classification accuracy on the test set reached approximately 74%, a commendable result given the relatively uncomplicated nature of the model. The article discusses various avenues for potential improvement, indicating that the obtained results offer insights into addressing the fake news detection problem using artificial intelligence methods.

Mahabub (2020) introduces an intelligent detection system for news classification, addressing both real and fake news tasks, utilizing an Ensemble Voting Classifier. The approach involves the incorporation of eleven well-established machine-learning algorithms, including Naïve Bayes, K-NN, SVM, Random Forest, Artificial Neural Network, Logistic Regression, Gradient Boosting, Ada Boosting, among others. Through cross-validation, the top three performing machine-learning algorithms are selected for integration into the Ensemble Voting Classifier. The experimental results validate the efficacy of the proposed framework, achieving an impressive accuracy rate of approximately 94.5%. Additionally, other key metrics such as ROC score, precision, recall, and F1 demonstrate outstanding performance. The proposed detection framework not only attains high accuracy but also effectively identifies crucial features within news data. These identified features hold promise for implementation in other classification techniques, extending the utility of the system to detect fake profiles and messages.

With the advent of deep learning, researchers explored the application of neural networks, (Kong et al., 2020; Kumar et al., 2020; Hiramath and Deshpande, 2019; Yigezu et al., 2022; Tash et al., 2023). These deep learning models demonstrated improved performance in capturing sequential dependencies within textual data.

To tackle the issue of fake news, the Thota et al. (2018) propose a neural network architecture designed to precisely predict the stance between a provided pair of headline and article body. Their model surpasses the performance of existing architectures by 2.5%, achieving an impressive accuracy rate of 94.21% on the test data.

The authors Sahoo and Gupta (2021) present an innovative approach to automatic fake news detection within the Chrome environment, enabling the detection of fake news on Facebook. Their methodology involves the utilization of various features linked to a Facebook account, coupled with certain news content features, to analyze account behavior through deep learning techniques. Through experimental analysis on real-world data, the authors demonstrate that their proposed fake news detection approach attains higher accuracy compared to existing state-of-the-art techniques.

In response to the proliferation of fake news, the imperative for computational methods to detect them has become increasingly apparent. The primary objective of fake news detection is to empower users to discern various forms of fabricated information. The determination of the news veracity hinges on a decision-making process influenced by previously encountered instances of fake or authentic news. Various models can be employed to discern deceptive news circulating on social media platforms. Kaliyar (2018) makes a two fold contribution to the field. Firstly, the authors introduce datasets encompassing both fake and real news, undertaking diverse experiments to design effective fake news detectors. Leveraging Natural Language Processing, Machine Learning, and deep learning techniques, they classify the datasets, providing a comprehensive assessment of fake news detection.

Their contribution extends to encompass fake news categorization, incorporating existing algorithms derived from machine learning techniques.

In this research Chauhan and Palivela (2021), a profound exploration into distinguishing false news from authentic sources is conducted through a deep learning-based approach. The cornerstone of the proposed model is a LSTM neural network. Complementing the neural network, a GloVe word embedding is employed to represent textual words as vectors. Additionally, tokenization is utilized for feature extraction or vectorization, enhancing the model's capacity. The integration of N-grams further refines the proposed approach. A comprehensive comparative analysis of multiple fake news detection techniques is undertaken. The results of the proposed model are meticulously evaluated using accuracy metrics, revealing an exceptional performance with an accuracy rate of 99.88%. This underscores the effectiveness of the LSTM-based model and its ability to discern false news with an exceedingly high level of accuracy.

3 Description of tasks and Dataset

There is an escalating demand for the detection of fake news within social media texts. The dataset for this crucial task has been generously provided by the organizers of the Fake News Detection in Dravidian Languages- DravidianLangTech@EACL 2024 (Subramanian et al., 2023) and our team, Habesha, actively participated in this shared endeavor.

Throughout our involvement in this collaborative initiative, we immersed ourselves in two distinctive tasks. The primary task aimed to classify social media texts as either original or fake. The data sources encompassed various social media platforms such as Twitter and Facebook. Given a social media post, the shared task mandated the classification of the content as either fake or authentic news.

In the second task, namely the Fake News Detection from Malayalam News (FakeDetect-Malayalam) shared task, researchers were provided with a platform to address the formidable challenge of identifying and flagging fake news within the realm of Malayalam-language news articles. Accurate misinformation detection is crucial for fostering trustworthy communication in an era of information overload. The core objective of the FakeDetect-Malayalam shared task was to inspire participants to develop effective models capable of accurately detecting and categorizing fake news articles in the Malayalam language into different categories. In this context, we considered five fake categories - False, Half True, Mostly False, Partly False, and Mostly True.

Through our engagement with these two tasks, our goal was to contribute to a comprehensive understanding of fake news detection, with a specific emphasis on addressing the nuances associated with YouTube comments in both tasks.

We utilized a total of 4,072 data points for training in Task 1, which involves classifying fake and original content. Additionally, 1,019 data points were allocated for evaluating the model's performance. In Task 2, focusing on fake news detection from Malayalam News, we employed 1,669 data points for training and reserved 250 data points for evaluation purposes. For a more comprehensive overview of the statistics related to these specific datasets, kindly refer to Figure 1 for Task 1 and Figure 2 for Task 2.

Figure 1: Task 1 data set statistics

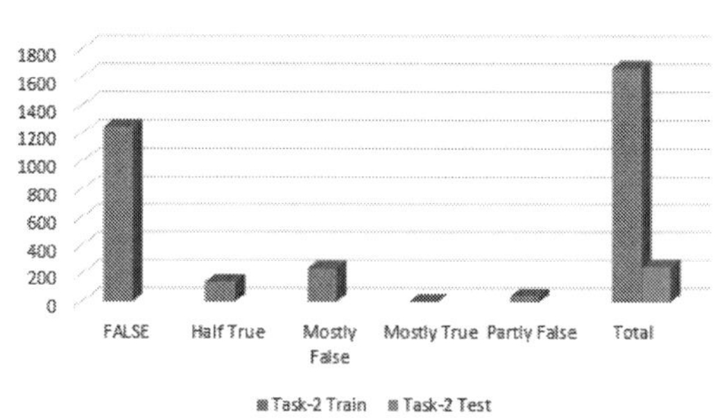

Figure 2: Task 2 data set statistics

In Figure 1, we observe an unbalanced distribution within the two-class dataset, indicating an uneven representation of the classes. In the meantime, Figure 2 shows that Task 2 is a multi-label assignment with five classes, which shows how the data is spread out in a very different way. This imbalance poses a significant challenge, potentially resulting in biased predictions and impacting the overall performance of the trained model. Recognizing and addressing such imbalances becomes imperative for fostering a more robust and unbiased predictive model (Yigezu et al., 2023b; Tonja et al., 2022; Bade and Seid, 2018).

4 Methodology

This section offers an in-depth insight into the methodology applied in this study, with a specific emphasis on data preprocessing and the adoption of a deep learning approach for fake news detection. Our primary goal was to perform fake news detection for both tasks.

Initiating our analysis, we acknowledged the significance of meticulous data preprocessing. This critical step involved purifying and formatting the raw data to optimize its appropriateness for subsequent stages in our model.

4.1 Experiment

In our methodology for detecting fake news in both shared tasks, we implemented a deep learning approach, specifically utilizing Recurrent Neural Networks (RNN). The process involved several crucial stages to ensure a thorough and accurate analysis. We used Long Short-Term Memory (LSTM) layers to model sequential dependencies in the text, dropout layers to stop overfitting during training, and a sigmoid activation function to tell the difference between fake and real news. This helped us capture semantic relationships.

We used the task organizer's training and development datasets, the Adam Optimizer, the cross-entropy loss function, and test data to evaluate the results of the model training. A grid search was conducted to automate hyperparameter tuning, systematically exploring different configurations, including varying numbers of hidden units and epochs. This rigorous approach aimed to optimize the model's performance and enhance its ability to generalize to diverse datasets.

5 Results and Discussion

As outlined in Section 4.1, we implemented the Recurrent Neural Network (RNN) model for both shared tasks. Our outcomes revealed a macro-F1 score of 0.82 for task 1 and 0.32 for task 2.

In task one, our model exhibited promising performance by effectively distinguishing between fake and original news, resulting in a superior outcome compared to task two. This discrepancy in performance can be attributed to the nature of task two, involving multi-label classification with an unbalanced data set, which presented challenges for achieving satisfactory results. The inherent complexity of addressing multiple classes in task 2 posed difficulties, leading to suboptimal performance in contrast to the binary classification nature of task 1.

6 Conclusion and Future work

The dissemination of fake news or misinformation poses a significant challenge, steering information in undesired directions and impeding the acquisition of reliable and timely information. To address this issue, we employed the deep learning approach, specifically RNN-LSTM. For optimal model training, we utilized grid search methods to fine-tune hyper parameters.

In binary classification, our approach yielded favorable results, showcasing its effectiveness in distinguishing between genuine and fake information. However, the application of multi-label classification suffered from the presence of unbalanced data, which led to less than ideal results.

As a recommendation for researchers aiming to extend this task, we suggest incorporating data balancing techniques. By addressing the imbalance in the dataset, more robust and accurate results can be achieved in the context of multi-label classification, enhancing the model's ability to handle diverse and nuanced information effectively.

Acknowledgments

The work was done with partial support from the Mexican Government through the grant A1-S-47854 of CONACYT, Mexico, grants 20241816, 20241819, and 20240951 of the Secretaría de Investigación y Posgrado of the Instituto Politécnico Nacional, Mexico. The authors thank the CONACYT for the computing resources brought to them through the Plataforma de Aprendizaje Profundo para Tecnologías del Lenguaje of the Laboratorio de Supercómputo of the INAOE, Mexico and acknowledge the support of Microsoft through the Microsoft Latin America PhD Award.

References

Hadeer Ahmed, Issa Traore, and Sherif Saad. 2017. Detection of Online Fake News using N-gram analysis and Machine Learning Techniques. In *Intelligent, Secure, and Dependable Systems in Distributed and Cloud Environments: First International Conference, ISDDC 2017, Vancouver, BC, Canada, October 26-28, 2017, Proceedings 1*, pages 127–138. Springer.

Muhammad Arif, Atnafu Lambebo Tonja, Iqra Ameer, Olga Kolesnikova, Alexander Gelbukh, Grigori Sidorov, and Abdul Gafar Manuel Meque. 2022. CIC at CheckThat! 2022: Multi-class and Cross-lingual Fake News Detection. *Working Notes of CLEF*.

Girma Yohannis Bade. 2021. Natural Language Processing and Its Challenges on Omotic Language Group of Ethiopia. *Journal of Computer Science Research*, 3(4):26–30.

Girma Yohannis Bade and Akalu Assefa Afaro. 2018. Object Oriented Software Development for Artificial Intelligence. *American Journal of Software Engineering and Applications*, 7(2):22–24.

Girma Yohannis Bade and Hussien Seid. 2018. Development of Longest-Match Based Stemmer for Texts of Wolaita Language. *vol*, 4:79–83.

Tavishee Chauhan and Hemant Palivela. 2021. Optimization and Improvement of Fake News Detection using Deep Learning Approaches for Societal Benefit. *International Journal of Information Management Data Insights*, 1(2):100051.

Mykhailo Granik and Volodymyr Mesyura. 2017. Fake News Detection using Naive Bayes Classifier. In *2017 IEEE first Ukraine conference on electrical and computer engineering (UKRCON)*, pages 900–903. IEEE.

Chaitra K Hiramath and GC Deshpande. 2019. Fake News Detection using Deep Learning Techniques. In *2019 1st International Conference on Advances in Information Technology (ICAIT)*, pages 411–415. IEEE.

Rohit Kumar Kaliyar. 2018. Fake News Detection using a Deep Neural Network. In *2018 4th international conference on computing communication and automation (ICCCA)*, pages 1–7. IEEE.

Sheng How Kong, Li Mei Tan, Keng Hoon Gan, and Nur Hana Samsudin. 2020. Fake News Detection using Deep Learning. In *2020 IEEE 10th symposium on computer applications & industrial electronics (ISCAIE)*, pages 102–107. IEEE.

Sachin Kumar, Rohan Asthana, Shashwat Upadhyay, Nidhi Upreti, and Mohammad Akbar. 2020. Fake News Detection using Deep Learning Models: A novel approach. *Transactions on Emerging Telecommunications Technologies*, 31(2):e3767.

Yang Liu and Yi-Fang Wu. 2018. Early detection of Fake News on Social Media Through Propagation Path Classification with Recurrent and Convolutional Networks. In *Proceedings of the AAAI conference on artificial intelligence*, volume 32.

Atik Mahabub. 2020. A Robust Technique of Fake News Detection using Ensemble Voting Classifier and Comparison with Other Classifiers. *SN Applied Sciences*, 2(4):525.

Julio CS Reis, André Correia, Fabrício Murai, Adriano Veloso, and Fabrício Benevenuto. 2019. Supervised Learning for Fake News Detection. *IEEE Intelligent Systems*, 34(2):76–81.

Somya Ranjan Sahoo and Brij B Gupta. 2021. Multiple Features Based Approach for Automatic Fake News Detection on Social Networks using Deep Learning. *Applied Soft Computing*, 100:106983.

Moein Shahiki-Tash, Jesús Armenta-Segura, Zahra Ahani, Olga Kolesnikova, Grigori Sidorov, and Alexander Gelbukh. 2023. Lidoma at Homo-Mex2023@ Iberlef: Hate Speech Detection Towards the Mexican Spanish-Speaking LGBT+ Population. the importance of preprocessing before using bert-based models. In *Proceedings of the Iberian Languages Evaluation Forum (IberLEF 2023)*.

Kai Shu, Amy Sliva, Suhang Wang, Jiliang Tang, and Huan Liu. 2017. Fake News Detection on Social Media: A Data Mining Perspective. *ACM SIGKDD explorations newsletter*, 19(1):22–36.

Naman Singh, Tushar Sharma, Abha Thakral, and Tanupriya Choudhury. 2018. Detection of Fake Profile in Online Social Networks Using Machine Learning. In *2018 International Conference on Advances in Computing and Communication Engineering (ICACCE)*, pages 231–234. IEEE.

Malliga Subramanian, Bharathi Raja Chakravarthi, Kogilavani Shanmugavadivel, Santhiya Pandiyan, Prasanna Kumar Kumaresan, Balasubramanian Palani, Premjith B, Sandhiya Raja, Vanaja, Mithunajha S, Devika K, Hariprasath S.B, Haripriya B, and Vigneshwar E. 2024. Overview of the Second Shared Task on Fake News Detection in Dravidian Languages. In *Proceedings of the Fourth Workshop on Speech, Vision, and Language Technologies for Dravidian Languages*, Malta. European Chapter of the Association for Computational Linguistics.

Malliga Subramanian, Bharathi Raja Chakravarthi, Kogilavani Shanmugavadivel, Santhiya Pandiyan, Prasanna Kumar Kumaresan, Balasubramanian Palani, Muskaan Singh, Sandhiya Raja, Vanaja, and Mithunajha S. 2023. Overview of the Shared Task on Fake News Detection from Social Media Text. In *Proceedings of the Third Workshop on Speech and Language Technologies for Dravidian Languages*, Varna, Bulgaria. Recent Advances in Natural Language Processing.

M Shahiki Tash, Z Ahani, Al Tonja, M Gemeda, N Hussain, and O Kolesnikova. 2022. Word Level Language Identification in Code-mixed Kannada-English Texts using traditional machine learning algorithms. In *Proceedings of the 19th International Conference on Natural Language Processing (ICON): Shared Task on Word Level Language Identification in Code-mixed Kannada-English Texts*, pages 25–28.

Moein Tash, Jesus Armenta-Segura, Zahra Ahani, Olga Kolesnikova, Grigori Sidorov, and Alexander Gelbukh. 2023. LIDOMA@ DravidianLangTech: Convolutional Neural Networks for Studying Correlation Between Lexical Features and Sentiment Polarity in Tamil and Tulu Languages. In *Proceedings of the Third Workshop on Speech and Language Technologies for Dravidian Languages*, pages 180–185.

Aswini Thota, Priyanka Tilak, Simrat Ahluwalia, and Nibrat Lohia. 2018. Fake News Detection: a Deep Learning Approach. *SMU Data Science Review*, 1(3):10.

Atnafu Lambebo Tonja, Mesay Gemeda Yigezu, Olga Kolesnikova, Moein Shahiki Tash, Grigori Sidorov, and Alexander Gelbuk. 2022. Transformer-Based Model for Word Level Language Identification in Code-mixed Kannada-English Texts. *arXiv preprint arXiv:2211.14459*.

Mesay Gemeda Yigezu, Girma Yohannis Bade, Olga Kolesnikova, Grigori Sidorov, and Alexander Gelbukh. 2023a. Multilingual Hope Speech Detection using Machine Learning.

Mesay Gemeda Yigezu, Selam Kanta, Olga Kolesnikova, Grigori Sidorov, and Alexander Gelbukh. 2023b. Habesha@ DravidianLangTech: Abusive Comment Detection using Deep Learning Approach. In *Proceedings of the Third Workshop on Speech and Language Technologies for Dravidian Languages*, pages 244–249.

Mesay Gemeda Yigezu, Tadesse Kebede, Olga Kolesnikova, Grigori Sidorov, and Alexander Gelbukh. 2023c. Habesha@ DravidianLangTech: Utilizing Deep and Transfer Learning Approaches for Sentiment Analysis. In *Proceedings of the Third Workshop on Speech and Language Technologies for Dravidian Languages*, pages 239–243.

Mesay Gemeda Yigezu, Olga Kolesnikova, Grigori Sidorov, and Alexander Gelbukh. 2023d. Transformer-Based Hate Speech Detection for Multi-Class and Multi-Label Classification.

Mesay Gemeda Yigezu, Moges Ahmed Mehamed, Olga Kolesnikova, Tadesse Kebede Guge, Alexander Gelbukh, and Grigori Sidorov. 2023e. Evaluating the Effectiveness of Hybrid Features in Fake News Detection on Social Media. In *2023 International Conference on Information and Communication Technology for Development for Africa (ICT4DA)*, pages 171–175. IEEE.

Mesay Gemeda Yigezu, Atnafu Lambebo Tonja, Olga Kolesnikova, Moein Shahiki Tash, Grigori Sidorov, and Alexander Gelbukh. 2022. Word Level Language Identification in Code-mixed Kannada-English Texts using Deep Learning Approach. In *Proceedings of the 19th International Conference on Natural Language Processing (ICON): Shared Task on Word Level Language Identification in Code-mixed Kannada-English Texts*, pages 29–33.

WordWizards@DravidianLangTech 2024:Fake News Detection in Dravidian Languages using Cross-lingual Sentence Embeddings

Akshatha Anbalagan[1], Priyadharshini T[1], Niranjana A[1], Shreedevi Seluka Balaji[1], Durairaj Thenmozhi[1]

akshatha2210397@ssn.edu.in , priyadharshini2210228@ssn.edu.in , niranjana2210379@ssn.edu.in , shreedevi2210389@ssn.edu.in , theni_d@ssn.edu.in

[1]**Sri Sivasubramaniya Nadar College of Engineering, Tamil Nadu, India**

Abstract

The proliferation of fake news in digital media has become a significant societal concern, impacting public opinion, trust, and decision-making. This project focuses on the development of machine learning models for the detection of fake news. Leveraging a dataset containing both genuine and deceptive news articles, the proposed models employ natural language processing techniques, feature extraction and classification algorithms.

This paper provides a solution to Fake News Detection in Dravidian Languages - DravidianLangTech 2024 [1]. There are two sub tasks: Task 1 - The goal of this task is to classify a given social media text into original or fake. We propose an approach for this with the help of a supervised machine learning model – SVM (Support Vector Machine). The SVM classifier achieved a macro F1 score of 0.78 in test data and a rank 11. The Task 2 is classifying fake news articles in Malayalam language into different categories namely False, Half True, Mostly False, Partly False and Mostly True.We have used Naive Bayes which achieved macro F1-score 0.3517 in test data and a rank 6.

1 Introduction

Fake News refers to false or misleading information presented as genuine news. This misinformation is often disseminated through traditional media, social media platforms, or other online channels. The intent behind fake news is typically to deceive and manipulate public opinion, influence political processes, or generate click-throughs for financial gain. In 2017, fake news has been seen to have influenced the US elections and the British Brexit vote, and locally in South Africa Finance Minister Pravin Gordhan, newspaper editors and journalists have become targets for fake news peddlers. In other instances breaking news on social media has turned out to be false and based on hoaxes and hearsay (Shu et al., 2017).

Following this, the task of Fake News Detection in Dravidian Language DravidianLangTech 2024 (Chakravarthi et al., 2021; Subramanian et al., 2023) aims to classify a set of social media texts and news articles using principles of feature extraction and machine learning.

The subsequent sections of this paper are structured as follows: Section 2 reviews relevant literature identified through a thorough literature survey. Section 3 presents an overview of the dataset, while Section 4 elaborates on the methodology employed for the task at hand. Section 5 delves into the discussion of results, and Section 6 concludes the paper.

2 Related Works

In recent years, there has been significant research in the domain of fake news detection, with a predominant focus on examining and identifying hoaxes within their primary dissemination channel: social media. The prevalent approach involves assessing the likelihood of a particular post being false by analyzing its inherent characteristics, such as likes, followers, shares, etc. This analysis typically employs traditional machine learning methods like classification trees, SVM, and similar techniques (Rodríguez and Iglesias, 2019).

In Natural Language Processing (NLP), there are many ways to approach the subject, and researchers have documented several methods in well-known literature. Recently, with advancements in turning image and speech into text, researchers have worked on creating and testing models that are both fast and accurate.

In the cited paper (Sharma et al., 2020), authors employed Artificial Intelligence, Natural Language Processing and Machine Learning for binary classification of news articles as fake or original. They assessed website authenticity using a two-step pro-

[1]https://sites.google.com/view/dravidianlangtech-2024/home

Proceedings of the Fourth Workshop on Speech, Vision, and Language Technologies for Dravidian Languages, pages 162–166
March 22, 2024

cess: Static Search (training Naive Bayes, Random Forest, and Logistic Regression) and Dynamic Search (with three search fields).

In this work (Adiba et al., 2020), Naive Bayes Classifier, a Bayesian approach of Machine Learning algorithm has been applied to identify the fake news. The researchers showed how the wealth of corpora can assist algorithm to improve the performance. The dataset collected from an open-source, has been used to classify whether the news is authenticated or not. Initially,they achieved classification accuracy about 87 percent which is higher than previously reported accuracy and then 92 percent by the same Naive Bayes Algorithm with enriched corpora.

In the cited paper (Khanam et al., 2021), authors utilized Python's scikit-learn library for tokenization, feature extraction, and vectorization, employing tools like Count Vectorizer and Tiff Vectorizer. They conducted feature selection methods based on confusion matrix results to determine the most fitting features for achieving the highest precision. The study revealed that many research papers favored the Naive Bayes algorithm, achieving prediction precision within the range of 70-76 percent. Qualitative analysis, relying on sentiment analysis, titles, and word frequency repetition, was commonly employed in these studies.

3 Dataset

The dataset of Task 1 is a list of social media comments in English and Malayalam with the labels either fake or original. The sources of data are various social media platforms such as Twitter and Facebook. Figure 1 describes the data distribution of this task.

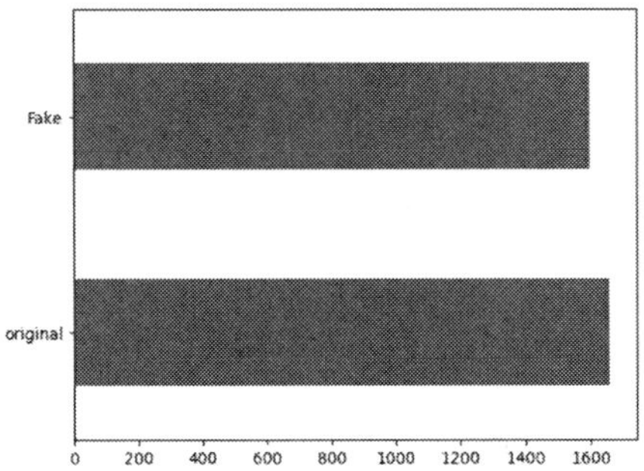

Figure 1:Task 1 dataset distribution

The dataset of Task 2 consists of news articles in Malayalam with the labels - False, Half True, Mostly False, Partly False and Mostly True. Figure 2 shows the data distribution of this task.

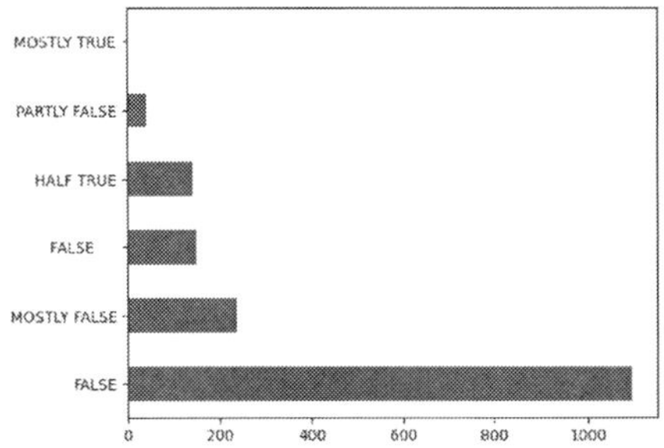

Figure 2:Task 2 dataset distribution

4 Methodology

4.1 Preprocessing

Preprocessing of given data involves cleaning, transforming, and organizing raw data into a format that is suitable for analysis or model training. The goal of data preprocessing is to improve the quality and usability of the data.

1. The elimination of punctuation marks and special characters serves to diminish noise and variations in the data, facilitating a clearer focus on the essential content making it easy for the model to learn the features.

2. Data reduction involves eliminating a significant portion of fillers or stop words present in any text which lack essential information for text analysis tasks. We have used a custom list of stop words in Malayalam and NLTK's English stop words list to remove such non-informative words from the text.

3. Vectorization is the method of representing words as vectors and is commonly referred to as word vector representations or word embeddings. In this paper, we experiment with the below mentioned word vector representations:

TF-IDF (term frequency-inverse document frequency) is a statistical measure that evaluates how relevant a word is to a document in a collection of documents. It helps to identify the most important words in a document by taking into account both the frequency of the word in the document and the rarity of the word in the entire collection of documents. This technique was used for Task-1.

CountVectorizer converts a collection of text documents into a matrix of token counts. It is used to transform a corpus of text to a vector of term/token counts. The vocabulary of known words is formed, which is subsequently used for encoding unseen text later. This method was utilized for Task-2.

A particular limitation faced here is that of the data set being in the Malayalam language, for which comparatively less resources are available. Thus a lot preprocessing techniques like lemmatisation and stemming could not be performed. The model may struggle to capture the subtleties of language use in different contexts.

4.2 LaBSE Feature Extraction

Feature extraction is a process that reduces the number of dimensions needed to define a large dataset by creating a smaller set of new features while discarding many existing ones. This involves transforming raw data into numerical features for further processing.

Language-agnostic BERT Sentence Embedding, or LaBSE, stands out as a multilingual language model developed by Google, building upon the BERT model.(Feng et al., 2020) In its pre-training process, LaBSE combines masked language modeling with translation language modeling. It is designed to be language-agnostic and has demonstrated superior performance compared to other existing sentence embedders.

This model proves useful for obtaining multilingual sentence embeddings and for bi-text retrieval. Recognized as the state-of-the-art in sentence embedding, LaBSE encodes sentences into a shared embedding space, ensuring that similar sentences are positioned closer to each other.

4.3 Models Used

Different researchers used different machine learning classifiers for checking the authenticity of news. According to their experiments the SVM and Naïve Bayes classifiers are best for detecting fake news. These two are better than other classifiers on the basis of accuracy they provide (Al Ayub Ahmed et al., 2021).

SVM: Support Vector Machine, is a supervised learning method that works for both classification and regression tasks. It is like a tool we use to organize information. SVM helps us find a special line, called a hyperplane, in a space with many different aspects or features (we call this space N-dimensional, where N is the number of features).

The idea behind SVM is to make decisions based on differences. Imagine some points in our data that are very important for making decisions; these are called support vectors. They are the ones closest to our decision line, or hyperplane (Patel et al., 2022).

SVM does its job by transforming our data into a space with many dimensions. This makes it better at figuring out patterns and making predictions, especially when our data is not easily separated in a straight line.

Naive Bayes: This classification technique is based on Bayes theorem, which assumes that the presence of a particular feature in a class is independent of the presence of any other feature. It provides way for calculating the posterior probability.

$$P(c|x) = \frac{P(x|c)P(c)}{P(x)}$$

P(clx) = posterior probability of class given predictor

P(c) = prior probability of class

P(xlc) = likelihood (probability of predictor given class)

P(x) = prior probability of predictor

(Ranjan, 2018)

5 Result And Analysis

5.1 Performance Metrics

We evaluate our model using the classification report which provides a summary of the performance metrics for a machine learning model, typically used for binary or multiclass classification tasks.

Precision: Precision is the ratio of correctly predicted positive observations to the total predicted positives.

$$\text{Precision} = \frac{\text{True Positive}}{\text{True Positive} + \text{False Positive}}$$

Recall (Sensitivity or True Positive Rate): Recall is also known as sensitivity or true positive rate and is defined as the ratio of correctly predicted positive observations to the all observations in the actual class.

$$\text{Recall} = \frac{\text{True Positive}}{\text{True Positive} + \text{False Negative}}$$

Macro Average and Weighted Average: Macro average calculates metrics independently for each class and then takes the unweighted average. It treats all classes equally. Weighted average calculates metrics for each class but uses the support of each class as weights when averaging. It considers class imbalance.

F1-Score: F1-score is the weighted average of precision and recall, providing a balance between the two metrics.

$$\text{F1 Score} = \frac{2 * \text{Precision} * \text{Recall}}{\text{Precision} + \text{Recall}}$$

In summary, precision, recall, and F1-score are key metrics to evaluate the model's performance, considering aspects of true positives, false positives, and false negatives.

5.2 Analysis

Table 1 shows the Classification Report obtained from the train data using SVM that was used for Task 1.

Table 1: Task 1 Training Report

Label	Precision	Recall	F1 score
original	0.75	0.85	0.80
fake	0.83	0.70	0.76

Table 2: Task 1 Development Report

Label	Precision	Recall	F1 score
original	0.85	0.96	0.90
fake	0.95	0.83	0.89

The development data was used to evaluate the model after the training phase.The predictions on the development data gave a macro F1 score of 0.89 as shown in Table 2. Table 3 shows the Classification Report obtained from the train data using Naive Bayes Model which was used for Task 2.

5.3 Result

The training and development data has been used to train and evaluate the models. Predictions of labels is done on the test data.

Table 4 and Table 5 describe the macro F1-score of the prediction and the rank secured in the competition.

Table 3: Task 2 Training Report

Label	Precision	Recall	F1 score
False	0.81	0.99	0.89
Half True	0.90	0.33	0.49
Mostly False	0.95	0.37	0.53
Partly False	0.67	0.10	0.17
Mostly True	0.80	0.00	0.00

Table 4: Rank Secured in Task 1

Team Name	Macro F1-Score	Rank
CUETDUO	0.88	1
PunnyPunctuators	0.87	2
WordWizard	**0.78**	**11**

6 Conclusion

In this research paper, we present a solution to the Fake News Detection in Dravidian Languages-DravidianLangTech 2024. Our approach involves classifying the text data into categories such as original and fake and False, Half True, Mostly False, Partly False and Mostly True. We leverage a Language-agnostic Sentence Embedder known as LaBSE and machine learning models, SVM (Support Vector Machine) and Naive Bayes. The models demonstrated good F1-scores and accuracy signifying their effectiveness in accurately identifying deceitful news from original news as the rankings are shown in Table 4 and Table 5.

These findings underscore the potential of Natural Language Processing (NLP) in automating fake news detection. This contribution has great implications in the society and politics since people are not influenced by fake news.

Table 5: Rank Secured in Task 2

Team Name	Macro F1-Score	Rank
CUETBinaryHackers	0.5191	1
CUETSentimentSilles	0.4964	2
WordWizard	**0.3517**	**6**

Limitations

Fake news is constantly evolving, and new tactics are regularly employed to keep a check on them. A model trained on historical data may struggle to adapt to emerging patterns of misinformation. Thus dynamic nature of fake news poses a limitation to the project.

Identifying relevant features for effective model training can be challenging, especially when dealing with a language like Malayalam which has unique linguistic features which are not well-captured by standard NLP techniques.

Ethics Statement

Ethical fake news detection is crucial for safeguarding information integrity and preserving the societal fabric. Detecting and combatting misinformation helps maintain public trust in media and democratic processes, preventing the erosion of confidence in reliable sources. Moreover, ethical efforts contribute to preventing harm by curtailing the dissemination of false information that can lead to negative consequences such as violence. By promoting informed decision-making, ethical fake news detection empowers individuals to make choices based on accurate and reliable information, ultimately fostering a more responsible and well-informed society.

References

Farzana Islam Adiba, Tahmina Islam, M Shamim Kaiser, Mufti Mahmud, and Muhammad Arifur Rahman. 2020. Effect of corpora on classification of fake news using naive bayes classifier. *International Journal of Automation, Artificial Intelligence and Machine Learning*, 1(1):80–92.

Alim Al Ayub Ahmed, Ayman Aljabouh, Praveen Kumar Donepudi, and Myung Suh Choi. 2021. Detecting fake news using machine learning: A systematic literature review. *arXiv e-prints*, pages arXiv–2102.

Bharathi Raja Chakravarthi, Gaman Mihaela, Radu Tudor Ionescu, Heidi Jauhiainen, Tommi Jauhiainen, Krister Lindén, Nikola Ljubešić, Niko Partanen, Ruba Priyadharshini, Christoph Purschke, Eswari Rajagopal, Yves Scherrer, and Marcos Zampieri. 2021. Findings of the VarDial evaluation campaign 2021. In *Proceedings of the Eighth Workshop on NLP for Similar Languages, Varieties and Dialects*, pages 1–11, Kiyv, Ukraine. Association for Computational Linguistics.

Fangxiaoyu Feng, Yinfei Yang, Daniel Cer, Naveen Arivazhagan, and Wei Wang. 2020. Language-agnostic bert sentence embedding. *arXiv preprint arXiv:2007.01852*.

Z Khanam, BN Alwasel, H Sirafi, and Mamoon Rashid. 2021. Fake news detection using machine learning approaches. In *IOP conference series: materials science and engineering*, volume 1099, page 012040. IOP Publishing.

Alpna Patel, Arvind Kumar Tiwari, and SS Ahmad. 2022. Fake news detection using support vector machine.

Aayush Ranjan. 2018. *Fake news detection using machine learning*. Ph.D. thesis.

Álvaro Ibrain Rodríguez and Lara Lloret Iglesias. 2019. Fake news detection using deep learning. *arXiv preprint arXiv:1910.03496*.

Uma Sharma, Sidarth Saran, and Shankar M Patil. 2020. Fake news detection using machine learning algorithms. *International Journal of Creative Research Thoughts (IJCRT)*, 8(6):509–518.

Kai Shu, Amy Sliva, Suhang Wang, Jiliang Tang, and Huan Liu. 2017. Fake news detection on social media: A data mining perspective. *ACM SIGKDD explorations newsletter*, 19(1):22–36.

Malliga Subramanian, Bharathi Raja Chakravarthi, Kogilavani Shanmugavadivel, Santhiya Pandiyan, Prasanna Kumar Kumaresan, Balasubramanian Palani, Muskaan Singh, Sandhiya Raja, Vanaja, and Mithunajha S. 2023. Overview of the shared task on fake news detection from social media text. In *Proceedings of the Third Workshop on Speech and Language Technologies for Dravidian Languages*, Varna, Bulgaria. Recent Advances in Natural Language Processing.

Sandalphon@DravidianLangTech-EACL2024: Hate and Offensive Language Detection in Telugu Code-mixed Text using Transliteration-Augmentation

Nafisa Tabassum, Mosabbir Hossain Khan, Shawly Ahsan
Jawad Hossain, and Mohammed Moshiul Hoque
Department of Computer Science and Engineering
Chittagong University of Engineering and Technology
{u1804066,u1704085,u1704057,u1704039}@student.cuet.ac.bd
moshiul_240@cuet.ac.bd

Abstract

Hate and offensive language in online platforms pose significant challenges, necessitating automatic detection methods. Particularly in the case of codemixed text, which is very common in social media, the complexity of this problem increases due to the cultural nuances of different languages. DravidianLangTech-EACL2024 organized a shared task on detecting hate and offensive language for Telugu. To complete this task, this study investigates the effectiveness of transliteration-augmented datasets for Telugu code-mixed text. In this work, we compare the performance of various machine learning (ML), deep learning (DL), and transformer-based models on both original and augmented datasets. Experimental findings demonstrate the superiority of transformer models, particularly Telugu-BERT, achieving the highest f_1-score of 0.77 on the augmented dataset, ranking the 1st position in the leaderboard. The study highlights the potential of transliteration-augmented datasets in improving model performance and suggests further exploration of diverse transliteration options to address real-world scenarios.

1 Introduction

In recent years, the growing problem of offensive language in user-generated content on online platforms and its harmful impacts has become a primary concern. The vast amount of daily user-generated content poses a significant challenge in the fight against offensive language. Consequently, automated methods are necessary for handling this task. Understanding code-mixed data is difficult due to several factors. First, it requires a deep understanding of the different linguistic levels involved. Second, the complex structure of code-mixed language makes it challenging to analyze. Finally, there needs to be more training data available for code-mixed languages, which hinders the development of effective classification systems. These challenges can lead to inaccurate classifications, mainly when using systems trained only on monolingual data. When a system trained on a single language encounters code-mixed data, it may be unable to accurately identify the different languages or understand the complex grammar rules involved. These challenges were addressed in the studies of Priyadharshini et al. (2023), which introduced a shared task for detecting hate and offensive language in Telugu. This paper contributes to the ongoing research efforts explored at the DravidianLangTech-EACL2024 (B et al., 2024).

The primary contributions of this work are illustrated in the following:

- Developed a transliteration-based augmentation scheme to help transformer models detect code-mixed Telugu offensive texts with high fidelity.
- Investigated various Ml, DL, and transformer-based techniques for the task and analyzed their performance in augmented and non-augmented datasets.

2 Related Work

Social media can often spread negativity and hurtful content. It is important to recognize such content because it can offend individuals and groups based on race, gender, or religion (Das et al., 2022). To maintain the integrity of the social media ecosystem, researchers and stakeholders must focus on creating computational models capable of swiftly

Proceedings of the Fourth Workshop on Speech, Vision, and Language Technologies for Dravidian Languages, pages 167–172
March 22, 2024

detecting and categorizing offensive content (Sharif et al., 2021). Hence, to address this growing concern on social media platforms, earlier research utilized diverse machine learning algorithms such as Linear Regression, Support Vector Machine, and Naive Bayes for the automated identification of hate speech (Abro et al., 2020). The performance of these models falls short as they need help to capture the semantic and contextual information present in textual data. Utilizing a publicly available dataset of tweets, Wei et al. (2021) suggests a methodology for automating tweets into three classes: Hate, Offensive, and Neither. Their approach utilizes BiLSTM models with blank embedding and pre-trained Glove embeddings to identify Offensive Language and Hate Speech. In recent years, pre-trained models have demonstrated remarkable accuracy in classifying code-mixed texts across various languages (Hande et al., 2020). The current focus of research in text analysis is within the transliteration domain, which holds the potential for achieving superior results (Shekhar et al., 2023).

3 Task and Dataset Descriptions

This task aimed to develop a model that successfully detects code-mixed offensive texts. To implement such a model, we utilized the Telugu-English code-mixed corpus that the organizers[1] provided to the participants. The dataset contains labels of two classes: *hate* and *non-hate*.

Label	Train	Augmented	Test	W_T
hate	1939	5816	250	18094
non-hate	2061	6181	250	21378
Total	4000	11997	500	39492

Table 1: Distribution of datasets, where W_T denotes total words in the train dataset

Table 1 shows the distribution of different classes across the train and test datasets. Both the train and test datasets are well-balanced. The texts in both the train and test dataset were preprocessed and cleaned to remove any unwanted symbols, emojis and punctuation marks before the development of the system.

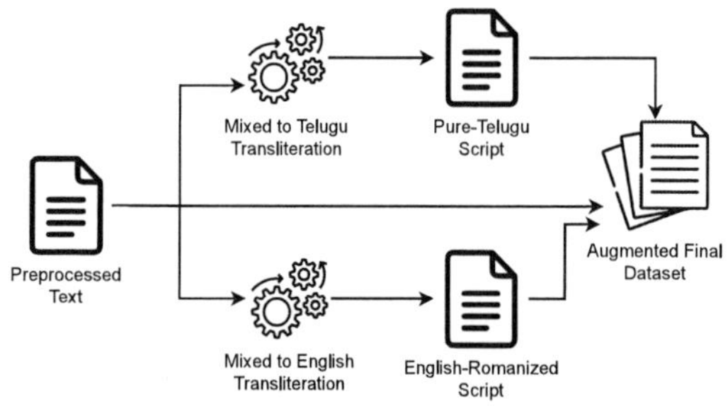

Figure 1: Augmentation process using transliteration

3.1 Data Augmentation with Transliteration

After cleaning, the dataset was augmented through transliteration. Transliteration handles code-mixed data since the dataset includes words in pure Telugu and English-romanized scripts. The proposed approach involves converting words between these scripts and translating code-mixed text to pure Telugu and English-romanized forms. Expanding vocabulary and providing context helps the model better understand the meaning of code-mixed text. We used AI4Bharat/IndicXlit[2] transformer model (Madhani et al., 2022) to first transliterate every single text from the cleaned dataset, to pure-Telugu text, as shown in Figure 1. Afterward, the cleaned texts were again transliterated, but this time to English-romanized text. These two new sets of texts are added to the original training dataset. In this way, every word in the original train dataset is guaranteed to appear at least twice in the augmented dataset: once in pure Telugu form and once in English-romanized form. This makes many common words reappear in both pure Telugu and English-romanized forms in the dataset, which ensures our model can learn from both forms of the exact text. The reason behind using this transliteration tool is that it has been trained on the Aksharantar (Madhani et al., 2023) dataset, which is, at the time of writing, the most extensive publicly available corpus on Indic languages. From the analysis of the authors of this tool, its performance in the Telugu language shows good potential. Hence, we chose this to generate synthetic transliterated texts.

4 Methodology

Figure 2 illustrates the overall process, including all employed models for the task. Various techniques are used to extract textual features for training the

[1] https://codalab.lisn.upsaclay.fr/competitions/16095

[2] https://pypi.org/project/ai4bharat-transliteration/

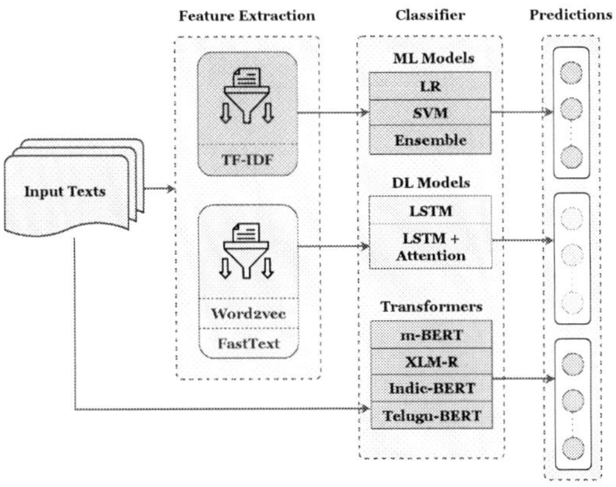

Figure 2: Abstract process of hate and offensive language detection in Telegu

respective ML and DL models. This work also utilized transformer-based techniques, such as m-BERT, XLM-R, Indic-BERT, and Telugu-BERT.

4.1 Feature Extraction

Following the approach of Tokunaga and Iwayama (1994), we utilized the TF-IDF (Term Frequency-Inverse Document Frequency) technique to extract unigram features. TF-IDF assigns word weights based on frequency within a document and across the entire corpus. This helps capture the importance of each word for distinguishing documents. We leveraged two widely used word embedding techniques for DL models: Word2Vec (Mikolov et al., 2013) and FastText (Grave et al., 2018). We implemented Word2Vec using the Keras embedding layer with an embedding dimension of 100 for both original and augmented datasets. Also, we utilized pre-trained FastText embedding matrices for each dataset. This pre-trained information incorporates subword information, potentially capturing more nuanced semantic relationships than Word2Vec.

4.2 ML Models

The 'lbgfs' optimizer was chosen for LR models, with C values 1.0 for both datasets. SVM models are configured with the linear kernel and $C = 1.0$ for both datasets.

4.3 DL Models

This research utilized a Bidirectional LSTM (BiLSTM) architecture with 100 cells per direction. To ensure robust generalization and prevent overfitting, we leveraged a dropout technique with a rate of 0.2. This technique randomly discards a small percentage of neurons during training. This promotes the network to learn relevant features across diverse data samples. Finally, the output of the BiLSTM layer is fed into a softmax layer for the final prediction. Inspired by the work of Vaswani et al. (2023), the DL model incorporated an attention mechanism to highlight impactful words in the input text. This attention layer, consisting of 20 neurons, was added to a BiLSTM layer. The BiLSTM output was then combined with the attention vector and fed into a softmax layer for the final prediction. We employed identical architectures for both datasets and utilized the 'sparse categorical cross-entropy' loss function. The model was trained with the 'Adam' optimizer (learning rate = $1e^3$, batch size = 32) for 15 epochs.

Transformer models often achieve the best results on various NLP benchmarks. Recognizing their strength, we employed four pre-trained transformer models: m-BERT (Devlin et al., 2019), XLM-R (Conneau et al., 2020), Indic-BERT (Kakwani et al., 2020) and Telugu-BERT (Joshi, 2023). All the transformer models were obtained from Huggingface[3] and fine-tuned with our original and augmented test set using the ktrain library (Maiya, 2020). In both datasets, we used a learning rate of $2e^{-5}$ in all the models and applied the method `fit_onecycle()` from the training library. The original dataset was trained with batch size 12, whereas the augmented dataset was trained with batch size 16 for all the models. Both datasets were used to fine-tune the transformer models for six epochs.

5 Results and Analysis

This section analyzes the effectiveness of different models for detecting hate speech and offensive language in Telugu code-mixed texts. The performance of the models is evaluated based on macro-averaged f_1-score. The evaluation result report is shown in Table 2, where the performance is presented in four cases: the original dataset (Non-Aug.), the original dataset augmented with Roman-transliterated texts (Roman-Aug.), the original dataset augmented with Telugu-transliterated texts (Telugu-Aug.), and finally, the intended, fully augmented dataset (Full-Aug.), which contains the combination of original, Roman-transliterated, and

[3] https://huggingface.co/docs/transformers/index

Classifiers	Non-Aug.			Roman-Aug.			Telugu-Aug.			Full-Aug.		
	P	**R**	**F**	**P**	**R**	**F**	**P**	**R**	**F**	**P**	**R**	**F**
LR	0.65	0.65	0.65	0.65	0.65	0.65	0.69	0.68	0.68	0.71	0.71	0.71
SVM	0.66	0.66	0.66	0.66	0.66	0.66	0.71	0.71	0.71	0.70	0.70	0.70
LSTM (Word2vec)	0.65	0.65	0.65	0.66	0.67	0.66	0.71	0.72	0.71	0.69	0.69	0.69
LSTM (FastText)	0.48	0.47	0.43	0.48	0.48	0.45	0.47	0.46	0.44	0.60	0.65	0.56
LSTM + Attention	0.62	0.62	0.62	0.62	0.62	0.62	0.64	0.64	0.64	0.67	0.67	0.67
m-BERT	0.67	0.67	0.67	0.65	0.65	0.65	0.71	0.71	0.71	0.72	0.72	0.72
XLM-R	0.73	0.72	0.72	0.53	0.52	0.51	0.72	0.72	0.72	0.76	0.75	0.75
Indic-BERT	0.67	0.66	0.66	0.67	0.66	0.66	0.69	0.68	0.68	0.67	0.66	0.65
Telugu-BERT	**0.74**	**0.73**	**0.73**	**0.73**	**0.73**	**0.73**	**0.77**	**0.76**	**0.76**	**0.78**	**0.77**	**0.77**

Table 2: Evaluation results obtained from models on four cases: original, only Roman-transliterated, only Telugu-transliterated, and fully-augmented test sets. P, R, and F denote macro-averaged precision, recall, and f_1 score. Here, "Aug." is used as shorthand for the word augmented.

Telugu-transliterated texts.

5.1 Discussion

The results indicated that ML models performed better than all DL models when using a fully augmented dataset. Word embeddings may not be able to capture the cultural subtleties and context of hate speech in code-mixed text as they are not trained on multilingual data. This might be a possible reason for such poor performance in DL classifiers. Still, the best result from ML and the best result from DL when applied to the Telugu-transliterated dataset was similar (0.71).

The transformer models' performance is outstanding compared to ML and DL models. All the transformer models except Indic-BERT for the original training dataset exceed the f_1 score previously obtained from ML and DL techniques. Among all the transformer models, Telugu-BERT shows the best result, with the highest f_1 score (0.73) achieved on the original train set and f_1 score of 0.77 in the fully augmented dataset. Although Indic-BERT was trained in Indic languages, it came last in performance, possibly due to many reasons. Alternatively, Telugu-English code mixed data might contain words in English rather than in the Telugu language written in a Roman script. Indic-BERT might need help finding word relationships better than XLM-Roberta or m-bert. Another reason might be because of data quality and context. XLM-Roberta and m-BERT, since they are trained on huge datasets, might capture hate-speech-related contexts better than Indic-BERT.

The results revealed the effect of various transliteration approaches. When only English-Romanized transliteration was applied, there needed to be more improvement in the performance. Compared to that, almost all classifiers performed better when Telugu transliteration was applied. Finally, in the fully augmented dataset, where both English-Romanized transliteration and Telugu transliteration were combined, we can see most of these classifiers show a slight performance improvement, which can be because this dataset is more extensive than all of the datasets above. Hence, relating different words between Roman script and Telugu script is easier. Also, the fully augmented dataset might give better context to the classifier due to many similar words appearing in both languages, and the two-way transliteration makes all forms of the similar words known to the classifiers. On the other hand, the IndicXlit transliteration tool is not perfect, and it might not always produce the best transliteration of every single word, so it hurts the performance.

The results showed that the proposed approach produces better f_1 scores when trained under the augmented dataset. The Telugu-BERT model trained on the augmented train set was chosen as the best overall performer.

5.2 Error Analysis

We conducted a comprehensive error analysis of quantitative and qualitative ways to gain an in-depth understanding of the best-performing model (Telugu-BERT).

Quantitative Analysis: It is shown that the best-performing model (Telugu-BERT) produced a maximum f_1 score of 0.77 (Table 2). Figure 3 represents the confusion matrix of this model. Among

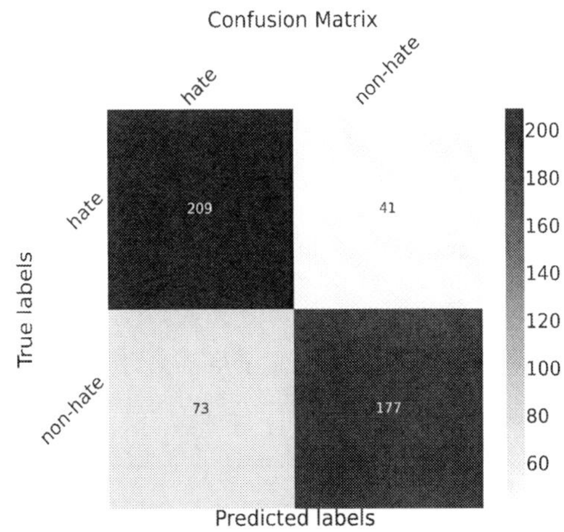

Figure 3: Confusion matrix of the best model (Telugu-BERT) on fully augmented dataset

the two classes, the hate class has the highest True-Positive Rate (TPR) of 83.6%, while the non-hate class has a lower TPR of 70.8%. This might indicate a slight bias towards detecting hate speech since a higher percentage of non-hate text (29.2%) was predicted to be from the hate speech class. Compared to that, 16.4% of actual offensive texts were predicted to be not offensive.

Qualitative Analysis: Figure 4 represents some predictions of the best-performing model compared to the actual labels. We generated the translations shown in the figure with the help of Google Translate[4]. The first sample was predicted accurately, entirely made up of pure Telugu script. Although the second sample had only Telugu script, it was not predicted accurately since it was a hate or offensive text, but Telegu-BERT labeled it *non-hate*. The third script was comprised of Telugu text in an English-Roman script, and Telegu-BERT was able to label it accurately. The fourth sample was of a code-mixed text, which mostly has text from Telugu script, with a minimal amount of English script. It was not predicted accurately. The final sample also consists of code-mixed text, with an English-script majority, but our model was able to predict its label accurately.

Limitations

The presented approach relies heavily on transliteration accuracy. Errors in transliteration can introduce misleading information, which can impact model performance. Furthermore, the diverse ways

Text	Actual	Predicted
ఎన్ని సార్లు అయిన వినాలని ఉంది చిట్టి తల్లి సూపర్ మా,, (How many times do you want to hear Chitti Mata Super Maa?)	non-hate	non-hate
ఇది బెండపూడి గవ్నమెంట్ స్టూడెంట్స్ కి మాత్రమే సాధ్యం. (This is only possible for Bendapudi Government students.)	hate	non-hate
dennichusthe chi daridram (If you look at this, you are poor)	hate	hate
నిజంగానే బుద్దిలేకుండా గెలిపించుకున్నాము worst CM (We really elected the worst CM without any intelligence.)	non-hate	hate
ఇప్పుడు YCP ki antha seen ledhu బులుగు batch dhammunte yedhi prnchakunda వుంటారా (The YCP doesn't have much of a chance now. Will they not be scared if the Bulugu batch attacks?)	hate	hate

Figure 4: Predicted outputs for some sample texts using the proposed (Telugu-BERT) model on fully augmented dataset

to transliterate a word in real-world scenarios highlight the importance of exploring methods to incorporate multiple transliteration options.

6 Conclusion

This paper explored various ML, DL, and transformer-based approaches for hate and offensive language detection in Telugu code-mixed text and demonstrated the effectiveness of transliteration-augmented datasets. In most cases, transformer models outperformed ML and DL methods. Telugu-BERT, trained explicitly on Telugu text, achieved an impressive f_1 score of 0.77. Investigating further augmentation methods and their combinations presents an exciting future direction to enhance the dataset and improve performance.

References

Sindhu Abro, Sarang Shaikh, Zahid Hussain Khand, Ali Zafar, Sajid Khan, and Ghulam Mujtaba. 2020. Automatic hate speech detection using machine learning: A comparative study. *International Journal of Advanced Computer Science and Applications*, 11(8).

Premjth B, Bharathi Raja, Prasanna Kumar Kumaresan, Saranya Rajiakodi, Sai Prashanth Karnati, Sai Rishith Reddy Mangamuru, and Janakiram Chandu. 2024. Findings of the shared task on hate and offensive language detection in telugu codemixed text (hold-telugu). In *Proc. of the Fourth Workshop on Speech, Vision, and Language Technologies for Dravidian Languages*, Malta. European Chapter of the Association for Computational Linguistics.

Alexis Conneau, Kartikay Khandelwal, Naman Goyal, Vishrav Chaudhary, Guillaume Wenzek, Francisco Guzmán, Edouard Grave, Myle Ott, Luke Zettlemoyer, and Veselin Stoyanov. 2020. Unsupervised cross-lingual representation learning at scale.

[4] https://translate.google.com/

Mithun Das, Somnath Banerjee, Punyajoy Saha, and Animesh Mukherjee. 2022. Hate speech and offensive language detection in bengali. *arXiv preprint arXiv:2210.03479*.

Jacob Devlin, Ming-Wei Chang, Kenton Lee, and Kristina Toutanova. 2019. Bert: Pre-training of deep bidirectional transformers for language understanding.

Edouard Grave, Piotr Bojanowski, Prakhar Gupta, Armand Joulin, and Tomas Mikolov. 2018. Learning word vectors for 157 languages. In *Proceedings of the Eleventh International Conference on Language Resources and Evaluation (LREC 2018)*, Miyazaki, Japan. European Language Resources Association (ELRA).

Adeep Hande, Ruba Priyadharshini, and Bharathi Raja Chakravarthi. 2020. KanCMD: Kannada CodeMixed dataset for sentiment analysis and offensive language detection. In *Proceedings of the Third Workshop on Computational Modeling of People's Opinions, Personality, and Emotion's in Social Media*, pages 54–63, Barcelona, Spain (Online). Association for Computational Linguistics.

Raviraj Joshi. 2023. L3cube-hindbert and devbert: Pre-trained bert transformer models for devanagari based hindi and marathi languages.

Divyanshu Kakwani, Anoop Kunchukuttan, Satish Golla, Gokul N.C., Avik Bhattacharyya, Mitesh M. Khapra, and Pratyush Kumar. 2020. IndicNLPSuite: Monolingual Corpora, Evaluation Benchmarks and Pre-trained Multilingual Language Models for Indian Languages. In *Findings of EMNLP*.

Yash Madhani, Sushane Parthan, Priyanka Bedekar, Gokul NC, Ruchi Khapra, Anoop Kunchukuttan, Pratyush Kumar, and Mitesh M. Khapra. 2023. Aksharantar: Open indic-language transliteration datasets and models for the next billion users.

Yash Madhani, Sushane Parthan, Priyanka A. Bedekar, Ruchi Khapra, Vivek Seshadri, Anoop Kunchukuttan, Pratyush Kumar, and Mitesh M. Khapra. 2022. Aksharantar: Towards building open transliteration tools for the next billion users. *ArXiv*, abs/2205.03018.

Arun S. Maiya. 2020. ktrain: A low-code library for augmented machine learning. *arXiv preprint arXiv:2004.10703*.

Tomas Mikolov, Ilya Sutskever, Kai Chen, Greg Corrado, and Jeffrey Dean. 2013. Distributed representations of words and phrases and their compositionality.

Ruba Priyadharshini, Bharathi Raja Chakravarthi, Malliga S, Subalalitha CN, Kogilavani S V, Premjith B, Abirami Murugappan, and Prasanna Kumar Kumaresan. 2023. Overview of shared-task on abusive comment detection in tamil and telugu. In *Proceedings of the Third Workshop on Speech and Language Technologies for Dravidian Languages*, Varna, Bulgaria. Recent Advances in Natural Language Processing.

Omar Sharif, Eftekhar Hossain, and Mohammed Moshiul Hoque. 2021. Nlp-cuet@ dravidianlangtech-eacl2021: Offensive language detection from multilingual code-mixed text using transformers. *arXiv preprint arXiv:2103.00455*.

Shashi Shekhar, Hitendra Garg, Rohit Agrawal, Shivendra Shivani, and Bhisham Sharma. 2023. Hatred and trolling detection transliteration framework using hierarchical lstm in code-mixed social media text. *Complex & Intelligent Systems*, 9(3):2813–2826.

Takenobu Tokunaga and Makoto Iwayama. 1994. Text categorization based on weighted inverse document frequency.

Ashish Vaswani, Noam Shazeer, Niki Parmar, Jakob Uszkoreit, Llion Jones, Aidan N. Gomez, Lukasz Kaiser, and Illia Polosukhin. 2023. Attention is all you need.

Bencheng Wei, Jason Li, Ajay Gupta, Hafiza Umair, Atsu Vovor, and Natalie Durzynski. 2021. Offensive language and hate speech detection with deep learning and transfer learning. *arXiv preprint arXiv:2108.03305*.

CUET_Binary_Hackers@DravidianLangTech EACL2024: Fake News Detection in Malayalam Language Leveraging Fine-tuned MuRIL BERT

Salman Farsi, Asrarul Hoque Eusha, Ariful Islam, Hasan Mesbaul Ali Taher
Jawad Hossain, Shawly Ahsan, Avishek Das and **Mohammed Moshiul Hoque**
Department of Computer Science and Engineering
Chittagong University of Engineering & Technology, Chattogram-4349, Bangladesh
{salman.cuet.cse, asrar2860, arif.cse18cuet, Hasanmesbaul440}@gmail.com
{u1704039, u1704057}@student.cuet.ac.bd, {avishek, moshiul_240}@cuet.ac.bd

Abstract

Due to technological advancements, various methods have emerged for disseminating news to the masses. The pervasive reach of news, however, has given rise to a significant concern: the proliferation of fake news. In response to this challenge, a shared task in Dravidian-LangTech EACL2024 was initiated to detect fake news and classify its types in the Malayalam language. The shared task consisted of two sub-tasks. Task 1 focused on a binary classification problem, determining whether a piece of news is fake or not. Whereas task 2 delved into a multi-class classification problem, categorizing news into five distinct levels. Our approach involved the exploration of various machine learning (RF, SVM, XGBoost, Ensemble), deep learning (BiLSTM, CNN), and transformer-based models (MuRIL, Indic-SBERT, m-BERT, XLM-R, Distil-BERT) by emphasizing parameter tuning to enhance overall model performance. As a result, we introduce a fine-tuned MuRIL model that leverages parameter tuning, achieving notable success with an F1-score of 0.86 in task 1 and 0.5191 in task 2. This successful implementation led to our system securing the 3rd position in task 1 and the 1st position in task 2. The source code will be found in the GitHub repository at this link: https://github.com/Salman1804102/DravidianLangTech-EACL-2024-FakeNews.

1 Introduction

Social media has gradually become an integral part of our lives, with regular posting and commenting being commonplace. Unfortunately, this platform is often misused, as individuals spread rumors by purposefully posting fake news to attack others and cause harm (Fowler, 2022; Medzerian, 2023). Given the importance of accurate information, it becomes crucial to curb the pervasiveness of fake news for the greater good. The widespread dissemination of false information carries catastrophic implications and potential dangers, particularly in the political and social spheres (De Paor and Heravi, 2020). A statistical analysis of the American public's aptitude for discerning between authentic and false news indicates a troubling pattern, as only 26% of survey participants express a high level of confidence in their ability to make this distinction (Watson, 2023). This low number underscores the urgent need for an automated system to detect fake news.

Numerous studies have been established for detecting fake news in high-resourced languages like English, Arabic, Spanish, French, German, etc. (Ahuja and Kumar, 2023; Mohawesh et al., 2023; Zhou et al., 2023; Al-Yahya et al., 2021; Guibon et al., 2019). But there is still much work to be done, especially for low-resourced languages like Malayalam, particularly in codemixed text (Thara and Poornachandran, 2021). Besides, in contrast to other Dravidian languages, Malayalam presents unique linguistic intricacies, encompassing dialect variations, nuanced word semantics, idiomatic expressions, and more (Coelho et al., 2023). These intricacies pose challenges in processing and analyzing Malayalam text. This shared task addresses precisely this issue, aiming to develop an automated system for detecting fake news and classifying its severity by categorizing news into various types. As participants in this shared task, the contributions of this paper are outlined as follows:

- We conducted a comprehensive comparative analysis of machine learning, deep learning, and transformer-based models through parameter tuning.
- We propose a fine-tuned MuRIL model that efficiently detects fake news, addresses class imbalance and performs news classification.

The rest of the paper follows this structure: Section 3 presents the task and dataset description, Section 4 discusses the methodology, Section 5

Proceedings of the Fourth Workshop on Speech, Vision, and Language Technologies for Dravidian Languages, pages 173–179
March 22, 2024 ©2024 Association for Computational Linguistics

covers the results and error analysis, and Section 6 describes the conclusion and outlines future work.

2 Literature Review

The surge in fake news incidents prompted extensive research, initially relying on machine learning for detection. A specific study (Ahmed et al., 2017) harnessed machine learning and n-gram analysis, achieving a notable 92% accuracy on real news articles collected from Reuters. In the DravidianLangTech@RANLP 2023[1] shared task, the team 'MUCS' (Coelho et al., 2023) excelled with an impressive F1-score of 0.830. They employed ensemble models that combined Multinomial Naive Bayes (MNB), Logistic Regression (LR), and Support Vector Machine (SVM) to detect fake news in low-resourced Malayalam. As the dataset size expanded and the need for intricate detection across multiple languages arose, the forefront shifted towards employing deep learning methods. This is due to their efficiency in handling increased complexity. Incorporating four diverse datasets consisting of English-language news articles, this study (Sastrawan et al., 2022) utilized CNN, BiLSTM, and ResNet. It used popular word embeddings like Word2Vec, GloVe, and fastText. The results highlighted the consistent superiority of BiLSTM across all datasets. In a parallel investigation, Kumar and Singh (2022) addressed the proliferation of fake news in Hindi, drawing from diverse news articles. The author utilized NB, LR, and LSTM classifiers. With LSTM emerging as the most effective model for fake news detection, they achieved an impressive accuracy of 92.36%.

However, the shift from deep learning to transformer-based models like BERT has notably improved fake news detection accuracy, especially in code-mixed-text contexts (Kaliyar et al., 2021; Malliga et al., 2023). A study (Rahman et al., 2022) on a Bengali fake news dataset revealed XLM-R's superior accuracy of 98%. Whereas in the multilingual fake news classification scheme, Hariharan and Anand Kumar (2022) focused on low-resourced Tamil and Malayalam. They assessed the effectiveness of transformer-based models like m-BERT, XLM-R, and MuRIL. The focus on the low-resourced Dravidian languages has continuously increased. Sivanaiah et al. (2022) achieved an impressive F1-score of approximately 95% utilizing LR and 98% utilizing BERT models in one of the fake news detection endeavors for several Indian low-resourced languages like Tamil, Kannada, Gujarati, and Malayalam. The author (Thara and Poornachandran, 2021) in this study delved into the use of a dataset sourced from YouTube comments featuring Malayalam-English code-mixed text. The study explored the effectiveness of Camem-BERT, Distil-BERT, ELECTRA, and XLM-R models in this context. Remarkably, ELECTRA achieved an impressive F1-score of 99.33%. In another DravidianLangTech@RANLP 2023 study, Bala and Krishnamurthy (2023) implemented the MuRIL base variant model and achieved a notable F1-score of 87% for Malayalam code-mixed text. Within the context of fake news detection, addressing multi-class classification scenarios where news articles encompass varying degrees of truthfulness becomes crucial (Kaliyar et al., 2019; Karimi et al., 2018). A recent study (Shushkevich et al., 2023) has delved into this challenge, addressing the multi-class classification of fake news with labels such as 'True', 'Partially False', 'False', and others. To handle class imbalance, the researchers experimented with ChatGPT-based data augmentation, achieving an F1-score of 23% with m-BERT proving to be the most effective.

[1] https://dravidianlangtech.github.io/2023/

3 Task and Dataset Description

This shared task (Subramanian et al., 2024) on 'Fake News Detection in Dravidian Languages' consisted of two separate sub-tasks. In task 1, participants aimed to distinguish whether a post or comment is 'original' or 'fake'. Task 2 involved a more nuanced challenge, requiring participants to categorize news into five distinct labels: 'FALSE' (F), 'MOSTLY FALSE' (MF), 'PARTLY FALSE' (PF), 'MOSTLY TRUE' (MT), and 'HALF TRUE' (HT).

The competition organizers provided a dataset (Malliga et al., 2023) in multilingual and code-mixed Malayalam for these tasks. Task 1 comprised three distinct datasets (train, dev, and test), while task 2 involved two separate datasets (train and test). The training dataset in task 1 demonstrated a near balance, but task 2's training dataset exhibited a significant imbalance, with only a single occurrence of the MT class. The 'FALSE' class constituted about three-fourths of the samples. However, task 2 lacked a dedicated dev set. Further dataset statistics are detailed in Table 1.

Data	Class	Task 1 SC	Task 1 UW	Task 1 AL	Class	Task 2 SC	Task 2 UW	Task 2 AL
Train	Original	1,658	18,526	11	F	1,246	9,371	10
					MF	239		
					HT	141		
	Fake	1,599			PF	42		
					MT	1		
Dev	Original	409	5,581	11	Dev set is not present			
	Fake	406						
Test	Orignal	512	6,738	11	F	149	1,888	11
					MF	63		
					HT	24		
	Fake	507			PF	14		
					MT	0		

Table 1: Dataset statistics for both tasks, with acronyms SC, UW, and AL representing sample count, unique words, and average length, respectively.

4 Methodology

This section outlines the model framework devised to tackle the issue detailed in Section 2. Initially, to preprocess the text, we conducted several steps including the removal of emoticons, pictographs, URLs, and brackets. Following this, we employed feature extraction techniques to retrieve essential information. Our choice of feature extraction techniques was driven by the linguistic nuances inherent in such languages. TF-IDF (Takenobu, 1994) was selected for the ML models to effectively weigh term importance based on frequency, aligning with the need for interpretability in the context of fake news detection. On the other hand, GloVe embeddings (Pennington et al., 2014) were employed for the DL models, as they excel in capturing semantic relationships and contextual nuances within the text. This choice aimed to enhance the models' understanding of the intricacies present in Malayalam, contributing to more effective fake news classification. The overview of the proposed methodology is shown in figure 1.

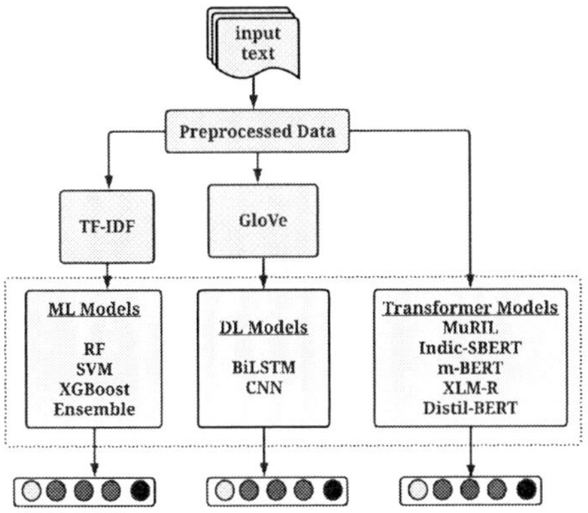

Figure 1: Overview of the methodology.

4.1 Machine Learning Approaches

In our exploration, we delved into several machine learning approaches, including Random Forest (RF), Support Vector Machine (SVM), eXtreme Gradient Boosting (XGBoost), and ensembles comprised of decision trees, SVM, and logistic regression. We used the TF-IDF feature extraction method for all ML models. To address the imbalanced dataset issue in Task 2, we assigned a class weight of type 'balanced' to all our ML approaches. The implementation of ML models was facilitated through the 'scikit-learn'[2] library for ease and efficiency. For our RF model, we set the 'n_estimators' to 100. With SVM, we utilized a 'linear' kernel with a regularization parameter C set to 1. Additionally, a tolerance of $1e^{-3}$ was employed as the stopping criterion. On the other hand, XGBoost was implemented with a 'multi:softmax' objective. For XGBoost, we used a learning rate of 0.3, 'n_estimators' of 100, and a maximum depth of 6. Lastly, an ensemble model consisting of LR, DT and SVM was utilized with a majority voting scheme.

4.2 Deep Learning Approaches

Deep learning models, BiLSTM and CNN, were implemented with a learning rate of $1e^{-3}$, 'Adam' as optimizer, and 'sparse_categorical_crossentropy' loss function. Class weights were employed to address the imbalanced data in task 2. The Bidirectional Long Short-Term Memory network (BiLSTM) was configured with a batch size of 64 and a single layer comprising 200 units. The Convolutional Neural Network (CNN) was designed with one layer containing 128 units and a batch size of 32. Both BiLSTM and CNN used the GloVe word embedding technique for feature extraction.

4.3 Transformer-based Approaches

We explored five transformer-based models, namely MuRIL (Khanuja et al., 2021), Indic-SBERT (Deode et al., 2023), m-BERT (Devlin et al., 2018), XLM-R (Conneau et al., 2020), and Distil-BERT (Sanh et al., 2019). All pre-trained transformer models were imported from 'Hugging Face' (Wolf et al., 2019) [3] and implemented using the ktrain library (Maiya, 2022). Subsequently, we fine-tuned these models on the provided datasets and utilized hyperparameter tuning to enhance

[2] https://scikit-learn.org/
[3] https://huggingface.co/

Method	Classifiers	Task 1			Task 2		
		P	R	F	P	R	F
ML models	RF (TF-IDF)	0.76	0.75	0.75	0.91	0.42	0.47
	SVM (TF-IDF)	0.76	0.76	0.76	0.58	0.44	0.45
	XGBoost (TF-IDF)	0.73	0.72	0.72	0.74	0.40	0.44
	Ensemble (TF-IDF)	0.77	0.77	0.77	0.51	0.29	0.31
DL models	BiLSTM (GloVe)	0.25	0.50	0.33	0.59	0.10	0.16
	CNN (GloVe)	0.31	0.46	0.29	0.43	0.18	0.17
Transformer models	**MuRIL**	0.86	0.86	**0.86**	0.66	0.48	**0.52**
	Indic-SBERT	0.86	0.86	0.86	0.33	0.24	0.17
	m-BERT	0.85	0.85	0.85	0.11	0.26	0.15
	XLM-R	0.86	0.86	0.86	0.12	0.25	0.16
	Distil-BERT	0.84	0.84	0.84	0.50	0.43	0.46

Table 2: Performance comparison of the proposed system over test data. Here P, R, and F stand for precision, recall, and macro F1-score respectively.

their performance. Specifically, in task 2, class weight augmentation was employed during the training of each transformer-based model to address class imbalance issues. We utilized the 'compute_class_weight' function imported from 'scikit-learn' for this purpose. The training configurations included a learning rate of $3e^{-5}$, batch size of 12 and 15 epochs for each respective model. For task 1 and task 2, we set the 'maxlen' parameter to 60 and 30, respectively. The rationale for choosing these parameters is grounded in a series of experiments conducted and GPU resource availability.

5 Results and Error Analysis

This section delves into the results and error analysis of the proposed fake news detection system. A detailed performance analysis is shown in Table 2.

5.1 Performance Analysis of Models

In task 1, among the different ML models, the Ensemble model outperformed others by achieving an F1-score of 0.77. Ensembling yielded improved performance by leveraging diverse strengths, enhancing generalization, and mitigating individual model weaknesses. Transformer-based models showcased superior performance in this task, and MuRIL turned out to be the best model by outperforming others. At the same time, the Indic-SBERT and XLM-R both displayed better results. As binary classification is inherently more straightforward for transformer-based models, this might contribute to the transformer models' effectiveness.

In task 2, ML models exhibited superior performance compared to transformer-based models except MuRIL. Mentionably, m-BERT's prediction skewed towards the 'HALF TRUE' class, and XLM-R consistently categorized maximum samples as 'FALSE' which led to extensive misclassification and poor performance. Since task 2 resembles a significant class imbalance, this issue also contributes to the differing performance of models. The ML models, being less complex, could potentially navigate the imbalanced dataset more effectively, resulting in superior performance compared to transformer-based models. Meanwhile, DL models encountered some specific challenges in both tasks. The poor performance of DL models in both tasks could be attributed to their sensitivity to the complexity and nuances of the Malayalam language. Apart from that, DL models, with their deep architectures, may overfit certain patterns in the training data, leading to a biased prediction tendency. Employing 'balanced' class weights in ML models was found to be better than using the 'compute_class_weight' function imported from 'scikit-learn' in the case of transformer-based models and DL models.

5.2 Error Analysis

Figure 2 shows the confusion matrix for task 1. It reveals that 433 fake news samples were correctly predicted, while 74 were misclassified. Similarly, 443 original news samples were accurately predicted, but 69 were erroneously classified as fake news in this task.

Moving to Figure 3, the confusion matrix for task 2 reveals insights into the model's performance on task 2. Among the 149 samples labeled as

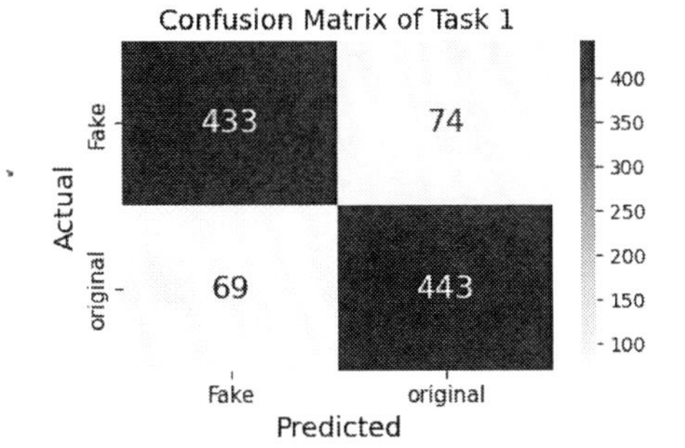

Figure 2: Confusion Matrix of task 1 for the MuRIL BERT.

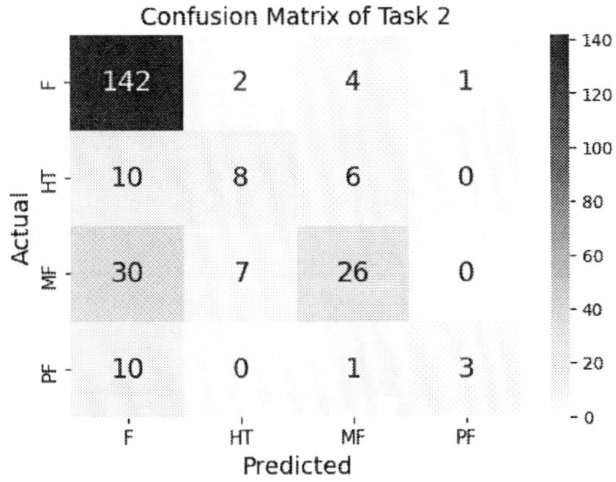

Figure 3: Confusion Matrix of task 2 for the MuRIL BERT.

'FALSE' in the test set, the model accurately predicted 142, with 7 misclassifications. However, for the 24 'HALF TRUE' samples, the model faced challenges, misclassifying 16 and achieving only 8 correct classifications. Among the 'MOSTLY FALSE' samples, 41.27% (26 out of 63) were accurately classified, while the remaining 58.73% faced misclassification. Notably, among the 'PARTLY FALSE' samples, 78.57% (11 out of 14) were misclassified. The elevated misclassification rates in these classes can be attributed to their limited number of instances in the dataset.

In summary, it appears the model predominantly predicted samples as 'FALSE', potentially influenced by the training data, where 'FALSE' samples comprised three-fourths of the dataset. A potential solution to address this issue could involve adjusting the efficient class weights mechanism, reducing the weight of the 'FALSE' class, and augmenting the weights of other classes for better model performance. However, some sample predictions for both tasks are provided in Appendix A.

5.3 Performance Comparison

Tables 3 and 4 show our position in the rank list.

Team Name	Score	Rank
CUET_DUO	0.88	1
Punny_Punctuators	0.87	2
CUET_Binary_Hackers	**0.86**	**3**

Table 3: A short rank list for task 1.

Team Name	Score	Rank
CUET_Binary_Hackers	**0.5191**	**1**
CUETSentimentSillies	0.4964	2
Quartlet	0.4797	3

Table 4: A short rank list for task 2.

Limitations

- The system is built on fine-tuning transformer-based models. It doesn't generalize to other languages and is not proven to give better results for a language that is not included in the training of MuRIL.
- Due to the GPU resource limitation, transformer ensembling couldn't be done.

6 Conclusion

This paper introduces a fake news detection system tailored for code-mixed Malayalam. It encompasses diverse models including ML, DL, and transformer-based models. Through extensive experimentation, evaluation, fine-tuning, and hyperparameter adjustments, the system showcases promising outcomes. Across both tasks, MuRIL emerges as the top performer, demonstrating its superior ability to handle code-mixed and transliterated Malayalam. The system achieves noteworthy F1-scores of 0.86 and 0.519, securing the 3rd and 1st positions in task 1 and task 2, respectively.

In the future, the exploration of fake news detection in other low-resourced Dravidian languages could be a worthwhile pursuit. Implementing data augmentation instead of relying solely on class weight adjustments for managing highly imbalanced datasets might prove more effective. Additionally, the utilization of hybrid models, combining transformers and DL models, holds the potential to yield improved results. Furthermore, exploring ensembles of transformer-based models could lead to superior performance.

References

Hadeer Ahmed, Issa Traore, and Sherif Saad. 2017. Detection of online fake news using n-gram analysis and machine learning techniques. In *Intelligent, Secure, and Dependable Systems in Distributed and Cloud Environments: First International Conference, ISDDC 2017, Vancouver, BC, Canada, October 26-28, 2017, Proceedings 1*, pages 127–138. Springer.

Nishtha Ahuja and Shailender Kumar. 2023. Mul-FaD: attention based detection of multiLingual fake news. *Journal of Ambient Intelligence and Humanized Computing*, 14(3):2481–2491.

Maha Al-Yahya, Hend Al-Khalifa, Heyam Al-Baity, Duaa AlSaeed, and Amr Essam. 2021. Arabic fake news detection: a comparative study of neural networks and transformer-based approaches. *Complexity*, 2021:1–10.

Abhinaba Bala and Parameswari Krishnamurthy. 2023. AbhiPaw@ DravidianLangTech: Fake News Detection in Dravidian Languages using Multilingual BERT. In *Proceedings of the Third Workshop on Speech and Language Technologies for Dravidian Languages*, pages 235–238.

Sharal Coelho, Asha Hegde, G Kavya, and Hosahalli Lakshmaiah Shashirekha. 2023. Mucs@ dravidianlangtech2023: Malayalam fake news detection using machine learning approach. In *Proceedings of the Third Workshop on Speech and Language Technologies for Dravidian Languages*, pages 288–292.

Alexis Conneau, Kartikay Khandelwal, Naman Goyal, Vishrav Chaudhary, Guillaume Wenzek, Francisco Guzmán, Edouard Grave, Myle Ott, Luke Zettlemoyer, and Veselin Stoyanov. 2020. Unsupervised Cross-lingual Representation Learning at Scale. In *Proceedings of the 58th Annual Meeting of the Association for Computational Linguistics*, pages 8440–8451, Online. Association for Computational Linguistics.

Saoirse De Paor and Bahareh Heravi. 2020. Information literacy and fake news: How the field of librarianship can help combat the epidemic of fake news. *The Journal of Academic Librarianship*, 46(5):102218.

Samruddhi Deode, Janhavi Gadre, Aditi Kajale, Ananya Joshi, and Raviraj Joshi. 2023. L3Cube-IndicSBERT: A simple approach for learning cross-lingual sentence representations using multilingual BERT. *arXiv preprint arXiv:2304.11434*.

Jacob Devlin, Ming-Wei Chang, Kenton Lee, and Kristina Toutanova. 2018. BERT: Pre-training of deep bidirectional transformers for language understanding. *arXiv preprint arXiv:1810.04805*.

Gary Fowler. 2022. Council Post: Fake News, Its Impact And How Tech Can Combat Misinformation. Accessed on December 12, 2023.

Gaël Guibon, Liana Ermakova, Hosni Seffih, Anton Firsov, and Guillaume Le Noé-Bienvenu. 2019. Multilingual fake news detection with satire. In *International Conference on Computational Linguistics and Intelligent Text Processing*, pages 392–402. Springer.

RamakrishnaIyer LekshmiAmmal Hariharan and Madasamy Anand Kumar. 2022. Impact of Transformers on Multilingual Fake News Detection for Tamil and Malayalam. In *International Conference on Speech and Language Technologies for Low-resource Languages*, pages 196–208. Springer.

Rohit Kumar Kaliyar, Anurag Goswami, and Pratik Narang. 2019. Multiclass fake news detection using ensemble machine learning. In *2019 IEEE 9th international conference on advanced computing (IACC), pages=103–107*. IEEE.

Rohit Kumar Kaliyar, Anurag Goswami, and Pratik Narang. 2021. FakeBERT: Fake news detection in social media with a BERT-based deep learning approach. *Multimedia tools and applications*, 80(8):11765–11788.

Hamid Karimi, Proteek Roy, Sari Saba-Sadiya, and Jiliang Tang. 2018. Multi-Source Multi-Class Fake News Detection. In *Proceedings of the 27th International Conference on Computational Linguistics*, pages 1546–1557, Santa Fe, New Mexico, USA. Association for Computational Linguistics.

Simran Khanuja, Diksha Bansal, Sarvesh Mehtani, Savya Khosla, Atreyee Dey, Balaji Gopalan, Dilip Kumar Margam, Pooja Aggarwal, Rajiv Teja Nagipogu, Shachi Dave, et al. 2021. MuRIL: Multilingual representations for Indian languages. *arXiv preprint arXiv:2103.10730*.

Sudhanshu Kumar and Thoudam Doren Singh. 2022. Fake news detection on Hindi news dataset. *Global Transitions Proceedings*, 3(1):289–297.

Arun S Maiya. 2022. ktrain: A low-code library for augmented machine learning. *The Journal of Machine Learning Research*, 23(1):7070–7075.

S Malliga, Bharathi Raja Chakravarthi, SV Kogilavani, Santhiya Pandiyan, Prasanna Kumar Kumaresan, Balasubramanian Palani, and Muskaan Singh. 2023. Overview of the shared task on Fake News Detection from Social Media Text. In *Proceedings of the Third Workshop on Speech and Language Technologies for Dravidian Languages*, pages 59–63.

David Medzerian. 2023. Study Reveals Key Reason Why Fake News Spreads on Social Media. Accessed on December 12, 2023.

Rami Mohawesh, Sumbal Maqsood, and Qutaibah Althebyan. 2023. Multilingual deep learning framework for fake news detection using capsule neural network. *Journal of Intelligent Information Systems*, pages 1–17.

Jeffrey Pennington, Richard Socher, and Christopher D Manning. 2014. Glove: Global vectors for word representation. In *Proceedings of the 2014 conference on empirical methods in natural language processing (EMNLP)*, pages 1532–1543.

MD Sijanur Rahman, Omar Sharif, Avishek Das, Sadia Afroze, and Mohammed Moshiul Hoque. 2022. FaND-X: Fake News Detection using Transformer-based Multilingual Masked Language Model. In *2022 IEEE International Women in Engineering (WIE) Conference on Electrical and Computer Engineering (WIECON-ECE)*, pages 153–158. IEEE.

Victor Sanh, Lysandre Debut, Julien Chaumond, and Thomas Wolf. 2019. DistilBERT, a distilled version of BERT: smaller, faster, cheaper and lighter. *arXiv preprint arXiv:1910.01108*.

I Kadek Sastrawan, IPA Bayupati, and Dewa Made Sri Arsa. 2022. Detection of fake news using deep learning CNN–RNN based methods. *ICT Express*, 8(3):396–408.

Elena Shushkevich, Mikhail Alexandrov, and John Cardiff. 2023. Improving Multiclass Classification of Fake News Using BERT-Based Models and ChatGPT-Augmented Data. *Inventions*, 8(5):112.

Rajalakshmi Sivanaiah, Nishaanth Ramanathan, Shajith Hameed, Rahul Rajagopalan, Angel Deborah Suseelan, and Mirnalinee Thanka Nadar Thanagathai. 2022. Fake News Detection in Low-Resource Languages. In *International Conference on Speech and Language Technologies for Low-resource Languages*, pages 324–331. Springer.

Malliga Subramanian, Bharathi Raja Chakravarthi, Kogilavani Shanmugavadivel, Santhiya Pandiyan, Prasanna Kumar Kumaresan, Balasubramanian Palani, Premjith B, Sandhiya Raja, Vanaja, Mithunajha S, Devika K, Hariprasath S.B, Haripriya B, and Vigneshwar E. 2024. Overview of the Second Shared Task on Fake News Detection in Dravidian Languages. In *Proceedings of the Fourth Workshop on Speech, Vision, and Language Technologies for Dravidian Languages*, Malta. European Chapter of the Association for Computational Linguistics.

Tokunaga Takenobu. 1994. Text categorization based on weighted inverse document frequency. *Information Processing Society of Japan, SIGNL*, 94(100):33–40.

S Thara and Prabaharan Poornachandran. 2021. Transformer based language identification for Malayalam-English code-mixed text. *IEEE Access*, 9:118837–118850.

Amy Watson. 2023. Confidence in Ability to Recognize Fake News in the U.S. Accessed on December 16, 2023.

Thomas Wolf, Lysandre Debut, Victor Sanh, Julien Chaumond, Clement Delangue, Anthony Moi, Pierric Cistac, Tim Rault, Rémi Louf, Morgan Funtowicz, et al. 2019. Huggingface's transformers: State-of-the-art natural language processing. *arXiv preprint arXiv:1910.03771*.

Lina Zhou, Jie Tao, and Dongsong Zhang. 2023. Does fake news in different languages tell the same story? An analysis of multi-level thematic and emotional characteristics of news about COVID-19. *Information Systems Frontiers*, 25(2):493–512.

A Appendix

Figures 4 and 5 depict predictions corresponding to randomly selected samples from the dataset. The English translation of the Malayalam samples was generated using Google Translator.

Text Sample	Predicted	Actual
Sample 1: Ede sagavu endina epo America poyadu keraliti... (This is not going to continue, AP went to America, Keralite...)	original	fake
Sample 2: മോളെ. ഇത് കോമഡി സ്റ്റാർസ് അല്ല. ചിരിച്ചും കളിച... (Molly It's not comedy stars. Laugh and play...)	fake	original
Sample 3: Evar oke ntena verte virus nne indakan nadakn (Who knows when and where the virus will strike)	fake	original
Sample 4: Ethil appuram നാണക്കേഢ് വന്നിട്ടില്ല cpmne a... (After this, haven't seen the CPM around here, haha)	original	original
Sample 5: 2ദിവസം കൂടി കഴിഞ്ഞാൽ എല്ലാവർക്കും കൂടി വീട്ടിൽ... (If two days pass, everyone should stay at home together...)	original	original
Sample 6: ഇയാളെ കൊറോണ. രോഗികൾ കിടയിൽ. ഇടാമായിരുന്നു---!! (He got Corona. Patients are increasing. Be cautious---!!)	fake	fake

Figure 4: Sample predictions for task 1 by MuRIL

Text Sample	Predicted	Actual
Sample 1: കണ്ണൂർ എയർപോർട്ടിന് ഭൂമി ഏറ്റെടുക്കുന്നതിന് എത... (What is the reason for acquiring land for Kannur Airport?)	Partly False	False
Sample 2: പലസ്തീൻ പതാകയണിഞ്ഞ് ക്രിസ്റ്റ്യാനോ റൊണാൾഡോ. (Cristiano Ronaldo wearing the Palestinian flag.)	Half True	False
Sample 3: മലാപറമ്പ്-പുതുപ്പാടി റോഡ് നവീകരണം സംസ്ഥാന സർ.. (Malaparamp-Puthuppady Road Upgradation State Sir..)	Half True	Mostly Fales
Sample 4: പാലക്കാട് കൊലപാതകങ്ങളുടെ പശ്ചാത്തലിൽ ആഭ്യന്ത... (In the context of the Palakkad murders, domestic...	False	False
Sample 5: പാലക്കാട് ഇരുചക്രവാഹനങ്ങളിൽ പുരുഷന്മാരുടെ പിൻസ... (Men's rear in Palakkad two-wheeler...)	Half True	Half True
Sample 6: ബിവറേജസ് ഔട്ട്‌ലെറ്റുകൾ തുറന്ന ആദ്യ ദിനത്തില... (On the first day of opening of the Beverages outlets...)	Mostly False	Mostly False

Figure 5: Sample predictions for task 2 by MuRIL

Punny_Punctuators@DravidianLangTech-EACL2024: Transformer-based Approach for Detection and Classification of Fake News in Malayalam Social Media Text

Nafisa Tabassum*, **Sumaiya Rahman Aodhora***, **Rowshon Akter**
Jawad Hossain, Shawly Ahsan and Mohammed Moshiul Hoque
Department of Computer Science and Engineering
Chittagong University of Engineering and Technology
{u1804066, u1804127, u1804003, u1704039, u1704057}@student.cuet.ac.bd
moshiul_240@cuet.ac.bd

Abstract

The alarming rise of fake news on social media poses a significant threat to public discourse and decision-making. While automatic detection of fake news offers a promising solution, research in low-resource languages like Malayalam often falls behind due to limited data and tools. This paper presents the participation of team Punny_Punctuators in the Fake News Detection in Dravidian Languages shared task at DravidianLangTech@EACL 2024, addressing this gap. The shared task focuses on two subtasks: 1. classifying social media texts as original or fake, and 2. categorizing fake news into 5 categories. We experimented with various machine learning (ML), deep learning (DL) and transformer-based models as well as processing techniques such as transliteration. Malayalam-BERT achieved the best performance on both sub-tasks, which obtained us 2nd place with a macro f_1-score of 0.87 for the subtask-1 and 11th place with a macro f_1-score of 0.17 for the subtask-2. Our results highlight the potential of transformer models for low-resource languages in fake news detection and pave the way for further research in this crucial area.

1 Introduction

In the current digital era, fake news and the spread of false information are widespread issues that have negative effects on people, communities, and countries (Raja et al., 2023). People can be misled and deceived by fake news, which can cause them to lose trust in organizations and information sources. The dissemination of misleading narratives and the promotion of biased opinions can cause societal division and conflict (Wani et al., 2023). Therefore, using cutting-edge natural language processing (NLP) techniques, academics, policymakers, and stakeholders are working to construct strong computational systems to prevent the dissemination of fake content (Hossain et al., 2022b).

Researchers have actively pursued the development of effective solutions to detect fake news across multiple languages in recent years (LekshmiAmmal et al., 2022). Fake news detection systems predominantly focus on high-resource languages like Spanish and English, neglecting low-resource Dravidian languages like Tulu, Malayalam, Tamil, Telugu, and Kannada due to resource scarcity (Hegde and Shashirekha, 2021). Despite the widespread use of the Malayalam language in Kerala, there is a lack of research on this language, necessitating the development of robust models for detecting fake news in Malayalam (Coelho et al., 2023). Malayalam's unique linguistic complexities, such as dialect variations, word semantics, and idiomatic expressions, make it challenging to process and analyze its text (Coelho et al., 2023). This work aims to develop a classification system for detecting fake news in Malayalam using various language technologies, aiming to identify fake articles written in the Malayalam language accurately. To effectively address the challenge, this work's major contributions are demonstrated by the following:

- Developed several machine learning (ML), deep learning (DL), and transformer-based models to identify fake news in the Malayalam language.
- Investigated and assessed the performance of the models using a variety of metrics to determine the best approach for the classification of fake news.

2 Related Work

The widespread use of social media and accessible internet access has resulted in the creation of mil-

*Authors have contributed equally to this work

Proceedings of the Fourth Workshop on Speech, Vision, and Language Technologies for Dravidian Languages, pages 180–186
March 22, 2024 ©2024 Association for Computational Linguistics

lions of posts and comments per minute (Hossain et al., 2022a). Fake news on social media leads to wrong judgments, prompting studies on various machine learning and deep learning models using different word embedding techniques (Sharif et al., 2021). The best score f_1-score they obtained using SVM was 94.39% in task-A. Rasel et al., 2022 achieved 95.9% accuracy by building a dataset with 4678 distinct news and improved the existing dataset accuracy from 1.4% to 3.4% using CNN. Roy et al., 2019 developed CNN and BiLSTM networks individually, then fed them into a Multi-layer Perceptron Model (MLP) which resulted in 44.87% accuracy. Rai et al., 2022 proposed a BERT model with a feed-forward network with 768 hidden sizes connected to an LSTM layer for fake news classification, outperforming the vanilla pre-trained model on two datasets with a 2.50% and 1.10% increase in accuracy. Research primarily focuses on high-resource languages, with few studies on detecting abusive language in low-resource languages like Malayalam. Coelho et al., 2023 achieved 0.831 macro f_1-score through applying TF-IDF as a feature extraction technique and ensembling three machine learning models (MNB, LR, SVM) with majority voting. Bala and Krishnamurthy, 2023 fine-tuned the MURIL variant named "mural-base-cased" in detecting fake news in Dravidian languages resulting accuracy of 87%. Wani et al., 2023 in their work, identify toxic fake news to save time on assessing non-toxic instances. Traditional and transformer-based machine learning techniques were employed and the linear SVM method outperformed BERT SVM, RF, and BERT RF with an accuracy of 92%. Using a newly annotated dataset, another study (Chakravarthi et al., 2023) showed MURIL as a multilingual transformer by effectively detecting abusive comments in the low-resource Tamil language. Several machine learning, deep neural networks, and transformer-based approaches were utilezed by Rahman et al., 2022 to analyze 5K fake news data, achieving a maximum f_1-score of 98% using XLM-R.

3 Task and Dataset Descriptions

For shared task-1, the task organizer[1] created a benchmark corpus for fake news detection (Subramanian et al., 2023). We utilized the corpus provided by the shared task-1 organizer to create the fake news detection classifier model. There are two subtasks in this shared task: subtask-1 and subtask-2. The goal of subtask-1 is to determine if a social media text is original or fake in the Malayalam language. In subtask-2, the objective is to create efficient models that can precisely identify and categorize fake news articles in Malayalam into five distinct classes. This subtask-2 offers five classes, including False, Half True, Mostly False, Partly False, and Mostly True. For subtask-1, the train, valid, and test splits of this dataset comprise 3257, 815 and 1019 texts respectively. Class-wise samples and dataset statistics are provided in Table 1. For Subtask 2, the train and test splits of this dataset comprise 1669 and 250 texts. Table 2 provides class-wise samples and dataset statistics of subtask-2. Because of the imbalance class distribution, we augmented the training dataset for further process.

Classes	Train	Valid	Test	W_T
Original	1658	409	512	13268
Fake	1599	406	507	21420
Total	3257	815	1019	34688

Table 1: Class-wise distribution of train, validation and test set for subtask-1, where W_T denotes total words in the Train dataset

Classes	Train	Test	W_T
False	1246	149	12183
Mostly False	239	63	2380
Half True	141	24	1462
Partly False	42	14	363
Mostly True	1	0	8
Total	1669	250	16396

Table 2: Class-wise distribution of train and test set for subtask-2, where W_T denotes total words in Train dataset

In the pre-processing stage, we filter out URLs, emojis, and assorted symbols present within the provided dataset.

4 Methodology

This section provides a brief overview of the methods and approaches used to solve the problem mentioned in the previous section. Several machine learning and deep learning approaches were em-

[1] https://sites.google.com/view/dravidianlangtech-2024/shared-tasks-2024?authuser=0

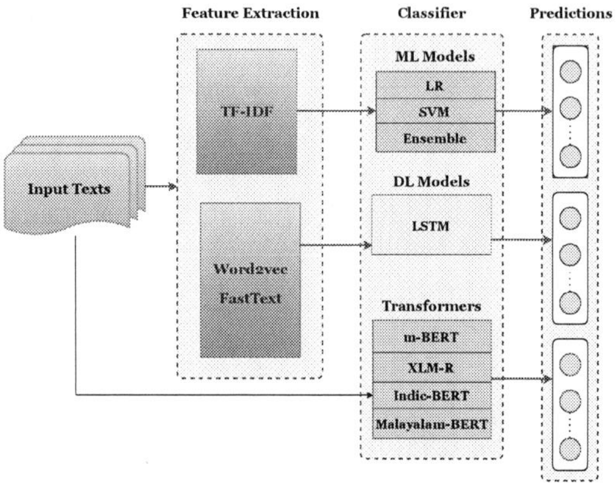

Figure 1: Abstract process of fake news detection

ployed for developing the baseline models. Performance of the classification of both tasks improved significantly by fine-tuning the transformer-based models. To identify fake news, this work employed four pre-trained transformer-based models: XLM-R, Malayalam BERT, mBERT, and Indic-BERT. To be more specific, we fine-tuned the Huggingface transformer[2] library's “XLM-RoBERTa-base" (Conneau et al., 2019), “l3cube-pune / Malayalam BERT”(Joshi, 2022), "BERT-base-multilingual-cased”(Devlin et al., 2018) and “Indic-BERT”(Kakwani et al., 2020). Figure 1 depicts the developed system's schematic process.

4.1 Pre-processing

During pre-processing, noises like punctuation, alphanumeric letters, and special characters (slash, brackets, ampersands, etc.) are eliminated from Malayalam code-mixed data and transliterated (Raihan et al., 2023).

4.2 Machine Learning Models

The feature vector has been extracted for machine learning techniques using Word2Vec and TF-IDF word embedding in subtask-1 (Mikolov et al., 2013). To establish a fake news detection system, we start by using conventional machine learning techniques like Logistic Regression (LR), Support Vector Machine (SVM) and Random Forest (RF). The application of an ensemble of machine learning classifiers was further enhanced for improved results. Ensemble technique was explored by subtask-1 using Random Forest (RF) and Decision Tree (DT) classifiers in conjunction with LR and SVM, whereas ‘n estimators = 100’ were utilized for DT and RF. Majority voting technique is applied to achieve the prediction from the ensemble method.

4.3 Deep Learning Models

For classification tasks, DL algorithms performed better. Two different deep learning models were used to classify fake news: LSTM (Word2Vec)and LSTM (FastText) in subtask-1. LSTM is widely recognized for its proficiency in capturing both the semantic details and sustained dependencies over the long term. While Bidirectional LSTM (BiLSTM) takes advantage of both past and future states, LSTM records semantic information and long-term dependencies. The models were trained using the Adam optimizer with a learning rate of 1e-3 and batch size of 32. To obtain the predictions, a sigmoid layer was employed at the end.

4.4 Transformer Models

In the past few years, transformers have gained increasing recognition due to their exceptional capabilities across different areas of natural language processing (NLP). We investigated four transformers XLM-R, m-BERT, Malayalam-BERT, and Indic-BERT pre-trained models to fine-tune on Malayalam fake news detection dataset. A self-supervised training method for cross-lingual comprehension, known as XLM-R (Conneau et al., 2019), is especially useful for low-resource languages. A transformer model called m-BERT (Devlin et al., 2018) has been pre-trained on 104 different languages; Malayalam-BERT (Joshi, 2022) has been pre-trained only on the Malayalam language. A multilingual ALBERT model embracing 12 main Indian languages, IndicBERT (Kakwani et al., 2020) were trained on a large corpus. The ktrain package is used to refine these models, which are selected from the Pytorch Huggingface transformers library. Each model has been trained for a maximum of 10 epochs using a batch size of 9 for Malayalam-BERT and 16 for XLM-R and m-BERT.

5 Results and Analysis

This section evaluates the performance of different models in recognizing fake news detection in Dravidian languages.

5.1 Evaluation Metrics

Model performance was measured using the macro-averaged F1 score. Table 3 and Table 4 present the

[2]`https://huggingface.co/docs/transformers/index`

Classifiers	Original			Transliterated		
	P	R	F	P	R	F
LR	0.82	0.82	0.82	0.82	0.82	0.82
SVM	0.80	0.80	0.80	0.83	0.83	0.83
RF	0.77	0.77	0.77	0.83	0.83	0.83
Ensemble	0.79	0.80	0.78	0.83	0.83	0.83
LSTM (Word2vec)	0.80	0.79	0.79	0.84	0.85	0.84
LSTM (Fasttext)	0.78	0.79	0.78	0.81	0.81	0.81
Indic-BERT	0.75	0.75	0.75	0.81	0.81	0.81
M-BERT	0.84	0.84	0.84	0.85	0.85	0.85
XLM-R	0.86	0.86	0.86	0.87	0.87	0.87
Malayalam-BERT	**0.86**	**0.86**	**0.86**	**0.87**	**0.87**	**0.87**

Table 3: Performance of various models on the test set of subtask-1. Here P, R, and F1 denotes macro Precision, macro Recall, and macro F1-Score respectively.

Classifiers	Original			Transliterated		
	P	R	F	P	R	F
Indic-BERT	0.14	0.25	0.12	0.02	0.25	0.04
XLM-R	0.14	0.25	0.12	0.07	0.25	0.11
M-BERT	0.12	0.25	0.14	0.21	0.23	0.16
Malayalam-BERT	**0.22**	**0.20**	**0.16**	**0.17**	**0.21**	**0.17**

Table 4: Performance of various models on the test set of subtask-2. Here P, R, and F1 denotes macro Precision, macro Recall, and macro F1-Score respectively.

performance of each classifier, trained on both the original and augmented training datasets.

5.2 Comparative Analysis

Regarding subtask-1, the f_1-scores highlight LR model sustained proficiency with a consistent f_1-score of 0.82 in both original and transliterated datasets. In the original dataset, SVM and RF demonstrate parallel performance, achieving f_1-scores of 0.80 and 0.77, respectively. Interestingly, in the transliterated dataset, both SVM and RF experience a slight boost in f_1-score to 0.83. The ensemble method exhibits robustness across both datasets, maintaining f_1-score of 0.79 in the original dataset and a commendable improvement (0.83) in the transliterated dataset.

Moving to deep learning techniques, LSTM with Word2Vec consistently outperformed others, achieving macro f_1-scores of 0.79 and 0.84 on the original and transliterated sets, respectively. FastText, however, yielded lower scores of 0.78 and 0.81 in the original and augmented datasets.

Transformer models outperformed both machine learning and deep learning models in each task. On the original dataset, all transformers, except Indic-BERT, surpassed the highest macro f_1-score (0.82) achieved by SVM. Malayalam-BERT emerged as the top performer with a leading score of 0.86. In the transliterated set, excluding Indic-BERT, all transformers excelled beyond the 0.82 macro f_1-score from machine learning and deep learning models, with Malayalam-BERT achieving the highest macro f_1-score of 0.87 in the augmented training set. This suggests the consistent superiority of transformers, particularly Malayalam-BERT, in Malayalam fake news identification.

In subtask-2, with the original dataset, Indic-BERT and XLM-R exhibit similar macro f_1-score of 0.12, indicating relatively low performance overall, while M-BERT and Malayalam-BERT achieved macro f_1-scores of 0.14 and 0.16, respectively. However, in the augmented dataset, there are notable improvements for some classifiers. M-BERT and Malayalam-BERT show increased macro f_1-scores of 0.16 and 0.17. respectively, suggesting a boost in performance. Malayalam-BERT remains the best performer even in the transliterated dataset.

5.3 Error Analysis

A thorough examination of error analysis is conducted both quantitatively and qualitatively to offer

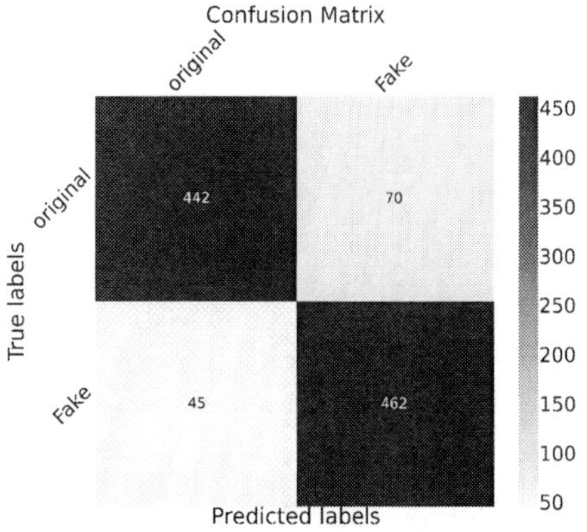

Figure 2: Confusion matrix of the best model, Malayalam-BERT, after running on the subtask-1 dataset

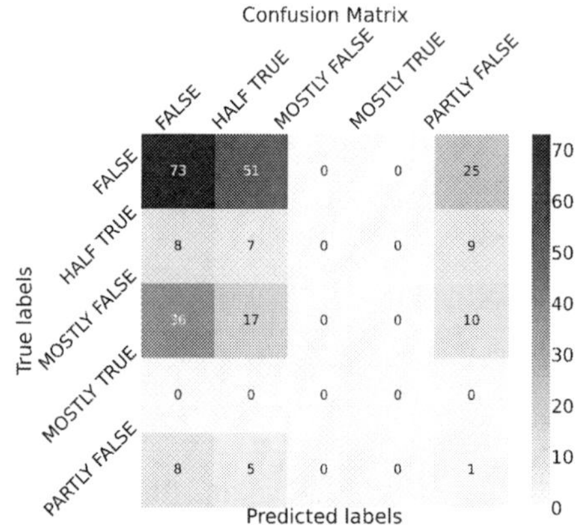

Figure 3: Confusion matrix of the best model, Malayalam-BERT, after running on the subtask-2 dataset

comprehensive insights into the effectiveness of the suggested model.

5.3.1 Quantitative Analysis

We can see the best performing model was Malayalam-BERT in subtask-1 which produced an f_1 score of 0.87 from Table 3. Figure 2 represents the confusion matrix of this model. From the confusion matrix, we can carry out an error analysis for this model. Among the two classes, the fake class has the highest True-Positive Rate (TPR) of 91.12%, while the original class has a lower TPR of 86.32%.

Figure 3 represents the confusion matrix of subtask-2. The FALSE class dominates with the highest True Positive Rate (TPR), closely followed by HALF TRUE. However, the discrimination is glaring as MOSTLY FALSE and MOSTLY TRUE struggle to detect any data accurately. Particularly, PARTLY FALSE suffers from a remarkably low detection rate for the True class. This bias stems from the dataset's imbalance, accentuating the need for a more equitable distribution for improved model performance.

5.3.2 Qualitative Analysis

Figure 4 and 5 in Appedix 8 provide illustrations of predicted outcomes by the best-performing model, Malayalam-BERT.

The model accurately predicts the outcomes for the 1st, 2nd, and 5th text samples in subtask-1. However, it encounters challenges in predicting the 3rd and 4th text samples, where its performance is not as successful for subtask-1. In subtask-2 the model correctly predicts text samples 1 and 2, however, it has trouble predicting text samples 3 and 4. The problem of class imbalance might be the cause of incorrect predictions.

6 Limitations

Our models depend on accurately turning words from one language into another (transliteration). Even small mistakes can significantly impact the information, affecting how well our models work. Furthermore, in subtask-2, the data was quite imbalanced, and no methods were applied to balance the data. Future exploration of methods with multiple transliteration options, as well as augmentation for balancing the dataset can be investigated to further enhance the accuracy of our approach.

7 Conclusion

This work aimed to detect and classify fake news from Malayalam social media text. We have thoroughly investigated several machine learning (ML), and deep learning (DL) and transformer-based models for Malayalam fake news identification and classification. The Malayalam-BERT model has proven to be more effective than the others, as evidenced by its highest macro F1-Score of 0.87 for subtask-1 and 0.17 for subtask-2. In subtask-1, the model excels, securing the 2nd position with a noteworthy macro f_1-score of 0.87. In contrast, in subtask-2, it ranks 11th with a macro f_1-score of 0.17. To improve model performance in the future, we want to look at different architectures and use ensemble techniques. We'll explore different ways to tackle problems that come from imbalanced datasets.

References

Abhinaba Bala and Parameswari Krishnamurthy. 2023. Abhipaw@ dravidianlangtech: Fake news detection in dravidian languages using multilingual bert. In *Proceedings of the Third Workshop on Speech and Language Technologies for Dravidian Languages*, pages 235–238.

Bharathi Raja Chakravarthi, Ruba Priyadharshini, Shubanker Banerjee, Manoj Balaji Jagadeeshan, Prasanna Kumar Kumaresan, Rahul Ponnusamy, Sean Benhur, and John Philip McCrae. 2023. Detecting abusive comments at a fine-grained level in a low-resource language. *Natural Language Processing Journal*, 3:100006.

Sharal Coelho, Asha Hegde, G Kavya, and Hosahalli Lakshmaiah Shashirekha. 2023. Mucs@ dravidianlangtech2023: Malayalam fake news detection using machine learning approach. In *Proceedings of the Third Workshop on Speech and Language Technologies for Dravidian Languages*, pages 288–292.

Alexis Conneau, Kartikay Khandelwal, Naman Goyal, Vishrav Chaudhary, Guillaume Wenzek, Francisco Guzmán, Edouard Grave, Myle Ott, Luke Zettlemoyer, and Veselin Stoyanov. 2019. Unsupervised cross-lingual representation learning at scale. *arXiv preprint arXiv:1911.02116*.

Jacob Devlin, Ming-Wei Chang, Kenton Lee, and Kristina Toutanova. 2018. Bert: Pre-training of deep bidirectional transformers for language understanding. *arXiv preprint arXiv:1810.04805*.

Asha Hegde and Hosahalli Lakshmaiah Shashirekha. 2021. Urdu fake news detection using ensemble of machine learning models. In *CEUR Workshop Proceedings*, pages 132–141.

Alamgir Hossain, Mahathir Bishal, Eftekhar Hossain, Omar Sharif, and Mohammed Moshiul Hoque. 2022a. Combatant@ tamilnlp-acl2022: Fine-grained categorization of abusive comments using logistic regression. In *Proceedings of the Second Workshop on Speech and Language Technologies for Dravidian Languages*, pages 221–228.

Alamgir Hossain, Mahathir Bishal, Eftekhar Hossain, Omar Sharif, and Mohammed Moshiul Hoque. 2022b. COMBATANT@TamilNLP-ACL2022: Fine-grained categorization of abusive comments using logistic regression. In *Proceedings of the Second Workshop on Speech and Language Technologies for Dravidian Languages*, pages 221–228, Dublin, Ireland. Association for Computational Linguistics.

Raviraj Joshi. 2022. L3Cube-MahaCorpus and MahaBERT: Marathi monolingual corpus, Marathi BERT language models, and resources. In *Proceedings of the WILDRE-6 Workshop within the 13th Language Resources and Evaluation Conference*, pages 97–101, Marseille, France. European Language Resources Association.

Divyanshu Kakwani, Anoop Kunchukuttan, Satish Golla, NC Gokul, Avik Bhattacharyya, Mitesh M Khapra, and Pratyush Kumar. 2020. Indicnlpsuite: Monolingual corpora, evaluation benchmarks and pre-trained multilingual language models for indian languages. In *Findings of the Association for Computational Linguistics: EMNLP 2020*, pages 4948–4961.

Hariharan LekshmiAmmal, Manikandan Ravikiran, and Anand Kumar Madasamy. 2022. NITK-IT_NLP@TamilNLP-ACL2022: Transformer based model for toxic span identification in Tamil. In *Proceedings of the Second Workshop on Speech and Language Technologies for Dravidian Languages*, pages 75–78, Dublin, Ireland. Association for Computational Linguistics.

Tomas Mikolov, Ilya Sutskever, Kai Chen, Greg S Corrado, and Jeff Dean. 2013. Distributed representations of words and phrases and their compositionality. *Advances in neural information processing systems*, 26.

MD Sijanur Rahman, Omar Sharif, Avishek Das, Sadia Afroze, and Mohammed Moshiul Hoque. 2022. Fand-x: Fake news detection using transformer-based multilingual masked language model. In *2022 IEEE International Women in Engineering (WIE) Conference on Electrical and Computer Engineering (WIECON-ECE)*, pages 153–158. IEEE.

Nishant Rai, Deepika Kumar, Naman Kaushik, Chandan Raj, and Ahad Ali. 2022. Fake news classification using transformer based enhanced lstm and bert. *International Journal of Cognitive Computing in Engineering*, 3:98–105.

Md Nishat Raihan, Umma Hani Tanmoy, Anika Binte Islam, Kai North, Tharindu Ranasinghe, Antonios Anastasopoulos, and Marcos Zampieri. 2023. Offensive language identification in transliterated and code-mixed bangla. *arXiv preprint arXiv:2311.15023*.

Eduri Raja, Badal Soni, and Sami Kumar Borgohain. 2023. nlpt malayalm@ dravidianlangtech: Fake news detection in malayalam using optimized xlm-roberta model. In *Proceedings of the Third Workshop on Speech and Language Technologies for Dravidian Languages*, pages 186–191.

Risul Islam Rasel, Anower Hossen Zihad, Nasrin Sultana, and Mohammed Moshiul Hoque. 2022. Bangla fake news detection using machine learning, deep learning and transformer models. In *2022 25th International Conference on Computer and Information Technology (ICCIT)*, pages 959–964. IEEE.

Arjun Roy, Kingshuk Basak, Asif Ekbal, and Pushpak Bhattacharyya. 2019. A deep ensemble framework for fake news detection and multi-class classification of short political statements. In *Proceedings of the 16th International Conference on Natural Language Processing*, pages 9–17.

Omar Sharif, Eftekhar Hossain, and Mohammed Moshiul Hoque. 2021. Combating hostility: Covid-19 fake news and hostile post detection in social media. *CoRR*, abs/2101.03291.

Malliga Subramanian, Bharathi Raja Chakravarthi, Kogilavani Shanmugavadivel, Santhiya Pandiyan, Prasanna Kumar Kumaresan, Balasubramanian Palani, Muskaan Singh, Sandhiya Raja, Vanaja, and Mithunajha S. 2023. Overview of the shared task on fake news detection from social media text. In *Proceedings of the Third Workshop on Speech and Language Technologies for Dravidian Languages*, Varna, Bulgaria. Recent Advances in Natural Language Processing.

Mudasir Ahmad Wani, Mohammad ELAffendi, Kashish Ara Shakil, Ibrahem Mohammed Abuhaimed, Anand Nayyar, Amir Hussain, and Ahmed A Abd El-Latif. 2023. Toxic fake news detection and classification for combating covid-19 misinformation. *IEEE Transactions on Computational Social Systems*.

8 Appendix

Text Sample	Actual	Predicted
മൊഴി മുത്തുകളായ വരികൾ (Lines that are pearls of expression)	Original	Original
Shame for entire Woman&#39	Original	Original
വിമർശിക്കുന്നു(Criticizing)	Fake	Original
They revised the social distancing from 2M to 2cm so it's fine.	Original	Fake
എല്ലാം വരുടെയും പ്രാത്ഥന മൂലം ആണ് (Everything is due to the prayer of the bridegroom)	Fake	Fake

Figure 4: Few examples of predicted outputs by the proposed (Malayalam-BERT) model for subtask-1

Text Sample	Actual	Predicted
കീർത്തി സുരേഷ് ഫർഹാൻ എന്ന മുസ്ലിം യുവാവിനെ കല്യാണം കഴിയ്ക്കുന്നു (Keerthi is getting married to a young Muslim named Suresh Farhan)	False	False
വാരിയം കുന്നനെ അറസ്റ്റ് ചെയ്തതായി മലയാള മനോരമ നൽകിയ വാർത്ത (Malayalam Manorama reported that Variyam Kunnan was arrested.)	Mostly False	Mostly False
ചന്ദനക്കുറിയണിഞ്ഞ് വിഎസ് അച്യുതാനന്ദൻ.(VS Achuthanandan dressed in sandalwood.)	False	Mostly True
പലസ്തീൻ പതാകയണിഞ്ഞ് ക്രിസ്ത്യാനോ റൊണാൾഡോ (Cristiano Ronaldo wearing the Palestinian flag)	Half True	Mostly False

Figure 5: Few samples of the predicted outcomes of the proposed (Malayalam-BERT) model for subtask-2

CUET_NLP_GoodFellows@DravidianLangTech EACL2024: A Transformer-Based Approach for Detecting Fake News in Dravidian Languages

Md Osama, Kawsar Ahmed, Hasan Mesbaul Ali Taher, Jawad Hossain, Shawly Ahsan and **Mohammed Moshiul Hoque**
Department of Computer Science and Engineering
Chittagong University of Engineering & Technology, Chattogram-4349, Bangladesh
{u1804039, u1804017, u1804038, u1704039, u1704057}@student.cuet.ac.bd
moshiul_240@cuet.ac.bd

Abstract

In this modern era, many people have been using Facebook and Twitter, leading to increased information sharing and communication. However, a considerable amount of information on these platforms is misleading or intentionally crafted to deceive users, which is often termed as fake news. A shared task on fake news detection in Malayalam organized by DravidianLangTech@EACL 2024 allowed us for addressing the challenge of distinguishing between original and fake news content in the Malayalam language. Our approach involves creating an intelligent framework to categorize text as either fake or original. We experimented with various machine learning models, including Logistic Regression, Decision Tree, Random Forest, Multinomial Naive Bayes, SVM, and SGD, and various deep learning models, including CNN, BiLSTM, and BiLSTM + Attention. We also explored Indic-BERT, MuRIL, XLM-R, and m-BERT for transformer-based approaches. Notably, our most successful model, m-BERT, achieved a macro F1 score of 0.85 and ranked 4th in the shared task. This research contributes to combating misinformation on social media news, offering an effective solution to classify content accurately.

1 Introduction

In recent years, there has been an unprecedented surge in user participation on social media platforms such as Facebook and Twitter, as individuals increasingly utilize these platforms (Sharif et al., 2021). The users engage in the exchange of information, communication, and the continuous monitoring of current events. Conversely, a significant portion of the recent information disseminated on these platforms is inaccurately represented and, at times, deliberately crafted to misguide users. This content category is commonly identified as "fake news," encompassing any deceptive or false information presented as authentic news (Subramanian et al., 2024). The anonymity afforded to users on social media provides an opportunity for disseminators of fake news to manipulate people's beliefs, trust, and opinions by intentionally spreading false information. Rumors and misinformation propagate swiftly, adversely affecting personal relationships and social connections. Moreover, they have the potential to induce anxiety and emotional distress by fostering unfavorable perceptions, subjecting individuals to public scrutiny, and contributing to social isolation (Coelho et al., 2023). Moreover, current news often makes statements without confirmed evidence. To determine if these real-time claims are true, we heavily depend on how well they match information from other sources. The shared task (Subramanian et al., 2024) organized by DravidianLangTech@EACL 2024[1] provided us with an opportunity to address this significant challenge. This task aims to categorize a given social media text as either original or fake. The data sources include diverse social media platforms like Twitter and Facebook. The objective of this research work is to develop a system capable of discerning whether a news sample is original or fake. The key contributions of this endeavor are outlined below:

- Explored the efficacy of various ML, DL, and transformer models in detecting fake news and analyzing errors to gain valuable insights into the detection process.
- Proposed a transformer-based model that can classify a Malayalam news sample into two classes: fake and original.

2 Related work

The detection of fake news in low-resource languages, including code-mixed texts, is gaining increasing attention. Researchers have investigated

[1] https://sites.google.com/view/dravidianlangtech-2024/home

Proceedings of the Fourth Workshop on Speech, Vision, and Language Technologies for Dravidian Languages, pages 187–192

various techniques for identifying fake news using benchmarked corpora in low-resourced languages. In this section, we provide a concise overview of relevant studies in this domain. Coelho et al. (2023) addressed the challenge of detecting fake news through three machine learning models (MNB, LR, and Ensemble) trained on code-mixed Malayalam text using Term Frequency - Inverse Document Frequency (TF-IDF). They achieved a notable macro F1-score of 0.831 and secured 3rd rank in the "Fake News Detection in Dravidian Languages" shared task at DravidianLangTech@RANLP 2023. In response to the urgent need for robust defenses against machine-generated fake news, Fung et al. (2021) created a benchmark dataset and identified fake news using cross-media consistency checking. Their proposed methodology surpassed the state-of-the-art models and achieved up to a 16.8% gain in accuracy. Rasel et al. (2022) constructed a comprehensive Bangla fake news dataset and have employed various machine learning, deep neural networks, and transformer models. The best performing models, CNN, CNN-LSTM, and BiLSTM, achieved notable accuracies of 95.9%, 95.5%, and 95.3%, respectively. Li et al. (2021) outlined the system for the AAAI 2021 shared task on COVID-19 fake news detection in English, securing the 3rd position with a weighted score of 0.9859 on the test set. They constructed an ensemble of pre-trained language models, including BERT, Roberta, and Ernie, and employed diverse training strategies like a warm-up, a learning rate schedule, and k-fold cross-validation. Shu et al. (2019) addressed the challenge of fake news detection on social media by introducing the TriFN framework, a novel approach leveraging the inherent tri-relationship among publishers, news pieces, and users during dissemination. Unlike traditional algorithms focusing solely on news content, TriFN concurrently models publisher-news relations and user-news interactions. Zhou and Zafarani (2020) addressed the pressing issue of fake news, emphasizing its detrimental impact on democracy, justice, and public trust. Evaluating detection methods from multiple perspectives, including false knowledge, writing style, propagation patterns, and source credibility, the survey encourages interdisciplinary research. Sharif et al. (2021) presented a detailed description of a system developed for encompassing COVID-19 fake news detection in English (Task-A) and hostile post detection in Hindi (Task-B) using SVM, CNN, BiLSTM, and CNN+BiLSTM with TF-IDF and Word2Vec embedding. Their system achieved notable results, with the highest weighted F1 score of 94.39% in Task-A and 86.03% coarse-grained and 50.98% fine-grained F1 scores in Task-B.

3 Task and Dataset Description

The surge in online social media usage has revolutionized communication, enabling users to exchange information, engage in conversations, and stay informed about current events. However, this convenience has also led to the widespread dissemination of false information, commonly known as fake news, aiming to mislead users. This shared task (Subramanian et al., 2024) focuses on classifying social media texts as either original or fake news. The dataset comprises of text samples collected from diverse social media platforms, including Twitter and Facebook. It is organized into two distinct classes: "Fake" and "Original". The following outlines the definitions of the classes:

- **Fake:** Fake news refers to information deliberately crafted to mislead or deceive. These texts often contain intentionally false or misleading content that is presented as genuine.
- **Original:** Original news represents authentic and accurate information that reflects truthful and unbiased content. These texts are not manipulated or intentionally misleading, providing a reliable representation of real-world information.

Table 1 provides the distribution of samples in training, validation, and test sets across all the classes.

Classes	Train	Valid	Test
Fake	1,599	406	507
Original	1,658	409	512
Total	3,257	815	1,019

Table 1: Distribution of the dataset

4 Methodology

To address the issue at hand, we conducted an extensive exploration of various machine learning (ML), deep learning (DL), and transformer-based models. Through careful analysis, our research recommends utilizing a transformer-based model employing m-BERT (Jacob Devlin and Ming-Wei

Chang and Kenton Lee and Kristina Toutanova, 2018). Figure 1 provides a concise visualization of our methodology, outlining the key steps involved in our approach.

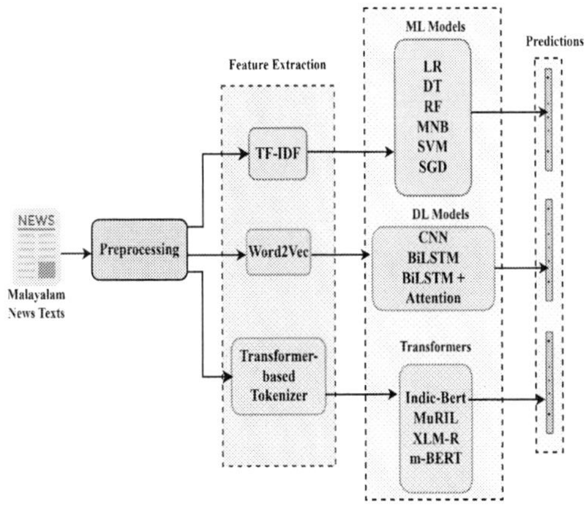

Figure 1: Abstract view of our methodology

4.1 Preprocessing

In the initial phase of our approach, we systematically executed essential preprocessing steps to refine the input data. This involved the meticulous removal of emojis, punctuation marks, URLs, and white spaces. By undertaking these measures, our objective was to optimize the quality and consistency of the dataset.

4.2 Feature Extraction

We employed a diverse set of techniques to capture and represent the underlying information within our textual data. The feature extraction techniques are as follows:

- **TF-IDF:** This technique (Qaiser and Ali, 2018) considers both the frequency of a term in a document and its rarity across the entire dataset, providing a robust representation of each document's content.
- **Word2Vec:** Leveraging the Word2Vec (Mikolov et al., 2013) technique, we transformed words into high-dimensional vectors, preserving semantic relationships and capturing context.
- **Transformer-based Tokenizer:** Leveraging transformer models, we used a transformer-based tokenizer to encode and tokenize our text data, benefiting from contextual information and hierarchical representations.

4.3 Model Building

In our research, we delved into a variety of models, including machine learning (ML), deep learning (DL), and transformer-based approaches.

4.3.1 ML models

In the realm of machine learning, our investigation involved the exploration and utilization of various classical models with TF-IDF. Specifically, we employed Logistic Regression, Decision Tree, Random Forest, Multinomial Naive Bayes, Support Vector Machine (SVM), and Stochastic Gradient Descent (SGD). Each of these models was strategically selected to harness different strengths and characteristics in addressing the complexities of this problem.

4.3.2 DL models

In this research work, we delved into the realm of deep learning models to get a better result with the word2vec word embedding technique. We experimented with a set of models, including CNN, BiLSTM (Huang et al., 2015), and BiLSTM + Attention (Vaswani et al., 2023), all incorporating word2vec embedding. Each model was chosen thoughtfully to extract unique insights and patterns from the data, contributing to a well-rounded analysis.

4.3.3 Transformer-based models

Finally, we delved into transformer-based models, specifically leveraging Indic-BERT (Jain et al., 2020), MuRIL (Khanuja et al., 2021), XLM-R (Conneau et al., 2019), and m-BERT (Jacob Devlin and Ming-Wei Chang and Kenton Lee and Kristina Toutanova, 2018) to enhance our outcomes. For these transformer models, we initially obtained them from the Hugging Face[2] library and fine-tuned them using our dataset. During testing, we streamlined the process using Hugging Face APIs, ultimately achieving accurate predictions.

5 Results

In this section, we provide comparisons of the performance achieved by different machine learning, deep learning, and transformer-based methods.

The performance evaluation of various classifiers for fake news detection showcases intriguing

[2]https://huggingface.co

Classifier	P	R	MF1
LR	0.67	0.65	0.64
DT	0.69	0.69	0.69
RF	0.71	0.71	0.71
MNB	0.72	0.71	0.71
SVM	0.70	0.69	0.69
SGD	0.73	0.73	0.73
CNN	0.78	0.72	0.71
BiLSTM	0.81	0.72	0.70
BiLSTM + Attention	0.80	0.72	0.71
Indic-BERT	0.67	0.64	0.66
MuRIL	0.74	0.76	0.75
XLM-R	0.84	0.83	0.84
m-BERT	**0.87**	**0.83**	**0.85**

Table 2: Performance of different models on test set

insights into their predictive capabilities. A detailed summary of the precision (P), recall (R), and macro-F1 (MF1) scores attained by each model on the test set is provided in Table 2.

Among the traditional ML classifiers, Stochastic Gradient Descent (SGD) demonstrated the highest precision (P), recall (R), and macro-F1 (MF1) scores of 0.73, demonstrating consistent performance across all criteria.

Transitioning to deep learning architectures, CNN, BiLSTM, and BiLSTM + Attention exhibited competitive performances. While BiLSTM showed slightly higher precision (P), BiLSTM + Attention demonstrated better recall (R), underscoring the importance of attention mechanisms for discerning subtle patterns.

However, the standout performers were the transformer-based models, XLM-R and m-BERT. Outperforming other models in precision (P), recall (R), and macro-F1 (MF1) scores, m-BERT emerged as the top performer with the highest scores across all metrics, achieving a macro-F1 (MF1) score of 0.85.

5.1 Error Analysis

5.1.1 Quantitative Analysis

The results underscore the efficacy of transformer-based architectures, especially m-BERT, in detecting fake news. m-BERT's ability to leverage contextual information and encode multilingual text representations is pivotal in distinguishing between original and fake news samples.

This suggests that incorporating contextual embeddings from pre-trained language models, like m-BERT, significantly enhances the accuracy and robustness of fake news detection systems. Figure 2 represents the basic analysis with a confusion matrix. This matrix provides a quantitative breakdown of our model's predictions. The analysis reveals that our model accurately identifies 415 fake news articles and 449 original ones. However, there is a slight challenge in instances where the model misclassifies 92 fake news as original and 63 originals as fake. This occurrence is attributed to the presence of code-mixed text in certain samples of our dataset, leading to moments of confusion for the model.

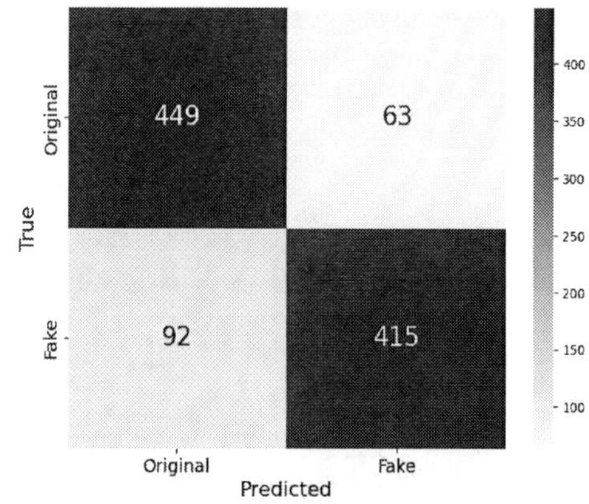

Figure 2: Confusion matrix of the m-BERT model for test set

5.1.2 Qualitative Analysis

Figure 3 showcases some sample predictions made by our model. Among these, samples 1, 2, and 4 are correctly classified. However, there are instances where the model misclassifies the samples, such as sample 3 being labeled as original when it

Text Sample	Actual	Predicted
Sample1: ഈ പാട്ടിനു ആടിയ ചേച്ചിസിന്റെ തൊലിക്കട്ടി. (The skin of Chechis who swayed to this song.)	original	original
Sample2: താത്വിക ആചാര്യന്മാർക്ക് ഒരു കയ്യബദ്ധം... നാറ്റിക്കരുത് (A handout for philosophical teachers...don't be a jerk)	original	original
Sample3: ഇതൊക്കെ ഉള്ളത് തന്നെ.. (All this is there..)	Fake	original
Sample4: ചൈനയിലെ മരണ സംഖ്യ യൂറോ പ്പിനെക്കാൾ വലുതാണ് (China's death toll is higher than Europe's)	Fake	Fake
Sample5: ലോകമെന്നാൽ കണ്ണൂരും പരിസരപ്രദേശവുമായി ചുരുങ്ങിയോ? (Is the world reduced to Kannur and its surroundings?)	original	Fake

Figure 3: Some examples of predicted outputs by the best model. Here, corresponding English texts are translated using "Google Translator"

is actually fake, and sample 5 being inaccurately classified as fake being confused with code-mixed Malayalam texts. An imbalanced dataset might be the cause for this. Also, the use of code-mixed data in the corpus made it more difficult for the model to classify the text. These nuances highlight the importance of qualitative analysis in understanding the model's performance in specific cases.

Limitations

While our model achieved a commendable score in detecting fake news in Malayalam, certain limitations need consideration. These include the scarcity of diverse training data for Dravidian languages, potential linguistic nuances impacting model performance, and the model's focus primarily on textual content, neglecting multimedia elements often present in fake news. Additionally, the dynamic nature of misinformation tactics, the ethical implications of misclassification, cultural influences, and the need for explainability in model decisions pose ongoing challenges. Addressing these limitations will be crucial for refining the model's accuracy, adaptability, and ethical considerations in combating fake news effectively.

6 Conclusion

In our study, we set out to tackle the task of classifying fake and original news. Through a detailed comparison of various machine learning (ML), deep learning (DL), and transformer-based models, we found that m-BERT delivered the most impressive performance, boasting a macro F1 score of 0.85, surpassing all other models. Looking ahead, we plan to refine our approach further by exploring ensemble techniques in future research endeavors, aiming for an even more effective solution to combat misinformation.

References

Sharal Coelho, Asha Hegde, Kavya G, and Hosahalli Lakshmaiah Shashirekha. 2023. MUCS@DravidianLangTech2023: Malayalam Fake News Detection Using Machine Learning Approach. In *Proceedings of the Third Workshop on Speech and Language Technologies for Dravidian Languages*, pages 288–292, Varna, Bulgaria. INCOMA Ltd., Shoumen, Bulgaria.

Alexis Conneau, Kartikay Khandelwal, Naman Goyal, Vishrav Chaudhary, Guillaume Wenzek, Francisco Guzmán, Edouard Grave, Myle Ott, Luke Zettlemoyer, and Veselin Stoyanov. 2019. Unsupervised Cross-lingual Representation Learning at Scale. *CoRR*, abs/1911.02116.

Yi Fung, Christopher Thomas, Revanth Gangi Reddy, Sandeep Polisetty, Heng Ji, Shih-Fu Chang, Kathleen McKeown, Mohit Bansal, and Avirup Sil. 2021. InfoSurgeon: Cross-Media Fine-grained Information Consistency Checking for Fake News Detection. In *Proceedings of the 59th Annual Meeting of the Association for Computational Linguistics and the 11th International Joint Conference on Natural Language Processing (Volume 1: Long Papers)*, pages 1683–1698.

Zhiheng Huang, Wei Xu, and Kai Yu. 2015. Bidirectional LSTM-CRF Models for Sequence Tagging.

Jacob Devlin and Ming-Wei Chang and Kenton Lee and Kristina Toutanova. 2018. BERT: Pre-training of Deep Bidirectional Transformers for Language Understanding. *CoRR*, abs/1810.04805.

Kushal Jain, Adwait P. Deshpande, Kumar Shridhar, Felix Laumann, and Ayushman Dash. 2020. Indic-Transformers: An Analysis of Transformer Language Models for Indian Languages. *CoRR*, abs/2011.02323.

Simran Khanuja, Diksha Bansal, Sarvesh Mehtani, Savya Khosla, Atreyee Dey, Balaji Gopalan, Dilip Kumar Margam, Pooja Aggarwal, Rajiv Teja Nagipogu, Shachi Dave, Shruti Gupta, Subhash Chandra Bose Gali, Vish Subramanian, and Partha P. Talukdar. 2021. MuRIL: Multilingual Representations for Indian Languages. *CoRR*, abs/2103.10730.

Xiangyang Li, Yu Xia, Xiang Long, Zheng Li, and Sujian Li. 2021. Exploring Text-Transformers in AAAI 2021 Shared Task: COVID-19 Fake News Detection in English. In *Combating Online Hostile Posts in Regional Languages during Emergency Situation*, pages 106–115, Cham. Springer International Publishing.

Tomas Mikolov, Kai Chen, Greg Corrado, and Jeffrey Dean. 2013. Efficient estimation of word representations in vector space. *arXiv preprint arXiv:1301.3781*.

Shahzad Qaiser and Ramsha Ali. 2018. Text mining: use of TF-IDF to examine the relevance of words to documents. *International Journal of Computer Applications*, 181(1):25–29.

Risul Islam Rasel, Anower Hossen Zihad, Nasrin Sultana, and Mohammed Moshiul Hoque. 2022. Bangla Fake News Detection using Machine Learning, Deep Learning and Transformer Models. In *2022 25th International Conference on Computer and Information Technology (ICCIT)*, pages 959–964.

Omar Sharif, Eftekhar Hossain, and Mohammed Moshiul Hoque. 2021. Combating hostility: Covid-19 fake news and hostile post detection in social media. *arXiv preprint arXiv:2101.03291*.

Kai Shu, Suhang Wang, and Huan Liu. 2019. Beyond News Contents: The Role of Social Context for Fake News Detection. In *Proceedings of the Twelfth ACM International Conference on Web Search and Data Mining*, WSDM '19, page 312–320, New York, NY, USA. Association for Computing Machinery.

Malliga Subramanian, Bharathi Raja Chakravarthi, Kogilavani Shanmugavadivel, Santhiya Pandiyan, Prasanna Kumar Kumaresan, Balasubramanian Palani, Premjith B, Sandhiya Raja, Vanaja, Mithunajha S, Devika K, Hariprasath S.B, Haripriya B, and Vigneshwar E. 2024. Overview of the Second Shared Task on Fake News Detection in Dravidian Languages. In *Proceedings of the Fourth Workshop on Speech, Vision, and Language Technologies for Dravidian Languages*, Malta. European Chapter of the Association for Computational Linguistics.

Ashish Vaswani, Noam Shazeer, Niki Parmar, Jakob Uszkoreit, Llion Jones, Aidan N. Gomez, Lukasz Kaiser, and Illia Polosukhin. 2023. Attention Is All You Need.

Xinyi Zhou and Reza Zafarani. 2020. A Survey of Fake News: Fundamental Theories, Detection Methods, and Opportunities. *ACM Comput. Surv.*, 53(5).

CUET_Binary_Hackers@DravidianLangTech EACL2024: Hate and Offensive Language Detection in Telugu Code-Mixed Text Using Sentence Similarity BERT

Salman Farsi, Asrarul Hoque Eusha
Jawad Hossain, Shawly Ahsan, Avishek Das and **Mohammed Moshiul Hoque**
Department of Computer Science and Engineering
Chittagong University of Engineering & Technology, Chattogram-4349, Bangladesh
{salman.cuet.cse, asrar2860}@gmail.com
{u1704039, u1704057}@student.cuet.ac.bd, {avishek, moshiul_240}@cuet.ac.bd

Abstract

With the continuous evolution of technology and widespread internet access, various social media platforms have gained immense popularity, attracting a vast number of active users globally. However, this surge in online activity has also led to a concerning trend by driving many individuals to resort to posting hateful and offensive comments or posts, publicly targeting groups or individuals. In response to these challenges, we participated in this shared task. Our approach involved proposing a fine-tuning-based pre-trained transformer model to effectively discern whether a given text contains offensive content that propagates hatred. We conducted comprehensive experiments, exploring various machine learning (LR, SVM, and Ensemble), deep learning (CNN, BiLSTM, CNN+BiLSTM), and transformer-based models (Indic-SBERT, m-BERT, MuRIL, Distil-BERT, XLM-R), adhering to a meticulous fine-tuning methodology. Among the models evaluated, our fine-tuned L3Cube-Indic-Sentence-Similarity-BERT or Indic-SBERT model demonstrated superior performance, achieving a macro-average F1-score of 0.7013. This notable result positioned us at the 6th place in the task. The implementation details of the task will be found in the GitHub repository [1].

1 Introduction

The contemporary digital landscape is heavily influenced by the pervasive role of social media in facilitating online communication. Platforms such as YouTube, Instagram, Facebook, and Twitter have not only provided users with avenues for creating and sharing content but have also become arenas where individuals can freely express their views and thoughts at any given moment (Taprial and Kanwar, 2012). The evolution of social media has brought forth a darker side, where individuals are defamed, targeted, and marginalized based on factors such as religion, physical appearance, or sexual orientation (Raja Chakravarthi et al., 2021). Given the impracticality of manually identifying offensive texts at scale, there arises a crucial need for an automated system capable of detecting hate speech. Such a system can empower relevant authorities to take necessary actions against offensive content. Natural Language Processing (NLP) emerges as a pivotal solution, offering various techniques to address these challenges effectively (Khurana et al., 2023). While the problem of identifying offensive language has been tackled from multiple angles, including detecting cyberbullying, aggression, toxicity, and abusive language (Fortuna et al., 2020; Mazari et al., 2023; Sharif et al., 2022; Hossain et al., 2022; Sharif and Hoque, 2021), there is a pressing need for more focused attention on hate-specific contexts in diverse languages.

Over the past few years, numerous studies have been conducted on detecting hate and offensive content in several high-resource languages such as English, Spanish, Arabic (Omar et al., 2020; Plaza-del Arco et al., 2021), and others that have ample linguistic resources, datasets, and related facilities. However, the challenge persists in addressing this issue efficiently for low-resource languages (Magueresse et al., 2020). In this particular task (B et al., 2024), the organizers presented a Telugu code-mixed hate speech dataset (Priyadharshini et al., 2023), framing it as a binary classification problem. The objective is to discern whether a given text represents any hate and offensive speech or not. This task serves as a crucial step toward addressing the gap in efficient hate speech detection for low-resource languages like Telugu, especially in the context of code-mixed text. As part of the participants in this task, the main contributions of our work are outlined below:

- We explored different ML, DL, and transformer-based models for hate speech de-

[1] https://github.com/Salman1804102/DravidianLangTech-EACL-2024-HOLD

Proceedings of the Fourth Workshop on Speech, Vision, and Language Technologies for Dravidian Languages, pages 193–199
March 22, 2024 ©2024 Association for Computational Linguistics

tection. And boosted the model's performance by determining the optimal hyper-parameters.

- Contributed to the field by conducting a comprehensive comparison of different models and evaluating the performance of these models.

We organized the rest of our presentation as follows: section 2 delves into related work, section 3 describes the task and dataset, section 4 outlines our methodology, section 5 describes the experimental setup, section 6 presents the results analysis, section 7 conducts an in-depth error analysis, and finally, section 8 concludes with insights and outlines directions for future work.

2 Related Work

In the evolving landscape of hate and offensive text detection, researchers have explored a spectrum of techniques, each contributing to the continuous refinement of models. An influential Bengali abusive text detection endeavor was conducted (Eshan and Hasan, 2017) assessing the efficacy of Support Vector Machine (SVM), Random Forest (RF), and Naive Bayes (NB) classifiers. Their framework, achieving an accuracy of approximately 95%, laid a foundation for subsequent investigations into more advanced methodologies. Saumya et al. (2021) investigated offensive language identification in social media code-mixed Tanglish (Tamil+English) and Manglish (Malayalam+English) text, as well as Malayalam script-mixed. The N-gram TF-IDF-based MNB classifier achieved a weighted F1-score of 0.90 in Tamil code-mixed text whereas LR led with 0.78 for Malayalam code-mixed content. The Vanilla Neural Network (VNN) outperformed in handling Malayalam script-mixed text, achieving an impressive weighted F1-score of 0.95.

As the field matured, a notable shift emerged from traditional machine learning to deep learning, exemplified by Omar et al. (2020)'s work on the detection of Arabic hate speech. Using Recurrent Neural Networks (RNN), they achieved an exceptional 98.7% accuracy which outperformed Convolutional Neural Networks (CNN). Another study (Mazari et al., 2023) employed a multi-label approach for hate speech detection on social media, utilizing pre-trained BERT and ensemble learning architectures that include BiLSTM and BiGRU models. Integrating recent word embedding techniques and DL models, the proposed approach achieved a remarkable ROC-AUC score of 98.63%.

The exploration of transformer-based models added a layer of complexity to hate speech detection. A weighted ensemble technique (Sharif et al., 2022), incorporating m-BERT, Distil-BERT, and Bangla-BERT, demonstrated the adaptability of these models in handling diverse linguistic nuances, particularly in Bengali aggressive text datasets. In DravidianLangTech2021[2], the author (Sharif et al., 2021) addressed the challenge of detecting offensive text in code-mixed social media data, employing effective transformer-based models like XLM-R, m-BERT, and Indic-BERT for Tamil, Kannada, and Malayalam languages. Extending this exploration, another study (Saha et al., 2021) within the same task also delved into a diverse set of transformer-based models, including MuRIL, Distil-BERT, and others. In HASOC 2023[3], a study (Joshi and Joshi, 2023) evaluated the efficacy of various sentence-BERT models, including Bengali-SBERT, Gujarati-SBERT, Assamese-BERT, and L3Cube Indic-SBERT, showcasing state-of-the-art results in detecting hate speech within Indian linguistic contexts.

3 Task and Dataset Description

In this shared task (B et al., 2024), a Telugu code-mixed dataset was introduced for the detection of hate and offensive language (Priyadharshini et al., 2023). The dataset, designed for binary classification, comprises diverse social media posts and comments containing both hate/offensive text and non-hate/non-offensive text. For participants, both the training and test datasets were provided, without any separate validation set. The training dataset consisted of 4,000 samples, comprising 2,061 non-hate-labeled and 1,939 hate-labeled samples, demonstrating a well-balanced distribution. Some other useful insights are mentioned in Table 1.

Set	Class	Sample Count	UW	MxL	AL	OOV
Train	Hate	2,061	17,097	71	10	1,167
	Non-Hate	1,939				
Test	Hate	1,939	2,365	18	7	
	Non-Hate	1,939				

Table 1: Dataset statistics, including UW (unique words), MxL (maximum length), AL (average length), and OOV (out-of-vocabulary) words in texts

[2] https://dravidianlangtech.github.io/2021/index.html
[3] https://hasocfire.github.io/hasoc/2023/

4 Methodology

In this section, we will delineate our methodology step by step. Figure 1 shows a schematic diagram of the methodology.

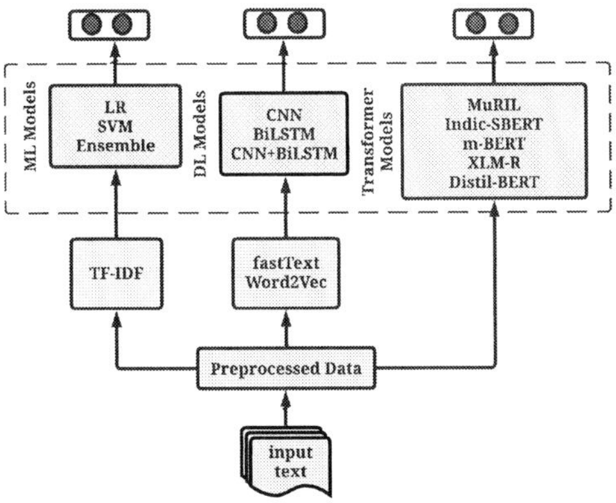

Figure 1: A schematic diagram of the methodology.

4.1 Data Pre-processing

Given that the dataset is code-mixed and sourced from social media, it inherently includes a substantial amount of extraneous and redundant content. Therefore, as an initial step, we conducted thorough data pre-processing. This involved the removal of emojis, symbols, signs, numbers, and certain unnecessary punctuation marks from the text.

4.2 Feature Extraction

In selecting feature extraction methods, our rationale is rooted in enhancing the interpretability and efficiency of ML and DL models for text data comprehension. TF-IDF was chosen for ML to capture important unigram features and highlight their significance in the context of our study (Das et al., 2023). For DL models, fastText and Word2Vec were employed to harness semantic relationships and context within the text. The implementation choices, such as the dimensionality of 300 for both Word2Vec and fastText, were made to strike a balance between computational efficiency and representation effectiveness, as supported by existing literature (Bojanowski et al., 2017; Mikolov et al., 2013). This approach ensures a comprehensive understanding of the textual content by both ML and DL models.

4.3 ML Models

To identify instances of hate speech, our initial approach involved the utilization of fundamental machine learning (ML) models. Specifically, we employed LR, SVM, and subsequently applied an ensemble technique incorporating RF, LR, SVM, and Decision Tree (DT) (Sarker, 2021). To train the LR model, we selected 'liblinear' as the solver, and set the parameter value of C to 1. For SVM, 'sigmoid' was chosen as the optimizer, and the C value was set to 1. This systematic deployment of basic ML models and an ensemble approach formed the initial exploration of our hate speech detection task.

4.4 DL Models

To leverage the proven efficacy of deep learning (DL) methods in handling sequence data, we incorporated three distinct approaches: Bidirectional Long Short Term Memory (BiLSTM) (Hochreiter and Schmidhuber, 1997), Convolutional Neural Network (CNN) (O'Shea and Nash, 2015) and a combination of CNN and BiLSTM (Sharif and Hoque, 2021). Each of these models was trained with both fastText and Word2Vec embeddings. The CNN model includes a 1D convolutional layer with 128 filters and a kernel size of 5, followed by global max pooling for feature extraction.

Meanwhile, in our combined CNN + BiLSTM (Khan et al., 2022) methodology, the CNN layer processed the initial embedding features using 128 filters. Subsequently, a max-pooling operation with a window size of 2 was applied to distill relevant features. The resultant vector underwent processing in the BiLSTM layer, which featured 200 bidirectional cells to adeptly capture long-term dependencies. To address overfitting concerns, a dropout technique with a 0.2 rate was implemented in the BiLSTM layer. The final step involved feeding the concatenated output of the BiLSTM layer into a sigmoid layer for prediction.

4.5 Transformer-based Models

Transformer-based models, particularly the latest addition preceding GPT, have revolutionized text classification and various problem domains (Gasparetto et al., 2022). Our method capitalizes on the versatility of pre-trained transformer-based models, evaluating their performance across different hyper-parameters. All the transformer-based models were trained using ktrain (Maiya, 2022) and imported from the 'Hugging Face'[4] (Wolf et al., 2019) library by incorporating a random seed for

[4]https://huggingface.co/

result reproducibility. Specifically, we employed m-BERT (Devlin et al., 2019), Distil-BERT (Sanh et al., 2019), MuRIL (Sakorikar et al., 2021), Indic-SBERT (Deode et al., 2023), and XLM-R (Conneau et al., 2020).

L3Cube Indic-SBERT, a multilingual Sentence-BERT model, is customized for Indian languages through fine-tuning vanilla BERT (Gao et al., 2019) models with a synthetic corpus. Demonstrating outstanding cross-lingual performance, it outperforms alternatives like LaBSE (Feng et al., 2020) and LASER (Artetxe and Schwenk, 2019) in sentence similarity tasks across diverse Indian languages, providing a valuable resource for natural language understanding in the Indian multilingual context.

5 Experimental Setup

The hyper-parameters used in this task were determined through an iterative process involving frequent trials. The choice of the parameters depicted in Table 2 also aligns with common practices in binary classification tasks for DL models (Plested et al., 2021; Roy et al., 2023). On the other hand, the hyper-parameters for transformer-based models are shown in Table 3. This meticulous experimentation aimed to optimize model performance, ensuring the chosen hyperparameters strike a balance between convergence and computational efficiency. The consistent application of these settings across all models facilitates a fair and meaningful comparison, allowing us to isolate the impact of architectural variances on overall performance.

Parameter	Value
Optimizer	Adam
Loss Function	Binary Crossentropy
Activation (Hidden Layer)	ReLU
Activation (Output Layer)	Sigmoid
Learning Rate	$1e^{-3}$
Batch Size	32
Epochs	30
MaxLen	80
Dropout	0.2

Table 2: Experimental setup for the DL models.

Parameter	Value
Optimizer	AdamW
Learning Rate	$3e^{-5}$
Batch Size	16
Maxlen	100
Epochs	10

Table 3: Experimental setup for the transformer-based models.

6 Result Analysis

The results in Table 4 unveil significant patterns and challenges across the evaluated models. In the ML category, LR and SVM classifiers demonstrate competitive precision, recall, and F1 scores, with SVM achieving the highest F1-score of 0.65. However, the ensemble method, while achieving a comparable F1 score, shows slightly lower precision and recall, suggesting potential challenges in integrating diverse ML models. Moving to DL models, those utilizing fastText embeddings consistently outperform Word2Vec counterparts. The best-performing model using Word2Vec embeddings was the hybrid CNN+BiLSTM, achieving an F1-score of 0.42. In contrast, the BiLSTM model achieved an F1-score of 0.60 using fastText word embeddings. The stark difference in F1-score among models using these two embeddings may be attributed to Word2Vec's struggle to capture the rich semantic information present in code-mixed text. The intricacies of code-mixing, where multiple languages coexist, pose a challenge for traditional embeddings, impacting their ability to represent nuanced meanings effectively.

Methods	Classifiers	P	R	F1
ML	LR	0.63	0.63	0.63
	SVM	0.65	0.65	0.65
	Ensemble	0.60	0.60	0.59
DL	CNN(Word2Vec)	0.54	0.51	0.40
	BiLSTM(Word2Vec)	0.58	0.52	0.41
	CNN+BiLSTM(Word2Vec)	0.56	0.52	0.42
	CNN(fastText)	0.64	0.60	0.57
	BiLSTM(fastText)	0.68	0.63	0.60
	CNN+BiLSTM(fastText)	0.65	0.60	0.55
TransF	m-BERT (uncased)	0.65	0.65	0.65
	m-BERT (cased)	0.69	0.69	0.69
	MuRIL	0.68	0.69	0.69
	XLM-R	**0.70**	0.69	**0.70**
	Distil-BERT	0.67	0.67	0.67
	Indic-SBERT	**0.70**	**0.70**	**0.70**

Table 4: Result comparison on test data where P, R and F1 denote precision, recall, macro F1-score and TransF denotes transformer-based model.

However, transformer-based models exhibited promising performance compared to both ML and DL models. XLM-R and Indic-SBERT both achieved the highest F1 score of 0.70. Due to the higher recall value of 0.70 in the case of Indic-SBERT, it was selected as the best model for our task, showcasing its adaptability to the complexities of code-mixed language. Table 5 illustrates the impressive performance of this model, among the other participating teams.

Team Name	Run	F1-Score	Rank
Sandalphon	1	0.7711	1
Selam	2	0.7711	2
CUET_Binary_Hackers	**2**	**0.7013**	**6**
MUCS	3	0.6501	15

Table 5: A brief ranking of participating teams.

In summary, DL models performed less effectively compared to ML and transformer-based models. The reason for this weaker performance is the extensive appearance of cross-lingual words in the text. As a result, Word2Vec and fastText embeddings failed to create appropriate feature mappings among the words (Sharif et al., 2021). Thus, LSTM and CNN-based models may not have found sufficient relational dependencies among the features, performing below expectations. However, Indic-SBERT outperformed other models, due to its ability to capture intricate semantic relationships and contextual nuances inherent in the language mixture. Sentence-BERT models, like Indic-SBERT, excel in understanding the semantic similarity between sentences, making them well-suited for code-mixed text comprehension. The model's robust encoding of semantic information enables it to effectively navigate the intricacies of Telugu code-mixing, contributing to its superior performance in this specific linguistic context.

7 Error Analysis

To comprehensively analyze the performance of L3Cube Indic-SBERT, we provide a detailed error analysis in this section, utilizing a confusion matrix depicted in Figure 2. Out of 250 samples, 179 hate speech and 172 non-hate speech samples were correctly classified. However, there were 71 misclassified hate speech samples and 78 misclassified non-hate speech samples. The misclassification rates for both hate and non-hate classes are 28.4% and 31.2% respectively. The minimal difference suggests a close misclassification rate between the two labels, potentially influenced by slight variations in the number of types of training samples.

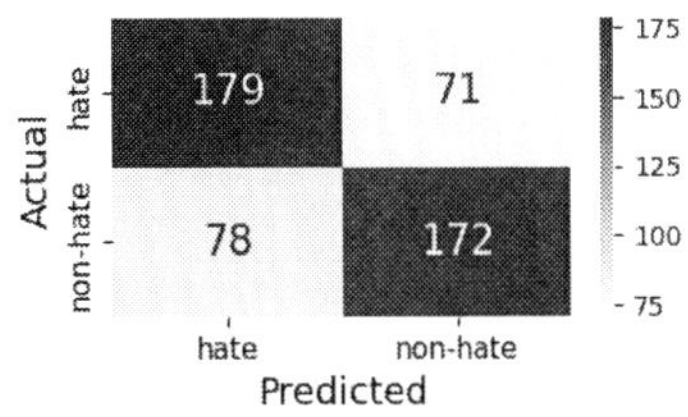

Figure 2: Confusion matrix for the Indic-SBERT model.

Additionally, similar code-mixed words between the two classes may contribute to this issue when the model attempts to understand the text's meaning. To reduce misclassification, a detailed analysis of each word in misclassified samples using the Named Entity Recognition (NER) method can be done to remove redundant codemixed words.

Limitations

- Our work relies on pre-trained transformer-based models, which may pose challenges in scenarios where the context significantly deviates from the model's training data.
- The employed DL models didn't perform well. It requires further investigation using other embeddings and building better models.
- GPU limitations hindered us from experimenting with the ensemble of transformers.

8 Conclusion and Future Work

This paper delves into the exploration and evaluation of various ML, DL, and transformer-based approaches. Our initial investigation involved TF-IDF and embedding features (Word2Vec & fastText), followed by systematic experiments with ML and DL methods. The results indicate that SVM outperformed other ML and DL models with an F1-score of 0.65. However, incorporating the transformer model significantly enhanced overall performance. Specifically, Indic-SBERT, stood out by achieving the highest F1-score of 0.70. Future exploration can involve incorporating contextualized embeddings like GPT, ELMO, and FLAIR, or experimenting with ensembling transformers and fusion models tailored to hate speech contexts. Besides, alternative embedding techniques such as GloVe and BERT-based embeddings can be applied to enhance the performance of DL models.

References

Mikel Artetxe and Holger Schwenk. 2019. Massively multilingual sentence embeddings for zero-shot cross-lingual transfer and beyond. *Transactions of the Association for Computational Linguistics*, 7:597–610.

Premjith B, Bharathi Raja, Prasanna Kumar Kumaresan, Saranya Rajiakodi, Sai Prashanth Karnati, Sai Rishith Reddy Mangamuru, and Janakiram Chandu. 2024. Findings of the Shared Task on Hate and Offensive Language Detection in Telugu Codemixed Text (HOLD-Telugu). In *Proceedings of the Fourth Workshop on Speech, Vision, and Language Technologies for Dravidian Languages*, Malta. European Chapter of the Association for Computational Linguistics.

Piotr Bojanowski, Edouard Grave, Armand Joulin, and Tomas Mikolov. 2017. Enriching word vectors with subword information. *Transactions of the association for computational linguistics*, 5:135–146.

Alexis Conneau, Kartik Khandelwal, Naman Goyal, Vishrav Chaudhary, Guillaume Wenzek, Francisco Guzmán, Edouard Grave, Myle Ott, Luke Zettlemoyer, and Veselin Stoyanov. 2020. Unsupervised Cross-lingual Representation Learning at Scale. In *Proceedings of the 58th Annual Meeting of the Association for Computational Linguistics*. Association for Computational Linguistics.

Udoy Das, Karnis Fatema, Md Ayon Mia, Mahshar Yahan, Md Sajidul Mowla, Md Fayez Ullah, Arpita Sarker, and Hasan Murad. 2023. EmptyMind at BLP-2023 Task 1: A Transformer-based Hierarchical-BERT Model for Bangla Violence-Inciting Text Detection. In *Proceedings of the First Workshop on Bangla Language Processing (BLP-2023)*, pages 174–178, Singapore. Association for Computational Linguistics.

Samruddhi Deode, Janhavi Gadre, Aditi Kajale, Ananya Joshi, and Raviraj Joshi. 2023. L3Cube-IndicSBERT: A simple approach for learning cross-lingual sentence representations using multilingual BERT. *arXiv preprint arXiv:2304.11434*.

Jacob Devlin, Ming-Wei Chang, Kenton Lee, and Kristina Toutanova. 2019. BERT: Pre-training of Deep Bidirectional Transformers for Language Understanding. In *Proceedings of the 2019 Conference of the North American Chapter of the Association for Computational Linguistics: Human Language Technologies, Volume 1 (Long and Short Papers)*. Association for Computational Linguistics.

Shahnoor C Eshan and Mohammad S Hasan. 2017. An application of machine learning to detect abusive Bengali text. In *2017 20th International Conference of Computer and Information Technology (ICCIT)*, pages 1–6. IEEE.

Fangxiaoyu Feng, Yinfei Yang, Daniel Cer, Naveen Arivazhagan, and Wei Wang. 2020. Language-agnostic BERT sentence embedding. *arXiv preprint arXiv:2007.01852*.

Paula Fortuna, Juan Soler, and Leo Wanner. 2020. Toxic, hateful, offensive or abusive? what are we really classifying? an empirical analysis of hate speech datasets. In *Proceedings of the Twelfth Language Resources and Evaluation Conference*, pages 6786–6794, Marseille, France. European Language Resources Association.

Zhengjie Gao, Ao Feng, Xinyu Song, and Xi Wu. 2019. Target-dependent sentiment classification with BERT. *Ieee Access*, 7:154290–154299.

Andrea Gasparetto, Matteo Marcuzzo, Alessandro Zangari, and Andrea Albarelli. 2022. A survey on text classification algorithms: From text to predictions. *Information*, 13(2):83.

Sepp Hochreiter and Jürgen Schmidhuber. 1997. Long short-term memory. *Neural computation*, 9(8):1735–1780.

Alamgir Hossain, Mahathir Bishal, Eftekhar Hossain, Omar Sharif, and Mohammed Moshiul Hoque. 2022. COMBATANT@TamilNLP-ACL2022: Fine-grained categorization of abusive comments using logistic regression. In *Proceedings of the Second Workshop on Speech and Language Technologies for Dravidian Languages*, pages 221–228, Dublin, Ireland. Association for Computational Linguistics.

Ananya Joshi and Raviraj Joshi. 2023. Harnessing Pre-Trained Sentence Transformers for Offensive Language Detection in Indian Languages. *arXiv preprint arXiv:2310.02249*.

Shakir Khan, Mohd Fazil, Vineet Kumar Sejwal, Mohammed Ali Alshara, Reemiah Muneer Alotaibi, Ashraf Kamal, and Abdul Rauf Baig. 2022. BiCHAT: BiLSTM with deep CNN and hierarchical attention for hate speech detection. *Journal of King Saud University-Computer and Information Sciences*, 34(7):4335–4344.

Diksha Khurana, Aditya Koli, Kiran Khatter, and Sukhdev Singh. 2023. Natural language processing: State of the art, current trends and challenges. *Multimedia tools and applications*, 82(3):3713–3744.

Alexandre Magueresse, Vincent Carles, and Evan Heetderks. 2020. Low-resource languages: A review of past work and future challenges. *arXiv preprint arXiv:2006.07264*.

Arun S Maiya. 2022. ktrain: A low-code library for augmented machine learning. *The Journal of Machine Learning Research*, 23(1):7070–7075.

Ahmed Cherif Mazari, Nesrine Boudoukhani, and Abdelhamid Djeffal. 2023. BERT-based ensemble learning for multi-aspect hate speech detection. *Cluster Computing*, pages 1–15.

Tomas Mikolov, Ilya Sutskever, Kai Chen, Greg S Corrado, and Jeff Dean. 2013. Distributed representations of words and phrases and their compositionality. *Advances in neural information processing systems*, 26.

Ahmed Omar, Tarek M Mahmoud, and Tarek Abd-El-Hafeez. 2020. Comparative performance of machine learning and deep learning algorithms for Arabic hate speech detection in osns. In *Proceedings of the International Conference on Artificial Intelligence and Computer Vision (AICV2020)*, pages 247–257. Springer.

Keiron O'Shea and Ryan Nash. 2015. An introduction to convolutional neural networks. *arXiv preprint arXiv:1511.08458*.

Flor Miriam Plaza-del Arco, M Dolores Molina-González, L Alfonso Urena-López, and M Teresa Martín-Valdivia. 2021. Comparing pre-trained language models for Spanish hate speech detection. *Expert Systems with Applications*, 166:114120.

Jo Plested, Xuyang Shen, and Tom Gedeon. 2021. Rethinking binary hyperparameters for deep transfer learning. In *Neural Information Processing: 28th International Conference, ICONIP 2021, Sanur, Bali, Indonesia, December 8–12, 2021, Proceedings, Part II 28*, pages 463–475. Springer.

Ruba Priyadharshini, Bharathi Raja Chakravarthi, Malliga S, Subalalitha Cn, Kogilavani S V, Premjith B, Abirami Murugappan, and Prasanna Kumar Kumaresan. 2023. Overview of Shared-task on Abusive Comment Detection in Tamil and Telugu. In *Proceedings of the Third Workshop on Speech and Language Technologies for Dravidian Languages*, pages 80–87, Varna, Bulgaria. INCOMA Ltd., Shoumen, Bulgaria.

Bharathi Raja Chakravarthi, Dhivya Chinnappa, Ruba Priyadharshini, Anand Kumar Madasamy, Sangeetha Sivanesan, Subalalitha Chinnaudayar Navaneethakrishnan, Sajeetha Thavareesan, Dhanalakshmi Vadivel, Rahul Ponnusamy, and Prasanna Kumar Kumaresan. 2021. Developing Successful Shared Tasks on Offensive Language Identification for Dravidian Languages. *arXiv e-prints*, pages arXiv–2111.

Sunita Roy, Ranjan Mehera, Rajat Kumar Pal, and Samir Kumar Bandyopadhyay. 2023. Hyperparameter Optimization for Deep NeuralNetwork Models: A Comprehensive Study onMethods and Techniques.

Debjoy Saha, Naman Paharia, Debajit Chakraborty, Punyajoy Saha, and Animesh Mukherjee. 2021. Hate-alert@DravidianLangTech-EACL2021: Ensembling strategies for transformer-based offensive language detection. In *Proceedings of the First Workshop on Speech and Language Technologies for Dravidian Languages*, pages 270–276, Kyiv. Association for Computational Linguistics.

Tushar Sakorikar, Pushpak Bhattacharyya, Surya Jauhar, and Mohit Neogi. 2021. MuRIL: Multilingual Representations for Indian Languages. *arXiv preprint arXiv:2103.09974*.

Victor Sanh, Lysandre Debut, Julien Chaumond, and Thomas Wolf. 2019. DistilBERT, a Distilled Version of BERT: Smaller, Faster, Cheaper and Lighter. In *Proceedings of the 2nd Workshop on Neural Machine Translation and Generation*. Association for Computational Linguistics.

Iqbal H Sarker. 2021. Machine learning: Algorithms, real-world applications and research directions. *SN computer science*, 2(3):160.

Sunil Saumya, Abhinav Kumar, and Jyoti Prakash Singh. 2021. Offensive language identification in Dravidian code mixed social media text. In *Proceedings of the First Workshop on Speech and Language Technologies for Dravidian Languages*, pages 36–45, Kyiv. Association for Computational Linguistics.

Omar Sharif and Mohammed Moshiul Hoque. 2021. Identification and classification of textual aggression in social media: Resource creation and evaluation. In *International Workshop on Combating Online Hostile Posts in Regional Languages during Emergency Situation*, pages 9–20. Springer.

Omar Sharif, Eftekhar Hossain, and Mohammed Moshiul Hoque. 2021. NLP-CUET@DravidianLangTech-EACL2021: Offensive language detection from multilingual code-mixed text using transformers. In *Proceedings of the First Workshop on Speech and Language Technologies for Dravidian Languages*, pages 255–261, Kyiv. Association for Computational Linguistics.

Omar Sharif, Eftekhar Hossain, and Mohammed Moshiul Hoque. 2022. M-BAD: A multilabel dataset for detecting aggressive texts and their targets. In *Proceedings of the Workshop on Combating Online Hostile Posts in Regional Languages during Emergency Situations*, pages 75–85, Dublin, Ireland. Association for Computational Linguistics.

Varinder Taprial and Priya Kanwar. 2012. *Understanding social media*. Bookboon.

Thomas Wolf, Lysandre Debut, Victor Sanh, Julien Chaumond, Clement Delangue, Anthony Moi, Pierric Cistac, Tim Rault, Rémi Louf, Morgan Funtowicz, et al. 2019. Huggingface's transformers: State-of-the-art natural language processing. *arXiv preprint arXiv:1910.03771*.

TechWhiz@DravidianLangTech 2024: Fake News Detection Using Deep Learning Models

Madhumitha M, Kunguma Akshatra M, Tejashri J, C Jerin Mahibha
Meenakshi Sundararajan Engineering College, Chennai, India
madhumithamurthy2002@gmail.com, kungumaakshatra@gmail.com,
tejashrijayachandran@gmail.com, jerinmahibha@gmail.com

Abstract

The ever-evolving landscape of online social media has initiated a transformative phase in communication, presenting unprecedented opportunities alongside inherent challenges. The pervasive issue of false information, commonly termed fake news, has emerged as a significant concern within these dynamic platforms. This study delves into the domain of Fake News Detection, with a specific focus on Malayalam. Utilizing advanced transformer models like mBERT, ALBERT, and XMLRoBERTa, our research proficiently classifies social media text into original or fake categories. Notably, our proposed model achieved commendable results, securing a rank of 3 in Task 1 with macro F1 scores of 0.84 using mBERT, 0.56 using ALBERT, and 0.84 using XMLRoBERTa. In Task 2, the XMLRoBERTa model excelled with a rank of 12, attaining a macro F1 score of 0.21, while mBERT and BERT achieved scores of 0.16 and 0.11, respectively. This research aims to develop robust systems capable of discerning authentic from deceptive content, a crucial endeavor in maintaining information reliability on social media platforms amid the rampant spread of misinformation.

1 Introduction

Navigating the digital realm, social media emerges as a pivotal force in disseminating information, presenting both opportunities and challenges. The surge in fake news instigated the initiation of the Fake News Detection in Dravidian Languages task(Subramanian et al., 2023), slated for presentation at DravidianLangTech@EACL in 2024 [1]. Task 1 plays a crucial role, concentrating on categorizing social media text to meticulously distinguish between original and fake news. The challenge lies in discerning genuine content from misleading information. Task 2 shifts focus to detecting fake news in Malayalam-language articles, aiming to develop models classifying misinformation into five distinct types. Beyond bolstering natural language processing capabilities, the initiative actively contributes to fostering a more informed and reliable digital environment. This effort not only upholds information integrity but also reinforces the pillars of a trustworthy digital space, marking a beacon for responsible technological advancements and ethical digital communication practices.

[1] https://sites.google.com/view/dravidianlangtech-2024

2 Related Works

Different deep learning models, including CNNs, LSTMs, ensembles, and attention mechanisms had been employed for fake news detection by kum (2020). The CNN + bidirectional LSTM ensembled network with attention had achieved the highest accuracy. Jwa et al. (2019) had proposed "exbake", a model for detecting fake news that uses Bidirectional Encoder Representations from Transformers (BERT). The model had outperformed previous models in terms of F1-score by effectively analysing the relationship between news headlines and body text. Raza and Ding (2022) had addressed early detection challenges and labelled data scarcity in fake news. The proposed transformer-based framework had taken into account both news content and social contexts, resulting in greater accuracy shortly after news dissemination. They had emphasised the significance of incorporating multiple features for better classification. Schütz et al. (2021) had made a contribution to the detection of disinformation by presenting a content-based classification approach based on pre-trained transformer models. Their experiments with models such as XLNet, BERT, and RoBERTa had yielded promising results, highlighting the effectiveness of transformers in achieving high accuracy even with small datasets. The Transformer-based fake news detection framework proposed by Raza and Ding (2022) had demonstrated higher accuracy in early detec-

Proceedings of the Fourth Workshop on Speech, Vision, and Language Technologies for Dravidian Languages, pages 200–204
March 22, 2024

Category	Training Dataset	Evaluation Dataset
Fake	1,599	1,658
Original	406	409

Table 1: Data Distribution for task 1

Category	Training Dataset
Half true	141
Mosty false	239
Mostly true	1
Partly false	42
False	1,246

Table 2: Data Distribution for task 2

tion, addressing label shortage challenges with effective features and a novel labelling technique. Application of Cross Lingual model for sentiment classification on Tamil-English code mixed data had been proposed by (Jerin et al., 2021).

Qazi et al. (2020) had employed an attention-based transformer model for social media fake news detection, discovering a 15 percentage improvement with a hybrid CNN model, underscoring the significance of attention mechanisms. Kula et al. (2021) had explored transformer-based neural network models, showcasing effectiveness in fake news detection using precision, F1-score, and recall metrics. Kumar et al. (2021) proposed an XLNet fine-tuning model, outperforming existing models in multi-class and binary-class fake news detection. The KATMF framework by Song et al. (2021), integrating Knowledge augmented transformer, had excelled in multimodal fake news detection on a real-world dataset. TRANSFAKE, a multi-task transformer model introduced by Jing et al. (2021) had outperformed competitors by jointly modeling body content and comments, emphasizing the importance of considering multiple modalities for comprehensive fake news analysis.

3 Data set

The datasets utilized for implementing fake news detection in Task 1 comprised the training, evaluation, and test datasets provided by the shared task organizers (Subramanian et al., 2024). Each instance in the training dataset was labeled to specify whether the text is fake or original. For Task 2, the datasets used for fake news detection included the training and test datasets from the task organizers. Each instance in the Task 2 training dataset was labeled to indicate one of the five fake categories: False, Half True, Mostly False, Partly False, and Mostly True. Table 1 illustrates the data distribution for the training and development datasets in Task 1, while Table 2 presents the distribution for Task 2. In Task 1, the training dataset consisted of 3,257 instances, with 1,599 falling under the fake category and 1,658 under the original category. The Malayalam development dataset comprised 815 instances, including 406 in the fake category and the remainder in the original category, highlighting data imbalance. The Malayalam test dataset contained 1,019 instances for evaluating model predictions. For Task 2, the training dataset encompassed 1,669 instances across five categories: Half True (141 instances), Mostly False (239 instances), Mostly True (1 instance), Partly False (42 instances), and False (1,246 instances), providing a diverse set for model training and evaluation. The Malayalam test dataset for Task 2 included 250 instances for evaluating model predictions.

4 System Description

In Task 1, social media text was classified as original or fake using XLM-RoBERTa, ALBERT, and mBERT. The methodology involved preprocessing data by removing unwanted characters and training models on datasets from the task organizers. XLM-RoBERTa, with the highest development accuracy, was chosen for final predictions. Task 2 addressed the FakeDetect-Malayalam challenge, focusing on five fake news categories. Transformer models (XLM-RoBERTa, mBERT, and BERT) handled data encoding and tokenization. In the absence of a designated development dataset, training data was split for validation. Optimization with AdamW and cross-entropy loss during training led to mBERT achieving the highest accuracy, highlighting the importance of precise classification in streamlined preprocessing, training, and model selection. Figure 1 illustrates the proposed architecture for both tasks.

4.1 XLM-RoBERTa Model

The XLM-RoBERTa model Conneau et al. (2019), developed by Facebook AI, stands as a pioneering advancement in natural language processing (NLP). Tailored for cross-lingual tasks, it exhibits remarkable proficiency in comprehending and processing text across diverse languages. Leveraging extensive

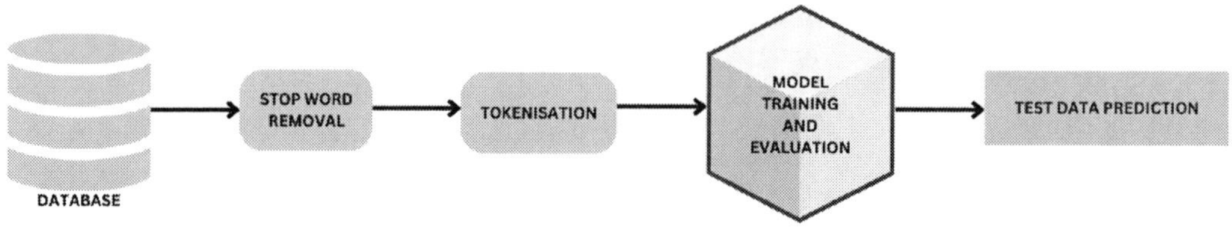

Figure 1: System Architecture

pre-training on multilingual datasets and the transformative potential of the transformer architecture, XLM-RoBERTa is optimized for Malayalam by Raja et al. (2023). This enhancement strengthens fake news detection, emphasizing the model's multilingual capabilities and performance, establishing XLM-RoBERTa as a crucial asset for identifying deceptive content in the digital communication landscape.

4.2 mBERT Model

mBERT (Multilingual BERT) Devlin et al. (2018), a transformer-based language model for multilingual natural language processing, excels in cross-lingual tasks. Inspired by BERT, its architecture, featuring multiple transformer layers and 768 hidden units, is particularly adept at capturing linguistic nuances ("c" model). In his 2022 PhD thesis, "Multi Languages Fake News Detection," Ali (2022) enhances accuracy in identifying and combating fake news across diverse languages using mBERT. This resonates with our focus on Fake News Detection Using Deep Learning Models, underscoring mBERT's multilingual capabilities and effectiveness in addressing specific linguistic nuances.

4.3 ALBERT Model

The ALBERT Model (A Lite BERT) (Lan et al., 2019), a transformative language model by Google Research, uniquely balances efficiency and performance. Employing parameter-sharing techniques, it achieves a compact yet accurate architecture. Widely adopted, Wang et al. (2022) leverage ALBERT for fake news detection, combining its advanced capabilities with multi-modal circulant fusion for robust performance in handling the complexities of identifying deceptive content in textual data.

4.4 BERT Model

The BERT Model Devlin et al. (2018), a transformative force in natural language processing, excels in understanding context and relationships. Developed by Google, BERT's bidirectional approach and attention mechanisms capture nuanced nuances. In BERT model for fake news detection based on social bot activities in the COVID-19 pandemic, Heidari et al. (2021) utilize BERT to scrutinize social bot behaviors, enhancing fake news identification during the pandemic. This emphasizes BERT's versatile application in addressing contemporary challenges related to misinformation.

Model	F1-Score	Accuracy
XLMRoBERTa	0.84	0.84
ALBERT	0.56	0.58
mBERT	0.84	0.84

Table 3: Performance Score for Task 1

Model	F1-Score	Accuracy
XLMRoberta	0.21	0.74
BERT	0.11	0.25
mBERT	0.16	0.63

Table 4: Performance Score for Task 2

5 Result

The evaluation of task performance focused on the macro-F1 score. In Task 1 of Dravidian-LangTech@EACL 2024, fake news detection assessment relied on macro F1-Score and Accuracy. XLMRoBERTa secured 3rd position on the leaderboard with a notable macro F1-Score of 0.84 and accuracy of 0.84. Despite similar Task 1 scores, XLMRoBERTa's overall excellence, especially in cross-lingual tasks, pre-training, and adaptability, influenced its preference over mBERT. Models like XLMRoBERTa, ALBERT, and mBERT made unique contributions, as depicted in Table 3. In Task 2, XLMRoBERTa maintained superiority, securing 11th position on the leaderboard with a macro F1-Score of 0.21 and accuracy of 0.74, while

Text	Model	Predicted Label	Actual Label
Athippo avark evde venelm aavamloo Thabileegenedirey 100 video ittu...	m-BERT	Fake	Original
Ithiney kurich onnenkilum ittallo	ALBERT	Original	Fake

Table 5: Error Analysis

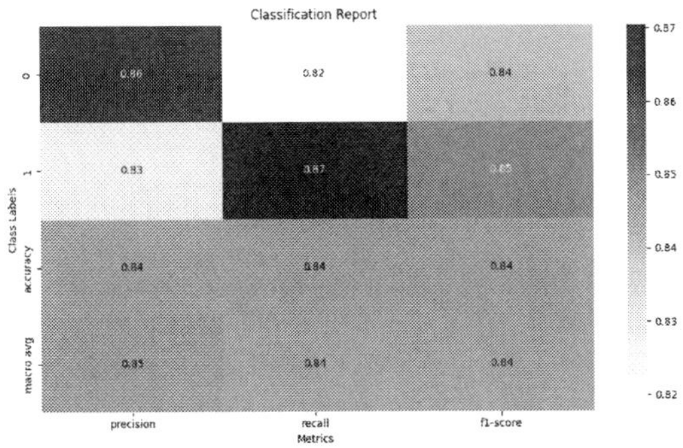

Figure 2: Classification Report - Task 1 XLMRoBERTa Model

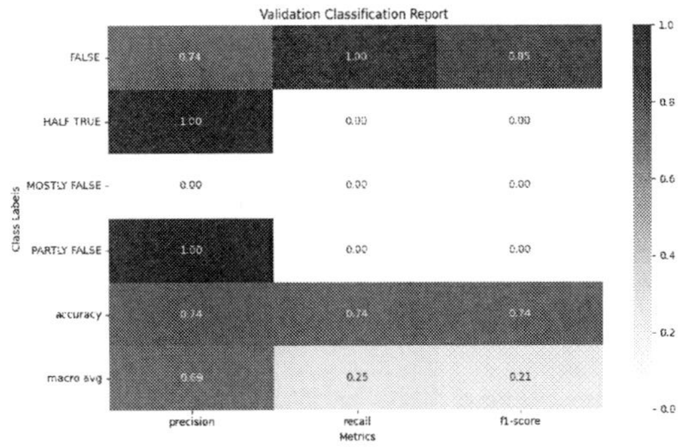

Figure 3: Classification Report - Task 2 XLMRoBERTa Model

mBERT and BERT exhibited lower scores, summarized in Table 4. Figures 2 and 3 depict the classification reports for Task 1 and Task 2, respectively. The classification reports for both tasks showcase the performance of the XLM-RoBERTa model, which outperformed all other models.

6 Error Analysis

The F1 score from the XLMRoBERTa model for both Task 1 and Task 2 exposes false positive and false negative prevalence, linked to inherent data imbalance. Class "false" with more instances, exhibits a high F1 score, precision, and recall, indicating Fake News. Lower training instances intensify misclassifications, highlighting the data imbalance impact. To address this, data augmentation is suggested for enhanced model performance. Misclassified Malayalam texts due to data imbalance are detailed in Table 5, emphasizing the need for strategies to overcome these challenges in Fake News detection.

7 Limitation

XLMRoberta, ALBERT, and mBERT excel but face hurdles: cross-lingual challenges, biased predictions due to data imbalances, uncertainties in generalizing to new datasets, resource-intensive fine-tuning for diverse languages, interpretability issues, and a textual focus overlooking multimodal fake news complexities. Recognizing and addressing these constraints is essential for refining approaches and ensuring robust fake news detection in transformer-based models.

8 Conclusion

The DravidianLangTech@EACL 2024 initiative, focused on fake news detection in Dravidian languages, signifies a critical step in countering misinformation on social media. Task 1, employing mBERT, ALBERT, and XMLRoBERTa, revealed XMLRoBERTa as the optimal model, showcasing its prowess in discerning authenticity. In Task 2, where XMLRoBERTa, mBERT, and BERT were employed, XMLRoBERTa consistently outperformed, emphasizing its effectiveness in classifying Malayalam-language articles. This collective effort not only advances natural language processing but also reinforces the importance of reliable information dissemination in the digital age. The XMLRoBERTa model's dual-task success highlights its pivotal role in navigating the challenges of fake news, setting the stage for continued innovation in Dravidian language technology.

References

2020. Fake News Detection using Deep Learning Models: A Novel Approach, author=Kumar, Sachin and Asthana, Rohan and Upadhyay, Shashwat and

Upreti, Nidhi and Akbar, Mohammad. *Transactions on Emerging Telecommunications Technologies*, 31(2):e3767.

Md Monsur Ali. 2022. *Multi Languages Fake News Detection*. Ph.D. thesis, Hochschule Rhein-Waal.

Alexis Conneau, Kartikay Khandelwal, Naman Goyal, Vishrav Chaudhary, Guillaume Wenzek, Francisco Guzmán, Edouard Grave, Myle Ott, Luke Zettlemoyer, and Veselin Stoyanov. 2019. Unsupervised Cross-lingual Representation Learning at Scale. *CoRR*, abs/1911.02116.

Jacob Devlin, Ming-Wei Chang, Kenton Lee, and Kristina Toutanova. 2018. BERT: Pre-training of Deep Bidirectional Transformers for Language Understanding. *CoRR*, abs/1810.04805.

Maryam Heidari, Samira Zad, Parisa Hajibabaee, Masoud Malekzadeh, SeyyedPooya HekmatiAthar, Ozlem Uzuner, and James H Jones. 2021. BERT Model for Fake News Detection Based on Social Bot Activities in the COVID-19 Pandemic. In *2021 IEEE 12th Annual Ubiquitous Computing, Electronics & Mobile Communication Conference (UEMCON)*, pages 0103–0109. IEEE.

Mahibha Jerin, Kayalvizhi Sampath, and Thenmozhi Durairaj. 2021. Sentiment Analysis using Cross Lingual Word Embedding Model. In *Proceedings of Forum for Information Retrieval Evaluation-FIRE 2021*.

Quanliang Jing, Di Yao, Xinxin Fan, Baoli Wang, Haining Tan, Xiangpeng Bu, and Jingping Bi. 2021. TRANSFAKE: Multi-Task Transformer for Multimodal Enhanced Fake News Detection. In *2021 International Joint Conference on Neural Networks (IJCNN)*, pages 1–8. IEEE.

Heejung Jwa, Dongsuk Oh, Kinam Park, Jang Mook Kang, and Heuiseok Lim. 2019. exBAKE: Automatic Fake News Detection model based on Bidirectional Encoder Representations from Transformers (BERT). *Applied Sciences*, 9(19):4062.

Sebastian Kula, Rafał Kozik, Michał Choraś, and Michał Woźniak. 2021. Transformer Based Models in Fake News Detection. In *International Conference on Computational Science*, pages 28–38. Springer.

Ashok Kumar, Tina Esther Trueman, and Erik Cambria. 2021. Fake news detection using XLNet fine-tuning model. In *2021 International Conference on Computational Intelligence and Computing Applications (ICCICA)*, pages 1–4. IEEE.

Zhenzhong Lan, Mingda Chen, Sebastian Goodman, Kevin Gimpel, Piyush Sharma, and Radu Soricut. 2019. Albert: A lite bert for self-supervised learning of language representations. *arXiv preprint arXiv:1909.11942*.

Momina Qazi, Muhammad US Khan, and Mazhar Ali. 2020. Detection of Fake nNews using Transformer Model. In *2020 3rd international conference on computing, mathematics and engineering technologies (iCoMET)*, pages 1–6. IEEE.

Eduri Raja, Badal Soni, and Sami Kumar Borgohain. 2023. nlpt malayalm@ DravidianLangTech: Fake News Detection in Malayalam using Optimized XLM-RoBERTa Model. In *Proceedings of the Third Workshop on Speech and Language Technologies for Dravidian Languages*, pages 186–191.

Shaina Raza and Chen Ding. 2022. Fake News Detection based on News Content and Social Contexts: a Transformer-based approach. *International Journal of Data Science and Analytics*, 13(4):335–362.

Mina Schütz, Alexander Schindler, Melanie Siegel, and Kawa Nazemi. 2021. Automatic Fake News Detection with Pre-Trained Transformer Models. In *Pattern Recognition. ICPR International Workshops and Challenges: Virtual Event, January 10-15, 2021, Proceedings, Part VII*, pages 627–641. Springer.

Chenguang Song, Nianwen Ning, Yunlei Zhang, and Bin Wu. 2021. Knowledge Augmented Transformer for Adversarial Multidomain Multiclassification Multimodal Fake News Detection. *Neurocomputing*, 462:88–100.

Malliga Subramanian, Bharathi Raja Chakravarthi, Kogilavani Shanmugavadivel, Santhiya Pandiyan, Prasanna Kumar Kumaresan, Balasubramanian Palani, Premjith B, Sandhiya Raja, Vanaja, Mithunajha S, Devika K, Hariprasath S.B, Haripriya B, and Vigneshwar E. 2024. Overview of the Second Shared Task on Fake News Detection in Dravidian Languages. In *Proceedings of the Fourth Workshop on Speech, Vision, and Language Technologies for Dravidian Languages*, Malta. European Chapter of the Association for Computational Linguistics.

Malliga Subramanian, Bharathi Raja Chakravarthi, Kogilavani Shanmugavadivel, Santhiya Pandiyan, Prasanna Kumar Kumaresan, Balasubramanian Palani, Muskaan Singh, Sandhiya Raja, Vanaja, and Mithunajha S. 2023. Overview of the Shared Task on Fake News Detection from Social Media Text. In *Proceedings of the Third Workshop on Speech and Language Technologies for Dravidian Languages*, Varna, Bulgaria. Recent Advances in Natural Language Processing.

Xingang Wang, Xiaomin Li, Xiaoyu Liu, and Honglu Cheng. 2022. Using ALBERT and Multi-modal Circulant Fusion for Fake News Detection. In *2022 IEEE International Conference on Systems, Man, and Cybernetics (SMC)*, pages 2936–2942. IEEE.

CUET_Binary_Hackers@DravidianLangTech-EACL 2024: Sentiment Analysis using Transformer-Based Models in Code-Mixed and Transliterated Tamil and Tulu

Asrarul Hoque Eusha, Salman Farsi, Ariful Islam
Jawad Hossain, Shawly Ahsan and **Mohammed Moshiul Hoque**
Department of Computer Science and Engineering
Chittagong University of Engineering & Technology, Chattogram-4349, Bangladesh
{asrar2860, salman.cuet.cse, arif.cse18cuet}@gmail.com
{u1704039, u1704057}@student.cuet.ac.bd, moshiul_240@cuet.ac.bd

Abstract

Textual Sentiment Analysis (TSA) delves into people's opinions, intuitions, and emotions regarding any entity. Natural Language Processing (NLP) serves as a technique to extract subjective knowledge, determining whether an idea or comment leans positive, negative, neutral, or a mix thereof toward an entity. In recent years, it has garnered substantial attention from NLP researchers due to the vast availability of online comments and opinions. Despite extensive studies in this domain, sentiment analysis in low-resourced languages such as Tamil and Tulu needs help handling code-mixed and transliterated content. To address these challenges, this work focuses on sentiment analysis of code-mixed and transliterated Tamil and Tulu social media comments. It explored four machine learning (ML) approaches (LR, SVM, XGBoost, Ensemble), four deep learning (DL) methods (BiLSTM and CNN with fastText and Word2Vec), and four transformer-based models (m-BERT, MuRIL, L3Cube-IndicSBERT, and Distilm-BERT) for both languages. For Tamil, L3Cube-IndicSBERT and ensemble approaches outperformed others, while m-BERT demonstrated superior performance among the models for Tulu. The presented models achieved the 3rd and 1st ranks by attaining macro F1-scores of 0.23 and 0.58 in Tamil and Tulu, respectively.

1 Introduction

TSA plays a crucial role in production and content creation, offering insights into how consumers perceive offerings and providing immediate feedback. Utilizing the internet and social media, studies focus on sentiment analysis in monolingual comments, achieving high accuracy levels (Wankhade et al., 2022). While research addresses multilingual, code-mixed, and code-switched text, extensive exploration focuses on well-resourced languages like English and Chinese (Xu et al., 2022). In contrast, low-resourced languages such as Tamil and Tulu need more exploration, particularly in code-mixed and code-switched contexts. The challenge arises from comments written in English letters, like Romanized Tamil or Tulu, attracting recent attention from academia (S. K. et al., 2024a).

ML and DL approaches like LSTM and BiLSTM, and transformer-based models like BERT, m-BERT, XLMR, and Distilm-BERT have been extensively studied for monolingual and multilingual text, encompassing code-mixed, code-switched, and Romanized formats in low-resource languages (Sharif et al., 2019; Kalaivani and Thenmozhi, 2021). Researchers focus on enhancing accuracy, particularly in Tamil-English and Tulu-English. Transformer-based models exhibit proficiency in handling sequence dependencies, motivating deeper exploration in these languages for improved contextual understanding.

The critical contributions of this research work are outlined below:

- Investigate several ML, DL, and transformer-based models with fine-tuning to classify sentiment in Tamil and Tulu languages into four classes: Positive, Neutral, Mixed, and Negative.
- Explored the suitable model for identifying textual sentiment from Tamil and Telegu texts on the available dataset.

2 Related Work

Understanding audience feedback is critical for social media content creators, fostering self-improvement and broader outreach. Similarly, grasping user sentiment in the restaurant industry is vital for improving services and cuisine quality (Sharif et al., 2019). The study examines several

Proceedings of the Fourth Workshop on Speech, Vision, and Language Technologies for Dravidian Languages, pages 205–211
March 22, 2024 ©2024 Association for Computational Linguistics

ML models, such as DT, RF, and MNB models, for classifying user reviews, where MNB achieved the highest accuracy (80.48%). SA on Bengali book reviews using a MNB attained an accuracy of 84% (Hossain et al., 2021). Moreover, a study on TSA in Tamil and Tulu code-mixed texts, utilizing SVM and ensemble models with fastText and TF-IDF, obtained F1 scores of 0.14 and 0.204, respectively (Rachana et al., 2023). Numerous DL methods have been explored for TSA across various high-resourced languages. For instance, an Arabic aspect-based sentiment analysis employed bidirectional GRU, achieving F1 scores of 70.76% and 83.98% for aspect-based sentiment and sentiment polarity classification, respectively (Abdelgwad et al., 2022). Additionally, a fusion-based deep learning model analyzed sentiment in COVID-19 tweets, outperforming individual models like CNN, BiGRU, and DistilBERT (Basiri et al., 2021).

Recent studies have explored transformer-based models for sentiment analysis. For instance, a proposed aspect-category sentiment analysis based on RoBERTa integrated 1D CNN, cross-attention, document attention, and fully connected layers for classification (Liao et al., 2021). Another study introduced a BERT-based sentiment analysis model focusing on software engineering, fine-tuning BERT, ALBERT, and RoBERTa models, and employing an ensemble of these models (Batra et al., 2021). Additionally, a hybrid model combining RoBERTa and LSTM layers demonstrated effectiveness in sentiment analysis (Tan et al., 2022). In multilingual sentiment analysis, a study utilizing multilingual BERT achieved notable F1 scores in Tamil, Malayalam, and Kannada, including English code-mixed text (Kalaivani and Thenmozhi, 2021). Similarly, sentiment analysis on a code-mixed Tamil-English dataset using transformer-based models revealed the superiority of XLM-RoBERTa over BERT and RoBERTa models (Sangeetha and Nimala, 2023). Furthermore, an investigation into sentiment analysis in Tamil and Tulu code-mixed text highlighted the efficacy of fine-tuned transformer-based models across various scenarios (Hegde et al., 2023).

3 Task and Dataset Descriptions

In the shared task on 'Sentiment Analysis in Tamil and Tulu' (S. K. et al., 2024b), participants were tasked with exploring distinct models for each language. Using the provided datasets, we conducted multi-class classification to discern whether a given comment falls into categories such as 'Positive,' 'Neutral,' 'Negative,' or 'Mixed' within the Tamil-English code-mixed dataset developed by Chakravarthi et al. (2020). Similarly, Hegde et al. (2022) developed Tulu-English code-mixed dataset SA containing the same classes as Tamil. These gold standard datasets encompass code-mixed Tamil-English, Romanized Tamil, code-mixed Tulu-English, and Romanized Tulu texts. Each corpus consists of distinct training, validation, and test sets.

Table 1 displays Tamil's dataset details for sentiment analysis. In this task, the training set contains 90704 unique words, and the test set contains 4832 unique words, with 2330 out-of-vocabulary words. The average lengths of samples are 10, 10, and 13 in the training, validation, and test sets, respectively.

Data	Class	SC	UWC	OOV	AL
Train	Positive	20,070	90,704		10
	Neutral	5,628			
	Mixed	4,020			
	Negative	4,271			
Validation	Positive	2,257	16,111	2,330	10
	Neutral	611			
	Mixed	438			
	Negative	480			
Test	Positive	73	4,832		13
	Neutral	137			
	Mixed	101			
	Negative	338			

Table 1: Detailed dataset statistics of sentiment analysis in Tamil. The acronyms SC, UWC, OOV, and AL denote sample count, unique word count, out-of-vocabulary words, and average sample length, respectively.

Table 2 presents the dataset details for the sentiment analysis task in Tulu. Here, the majority of training samples belong to the positive class. The unique word counts in the training, validation, and test sets are 18056, 2004, and 2145, respectively. These statistics indicate that out of 2145 unique words in the test samples, 1094 are out-of-vocabulary words unseen by the models during training. The average sample lengths are 7, 6, and 7 in the training, validation, and test sets.

Notably, in both the Tamil and Tulu test sets, the 'Positive' class accounted for nearly two-thirds of the samples in the training set, resulting in highly imbalanced datasets.

Data	Class	SC	UWC	OOV	AL
Train	Positive	3,352	18,056		7
	Neutral	1,854			
	Mixed	1,041			
	Negative	698			
Validation	Positive	231	2,004	1,094	6
	Neutral	124			
	Mixed	90			
	Negative	55			
Test	Positive	248	2,145		7
	Neutral	140			
	Mixed	70			
	Negative	43			

Table 2: Detailed dataset statistics of sentiment analysis in Tulu.

4 Methodology

The developed SA method starts with the text undergoing preprocessing to eliminate unwanted special characters, spaces, line breaks, and emojis. For ML, we employed TF-IDF (Takenobu, 1994), while pre-trained fastText (Bojanowski et al., 2017) and Word2Vec (Mikolov et al., 2013) word embeddings were utilized for DL. Figure 1 shows an abstract process and employed models for TSA.

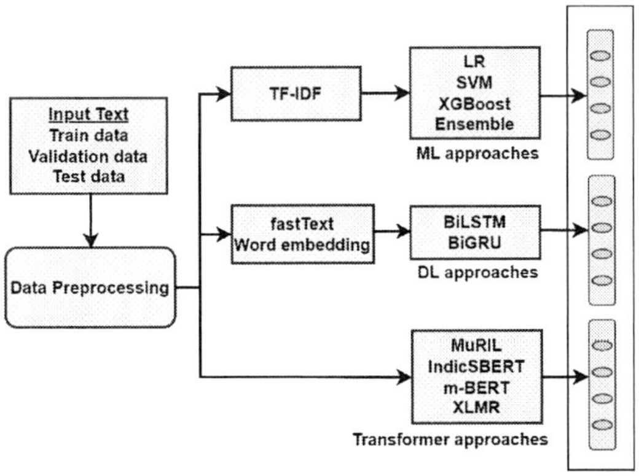

Figure 1: Schematic process of sentiment analysis in Tamil and Tulu

TF-IDF, a statistical method, is an information retrieval technique for words within text commonly used in NLP tasks. In this work, we used word-level n-grams for feature extraction using TF-IDF. On the other hand, word embeddings transform words into numerical representations, enabling the capture of semantic meaning and relationships within a continuous vector space. This work utilized the 300 dimensions for both fastText and Word2Vec.

4.1 Classifiers

This work explored several ML, DL, and transformer-based approaches to classify sentiment from Tamil and Tule texts.

ML Approaches: Logistic Regression (LR) is developed using a 'balanced' class weight approach to handle imbalanced datasets. It employs an 'l2' penalty for L2 regularization and the 'lbfgs' solver, with a maximum iteration set to 200 and a regularization parameter C kept at 1.0. Support Vector Machine (SVM) was used with a 'linear' kernel and applied 'balanced' class weights. The ensemble method combined multiple ML-based classifiers to generate a new classifier. Its superior performance in classification tasks over individual ML models has already been established (Roy et al., 2018). We constructed an ensemble method using DT, RF, SVM, and LR, implementing majority voting for prediction. We set the class weight to 'balanced' and utilized the 'gini' criterion for RF and DT. For RF, we used a value of 100 for 'n_estimators.' The parameters for SVM and LR remain consistent with their previous settings. XGBoost was employed with the 'multi:softmax' objective, employing 'n_estimators' of 200, a learning rate of 0.3, and a maximum depth of 6.

DL Approaches: This work developed the BiLSTM model (Hameed and Garcia-Zapirain, 2020) using Word2Vec and fastText. They consist of a single BiLSTM layer featuring 100 units. For classification within the output layer, we applied softmax activation. During training, we set a learning rate of $3e^{-3}$, a batch size of 32, utilized 15 epochs, and introduced a dropout of 0.2 to prevent overfitting. We employed the CNN model (O'Shea and Nash, 2015) utilizing Word2Vec and fastText. Our approach involved a single layer of CNN, comprising 128 units with max-pooling. All other parameters were configured identically to those of the BiLSTM.

Transformer-based Appraches: We selected several pre-trained transformer models available through HuggingFace[1] (Wolf et al., 2019), including m-BERT, Distil-mBERT, L3Cube-IndicSBERT, and MuRIL. The task dataset contains code-mixed multilingual text, so these models proved particularly suitable. We fine-tuned these four models, adjusting hyperparameters to attain optimal results, utilizing a maximum length of 50, a batch size of 16, and a learning rate of $5e^{-6}$. Also utilized the

[1] https://huggingface.co/

number of epochs 10 and 15 for Tamil and Tulu, respectively.

MuRIL is a pre-trained BERT model on 17 major Indian languages, including their transliterated counterparts (Khanuja et al., 2021). L3Cube-IndicSBERT (Deode et al., 2023) utilizes the MuRIL approach, trained on NLI datasets encompassing 10 primary Indian languages, Tamil and Tulu included. m-BERT (Devlin et al., 2018) is a pre-trained model trained on a vast multilingual corpus, covering 104 languages in a self-supervised manner. We employed 'bert-base-multilingual-cased.' We also employed Distil-mBERT, a multilingual variant of DistilBERT (Sanh et al., 2019). It serves as a smaller and faster iteration of m-BERT. We used 'distilbert-base-multilingual-cased.'

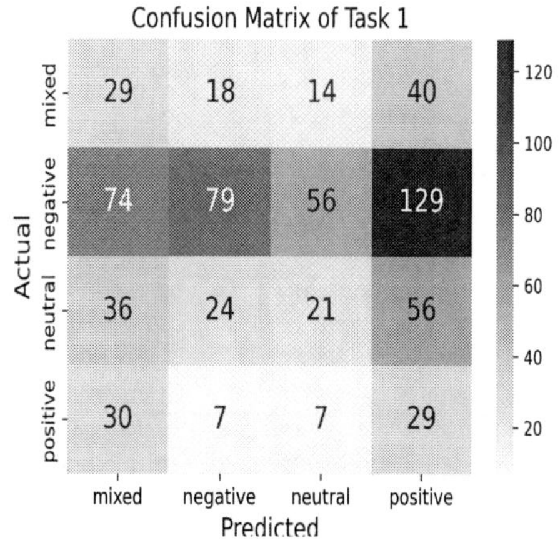

Figure 2: Confusion matrix for sentiment analysis in Tamil using an ensemble of ML techniques

5 Results and Analysis

This section details the performance analysis of the proposed system, trained and evaluated on separate corpora. The best models were employed for test data predictions and evaluated using the macro-averaged F1-score. Table 3 shows the results of all ML, DL, and transformer-based models.

The ensemble approach in Tamil sentiment analysis outperformed most DL and transformer models, except L3Cube-IndicSBERT, achieving a precision (P) of 0.28, a recall (R) of 0.26, and a macro F1-score (F) of 0.23. Meanwhile, L3Cube-IndicSBERT achieved a similar macro F1-score with a precision of 0.24 and a recall of 0.28. XGBoost showed poor performance, possibly due to overfitting. In Tulu code-mixed sentiment analysis, m-BERT excelled with precision of 0.59, recall of 0.58, and a macro F1-score of 0.58, surpassing other models.

5.1 Error Analysis

The best-performed models, ensemble (for Tamil) and m-BERT (for Tulu), are further investigated using quantitative and qualitative analysis for more insights regarding their performance.

Quantitative Analysis: Figure 2 illustrates that the model misclassified a significant portion of the test samples in the TSA task in Tamil. This misclassification stems from the fact that while two-thirds of the training samples were 'Positive,' the test set comprised half as 'Negative,' a classless frequency in the training set. Consequently, the models predominantly predicted test samples as 'Positive,' leading to increased misclassification.

The developed m-BERT model (for Tulu) shows promise, but there is room for improvement. Figure 3 shows that most 'Mixed' and 'Negative' test samples and a notable portion of 'Neutral' samples are misclassified. Imbalanced datasets during training could be the cause. Adjusting class weights could enhance results.

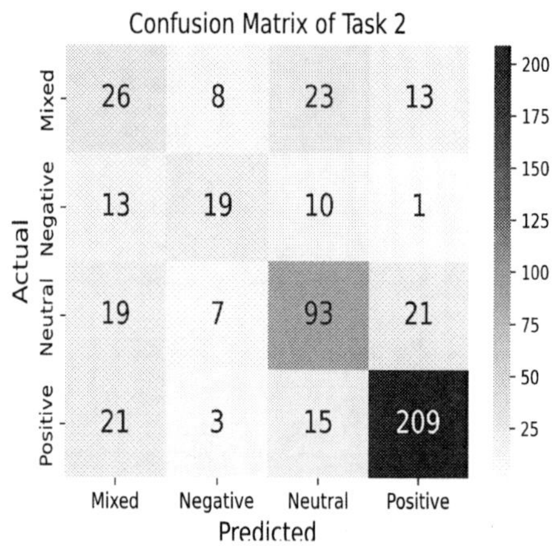

Figure 3: Confusion matrix for sentiment analysis in Tulu using m-BERT

Qualitative Analysis: Figure 4 displays predicted outcomes from the ensemble model for text samples 2 and 3, which align with the actual classes in the TSA task in Tamil. However, for samples 1, 4, and 5, misclassification of text occurs. Figure 5, concerning the TSA in Tulu, shows that m-BERT misclassified samples 2, 3, and 5. Whereas samples 1 and 4 were predicted to match the actual labels. It is noted that English translations of Tamil texts are

Methods	Classifiers	Tamil			Tulu		
		P	R	F	P	R	F
ML	LR	0.29	0.26	0.14	0.53	0.53	0.53
	SVM	0.27	0.24	0.12	0.53	0.54	0.53
	XGBoost	0.22	0.21	0.09	0.24	0.24	0.23
	Ensemble	0.28	0.27	**0.23**	0.53	0.54	0.53
DL	BiLSTM + WV	0.27	0.27	0.22	0.27	0.26	0.26
	BiLSTM + FT	0.27	0.24	0.19	0.25	0.24	0.21
	CNN + WV	0.26	0.25	0.21	0.26	0.26	0.26
	CNN + FT	0.25	0.25	0.19	0.24	0.23	0.21
Transformer	MuRIL	0.25	0.29	0.21	0.54	0.53	0.53
	Indic-SBERT	0.24	0.28	0.23	0.55	0.56	0.56
	m-BERT	0.29	0.26	0.20	0.59	0.58	**0.58**
	Distil-mBERT	0.29	0.26	0.18	0.53	0.53	0.52

Table 3: Evaluation results on the test set using various ML, DL, and transformer-based models. P, R, F1, WV, and FT represents precision, recall, macro F1-score, Word2Vec, and fastText respectively

Text Sample	Actual	Predicted
Sample 1. இப்போது இந்த 9தொல்லை அதிகமாக ஆயிருச்சு (Now this 9 trouble is more)	Negative	Mixed
Sample 2. இது புதுவகை கொள்ளை கூட்டம் (This is a new type of robbery)	Neutral	Neutral
Sample 3. என்று சொல்லாதீர்கள் திருநங்கை என்று கூறுங்கள் முதலில்.(Don't say that, say transgender first)	Positive	Positive
Sample 4. Romba thollai pannuthunga yaarume ketka matangala (No one bothers to listen to religions.)	Negative	Positive
Sample 5. காவல்துறை கண்டிப்பாக நடவடிக்கை எடுக்க வேண்டும். (Police must take action.)	Neutral	Positive

Figure 4: Some predicted samples in Tamil using ensemble

Text Sample	Actual	Predicted
Sample 1. ಥರ್ಡ್ ಕ್ಲಾಸ್ ಕಾಮಿಡಿ (Third Class Comedy)	Negative	Negative
Sample 2. ಈ ಪೊಣ್ಣುಗ್ ಪನ್ಪಿನಗುಲ್ ಯೇ ಲಾರ್ ಇಜ್ಜೆರ (This girl is very beautiful.)	Negative	Mixed
Sample 3. ಕುಸಾಸ್ ಇತ್ತುಂಡು. ಪ್ರಾಕ್ಟಿಸ್ ಕಮ್ಮಿ. ಒಟ್ಟುಗ್ ಓಕೆ. (Having fun. Practice together. All okay.)	Mixed	Neutral
Sample 1. ಸರ್ ಮಸ್ತ್ ಧನ್ಯವಾದ ರಡ್ ಜನಕ್ಲೆಗ್ಲ ನಿಕ್ಲೆಗ್ ಬೊಕ್ಕ ಈರ್ನ ಟೀಮ್ದುಲ ಕಾಫಿ ನಾಡುನ್ ಎಡ್ಡೆ ತೋಜಿದರ್ಬ (Sir, thank you very much, for those people who came out, and for the team.)	Positive	Positive
Sample 5. Vol ittar anna onji vaara.. (Can you give me a little time..)	Neutral	Positive

Figure 5: Few predictions in Tulu using m-BERT

accomplished with Google Translate, and ChatGPT does English translations of Tulu texts.

6 Limitations

The developed systems suffered some significant limitations.

- The DL and transformer-based models rely on extensive training data. Limited or biased datasets can notably impact results, especially when dealing with diverse or uncommon sentiment expressions.

- The system encountered difficulty effectively managing class imbalances in both tasks.

7 Conclusion and Future Work

This paper explored sentiment analysis on code-mixed Tamil and Tulu datasets, investigating various ML, DL, and transformer-based models. For improved performance, this work delved into experiments with transformer-based models such as m-BERT, L3Cube-IndicSBERT, Distilm-BERT, and MuRIL. In the case of Tamil, both the ensemble and L3Cube-IndicSBERT outperformed, achieving macro F1-scores of 0.23. Conversely, m-BERT exhibited superior performance for Tulu with a macro F1-score of 0.58.

Future research should explore adaptive learning rates, ensembles comprising different BERT models, and advanced word embedding techniques (ELMO, ULMFiT). Lastly, developing a fair model applicable across languages can improve accuracy.

References

Mohammed M Abdelgwad, Taysir Hassan A Soliman, Ahmed I Taloba, and Mohamed Fawzy Farghaly. 2022. Arabic aspect based sentiment analysis using bidirectional GRU based models. *Journal of King Saud University-Computer and Information Sciences*, 34(9):6652–6662.

Mohammad Ehsan Basiri, Shahla Nemati, Moloud Abdar, Somayeh Asadi, and U Rajendra Acharrya. 2021. A novel fusion-based deep learning model for sentiment analysis of COVID-19 tweets. *Knowledge-Based Systems*, 228:107242.

Himanshu Batra, Narinder Singh Punn, Sanjay Kumar Sonbhadra, and Sonali Agarwal. 2021. BERT-based sentiment analysis: A software engineering perspective. In *Database and Expert Systems Applications: 32nd International Conference, DEXA 2021, Virtual Event, September 27–30, 2021, Proceedings, Part I 32*, pages 138–148. Springer.

Piotr Bojanowski, Edouard Grave, Armand Joulin, and Tomas Mikolov. 2017. Enriching word vectors with subword information. *Transactions of the association for computational linguistics*, 5:135–146.

Bharathi Raja Chakravarthi, Vigneshwaran Muralidaran, Ruba Priyadharshini, and John P McCrae. 2020. Corpus creation for sentiment analysis in code-mixed Tamil-English text. *arXiv preprint arXiv:2006.00206*.

Samruddhi Deode, Janhavi Gadre, Aditi Kajale, Ananya Joshi, and Raviraj Joshi. 2023. L3Cube-IndicSBERT: A simple approach for learning cross-lingual sentence representations using multilingual BERT. *arXiv preprint arXiv:2304.11434*.

Jacob Devlin, Ming-Wei Chang, Kenton Lee, and Kristina Toutanova. 2018. BERT: Pre-training of deep bidirectional transformers for language understanding. *arXiv preprint arXiv:1810.04805*.

Zabit Hameed and Begonya Garcia-Zapirain. 2020. Sentiment classification using a single-layered BiLSTM model. *Ieee Access*, 8:73992–74001.

Asha Hegde, Mudoor Devadas Anusha, Sharal Coelho, Hosahalli Lakshmaiah Shashirekha, and Bharathi Raja Chakravarthi. 2022. Corpus creation for sentiment analysis in code-mixed Tulu text. In *Proceedings of the 1st Annual Meeting of the ELRA/ISCA Special Interest Group on Under-Resourced Languages*, pages 33–40, Marseille, France. European Language Resources Association.

Asha Hegde, Bharathi Raja Chakravarthi, Hosahalli Lakshmaiah Shashirekha, Rahul Ponnusamy, Subalalitha Cn, SK Lavanya, Durairaj Thenmozhi, Martha Karunakar, Shreya Shreeram, and Sarah Aymen. 2023. Findings of the shared task on sentiment analysis in Tamil and Tulu code-mixed text. In *Proceedings of the Third Workshop on Speech and Language Technologies for Dravidian Languages*, pages 64–71.

Eftekhar Hossain, Omar Sharif, and Mohammed Moshiul Hoque. 2021. Sentiment polarity detection on Bengali book reviews using multinomial naive bayes. In *Progress in Advanced Computing and Intelligent Engineering: Proceedings of ICACIE 2020*, pages 281–292. Springer.

Adaikkan Kalaivani and Durairaj Thenmozhi. 2021. Multilingual Sentiment Analysis in Tamil Malayalam and Kannada code-mixed social media posts using MBERT. In *FIRE (Working Notes)*, pages 1020–1028.

Simran Khanuja, Diksha Bansal, Sarvesh Mehtani, Savya Khosla, Atreyee Dey, Balaji Gopalan, Dilip Kumar Margam, Pooja Aggarwal, Rajiv Teja Nagipogu, Shachi Dave, et al. 2021. MuRIL: Multilingual representations for Indian languages. *arXiv preprint arXiv:2103.10730*.

Wenxiong Liao, Bi Zeng, Xiuwen Yin, and Pengfei Wei. 2021. An improved aspect-category sentiment analysis model for text sentiment analysis based on RoBERTa. *Applied Intelligence*, 51:3522–3533.

Tomas Mikolov, Kai Chen, Greg Corrado, and Jeffrey Dean. 2013. Efficient estimation of word representations in vector space. *arXiv preprint arXiv:1301.3781*.

Keiron O'Shea and Ryan Nash. 2015. An introduction to convolutional neural networks. *arXiv preprint arXiv:1511.08458*.

K Rachana, M Prajnashree, Asha Hegde, and HL Shashirekha. 2023. MUCS@ Dravidian-LangTech2023: Sentiment Analysis in Code-mixed Tamil and Tulu Texts using fastText. In *Proceedings of the Third Workshop on Speech and Language Technologies for Dravidian Languages*, pages 258–265.

Arjun Roy, Prashant Kapil, Kingshuk Basak, and Asif Ekbal. 2018. An ensemble approach for aggression identification in English and Hindi text. In *Proceedings of the first workshop on trolling, aggression and cyberbullying (TRAC-2018)*, pages 66–73.

Lavanya S. K., Asha Hegde, Bharathi Raja Chakravarthi, Hosahalli Lakshmaiah Shashirekha, Rajeswari Natarajan, Sajeetha Thavareesan, Ratnasingam Sakuntharaj, Thenmozhi Durairaj, and Rajkumar Charmathi Kumaresan, Prasanna Kumar. 2024a. Overview of Second Shared Task on Sentiment Analysis in Code-mixed Tamil and Tulu. In *Proceedings of the Fourth Workshop on Speech, Vision, and Language Technologies for Dravidian Languages*, Malta. European Chapter of the Association for Computational Linguistics.

Lavanya S. K., Asha Hegde, Bharathi Raja Chakravarthi, Hosahalli Lakshmaiah Shashirekha, Rajeswari Natarajan, Sajeetha Thavareesan, Ratnasingam Sakuntharaj, Thenmozhi Durairaj, and Rajkumar Charmathi Kumaresan, Prasanna Kumar. 2024b. Overview of Second Shared Task on Sentiment Analysis in Code-mixed Tamil and Tulu. In *Proceedings of the Fourth Workshop on Speech, Vision, and Language Technologies for Dravidian Languages*, Malta. European Chapter of the Association for Computational Linguistics.

M Sangeetha and K Nimala. 2023. Sentiment Analysis on Code-Mixed Tamil-English Corpus: A Comprehensive Study of Transformer-Based Models.

Victor Sanh, Lysandre Debut, Julien Chaumond, and Thomas Wolf. 2019. DistilBERT, a Distilled Version of BERT: Smaller, Faster, Cheaper and Lighter. In *Proceedings of the 2nd Workshop on Neural Machine Translation and Generation*. Association for Computational Linguistics.

Omar Sharif, Mohammed Moshiul Hoque, and Eftekhar Hossain. 2019. Sentiment analysis of Bengali texts on online restaurant reviews using multinomial Naïve Bayes. In *2019 1st international conference on advances in science, engineering and robotics technology (ICASERT)*, pages 1–6. IEEE.

Tokunaga Takenobu. 1994. Text categorization based on weighted inverse document frequency. *Information Processing Society of Japan, SIGNL*, 94(100):33–40.

Kian Long Tan, Chin Poo Lee, Kalaiarasi Sonai Muthu Anbananthen, and Kian Ming Lim. 2022. RoBERTa-LSTM: a hybrid model for sentiment analysis with transformer and recurrent neural network. *IEEE Access*, 10:21517–21525.

Mayur Wankhade, Annavarapu Chandra Sekhara Rao, and Chaitanya Kulkarni. 2022. A survey on sentiment analysis methods, applications, and challenges. *Artificial Intelligence Review*, 55(7):5731–5780.

Thomas Wolf, Lysandre Debut, Victor Sanh, Julien Chaumond, Clement Delangue, Anthony Moi, Pierric Cistac, Tim Rault, Rémi Louf, Morgan Funtowicz, et al. 2019. Huggingface's transformers: State-of-the-art natural language processing. *arXiv preprint arXiv:1910.03771*.

Yuemei Xu, Han Cao, Wanze Du, and Wenqing Wang. 2022. A survey of cross-lingual sentiment analysis: Methodologies, models and evaluations. *Data Science and Engineering*, 7(3):279–299.

Binary_Beasts@DravidianLangTech-EACL 2024: Multimodal Abusive Language Detection in Tamil based on Integrated Approach of Machine Learning and Deep Learning Techniques

Md. Tanvir Rahman, Abu Bakkar Siddique Raihan, Tanzim Rahman, Shawly Ahsan, Jawad Hossain, Avishek Das and **Mohammed Moshiul Hoque**
Department of Computer Science and Engineering
Chittagong University of Engineering & Technology, Chattogram-4349, Bangladesh
{u1804002, u1804004, u1804015, u1704057, u1704039}@student.cuet.ac.bd
{avishek, moshiul_240}@cuet.ac.bd

Abstract

Detecting abusive language on social media is a challenging task that needs to be solved effectively. This research addresses the formidable challenge of detecting abusive language in Tamil through a comprehensive multimodal approach, incorporating textual, acoustic, and visual inputs. This study utilized ConvLSTM, 3D-CNN, and a hybrid 3D-CNN with BiLSTM to extract video features. Several models, such as BiLSTM, LR, and CNN, are explored for processing audio data, whereas for textual content, MNB, LR, and LSTM methods are explored. To further enhance overall performance, this work introduced a weighted late fusion model amalgamating predictions from all modalities. The fusion model was then applied to make predictions on the test dataset. The ConvLSTM+BiLSTM+MNB model yielded the highest macro F1 score of **71.43%**. Our methodology allowed us to achieve **1st** rank for multimodal abusive language detection in the shared task.

1 Introduction

Recently, the proliferation of social media platforms has played a pivotal role in facilitating the global exchange of ideas, opinions, and information. Although this interconnectedness has engendered a rich diversity of conversations, it has concurrently presented challenges, as noted by Das et al. (2021). The widespread occurrence of abusive language, hate speech, and offensive content exemplifies these challenges. Among the myriad languages employed on these platforms, one notable example is Tamil, a Dravidian language predominantly spoken in South India. The need for effective detection and mitigation of abusive language in Tamil is imperative to ensure a secure and inclusive online environment. Yasaswini et al. (2021) addressed this pressing concern by exploring a multimodal approach to abusive language detection in Tamil. By incorporating multiple modalities, such as text, video, and audio, we aim to enhance the accuracy and robustness of the detection system in the Tamil-speaking digital landscape.

Although studies have been conducted on these issues for multimodal data in the English language, there needs to be more research explicitly looking at abusive language recognition in the context of Dravidian languages (Barman and Das, 2023; Bala and Krishnamurthy, 2023). Limited research on abusive language identification in these languages presents unique challenges. As part of our effort, we investigated abusive language detection in Tamil. The task entails the development of models capable of analyzing the textual, speech, and visual elements within social media videos to predict their classification as either abusive or non-abusive. The main contributions of this work are:

- Implement a weighted late fusion model that effectively amalgamates predictions from text, video, and audio modalities.
- Investigate various Machine Learning (ML), Deep Learning (DL), and their integrated approaches to find a suitable solution for detecting multimodal abusive language in Tamil.

2 Related Work

Online abuse poses a significant threat, prompting the need for sophisticated measures. Multimodal strategies, integrating text, acoustic, and visual analysis, are at the forefront of enhancing content moderation efficacy. Premjith et al. (2023) provides an overview of the shared task on multimodal abusive language detection and sentiment analysis in Dravidian languages, carried out during the third Workshop on Speech and Language Technologies for Dravidian Languages at RANLP 2023. This study covers the word vector enhancement techniques given by Bojanowski et al. (2017), which may help understand word representations in Dravidian languages. In their survey of recent

Proceedings of the Fourth Workshop on Speech, Vision, and Language Technologies for Dravidian Languages, pages 212–217
March 22, 2024 ©2024 Association for Computational Linguistics

advancements in multimodal sentiment analysis (text, audio, and video/image), Chandrasekaran et al. (2021) presented a thorough analysis of sentiment datasets, feature extraction algorithms, data fusion techniques, and the effectiveness of various classification strategies. A more comprehensive presentation of multimodal and multilingual hate speech detection was given by Chhabra and Vishwakarma (2023).

In a multilingual social media setting, Sharon et al. (2022) presented MADA, a multimodal technique for abuse detection in conversational audio. (Mozafari et al., 2020) used a range of methods using various architectures, including multi-modal models, video-based models, text-based models, and image-based models. Poria et al. (2018) developed a Multimodal EmotionLines Dataset (MELD) to improve and expand EmotionLines. A novel approach to multimodal sentiment analysis was presented by Poria et al. (2016), which used textual, visual, and audio modalities to extract sentiments from web videos. They combined adequate data from several sources using feature and decision-level fusion techniques. Several methods are used for categorizing audio, video, and natural language text that identify the emotions conveyed as Positive, Negative, or Neutral by Mahendhiran and Kannimuthu (2018). In their analysis of the growth of multimedia communication apps, Soni and Singh (2018) noted both the dangers of cyberbullying and the potential for improved user engagement and natural communication. Few studies have been conducted on multimodal social media data analysis in Dravidian languages. Barman and Das (2023) proposed various unimodal models and introduced a fusion model. Their investigation highlighted mBERT and MFCC's efficacy in classifying abusive language. Furthermore, the Vision Transformer (ViT) demonstrated notable success in sentiment analysis for Tamil and Malayalam, achieving an F1-score (macro) of 57.86% (Barman and Das, 2023). Bala and Krishnamurthy (2023) conducted a study focused on detecting abusive language that amalgamated visual, auditory, and textual features, culminating in an F1-score (macro) of 33%, indicative of the achieved performance in this multimodal endeavor.

3 Task and Dataset Description

The task aims to develop advanced models for detecting abusive content in Tamil videos on social media, particularly YouTube. These models scrutinize diverse video elements to predict whether the content is abusive or non-abusive. Abusive content includes offensive language or visuals intended to cause harm, distress, or discomfort, while non-abusive content aligns with guidelines promoting respectful and positive engagement. The organizers of the competition, DravidianLangTech@EACL 2024, have released a Tamil language dataset for abusive content detection (Chakravarthi et al., 2021; Premjith et al., 2022; B et al., 2024). Table 1 illustrates the training and test set distribution for all three modalities.

Dataset	Abusive	Non-Abusive	Total
Train	38	32	70
Test	9	9	18

Table 1: Summary of abusive language detection dataset

The provided dataset included components encompassing video, audio, and extracted text. In the training dataset, the duration for both audio and video spans from a minimum of 23.38 seconds to a maximum of 86.36 seconds, with an average time of 47.90 seconds. The extracted text data contains 19,743 words, consisting of 642 unique words. After removing stopwords, the number of unique words reduces to 588. The text samples exhibit a minimum of 65 words, a maximum of 500 words, and an average of 282.04 words.

4 Methodology

The proposed work starts by examining the videos' visual elements and then investigates the audio data before moving on to the textual aspects of the modeling. To combine the textual, audio, and visual elements, we employed weighted late fusion to create a more reliable classification of abusive and non-abusive content. Figure 1 displays the schematic framework for detecting multimodal abusive language in Tamil.

4.1 Visual Approach

This study targets the detection of abusive content in videos. Using OpenCV, we extract 15 sequential frames from each video, each being 128x128 in size. The extracted frames are normalized for consistent pixel value comparison in subsequent analysis. These frames are then input into three distinct models: ConvLSTM, 3D-CNN, and 3D-CNN combined with BiLSTM. To extract spatial and

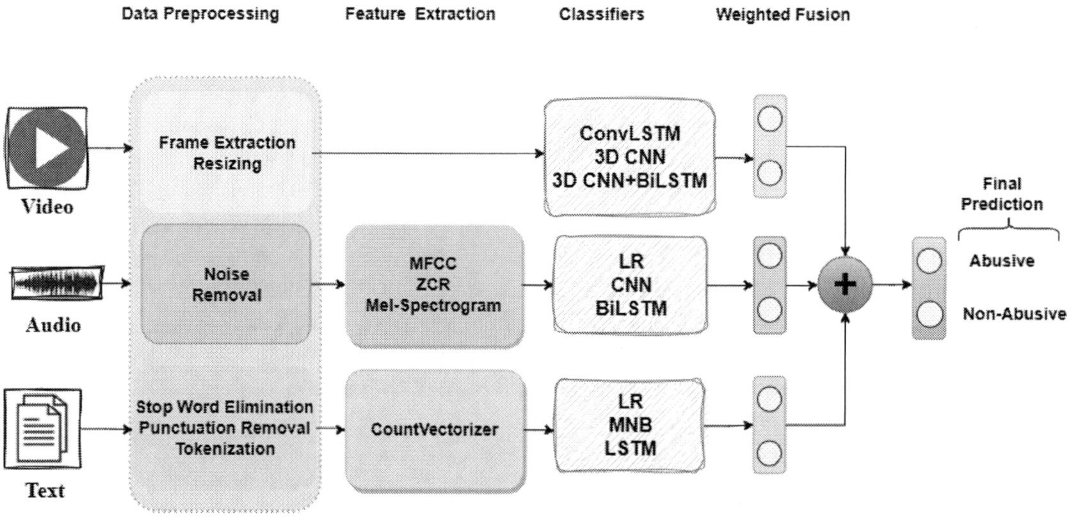

Figure 1: Schematic framework for Tamil abusive language detection

temporal features simultaneously, we employed ConvLSTM, which combines CNNs and LSTMs. We also used a hybrid model combining 3D-CNNs with LSTM to use their complementary abilities for improved abusive content identification. Additionally, standalone 3D-CNNs are used for extracting direct spatiotemporal features. The experimental setup for the deep learning models employed in video is outlined in Table 2.

Parameter	Value
Optimizer	adam
Loss function	categorical_crossentropy
Activation_function (hidden layer)	tanh
Activation_function (output layer)	softmax
Batch size	4
Learning rate	0.001
Epochs	100
Drop-out	0.3

Table 2: Experimental setup for the DL models for video

4.2 Acoustic Approach

This research prioritized noise removal as a preliminary step to refine the audio data. Employing effective noise reduction methods enhances the clarity of the audio signals. Subsequently, we extracted features from each audio sample to discern abusive content. The features include Mel-frequency spectrogram (Mel), Zero Crossing Rate (ZCR), Spectral Contrast, and Mel-frequency Cepstral Coefficients (MFCC). Each feature serves a specific purpose—Spectral Contrast captures spectral texture changes, Mel reflects frequency distribution, ZCR denotes the rate of signal crossings, and MFCC records detailed spectral features. Following extracting these discriminative features, we employed a diverse set of models, namely LR, CNN, and BiLSTM, for a nuanced and thorough analysis leading to the classification of abusive content.

4.3 Textual Approach

In this work, we preprocessed the text using punctuation and Tamil stop-word removal to identify abusive content in text data. We extracted features using CountVectorizer to convert text data into vectorized tokens. The study examined the influence of various preprocessing methods on the performance of conventional machine learning models, such as Logistic Regression (LR) and Multinomial Naive Bayes (MNB). Concurrently, the deep learning model LSTM was also employed. The preprocessed data was utilized to train these models, renowned for their sequential processing capabilities, to discern intricate dependencies and temporal nuances within the text sequences.

4.4 Weighted Late Fusion Approach

This research adopted a weighted late fusion methodology (Pasqualino et al., 2020), wherein distinct models are trained independently for each modality (text, audio, and video). The predictions generated by these individual models are subsequently combined later, employing uniform weights for each modality. This late fusion ap-

Approach	Models	P	R	F1
Visual	ConvLSTM	0.56	0.56	0.56
	3D CNN	0.56	0.56	0.56
	3D CNN+BiLSTM	0.50	0.50	0.50
Acoustic	BiLSTM	0.75	0.72	0.71
	CNN	0.80	0.67	0.62
	LR	0.62	0.61	0.60
Textual	LSTM	0.25	0.50	0.33
	MNB	0.66	0.61	0.58
	LR	0.66	0.61	0.58
Multimodal	**ConvLSTM+BiLSTM+MNB**	0.75	0.72	**0.71**
	ConvLSTM+CNN+LR	0.71	0.67	0.65
	3DCNN+CNN+LSTM	0.62	0.61	0.60
	(3DCNN+BiLSTM)+BiLSTM+MNB	0.71	0.67	0.65

Table 3: Performance of different unimodal and multimodal approaches on the test set, where P, R, and F1 denotes precision, recall and macro F1-score respectively

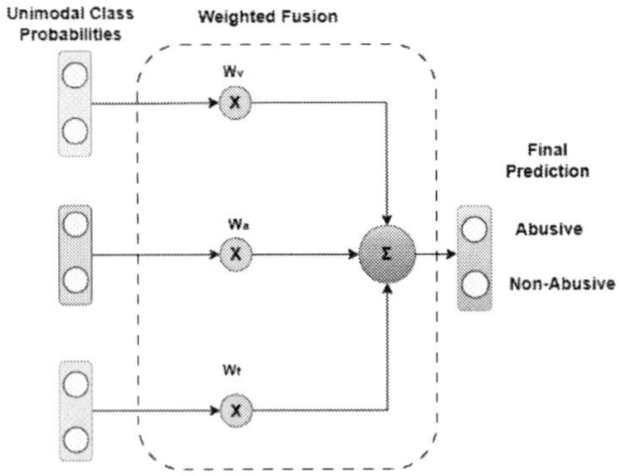

Figure 2: Schematic framework for weighted late fusion

proach allows us to leverage each modality's unique features and effectively amalgamate their contributions. Figure 2 depicts the schematic framework for weighted late fusion for multimodal abusive language detection in Tamil. Mathematically, the late fusion process's final prediction (P) can be expressed 1.

$$P = w_t \cdot P_{text} + w_a \cdot P_{audio} + w_v \cdot P_{video} \quad (1)$$

Here, *P* is the ultimate output of the late fusion model. The equitable allocation of uniform weights (w_t, w_a, w_v), each assigned a weight of 0.333, guarantees an even contribution from every modality. This approach facilitates a harmonized integration of information originating from text, audio, and video sources within the framework of our weighted late fusion methodology.

5 Results

Precision (P), recall (R), and macro F1-score (F1) are used to assess the model's performance. Results on the test dataset demonstrate that the combined model (ConvLSTM+BiLSTM+MNB) achieved preeminence, securing the topmost performance with a notable F1 (macro) score of 0.7143, as detailed in Table 3.

Table 4 compares the other team's performance with the rank participating in the shared task, where it is evident that our proposed method has achieved the highest F1-score among all participating teams.

Team	F1-(macro	Rank
Binary_Beasts	**0.7143**	**1**
Wit Hub	0.4156	2

Table 4: Competition rank list for Tamil abusive language detection

5.1 Error Analysis

A thorough evaluation of the model's performance on the test data is provided through the presentation of the confusion matrix in Figure 3. The examination of the confusion matrix reveals nearly flawless detection accuracy for abusive content, whereas the performance for non-abusive content is comparatively lower. This discrepancy may be attributed to the model incorrectly predicting non-abusive instances as abusive, potentially due to shared features between the two classes, or it could be a consequence of inadequate training data leading to

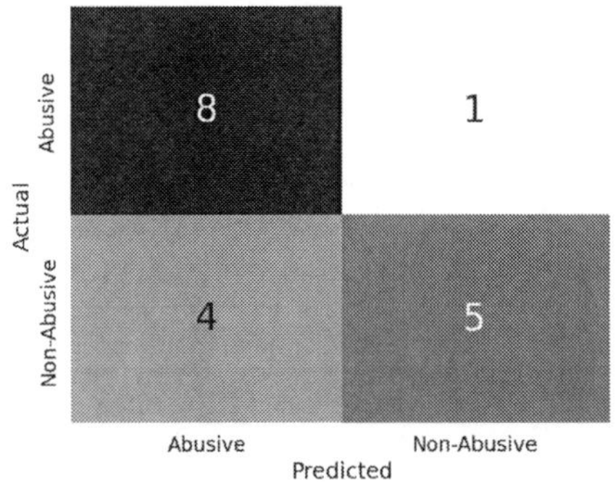

Figure 3: Confusion matrix of the proposed model (**ConvLSTM+BiLSTM+MNB**)

Test sample	Actual	Predicted
test1.txt test1.mp3 test1.mp4	Abusive	Abusive
test2.txt test2.mp3 test2.mp4	Abusive	Non-Abusive
test10.txt test10.mp3 test10.mp4	Non-Abusive	Non-Abusive
test15.txt test15.mp3 test15.mp4	Non-Abusive	Non-Abusive
test16.txt test16.mp3 test16.mp4	Non-Abusive	Abusive

Table 5: Few examples of predicted outputs by the proposed model (**ConvLSTM+BiLSTM+MNB**)

challenges in generalizing to diverse contexts.

Table 5 illustrates some correct and incorrect predicted outcomes by the best-performed model (**ConvLSTM+BiLSTM+MNB**).

Limitations

The current work encountered several hurdles, including:

- Concerns exist about the efficacy of the uniform weighting strategy, potentially compromising the model's responsiveness to specific features.
- The study concentrated on content detection in Tamil, prompting the need to explore the generalizability of the approach to other linguistic domains.
- The dataset's composition and size could influence the model's robustness, necessitating exploration across diverse datasets to validate adaptability in varied contextual settings.

6 Conclusion

This paper endeavors to advance the field of abusive content classification in the Tamil language by employing a multimodal approach that integrates textual, auditory, and visual information. Implementing a weighted late fusion strategy (with an integrated approach of ConvLSTM, BiLSTM, and MNB models), where each modality is assigned a uniform weight, has demonstrated a noteworthy improvement in F1-score compared to unimodal techniques. This outcome underscores the synergistic benefits achieved through the comprehensive analysis of multiple modalities, enhancing the robustness and discriminatory power of our abusive content detection model. Future research endeavors may encompass the refinement of weighting mechanisms and alternative fusion techniques, including the adoption of transformer-based approaches, to enhance modality integration.

References

Premjth B, Jyothish Lal G, Sowmya V, Bharathi Raja Chakravarthi, Nandhini K, Rajeswari Natarajan, Abirami Murugappan, Bharathi B, Saranya Rajiakodi, Rahul Ponnusamy, Jayanth Mohan, and Spandana Reddy Mekapati. 2024. Findings of the shared task on multimodal social media data analysis in dravidian languages (msmda-dl). In *Proceedings of the Fourth Workshop on Speech, Vision, and Language Technologies for Dravidian Languages*, Malta. European Chapter of the Association for Computational Linguistics.

Abhinaba Bala and Parameswari Krishnamurthy. 2023. Abhipaw@ dravidianlangtech: Multimodal abusive language detection and sentiment analysis. In *Proceedings of the Third Workshop on Speech and Language Technologies for Dravidian Languages*, pages 140–146.

Shubhankar Barman and Mithun Das. 2023. hate-alert@ dravidianlangtech: Multimodal abusive language detection and sentiment analysis in dravidian languages. In *Proceedings of the Third Workshop on Speech and Language Technologies for Dravidian Languages*, pages 217–224.

Piotr Bojanowski, Edouard Grave, Armand Joulin, and Tomas Mikolov. 2017. Enriching word vectors with subword information. *Transactions of the association for computational linguistics*, 5:135–146.

Bharathi Raja Chakravarthi, KP Soman, Rahul Ponnusamy, Prasanna Kumar Kumaresan, Kingston Pal Thamburaj, John P McCrae, et al. 2021. Dravidianmultimodality: A dataset for multi-modal sentiment analysis in tamil and malayalam. *arXiv preprint arXiv:2106.04853*.

Ganesh Chandrasekaran, Tu N Nguyen, and Jude Hemanth D. 2021. Multimodal sentimental analysis for social media applications: A comprehensive review. *Wiley Interdisciplinary Reviews: Data Mining and Knowledge Discovery*, 11(5):e1415.

Anusha Chhabra and Dinesh Kumar Vishwakarma. 2023. A literature survey on multimodal and multilingual automatic hate speech identification. *Multimedia Systems*, pages 1–28.

Mithun Das, Punyajoy Saha, Ritam Dutt, Pawan Goyal, Animesh Mukherjee, and Binny Mathew. 2021. You too brutus! trapping hateful users in social media: Challenges, solutions & insights. In *Proceedings of the 32nd ACM Conference on Hypertext and Social Media*, pages 79–89.

PD Mahendhiran and SJIJoIT Kannimuthu. 2018. Deep learning techniques for polarity classification in multimodal sentiment analysis. *International Journal of Information Technology & Decision Making*, 17(03):883–910.

Marzieh Mozafari, Reza Farahbakhsh, and Noel Crespi. 2020. A bert-based transfer learning approach for hate speech detection in online social media. In *Complex Networks and Their Applications VIII: Volume 1 Proceedings of the Eighth International Conference on Complex Networks and Their Applications COMPLEX NETWORKS 2019 8*, pages 928–940. Springer.

Giovanni Pasqualino, Stefano Scafiti, Antonino Furnari, and Giovanni Maria Farinella. 2020. Localizing visitors in natural sites exploiting modality attention on egocentric images and gps data. In *VISIGRAPP (5: VISAPP)*, pages 609–617.

Soujanya Poria, Erik Cambria, Newton Howard, Guang-Bin Huang, and Amir Hussain. 2016. Fusing audio, visual and textual clues for sentiment analysis from multimodal content. *Neurocomputing*, 174:50–59.

Soujanya Poria, Devamanyu Hazarika, Navonil Majumder, Gautam Naik, Erik Cambria, and Rada Mihalcea. 2018. Meld: A multimodal multi-party dataset for emotion recognition in conversations. *arXiv preprint arXiv:1810.02508*.

B Premjith, Bharathi Raja Chakravarthi, Malliga Subramanian, B Bharathi, Soman Kp, V Dhanalakshmi, K Sreelakshmi, Arunaggiri Pandian, and Prasanna Kumaresan. 2022. Findings of the shared task on multimodal sentiment analysis and troll meme classification in dravidian languages. In *Proceedings of the Second Workshop on Speech and Language Technologies for Dravidian Languages*, pages 254–260.

B Premjith, V Sowmya, Bharathi Raja Chakravarthi, Rajeswari Natarajan, K Nandhini, Abirami Murugappan, B Bharathi, M Kaushik, Prasanth Sn, et al. 2023. Findings of the shared task on multimodal abusive language detection and sentiment analysis in tamil and malayalam. In *Proceedings of the Third Workshop on Speech and Language Technologies for Dravidian Languages*, pages 72–79.

Rini Sharon, Heet Shah, Debdoot Mukherjee, and Vikram Gupta. 2022. Multilingual and multimodal abuse detection. *arXiv preprint arXiv:2204.02263*.

Devin Soni and Vivek K Singh. 2018. See no evil, hear no evil: Audio-visual-textual cyberbullying detection. *Proceedings of the ACM on Human-Computer Interaction*, 2(CSCW):1–26.

Konthala Yasaswini, Karthik Puranik, Adeep Hande, Ruba Priyadharshini, Sajeetha Thavareesan, and Bharathi Raja Chakravarthi. 2021. Iiitt@ dravidianlangtech-eacl2021: Transfer learning for offensive language detection in dravidian languages. In *Proceedings of the First Workshop on Speech and Language Technologies for Dravidian Languages*, pages 187–194.

WordWizards@DravidianLangTech 2024: Sentiment Analysis in Tamil and Tulu using Sentence Embedding

Shreedevi Seluka Balaji[1], Akshatha Anbalagan[1], Priyadharshini T[1], Niranjana A[1], Durairaj Thenmozhi[1]

[1]**Sri Sivasubramaniya Nadar College of Engineering, Tamil Nadu, India**
shreedevi2210389@ssn.edu.in , akshatha2210397@ssn.edu.in ,
priyadharshini2210228@ssn.edu.in , niranjana2210379@ssn.edu.in , theni_d@ssn.edu.in

Abstract

Sentiment Analysis of Dravidian Languages has begun to garner attention recently as there is more need to analyze emotional responses and subjective opinions present in social media text. As this data is code-mixed and there are not many solutions to code-mixed text out there, we present to you a stellar solution to DravidianLangTech 2024: Sentiment Analysis in Tamil and Tulu task [1]. To understand the sentiment of social media text, we used pre trained transformer models and feature extraction vectorizers to classify the data with results that placed us 11th in the rankings for the Tamil task and 8th for the Tulu task with a accuracy F1 score of 0.12 and 0.30 which shows the efficiency of our approach.

1 Introduction

Social media transcends borders, fostering global communication with user-generated content expressing emotions. Research, like Wang et al.'s study (Wang et al., 2022), uses ensemble models to detect depression signs from social media. The surge in platforms underscores the importance of sentiment analysis in local languages, as seen in the study on Dravidian languages like Tamil (Chakravarthi et al., 2021). English intertwining with native scripts poses challenges, and Natural Language Processing techniques are suggested for effective sentiment analysis, focusing on specific subjects. The task involves classifying YouTube comments into labels for Tulu and Tamil, aligning with findings that sentiment analysis in code-mixed text requires careful consideration of linguistic nuances in multilingual contexts. The rest of the paper is organized as follows. Section 2 outlines the related works emphasizing Sentiment Analysis in Dravidian languages. Section 3 presents a description of the dataset. Section 4 describes the methodology used for the shared task. Section 5 discusses the result and analysis of the task assigned. In Section 6 concludes the paper followed by ethics statement in Section 7.

[1]https://sites.google.com/view/dravidianlangtech-2024/home

2 Related Works

Sentiment analysis is vital amid the vast data on social media. Approaches include lexicon-based methods, using dictionaries like Sentiwordnet and TF-IDF (Term Frequency-Inverse Document Frequency), and machine learning methods employing SVM and Naïve Bayes models. Combining these methods enhances efficiency, addressing unstructured data effectively (Jada et al., 2021; Drus and Khalid, 2019). Research on sentiment analysis of Dravidian languages, exemplified by Chakravarthi et al.'s study (Chakravarthi et al., 2021), explores challenges in linguistic diversity and code-mixing, emphasizing the need for tools handling code-mixed text (S. K. et al., 2024). The findings underscore the importance of linguistic considerations in capturing sentiments in Dravidian languages and English on social media (Chakravarthi et al., 2021; Hegde et al., 2023), providing valuable insights into public opinion, cultural discourse, and community dynamics. This highlights the necessity of language-specific sentiment analysis tools for understanding sentiments in diverse linguistic communities.

3 Dataset

The datasets provided were comments from social media and each comment corresponded to a particular label. The labels were Positive for comments that were appreciative, Negative for hate speech and other detected signs on aggression, Mixed feeling/feelings for comments on the fence and Neutral/unknown_state for comments that were neither positive nor negative. The dataset was divided into three parts namely train,test and dev. The train and dev datasets had *text* and *category* as labels while the test dataset had *id* and *text* as labels for

Proceedings of the Fourth Workshop on Speech, Vision, and Language Technologies for Dravidian Languages, pages 218–222
March 22, 2024

Tamil (Chakravarthi et al., 2020). The train and dev datasets had *Text* and *Annotations* as labels while the test dataset had *ID* and *Text* as labels (Hegde et al., 2022) for Tulu. The test data for both languages was not labeled and we had to find and classify the test data as part of the task. The train dataset consisted of 33,988 rows of which
Positive: 20,070
Unknown State: 5,628
Negative: 4,271
Mixed Feelings: 4,020 for Tamil and 6945 rows of which
Positive: 3,352
Neutral: 1,854
Mixed Feeling: 1,041
Negative: 698 for Tulu. The dev dataset consisted of 3,785 rows for Tamil and 500 rows for Tulu. The test dataset consisted of 650 rows for Tamil and 502 rows for Tulu.

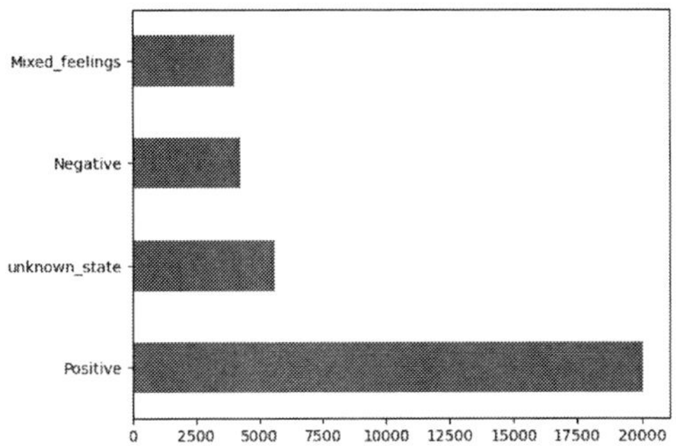

Figure 1: Category Metrics

4 Methodology

4.1 Preprocessing

Preprocessing refers to the ways in which we can clean data and remove noise (inconsistencies). These methods are applied to raw data so we may process them better later on. Preprocessing involves many steps which include:

1.Tokenisation to breakdown sentences into words or subwords.

2.Converting all text to lowercase.

3.Removing stopwords which are words that do not add any value to the meaning of the sentence. This is done using a list of stopwords, provided by the Python package NLTK and enhancing the list with our own Tamil and Tulu stopwords, which can be iterated through each row and removed.

4.De-emojify using the re package to remove emoticons, flags in iOS, symbols and pictographs, transport and map symbols.

4.2 Feature Extraction

LaBSE, or Language-agnostic BERT Sentence Embedding, is a multilingual variant of BERT designed for cross-lingual natural language processing tasks. Unlike traditional BERT models that are trained on individual languages, LaBSE is trained to generate language-agnostic sentence embeddings, making it effective for applications where text spans multiple languages(Feng et al., 2020).

The key innovation in LaBSE lies in its training approach. It utilizes a parallel data mining strategy, leveraging publicly available parallel sentences in multiple languages. This allows LaBSE to learn cross-lingual representations by aligning sentence embeddings across languages in a shared embedding space. The model is trained to map semantically similar sentences in different languages to nearby points in the embedding space.

The training process involves encoding sentences into fixed-dimensional vectors, ensuring that semantically equivalent sentences in different languages are close to each other in the embedding space. This shared embedding space enables LaBSE to capture universal semantic features across languages, facilitating effective cross-lingual understanding.

The feature extraction process with LaBSE involves encoding a given sentence into a dense vector representation. This vector, often referred to as a sentence embedding, encapsulates the semantic meaning of the input sentence. These embeddings can then be used for various downstream tasks, such as cross-lingual document retrieval, sentiment analysis, or machine translation.

LaBSE's effectiveness stems from its ability to generate language-agnostic representations, making it particularly useful for scenarios where language boundaries are fluid or when dealing with multilingual datasets. It allows practitioners to perform cross-lingual tasks without the need for language-specific models, offering a unified approach for diverse linguistic contexts.

4.3 Models Used

Support Vector Machine (SVM)

Support Vector Machine (SVM) is a powerful machine learning algorithm employed for classification and regression tasks by finding a hyperplane that maximizes the margin between data points of different classes. Its effectiveness in handling high-dimensional data and capability to identify complex decision boundaries make SVM widely applied across diverse domains (Cortes and Vapnik, 1995).

K-Nearest Neighbors (KNN)

K-Nearest Neighbors (KNN) is a versatile algorithm utilized for classification and regression, making predictions by considering the majority class or average of the k-nearest data points in the feature space. Renowned for its simplicity and ease of implementation, KNN is widely adopted in applications such as pattern recognition and recommendation systems (Altman, 1992).

Naive Bayes

Naive Bayes, a probabilistic classification algorithm founded on Bayes' theorem with the assumption of feature independence, has demonstrated remarkable effectiveness in tasks like text classification, spam filtering, and sentiment analysis. Its computational efficiency, minimal training data requirement, and suitability for high-dimensional datasets make Naive Bayes widely employed (Rish et al., 2001).

4.4 KNN

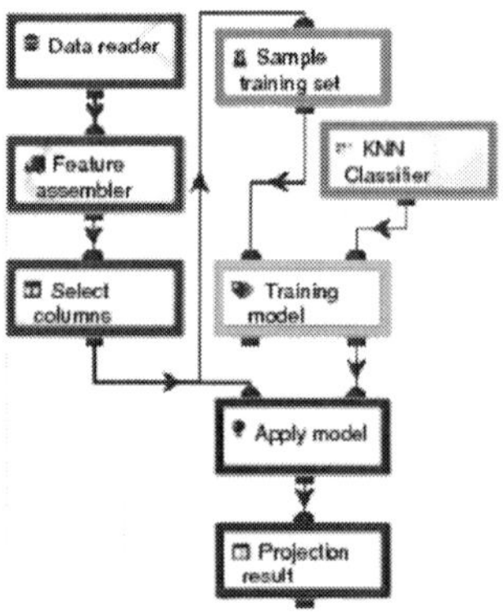

Figure 2: Workflow of KNN Model

The KNN workflow, illustrated in the figure, encompasses a sequence of operations. This includes a step for reading and preprocessing data, a subsequent step for sampling data intended for training a K Nearest Neighbors classifier, and a final step for applying the model to the dataset. In the end, the model that prevailed, with the best results was the K-Nearest Neighbors model with an overall macro F1 score of 0.62 for the Tamil train and dev datasets with an accuracy of 0.12 and a macro F1 score of 0.07 with the test dataset, placing us 11th on the ranklist and for the Tulu dataset, a macro F1 score of 0.66 and 0.67 on the training and dev datasets and a macro F1 score of 0.26 and an accuracy 0.30 with the test dataset, placing us 8th on the ranklist.

5 Results

5.1 Analysis

Here are the comparison metrics of the models applied to the training dataset for Tamil.

Metric	0	1	2	3
Precision	0.56	0.80	0.74	0.73
Recall	0.71	0.90	0.32	0.45

Table 1: Precision and Recall on Tamil Training Data

Label 0- unknown_state: Precision score 0.56 means that whenever the model predicts Unknown state, it is correct around 56% of the time. Recall 0.71 means that it identify 71% of the actual instances belonging to class 0.

Label 1- Positive: Precision score 0.80 means that whenever the model predicts Positive, it is correct around 80% of the time. Recall 0.90 means that it identify 90% of the actual instances belonging to class 1.

Label 2- Mixed_feelings: Precision score 0.74 means that whenever the model predicts Positive, it is correct around 74% of the time. Recall 0.83 means that it identify 83% of the actual instances belonging to class 2.

Label 3- Negative: Precision score 0.73 means that whenever the model predicts Positive, it is correct around 73% of the time. Recall 0.45 means that it identify 45% of the actual instances belonging to class 0.

Metric	Support Vector Machine	Naive Bayes	KNN
Accuracy	0.61	0.56	0.74
Macro Average F1 score	0.30	0.44	0.62

Table 2: Comparison of metrics on Tamil Training Data

The model demonstrates an overall performance, as indicated by the weighted average F1-score of 0.73, considering the support (number of instances) for each class. The accuracy, standing at 0.74, reflects the percentage of correctly classified instances across all classes. The macro average F1-score, measuring 0.62, provides an assessment of the model's performance across all classes while treating them equally, irrespective of class imbalances.

Metric	Support Vector Machine	Naive Bayes	KNN
Accuracy	0.65	0.35	0.77
Macro Average F1 score	0.54	0.32	0.66

Table 3: Comparison of metrics on Tulu Training Data

Tests conclude that the KNN model has an overall F1 score accuracy of 0.30 with the test data for Tulu along with a 0.70 precision for the Positive label.

6 Conclusion

This study explores sentiment analysis in Dravidian languages, Tamil and Tulu, using LaBSE for feature extraction and KNN for classification. Achieving competitive rankings in the DravidianLangTech 2024 competition (11th for Tamil, 8th for Tulu), our model demonstrated promising precision and recall, particularly excelling in handling uncertain sentiments in the "Unknown State" class for Tamil. While acknowledging limitations and scalability challenges, we emphasize ethical considerations, including privacy and cultural sensitivity. In conclusion, our research provides insights into effective strategies for sentiment analysis in code-mixed social media text in Dravidian languages, showcasing the viability of LaBSE and KNN in culturally diverse contexts.

Label	Precision	Recall	F1 score
Mixed Feeling	0.15	0.23	0.18
Negative	0.10	0.21	0.14
Neutral	0.27	0.39	0.32
Positive	0.70	0.28	0.40

Table 4: Classification Report of Tulu Test Set

7 Limitations

Performing sentiment analysis on YouTube comments faces challenges due to their diverse language styles and informal expressions, making traditional models like K-Nearest Neighbors (KNN) and TF-IDF less effective in capturing nuanced semantics. The scalability of KNN becomes a concern with large datasets, and the presence of multilingual text further complicates sentiment representation. These limitations highlight the need for more sophisticated, context-aware approaches in future research to better handle the diverse nature of YouTube comments.

Label	Precision	Recall	F1 score
Mixed_feelings	0.14	0.01	0.02
Negative	0.42	0.01	0.03
Positive	0.11	0.92	0.20
unknown_state	0.18	0.03	0.05

Table 5: Classification Report of Tamil Test Set

8 Ethics Statement

Ethical considerations in conducting sentiment analysis on YouTube comments are crucial for maintaining responsible research practices. Privacy, consent, and the handling of sensitive content should be prioritized throughout the research process. Transparent data collection practices, coupled with efforts to mitigate biases, are paramount to ensure the ethical treatment of user-generated content.

Respecting privacy rights involves anonymizing and securing user information, especially when dealing with publicly available but personally identifiable data. Seeking consent for data usage is essential, and researchers should be transparent about the purpose and scope of their analysis when working with comments from public platforms. Sensitivity to cultural nuances and potential biases in sentiment analysis algorithms is crucial to avoid perpetuating stereotypes or misrepresenting sentiments across diverse communities.

Fairness should be a guiding principle in sentiment analysis, ensuring that the models do not disproportionately favor or disadvantage any particular group. Acknowledging the broader societal implications of sentiment analysis on YouTube comments is vital, as the findings may impact public opinion, shape narratives, and influence decision-making. Upholding ethical standards in this research involves navigating privacy, consent, sensitivity, fairness, and cultural considerations to contribute responsibly to the evolving field of sentiment analysis on social media platforms.

References

Naomi S Altman. 1992. An Introduction to Kernel and Nearest-Neighbor Nonparametric Regression. *The American Statistician*, 46(3):175–185.

Bharathi Raja Chakravarthi, Vigneshwaran Muralidaran, Ruba Priyadharshini, and John Philip McCrae. 2020. Corpus creation for sentiment analysis in code-mixed Tamil-English text. In *Proceedings of the 1st Joint Workshop on Spoken Language Technologies for Under-resourced languages (SLTU) and Collaboration and Computing for Under-Resourced Languages (CCURL)*, pages 202–210, Marseille, France. European Language Resources association.

Bharathi Raja Chakravarthi, Ruba Priyadharshini, Sajeetha Thavareesan, Dhivya Chinnappa, Durairaj Thenmozhi, Elizabeth Sherly, John P McCrae, Adeep Hande, Rahul Ponnusamy, Shubhanker Banerjee, et al. 2021. Findings of the Sentiment Analysis of Dravidian Languages in Code-Mixed Text. *arXiv preprint arXiv:2111.09811*.

Corinna Cortes and Vladimir Vapnik. 1995. Support-Vector Networks. *Machine learning*, 20:273–297.

Zulfadzli Drus and Haliyana Khalid. 2019. Sentiment analysis in social media and its application: Systematic literature review. *Procedia Computer Science*, 161:707–714.

Fangxiaoyu Feng, Yinfei Yang, Daniel Cer, Naveen Arivazhagan, and Wei Wang. 2020. Language-agnostic BERT sentence embedding. *arXiv preprint arXiv:2007.01852*.

Asha Hegde, Mudoor Devadas Anusha, Sharal Coelho, Hosahalli Lakshmaiah Shashirekha, and Bharathi Raja Chakravarthi. 2022. Corpus creation for sentiment analysis in code-mixed Tulu text. In *Proceedings of the 1st Annual Meeting of the ELRA/ISCA Special Interest Group on Under-Resourced Languages*, pages 33–40, Marseille, France. European Language Resources Association.

Asha Hegde, Bharathi Raja Chakravarthi, Hosahalli Lakshmaiah Shashirekha, Rahul Ponnusamy, SUBALALITHA CN, Lavanya S K, Durairaj Thenmozhi, Martha Karunakar, Shreya Shreeram, and Sarah Aymen. 2023. Findings of the Shared Task on Sentiment Analysis in Tamil and Tulu Code-Mixed Text. In *Proceedings of the Third Workshop on Speech and Language Technologies for Dravidian Languages*, Varna, Bulgaria. Recent Advances in Natural Language Processing.

Pawan Kalyan Jada, D Sashidhar Reddy, Konthala Yasaswini, Arunaggiri Pandian K, Prabakaran Chandran, Anbukkarasi Sampath, and Sathiyaraj Thangasamy. 2021. Transformer based Sentiment Analysis in Dravidian Languages. In *FIRE (Working Notes)*, pages 926–938.

Irina Rish et al. 2001. An empirical study of the Naive Bayes classifier. In *IJCAI 2001 workshop on empirical methods in artificial intelligence*, volume 3, pages 41–46.

Lavanya S. K., Asha Hegde, Bharathi Raja Chakravarthi, Hosahalli Lakshmaiah Shashirekha, Rajeswari Natarajan, Sajeetha Thavareesan, Ratnasingam Sakuntharaj, Durairaj Thenmozhi, and Rajkumar Charmathi Kumaresan, Prasanna Kumar. 2024. Overview of Second Shared Task on Sentiment Analysis in Code-mixed Tamil and Tulu. In *Proceedings of the Fourth Workshop on Speech, Vision, and Language Technologies for Dravidian Languages*, Malta. European Chapter of the Association for Computational Linguistics.

Wei-Yao Wang, Yu-Chien Tang, Wei-Wei Du, and Wen-Chih Peng. 2022. NYCU_TWD@ LT-EDI-ACL2022: Ensemble models with VADER and contrastive learning for detecting signs of depression from social media. In *Proceedings of the second workshop on language technology for equality, diversity and inclusion*, pages 136–139.

CUET_DUO@DravidianLangTech EACL2024: Fake News Classification Using Malayalam-BERT

Tanzim Rahman, Abu Bakkar Siddique Raihan, Md. Tanvir Rahman, Jawad Hossain, Shawly Ahsan, Avishek Das and **Mohammed Moshiul Hoque**
Department of Computer Science and Engineering
Chittagong University of Engineering & Technology, Chattogram-4349, Bangladesh
{u1804015, u1804004, u1804002, u1704039, u1704057}@student.cuet.ac.bd
{avishek, moshiul_240}@cuet.ac.bd

Abstract

Identifying between fake and original news in social media demands vigilant procedures. This paper introduces the significant shared task on 'Fake News Detection in Dravidian Languages - DravidianLangTech@EACL 2024'. With a focus on the Malayalam language, this task is crucial in identifying social media posts as either fake or original news. The participating teams contribute immensely to this task through their varied strategies, employing methods ranging from conventional machine-learning techniques to advanced transformer-based models. Notably, the findings of this work highlight the effectiveness of the Malayalam-BERT model, demonstrating an impressive macro F1 score of **0.88** in distinguishing between fake and original news in Malayalam social media content, achieving a commendable rank of **1**st among the participants.

1 Introduction

A growing number of people are choosing to get their news from social media platforms rather than traditional news outlets in an era where online interactions are becoming more common. News consumption on social media differs from traditional media, such as newspapers and television, regarding timeliness and affordability. Social media preference is also influenced by the ease with which news can be shared, commented on, and discussed with friends and other readers. However, the ease of sharing content via social media and the cost-effectiveness of online news distribution have led to the massive spread of fake news. This trend is particularly pertinent in the context of our paper on Fake News Detection in the Malayalam language. Kumari and Kumar (2021) introduced ensemble-based models for detecting offensive language in mixed-script social media posts. Many task formulations, datasets, and natural language processing (NLP) solutions have been used to investigate the intricacies of identifying fake news in the literature (Oshikawa et al., 2018).

This paper discusses the challenges of identifying fake news, focusing on the Malayalam language. The aim is to curb the spread of misinformation in this language space by providing culturally sensitive insights and solutions by exploring methodologies. Recent data on the impact of Facebook referrals, which shows that 20% of traffic goes to reliable websites and 50% goes to fake news sites, underscores the pressing nature of the problem. Considering that 62% of American adults get their news from social media, recognizing and mitigating the influence of fake content in online sources is more crucial than ever (Purcell et al., 2010).

This research contributes to the domain of fake news detection in the Malayalam language through the following key aspects:

- Investigate various machine learning, deep learning, and fine-tuned transformer models (m-BERT and Malayalam-BERT) to find the superior model for identifying fake news using relevant datasets.
- A comprehensive analysis of the proposed model to gain a nuanced understanding of its efficacy in recognizing fake news in Malayalam code-mixed social media content.

2 Related Work

Sivanaiah et al. (2022) prepared fake news datasets for several low-resource languages and applied Logistic Regression and BERT models for fake news classification. It was demonstrated through rigorous experiments that 'BERT-based-multilingual-cased' achieved a maximum F1 score of around 98%. At the same time, Logistic Regression reached approximately 95% in low-resource Indian languages such as Malayalam, Gujarati, and Tamil. Hariharan and Anand Kumar (2022) created a

Proceedings of the Fourth Workshop on Speech, Vision, and Language Technologies for Dravidian Languages, pages 223–228
March 22, 2024 ©2024 Association for Computational Linguistics

multilingual low-resource fake news classification dataset and examined the impact of transformer-based models, such as multilingual BERT, XLM-RoBERTa, and MuRIL. For Telugu, Kannada, Tamil, and Malayalam, they assessed four transformer models: mBERT, XLM-RoBERTa, IndicBERT, and MuRIL. However, Raja et al. (2022) demonstrated that, for these low-resource languages, MuRIL had a higher accuracy in identifying fake news.

The DravidianLangTech@RANLP (Amjad et al., 2022) 2023 session "Fake News Detection in Dravidian Languages" concentrated on Malayalam content. In particular, the XLMRoBERTa-based model performed exceptionally well, obtaining a macro F1-score of 0.90. In DravidianLangTech-2023, Balaji et al. (2023) proposed transformer models such as M-BERT, ALBERT, BERT, and XLNET. M-BERT outperformed competitors with a robust F1 score of 0.74, surpassing XLNET and ALBERT, which achieved accuracy scores of 0.71 and 0.66, respectively. Using transformer-based models for language analysis, the study (Bala and Krishnamurthy, 2023) explored the nuances of identifying fake news. The *mural-base-cased* version of MuRIL was refined using a Dravidian language-curated dataset.

Rasel et al. (2022) addressed the scarcity of resources for the Bangla language in fake news detection by constructing a dataset of 4678 distinct news instances. Employing various machine learning, deep neural network, and transformer models, including CNN, CNN-LSTM, and BiLSTM, they achieved state-of-the-art accuracy ranging from 95.3% to 95.9%, showcasing notable improvements in accuracy and recall compared to previous studies when tested on both newly collected and existing datasets. Rahman et al. (2022) created the BFNC dataset containing 5,000 instances of fake news and presented the FaND-X framework using transformer-based and neural network-based techniques. With a maximum F1-score of 98% on the test data, experimental results showed that XLM-R outperformed other methods, demonstrating its efficacy in detecting fake news.

Abedalla et al. (2019) conducted a comparison of various BiLSTM models for detecting false information. This research demonstrates the efficacy of sequential models in text classification and identifying deceptive information, suggesting a potential future evaluation compared to BERT. In a similar application, the artificial intelligence initiative by Facebook (Kurasinski and Mihailescu, 2020) incorporates BERT as an integral component of its machine-learning strategy for detecting hate speech. In the past few years, pre-established models leveraging the Transformer architecture introduced (Vaswani et al., 2017) have gained prominence and serve a crucial function in sequence encoding and decoding. The effectiveness of these models in generating condensed contextualized embeddings for diverse texts inspired us to develop a system for detecting deceptive information based on these models.

3 Task and Dataset Descriptions

For the goal of fake news identification in the Malayalam language, the organizers created an almost balanced and standardized dataset. The primary purpose is to design a system that appropriately differentiates between fake and original news from social media posts in Malayalam. The dataset utilized in this challenge is derived from the corpus given by the workshop organizers (Subramanian et al., 2024). The work entails sorting social media statements into two predetermined classes: Fake and original news. Table 1 displays the distribution

Classes	Train	Test	Dev	TW
Original	1658	512	409	14031
Fake	1599	507	406	23198
Total	3257	1019	815	37229

Table 1: Distribution of Malayalam fake news dataset, where TW denote total words

of samples across the train, development (dev), and test sets for each class. Notably, the dataset is almost balanced, ensuring nearly equal instances for original and fake news classes.

4 Methodology

The proposed method experimented with several machine learning (ML), DL, and transformer-based baselines with fine-tuning the hyperparameters. Figure 1 demonstrates a schematic process of the employed models.

4.1 Feature Extraction

This work used TF-IDF (Sundaram et al., 2021) and Word2Vec embeddings (Rashid et al., 2020) for extracting textual features. The Keras embedding layer plays a crucial role in generating 100-

Method	Classifier	P	R	F1	A
	LR	0.92	0.26	0.41	0.62
ML	DT	0.84	0.31	0.45	0.63
	NB	0.78	0.79	0.78	0.78
	CNN	0.77	0.76	0.75	0.76
DL	BiLSTM	0.80	0.79	0.81	0.80
	CNN+BiLSTM	0.82	0.81	0.82	0.82
Transformers	m-BERT	0.73	0.52	0.38	0.52
	Malayalam-BERT	0.88	0.88	**0.88**	**0.88**

Table 2: Performance of various models for fake news classification in Malayalam, where P, R, F1, and A denotes precision, recall, macro F1-score, and accuracy, respectively

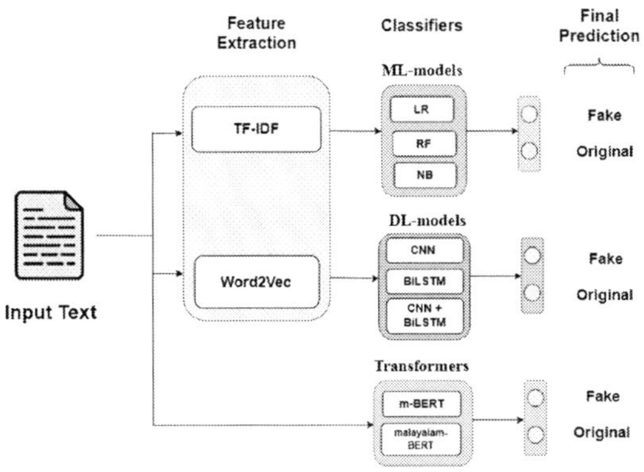

Figure 1: Schematic process of fake news identification

dimensional embedding vectors, enhancing the models' ability to identify and capture complex patterns in information, thereby improving the effectiveness of fake news detection.

4.2 ML Approaches

Various ML techniques, such as Logistic Regression (LR), Decision Tree (DT), and Naïve Bayes (NB), are explored for the task. This comprehensive approach involved meticulous parameterization to optimize the effectiveness of each algorithm. Specifically, the LR model underwent fine-tuning with a regularization value set at 0.01, while the DT is designed with a maximum depth of 10. Integrating NB included applying a radial basis function (RBF) kernel with a gamma value set to 0.001.

4.3 DL Approaches

A hybrid Convolutional Neural Network (CNN) and Long Short-Term Memory (LSTM) architecture (Wu et al., 2020) was applied, featuring seven layers. Additionally, individual CNN and BiLSTM models were implemented as part of the broader hybrid architecture. The sequence vector of length 200 is input to the embedding layer, followed by two convolution layers with 'relu' activation and downsampling via max-pooling. The Bidirectional LSTM (BiLSTM) layer, with 128 units, captures intricate patterns, mitigating overfitting with a 0.5 dropout rate. The final layer uses a sigmoid activation function for binary classification, with variations exploring pre-trained word vectors. The 'Adam' optimizer employs a $1e^{-4}$ learning rate and binary cross-entropy as the loss function. Training spans 20 epochs with a batch size of 64, balancing performance and computational efficiency in fake news identification.

4.4 Transformer Models

This work applied two pre-trained transformer models, particularly M-BERT (Devlin et al., 2018), Malayalam-BERT (Joshi, 2022). These models, sourced from the Hugging Face transformers library [1] , underwent fine-tuning on the fake news corpus using the Ktrain (Maiya, 2022) package. The maximum sequence length was set at 100 with a batch size of 16. The models underwent training for three epochs, with a learning rate ($1e^{-4}$), enhancing their performance for the specific goal of fake news identification.

5 Results and Analysis

Table 2 illustrates the performance of the employed models for the fake news classification in Malayalam. Table 3 provides a comprehensive comparison of the performance across all participating teams. Our proposed model, Malayalam-BERT, has demonstrated superior performance, achieving the highest F1-score of **0.88** when compared to

[1] https://huggingface.co/

all other participating teams. illustrates a comparison of the performance of the opposing team with their respective ranks in the shared task. Among ML models, NB shines out with good accuracy of 0.78 and an impressive macro F1-score (0.78). On the other hand, CNN+BiLSTM achieved balanced accuracy (0.82), recall (0.81), and F1-score (0.82). Strategic modifications, including fine-

Team	F1_Score (Macro)	Rank
CUET_DUO	**0.88**	**1**
Punny_Punctuators	0.87	2
TechWhiz xlmr	0.86	3
CUET_Binary_Hackers	0.86	3
CUET_NLP_GoodFellows	0.85	4
CUETSentimentSilles	0.84	5

Table 3: Rank List of the Competition

tuning model hyperparameters and examining false positive occurrences, are proposed to increase the model's accuracy and overall efficacy in identifying fake news within the Malayalam language context.

6 Error Analysis

The fake news detection performance of the Malayalam-BERT model in Malayalam exhibits outstanding performance, especially evident in the high true positive count. Figure 2 shows the confusion matrix of the best-performed model (Malayalam-BERT) that highlighted the finest accuracy achieved by correctly tagging 442 out of 512 fake samples, demonstrating an effective capability to detect fake samples.

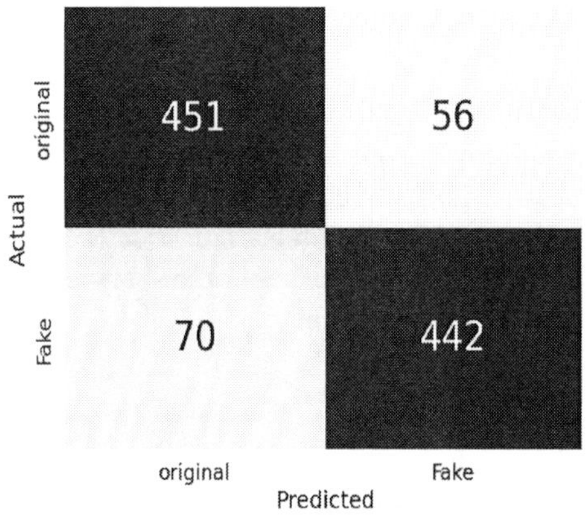

Figure 2: Confusion matrix of Malayalam-BERT model

However, a limitation arises in precision since 70 original samples were incorrectly identified as fake, indicating a vulnerability to false news detection. Less effective data preparation techniques could cause the misclassification. Addressing this issue through better preprocessing approaches may enhance precision and contribute to a more accurate classification. This observed pattern necessitates careful analysis and adjustment of the model's discriminatory capabilities. Further evaluations of the validation and test sets are essential to thoroughly examine the model's adaptability.

Figure 3 illustrates some predicted outcomes by the best-performed model (Malayalam-BERT).

Limitations

- The application of pre-trained transformers, specifically Malayalam-BERT, introduces a notable consideration in our fake news detection efforts. While leveraging pre-trained models can enhance contextual understanding, their effectiveness may be constrained by the specificity of the pre-training corpus. This may lead to a potential mismatch with the unique characteristics of fake news in Malayalam, highlighting the need for careful fine-tuning to ensure optimal performance.

Text Sample	Actual	Predicted
Sample1. കമ്മ്യൂണിസ്റ്റ് പൊളിഞ്ഞു തുടങ്ങി (The Communists began to collapse)	Original	Original
Sample2. ഇന്നെങ്കിലും ആ കണ്ണട മുഖത്ത് വെക്കാം എന്ന് കരുതി പക്ഷേ വീണ്ടും ഞാൻ ശശിയായി (I thought I would put those glasses on my face at least today, but I was disappointed again)	Fake	Original
Sample3. ചൈന ഉത്പന്നങ്ങൾ ബഹിഷ്കരിക്കുക (Boycott China products)	Fake	Fake
Sample4. റാന്നിക്കാരെ മാത്രം കുറ്റം പറഞ്ഞവർ എന്തിയേ? ഇപ്പോൾ ചില യാ ളുകൾ കേരളം മുഴുവൻ പരത്തിയപ്പോൾ ആർക്കും കുഴപ്പമില്ല (Why those who blamed only the Rannis? Now when some people have spread all over Kerala, no one has any problem)	Fake	Original
Sample5. കൊറോണ പോയി ഒന്ന് കൂടെ മെച്ചപ്പെട്ട് ഒമൈക്രോണായി വന്നപ്പോൾ നമ്മുടെ പിണുവിന്റെ നേതൃത്വത്തിൽ ഒരു സ്വീകരണം കൊടുത്തതല്ലേ (When Corona went away and got better and came back as Omicron, didn't we give a reception under the leadership of our Pinu)	Original	Fake

Figure 3: Few examples of predicted outputs by the proposed (Malayalam-BERT) model

- Additionally, the inherent linguistic complexities of Malayalam pose challenges that may impact the model's ability to discern subtle patterns, warranting further investigation and refinement.

7 Conclusion

This work addresses the challenges of fake news detection in Malayalam by exploiting three ML, three DL, and two transformer-based models. Experimental investigations on the test dataset revealed that Malayalam-BERT demonstrated superior performance among all models, achieving the highest macro F1 score (0.88). This finding highlights the proficiency of transformer-based strategies, precisely the efficiency of the Malayalam-BERT architecture, in excelling at the challenge of fake news identification. For future improvements, employing more language-specific preprocessing techniques and exploring ensemble models could enhance the overall performance of fake news detection in Malayalam. These strategies may contribute to refining the accuracy and robustness of the models in identifying misinformation effectively.

References

Ayat Abedalla, Aisha Al-Sadi, and Malak Abdullah. 2019. A closer look at fake news detection: A deep learning perspective. In *Proceedings of the 3rd International Conference on Advances in Artificial Intelligence*, pages 24–28.

Maaz Amjad, Sabur Butt, Hamza Imam Amjad, Alisa Zhila, Grigori Sidorov, and Alexander Gelbukh. 2022. Overview of the shared task on fake news detection in urdu at fire 2021. *arXiv preprint arXiv:2207.05133*.

Abhinaba Bala and Parameswari Krishnamurthy. 2023. Abhipaw@ dravidianlangtech: Fake news detection in dravidian languages using multilingual bert. In *Proceedings of the Third Workshop on Speech and Language Technologies for Dravidian Languages*, pages 235–238.

Varsha Balaji, B Bharathi, et al. 2023. Nlp_ssn_cse@ dravidianlangtech: Fake news detection in dravidian languages using transformer models. In *Proceedings of the Third Workshop on Speech and Language Technologies for Dravidian Languages*, pages 133–139.

Jacob Devlin, Ming-Wei Chang, Kenton Lee, and Kristina Toutanova. 2018. BERT: pre-training of deep bidirectional transformers for language understanding. *CoRR*, abs/1810.04805.

RamakrishnaIyer LekshmiAmmal Hariharan and Madasamy Anand Kumar. 2022. Impact of transformers on multilingual fake news detection for tamil and malayalam. In *International Conference on Speech and Language Technologies for Low-resource Languages*, pages 196–208. Springer.

Raviraj Joshi. 2022. L3cube-hindbert and devbert: Pre-trained bert transformer models for devanagari based hindi and marathi languages. *arXiv preprint arXiv:2211.11418*.

Jyoti Kumari and Abhinav Kumar. 2021. Offensive language identification on multilingual code mixing text. In *Working Notes of FIRE 2021-Forum for Information Retrieval Evaluation (Online). CEUR*.

Lukas Kurasinski and Radu-Casian Mihailescu. 2020. Towards machine learning explainability in text classification for fake news detection. In *2020 19th IEEE international conference on machine learning and applications (ICMLA)*, pages 775–781. IEEE.

Arun S Maiya. 2022. ktrain: A low-code library for augmented machine learning. *The Journal of Machine Learning Research*, 23(1):7070–7075.

Ray Oshikawa, Jing Qian, and William Yang Wang. 2018. A survey on natural language processing for fake news detection. *arXiv preprint arXiv:1811.00770*.

Kristen Purcell, Lee Rainie, Amy Mitchell, Tom Rosenstiel, and Kenny Olmstead. 2010. Understanding the participatory news consumer. *Pew Internet and American Life Project*, 1:19–21.

MD Sijanur Rahman, Omar Sharif, Avishek Das, Sadia Afroze, and Mohammed Moshiul Hoque. 2022. Fand-x: Fake news detection using transformer-based multilingual masked language model. In *2022 IEEE International Women in Engineering (WIE) Conference on Electrical and Computer Engineering (WIECON-ECE)*, pages 153–158. IEEE.

Eduri Raja, Badal Soni, and Samir Kumar Borgohain. 2022. Fake news detection in dravidian languages using transformer models. In *International Conference on Computer Vision, High-Performance Computing, Smart Devices, and Networks*, pages 515–523. Springer.

Risul Islam Rasel, Anower Hossen Zihad, Nasrin Sultana, and Mohammed Moshiul Hoque. 2022. Bangla fake news detection using machine learning, deep learning and transformer models. In *2022 25th International Conference on Computer and Information Technology (ICCIT)*, pages 959–964. IEEE.

Umar Rashid, Muhammad Waseem Iqbal, Muhammad Akmal Skiandar, Muhammad Qasim Raiz, Muhammad Raza Naqvi, and Syed Khuram Shahzad. 2020. Emotion detection of contextual text using deep learning. In *2020 4th International symposium on multidisciplinary studies and innovative technologies (ISMSIT)*, pages 1–5. IEEE.

Rajalakshmi Sivanaiah, Nishaanth Ramanathan, Shajith Hameed, Rahul Rajagopalan, Angel Deborah Suseelan, and Mirnalinee Thanka Nadar Thanagathai. 2022. Fake news detection in low-resource languages. In *International Conference on Speech and Language Technologies for Low-resource Languages*, pages 324–331. Springer.

Malliga Subramanian, Bharathi Raja Chakravarthi, Kogilavani Shanmugavadivel, Santhiya Pandiyan, Prasanna Kumar Kumaresan, Balasubramanian Palani, Premjith B, Sandhiya Raja, Vanaja, Mithunajha S, Devika K, Hariprasath S.B, Haripriya B, and Vigneshwar E. 2024. Overview of the Second Shared Task on Fake News Detection in Dravidian

Languages. In *Proceedings of the Fourth Workshop on Speech, Vision, and Language Technologies for Dravidian Languages*, Malta. European Chapter of the Association for Computational Linguistics.

Varun Sundaram, Saad Ahmed, Shaik Abdul Muqtadeer, and R Ravinder Reddy. 2021. Emotion analysis in text using tf-idf. In *2021 11th International Conference on Cloud Computing, Data Science & Engineering (Confluence)*, pages 292–297. IEEE.

Ashish Vaswani, Noam Shazeer, Niki Parmar, Jakob Uszkoreit, Llion Jones, Aidan N Gomez, Łukasz Kaiser, and Illia Polosukhin. 2017. Attention is all you need. *Advances in neural information processing systems*, 30.

Jheng-Long Wu, Yuanye He, Liang-Chih Yu, and K Robert Lai. 2020. Identifying emotion labels from psychiatric social texts using a bi-directional lstm-cnn model. *IEEE Access*, 8:66638–66646.

Wit Hub@DravidianLangtech-2024:Multimodal Social Media Data Analysis in Dravidian Languages using Machine Learning Models

Anierudh H S [1], **Abhishek R**[2], **Ashwin V Sundar**[3], **Amrit Krishnan**[4]&**B. Bharathi**[5]
Department of Computer Science And Engineering
Sri Sivasubramaniya Nadar College of Engineering,
Tamil Nadu, India
anierudh2210395@ssn.edu.in[1]
abhishek2210170@ssn.edu.in[2]
ashwin2210412@ssn.edu.in[3]
amrit2210213@ssn.edu.in[4]
bharathib@ssn.edu.in[5]

Abstract

The main objective of the task is categorised into three subtasks. Subtask 1 Build models to determine the sentiment expressed in multimodal posts (or videos) in Tamil and Malayalam languages, leveraging textual, audio, and visual components. The videos are labelled into five categories: highly positive, positive, neutral, negative and highly negative. Subtask 2 Design machine models that effectively identify and classify abusive language within the multimodal context of social media posts in Tamil. The data are categorized into abusive and non-abusive categories. Subtask 3 Develop advanced models that accurately detect and categorize hate speech and offensive language in multimodal social media posts in Dravidian languages. The data points are categorized into caste, offensive, racist and sexist classes. In this session, the focus is primarily on Tamil language text data analysis. Various combination of machine learning models have been used to perform each tasks and do oversampling techniques to train models on biased dataset.

1 Introduction

The digital age has fundamentally transformed our information landscape, with social media emerging as a dominant force shaping how we interact and engage with the world. While its benefits are undeniable, the rapid spread of online hate has become a pressing concern, posing significant threats to trust, democracy, and societal cohesion. Unrestricted access to post any data that may be offensive or abusive is a very important con of social media. This issue is particularly acute in Dravidian languages, where the lack of dedicated tools and resources exacerbates the impact of negativity in social media.

To address this challenge, significant research efforts have been directed towards developing advanced models capable of effectively detecting and categorizing various forms of harmful content in online spaces. This paper delves into the development of such models within the context of Tamil text data, focusing on three critical tasks:

1. Multimodal Sentiment Analysis : This allows for a nuanced understanding of expressed sentiment, ranging from highly positive to highly negative, offering valuable insights into online interactions and fostering constructive dialogue. It is trained with movie reviews and a supervised learning mode.

2. Multimodal Abusive Language Detection : Recognizing the prevalence of online abuse, this task focuses on building robust models that accurately identify and classify abusive language within Tamil text contexts. The models aim to improve detection accuracy and create a safer online environment by combating harmful interactions.

3. Multimodal Hate and Offensive Language Detection : Expanding beyond binary classification, this task delves into the complexities of offensive language by developing sophisticated models capable of accurately identifying and categorizing diverse forms of harmful content in Tamil text data. This includes nuanced distinctions between subtle categories like caste-based discrimination, general offensiveness, racism, and sexism, ultimately paving the way for a more inclusive and respectful online experience.

Through these tasks, the research presented in this paper highlights the immense potential of multimodal NLP and deep learning techniques in analyzing the complexities of communication within Tamil text data. The developed models offer practical solutions for combating misinformation, fostering trust, and promoting healthy online spaces.

The model traverses through different models employed for each model, such as LSTM, K-nearest neighbors, Linear Regression, Multinomial Naive Bayes and others and explains the purpose

Proceedings of the Fourth Workshop on Speech, Vision, and Language Technologies for Dravidian Languages, pages 229–233
March 22, 2024

for each method. Firstly the methodology and data is analysed, which includes model description, previous models and disadvantages,then an overview of obtained results, limitations, and conclusion with the findings. The datasets that have been used are (Premjith et al., 2023) , (Premjith et al., 2022) , (Chakravarthi et al., 2021). The overview of the shared task is given in Findings of the Shared Task on Multimodal Social Media Data Analysis in Dravidian Languages (MSMDA-DL) (B et al., 2024).

2 Related work

Banerjee (Banerjee et al., 2020), has used an autoregressive XLNet model to perform sentiment analysis on code-mixed Tamil-English and Malayalam-English datasets.

DravidianMultiModality: A Dataset for Multimodal Sentiment Analysis in Tamil and Malayalam is a paper (Chakravarthi et al., 2021), where the product or movies review videos were downloaded from YouTube for Tamil and Malayalam. Next, the captions were created for the videos with the help of annotators and the videos were labelled for sentiment.

In the paper (Ofli et al., 2020), they are doing analysis on social media data using multi modal deep learning for disaster response. They have used CNN, image modality and others. By using these models, they performed 2 tasks, Informativeness classification task and humanitarian classification task with F1 score 84.2 and 78.3 respectively.

3 Methodology and Data

3.1 Multimodal Sentiment Analysis

The fundamental goal of sentiment analysis using machine learning (ML) classification is to create reliable and accurate models that can distinguish between positive, negative, highly negative, highly positive and neutral comments. The model is restricted to testing and training only on Tamil dataset. The objective is to use labeled datasets with examples ranging from highly positive to highly negative to train the models. The primary goal of the model is to develop algorithms that can apply the trained features onto any Tamil text content and determine the sentiment accurately.

The following dataset contains various movie reviews of Tamil movies in Tamil text. The dataset consists of 2 attributes namely the TextContent and the corresponding sentiment label.

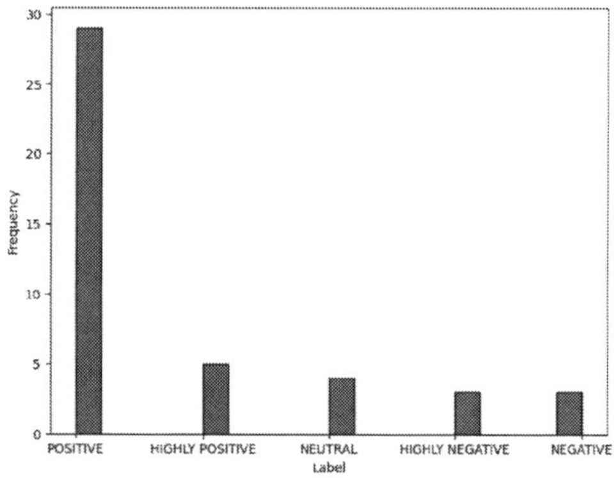

Figure 1: Training Data Bias

The dataset was very biased with high datapoints corresponding to positive reviews and very few for the others as shown in Figure-1.

With such a biased dataset, the two available options to train the model were to use OverSampling such as Smote Analysis and test on development data to test the best model, or to concatenate training and development data and obtain a train test split to train the model and test it.

3.1.1 Trial 1 (Random Forest with SMOTE)

Methods: 1. Text preprocessing: removing punctuation and converting to lowercase. 2. TF-IDF vectorization for text features. 3. SMOTE for oversampling imbalanced classes. 4. Random Forest Classifier for prediction. In this model some basic text preprocessing on train and development data has been applied. Oversampled training data has been used to train. Next using TF-IDF vectorizer text features are extracted. SMOTE is applied onto the training data to oversample. Then a random-forest classifier has been used and the model has been trained and tested on development data to find F1 score. This method is likely suitable for simple text classification tasks but may not capture long-range dependencies or word order. And SMOTE has its disadvantages in classification tasks. SMOTE involves creating synthetic examples, which increases the size of the dataset. This larger dataset can lead to increased computational complexity, especially for algorithms that scale poorly with the number of instances.

3.1.2 Trial 2 (K-Nearest Neighbors with SMOTE)

Methods: 1. Text preprocessing: removing punctuation and converting to lowercase. 2. TF-IDF vectorization for text features. 3. SMOTE for oversampling imbalanced classes. 4. K nearest neighbor for prediction. This method is very similar to Trial 1 and thus follows a few disadvantages of Trial-1 such as not being able to capture word order. SMOTE focuses on generating synthetic instances for the minority class. While this helps balance class distribution, it does not address potential imbalances within the majority class, and synthetic instances may not accurately capture the characteristics of the majority class. And also KNN can be sensitive to noisy data and may lack interpretability compared to other models.

3.1.3 Final Method (LSTM,KNN and Linear Regression)

Methods: 1.Text preprocessing 2.Tokenization and padding for LSTM input 3.K-Means clustering of LSTM model predictions to extract high-level features. 4.KNN classifier trained on clustered features for added robustness. 5.Linear Regression on clustered features for another prediction perspective. 6.Model saving and loading for prediction on new data. In this model, considering the limitations of Smote in classification tasks, training and development data are merged and train test split is done onto the concatenated dataset. This model combines LSTM for capturing complex text patterns with K-Means clustering for identifying latent features and Linear Regression for class prediction. LSTM offers an unfair advantage over other models as it is implemented using neural network and takes into account word order for determining patterns in the data. So it is best for feature extraction. Then the outputs are clustered and offered into a linear model for accurate prediction of test data.

3.1.4 Comparison of F1 scores

Table 1 shows the F1 scores for different models on training and development data. The results are evident to prove that the chosen model is advanced in performance.

Model used	F1 Score
Trial 1	0.228
Trial 2	0.228
Final Model	0.603

Table 1: Output Comparison

3.2 Multimodal Abusive Language Detection

In this subtask machine models are built such that they effectively identify and classify abusive language within the multimodal context of social media posts in Tamil. The dataset is classified into abusive and non-abusive texts. Figure 2 shows the provided dataset from codalab which is unbiased.

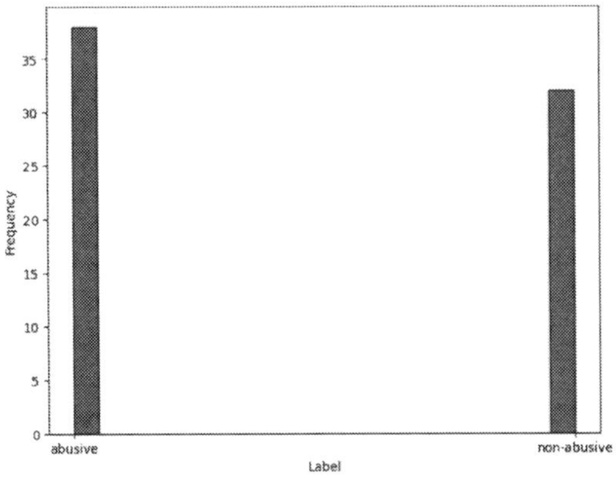

Figure 2: Task2 dataset

3.2.1 Model using LSTM, KMeans, KNN, Logistic Regression

In this method, LSTM (Long short term memory) has been used to identify sequence of words that may be abusive, the features have been clustered using K-Means and logistic regression has been applied as it is a binary classification task. This is a pretty decent model but does have a few limitations. The model might be effective for complex abusive language patterns but requires significant training data and computation. Since the training dataset is small, it may not be the perfect model. The model is best suited for large datasets for its faster adaptability.

3.2.2 Final Model using MNB

MultiNomial Naive Bayes is used for this task. It is a lightweight probabilistic classifier based on word frequency in different classes. The reason this model is chosen is because the main reason a statement can be found abusive is due to the presence of a single or a few offensive words and not on the sequence of words. Thus a model using MNB is better for this scenario. It can be easily integrated into online systems because of its lightweight nature.It also provides insights into the words and phrases that contribute to the classification through word frequency analysis.

3.2.3 Output classification

Table 2 will provide an insight onto the obtained f1 scores of training and testing after a train test split and shows why the chosen model is better for a small dataset

.

Model used	F1 Score
Trial model	0.590
Final Model	0.791

Table 2: Output Comparison

3.3 Multimodal Hate and Offensive Language Detection

In this task advanced models that accurately detect and categorize hate speech and offensive language in multimodal social media posts in Dravidian languages are developed. The data points in the dataset are categorized into caste, offensive, racist and sexist classes.

3.3.1 Trial 1 (Multinomial Naive Bayes)

In this task, MNB is used in same pattern as in Subtask 2. The F1 score obtained is very less, around 0.16. The reasons for the inefficiency can be looked upon to the facts that the model may not capture complex language patterns. Thus this model is discarded and new model is used.

3.3.2 Final Code (Random Forest with combined TF-IDF and Count vectors)

In this model we use Random Forest with two feature sets: TF-IDF for term weighting and Count vectors for word frequency. The pros of the model lies in the capability to capture both term importance and word frequency through combined features. Though the F1 score obtained on train test split on the training data was not great, reflecting to the size and variability of dataset. Thus this model is preferred despite the difficulty in its complex training procedures.

3.3.3 Output Classification

Table 3 shows the classification of outputs of trial model and final model, hence proving its efficiency over others

Model	F1 score
Trial Model	0.166
Final Model	0.371

Table 3: Output Classification

Tamil Sentimental Analysis			
Team	Run	F1score(score)	Rank
WitHub	3	0.244	1
Tamil Hate Speech Detection			
Team	Run	F1score(score)	Rank
WitHub	3	0.288	1
Tamil Abusive Language Detection			
Team	Run	F1score(score)	Rank
BinaryBeasts	1	0.714	1
WitHub	1	0.415	2

Table 4: Results

4 Experimental Result and Performance Analysis

The prescribed models had been submitted to codalab and the runs on the test data had been submitted. The submissions were evaluated and and the results are as in Table 4. SubTask 1 got a F1 score of 0.244. Subtask 2 got a F1 score of 0.288 and Subtask 3 got a score of 0.415. From these scores and corresponding ranks, we infer that the prescribed models are very effective and adapted to the dataset.

5 Limitations

The model is trained only over a small sample of training data. There may be various other data that should be included for better performance of the model. And also, as linguistic trends change, the model may be ineffective over time. We need measures to prevent that too.

6 Conclusions

In conclusion, various models have been trained and tested for each subtask. These models have been trained only under a specific small dataset and are adapted to it. The models prescribed are best adapted to the small training datasets and are proven to produce a good F1 score for each task. The model can be improved by including online learning techniques and reinforcement learning to adapt to new data and trends and thus have an enhanced performance.

References

Premjth B, Jyothish Lal G, Sowmya V, Bharathi Raja Chakravarthi, Nandhini K, Rajeswari Natarajan, Abirami Murugappan, Bharathi B, Saranya Rajiakodi, Rahul Ponnusamy, Jayanth Mohan, and Spandana Reddy Mekapati. 2024. Findings of the shared task on multimodal social media data analysis in dravidian languages (msmda-dl). In *Proceedings of the Fourth Workshop on Speech, Vision, and Language Technologies for Dravidian Languages*, Malta. European Chapter of the Association for Computational Linguistics.

Shubhanker Banerjee, Arun Jayapal, and Sajeetha Thavareesan. 2020. Nuig-shubhanker@ dravidian-codemix-fire2020: Sentiment analysis of code-mixed dravidian text using xlnet. *arXiv preprint arXiv:2010.07773*.

Bharathi Raja Chakravarthi, KP Soman, Rahul Ponnusamy, Prasanna Kumar Kumaresan, Kingston Pal Thamburaj, John P McCrae, et al. 2021. Dravidianmultimodality: A dataset for multi-modal sentiment analysis in tamil and malayalam. *arXiv preprint arXiv:2106.04853*.

Ferda Ofli, Firoj Alam, and Muhammad Imran. 2020. Analysis of social media data using multimodal deep learning for disaster response. *arXiv preprint arXiv:2004.11838*.

B Premjith, Bharathi Raja Chakravarthi, Malliga Subramanian, B Bharathi, Soman Kp, V Dhanalakshmi, K Sreelakshmi, Arunaggiri Pandian, and Prasanna Kumaresan. 2022. Findings of the shared task on multimodal sentiment analysis and troll meme classification in dravidian languages. In *Proceedings of the Second Workshop on Speech and Language Technologies for Dravidian Languages*, pages 254–260.

B Premjith, V Sowmya, Bharathi Raja Chakravarthi, Rajeswari Natarajan, K Nandhini, Abirami Murugappan, B Bharathi, M Kaushik, Prasanth Sn, et al. 2023. Findings of the shared task on multimodal abusive language detection and sentiment analysis in tamil and malayalam. In *Proceedings of the Third Workshop on Speech and Language Technologies for Dravidian Languages*, pages 72–79.

CUETSentimentSillies@DravidianLangTech-EACL2024: Transformer-based Approach for Sentiment Analysis in Tamil and Tulu Code-Mixed Texts

Zannatul Fardaush Tripty, Md. Arian Al Nafis, Antu Chowdhury, Jawad Hossain, Shawly Ahsan, Avishek Das and **Mohammed Moshiul Hoque**
Department of Computer Science and Engineering
Chittagong University of Engineering and Technology, Bangladesh
{u1804030, u1804111, u1804112, u1704039, u1704057}@student.cuet.ac.bd,
{ avishek,moshiul_240}@cuet.ac.bd

Abstract

Sentiment analysis (SA) on social media reviews has become a challenging research agenda in recent years due to the exponential growth of textual content. Although several effective solutions are available for SA in high-resourced languages, it is considered a critical problem for low-resourced languages. This work introduces an automatic system for analyzing sentiment in Tamil and Tulu code-mixed languages. Several ML (DT, RF, MNB), DL (CNN, BiLSTM, CNN+BiLSTM), and transformer-based models (Indic-BERT, XLM-RoBERTa, m-BERT) are investigated for SA tasks using Tamil and Tulu code-mixed textual data. Experimental outcomes reveal that the transformer-based models XLM-R and m-BERT surpassed others in performance for Tamil and Tulu, respectively. The proposed XLM-R and m-BERT models attained macro F1-scores of 0.258 (Tamil) and 0.468 (Tulu) on test datasets, securing the 2nd and 5th positions, respectively, in the shared task.

1 Introduction

Social media has changed how people network and socialize, especially the younger generation, and multilingual user interfaces allow people to express their emotions in their native languages (Ahmad and Singla, 2021; Patra et al., 2018; Tarihoran and Sumirat, 2022). Sentiment analysis (SA) may help firms assess their brand's image and sentiment and make informed customer relationship management and marketing choices. It analyzes social media postings to detect user attitudes (Chakravarthi et al., 2020c). Code-mixed texts greatly concern sentiment analysis. Many multilingual societies use code-mixed texts, combining words, morphemes, and phrases from two or more languages (Chakravarthi et al., 2023). This behavior is problematic for SA systems, mainly when they utilize non-native scripts like Roman letters to represent languages written in other scripts (Hegde and Shashirekha, 2022). Coded language texts need specialized sentiment analysis due to language mixing and context-dependent emotions. Scholars are improving security awareness methods to govern virtual communication's growth (Chakravarthi et al., 2021; Hegde et al., 2023). The goal is to create a system that can classify code-mixed sentiment polarity in Tamil-English and Tulu-English code-mixed texts into four predetermined categories: positive, negative, mixed feeling, and neutral/unknown state. The main contributions of this study are:

- Developed numerous ML and DL methods and fine-tuned transformers to classify textual sentiment into four categories () for Tamil and Tulu code-mixed datasets.
- Investigated the effectiveness of the developed models for Tamil and Tulu subtasks, where XLM-RoBERTa exceeded other models for Tamil and m-BERT exceeded other models for the Tulu language.

2 Related Work

Researchers studying several SA techniques tend to focus on high-resource languages such as English and Spanish. However, SA is also being studied in code-mixed, low-resource languages. Shetty (2023) trained various ML models for SA of Tamil and Tulu code-mixed texts. The proposed method yielded F1 scores of 0.14 and 0.204 in Tamil and Tulu, respectively. To detect abusive comments in code-mixed Tamil text, Bharathi and Varsha (2022) employed BERT, m-BERT, and XLNet models. They obtained a weighted F1 score of 0.96 for Tamil-English code-mixed text and a weighted F1 score of 0.59 for Tamil text. Babu and Eswari (2021) improved sentiment analysis using Paraphrase XLM-R on Dravidian code-mixed YouTube comments. They trained the model using Tamil,

Proceedings of the Fourth Workshop on Speech, Vision, and Language Technologies for Dravidian Languages, pages 234–239
March 22, 2024 ©2024 Association for Computational Linguistics

Malayalam, and Kannada code-mixed language datasets and achieved F1 scores of 71.1, 75.3, and 62.5, respectively. Chakravarthi et al. (2020a) created a gold standard Tamil-English code-switched, sentiment-annotated corpus containing 15,744 comment posts from YouTube.

An m-BERT-based model utilized by Zhu and Dong (2020) for SA where self-attention was employed to assign a weight to the output of the BiLSTM. The proposed model achieved weighted average F1 scores of 0.73 and 0.64 in Malayalam and Tamil, respectively. Rakshitha et al. (2021) proposed a model that used Twitter APIs to collect consumer reviews. TextBlob rated these reviews and classified them as favorable, negative, or neutral using a text classification algorithm. Ehsan et al. (2023) developed BiLSTM network-based models for sentiment analysis of code-mixed Tamil and Tulu. ELMo embedding was trained on larger unannotated code-mixed text corpora. The proposed model achieved macro F1-scores of 0.2877 and 0.5133 on Tamil and Tulu code-mixed datasets, respectively.

3 Task and Dataset Descriptions

The goal of this task is sentiment analysis in Tamil and Tulu, explicitly focusing on determining sentiment polarity in social media comments. This task aimed to develop two systems that can individually identify sentiment polarity from a given set of texts in Tamil or Tulu. To achieve this, we utilized the corpora provided by the shared task organizers[1] for sentiment analysis in Tamil (Chakravarthi et al., 2020b) and Tulu (Hegde et al., 2022). The task required classifying texts into four predefined classes, positive, negative, mixed feeling, and neutral/unknown state, for Tamil and Tulu code-mixed texts.

Table 1 summarizes the Tamil dataset. The combined training and development sets for Tamil exhibited the highest number of samples for the positive class (22,327 texts). Subsequently, the unknown state category comprised 6,239 texts, while negative had 4,751 texts, and mixed feelings had 4,559 texts, each containing fewer instances than the positive class. The Tulu dataset was divided into three subsets: training, development, and testing, containing 6,945, 500, and 501 samples, respectively (Table 2). The dataset demonstrated an uneven distribution among classes, with the positive class having the most samples with 3,831 texts, neutral with 2,118 texts, negative with 796 texts, and mixed feelings with 1,201 texts having fewer samples. Text lengths in the dataset varied from one word to 261 words, with an average length of 7 words.

Classes	Train+Dev	Test	Total words
Positive	22327	73	208365
Positive (after augmentation)	22327	73	187294
Unknown state	6239	137	69311
Unknown state (after augmentation)	17135	137	177181
Negative	4751	338	51459
Negative (after augmentation)	14040	338	188356
Mixed feelings	4458	101	64844
Mixed feelings (after augmentation)	13461	101	133810

Table 1: Tamil dataset statistics before and after augmentation

Classes	Train	Dev	Test	Total words
Positive	3352	231	248	22298
Negative	698	55	43	4658
Neutral	1854	124	140	12738
Mixed feelings	1041	90	70	7033
Total	**6945**	**500**	**501**	**46727**

Table 2: Tulu Dataset Statistics

4 Methodology

This section summarized the methods and techniques applied for sentiment analysis in Tamil and Tulu. Figure 1 outlines the employed techniques for SA in Tamil and Tulu.

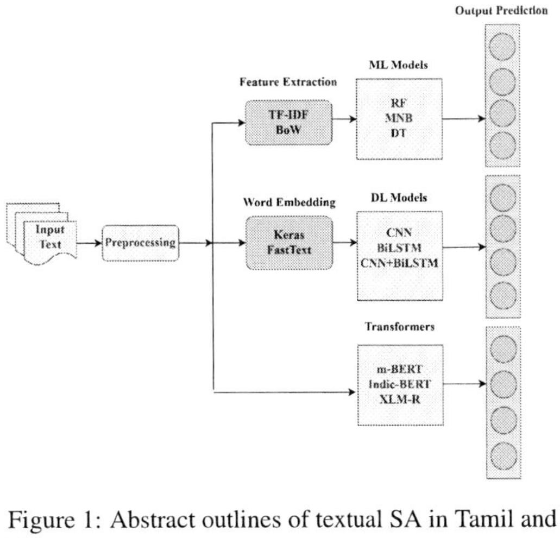

Figure 1: Abstract outlines of textual SA in Tamil and Tulu

[1] https://sites.google.com/view/dravidianlangtech-2024/home

4.1 Data Augmentation

The Tamil dataset 1 before augmentation exhibited an imbalance, specifically in the unknown state, negative, and mixed feelings classes, with fewer samples compared to the positive class. We merged the training and development sets to rectify this to minimize the class distribution gap. Additionally, we applied back translation using Google Translator for data augmentation. Google Translator was selected for its widespread availability and proven effectiveness in generating diverse language variations. The back translation process involved iteratively translating sentences from Tamil to another language and then back to Tamil, introducing nuanced variations. After augmentation, there were notable shifts in class distribution: the unknown state class increased to 17,135 texts, the negative class reached 14,040 texts, and the mixed feelings class grew to 13,461 texts. This combined strategy of merging datasets and the back translation method aimed to broaden the dataset's scope and ensure a more representative distribution of sentiment classes, specifically addressing data scarcity in the unknown-state, harmful, and mixed feelings categories. This precise approach enhanced the dataset's robustness and reliability for subsequent analysis and model development.

4.2 Preprocessing

The dataset obtained from YouTube comments underwent preprocessing to ensure that it was clear of irrelevant information. This process involved the elimination of emojis, punctuation, spaces, URLs, and numerical texts. English letters are transformed to lowercase. To enhance linguistic relevance, common stopwords were manually eliminated based on a curated list obtained from a Tamil stopwords repository on GitHub[2]. Similarly, for the Tulu language, English stop words were excluded. We also identified and removed Tamil and Tulu's ten most frequently occurring words.

4.3 Training

The initial step involved extracting features using various feature extraction techniques and applying different ML, DL, and transformer-based approaches.

ML Baselines: TF-IDF (Nayel, 2020) values were used as features for training ML models based on unigram features. Additionally, bag-of-words (BoW) representations are also utilized for feature extraction. Traditional ML-based methods, including RF, DT, and MNB, were employed for sentiment analysis. In the DT model, the regularization parameter was set to 2. RF was implemented with 100 estimators (n_estimator 100) to enhance its predictive performance.

DL Baselines: Three DL models, CNN, BiLSTM, and CNN+BiLSTM, along with FastText (Joulin et al., 2016) and Keras embeddings, were employed for sentiment analysis. In the CNN model, the process began with an embedding layer, followed by three convolutional layers featuring 64, 32, and 16 filters. MaxPooling layers were added after convolution layers for feature reduction. In the BiLSTM model, the embedding layer was followed by two BiLSTM layers with 32 and 16 units, respectively, capturing information bi-directionally. The resulting sequences were flattened, and a dense layer with softmax activation was added for classification. In the CNN+BiLSTM model, the embedding layer was followed by a convolutional layer with 128 filters and a kernel size of 5. A BiLSTM with 32 units and a dropout rate (0.2) is added after the convolution layer.

Transformers: Three transformer-based models, XLM-RoBERTA (Conneau et al., 2019), IndicBERT (Kakwani et al., 2020), and m-BERT (Devlin et al., 2018), were utilized for SA in Tamil and Tulu. This work used the same hyperparameters for Tamil and Tulu subtasks training. Specifically, during the training of all transformers, we used the Adafactor optimizer with a consistent learning rate of 2e-5 over 10 epochs, incorporating a warm-up ratio of 0.1 for a smoother initialization. To improve stability, gradient accumulation steps were doubled to 2. A weight decay of 0.01 was applied to regularize the training process. Fine-tuned hyperparameter values allowed us to do extensive training and optimization of the model parameters. The choice of a batch size of 16 facilitated efficient processing and updating of the model weights during each iteration.

5 Results and Analysis

Table 3 displays the results of various employed approaches for the SA task on the Tamil test set, with the XLM-RoBERTA model leading among transformers with a macro F1 score (0.258). The RF model with BoW surpassed other ML models, achieving the highest macro F1 score (0.248). No-

[2] https://gist.github.com/arulrajnet

tably, the CNN+BiLSTM model exhibited superior performance compared to other DL models.

Classifier	P	R	F
DT (TF-IDF)	0.247	0.251	0.237
RF (TF-IDF)	0.270	0.26	0.24
MNB (TF-IDF)	0.324	0.27	0.213
DT (BoW)	0.280	0.297	0.248
RF (BoW)	0.228	0.252	0.056
MNB (BoW)	0.282	0.248	0.185
CNN (Keras)	0.235	0.232	0.214
BiLSTM (Keras)	0.262	0.258	0.253
C+B (Keras)	0.250	0.257	0.241
CNN (FastText)	0.220	0.230	0.137
BiLSTM (FastText)	0.239	0.240	0.147
C+B (FastText)	0.234	0.236	0.148
m-BERT	0.275	0.269	0.255
XLM-RoBERTa	**0.288**	**0.27**	**0.258**
Indic-BERT	0.276	0.265	0.252

Table 3: Performance of various models on the Tamil test set where P, R, and F denote precision, recall, and macro F1-score, respectively, and C+B represents the CNN+BiLSTM model

For the Tulu test set, as shown in Table 4, the m-BERT model excelled among transformer models, attaining the highest macro F1 score of 0.468. Among ML models, the RF model with BoW stood out with the highest macro F1 score of 0.449, while within DL models, BiLSTM with Fasttext emerged as the top performer with macro F1 of 0.394.

5.1 Error Analysis

The best-performed models (XLM-RoBERTa for Tamil texts, and m-BERT for Tulu texts) are further investigated to understand better insights regarding the performance using quantitative and qualitative analysis.

Quantitative Analysis: The confusion matrix is used for error analysis for both Tamil (Figure 2) and Tulu (Figure 3) datasets.

In Tamil, we found that the model did well with TPR of 33.13% and 28.46% negative and unknown state, respectively. However, the positive class had a lower TPR of 20.54%, meaning the model struggled to identify positive sentiments. The confusion matrix for Tulu revealed a True Positive Rate (TPR) of 90.70% for the positive class. Conversely, the mixed feeling class exhibited the lowest TPR of 10%. Notably, the model misidentified 35 mixed-feeling class text samples as neutral, indicating difficulty distinguishing between texts conveying

Classifier	P	R	F
DT (TF-IDF)	0.442	0.449	0.443
RF (TF-IDF)	0.465	0.434	0.424
MNB (TF-IDF)	**0.565**	0.360	0.334
DT (BoW)	0.420	0.431	0.436
RF (BoW)	0.518	0.459	0.449
MNB (BoW)	0.514	0.428	0.427
CNN (Keras)	0.370	0.405	0.383
BiLSTM (Keras)	0.380	0.373	0.357
C+B (Keras)	0.379	0.374	0.367
CNN (Fasttext)	0.379	0.374	0.367
BiLSTM (Fasttext)	0.444	0.394	0.394
C+B (Fasttext)	0.379	0.374	0.367
m-BERT	0.512	**0.468**	**0.468**
XLM-RoBERTa	0.454	0.405	0.387
indic-BERT	0.307	0.399	0.344

Table 4: Performance of various models on the Tulu test set where P, R, and F denote precision, recall, and macro F1-score, respectively, and C+B represents the CNN+BiLSTM model

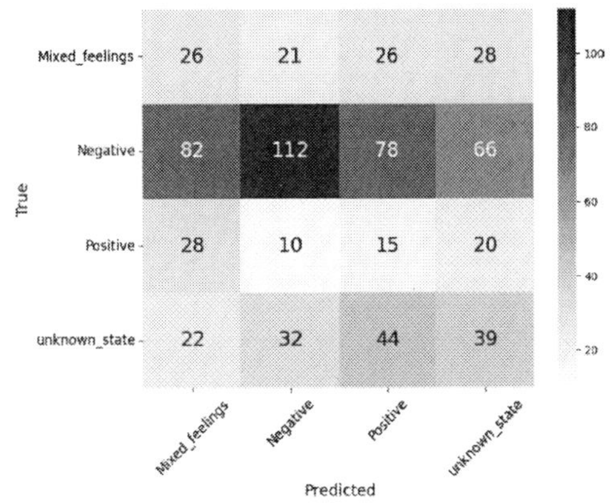

Figure 2: Confusion matrix of XLM-RoBERTA for Tamil test set

mixed feelings and those with neutral sentiments. This challenge arose due to the nuanced similarity in meaning between texts with mixed feelings and those that are neutral, leading to frequent misclassifications, primarily for the neutral class.

5.2 Qualitative Analysis:

Figure 4 illustrates some predicted outcomes by the best-performed model (XLM-RoBERTa) for Tamil SA task. It is revealed that the proposed model demonstrated accurate predictions for sample 2 while other samples were misclassified. It exhibited challenges in correctly categorizing text samples 1,3,4. Especially for texts of *mixed-feelings* and

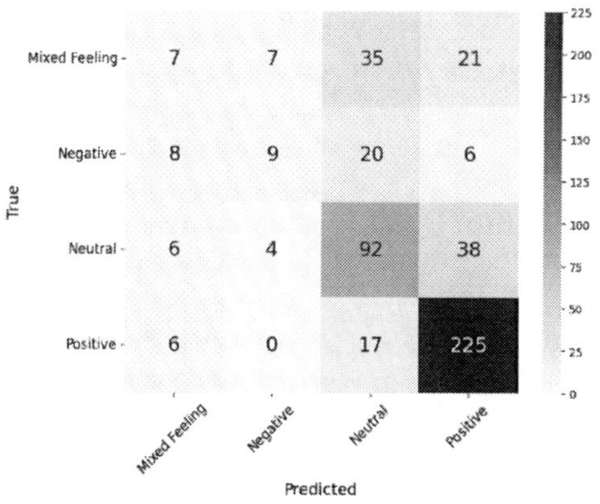

Figure 3: Confusion matrix of m-BERT for Tulu test set

unknown state categories. Because texts of these two categories were semantically analogous.

Text Sample	Actual	Predicted
Sample1: திரு நங்கைகளின் அட்டகாசம் அதிகமாகிக்கொண்டே போகிறது ரயில் நிலையம், பஸ்ஸில்...உடனே தமிழக அரசு நடவடிக்கை எடுக்க வேண்டும் .. (The violence of Mr. Nankais is increasing in railway station, bus.Tamil Nadu government should take action immediately.)	Positive	Negative
Sample 2: இவர்களை போலீஸ் கொண்டு போய் சூ லாடம் கட்டவேண்டும் (The police should take them and arrest them)	Negative	Negative
Sample 3:கடவுளின் சாபத்தில் வாழும் உங்க ளுக்கு இந்த அநியாயம் இருக்க கூடாது (You who live under God's curse should not have this injustice)	Unknown State	Mixed Feeling
Sample 4 : இவர்கள் அராஜகம் மிக அதிகம். போலீஸ்துறை கடுமையான நடவடிக்கை எடுக்க வேண்டும். (They are very anarchic. Police are strict Action should be taken.)	Mixed Feeling	Unknown State

Figure 4: A few examples of predicted output by the proposed (XLM-RoBERTa) model for Tamil SA task. The corresponding english texts were translated using 'Google Translator')

Figure 5 presents a few predicted samples by the best-performed model (m-BERT) for Tulu SA task. It is shown that the proposed model depicted correct predictions for text samples 1 and 3. However, it failed to classify *neutral* and *mixed-feelings* properly as their texts were semantically similar. Therefore, the proposed model classified *neutral* texts as *mixed feelings* and *mixed feelings* as *neutral*.

Limitations

Despite these developments, several obstacles, such as the need for pre-trained transformer models, limit our capacity to use current language representations effectively. Although a single pre-trained model has been identified and made available for Tamil, there needs to be a similar resource for Tulu

Text Sample	Actual	Predicted
Sample 1 : ಮಾತಾ ಬಿತ್ತಿಲ್u200cದ್u200cದ್ ಉಂಡು ಭಾರಿ ಚೋಕಾತ್ಂಡ್	Positive	Positive
Sample 2: ಈ ಪೊಣ್ಣುಗ್ ಪನ್ಪಿನಗುಲ್ ಯೇ ಲಾರ್ ಇಜ್ಜಿರ	Negative	Neutral
Sample 3: ಅರೆಗ್ ಎಂಡ ದಾನೆ ಪತೊಂದಿನ ಆತು	Neutral	Neutral
Sample 4: ಕುಸಾಸ್ ಇತ್ತುಂಡು. ಪ್ರಾಕ್ಟಿಸ್ ಕಮ್ಮಿ. ಒಟ್ಟುಗ್ ಓಕೆ.	Mixed Feeling	Neutral

Figure 5: Some examples of predicted output by the m-BERT model for Tulu SA task

presents a more significant obstacle, restricting the extent and effectiveness of language processing endeavors. Lower accuracy is also a result of the model's inability to learn patterns for minority classes due to the small sample size and notable class imbalance in the datasets. The lack of resources for data augmentation as back translation, particularly in Tulu's case, makes addressing this imbalance even more difficult.

6 Conclusion

This paper investigated different ML, DL, and transformer-based models for categorizing textual sentiment in Tamil and Tulu. The experimental results revealed that the XLM-RoBERTa model obtained the highest macro F1 score (0.258) for the Tamil textual comments, whereas the m-BERT model scored the best (0.468) for the Tulu texts. For future research, collaborative efforts are necessary to create resources, especially for low-resource languages like Tamil and Tulu, and add more diverse data to the existing corpora. Additionally, improving the performance of sentiment analysis models for these languages will depend heavily on developments in pre-training methods and the availability of more thorough language representations.

References

Gazi Imtiyaz Ahmad and Jimmy Singla. 2021. Sentiment analysis of code-mixed social media text (sacmsmt) in indian-languages. In *2021 International Conference on Computing Sciences (ICCS)*, pages 25–33. IEEE.

Yandrapati Prakash Babu and Rajagopal Eswari. 2021. Sentiment analysis on dravidian code-mixed youtube comments using paraphrase xlm-roberta model. *Working Notes of FIRE*.

B Bharathi and Josephine Varsha. 2022. Ssncse nlp@ tamilnlp-acl2022: Transformer based approach for detection of abusive comment for tamil language. In *Proceedings of the Second Workshop on Speech and Language Technologies for Dravidian Languages*, pages 158–164.

Bharathi Raja Chakravarthi, Manoj Balaji Jagadeeshan, Vasanth Palanikumar, and Ruba Priyadharshini. 2023. Offensive language identification in dravidian languages using mpnet and cnn. *International Journal of Information Management Data Insights*, 3(1):100151.

Bharathi Raja Chakravarthi, Vigneshwaran Muralidaran, Ruba Priyadharshini, and John P McCrae. 2020a. Corpus creation for sentiment analysis in code-mixed tamil-english text. *arXiv preprint arXiv:2006.00206*.

Bharathi Raja Chakravarthi, Vigneshwaran Muralidaran, Ruba Priyadharshini, and John Philip McCrae. 2020b. Corpus creation for sentiment analysis in code-mixed Tamil-English text. In *Proceedings of the 1st Joint Workshop on Spoken Language Technologies for Under-resourced languages (SLTU) and Collaboration and Computing for Under-Resourced Languages (CCURL)*, pages 202–210, Marseille, France. European Language Resources association.

Bharathi Raja Chakravarthi, Ruba Priyadharshini, Vigneshwaran Muralidaran, Shardul Suryawanshi, Navya Jose, Elizabeth Sherly, and John P McCrae. 2020c. Overview of the track on sentiment analysis for dravidian languages in code-mixed text. In *Proceedings of the 12th Annual Meeting of the Forum for Information Retrieval Evaluation*, pages 21–24.

Bharathi Raja Chakravarthi, Ruba Priyadharshini, Sajeetha Thavareesan, Dhivya Chinnappa, Durairaj Thenmozhi, Elizabeth Sherly, John P McCrae, Adeep Hande, Rahul Ponnusamy, Shubhanker Banerjee, et al. 2021. Findings of the sentiment analysis of dravidian languages in code-mixed text. *arXiv preprint arXiv:2111.09811*.

Alexis Conneau, Kartikay Khandelwal, Naman Goyal, Vishrav Chaudhary, Guillaume Wenzek, Francisco Guzmán, Edouard Grave, Myle Ott, Luke Zettlemoyer, and Veselin Stoyanov. 2019. Unsupervised cross-lingual representation learning at scale. *CoRR*, abs/1911.02116.

Jacob Devlin, Ming-Wei Chang, Kenton Lee, and Kristina Toutanova. 2018. BERT: pre-training of deep bidirectional transformers for language understanding. *CoRR*, abs/1810.04805.

Toqeer Ehsan, Amina Tehseen, Kengatharaiyer Sarveswaran, and Amjad Ali. 2023. Sentiment analysis of code-mixed tamil and tulu by training contextualized elmo representations. *RANLP'2023*, page 152.

Asha Hegde, Mudoor Devadas Anusha, Sharal Coelho, Hosahalli Lakshmaiah Shashirekha, and Bharathi Raja Chakravarthi. 2022. Corpus creation for sentiment analysis in code-mixed Tulu text. In *Proceedings of the 1st Annual Meeting of the ELRA/ISCA Special Interest Group on Under-Resourced Languages*, pages 33–40, Marseille, France. European Language Resources Association.

Asha Hegde, Bharathi Raja Chakravarthi, Hosahalli Lakshmaiah Shashirekha, Rahul Ponnusamy, Subalalitha Cn, SK Lavanya, Durairaj Thenmozhi, Martha Karunakar, Shreya Shreeram, and Sarah Aymen. 2023. Findings of the shared task on sentiment analysis in tamil and tulu code-mixed text. In *Proceedings of the Third Workshop on Speech and Language Technologies for Dravidian Languages*, pages 64–71.

Asha Hegde and Hosahalli Lakshmaiah Shashirekha. 2022. Leveraging dynamic meta embedding for sentiment analysis and detection of homophobic/transphobic content in code-mixed dravidian languages.

Armand Joulin, Edouard Grave, Piotr Bojanowski, and Tomas Mikolov. 2016. Bag of tricks for efficient text classification. *arXiv preprint arXiv:1607.01759*.

Divyanshu Kakwani, Anoop Kunchukuttan, Satish Golla, Gokul N.C., Avik Bhattacharyya, Mitesh M. Khapra, and Pratyush Kumar. 2020. IndicNLPSuite: Monolingual Corpora, Evaluation Benchmarks and Pre-trained Multilingual Language Models for Indian Languages. In *Findings of EMNLP*.

Hamada A Nayel. 2020. Nayel at semeval-2020 task 12: Tf/idf-based approach for automatic offensive language detection in arabic tweets. *arXiv preprint arXiv:2007.13339*.

Braja Gopal Patra, Dipankar Das, and Amitava Das. 2018. Sentiment analysis of code-mixed indian languages: An overview of sail_code-mixed shared task@ icon-2017. *arXiv preprint arXiv:1803.06745*.

Kakuthota Rakshitha, H M Ramalingam, M Pavithra, H D Advi, and Maithri Hegde. 2021. Sentimental analysis of indian regional languages on social media. *Global Transitions Proceedings*, 2(2):414–420.

Poorvi Shetty. 2023. Poorvi@ dravidianlangtech: Sentiment analysis on code-mixed tulu and tamil corpus. In *Proceedings of the Third Workshop on Speech and Language Technologies for Dravidian Languages*, pages 124–132.

Naf'an Tarihoran and Iin Ratna Sumirat. 2022. The impact of social media on the use of code mixing by generation z. *International Journal of Interactive Mobile Technologies (iJIM)*, 16(7):54–69.

Yueying Zhu and Kunjie Dong. 2020. Yun111@ dravidian-codemix-fire2020: Sentiment analysis of dravidian code mixed text. In *FIRE (Working Notes)*, pages 628–634.

Social Media Hate and Offensive Speech Detection Using Machine Learning Method

Girma Yohannis Bade, Olga Kolesnikova , Grigori Sidorov,
José Luis Oropeza
Instituto Politécnico Nacional (IPN), Centro de Investigación en Computación (CIC),
Mexico City, Mexico
Correspondence : girme2005@gmail.com

Abstract

Even though the improper use of social media is increasing nowadays, there is also technology that brings solutions. Here, improperness is posting hate and offensive speech that might harm an individual or group. Hate speech refers to an insult toward an individual or group based on their identities. Spreading it on social media platforms is a serious problem for society. The solution, on the other hand, is the availability of natural language processing(NLP) technology that is capable to detect and handle such problems. This paper presents the detection of social media's hate and offensive speech in the code-mixed Telugu language. For this, the task and golden standard dataset were provided for us by the shared task organizer (DravidianLangTech@EACL 2024)[1]. To this end, we have employed the TF-IDF technique for numeric feature extraction and used a random forest algorithm for modeling hate speech detection. Finally, the developed model was evaluated on the test dataset and achieved 0.492 macro-F1.

1 Introduction

The growth of communication technology over the past few decades has resulted in a ballooning user active participation on social media. Social media is highly utilized for a wide range of activities, including news, business, advertising, etc. However, it simultaneously raises hate and offensive speech (Saleh et al., 2023). One of the reasons for this prevalence is users post improper information on social media. Hate speech on the social media platform can be in the form of text, images, or videos. The text mode, particularly is the most prevalent type of harmful content on social media (Bade and Seid, 2018). Hate speech refers to an insult that is aimed toward an individual or group based on identities including race, gender, minorities, political parties, religion, nationality, and public figures (Yigezu et al., 2023d). Today, several federal and international organizations pledged to combat hate speech online (Yasaswini et al., 2021; Ghanghor et al., 2021). However, many communities use multiple languages and mix their opinion in text mode, so the identification becomes complicated manually. Telugu, one of the Dravidian languages experiences code-mixed practice and is subjected to this complication. Code mixing is the mingling of two or more languages, and it can be difficult to identify toxicity in the multilingual statements (Priyadharshini et al., 2023; Yigezu et al., 2023c). In this regard, a shared task(DravidianLangTech@EACL 2024) opened a door to participate in the detection of Telugu social media hate and offensive speech by providing golden standard datasets. This shared task offered an opportunity for researchers to come up with solutions leveraging existing technology to identify hate speech and objectionable pieces of information. This study aims to determine whether a given comment in code-mixed Telugu language contains hate and offensive content and anticipated that the study will improve the detecting efficiency and handle all aspects of language.

2 Related Works

Hate speech spreading on the internet is a serious problem for society, and platforms need to identify objectionable information (Okechukwu et al., 2023). Numerous studies have been conducted to identify hate speech using different approaches with different levels of performance measures (Okechukwu et al., 2023). Hate speech recognition work has been modeled in research as a text classification issue and determines a message's classes from its text as hate speech or non-hate (Madhu et al., 2023). The study (Al-Dabet et al., 2023) presents a transformer-based method to deal with the problem of offensive speech detection.

[1] https://codalab.lisn.upsaclay.fr/competitions/16095

Proceedings of the Fourth Workshop on Speech, Vision, and Language Technologies for Dravidian Languages, pages 240–244
March 22, 2024 ©2024 Association for Computational Linguistics

This model was validated using a combination of four benchmark Twitter Arabic datasets annotated for hate speech detection tasks including the workshop (OSACT5 2022) shared task dataset. The demonstrated model was able to recognize offensive speech in Arabic tweets with 87.15% accuracy and 83.6 % F1 score. Similarly, in the work conducted (Okechukwu et al., 2023), hate speech was detected using the Term Frequency-Inverse Document Frequency (TF-IDF) with a majority voting ensemble learning classification Model. The model's accuracy was 95%, and its F-Measure was 95%. It made use of a Kaggle.com dataset that was accessible to the public.

In the study (Abbes et al., 2023), a deep learning method for identifying harmful and hostile content on Arabic social media platforms like Facebook was proposed. The researchers collected 2,000 Facebook comments in the Tunisian dialect and created two models: a Bi-LSTM based on an attention mechanism combining the BERT for Facebook comment classification toward hate speech detection. After evaluating the suggested model, an accuracy of 98.89% was attained. The researchers used a transformer-based model in (Bilal et al., 2023) to categorize hate speech in Roman Urdu. Furthermore, the first Roman Urdu pre-trained BERT model, known as BERT-RU, was created in this work. This research utilized the BERT's capabilities starting from scratch and trained on the biggest Roman Urdu dataset, which consists of 173,714 text messages. With scores of 96.70%, 97.25%, 96.74%, and 97.89% in accuracy, precision, recall, and F-measure, respectively, the created transformer-based model has met the performance metrics.

3 System Description

In this section, we offer thorough information regarding the dataset and the details of experimental tools . Moreover, it dives into the format of datasets, preprocessing, and the experimental details.

3.1 Datasets

In the real world, the problems are always existing until the solutions are investigated. To investigate solutions for computational linguistic challenges, the availability of data is crucial (Bade, 2021; Bade and Afaro, 2018). The dataset for this particular task was provided on Codalab by the Shared_task (DravidianLangTech@EACL 2024) organizer (Premjth et al., 2024). The dataset is arranged in three different lists training, development, and test set. The training and development data sets are made available when we register for the competition on the Codalab and the test set was released when ten days left for the run submission deadline.

Table 1: Sample data statistics in both training and test data of Telugu language

Text	Label	Dataset lists	# of records
Jagan meeda jaganke visvasam ledu anduke Students tho adukovtam thappu Gudivada king true leader	hate non-hate non hate	training	4000
Anna gurinchi chili excellent ga cheppindi Arey budder khan nuvvu asalu	— —	Testing	500

Table 1 shows sample instances of both training and testing data, the class feature or label, and the record size in both lists. Telugu uses Arabic scripts in addition to Latin but the table skipped the Arabic text to sample due to Unicode issue.

3.2 Preprocessing

Preprocessing is the process of preparing raw data for machine learning algorithms by cleaning, converting, and organizing the data rendering it to the machine. It is the vital stage that fills in the gaps between raw data and useful insights because raw data is rarely in an ideal state (Tonja et al., 2022). During the data preparation phase of machine learning tasks, there are typical or standard activities that we should use. The following are some among others.

Importing dependency libraries:- There are two libraries that we must always bring in. A library containing mathematical functions is called NumPy and the library used to import and manage the 'CSV' data sets is called Pandas.

Loading the data set:- In most cases, data sets are offered in a csv format. Tabular data is stored in plain text in a CSV file. In a file, every line represents a data record. To read a local CSV file as a data frame, the pandas library's (read_csv) function was utilized.

Handling Missing Data:- In real-world datasets, handling missing data is a prevalent difficulty. Preprocessing methods like imputation and the removal of missing data or null values ensure that the model is fed accurate and comprehensive data. For a variety of reasons, data may be missing, and it must be handled to prevent our machine-learning model from performing worse (Tash et al.). In addition, we used "raw['category'].fillna(0, inplace=True)" to handle empty strings of class label.

Data Cleaning:- is finding and fixing inaccuracies or flaws in the data (Yigezu et al., 2023b). In this regard, researchers explored the dataset listing and applied all needed.
Handling Outliers:- Anomalies that drastically depart from the average might cause distortions in learning. Preprocessing techniques such as transformation or scaling lessen the negative effects of outliers on model performance (Shahiki-Tash et al., 2023).
Data Encoding:- Since machine learning algorithms usually operate on numerical data, it is necessary to properly encode our text inputs in numerical equivalent (Yigezu et al., 2023a). To do so we have specifically used the TF-IDF text vectorization technique. It preserves the semantics and instance positions in addition to converting the provided text into a numeric representation (Yigezu et al., 2023e). However, in the case of converting 'class label', we used the "to_numeric()" function as "raw['category'] = pd.to_numeric(raw['category'], errors='coerce')".

3.3 Model Selection and Experimentation

The selected machine learnig model for this study is random forest.This is because several decision trees are combined in random forest, an ensemble learning technique to produce predictions that are more reliable and accurate. In a random forest, every decision tree is trained using a random subset of features and a random subset of the data (bootstrap samples). The diversity among the individual trees is increased and overfitting is lessened by this randomization (Yigezu et al., 2023b). During prediction, the ultimate result is established by combining all of the trees' predictions, either by average (for regression) or by majority voting (for classification). The capacity to manage complicated datasets, high-dimensional data, and non-linear interactions is a well-known feature of random forests. They are also frequently utilized in machine learning applications and are less prone to overfitting than a single decision tree (Destaw et al., 2022).

Experimental setup:- This section discusses the details of the developmental tool and the dependency libraries we used. For this research, we used Jupyter Notebook3 which is the Integrated Development Environment(IDE) of Python. After the tool setup was finished, we imported the four basic dependency libraries known as pandas, TfidfVectorizer, RandomForest, Joblib. Among those, the first three(pandas, TfidfVectorizer, RandomForest) are found in the Sklearn module. At the usage level, Pandas library is used to read CSV files from the local drive to a Python-run environment, TfidfVectorizer is for converting text data inputs into a numerical representation, and RandomForest is the principal algorithm to train the input data based on the predefined class. Finally, joblib which is a standalone module for saving the trained model for later use.

4 Result and Discussion

The Random Forest algorithm-based model was developed and classified the test dataset into two classes as they are presented in training data.

Table 2: Class label test data overview of manually or by annotator classified and machine or our model classified classification distribution.

Class	Manually classified	**Machine classified**
Non-hate	250	**375**
Hate	250	**125**
Total	500	**500**

As we can see from Table 2, our model classified 125 instances of the class label "Hate" as a "Non-hate" incorrectly. It also indicates that the model is more biased toward the 'non-hate' category. The Figure 1 shows in more detail below.

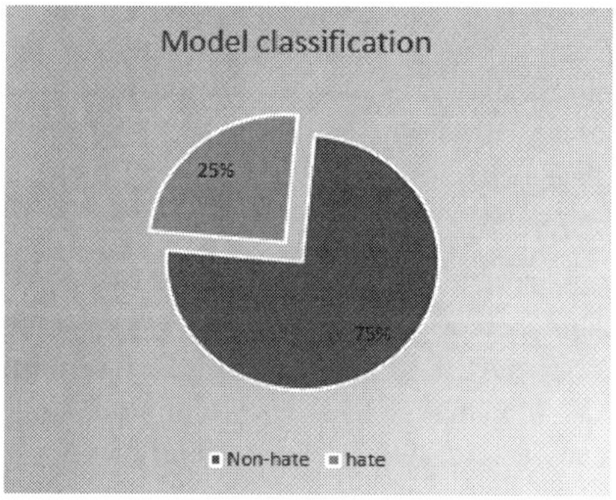

Figure 1: The diagrammatical representation of how the model classified the given test datasets.

According to the result published by the organizer, the model has also been evaluated in terms of macro-F1 scores to assess its performance and performed a 0.4921 macro-F1 score on the test dataset.

5 Conclusion

In this particular task, we have developed a model to classify social media posts into two binary classes hate and non-hate. The model has used the Random Forest algorithm method. The numeric features are extracted using TF-IDF techniques. The newly developed model has been evaluated with the new unseen test dataset and less performed on a selected algorithm for Telugu language text data.

6 Future work

Since social media posts that detect the posts of improper speech are critical, the jobs ought to be transferred into other various languages. Furthermore, by offering additional algorithms for the languages utilized here and expanding the number of dataset sizes, the performance of the suggested model in this study should be enhanced.

Acknowledgements

The work was done with partial support from the Mexican Government through the grant A1-S-47854 of CONACYT, Mexico, grants 20232138, 20231567, and 20232080 of the Secretaría de Investigación y Posgrado of the Instituto Politécnico Nacional, Mexico. The authors thank the CONACYT for the computing resources brought to them through the Plataforma de Aprendizaje Profundo para Tecnologías del Lenguaje of the Laboratorio de Supercómputo of the INAOE, Mexico and acknowledge the support of Microsoft through the Microsoft Latin America PhD Award.

7 Limitation and Ethics Statement

Finding words outside of one's lexicon or linguistic occurrences that were not taken into consideration during preprocessing are limitations. Code-mixing can bring linguistic variances that the current language processing algorithms may not be able to handle well enough, which could result in incorrect classifications. Future studies could improve the model's performance and generalization capacities by addressing these linguistic issues. Notably, out of all the participating systems, our method achieved the 24th rank in the shared job. Our model performs well in classifying hate and offensive comments in code-mixed text, even in the face of competition from other participants and obstacles in the competition. Furthermore, our work obeyed the computational ethics[2].

References

Mariem Abbes, Zied Kechaou, and Adel M. Alimi. 2023. Deep learning approach for Tunisian hate Speech detection on Facebook. In *2023 IEEE Symposium on Computers and Communications (ISCC)*, pages 739–744.

Saja Al-Dabet, Ahmed ElMassry, Ban Alomar, and Abdullah Alshamsi. 2023. Transformer-based Arabic Offensive Speech Detection. In *2023 International Conference on Emerging Smart Computing and Informatics (ESCI)*, pages 1–6.

Girma Yohannis Bade. 2021. Natural Language Processing and Its Challenges on Omotic Language Group of Ethiopia. *Journal of Computer Science Research*, 3(4):26–30.

Girma Yohannis Bade and Akalu Assefa Afaro. 2018. Object Oriented Software Development for Artificial Intelligence. *American Journal of Software Engineering and Applications*, 7(2):22–24.

Girma Yohannis Bade and Hussien Seid. 2018. Development of Longest-Match Based Stemmer for Texts of Wolaita Language. *vol*, 4:79–83.

Muhammad Bilal, Atif Khan, Salman Jan, Shahrulniza Musa, and Shaukat Ali. 2023. Roman Urdu hate speech detection using transformer-based model for cyber security applications. *Sensors*, 23(8):3909.

Tadesse Destaw, Seid Muhie Yimam, Abinew Ayele, and Chris Biemann. 2022. Question answering classification for Amharic social media community based questions. In *Proceedings of the 1st Annual Meeting of the ELRA/ISCA Special Interest Group on Under-Resourced Languages*, pages 137–145, Marseille, France. European Language Resources Association.

Nikhil Ghanghor, Rahul Ponnusamy, Prasanna Kumar Kumaresan, Ruba Priyadharshini, Sajeetha Thavareesan, and Bharathi Raja Chakravarthi. 2021. IIITK@ LT-EDI-EACL2021: Hope speech detection for equality, diversity, and inclusion in Tamil, Malayalam and English. In *Proceedings of the First Workshop on Language Technology for Equality, Diversity and Inclusion*, pages 197–203.

Hiren Madhu, Shrey Satapara, Sandip Modha, Thomas Mandl, and Prasenjit Majumder. 2023. Detecting offensive speech in conversational code-mixed dialogue on social media: A contextual dataset and benchmark experiments. *Expert Systems with Applications*, 215:119342.

Chukwuemeka Okechukwu, I Idris, JA Ojeniyi, Morufu Olalere, et al. 2023. Hate and Offensive Speech Detection Using Term Frequency-Inverse Document

[2]https://www.aclweb.org/portal/content/acl-code-ethics

Frequency (TF-IDF) and Majority Voting Ensemble Machine Learning Algorithms. 4th International Engineering Conference (IEC 2023).

Premjth, Bharathi Raja, Prasanna Kumar Kumaresan, Saranya Rajiakodi, Sai Prashanth Karnati, Sai Rishith Reddy Mangamuru, and Janakiram Chandu. 2024. Findings of the Shared Task on Hate and Offensive Language Detection in Telugu Codemixed Text (HOLD-Telugu). In *Proceedings of the Fourth Workshop on Speech, Vision, and Language Technologies for Dravidian Languages*, Malta. European Chapter of the Association for Computational Linguistics.

Bharathi Raja andS Malliga andCN SUBALALITHA Priyadharshini, Ruba andChakravarthi, Premjith and-Murugappan Abirami S V, Kogilavani andB, and Prasanna Kumar Kumaresan. 2023. Overview of Shared-task on Abusive Comment Detection in Tamil and Telugu. In *Proceedings of the Third Workshop on Speech and Language Technologies for Dravidian Languages*, Varna, Bulgaria. Recent Advances in Natural Language Processing.

Hind Saleh, Areej Alhothali, and Kawthar Moria. 2023. Detection of hate speech using BERT and hate speech word embedding with deep model. *Applied Artificial Intelligence*, 37(1):2166719.

Moein Shahiki-Tash, Jesús Armenta-Segura, Zahra Ahani, Olga Kolesnikova, Grigori Sidorov, and Alexander Gelbukh. 2023. Lidoma at homomex2023@ iberlef: Hate speech detection towards the mexican spanish-speaking lgbt+ population. the importance of preprocessing before using bert-based models. In *Proceedings of the Iberian Languages Evaluation Forum (IberLEF 2023)*.

M Shahiki Tash, Z Ahani, Al Tonja, M Gemeda, N Hussain, and O Kolesnikova. Word Level Language Identification in Code-mixed Kannada-English Texts using traditional machine learning algorithms. In *Proceedings of the 19th International Conference on Natural Language Processing (ICON): Shared Task on Word Level Language Identification in Code-mixed Kannada-English Texts*.

Atnafu Lambebo Tonja, Mesay Gemeda Yigezu, Olga Kolesnikova, Moein Shahiki Tash, Grigori Sidorov, and Alexander Gelbuk. 2022. Transformer-based model for word level language identification in code-mixed kannada-english texts. *arXiv preprint arXiv:2211.14459*.

Konthala Yasaswini, Karthik Puranik, Adeep Hande, Ruba Priyadharshini, Sajeetha Thavareesan, and Bharathi Raja Chakravarthi. 2021. IIITT@ DravidianLangTech-EACL2021: Transfer learning for offensive language detection in Dravidian languages. In *Proceedings of the First Workshop on Speech and Language Technologies for Dravidian Languages*, pages 187–194.

Mesay Gemeda Yigezu, Girma Yohannis Bade, Olga Kolesnikova, Grigori Sidorov, and Alexander Gelbukh. 2023a. Multilingual Hope Speech Detection using Machine Learning.

Mesay Gemeda Yigezu, Selam Kanta, Olga Kolesnikova, Grigori Sidorov, and Alexander Gelbukh. 2023b. Habesha@ DravidianLangTech: Abusive Comment Detection using Deep Learning Approach. In *Proceedings of the Third Workshop on Speech and Language Technologies for Dravidian Languages*, pages 244–249.

Mesay Gemeda Yigezu, Tadesse Kebede, Olga Kolesnikova, Grigori Sidorov, and Alexander Gelbukh. 2023c. Habesha@ DravidianLangTech: Utilizing Deep and Transfer Learning Approaches for Sentiment Analysis. In *Proceedings of the Third Workshop on Speech and Language Technologies for Dravidian Languages*, pages 239–243.

Mesay Gemeda Yigezu, Olga Kolesnikova, Grigori Sidorov, and Alexander Gelbukh. 2023d. Transformer-Based Hate Speech Detection for Multi-Class and Multi-Label Classification.

Mesay Gemeda Yigezu, Moges Ahmed Mehamed, Olga Kolesnikova, Tadesse Kebede Guge, Alexander Gelbukh, and Grigori Sidorov. 2023e. Evaluating the Effectiveness of Hybrid Features in Fake News Detection on Social Media. In *2023 International Conference on Information and Communication Technology for Development for Africa (ICT4DA), pages=171–175*. IEEE.

CUETSentimentSillies@DravidianLangTech EACL2024: Transformer-based Approach for Detecting and Categorizing Fake News in Malayalam Language

Zannatul Fardaush Tripty, Md. Arian Al Nafis, Antu Chowdhury, Jawad Hossain, Shawly Ahsan and **Mohammed Moshiul Hoque**
Department of Computer Science and Engineering
Chittagong University of Engineering and Technology, Bangladesh
{u1804030, u1804111, u1804112, u1704039, u1704057}@student.cuet.ac.bd
moshiul_240@cuet.ac.bd

Abstract

Fake news misleads people and may lead to real-world miscommunication and injury. Removing misinformation encourages critical thinking, democracy, and the prevention of hatred, fear, and misunderstanding. Identifying and removing fake news and developing a detection system is essential for reliable, accurate, and clear information. Therefore, a shared task was organized to detect fake news in Malayalam. This paper presents a system developed for the shared task of detecting and classifying fake news in Malayalam. The approach involves a combination of machine learning models (LR, DT, RF, MNB), deep learning models (CNN, BiLSTM, CNN+BiLSTM), and transformer-based models (Indic-BERT, XLM-R, Malayalam-BERT, m-BERT) for both subtasks. The experimental results demonstrate that transformer-based models, specifically m-BERT and Malayalam-BERT, outperformed others. The m-BERT model achieved superior performance in subtask 1 with macro F1-scores of 0.84, and Malayalam-BERT outperformed the other models in subtask 2 with macro F1-scores of 0.496, securing us the 5th and 2nd positions in subtask 1 and subtask 2, respectively.

1 Introduction

Social media has fundamentally transformed how we receive and exchange information in the digital era. But social media is also a source of false news, misinformation, and content emphasized by sensationalism, manipulation, and propaganda (Rohera et al., 2022). So the adoption of social media is very significant for awareness, but the authenticity of news is the cause of concern as some sources of news are not reliable (Choudhary and Arora, 2021). However, incorrect information may swiftly spread, sway public opinion, cause conflict, and advance agendas. Social media fake news undermines truth, democracy, and social unity (Bharathi et al., 2021). Propaganda raises public safety concerns. Financial losses and stock market fluctuations can result from rumors or false information about companies. So to maintain social cohesion, protect against cyber threats, and promote ethical journalism, it is important to detect fake news. Sometimes fake news can hamper the reputation of individuals, organizations, or businesses. So it is important to identify and correct false information to protect the integrity of affected people. Therefore, automated fake news identification is of utmost priority in today's digital age. Fake news detection has been a prominent subject of study, with academics examining different methodologies, databases, and NLP solutions to handle this issue (Oshikawa et al., 2018). This work aims to develop a system that can classify news into original and fake for subtask 1 and classify a text into four predefined categories for subtask 2. The key contributions of this work are illustrated in the following:

- Developed several ML and DL techniques to detect and categorize fake news.
- Investigated the performance of the models to find the right approach for the classification of social media text and performed in-depth error analysis, offering important insight into classifying text.

2 Related Work

Recent studies have made significant strides in detecting fake news in Dravidian languages. A Dravidian dataset was introduced by Raja et al. (2023), and they utilized unique adaptive learning to fine-tune transformer models. Their work demonstrated the effectiveness of transfer learning algorithms, with transformer models, particularly m-BERT and XLM-RoBERTa, outperforming other approaches. In another study, transformer models, including m-BERT, AL-BERT, BERT, and XLNet, were investigated by Balaji et al. (2023) to detect fraudulent

Proceedings of the Fourth Workshop on Speech, Vision, and Language Technologies for Dravidian Languages, pages 245–251
March 22, 2024 ©2024 Association for Computational Linguistics

content. Among these models, m-BERT exhibited the best performance.

Bala and Krishnamurthy (2023) employed Google's MuRIL model with a curated dataset of labeled Dravidian data to detect fake news. By leveraging fine-tuning techniques, their work showcased the effectiveness of the "mural-base-cased" model in identifying fake news. To detect fake news in Malayalam, Coelho et al. (2023) used LR, MNB, and an ensemble model (MNB, LR, and SVM). Among the three models, the ensemble model performed the best with a macro F1-score of 0.831.

Kumari et al. (2023) utilized fine-tuning techniques on the IndicBERT model (macro F1 score of 0.78) for detecting misinformation in Dravidian languages. They employed SBERT sentence embedding, DNN-based classification, and an ensemble classifier to accurately categorize text. Chakravarthi et al. (2023) focused on categorizing code-mixed social media comments and posts into offensive or not offensive at different levels and presented a multilingual MPNet and CNN fusion model with weighted average F1-scores of 0.85, 0.98, and 0.76 for Tamil, Malayalam, and Kannada, respectively.

Kaliyar et al. (2021) proposed FakeBERT, a BERT-based deep learning strategy, to identify bogus news. They also employed deep learning-based models, including CNN and LSTM. The proposed FakeBERT model outperformed the other models with an accuracy of 0.989. Hossain et al. (2022) employed Logistic Regression to detect the abusive language in Tamil text. The LR and CNN+BiLSTM models outperformed the others, with LR achieving a higher recall value (0.44) than CNN+BiLSTM (0.36).

For the fake news detection task in the Urdu language, Kalra et al. (2022) utilized an ensemble of transformer models. Tula et al. (2021) proposed a multilingual ensemble-based model for identifying offensive content in low-resource Dravidian languages. The mode achieved an F1-score of 0.97, 0.75, and 0.70 for the Malayalam, Tamil, and Kannada datasets, respectively. Monti et al. (2019) proposed a novel automatic fake news detection model based on geometric deep learning. The authors achieved high accuracy for fake news detection with an ROC AUC score of 92.7%.

3 Task and Dataset Description

This shared task Subramanian et al. (2024) was organized by the organizers to detect and classify fake news. The shared task[1] included two subtasks: subtask 1 focused on classifying text as 'Original' or 'Fake' news and subtask 2 targeted to categorize texts into 'False', 'Half True', 'Mostly False', 'Partly False' and 'Mostly True'. For subtask 1, a system was developed to classify texts as fake or original using a corpus created by Malliga et al. (2023). The dataset included 5091 texts from YouTube comments of varying lengths in the Malayalam language. The training, validation, and test sets contained 3257, 815, and 1019 texts, respectively, divided into 'Original' and 'Fake' categories. 'Original' texts comprise 14031 words, while fake texts contain 23198 words (Table 1).

Classes	Train	Valid	Test	Total Words
Original	1658	409	512	14031
Fake	1599	406	507	23198
Total	3257	815	1019	37229

Table 1: Dataset statistics of subtask 1

The aim of subtask 2 was to classify texts into five categories, each defined by the degree of misinformation. The dataset consisted of 1919 texts from Malayalam language YouTube comments. The training set had 1669 texts and the test set had 250 texts (Table 2). Text lengths varied from 3 to 36 words, with an average of 10 words.

Classes	Train	Test	Total Words
False	1246	149	12185
Mostly False	239	63	2380
Half True	141	24	1462
Partly False	42	14	363
Mostly True	1	0	8
Total	1669	250	16398

Table 2: Dataset statistics of subtask 2

4 Methodology

We developed a framework for detecting and classifying fake news in the Malayalam language. Initially, data preprocessing was conducted to clean the data. Features were extracted using TF-IDF

[1]https://codalab.lisn.upsaclay.fr/competitions/16055

(Nayel, 2020) for the machine learning (ML) models, while FastText (Joulin et al., 2016) embeddings were utilized for deep learning (DL) models. Various ML, DL, and transformer-based techniques were subsequently employed for classification purposes. The graphical representation of our methodology is depicted in Figure 1.

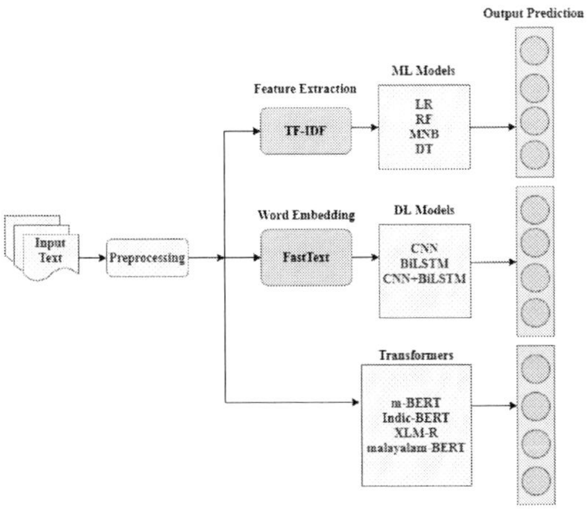

Figure 1: Proposed methodology for fake news detection and classification

4.1 Data Augmentation

In subtask 2, a noticeable class imbalance existed, particularly in the 'Mostly True' class, which contained only one sample. To tackle this, we adopted the back translation technique to augment all classes except the class of 'False'. This technique enhanced dataset balance by iteratively translating sentences from Malayalam to another language and back, as detailed in Table 3.

Classes	Train	Total Words
False	1246	12185
Mostly False	671	6819
Half True	399	4148
Partly False	122	1074
Mostly True	3	21
Total	2441	24247

Table 3: Training set statistics of subtask 2 after augmentation

4.2 Preprocessing

For effective training and evaluation, we conducted preprocessing on datasets, like removing emojis, punctuation, extra spaces, URLs, and numerical texts. We considered the five most frequent stopwords and removed them. For subtask 1, English stopwords in the corpus were also removed. This streamlined preprocessing ensured standardized and refined textual datasets for analysis.

4.3 Training

In this section, we provide a detailed overview of the architectures of various models. The first step in both cases was to extract features using different feature extraction techniques and then apply various machine learning (ML) and deep learning (DL) algorithms. Furthermore, as depicted in Figure 1, the system development also utilized different transformer models.

4.3.1 ML Baseline

TF-IDF values for unigram features have been used as features for training ML models. Various conventional machine learning methods were employed for the detection of fake news. These methods include Logistic Regression (LR), Random Forest (RF), Decision Tree (DT), and Multinomial Naive Bayes (MNB). In the LR and DT models, the regularization parameter (C value) was set to 2. For Random Forest, we implemented 100 estimators (n_estimators = 100) to enhance its predictive performance.

4.3.2 DL Baseline

Three deep learning models CNN, BiLSTM, and CNN+BiLSTM were employed for fake news detection and classification. In the CNN model, the embedding layer was followed by three convolutional layers featuring 64, 32, and 16 filters, each activated by ReLU. The convolution layers were followed by MaxPooling layers for feature reduction. For the BiLSTM model, the embedding layer was followed by two bidirectional LSTM layers with 32 and 16 units. The resulting sequences were flattened and directed into a dense layer with softmax activation for classification. In the CNN+BiLSTM hybrid model, the embedding layer was followed by a convolutional layer with 128 filters and a kernel of 5 and a BiLSTM layer with 32 units with a dropout rate of 0.2.

4.3.3 Transformers

Considering the current trend of transformers, we also utilized pre-trained transformer-based models including XLM-R (Conneau et al., 2019), m-BERT (Joshi, 2022), Indic-BERT (Kakwani et al., 2020), and Malayalam-BERT (Joshi, 2022). The learning rate was $2e^{-5}$ with a 0.1 warm-up ratio, and stability was improved by doubling gradient accumulation steps to 2. We applied a weight decay of 0.01 and used a linear learning rate scheduler over a 10-epoch training period. We employed the Adafactor optimizer and used a batch size of 16 for both training and evaluation.

5 Experiments and Results

The performance of various methods on the test set is presented in Table 4 and Table 5 for subtask 1 and subtask 2, respectively. From the results displayed in Table 4, it's evident that transformer-based models outperformed ML and DL models in subtask 1, with the m-BERT model achieving the highest macro F1 score of 0.84. Among the DL models, BiLSTM exhibited the highest macro F1 score of 0.782.

Classifier	P	R	F
LR	0.83	0.82	0.82
DT	0.75	0.74	0.74
RF	0.79	0.77	0.76
MNB	0.83	0.83	0.83
CNN	0.714	0.650	0.622
BiLSTM	0.785	0.782	0.782
CNN + BiLSTM	0.714	0.650	0.622
m-BERT	**0.84**	**0.84**	**0.84**
Indic-BERT	0.763	0.747	0.743
XLM-R	0.837	0.837	0.837

Table 4: Performance of various models for the subtask 1, where P, R, and F denote precision, recall, and macro F1-score, respectively

In subtask 2, Malayalam-BERT achieved the highest macro F1 score of 0.496 among transformer models, followed closely by m-BERT (0.467) and IndicBERT (0.309). Among machine learning models, Random Forest demonstrated the best macro F1 score of 0.476. Furthermore, among the deep learning models, the Convolutional Neural Network (CNN) attained the highest macro F1 score of 0.463 compared to the other models.

6 Error Analysis

6.1 Quantitative Analysis:

We utilized a confusion matrix for error analysis for both subtask 1 and subtask 2. The confusion matrix of subtask 1 (Figure 2) showed us a True Positive Rate (TPR) of 82.64% and 85.54% for the

Classifier	P	R	F
LR	0.785	0.360	0.384
DT	0.482	0.451	0.461
RF	**0.796**	0.426	0.476
MNB	0.663	0.366	0.386
CNN	0.466	0.463	0.463
BiLSTM	0.485	0.476	0.441
CNN+BiLSTM	0.353	0.369	0.109
m-BERT	0.529	0.453	0.467
Indic-BERT	0.382	0.314	0.309
Malayalam-BERT	0.589	**0.456**	**0.496**

Table 5: Performance of various models for the subtask 2, where P, R, and F denote precision, recall, and macro F1-score, respectively

'Fake' and 'Original' classes, respectively, which is an indicator that our applied model performed well overall in identifying both the original and fake cases.

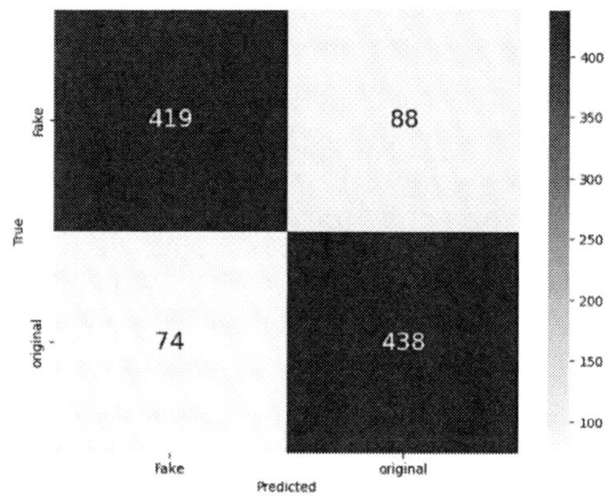

Figure 2: Confusion matrix of m-BERT for subtask 1

By analyzing the confusion matrix of subtask 2 (Figure 3), we found that the False class had the highest TPR of 79.86% due to an adequate amount of data. However, the classes 'Mostly False' and 'Partly False' had lower TPR of 32.26% and 28.57%, respectively. Since the texts of the classes 'Mostly False' and 'False' were similar in context, the model had a tendency to misclassify 'Mostly False' as 'False' and vice versa.

Furthermore, upon analyzing Table 3, we observed that the dataset for subtask 2 was imbalanced. This imbalance caused our model to misclassify instances with the wrong class.

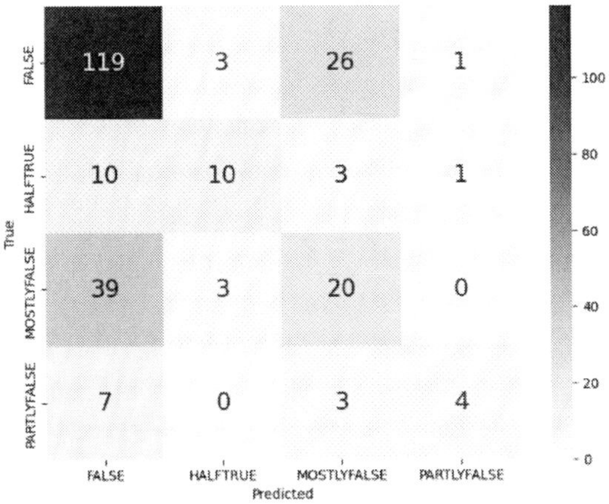

Figure 3: Confusion matrix of Malayalam-BERT for subtask 2

Text Sample	Actual	Predicted
Sample 1. അനുഭവിക്കുന്നത് പാവപ്പെട്ട സാധാരണക്കാരായ ജനങ്ങൾ ഇനി പുതിയ പ്രോട്ടോകോൾ വരും (It is the poor common people who are suffering now that the new protocol will come)	Original	Original
Sample 2. ഇവിടെ ഇപ്പോഴും നേരം വെളുക്കാത്ത അന്തങ്ങൾ ഉണ്ട് There are still dawning ends here	Fake	Original

Figure 4: A few examples of predicted outputs by the proposed (m-BERT) model for subtask 1 (here, corresponding english texts were translated using 'Google Translator')

6.2 Qualitative Analysis:

We analyzed some samples to understand the misclassifications made by our model. In Figure 4, the model demonstrated accurate prediction for sample 1, while sample 2 was misclassified. Further analysis of the confusion matrix in subtask 1, as depicted in Figure 2, revealed a lower TPR for the 'Fake' class than the 'Original' class. The model's inability to effectively detect fake news may be attributed to the semantic depth of the content, where the nuanced meanings closely resemble those found in the 'Original' news. Figure 5 illustrates the predicted labels and actual labels generated by the proposed model for subtask 2. Notably, the model demonstrated accurate classification for text samples 1 and 4. However, it exhibited challenges in correctly categorizing text samples 2 and 3. Specifically, text sample 2 was predicted as 'Partly False' instead of its true class, 'Half True', while text sample 4 was predicted as 'Mostly False' instead of its actual class, 'Partly False'. This misclassification can be attributed to a class imbalance within the dataset. The dataset was comprised of a limited number of examples for the 'Half True' (399 samples) and 'Partly False' (122 samples) classes, even after augmentation. In comparison, the classes 'False' and 'Mostly False' were more abundant. This scarcity of samples for 'Half True' and 'Partly False' may pose challenges for the model to effectively learn and generalize patterns associated with these classes, contributing to the observed misclassification.

Text Sample	Actual	Predicted
Sample 1. ചന്ദനക്കുറിയണിഞ്ഞ് വിഎസ് അച്യുതാനന്ദൻ. (VS Achuthanandan dressed in sandalwood.)	False	False
Sample 2. ടി പി ചന്ദ്രശേഖരൻ വധത്തിന് പിന്നിൽ സി.പി.ഐ.എം ആണെന്ന് കെ.ടി ജലീൽ ഏറ്റുപറയുന്നു (KT Jalil confesses that CPIM is behind the assassination of TP Chandrasekaran	Half True	Partly False
Sample 3. വിവിധ വാഹന ടാക്സ് നിരക്കുകൾ സംസ്ഥാന സർക്കാർ കൂട്ടി. (The state government has increased various vehicle tax rates.)	Partly False	Mostly False
Sample 4. ബഹ്റൈനിലെ ഇസ്രായേൽ എംബസിക്ക് പലസ്തീൻ അനുകൂലികൾ തീയിട്ടു. (Palestinian supporters set fire to Israel's embassy in Bahrain.)	Mostly False	Mostly False

Figure 5: A few examples of predicted outputs by the proposed (Malayalam-BERT) model for subtask 2 (here, corresponding english texts were translated using 'Google Translator')

7 Conclusion and Limitations

Our study explored a diverse range of models for detecting and classifying fake news. Through the investigation of four ML models, three DL models, and four transformer models, we gained valuable insights into their performance and effectiveness in these tasks. In subtask 1, m-BERT outperformed other transformer models, including ML and DL models, with a macro F1 score of 0.84, but surprisingly, the LR model with TF-IDF feature extraction came close to 0.82. In subtask 2, Malayalam-BERT outperformed the other ML, DL, and transformer models with a macro F1 score of 0.496. Some DL and ML models came close to this result. CNN with FastText feature extraction came close to it with a macro F1 score of 0.463. Although the system demonstrated strong performance in detecting Malayalam fake news, it faced a significant challenge in classifying multi-class fake news due to a potential data imbalance. To address this limitation, further research and strategies, such as advanced algorithms tailored for imbalanced datasets, are needed to enhance classification accuracy.

References

Abhinaba Bala and Parameswari Krishnamurthy. 2023. Abhipaw@ dravidianlangtech: Fake news detection in dravidian languages using multilingual bert. In *Proceedings of the Third Workshop on Speech and Language Technologies for Dravidian Languages*, pages 235–238.

Varsha Balaji, B Bharathi, et al. 2023. Nlp_ssn_cse@ dravidianlangtech: Fake news detection in dravidian languages using transformer models. In *Proceedings of the Third Workshop on Speech and Language Technologies for Dravidian Languages*, pages 133–139.

B Bharathi et al. 2021. Ssncse_nlp@ dravidianlangtech-eacl2021: Offensive language identification on multilingual code mixing text. In *Proceedings of the First Workshop on Speech and Language Technologies for Dravidian Languages*, pages 313–318.

Bharathi Raja Chakravarthi, Manoj Balaji Jagadeeshan, Vasanth Palanikumar, and Ruba Priyadharshini. 2023. Offensive language identification in dravidian languages using mpnet and cnn. *International Journal of Information Management Data Insights*, 3(1):100151.

Anshika Choudhary and Anuja Arora. 2021. Linguistic feature based learning model for fake news detection and classification. *Expert Systems with Applications*, 169:114171.

Sharal Coelho, Asha Hegde, G Kavya, and Hosahalli Lakshmaiah Shashirekha. 2023. Mucs@ dravidianlangtech2023: Malayalam fake news detection using machine learning approach. In *Proceedings of the Third Workshop on Speech and Language Technologies for Dravidian Languages*, pages 288–292.

Alexis Conneau, Kartikay Khandelwal, Naman Goyal, Vishrav Chaudhary, Guillaume Wenzek, Francisco Guzmán, Edouard Grave, Myle Ott, Luke Zettlemoyer, and Veselin Stoyanov. 2019. Unsupervised cross-lingual representation learning at scale. *CoRR*, abs/1911.02116.

Alamgir Hossain, Mahathir Bishal, Eftekhar Hossain, Omar Sharif, and Mohammed Moshiul Hoque. 2022. Combatant@ tamilnlp-acl2022: Fine-grained categorization of abusive comments using logistic regression. In *Proceedings of the Second Workshop on Speech and Language Technologies for Dravidian Languages*, pages 221–228.

Raviraj Joshi. 2022. L3cube-hindbert and devbert: Pre-trained bert transformer models for devanagari based hindi and marathi languages. *arXiv preprint arXiv:2211.11418*.

Armand Joulin, Edouard Grave, Piotr Bojanowski, and Tomas Mikolov. 2016. Bag of tricks for efficient text classification. *arXiv preprint arXiv:1607.01759*.

Divyanshu Kakwani, Anoop Kunchukuttan, Satish Golla, Gokul N.C., Avik Bhattacharyya, Mitesh M. Khapra, and Pratyush Kumar. 2020. IndicNLPSuite: Monolingual Corpora, Evaluation Benchmarks and Pre-trained Multilingual Language Models for Indian Languages. In *Findings of EMNLP*.

Rohit Kumar Kaliyar, Anurag Goswami, and Pratik Narang. 2021. Fakebert: Fake news detection in social media with a bert-based deep learning approach. *Multimedia tools and applications*, 80(8):11765–11788.

S Kalra, P Verma, Y Sharma, and GS Chauhan. 2022. Ensembling of various transformer based models for the fake news detection task in the urdu language.

Kirti Kumari, Shirish Shekhar Jha, Zarikunte Kunal Dayanand, and Praneesh Sharma. 2023. Ml&ai_iiitranchi@ dravidianlangtech: Leveraging transfer learning for the discernment of fake news within the linguistic domain of dravidian language. In *Proceedings of the Third Workshop on Speech and Language Technologies for Dravidian Languages*, pages 198–206.

S Malliga, Bharathi Raja Chakravarthi, SV Kogilavani, Santhiya Pandiyan, Prasanna Kumar Kumaresan, Balasubramanian Palani, and Muskaan Singh. 2023. Overview of the shared task on fake news detection from social media text. In *Proceedings of the Third Workshop on Speech and Language Technologies for Dravidian Languages*, pages 59–63.

Federico Monti, Fabrizio Frasca, Davide Eynard, Damon Mannion, and Michael M Bronstein. 2019. Fake news detection on social media using geometric deep learning. *arXiv preprint arXiv:1902.06673*.

Hamada A Nayel. 2020. Nayel at semeval-2020 task 12: Tf/idf-based approach for automatic offensive language detection in arabic tweets. *arXiv preprint arXiv:2007.13339*.

Ray Oshikawa, Jing Qian, and William Yang Wang. 2018. A survey on natural language processing for fake news detection. *arXiv preprint arXiv:1811.00770*.

Eduri Raja, Badal Soni, and Samir Kumar Borgohain. 2023. Fake news detection in dravidian languages using transfer learning with adaptive finetuning. *Engineering Applications of Artificial Intelligence*, 126:106877.

Dhiren Rohera, Harshal Shethna, Keyur Patel, Urvish Thakker, Sudeep Tanwar, Rajesh Gupta, Wei-Chiang Hong, and Ravi Sharma. 2022. A taxonomy of fake news classification techniques: Survey and implementation aspects. *IEEE Access*, 10:30367–30394.

Malliga Subramanian, Bharathi Raja Chakravarthi, Kogilavani Shanmugavadivel, Santhiya Pandiyan, Prasanna Kumar Kumaresan, Balasubramanian Palani, Premjith B, Sandhiya Raja, Vanaja, Mithunajha S, Devika K, Hariprasath S.B, Haripriya B, and Vigneshwar E. 2024. Overview of the Second Shared Task on Fake News Detection in Dravidian

Languages. In *Proceedings of the Fourth Workshop on Speech, Vision, and Language Technologies for Dravidian Languages*, Malta. European Chapter of the Association for Computational Linguistics.

Debapriya Tula, Prathyush Potluri, Shreyas Ms, Sumanth Doddapaneni, Pranjal Sahu, Rohan Sukumaran, and Parth Patwa. 2021. Bitions@ dravidianlangtech-eacl2021: Ensemble of multilingual language models with pseudo labeling for offence detection in dravidian languages. In *Proceedings of the first workshop on speech and language technologies for dravidian languages*, pages 291–299.

MUCS@DravidianLangTech-2024: Role of Learning Approaches in Strengthening Hate-Alert Systems for code-mixed text

Manavi K K[a], Sonali[b], Gauthamraj[c]
Kavya G[d], Asha Hegde [e], H L Shashirekha[f]
Department of Computer Science, Mangalore University, Mangalore, Karnataka, India
{[a]kkmanavi, [b]sonalikulal417, [c]gauthamrajdataspace}@gmail.com,
{[d]kavyamujk, [e]hegdekasha}@gmail.com, [f]hlsrekha@mangaloreuniversity.ac.in

Abstract

Hate and Offensive (HOF) language detection is the task of detecting HOF content targeting a person or a group of people. Detecting HOF content is essential for promoting safety and positive engagement in online spaces, while also upholding community standards and protecting users from harm. However, despite massive efforts, it still remains challenging to effectively detect HOF content on online platforms because of ever-growing creative users. In view of this, to address the identification of HOF content on social media platforms, this paper describes the learning models submitted by our team - MUCS to "Hate and Offensive Language Detection in Telugu Codemixed Text (HOLD-Telugu): Dravidian-LangTech@EACL" - a shared task organized at European Chapter of the Association for Computational Linguistics (EACL) 2024. Three models: i) Logistic Regression (LR) model - a Machine Learning (ML) algorithm trained with Term Frequency-Inverse Document Frequency (TF-IDF) of character and word sequences in the range (1, 5) and (1, 3) respectively, and sub-words, ii) Ensemble model - a combination of ML classifiers (Multinomial Naive Bayes (MNB), LR, and Gaussian Naive Bayes (GNB)) trained with CountVectorizer of character and word sequences in the range (1, 5) and (1, 3), respectively, and iii) HateExplain_TL - a model based on Transfer Learning (TL) approach using Bidirectional Encoder Representations from Transformers (BERT) variant, are submitted to the shared task for detecting HOF content in Telugu code-mixed text. The proposed LR model outperformed the other models with a macro F1 score of 0.65.

1 Introduction

Twitter, Facebook, LinkedIn, Instagram, and other social media platforms have become popular places for people to spend their time and communicate with each other (Dikshitha Vani and Bharathi, 2022). While social media platforms offers numerous benefits, it also comes with drawbacks, including the spread of harmful content such as hate speech, offensive, abusive, and fake news content. Hate speech refers to any type of communication that targets, disparages, or encourages violence against an individual or group of people (Velankar et al., 2021).

Disseminating hateful content about a group or a community has a detrimental effect on those who are targeted by it. These victims experience stress, depression, and other mental health issues, and in extreme circumstances, they might even commit suicide (Roy et al., 2022). Therefore, it is necessary to detect HOF content to maintain healthy online platforms. Usually HOF content on social media is written by mixing words or sub-words belonging to more than one language known as code-mixed text. The code-mixed nature of HOF content is challenging because of its linguistic diversity (Priyadharshini et al., 2023b).

"Hate and Offensive Language Detection in Telugu Codemixed Text (HOLD-Telugu)" (B et al., 2024; Priyadharshini et al., 2023a), encourages the researchers to develop models to detect the HOF content in Telugu code-mixed texts. We - team MUCS, describe the three distinct models: i) LR model - a ML classifier fed with TF-IDF of character and word sequences in the range (1, 5) and (1, 3) respectively, and sub-words, ii) Ensemble model - a combination of ML classifiers (MNB, LR, and GNB) trained with CountVectorizer of character and word sequences in the range (1, 5) and (1, 3), respectively, and iii) HateExplain_TL - a model based on TL approach using BERT variant[1], for detecting HOF content in Telugu code-mixed texts.

The rest of the paper is organized as follows: while Section 2 describes the literature on HOF language identification in social media text, Sec-

[1]https://huggingface.co/Hate-speech-CNERG/bert-base-uncased-hatexplain

Proceedings of the Fourth Workshop on Speech, Vision, and Language Technologies for Dravidian Languages, pages 252–256

tion 3 focuses on the description of the models submitted to the shared task followed by the experiments and results in Section 4. Conclusion and future works are included in Section 5.

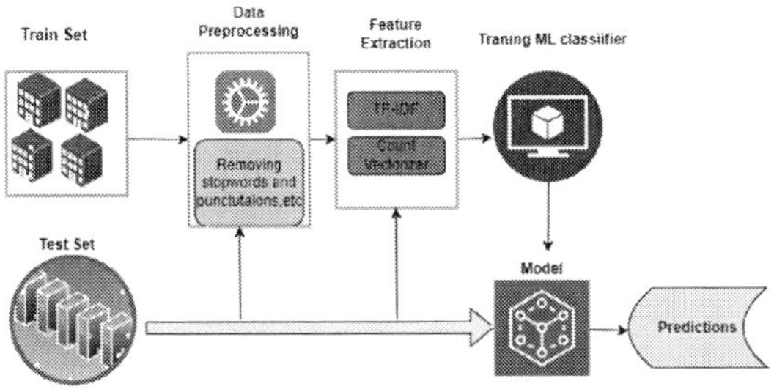

Figure 1: Framework of the proposed ML models

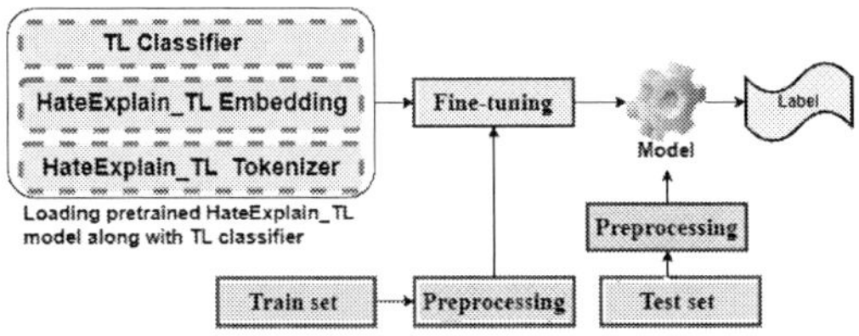

Figure 2: Framework of the proposed HateExplain_TL model

2 Related Work

HOF content detection in code-mixed text is a growing area of study and several researchers have contributed to this area. Some of the related works for detecting HOF language are described below: To identify HOF content in Malayalam and Tamil code-mixed texts, Pathak et al. (2021) presented ML models (Support Vector Classifier (SVC), MNB, LR, and Random Forest (RF)) trained with TF-IDF of character and word sequences in the range (1, 5) and (1, 2) respectively for Malayalam code-mixed text, and TF-IDF of character and word sequences in the range (1, 7) and (1, 4) respectively for Tamil code-mixed text. They also trained ML models concatenating character and word TF-IDF. Among their proposed models, SVC models outperformed other models obtaining macro F1 scores of 0.74 and 0.86 for Malayalam and Tamil code-mixed texts respectively. Bhawal et al. (2021) experimented with ML (LR, RF, NB, eXtreme Gradient Boosting (XGBoost) and Support Vector Machine (SVM)), Deep Learning (DL) (Deep Neural Network (DNN), Convolutional Neural Network (CNN), and Bidirectional Long Short-Term Memory (Bi-LSTM)), and Transfer Learning (TL) (multilingual BERT (mBERT), a multilingual ALBERT model (IndicBERT), and Multilingual Representations for Indian Languages (MuRIL)) models, for HOF content detection in Malayalam and Tamil code-mixed texts. Their proposed ML and DL models were trained with TF-IDF of word n-grams in the range (1, 5) and for TL models, the corresponding BERT-based embeddings are used as features for training the classifiers. Out of their proposed models, the MuRIL model performed better with weighted F1 scores of 0.636 and 0.734 for Tamil and Malayalam code-mixed texts respectively.

Hegde et al. (2023) proposed two distinct models: i) AbusiveML - a Linear Support Vector Classifier (LinearSVC) trained with TF-IDF of word and character n-grams both in the range (1, 3) and ii) AbusiveTL - a model based on TL based approach with three BERT variants (Distilled Multilingual BERT (DistilmBERT), Tamil BERT, and Telugu BERT), for HOF content detection in Tamil, Telugu and romanized Tamil (RTamil) code-mixed texts. Their proposed AbusiveTL model outperformed the other models with macro F1 scores of 0.46, 0.74, and 0.49 securing 1st, 1st, and 4th ranks for code-mixed Tamil, Telugu, and RTamil texts respectively. Banerjee et al. (2021) fine-tuned various BERT models (mBERT-base, Cross-lingual Language Model with Robustly Optimized BERT approach (XLMR) - large, XLMR-base) on code-mixed Hindi texts and Hindi and English languages for binary (Non Hate-Offensive (NOT), HOF (HOF)) and multi-class (Hate speech (HATE), Offensive (OFFN), Profane (PRFN), Non-Hate (NONE)) tasks. Their proposed XLMR-large model obtained macro F1 scores of 0.7107, 0.8006, and 0.6447 for code-mixed Hindi (four classes), English (four classes), and English (two classes) texts respectively. Further, mBERT-base model obtained a macro F1 score of 0.7797 for Hindi (two classes) text.

From the above literature, it is found that there are several techniques for detecting HOF content in code-mixed text. However, there are only few studies that focus on Telugu code-mixed text indicating the need for further research and innovation in this field.

3 Methodology

To identify the HOF content in code-mixed Telugu text three distinct models: i) LR model ii) Ensemble model, and iii) HateExplain_TL models are pro-

Sample Text	Translated Text	Label
ఈ పాట కన్న .. మీ మాటే బాగుంది..	Kanna this song.. your words are good..	Non-hate
నాగబాబు సెలక్షన్ సూపర్, గల్లి బాయ్స్ అదుర్స్	The day of breaking the wings of the Fan is near	Non-hate
టీవీ ఫైవ్ ఎప్పుడు తప్పుడు ప్రచారమే	TV Five is always a false advertisement	hate
పిచోళ్ళ గురించి వినడమే కాని చూడటం ఇదే ఫస్ట్ టైం	This is the first time to hear about Pichola but to see it	hate

Table 1: Sample Telugu text along with their English translations and corresponding labels

posed. The framework of the ML and TL models are shown in Figures 1 and 2. Pre-processing is the preliminary step in building learning models and it involves cleaning and transforming raw text data to a standardized format. Usually, text data contains noise in the form of: user mentions, hashtags, punctuation, digits, and hyperlinks, and eliminating this irrelevant information makes the data less complex and improves the performance of the classifier. Hence, in this work, punctuation, URLs, and stopwords are removed during pre-processing. Further, English stopwords available at NLTK library[2] and Telugu stopwords available at github[3] repository are used as references to remove English and Telugu stopwords from the given dataset. Further, the text in Roman script is converted to lowercase. The steps involved in building the proposed LR and Ensemble models are given below:

3.1 ML models

This section outlines the proposed LR and Ensemble models which are trained using feature vectors derived from n-grams of characters and words and sub-word tokens for identifying HOF content in code-mixed Telugu text and the steps are given below:

3.1.1 Feature Extraction

The role of feature extraction is to extract relevant features from the given data to train the learning models. Feature extraction techniques which are used to train LR and Ensemble models are described below:

- Character n-grams: are sequences of n consecutive characters. While one key stroke is enough to process each character in Roman script, characters in Indian languages like Telugu in its native script require more than one key stroke to process it. Therefore, in this work, to obtain character sequences for the given Telugu text where most of the text is in its native script, Telugu text is romanized using Indic transliterator[4] library. Subsequently, character n-grams in the range (1, 5) are obtained from the romanized Telugu text.
- Sub-word tokens: Sub-word tokenization algorithms prioritize breaking down rare words into smaller sub-word units, while leaving frequently used words (Bollegala et al., 2020). These algorithms are useful in representing both common and rare terms in a language. Therefore, this work utilizes Byte Pair Encoding algorithm to obtain sub-word tokens from the given Telugu text.
- Word n-grams: are sequences of 'n' consecutive words in a given text and these sequences capture the relationships between words. In this work, word sequences in the range (1, 3) are extracted from the given Telugu text.

The resultant character and word sequences and sub-words are vectorized using TFIDFVectorizer[5] and CountVectorizer[6] to construct the feature vectors.

3.1.2 Model Description

The proposed LR and Ensemble models are trained with the feature vectors obtained in the feature extraction step to classify the given code-mixed Telugu text as 'hate' or 'Non-hate' and description of each learning model is given below:

- **Logistic Regression (LR)** model: is used to predict the probability of certain classes based on dependent variables. The output of LR is always between (0 and 1), which is suitable for a binary classification task. Further, regularisation approaches in LR classifiers are useful for reducing overfitting in high dimensional space (Friedman et al., 2000).

[2]https://www.nltk.org/search.html?q=stopwords

[3]https://github.com/Xangis/extra-stopwords/blob/master/telugu

[4]https://github.com/libindic/indic-trans

[5]https://scikit-learn.org/stable/modules/generated/sklearn.feature_extraction.text.TfidfVectorizer.html

[6]https://scikit-learn.org/stable/modules/generated/sklearn.feature_extraction.text.CountVectorizer.html

Models	Development set			Test set		
	Precision	Recall	Macro F1 score	Precision	Recall	Macro F1 score
LR model	0.76	0.76	**0.76**	0.65	0.65	**0.65**
Ensemble model	0.73	0.73	0.72	0.55	0.54	0.53
HateExplain_TL	0.72	0.72	0.72	0.49	0.49	0.48

Table 2: Performances of the proposed models

Comment	English Translation	Actual Label	Predicted Label	Remarks
naani ee madhya Roja tho kalsi manchi punchlu vesthunnad ra, kaani avi pelaltla nagabaabugarru navvatla	Lately, Nani has been throwing good punches with Roja, but they are like the laughter of Naga Babu.	non-hate	hate	After removing the following stop words ('Lately', 'has', 'been', 'with', 'but', 'they', 'are', 'like', 'the', 'of') the content words, 'throwing' ,'punches', 'laughter' are associated with hate class and hence, the model has classified this comment as 'hate'.
అదే 420 పరిపాలన	Same 420 administration	hate	non-hate	'420' is a slang term that is often used in the negative tone and it is been removed during pre-processing. The remaining words are nothing to do with 'hate' class and hence may be the comment is classified as 'non-hate'

Table 3: Samples of misclassification for code-mixed Telugu texts with respect to LR model

- **Ensemble model**: is a strategy for building a new classifier from several heterogeneous base classifiers taking benefit of the strength of one classifier to overcome the weakness of another classifier to get better performance for the classification task (Li et al., 2018). In this work, three ML classifiers (MNB, LR, and GNB) are ensembled with hard voting for identifying HOF content in code-mixed Telugu text. MNB is a probability-based ML classifier suitable for classification problems involving text data with discrete characteristics like word frequency counts (Ali et al., 2021). GNB is a probabilistic ML algorithm that relies on the Bayes theorem. By assuming feature independence, GNB determines the likelihood that a sample will fall into each of the predefined classes (Jain and Sharma).

3.2 HateExplain_TL model

TL is a technique within the broader field of ML that leverages knowledge gained from one task to improve the performance of a related task. It involves using pretrained models as a starting point and fine-tuning them for a specific task or domain (Hegde et al., 2023). The proposed HateExplain_TL model utilizes a HateExplainBERT[7] model pretrained on Twitter and Human Rationales text data that contains hatred or offensive texts exclusively making this model suitable for detecting HOF content. This BERT variant is fine-tuned on the pre-processed Train set and is used to train transformer classifier (ClassificationModel) to make the predictions.

[7]https://huggingface.co/Hate-speech-CNERG/bert-base-uncased-hatexplain

4 Experiments and Results

The datasets provided by the shared task organizers for HOF content detection in Telugu code-mixed text consists of 2,061 samples belonging to 'Non-hate' class and 1,939 samples belonging to 'hate' class and 500 samples in the Test set. The sample code-mixed Telugu text, their English translations and the corresponding labels are shown in Table 1. Experiments are carried out, incorporating several feature combinations (sub-word count, word count, and character count), and classifiers (LR, SVM, k-Nearest Neighbors (k-NN), Ensemble (MNB, LR, and GNB), and HateExplain_TL). The models that showed considerable improvement on the Development set were subsequently tested on the Test set.

Predictions of the proposed models are evaluated based on macro F1 score and performances of the proposed models on Development and Test sets are shown in Table 2. The results reveal that LR model trained with TF-IDF of character and word sequences in the range (1, 5) and (1, 3) respectively, and sub-words, outperformed the other models with a macro F1 score of 0.65 securing 15th rank in the shared task. Few misclassified comments along with the actual and predicted labels (obtained from evaluating LR model on the given Test set) are shown in Table 3. It can be observed that most of the wrong classifications are due to removing stopwords and digits. Further, lack of context may also lead to misclassification in addition to rare words and wrong annotations.

5 Conclusion and Future Work

This paper describes the models submitted by our team - MUCS, to "Hate and Offensive Language Detection in Telugu Codemixed Text (HOLD-Telugu)" shared task at Dravidian-LangTech@EACL 2024, to identify HOF content in code-mixed Telugu text. Three models: i) LR model - a ML algorithm trained with TF-IDF of character and word sequences in the range (1, 5) and (1, 3) respectively and sub-words, ii) Ensemble model - a combination of ML classifiers (MNB, LR, and GNB) trained with CountVectorizer of character and word sequences in the range (1, 5) and (1, 3) respectively, iii) HateExplain_TL - a model based on TL approach with a BERT variant, are submitted to the shared task for detecting HOF content in Telugu code-mixed text. The proposed LR model outperformed the other models with a macro F1 score of 0.65 for Telugu code-mixed text. Effective feature extraction techniques and classifiers will be explored further.

References

Muhammad Z Ali, Sahar Rauf, Kashif Javed, Sarmad Hussain, et al. 2021. Improving Hate Speech Detection of Urdu Tweets Using Sentiment Analysis. In *IEEE Access*, volume 9, pages 84296–84305. IEEE.

Premjth B, Bharathi Raja, Prasanna Kumar Kumaresan, Saranya Rajiakodi, Sai Prashanth Karnati, Sai Rishith Reddy Mangamuru, and Janakiram Chandu. 2024. Findings of the shared task on hate and offensive language detection in telugu codemixed text (hold-telugu). In *Proceedings of the Fourth Workshop on Speech, Vision, and Language Technologies for Dravidian Languages*, Malta. European Chapter of the Association for Computational Linguistics.

Somnath Banerjee, Maulindu Sarkar, Nancy Agrawal, Punyajoy Saha, and Mithun Das. 2021. Exploring Transformer Based Models to Identify Hate Speech and Offensive Content in English and Indo-Aryan Languages. In *arXiv preprint arXiv:2111.13974*.

Snehaan Bhawal, Pradeep Roy, and Abhinav Kumar. 2021. Hate Speech and Offensive Language Identification on Multilingual Code-mixed Text using BERT. In *Working Notes of FIRE 2021-Forum for Information Retrieval Evaluation (Online). CEUR*.

Danushka Bollegala, Ryuichi Kiryo, Kosuke Tsujino, and Haruki Yukawa. 2020. Language-Independent Tokenisation Rivals Language-Specific Tokenisation for Word Similarity Prediction. In *arXiv preprint arXiv:2002.11004*.

V Dikshitha Vani and B Bharathi. 2022. Hate Speech and Offensive Content Identification in Multiple Languages using machine learning algorithms. In *Forum for Information Retrieval Evaluation (Working Notes)(FIRE). CEUR-WS. org*.

Jerome Friedman, Trevor Hastie, and Robert Tibshirani. 2000. Additive Logistic Regression: A Statistical View of Boosting (With Discussion and a Rejoinder by the Authors). In *The annals of statistics*, volume 28, pages 337–407. Institute of Mathematical Statistics.

Asha Hegde, G Kavya, Sharal Coelho, and Hosahalli Lakshmaiah Shashirekha. 2023. MUCS@DravidianLangTech2023: Leveraging Learning Models to Identify Abusive Comments in Code-mixed Dravidian Languages. In *Proceedings of the Third Workshop on Speech and Language Technologies for Dravidian Languages*, pages 266–274.

Archika Jain and Sandhya Sharma. Hasoc19: Hate Speech Detection on Multimodal Dataset.

Ming Li, Peilun Xiao, and Ju Zhang. 2018. Text Classification based on Ensemble Extreme Learning Machine. In *arXiv preprint arXiv:1805.06525*.

Varsha Pathak, Manish Joshi, Prasad Joshi, Monica Mundada, and Tanmay Joshi. 2021. KBCNMU-JAL@ HASOC-Dravidian-CodeMix-FIRE20: Using Machine Learning for Detection of Hate Speech and Offensive Code-mixed Social Media. In *arXiv preprint arXiv:2102.09866*.

Bharathi Raja andS Malliga andCN SUBALALITHA Priyadharshini, Ruba andChakravarthi, Premjith and-Murugappan Abirami S V, Kogilavani andB, and Prasanna Kumar Kumaresan. 2023a. Overview of shared-task on abusive comment detection in tamil and telugu. In *Proceedings of the Third Workshop on Speech and Language Technologies for Dravidian Languages*, Varna, Bulgaria. Recent Advances in Natural Language Processing.

Ruba Priyadharshini, Bharathi Raja Chakravarthi, S Malliga, Subalalitha Cn, SV Kogilavani, B Premjith, Abirami Murugappan, and Prasanna Kumar Kumaresan. 2023b. Overview of Shared-task on Abusive Comment Detection in Tamil and Telugu. In *Proceedings of the Third Workshop on Speech and Language Technologies for Dravidian Languages*, pages 80–87.

Pradeep Kumar Roy, Snehaan Bhawal, and Chinnaudayar Navaneethakrishnan Subalalitha. 2022. Hate Speech and Offensive Language Detection in Dravidian Languages using Deep Ensemble Framework. In *Computer Speech & Language*, volume 75, page 101386. Elsevier.

Abhishek Velankar, Hrushikesh Patil, Amol Gore, Shubham Salunke, and Raviraj Joshi. 2021. Hate and Offensive Speech Detection in Hindi and Marathi. In *arXiv preprint arXiv:2110.12200*.

MUCS@DravidianLangTech-2024: A Grid Search Approach to Explore Sentiment Analysis in Code-mixed Tamil and Tulu

Prathvi B[a], **Manavi K K**[b], **Subrahmanya**[c],
Asha Hegde[d], **Kavya G**[e], **H L Shashirekha**[f]
Department of Computer Science, Mangalore University, Mangalore, Karnataka, India
{[a]bprathvi968, [b]kkmanavi, [c]subrahmanyapoojary789}@gmail.com,
{[d]hegdekasha, [e]kavyamujk}@gmail.com, [f]hlsrekha@mangaloreuniversity.ac.in

Abstract

Sentiment Analysis (SA) is a field of computational study that analyzes users' reviews, opinions, and emotions, towards any entity on online platforms. As user sentiments play a major role in decision making, there is an increasing demand for the tools that can effectively analyze the user-generated sentiments. The availability of user-generated code-mixed sentiments in low-resource languages like Tamil and Tulu further necessitates the growing need for efficient SA tools. To address SA in code-mixed Tamil and Tulu text, this paper describes the Machine Learning (ML) models submitted by our team - MUCS to "Sentiment Analysis in Tamil and Tulu - DravidianLangTech" - a shared task organized at European Chapter of the Association for Computational Linguistics (EACL) 2024. Two models: i) Linear Support Vector Classifier (LinearSVC) and ii) Ensemble of ML classifiers (k Nearest Neighbour (kNN), Stochastic Gradient Descent (SGD), Logistic Regression (LR), LinearSVC, and Random Forest Classifier (RFC)) with hard voting, are trained individually with the features obtained by the concatenation of TfidfVectorizer and CountVectorizer of word and character n-grams, for SA in code-mixed Tamil and Tulu texts. Gridsearch method is employed to get the best hyperparameter values for the proposed classifiers. Among the two models, the proposed Ensemble models achieved macro F1 scores of 0.260 and 0.550 for Tamil and Tulu languages respectively.

1 Introduction

SA is the process of examining opinions, emotions, and reviews to recognise the sentiments expressed by the users regarding a topic, movie, song, product, etc., available on online platforms (Chakravarthi et al., 2021). This user-generated content is used by businesses and individuals to gain knowledge and make well-informed decisions regarding their content (Mahadzir et al., 2021). The user sentiments are usually available in code-mixed language where words and/or sub-words belong to more than one language. Processing the code-mixed user-generated content to develop SA models poses a significant challenge (Hegde and Shashirekha, 2022). This is especially notable when addressing SA in low-resource languages such as Tulu, Tamil, Malayalam, and Telugu (Ka et al., 2023).

To address the challenges of detecting SA in user-generated code-mixed low-resource languages, in this paper, we - team MUCS, describe ML models submitted to the shared task "Sentiment Analysis in Tamil and Tulu - DravidianLangTech@EACL-2024" (S. K. et al., 2024). This shared task is modeled as a multi-class text classification problem with two distinct models: i) LinearSVC and ii) Ensemble of ML classifiers (kNN, SGD, LR, LinearSVC, and RFC) with hard voting, trained individually with the features obtained by the concatenation of TfidfVectorizer[1] and CountVectorizer[2] of word and character n-grams, for SA in code-mixed Tamil and Tulu texts. In addition, the Gridsearch method is used to find the ideal values for the hyperparameters of these classifiers.

The rest of the paper is organized as follows: while Section 2 describes the related works of SA, Section 3 focuses on the description of the models submitted to the shared task followed by the experiments and results in Section 4. The conclusion and future works are included in Section 5.

2 Related Work

Several ML models are experimented with various features for SA of user-generated content in code-mixed low-resource languages (Hegde et al., 2023a). Some of the relevant works are outlined

[1]https://scikit-learn.org/stable/modules/generated/sklearn.feature_extraction.text.TfidfVectorizer.html

[2]https://scikit-learn.org/stable/modules/generated/sklearn.feature_extraction.text.CountVectorizer.html

Proceedings of the Fourth Workshop on Speech, Vision, and Language Technologies for Dravidian Languages, pages 257–261
March 22, 2024

below:
Ponnusamy et al. (2023) proposed ML models (LR, Multinomial Naive Bayes (MNB), and LinearSVC) trained with Term Frequency-Inverse Document Frequency (TF-IDF) of word unigrams for SA in Tamil and Tulu languages. Their proposed LR, MNB, and LinearSVC models obtained macro F1 scores of 0.43, 0.20, 0.41 and 0.51, 0.25, 0.49 for Tamil and Tulu languages respectively. Coelho et al. (2023) used ML models (LinearSVC, LR, and an Ensemble model (LR, Decision Tree (DT), and Support Vector Machine (SVM)) with hard voting), trained with TF-IDF of word unigrams achieving macro F1 scores of 0.189 and 0.508 for code-mixed Tamil and Tulu texts respectively. Ehsan et al. (2023) implemented Bidirectional Long Short-Term Memory (BiLSTM) networks for SA of code-mixed Tamil and Tulu text, utilizing contextualized Elmo representations and obtained macro F1 scores of 0.2877 and 0.5133 for Tamil and Tulu code-mixed datasets respectively. Hegde et al. (2023b) implemented three models: i) n-gramsSA (LinearSVC trained with TF-IDF, ii) EmbeddingsSA (LinearSVC trained with fastText and Byte Pair embeddings), and iii) BERTSA (a transformer classifier trained with Bidirectional Encoder Representations from Transformer (BERT) embeddings) and obtained macro F1 scores of 0.26 and 0.53 for Tamil using BERTSA model and for Tulu using EmbeddingsSA model respectively.

Puranik et al. (2021) fine-tuned: the Universal Language Model Fine-Tuning (ULMFiT) and multilingual BERT (mBERT) models, the two pre-trained models for SA in code-mixed Kannada, Tamil, and Malayalam and obtained macro F1 scores of 0.63, 0.65, and 0.70, respectively. Garain et al. (2020) presented the Support Vector Regression model (SVR) model with Grid Search approach, trained with TF-IDF of word unigrams and GloVe word vector features, for Hindi code-mixed sentences and obtained a macro F1 score of 0.662.

The related work reveals that the performances of SA models for code-mixed low-resource languages are still low, indicating the scope for developing models to improve the performance further.

3 Methodology

The proposed methodology for SA in code-mixed Tamil and Tulu texts include: Pre-processing, Feature Extraction (FE), and Classifier Construction. The framework of the proposed methodology is shown in Figure 1 and the steps are explained below:

Language	Sample Text	Label
Tamil	நம்ப நடே நாசாமா தான் போச்சி	Negative
	ennaya trailer Ku mudi Ellam nikkudhu... Vera	Positive
Tulu	Tulu panda enku masth ista i love tulu tulunadu	Positive
	Bega 2 nd part padle	Neutral

Table 1: Sample code-mixed Tamil and Tulu comments along with the corresponding labels

3.1 Pre-processing

During pre-processing, punctuation, digits, user mentions, and hashtags are removed to clean the text. English stopwords available at Natural Language Tool Kit (NLTK)[3] library and Tamil[4] stopwords from a GitHub repository are utilized as references for filtering out English and Tamil stopwords in Tamil dataset respectively and English stopwords from Tulu text. As the given dataset is code-mixed, English words will be present in the dataset. Additionally, emojis are converted to English text using the demoji library. The resulting pre-processed text is then used for FE.

3.2 Feature Extraction

FE involves extracting distinguishing characteristics from the given data and the performance of the classifiers depends on the quality of the features. n-grams refers to 'n' consecutive lexical units where th lexical units are words or characters. These word/character n-grams capture the local context by following sequential patterns, facilitating a deeper understanding of relationships between words/characters (Bahdanau et al., 2014). Choosing the right value for 'n' in n-grams is crucial for capturing contextual relationships between the words/characters and the selection of 'n' depends on the desired level of context. While the higher 'n' value provide more extensive context at the cost of increased computational complexity, lower 'n' value focus on shorter and more immediate relationships (Nagao and Mori, 1994). In this work, word n-grams in the range (1, 3) are obtained.

As the given Tamil and Tulu dataset includes text in native script, they are romanized using libindic[5] library and character n-grams in the range (1, 5)

[3]https://pythonspot.com/nltk-stop-words/
[4]https://gist.github.com/arulrajnet/e82a5a331f78a5cc9b6d372df13a919c
[5]https://github.com/libindic/indic-trans

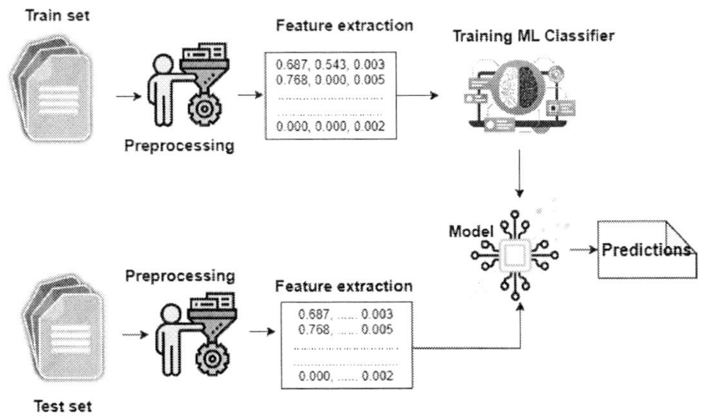

Figure 1: Framework of the proposed methodology

Classifier	Hyperparameters and values
LinearSVC	class_weight = balanced, C = 1
RFC	criterion = gini, max_depth = 8, max_features = log2, n_estimators = 200, class_weight = balanced
LR	C = 3, penalty = l2, class_weight = balanced,
kNN	n_neighbors = 7, p = 2, weights = distance
SGD	class_weight = balanced, loss = log, penalty = elasticnet, alpha = 4, l1_ratio = 0.1

Table 2: Hyperparameter values obtained from Gridsearch algorithm

	Labels	Tamil	Tulu
Train set	**Positive**	20,070	3,352
	Negative	4,271	698
	Unknown state	5,628	1,854
	Mixed Feeling	4,020	1,041
Dev set	**Positive**	2,257	231
	Negative	480	55
	Unknown state	611	124
	Mixed Feeling	438	90

Table 3: Class-wise distribution of Tamil and Tulu datasets

are obtained from the romanized Tamil and Tulu texts. The word and character n-grams are vectorized using TfidfVectorizer and CountVectorizer and the resulting vectors are concatenated to train the learning models. The sample code-mixed Tamil and Tulu comments along with their corresponding labels are shown in Table 1.

3.3 Classifier Construction

This work utilizes LinearSVC and an Ensemble of ML classifiers (RFC, LR, kNN, SGD), for SA in code-mixed Tamil and Tulu texts. A brief description of the classifiers is given below:

- LinearSVC - uses a linear kernel function, which calculates the dot product between data points in the feature space. This makes it particularly effective for high-dimensional datasets and situations where the relationship between features and classes is approximately linear (Hegde et al., 2023b).

- Ensemble - is a method of generating a new classifier using a pool of classifiers such that the strength of one classifier is used to overcome the weakness of other classifier, with the objective of obtaining a better classification performance (Hegde and Shashirekha, 2021). When compared to the performance of individual baseline classifier in the ensemble, this configuration of several classifiers will perform better. As the Ensemble model uses more than one classifier to predict class labels for an unlabeled sample, it is also called a voting classifier.

Optimal hyperparameter values are obtained by employing gridsearch[6] algorithm and the hyperparameters and their values used for the classifiers are shown in Table 2.

[6]https://scikit-learn.org/stable/modules/generated/sklearn.model_selection.GridSearchCV.html

Language	Model	Precision	Recall	Macro F1-score
Tamil	LinearSVC	0.284	0.263	0.252
	Ensemble	0.291	0.279	**0.260**
Tulu	LinearSVC	0.546	0.546	0.546
	Ensemble	0.548	0.554	**0.550**

Table 4: Performance of the proposed models for code-mixed Tamil and Tulu texts

4 Experiments and Results

Code-mixed Tamil and Tulu SA datasets are provided by the organizers of the shared task and statistics of the datasets are shown in Table 3. Using these datasets, several experiments were conducted by employing various FE techniques and classifiers. Combination of features and classifiers which gave good performance on the Development (Dev) sets are used to train the proposed models. The proposed models are evaluated on the Test set and the predictions are assessed by the organizers based on macro F1-score for the final evaluation and ranking. Performance of the proposed models for both Tamil and Tulu datasets are shown in Table 4. Ensemble models outperformed the LinearSVC models obtaining macro F1 scores of 0.260 and 0.550 securing 1st and 2nd ranks in the shared task for Tamil and Tulu languages respectively. Though class_weight is set to 'balanced' for both the classifiers, the extreme data imbalance in the given datasets has lead to low macro F1 scores.

4.1 Error Analysis

The confusion matrix reveals the percentage of classification error obtained by the learning model. As the Ensemble models performed better than the LinearSVC model, confusion matrix is shown for Ensemble model. The confusion matrix for code-mixed Tamil texts is shown in Figure 2. The results reveal that the Ensemble model exhibits a relatively weak True Positive Rate (TPR) of 38.61% for the 'Mixed Feelings' class (though it is the highest rate among the TPRs obtained across all the classes) indicating lower performance of the proposed model. This may be due to extreme data imbalance in the training set. Additionally, the model faces difficulty in identifying 'Unknown state' class by exhibiting a notably low TPR of 13% for this class, as the learning model fails to distinguish between 'Unknown state' and 'Mixed Feelings' sentiments.

The confusion matrix for code-mixed Tulu texts is shown in Figure 3. The results reveal that the Ensemble model exhibits a good performance with a TPR of 79.44% for the 'Positive' class. However, the model fails to distinguish between 'Mixed Feelings' and 'Neutral' sentiments, as reflected in a lower TPR of 37.14% for the 'Mixed Feelings' class.

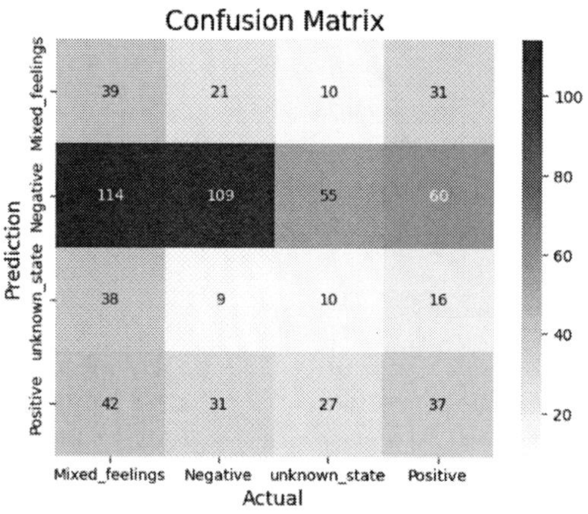

Figure 2: Confusion matrix of the proposed Ensemble model for code-mixed Tamil text

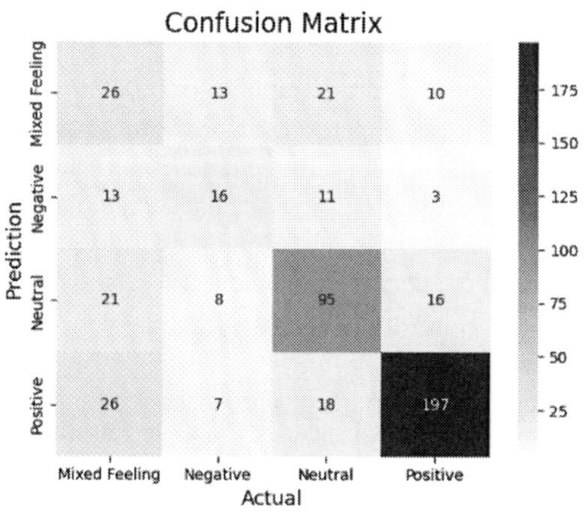

Figure 3: Confusion matrix of the proposed Ensemble model for code-mixed Tulu text

5 Conclusion and Future Work

This paper describes the models submitted by our team MUCS to "Sentiment Analysis in Tamil and Tulu - DravidianLangTech@EACL-2024" shared task. The proposed methodology consists of using LinearSVC and Ensemble of ML classifiers with hard voting, trained individually with the features obtained by the concatenation of TfidfVectorizer and CountVectorizer of word and character n-grams. Further, in order to get the optimal hyperparameter values for these classifiers, the Gridsearch method is used during training. The proposed Ensemble models exhibited macro F1 scores of 0.260 and 0.550 securing 1st and 2nd ranks in the shared task for Tamil and Tulu languages respectively. Suitable oversampling or text augmentation techniques will be explored further to improve the performance of the proposed models.

References

Dzmitry Bahdanau, Kyunghyun Cho, and Yoshua Bengio. 2014. Neural Machine Translation by Jointly Learning to Align and Translate. In *arXiv preprint arXiv:1409.0473*.

Bharathi Raja Chakravarthi, Ruba Priyadharshini, Sajeetha Thavareesan, Dhivya Chinnappa, Durairaj Thenmozhi, Elizabeth Sherly, John P McCrae, Adeep Hande, Rahul Ponnusamy, Shubhanker Banerjee, et al. 2021. Findings of the sentiment analysis of dravidian languages in code-mixed text. In *arXiv preprint arXiv:2111.09811*.

Sharal Coelho, Asha Hegde, Pooja Lamani, G Kavya, and Hosahalli Lakshmaiah Shashirekha. 2023. MUCSD@DravidianLangTech2023: Predicting Sentiment in Social Media Text using Machine Learning Techniques. In *Proceedings of the Third Workshop on Speech and Language Technologies for Dravidian Languages*, pages 282–287.

Toqeer Ehsan, Amina Tehseen, Kengatharaiyer Sarveswaran, and Amjad Ali. 2023. Sentiment Analysis of Code-Mixed Tamil and Tulu by Training Contextualized ELMo Representations. In *RANLP'2023*, page 152.

Avishek Garain, Sainik Kumar Mahata, and Dipankar Das. 2020. JUNLP@ SemEval-2020 Task 9: Sentiment Analysis of Hindi-English Code Mixed Data using Grid Search Cross Validation.

Asha Hegde, Bharathi Raja Chakravarthi, Hosahalli Lakshmaiah Shashirekha, Rahul Ponnusamy, Subalalitha Cn, SK Lavanya, Durairaj Thenmozhi, Martha Karunakar, Shreya Shreeram, and Sarah Aymen. 2023a. Findings of the Shared Task on Sentiment Analysis in Tamil and Tulu Code-Mixed Text. In *Proceedings of the Third Workshop on Speech and Language Technologies for Dravidian Languages*, pages 64–71.

Asha Hegde, G Kavya, Sharal Coelho, Pooja Lamani, and Hosahalli Lakshmaiah Shashirekha. 2023b. MUNLP@DravidianLangTech2023: Learning Approaches for Sentiment Analysis in Code-mixed Tamil and Tulu Text. In *Proceedings of the Third Workshop on Speech and Language Technologies for Dravidian Languages*, pages 275–281.

Asha Hegde and Hosahalli Lakshmaiah Shashirekha. 2021. Urdu Fake News Detection Using Ensemble of Machine Learning Models. In *CEUR Workshop Proceedings*, pages 132–141.

Asha Hegde and Hosahalli Lakshmaiah Shashirekha. 2022. Leveraging Dynamic Meta Embedding for Sentiment Analysis and Detection of Homophobic. In *Transphobic Content in Code-mixed Dravidian Languages*.

Rachana Ka, Prajnashree Mb, Asha Hegdec, and HL Shashirekhad. 2023. MUCS@ DravidianLangTech2023: Sentiment Analysis in Code-mixed Tamil and Tulu Texts using fastText. In *RANLP'2023*, page 258.

Nurul Husna Mahadzir et al. 2021. Sentiment Analysis of Code-Mixed Text: A Review. In *Turkish Journal of Computer and Mathematics Education (TURCOMAT)*, volume 12, pages 2469–2478.

Makoto Nagao and Shinsuke Mori. 1994. A New Method of N-gram Statistics for Large Number of n and Automatic Extraction of Words and Phrases from Large Text Data of Japanese. In *COLING 1994 Volume 1: The 15th International Conference on Computational Linguistics*.

Kishore Kumar Ponnusamy, Charmathi Rajkumar, Prasanna Kumar Kumaresan, Elizabeth Sherly, and Ruba Priyadharshini. 2023. VEL@ DravidianLangTech: Sentiment Analysis of Tamil and Tulu. In *Proceedings of the Third Workshop on Speech and Language Technologies for Dravidian Languages*, pages 211–216.

Karthik Puranik et al. 2021. IIITT@ DravidianCodeMix-FIRE2021: Transliterate or Translate? Sentiment Analysis of Code-mixed Text in Dravidian Languages. In *arXiv preprint arXiv:2111.07906*.

Lavanya S. K., Asha Hegde, Bharathi Raja Chakravarthi, Hosahalli Lakshmaiah Shashirekha, Rajeswari Natarajan, Sajeetha Thavareesan, Ratnasingam Sakuntharaj, Thenmozhi Durairaj, and Rajkumar Charmathi Kumaresan, Prasanna Kumar. 2024. Overview of Second Shared Task on Sentiment Analysis in Code-mixed Tamil and Tulu. In *Proceedings of the Fourth Workshop on Speech, Vision, and Language Technologies for Dravidian Languages*, Malta. European Chapter of the Association for Computational Linguistics.

InnovationEngineers@DravidianLangTech-EACL 2024: Sentimental Analysis of YouTube Comments in Tamil by using Machine Learning

Kogilavani Shanmugavadivel[1], Malliga Subramanian[1], Palanimurugan V[1], Pavul chinnappan D[1]
[1]Department of AI, Kongu Engineering College, Perundurai, Erode.
{kogilavani.sv, mallinishanth72}@gmail.com
{palanimuruganv.22aid, pavulchinnappand.22aid}@kongu.edu

Abstract

There is opportunity for machine learning and natural language processing research because of the growing volume of textual data. Although there has been little research done on trend extraction from YouTube comments, sentiment analysis is an intriguing issue because of the poor consistency and quality of the material found there.The purpose of this work is to use machine learning techniques and algorithms to do sentiment analysis on YouTube comments pertaining to popular themes.The findings demonstrate that sentiment analysis is capable of giving a clear picture of how actual events affect public opinion. This study aims to make it easier for academics to find high-quality sentiment analysis research publications.Data normalisation methods are used to clean an annotated corpus of 3200 citation sentences for the study.A system that uses the machine learning algorithms K-Nearest Neighbor (KNN), Naïve Bayes, SVC (Support Vector Machine), and RandomForest is constructed for classification. The accuracy of the system is evaluated using metrics such as the f1-score and correctness score.

1 Introduction

In the dynamic realm of social media, the role of sentiment analysis is increasingly crucial in comprehending the subtleties of user expressions. Traditionally designed for high-resource languages and individual utterances, sentiment analysis tools are encountering new challenges amid bilingual communities and code-mixed writing styles. This project addresses the growing significance of sentiment analysis, specifically focusing on code-mixed Tamil-English expressions prevalent across various social media platforms. Supervised learning approaches, traditionally reliant on annotated data, face limitations when applied to code-mixed languages. Notably, features based on lexical attributes, such as word dictionaries and parts of speech tagging, exhibit suboptimal performance in this multilingual context. To overcome these challenges, our research focuses on sentiment analysis within code-mixed Tamil-English contexts. Central to our approach is the implementation of the Decision Tree algorithm, which offers a robust solution for accurately classifying sentiments within this unique linguistic fusion. This project not only demonstrates exceptional accuracy using detailed metrics like precision, recall, and F1-score but also introduces a substantial corpus for under-resourced code- mixed Tanglish. Marked by high inter-annotator agreement, this dataset serves as a valuable resource for researchers delving into sentiment analysis and linguistic phenomena in code-mixed environments. Positioned at the intersection of sentiment analysis, machine learning, and code-mixed language research, our project extends beyond precise sentiment classification. It serves as a foundational resource for future investigations into the dynamic landscape of multilingual social media expressions.

2 Literature Survey

Certainly, here's a brief list of literature surveys by various authors focusing on sentiment analysis in Tamil Nadu:

The research paper work in Thavareesan and Mahesan (2021) demonstrates a sentiment analysis technique for Tamil texts utilising k-means clustering and k-nearest neighbour classifier. Despite different settings, the technique achieved an accuracy of 89.87% for the UJ_MovieReviews corpus utilising fastText and class-wise clustering. The main focus of the paper present in Kausikaa and Uma (2016) is sentiment analysis, a natural language processing task that involves determining the sentiment or emotion expressed in a given piece of text. In this case, the analysis is applied to tweets in both English and Tamil.It is discovered that the suggested system's F-measure accuracy value, which

Proceedings of the Fourth Workshop on Speech, Vision, and Language Technologies for Dravidian Languages, pages 262–265
March 22, 2024 ©2024 Association for Computational Linguistics

makes use of SVM, is 0.741. The primary focus of the paper work in Se et al. (2016)is on sentiment analysis, particularly suited to data with mixed Tamil codes. The term "code-mixing" describes the typical practice in multilingual cultures of combining two or more languages into a single statement or speech. SVM achieves 75.9% classification accuracy for Tamil movie reviews, a noteworthy achievement in Tamil language study. The primary focus of the paper repersent in Shanmugavadivel et al. (2022) is on sentiment analysis,particularly applicable to data with mixed Tamil codes. Code-mixing, a prevalent practice in multilingual cultures, is the blending of two or more languages inside a single statement or speech.The outcome shows that, with an accuracy of 0.66 using pre-processed Tamil code-mixed data, the hybrid deep learning model in particular, the CNN+BiLSTM model performs better than all the other models used.

The paper in Soumya and Pramod (2020) A review of machine learning methods for sentiment analysis of data with mixed Tamil codes This study examines the impact of pre-processing on Tamil code-mixed data using transfer learning, hybrid deep learning, deep learning, and traditional machine learning models. The study concentrates on removing emojis, punctuation, symbols, numerals, and repeating characters from the data. The hybrid deep learning model CNN+BiLSTM performs better with pre-processed Tamil code-mixed data, with an accuracy of 0.66. The study compares the performance of these models with the state-of-the-art methods, including IndicBERT, logistic regression, random forest, multinomial Naive Bayes, and linear support vector classification. In order to increase the accuracy of sentiment analysis on social media data, future research should focus on multimodal data sets and context-based algorithms.

The primary focus of the paper work in Se et al. (2016) is predicting sentiment in reviews related to Tamil movies using machine learning algorithms.with accurancy For categorising Tamil movie reviews, SVM yields a 75.9% accuracy rate.

The paper inChakravarthi et al. (2020b)The Dravidian-CodeMix-FIRE 2020 track focused on sentiment analysis for code-mixed Tamil and Malayalam in YouTube comments. Researchers aimed to classify sentiments using a weighted-F1 score, addressing linguistic complexities.

The primary focus of the paper work inChakravarthi et al. (2020a) sentiment in social media comments is crucial for decision-making. This study addresses challenges in sentiment analysis, especially in code-mixed text from low-resourced languages like Tamil, presenting a benchmark corpus and sentiment analysis results.

The paper in Hegde et al. (2022)Sentiment Analysis (SA) uses code-mixed data from social media for decision-making. However, low-resource languages like Tulu struggle with annotated data. A gold standard corpus of 7,171 Tulu comments is created, and Machine Learning algorithms are used to evaluate the dataset, showing encouraging performance.

3 Problem and System Description

The objective of the sentiment analysis project is to automatically analyse and categorize the sentiment expressed in a given text. The sentiment is classified into categories such as "Positive", "Negative" or "Unknown State." The project aims to leverage machine learning, specifically the KNN algorithm, to accurately predict the sentiment of textual data.

TEXT	CATEGORY
Thalavaa neenga veera level boss and neega thaan marana mass That bgm..	Positive
Do or Die	Negative
Sema trailer fun movie Comali blockbuster 90s kids like	Unknown_State

Table 1: Dataset Description

4 Dataset Description

The training dataset comprises 33990 samples of code-mixed Tamil-English language, spanning diverse topics, with sentiment labels including Positive, Negative, Mixed Feelings, and Unknown State. The text data underwent TF-IDF vectorization, resulting in the creation of the `train_tfdf` matrix. The Decision Tree classifier demonstrated exceptional accuracy, achieving approximately 99.97% on the training data. The test dataset comprises 649 samples of code-mixed Tamil-English language. Each sample includes a text segment unseen during training, serving to assess the model's generalization to new data. The dataset includes predicted sentiment labels generated by the trained Decision Tree classifier, indicating the model's predictions for the sentiments expressed in the text segments.

5 Predictions on Test Data

Text Segments: The test dataset consists of 649 text segments in code-mixed Tamil-English language. Prediction Labels: Predicted sentiment labels were generated using the trained Decision Tree classifier, categorizing each text segment into sentiments such as Positive, Negative, Mixed Feelings, or Unknown State. Model Generalization: The predictions on the test data showcase the model's ability to generalize its learned patterns to previously unseen text, providing insights into its performance on real-world, diverse language expressions. Evaluation: The predicted sentiment labels can be compared with the ground truth labels, if available, to assess the model's accuracy and performance on this new, independent dataset.

6 Workflow

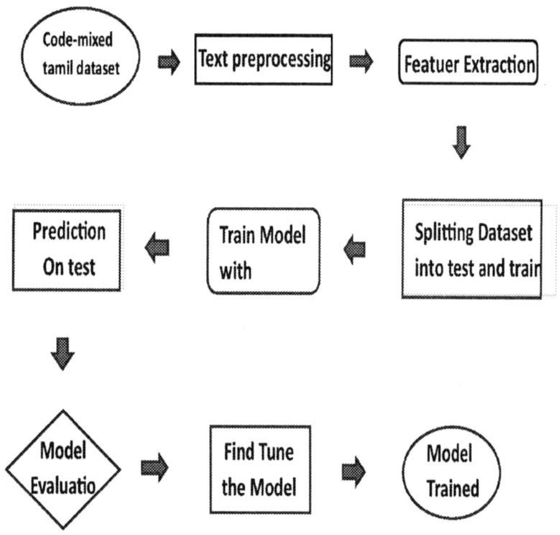

Figure 1: Processed workflow

7 Result

The sentiment is classified into categories such as Positive,Negative, or Unknown State by using different types of machine learning algorithm.

7.1 KNN report

Algorithm used	Accuracy
KNN	0.7345812952815269

Class Label	Precision	Recall	f1 score
Mixed Feelings	0.35	0.01	0.01
Positive	0.23	0.01	0.01
Negative	0.61	0.96	0.74
Unknown State	0.52	0.19	0.28

7.2 NAIVE BAYES report

Algorithm used	Accuracy
Naivebayes	0.598705501618123

Class Label	Precision	Recall	f1-score
Mixed Feelings	0.5	0.002	0.0024
Positive	0.78	0.029	0.056
Negative	0.596	0.99	0.746
Unknown State	0.76	0.031	0.060

7.3 SVC report

Algorithm used	Accuracy
SVC	0.6301853486319505

Class Label	Precision	Recall	f1-score
Mixed Feelings	0.537	0.035	0.066
Positive	0.535	0.148	0.233
Negative	0.634	0.963	0.765
Unknown State	0.632	0.232	0.339

7.4 Randomforest report

Algorithm used	Accuracy
Randomforest	0.99973589910195

Class Label	Precision	Recall	f1-score
Mixed Feelings	1.0	1.0	1.0
Positive	1.0	1.0	1.0
Negative	1.0	1.0	1.0
Unknown State	1.0	1.0	1.0

8 Conclusion

The project analyzes sentiment using the RandomForest Tree technique, and it achieves remarkable accuracy in a variety of classes. Important parameters including precision, recall, and F1-score are shown in its thorough classification report. The project has the potential to influence linguistic study and is a useful resource for code-mixed research with a carefully annotated dataset. Nonetheless, it encounters obstacles like as overfitting and broad generalization to other settings. Despite these, the project is a commendable addition to sentiment analysis in code-mixed languages because of its solid base and available resources.

References

Bharathi Raja Chakravarthi, Vigneshwaran Muralidaran, Ruba Priyadharshini, and John P McCrae. 2020a. Corpus creation for sentiment analysis in code-mixed tamil-english text. *arXiv preprint arXiv:2006.00206*.

Bharathi Raja Chakravarthi, Ruba Priyadharshini, Vigneshwaran Muralidaran, Shardul Suryawanshi, Navya Jose, Elizabeth Sherly, and John P McCrae. 2020b. Overview of the track on sentiment analysis for dravidian languages in code-mixed text. In *Proceedings of the 12th Annual Meeting of the Forum for Information Retrieval Evaluation*, pages 21–24.

Asha Hegde, Mudoor Devadas Anusha, Sharal Coelho, Hosahalli Lakshmaiah Shashirekha, and Bharathi Raja Chakravarthi. 2022. Corpus creation for sentiment analysis in code-mixed tulu text. In *Proceedings of the 1st Annual Meeting of the ELRA/ISCA Special Interest Group on Under-Resourced Languages*, pages 33–40.

N Kausikaa and V Uma. 2016. Sentiment analysis of english and tamil tweets using path length similarity based word sense disambiguation. *International Organization of Scientific Research Journal*, 1:82–89.

Shriya Se, R Vinayakumar, M Anand Kumar, and KP Soman. 2016. Predicting the sentimental reviews in tamil movie using machine learning algorithms. *Indian journal of science and technology*, 9(45):1–5.

Kogilavani Shanmugavadivel, Sai Haritha Sampath, Pramod Nandhakumar, Prasath Mahalingam, Malliga Subramanian, Prasanna Kumar Kumaresan, and Ruba Priyadharshini. 2022. An analysis of machine learning models for sentiment analysis of tamil code-mixed data. *Computer Speech & Language*, 76:101407.

S Soumya and KV Pramod. 2020. Sentiment analysis of malayalam tweets using machine learning techniques. *ICT Express*, 6(4):300–305.

Sajeetha Thavareesan and Sinnathamby Mahesan. 2021. Sentiment analysis in tamil texts using k-means and k-nearest neighbour. In *2021 10th International Conference on Information and Automation for Sustainability (ICIAfS)*, pages 48–53. IEEE.

KEC_HAWKS@DravidianLangTech 2024 : Detecting Malayalam Fake News using Machine Learning Models

Malliga Subramanian, Jayanth J R, Muthu Karuppan P,
KeerthiBala A T, Kogilavani Shanmugavadivel
Kongu Engineering College
Tamil Nadu
India
{mallisenthil.cse, jayanthjr.21cse, muthukaruppanp.21cse,
keerthibalaat.21cse, kogilavani.cse}@kongu.edu

Abstract

The proliferation of fake news in the Malayalam language across digital platforms has emerged as a pressing issue. By employing Recurrent Neural Networks (RNNs), a type of machine learning model, we aim to distinguish between Original and Fake News in Malayalam and achieved 9th rank in Task 1. RNNs are chosen for their ability to understand the sequence of words in a sentence, which is important in languages like Malayalam. Our main goal is to develop better models that can spot fake news effectively. We analyze various features to understand what contributes most to this accuracy. By doing so, we hope to provide a reliable method for identifying and combating fake news in the Malayalam language.

1 Introduction

In today's digital age, the proliferation of fake news has emerged as a significant challenge, disrupting the flow of accurate information and eroding public trust in media sources. In this study, the shared task is to determine the authenticity of news articles in the Malayalam language, distinguishing between fake and original news. Leveraging deep learning techniques, particularly Recurrent Neural Networks (RNNs), we preprocess the data using tokenization and padding techniques. Our model, built with RNNs known for capturing sequential dependencies in language, will be compiled, trained on the dataset shared as part of Fake News Detection in Dravidian Languages-DravidianLangTech@EACL 2024[1], and evaluated using metrics like accuracy score and classification report. Visualization techniques, including confusion matrix heatmaps, will provide insights into model performance. Ultimately, we aim to develop an effective tool for distinguishing between authentic and fake news articles, contributing to combating misinformation in the digital landscape. The following sections will delve into a comprehensive literature survey to understand existing approaches to fake news detection, followed by detailing the methods employed in our study. We will present the results of our experiments, analyze the performance metrics of the model, and finally, conclusions regarding the effectiveness of our approach and its implications for addressing the challenge of fake news in the Malayalam language.

The rest of the article is organized as follows: Section 2 provides a brief overview of existing works on fake news detection. The dataset used and the proposed model are discussed in Section 3. The results are presented in Section 4. Finally, we conclude our work in Section 5.

[1] https://codalab.lisn.upsaclay.fr/competitions/16055

2 Literature Survey

In the modern digital era, combating the rapid spread of misinformation has become a critical societal challenge, necessitating innovative strategies for detection and mitigation. This literature review critically assesses the landscape of fake news detection. Mykhailo and Volodymyr (2017) presents a straightforward method using a naive Bayes classifier, achieving a respectable accuracy of approximately 0.74 on Facebook news posts. Akshay and Amey (2018) utilizes a Naive Bayes classification model for predicting the authenticity of Facebook posts, with potential improvements discussed in the paper. Bijimol and Anit Sara (2023) focuses on detecting Malayalam fake news using a Passive Aggressive Classifier, while Murari et al. (2021) provides a comprehensive review of machine learning algorithms for fake news detection across var-

Proceedings of the Fourth Workshop on Speech, Vision, and Language Technologies for Dravidian Languages, pages 266–270
March 22, 2024 ©2024 Association for Computational Linguistics

ious social media platforms. Sumit and Jyoti (2022) combines SVM and Naive Bayes for detecting fake news with an accuracy of 0.84, while Rizwana Kallooravi and Mohamed (2021) emphasizes the importance of including more search engines for improved accuracy in fake news detection. Jasmine and Rupali (2021) specifically addresses the challenge of fake news detection in the Malayalam language, employing Recurrent Neural Networks (RNNs) for their ability to capture sequential dependencies and achieve high accuracy. Nihel Fatima and Abdelhamid (2021) proposes a machine learning-based system utilizing TF-IDF and SVM for effective fake news detection. Further, the results of various approaches proposed for detecting fake news have been reviewed and presented in Subramanian et al. (2024). Also, the performance of several methods proposed for the fake news shared task released during 2023 presented in Subramanian et al. (2023). In the quest to combat misinformation, the contribution of RNNs underscores their interdisciplinary nature in addressing linguistic and contextual complexities, aiming to deepen understanding and enhance countermeasures against fake news proliferation in the digital age.

3 Materials and Methods

3.1 Taskset Description

For this model we have taken taskset with different labels.Taskset are labeled as either 'Original' for presenting genuine and factual information or 'Fake' if they contain intentionally deceptive or fabricated content. This binary classification serves as a robust foundation for training models to discern between legitimate and misleading news in the Malayalam language. These refined labels contribute to the datasets' richness, fostering the development of sophisticated machine learning models capable of adeptly handling the intricacies of news classification and detection. Whether through nuanced truthfulness labels in task set or binary authenticity labels,these distinctions collectively enhance the depth and accuracy of the analyses conducted in their respective domains, while the sentence structure is adjusted for originality without altering the meaning.

3.2 Pre-processing and Feature Extraction

The model pre-processes textual data for training a Bidirectional Long Short-Term Memory (LSTM) model for binary classification. It starts with label encoding using the LabelEncoder to convert categorical labels ('Original' and 'Fake') into numerical values (0 and 1). Then, the Tokenizer class from Keras tokenizes the text data, limiting the vocabulary size based on word frequency. Sequences are padded or truncated to ensure uniform sequence length. An embedding layer is added to learn dense word representations, followed by two Bidirectional LSTM layers to capture information from past and future contexts. Dense layers with ReLU activation functions and a final sigmoid activation function for binary classification are included. A dropout layer mitigates overfitting, and the model is compiled using the Adam optimizer and binary cross-entropy loss function.

3.3 Methodology

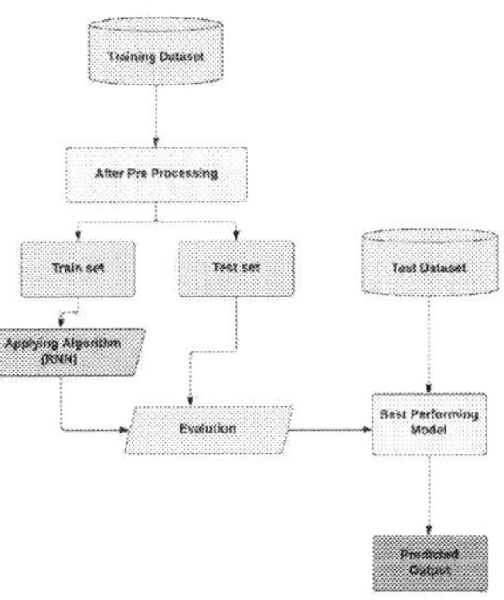

Figure 1: Flow diagram

3.4 Proposed Classifiers

For fake News detection, we propose utilizing a Recurrent Neural Network (RNN). RNNs are specifically designed for sequential data processing and are highly effective in natural language tasks. They have the ability to capture intricate dependencies within textual content by retaining memory from previous inputs. The proposed RNN model incorporates recurrent layers such as LSTM or GRU to effectively capture sequential patterns and identify offensive language patterns. This approach aims to

S.NO	NEWS	LABEL
1	Poda polayadi monea thooooo. Madar choot thooooo..	FAKE
2	e pennugalk vera valla panikum poikoode	ORIGINAL
3	Ee prandhane oke anu .....aadhyam naadu kadathande	FAKE
4	Cpm raja baranam pole aayi	ORIGINAL

Table 1: Task set

leverage the contextual understanding power of RNNs for robust offensive text detection. RNNs are selected for their strengths in handling the challenges of identifying offensive content within textual data.

4 Results and Discussion

The implementation of recurrent neural network (RNN) models in Task 1 run 1 and Task 1 run 2 for classifying Malayalam news articles as fake or original revealed critical limitations in accurately distinguishing between the two categories and achieved the overall accuracy of around 0.5833 and 0.5882. Despite training and evaluating the models on separate datasets, both runs exhibited a systemic issue where all instances were erroneously classified as original news, yielding zero true positives for fake news. This misclassification highlights fundamental flaws in the model's ability to discern meaningful patterns from the data. To address this, future improvements could involve exploring alternative model architectures incorporating attention mechanisms or more complex recurrent units, enhancing feature engineering techniques such as utilizing word embeddings or capturing semantic relationships, and mitigating data imbalance issues through oversampling or augmentation methods. Overall, these findings underscore the necessity for iterative refinement and experimentation to develop a more robust and effective classification system for combatting misinformation within the digital landscape of Malayalam news.

4.1 Performance Metrics

The evaluation of various classification models for detecting Malayalam fake news employed key metrics, including Accuracy, Precision, Recall, and F1-Score . These metrics are fundamental for assessing the classifiers' effectiveness in distinguishing between Original and Fake Malayalam NEWS.

Accuracy is calculated using the following formula:

$$\text{Accuracy} = \frac{TP + TN}{TP + TN + FP + FN}$$

Recall, also known as Sensitivity or True Positive Rate, is defined by the formula:

$$\text{Recall} = \frac{TP}{TP + FN}$$

Precision, or Positive Predictive Value, is given by the formula:

$$\text{Precision} = \frac{TP}{TP + FP}$$

F1-Score is the harmonic average of Precision and Recall, calculated as in the following formula:

$$\text{F1-Score} = \frac{2 \times \text{Precision} \times \text{Recall}}{\text{Precision} + \text{Recall}}$$

providing a balanced assessment of the model's performance.The performance metrics for each classifier on the test dataset, along with the confusion matrix. The confusion matrix visually illustrates correct and incorrect classifications, with the X-axis representing predicted classes and the Y-axis representing actual classes. Notably, the proposed models utilizing RNN accurately classifying Original and Fake Malayalam NEWS.

Model	Accuracy	Macro Precision	Macro Recall	Macro F1-Score	Weighted Precision	Weighted Recall	Weighted F1-Score
RNN	0.59	0.29	0.50	0.37	0.35	0.59	0.44

Table 2: Classification report for RNN

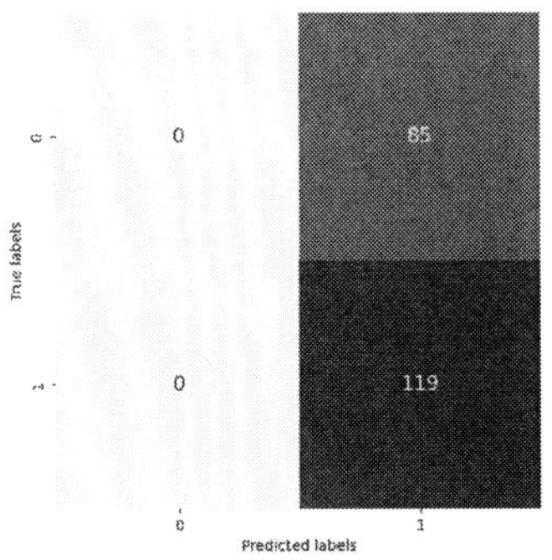

Figure 2: Confusion matrix for Malayalam fake NEWS detection Run1

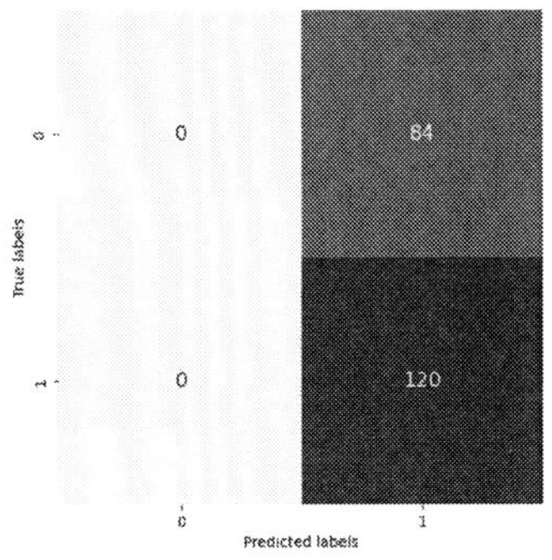

Figure 3: Confusion matrix for Malayalam fake NEWS detection Run2

Upon examining the confusion matrices in Figures 2 and 3, specific patterns emerge in the classification performance. For Taskset 1 Run 1 and Taskset 1 run 2 the RNN model exhibits a balanced performance, effectively identifying both Original and fake news.

5 Conclusion

In conclusion, the RNN model's performance in both Task 1 Run 1 and Task 1 Run 2 is characterized by an overall accuracy of around 0.5833 and 0.5882, respectively. While proficient in classifying original news instances, the model exhibits significant limitations in identifying potentially fake news. The precision for fake news is strikingly low, indicating a high number of false positives, and the recall is particularly deficient, especially in Task 1 Run 2 where it is zero.These findings underscore the imperative need for refinement, specifically in enhancing the model's ability to discern and accurately classify instances of potentially deceptive news. The observed patterns provide clear directions for future iterations, emphasizing the importance of addressing these limitations to elevate the model's effectiveness in distinguishing between original and fake news in Malayalam text.

References

Jain Akshay and Kasbe Amey. 2018. Fake News Detection. *2018 IEEE International Students' Conference on Electrical, Electronics and Computer Science (SCEECS).*

T K Bijimol and Santhosh Anit Sara. 2023. Malayalam Fake News Detection using Machine Learning. *National Conference on Emerging Computer Applications, 4(1)*, 4(1).

Shaikh Jasmine and Patil Rupali. 2021. Fake News Detection using Machine Learning. *2020 IEEE International Symposium on Sustainable Energy, Signal Processing and Cyber Security (iSSSC).*

Choudhary Murari, Prashant Deepika Saxena Shashank, Jha, and Singh Ashutosh Kumar. 2021. A Review of Fake News Detection using Machine Learning. *2021 2nd International Conference for Emerging Technology (INCET).*

Granik Mykhailo and Mesyura Volodymyr. 2017. Fake news detection using naive Bayes classifier. *2017 IEEE First Ukraine Conference on Electrical and Computer Engineering (UKRCON)).*

Baarir Nihel Fatima and Djeffal Abdelhamid. 2021. Fake News detection Using Machine Learning. *2020 2nd International Workshop on Human-Centric Smart Environments for Health and Wellbeing (IHSH).*

Thandil Rizwana Kallooravi and Muneer Mohamed, Basheer V K. 2021. Natural Language Processing of Malayalam Text for predicting its Authenticity. *Proceedings of the Yukthi 2021- The International Conference on Emerging Trends in Engineering - GEC Kozhikode, Kerala, India.*

Malliga Subramanian, Bharathi Raja Chakravarthi, Kogilavani Shanmugavadivel. Santhiya Pandiyan, Prasanna Kumar Kumaresan, Balasubramanian

Palani, Premjith B, Sandhiya Raja, Vanaja, Mithunajha S, Devika K, Hariprasath S.B, Haripriya B, and Vigneshwar E. 2024. Overview of the Second Shared Task on Fake News Detection in Dravidian Languages. In *Proceedings of the Fourth Workshop on Speech, Vision, and Language Technologies for Dravidian Languages*, Malta. European Chapter of the Association for ComputationalLinguistics.

Malliga Subramanian, Bharathi Raja Chakravarthi, Kogilavani Shanmugavadivel, Santhiya Pandiyan, Prasanna Kumar Kumaresan, Balasubramanian Palani, and Muskaan Singh. 2023. Overview of the Shared Task on Fake News Detection in Dravidian Languages. In *Proceedings of the Third Workshop on Speech, Vision, and Language Technologies for Dravidian Languages*, Bulgaria. European Chapter of the Association for ComputationalLinguistics.

kumar Sumit and Tiwari Jyoti. 2022. Implementing a hybrid method for fake news detection. *International Journal of Emerging Trends in Engineering Research.*

Author Index

Association for Computational Linguistics
209 N. Eighth Street
Stroudsburg, Pennsylvania 18360

ISBN 978-1-7138-9453-7

CURRAN ASSOCIATES INC.
proceedings.com